ENCYCLOPEDIA OF THE
LANGUAGES *of* EUROPE

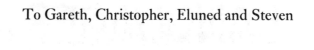
To Gareth, Christopher, Eluned and Steven

ENCYCLOPEDIA OF THE

LANGUAGES *of*
EUROPE

edited by
Glanville Price

Emeritus Professor of French
University of Wales Aberystwyth

Copyright © Blackwell Publishers Ltd 1998, 2000

Editorial matter and organization copyright © Glanville Price 1998, 2000

First published 1998
First published in paperback 2000

2 4 6 8 10 9 7 5 3 1

Blackwell Publishers Ltd
108 Cowley Road
Oxford OX4 1JF
UK

Blackwell Publishers Inc.
350 Main Street
Malden, Massachusetts 02148
USA

British Library Cataloguing in Publication Data

A CIP catalogue record for this book is available from the British Library.

Library of Congress Cataloging-in-Publication Data

Encyclopedia of the languages of Europe / edited by Glanville Price.
    p.   cm.
  Includes bibliographical references.
  ISBN 0–631–19286–7 (alk. paper) — ISBN 0–631–22039–9 (pbk)
   1. Europe—Languages—Encyclopedias. I. Price, Glanville.
P380.E53 1998
409'.4—dc21   97–29542
                                     CIP

Typeset in 11 on 13 pt Ehrhardt
By G&G Editorial, Brighton
Printed in Great Britain by MPG Books Ltd, Bodmin, Cornwall
This book is printed on acid-free paper

Contents

Figures

Maps

Contributors

†**A. J. Aitken**, former Editor, *A Dictionary of the Older Scottish Tongue*, Honorary Professor, University of Edinburgh.

Robin Allan, Senior Lecturer in Danish, University College London.

Michael P. Barnes, Professor of Scandinavian Studies, University College London.

Linara Bartkuvienė, Lecturer in English, Faculty of Philology, Vilnius University.

Ildikó Bellér-Hann, Research Fellow, University of Kent at Canterbury.

Paola Benincà, Professor of Linguistics, University of Padua.

Michael Branch, Professor of Finnish, School of Slavonic and East European Studies, University of London.

Maija Brēde, Lecturer in Linguistics, University of Latvia.

Joseph Cremona, Emeritus Lecturer in Romance Philology and Fellow of Trinity Hall, University of Cambridge.

Marie-José Dalbera-Stefanaggi, Professor, University of Corsica.

Peter V. Davies, Senior Lecturer in French, University of Glasgow.

Jim Dingley, Senior Lecturer in Ukrainian Studies, School of Slavonic and East European Studies, University of London.

Viv Edwards, Professor of Language and Education and Director of the Reading and Language Information Centre, University of Reading.

Katherine Forsyth, British Academy Institutional Research Fellow, Department of History, University College London.

Tourkhan Gandjeï, Emeritus Professor of Persian and Turkish Studies, University of London.

Monica Genesin, PhD in Albanian, University of Padua.

William Gillies, Professor of Celtic, University of Edinburgh.

Lewis Glinert, Professor of Hebrew, Dartmouth College, New Hampshire.

Nigel Gotteri, Senior Lecturer in Russian and Slavonic Studies, University of Sheffield.

Wolfgang Greller, Researcher, Centre for Bilingual Studies, Trinity College, Carmarthen.

Ian Hancock, Professor, Linguistics, English and Asian Studies, University of Texas at Austin.

Peter Herrity, Reader in Slavonic Languages, University of Nottingham.

Brian George Hewitt, Professor of Caucasian Languages, School of Oriental and African Studies, University of London.

Phil Holmes, Reader in Scandinavian Studies, University of Hull.

G. C. Horrocks, Professor of Comparative Philology, University of Cambridge.

Humphrey Lloyd Humphreys, Lecturer in French, University of Wales, Lampeter.

Sonia Kanikova, former teacher of Bulgarian language and literature, School of Slavonic and East European Studies, University of London.

Dovid Katz, Academic Director, East European Jewish Heritage Project, Oxford.

Paddy Ladd, researcher and writer on Deaf Studies.

David Mackenzie, Professor of Spanish, University College, Cork.

C. M. MacRobert, University Lecturer in Russian Philology and Comparative Slavonic Philology, University of Oxford, and Tutorial Fellow in Russian, Lady Margaret Hall.

Rory McTurk, Reader in Icelandic Studies, University of Leeds.

Martin Maiden, Professor of the Romance Languages, University of Oxford.

Peter Meredith, Professor of Medieval Drama, School of English, University of Leeds.

Georges Moracchini, Maître de conférences, University of Corsica.

Christopher Moseley, MPhil in Livonian Studies, University of London.

Vrej Nerses Nersessian, Curator in charge of the Christian Middle East Collections in the British Library, London.

Gerald Newton, Senior Lecturer in the Department of Germanic Studies and Director of the Centre for Luxemburg Studies, University of Sheffield.

Máirtín Ó Murchú, Senior Professor at the Dublin Institute for Advanced Studies.

Stephen Parkinson, Lecturer in Portuguese Language and Linguistics, University of Oxford.

Mair Parry, Senior Lecturer in Italian, University of Bristol.

Philip Payton, Reader in Cornish Studies and Director of the Institute of Cornish Studies, University of Exeter.

Ralph Penny, Professor of Romance Philology, Queen Mary and Westfield College, University of London.

J. G. F. Powell, Professor of Latin, University of Newcastle upon Tyne.

Glanville Price, Emeritus Professor of French, University of Wales Aberystwyth.

Catrin Redknap, School of European Studies, University of Wales Cardiff.

Reinier Salverda, Professor of Dutch Language and Literature, University College London.

Peter Schrijver, Lecturer in Comparative Indo-European Linguistics, Leiden University.

Stefan Schumacher, researcher, University of Halle-Wittenberg.

David Short, Senior Lecturer in Czech and Slovak, School of Slavonic and East European Studies, University of London.

Ingmar Söhrman, Reader in Romance Philology, Umeå University.

Gerald Stone, Fellow of Hertford College, Oxford.

R. L. Thomson, formerly Reader in Celtic, University of Leeds.

D. A. Trotter, Professor of French, University of Wales Aberystwyth.

Laura Vanelli, Associate Professor of Ladin Linguistics, University of Padua.

Roel Vismans, Senior Lecturer, Department of Dutch Studies, University of Hull.

Terence Wade, Professor Emeritus in Russian Studies, Research Fellow, University of Strathclyde.

Stephen J. Walton, Reader in Norwegian, University College London.

Jonathan West, Senior Lecturer in German, University of Newcastle upon Tyne.

Max W. Wheeler, Reader in Linguistics, University of Sussex.

Preface

The title of this volume, *Encyclopedia of the Languages of Europe*, calls for definition of the terms 'Europe' and 'language'.

The definition of Europe

Europe is not an established political entity with recognized borders (such as, say, the European Union or the former Soviet Union) and, in consequence, different reference works define it differently. Ideally, it would be preferable to adopt geographical or geological criteria rather than political ones but, in practice, this is not always possible.

Let us take the problematic areas one by one.

(1) Iceland is conventionally considered to be a European country and this is supported by geological criteria: the island is situated at the northern end of the mid-Atlantic ridge and, though its western part (including the capital, Reykjavik) is on the North American tectonic plate, the greater part is on the Eurasian plate and so, for this reason too, there is good cause to include Iceland in Europe (Greenland on the other hand is, according to all criteria, part of North America).

(2) Of the Portuguese Atlantic islands, in so far as they can properly be said to form part of any continent, the Azores, situated as they are on the Azores-Cape St Vincent ridge (Cape St Vincent being the south-westernmost point of Portugal), can plausibly be considered as part of Europe; Madeira, on the other hand, being situated well to the south of the ridge, can only be assigned to Africa; in practice, the question is of little importance for our purposes since the only language involved is Portuguese.

(3) Malta is not only conventionally considered to be a European country but is on a shelf extending southwards from Sicily and is closer to Sicily than to the North African coast; there is no good reason, therefore, not to consider it as forming part of Europe.

(4) In strictly non-political and non-cultural terms, there can be little doubt that Cyprus ought to be considered as part of Asia: it lies south of the eastern part of Asia Minor and, at its closest point, is little more than 100 km off the coast of Syria. However, Cyprus has conventionally been considered as a European country. Were we concerned only with the two major contemporary vernaculars of the island, Greek and Turkish, the matter would be of only secondary importance since both languages are in any case included in the encyclopedia. But the decision to follow convention and include Cyprus means that we have to take into account also both of the long-extinct languages of the island (see ***Cypriot scripts**) and of contemporary ***Cypriot Arabic**.

(5) As far as the south-eastern limit of Europe is concerned, the crest of the Caucasus Mountains offers an obvious dividing line between Europe and Asia, and

indeed is often taken as such. This, however, leaves Georgia, Armenia and Azerbaijan in Asia whereas the first two, at least, would almost certainly wish to be considered as European countries. The decision to include all three means that some forty other languages, mainly those belonging to the Caucasian language families (see ***Caucasian languages**), have to be included.

(6) For most of its length, the eastern border of Europe, namely the Ural mountains, is beyond contention. But between the southern end of the Urals (from, say, the city of Orsk where the Ural river turns westwards) and the Caspian Sea there is a gap from north-east to south-west of some 400 km. Here there is no agreement as to where Europe ends and Asia begins and at least three 'natural' lines have been suggested, namely:

(i)   the Volga river, which however seems too far west and, moreover, divides a number of constituent republics of the Russian Federation between the two continents;

(ii)   the Emba river, which, of all major waterways, continues the most directly the line of the Urals in a broadly south-westerly direction towards the Caspian; this, however, would divide the Republic of Kazakhstan, usually considered as an Asian state, between Asia and Europe and there seems no good reason to accept the Emba as constituting the border;

(iii)   between the Volga and the Emba is the Ural river which, if we were to decide on a 'natural' border, would perhaps be the most satisfactory of those proposed; this, however, would still leave a substantial part of Kazakhstan in Europe.

For the purposes of this encyclopedia, therefore, we have opted for a political border: the eastern border of Europe between the southern end of the Urals and the Caspian Sea is taken to be the frontier of the Republic of Kazakhstan.

The definition of 'language'

A second and even more intractable problem than that of defining 'Europe' is this: what is a language? More specifically: on what criteria can one decide whether a given speech-variety is to be considered as a language in its own right rather than as a dialect of some other language? The question is unanswerable in the sense that there are no universally applicable criteria that will enable us to decide objectively in every doubtful case. One can only approach the matter pragmatically: at one end of the scale, it is beyond doubt that, say, English, German and Latin are languages while, at the other end, there are no grounds for considering Yorkshire English, Austrian German and Medieval Latin, despite their defining characteristics, as separate languages. In practice, and after consultation with the relevant contributors, I have taken in controversial cases what seem to me to be defensible but, necessarily, not the only defensible decisions. I am well aware that there are those who will quarrel with the decision to recognize, say, Scots and Gascon as separate languages from English and Occitan respectively, and, on the other hand, those who will object to the fact that speech-varieties such as Asturian, Norman, Schwyzertüütsch and Valencian are considered as forms of Spanish, French, German and Catalan respectively and are therefore included under those headings rather than being accorded the status of 'languages'.

This problem arises with particular acuity in the case of some of the Romance vernaculars of Italy, such as (among others) Ligurian, Piedmontese, Sardinian and those speech-varieties of northern Italy (Dolomitic Ladin and Friulian) which are widely, but not in the view of all specialists, considered as varieties of a Rhaeto-Romance language. In this case, we have devoted one major and all-inclusive article, with contributions from four scholars, to the Romance vernaculars of Italy (including the Italian language itself).

Coverage

This is an encyclopedia of languages, not of linguistic communities. There are, therefore, no separate articles on, for example, the Swedish-speaking community in Finland, German-speaking communities in Belgium, Romania and elsewhere, or the partly Catalan-speaking port of Alghero in Sardinia. However, where distinctive terms are applied to such communities, cross-references or brief comments are provided.

A different problem is that of the measure of coverage to be accorded to what are now generally known, at least in Britain, as 'community languages' (otherwise known as 'immigrant languages'), i.e. the languages of reasonably settled communities of (in most cases recent) incomers from such areas as Asia, Africa or the Caribbean. If these are not, in the usual sense of the term, 'European languages', it seems difficult not to recognize them as having achieved the status of 'languages of Europe'. Given the impossibility in practice of referring to (or, indeed, identifying) every such community in Europe (for example, Viv Edwards points out in her contribution on community languages in Britain that a recent survey recorded no fewer than 172 languages spoken by schoolchildren in London), articles are devoted to the principal languages in question in each of three countries where their presence is perhaps particularly significant, namely Britain, France and the Netherlands. In general, communities of European origin, whose languages are in any case covered in the encyclopedia, are not discussed in these articles. (See also the entries on '***Greenlandic**', '***Creoles**' and '***Pidgin languages**'.)

The limits of the encyclopedia have been further extended to take in articles on 'Artificial languages' and 'Sign languages'.

The scope of the individual articles is what might be defined very broadly as the external history and sociolinguistic aspects of the language or languages covered. This can include such topics as origins and linguistic affiliations, earliest attestations, literary use (though no attempt is made to give potted histories of literature), standardization, scripts and orthography, geographical spread, contacts with and influence of other languages, and, where applicable, present situation (including demographic factors, official status, role in the media, education and public life generally, etc.). However, given the widely differing history and present position of the many languages covered, it seemed inadvisable to attempt to impose any kind of set pattern on the individual authors. In general, however, the presentation follows the order of the topics listed above, but not all the topics mentioned are covered in every article and, in some cases (for example, where it seems important to discuss dialects before standardization), a different order is followed.

Presentation

The books and articles listed at the end of entries are, in general, intended as references for further reading not as an acknowledgement of sources. All major articles and many shorter ones are signed (see list of contributors, pp. viii–x). Brief unsigned entries are by the editor.

In the bibliographies, titles in French and others whose meaning seems reasonably transparent in the context are left untranslated.

Acknowledgements

The editor, the relevant contributors and the publishers are grateful to the following for permission to reproduce or adapt the maps or figures indicated or for providing information on which a map is based: the Information Department of the Belgian Embassy (map 1); Blackwell (map 4, figs 6, 9 and 10 (a)); British Museum Press (fig. 10 (b)); Cambridge University Press (fig. 13); Anne Haavaldsen (fig. 12); Professor Kenneth MacKinnon (map 16); Oxford University Press (map 8); Scottish National Dictionary Association and Professor Robert J. Gregg (map 15); the Press and Information Department of the Swiss Embassy (map 20); University of Wales Press (map 21).

The editor also wishes to express his gratitude to Margaret Aherne whose excellent copy-editing saved us from many errors, inconsistencies and other infelicities.

Phonetic Transcriptions

Phonetic transcriptions used in a number of articles employ characters of the International Phonetic Alphabet (IPA) and are given in square brackets, [ ]. The widespread convention of adopting slashes, / /, to indicate phonemic transcriptions is not followed in this encyclopedia.

Unless otherwise stated below, consonant characters of the IPA indicate the sounds that they primarily indicate in English, French and Italian (and often in other western European languages using the Latin alphabet), e.g. [b], [t], [s], [v] correspond to the value of <b>, <t>, <s>, <v> (on the use of angle brackets, < >, see Conventions and Conventional Symbols, p. xviii) in English *boy*, French *beau*, Italian *bene*, English *ten*, French *table*, Italian *tale*, English *sing*, French, Italian *si*, English *very*, French *vie*, Italian *vita*, etc. (As narrow phonetic transcriptions are not given, differences between the various languages mentioned in the way the consonants in question are articulated are not taken in account.)

Other IPA characters that occur in the encyclopedia are the following:

Consonants and semi-consonants

g	voiced velar plosive, English *good*
q	voiceless uvular plosive (see *Caucasian languages)
G	voiced uvular plosive (see *Caucasian languages)
ʔ	glottal stop
ŋ	velar nasal, English *sing*
β	voiced bilabial fricative, Spanish *haber*
θ	voiceless dental fricative, English *thin*
ð	voiced dental fricative, English *then*
ɕ	voiceless alveolo-palatal fricative (see *Caucasian languages)
ʂ	voiceless retroflex fricative (see *Caucasian languages)
ʃ	voiceless postalveolar fricative, English *ship*, French *chat*
ʃ̡	palatalized [ʃ] (see *Russian)
ʒ	voiced postalveolar fricative, English *measure*, French *jaune*
ç	voiceless palatal fricative, German *ich*
j	voiceless palatal fricative or approximant, English *yes*, German *ja*
x	voiceless velar fricative, German *Bach*
ɣ	voiced velar fricative, Spanish *pagar*
χ	voiceless uvular fricative, Welsh *bach*
ʁ	uvular fricative r
ħ	voiceless pharyngeal fricative (see *Maltese)
ʕ	voiced pharyngeal fricative (see *Caucasian languages)
w	voiced labial-velar approximant, English *weave*
ɬ	voiceless lateral fricative, Welsh *llan*

ʎ   palatal lateral approximant, Spanish *llamar*, Italian *figlio*
ɫ   velarized or 'dark' *l*, southern English *cool*, *milk*

[ʷ]   indicates labialization, e.g. [tʷ]
[ʰ]   indicates aspiration, e.g. [tʰ]
[ʲ]   indicates palatalization, e.g. [tʲ]

Oral vowels

The quality of oral vowels (excluding those not needed for our purposes) is indicated in the following table:

		Unrounded			Rounded		
	Front	*Central*	*Back*		*Front*		*Back*
Close	i	ɨ			y		u
	ɪ				Y	ʊ	
Half-close	e	ə					o
Half-open	ɛ		ʌ				ɔ
	æ						
Open	a		ɑ				

Examples:
    Unrounded vowels: Fr., Ital. *si* [si], Russ. пыл [pɨl], Eng. *bit* [bɪt], Fr. *été* [ete], Eng. *ahead* [əhɛd], Fr. *petit* [pəti] (French [ə] is in fact a rounded vowel), Fr. *tête* [tɛt], Eng. *cut* [kʌt], Fr. *patte* [pat], Eng. *calf* [kɑːf] (for [ː], see below).
    Rounded vowels: Fr. *lune* [lyn], Fr *tout* [tu], Ger. *Sünde* [zʏndə], Eng. *put* [pʊt], Fr. *dos* [do], Ital. *dove* [dove], Fr. *botte* [bɔt], Ital. *posta* [pɔsta].

Nasal vowels

Nasal vowels are indicated by the symbol for the corresponding oral vowel surmounted by a tilde, [~], e.g. Fr. *main* [mɛ̃], *bon* [bɔ̃], Portuguese *bom* [bõ].

Additional conventions

[ː] indicates that the preceding consonant or vowel is long, e.g. Ital. *fatto* [fatːo], Fr. *rive* [riːv].
['] indicates that the preceding consonant is an ejective.
['] indicates that the following syllable is stressed, e.g. Eng. *above* [ə'bʌv], Ital. *vino* ['vino].

Conventions and Conventional Symbols

An asterisk before the name of a language, language family or script (e.g. '***Spanish**') indicates a cross-reference to the entry so headed.

An asterisk before a word or form quoted (e.g. 'Germanic **kuningaz*') indicates that the form is conjectural and not attested.

Characters of the International Phonetic Alphabet (see pp. xvi–xvii) are enclosed within square brackets, e.g. [ʃ].

Graphemes are enclosed within angle brackets, e.g. 'English <c> is pronounced either [k] or [s]'; 'In Danish, <å> has replaced earlier <aa>'; 'The Cyrillic character <в> is pronounced [v]'.

> = 'becomes' (e.g. 'Latin *cantare* > French *chanter*').

< = 'comes from' (e.g. 'French *chanter* < Latin *cantare*').

The Languages of Europe

A

Abaza (see under *Caucasian languages. II. North-West Causasian family*)

Abkhaz (see under *Caucasian languages. II. North-West Caucasian family*)

Adyghe (see *Circassian* under *Caucasian languages. II. North-West Caucasian family*)

Aequian

Aequian is the name applied to the language of one brief inscription found in the territory of the Aequi, who originally inhabited a small region in the mountainous interior of Italy, directly east of Rome, south of present-day Rieti and north of the Fucine lake (see map 10). Around 500 BC, the Aequi expanded to the west, threatening Rome and Latium. From around 430 BC until 300 BC, the Romans gradually broke their power and quickly Romanized them. The name of the Aequi servives in that of the district of *Cicolano* from *Aequiculanum*.

The one remaining inscription, in Latin script, is located on a stone slab at the bottom of a spring near Collemaggiore (Vetter 1953: 226). It is a dedication by a magistrate, Po(mpo?) Pomposiies, son of Gaius, to the Stata Mater, a deity associated with the extinguishing of fire. The language of the inscription is clearly of the **Osco-Umbrian* type. The position of the name of the father before rather than after the family name reflects an **Umbrian* rather than **Oscan* custom. As in the case of **Marsian, *Sabinian, *Vestinian, *Volscian, *Marrucinian, *Paelignian*, it is doubtful whether one should assign to Aequian the status of an independent Italic language: it was either a dialect of Oscan or Umbrian or a dialect intermediate between Oscan and Umbrian.

Coleman, R. 1986. The central Italic languages in the period of Roman expansion. *Transactions of the Philological Society* 1986: 100–31.
Vetter, E. 1953. *Handbuch der italischen Dialekte* ('Handbook of the Italic Dialects'). Heidelberg.

PETER SCHRIJVER

African languages (see under *Community languages (France)*)

Aghul (see under *Caucasian languages. IV. North-East Caucasian family*)

Akhvakh (see under *Caucasian languages. IV. North-East Caucasian family*)

Alanic

The Alans were an *Iranian-speaking tribe (considered to be ancestors of the present-day Ossetes of the Caucasus – see *Ossetic), some of whom moved westwards into Europe from the 3rd c. onwards. Bands of Alans, together with *Germanic-speaking Swabians and Vandals, crossed the Rhine on 31 December 406 and, in late 409, again with Swabians and Vandals, crossed the Pyrenees into Iberia. The Alans took as their share of the Peninsula an area corresponding to much of modern Portugal and the central Spanish plateau. Their dominion over these territories ended when they were defeated by the Visigoths in 416 and their last remnants crossed over into Africa in 429. Their language appears to have left no traces in the languages of the Peninsula but their presence is recalled in a handful of Spanish place-names such as *Puerto del Alano* (Huesca) and *Villalán* (Valladolid).

In the Middle Ages, other Alans from the Caucasus settled in Hungary (see *Yassic).

Albanian

Albanian (*gjuha shqipe*) is the sole surviving member of a branch of *Indo-European that may also (though this is still uncertain) have included *Illyrian and *Messapic. It is spoken mainly in the western Balkans, primarily in the Republic of Albania (*Shqipëria*), where there are two main varieties, Geg (northern) and Tosk (southern), and in adjacent parts of Serbia and Montenegro, with pockets elsewhere in the Balkans and in Italy.

History

The fact that there is considerable uncertainty about the areas occupied by the pre-Albanians means that it is very difficult to establish what their relations may have been with other ancient peoples of the Balkan peninsula (such as the Illyrians and the Thracians). Various views have been expressed about the early history of Albanian, particularly in connection with ancient elements common to Albanian and *Romanian. Many scholars uphold a 'theory of continuity' by placing the pre-Albanians in the territory now occupied by Albanians. Others claim that the lack of early maritime terminology argues persuasively against their having spread as far as the coast of the Adriatic. The scarcity of borrowings from (Doric) Greek also suggests that the proto-Albanians were to be found well north of the line fixed by C. Jireček who, on the basis of milestones, inscriptions and coins, tried to establish the limits of the Greek- and Latin-speaking areas. In that case, Albanian would derive from an ancient mixture of Balkan tongues, though this does not explain how the koine came into being.

Earliest texts

The earliest traces of written Albanian are represented by fragmentary documents and by isolated words and phrases found in non-Albanian texts. Though there is a suggestion by the Bishop of Antivari, Guillelmus Adae (Brocardus Monacus), writing in 1332, that the Latin alphabet was already used for writing Albanian, the earliest known examples are a short Catholic baptismal formula of 1462, in the northern (Geg) dialect (see below, 'Dialects'), in a Latin manuscript now in the Laurentian Library in Florence, and some verses of the New Testament, followed by a small fragment of an Orthodox Easter chant, also dating from the 15th c., both in the southern (Tosk) dialect, in a Greek manuscript now in the Ambrosian Library in Milan. These earliest attestations of Albanian in both Latin and Greek script provide evidence of the twofold relations both with the West and with the eastern European cultural tradition. Other 15th-c. documents are a sentence in Albanian in Thomas Medius's Latin comedy *Epirota* (1483) and a word-list compiled in 1496 by Arnold von Harff. The first printed book, and the first text to make substantial use of the language, is the so-called *Mëshari* ('Missal') of Gjon Buzuku, written in Geg and printed in 1554–5, now in the Vatican Library. Another important 16th-c. work is the earliest book in Tosk, a Catechism of 1592 by an Italo-Albanian priest, Lekë Matranga. In the 17th c. come Frang-Bardhi's Latin–Albanian dictionary (1635), Pjetër Budi's translations and adaptations of *Dottrina Christiana* (1618), *Rituale Romanum* and *Speculum Confessionis* (1621), and Pjetër Bogdani's monumental work, *Cuneus Prophetarum* (1685). Their works, together with folk-poetry on religious themes by the Italo-Albanian Varibobba, mark the beginning of Albanian belletristic writing. The authors were all Catholic clerics from northern Albania who wrote during the period of the Counter-Reformation.

Literary tradition

While, in northern Albania, literature with a (Catholic) religious content had already emerged in the 16th c., it was only later that other cultural centres developed in the southern Geg and northern Tosk areas which were influenced by the Orthodox tradition. In the 17th and 18th centuries, there flourished in southern Albania a movement, inspired by the so-called *Bejtexhínj* ('verse-makers'), that promoted a secular Islamic poetic culture. Because of Turkish hostility, in the 19th c. it was only outside the homeland that literature flourished, in Egypt, Romania, Greece, Bulgaria and Italy, where the Arbëreshë (see below, 'Outlying communities') played a significant part in the formation of the *Rilindja Kombëtare* (Albanian Renaissance Movement). The existence of a rich oral literature was also vitally important in fostering a sense of national identity and helping to maintain the survival of the native language.

Standard language

The 19th c. was characterized by two significant developments: the rise of several supradialectal varieties and the change from a prenational to a national language. Up until 1944, Albanian had a bidialectal literary tradition (see below, 'Dialects'), a polycentric system with two principal variants. Political and social instability and the colonial status of the country under the Ottoman regime prevented any dialect from assuming a pre-eminent national role. An attempt in 1917 to establish an official language for the whole country on the basis of the southern Geg dialect of Elbasan proved ineffective: many school grammars based on Tosk continued to be published and writers carried on writing in other varieties. After the Second World War, the task of standardizing the language was taken over by the state and was heavily influenced by political considerations. The central role assumed by communists from southern Albania in positions of authority was reflected in the emergence of a Tosk-based standard and Geg declined in literary use. With the demise of communism in 1991, however, and the consequent revival of Geg literature, it is possible that the question of standardization could be reopened at some future date.

Scripts

Albanian is now written in a homogeneous, phonetically based, version of the Latin alphabet. Before 1908, no fewer than four major scripts had been in use: Latin (in at least four variants), *Greek (in two variants), Turkish-Arabic, and *Cyrillic. In 1908, however, the Congress of Manastir (Bitola, in Macedonia) decided in favour of the adoption of the Latin alphabet which thereafter came to be gradually accepted by all Albanians.

Dialects

The river Shkumbini, which traverses central Albania from east to west, represents the historical dividing line between the Gegs, to the north, who represent about two-thirds of all Albanian speakers and who are either Catholic or Muslim, and, to the south, the Tosks, who are Muslim or Orthodox. At the beginning of the literary tradition, the gap between the two varieties was smaller than it was to become later. Each dialect has sub-varieties which form a continuum. The Geg area falls into three parts, a northern (subdivided into north-western and north-eastern areas by a line passing to the east of Theth (a village some 70 kilometres north-east of Shkodër), along the river Shalë, and running to the west of Pukë), a central, and a southern. Tosk is generally subdivided into northern and southern varieties, the latter having the two sub-varieties of Çamëria and Labëria (the two southernmost regions of Albania). Most of the Albanian-speaking communities outside *Shqipëria* speak Geg, though there are a few areas where Tosk is also used.

Foreign influences

Until the 20th c. Albanian was always subordinate to some other language. In particular, since the territory was ruled by Rome for some five centuries, lexis and word-formation were deeply marked by Latin. Political, economic and cultural relations with Italy lasted until modern times and an important role was played, particularly in Geg, by the Venetian Republic and the Catholic Church. The Byzantine world, mainly through the Orthodox Church, helped to spread Greek culture in Albania, as in other Balkan countries. This influence played an important part in (though it is by no means solely responsible for) the formation of the so-called 'Balkan Sprachbund', a term that refers to the presence in Albanian, *Macedonian, *Bulgarian, *Romanian and *Greek not only of shared lexical items and parallel phraseology but of correspondences at the phonological and morphosyntactic levels. From the 5th–6th c. onwards, the Slavs began to expand into the Balkans and for several centuries the area was subject to Slavonic migrations. Albanian–Slavonic relationships intensified when Albanian feudal dynasties were subject to Serbian rule and Serbian (see under *Serbo-Croat) and *Church Slavonic were used for official purposes. Finally, the Turks occupied the territory of modern Albania and ruled it for about 450 years until 1912. From the 19th c. onwards, Albanian has been purged of as many foreign (and particularly Turkish) words as possible but, in the last decades of the 20th c., a more tolerant attitude has prevailed since the language is so indebted lexically to foreign languages and cannot afford a large-scale purge for reasons of purism.

Present situation

The total number of Albanian-speakers can be estimated at some 6 million, of whom more than 3 million live in the Republic of Albania. Standard Albanian is the official language of the Republic. Since 1972, standard Albanian has also been accepted in the Kosovë region of Serbia (see below) which previously, since the Second World War, had adopted as an official language, alongside Serbian, the southern Geg variety.

Outlying communities

Outside the Republic of Albania itself, the main Albanian-speaking communities are those in adjacent areas, in particular Kosovë in southern Serbia (over 2 million) and Macedonia (nearly 380,000 in 1981), with substantial communities elsewhere in ex-Yugoslavia, including one at Arbanasi on the coast of Croatia where a northern Geg dialect was introduced in the 18th c. by immigrants from two villages near Bar (Tivar in Albanian).

A migration from the southernmost Albanian-speaking regions to central Greece and the Peloponnese took place from the 12th to the 14th centuries and, under pressure of Turkish domination, there was a further migration from Greece and Albania to southern Italy (Apulia, Calabria, Sicily, Campania) from the 15th to the 18th centuries. Other migrants from southern Albania settled during Ottoman times in Romania, Bulgaria (where only Mandrica, in the Kurdzhali region, survived the Second World War), Turkish Thrace, and Egypt. Splinters of this eastward trek live on in the village of Màndres, south of Kilkís in northern Greece, which was founded by migrants from Mandrica, and in three villages near Melitopol, in the southern Ukraine, where they moved in the 19th c. from Karakurt in the Odessa region. Some 100,000 Albanian-speakers (the Arbëreshë) remain in Italy. No figures are available for numbers of speakers in Greece and other parts of southern and eastern Europe. There are also small Albanian-speaking minorities in western Europe, Syria, North and South America, and in Australia among émigré colonies from Albanian enclaves in Italy and Greece.

Bucholz, O. and Fiedler, W. 1984. *Albanische Grammatik*. Leipzig.
Bucholz, O. Fiedler, W. and Uhlisch, G. 1977. *Wörterbuch Albanisch–Deutsch* ('Albanian–German Dictionary'). Leipzig.
Camaj, M. 1984. *Albanian Grammar*. Wiesbaden.

Hamp, E. P. 1972. Albanian. In Sebeok, T. A. (ed.), *Current Trends in Linguistics*, The Hague and Paris, vol. 9, pp. 1626–92.

Mann, S. E. 1948. *An Historical Albanian–English Dictionary*. London.

MONICA GENESIN

Alderney French (Auregnais)

The now extinct variety of *Channel Islands French spoken in the island of Alderney. It was closer than the other insular dialects to those of mainland Normandy and in particular to that of the peninsula of La Hague some eight miles away in the north-west of the Cotentin.

The Anglicization of Alderney probably began with the bringing in of large numbers of English-speaking labourers to work on the construction between 1845 and 1864 of extensive naval and military installations and the permanent presence thereafter of a large garrison. A dozen or so speakers remained at the outbreak of the Second World War in 1939 and even fewer still survived when the population, which was evacuated in 1940, returned after the war. The last native speakers died around 1960 but something of the language has been preserved (Le Maistre 1982) in the form of a passage of some 400 words recorded by a specialist on Jersey French, Frank Le Maistre, who, before the war, knew Alderney, a number of the last speakers, and its dialect. Auregnais never served as a written language and no systematic study of it was ever made.

Le Maistre, F. 1982. *The Language of Auregny* (cassette with accompanying 19-page booklet). [St Helier] (Jersey) and [St Anne] (Alderney).

GLANVILLE PRICE

Altaic languages

The Altaic languages, which are spoken widely in Siberia and central Asia and as far west as Turkey, fall into three subgroups:

(1) the *Turkic languages, including in Europe *Turkish, *Azeri and several others;
(2) the Mongolian languages, represented in Europe only by *Kalmyk;
(3) the Tungusic or Manchu-Tungus languages, which are not represented in Europe.

The common origin of all three branches is not considered by all scholars to be definitely established (see *Turkic languages).

Andi (see under *Caucasian languages. IV. North-East Caucasian family*)

Anglo-French, see *Anglo-Norman*

Anglo-Norman

The variety of *French which, as a result of the Norman Conquest, was in use in the British Isles from 1066 until at least the end of the 15th c.

From its base in England, and above all in SE England, Anglo-Norman was subsequently re-exported by the Normans as they invaded Wales, Scotland and Ireland, from all of which countries substantial documentary evidence of its use survives. This British, rather than English, dimension of Anglo-Norman has been almost entirely overlooked. It was, however, assumed, by an earlier generation, that the implantation of Anglo-Norman led to a sustained period of generalized bilingualism, widespread in all social classes and all areas of England; the consensus now is that bilingualism must have been limited in time as well as socially, with only the upper classes (the colonizing Norman nobility) continuing to use French as a vernacular, and then only for a limited period after the Conquest; for the vast majority of the population, French would have been either completely unknown or at best an acquired foreign language. In this, the development of Anglo-Norman follows the well-attested pattern of immigrant languages. In the later Middle Ages the main function of Anglo-Norman was no longer as a spoken vernacular, but as a written, vehicular language. A further long-standing assumption, now also questioned by modern scholarship, is that, with the loss of Normandy in 1204, Anglo-Norman went into irreversible decline, becoming increasingly isolated from its French roots, and in due course decaying into what is still too often thought of as a *faus franceis d'Angleterre* ('false French of England'). In fact, it is clear that Anglo-Norman was not so isolated, indeed that it served throughout the later Middle Ages as the medium of international trade and diplomacy for the English; and, far from being a degenerate jargon, it was used for a wide range of documentary purposes, and was one of the major languages of record at all levels, local and national, in medieval Britain.

From an early date – earlier, indeed, than in France itself – Anglo-Norman imaginative literature flourished, its precocity most probably a direct consequence of the fact that, in the British Isles, vernaculars (***Germanic** or ***Celtic**) had long co-existed with Latin as languages of culture, religion and record. This literature, in which conventional enough saints' lives, epics and romances figure prominently, drew extensively on French culture, and the language of the texts is almost certainly a more central form of French than would have been the language of the Anglo-Normans themselves, of which, of course, the literary texts are at best a pale and distant reflection. By the middle of the 14th c. this imaginative literature had largely disappeared, giving way to a mass of (literally) more prosaic documents of an administrative type. These bear lengthy, although not often eloquent, testimony to the importance of later Anglo-Norman as a documentary language; and many, too, amply exemplify the contact between languages which must have characterized the daily life of the literate elite in medieval Britain and Ireland. It is to this constant interaction that modern English owes most of its substantial ***Romance** (i.e. Anglo-Norman) element. It is, too, in this material that the evidence is to be found for Anglo-Norman's capacity to evolve independently of continental French, and above all for the autonomous semantic extension of its lexis in ways unknown to French itself. This development (when it is not simply a consequence of language contact) arose principally because the language was called on to operate in a different society, and to deal with different practices; and it is the semantic autonomy of

Anglo-Norman which gives rise to the majority of so-called *faux amis* ('false friends') in modern English and French. These are words which look the same or similar but mean different things (e.g. English *trick*, French *tricher* 'to cheat'; English *actual*, French *actuel* 'current, present').

The appellation 'Anglo-Norman' has the drawback of implying both an identifiable, and a homogeneous, dialectal base for the French used in Britain. It is patently absurd to suggest that there was no dialectal or social variation among the soldiers and administrators who arrived with the Conqueror. Not all came from Normandy proper; they were not socially uniform, but (as even the Bayeux tapestry reveals) came from divergent social classes and backgrounds. In later periods, too, the directly Norman connection had undoubtedly been weakened, and continental French itself was, at least in written documents – our only concrete evidence – increasingly centralized and standardized. For these reasons some scholars have preferred the term 'Anglo-French'. It is in any case questionable whether and to what extent Anglo-Norman may legitimately be considered a separate entity from medieval French in general. The study of later documents which are ostensibly Anglo-Norman suggests less and less which is particularly Norman, and more and more evidence of the influence of the Paris chancery. In particular, international documents in Anglo-Norman (that is, emanating from the Anglo-Norman *regnum*) show little divergence from those produced on the Continent. On the other hand, there are any number of documents drawn up for purely local consumption, and in which interference from English or Welsh is visible on a massive scale. It is in these documents that the most striking, but not necessarily most typical, Anglo-Norman features (lexical and syntactic) are to be found. The pattern which emerges is one of diaphasic or contextual variation, with (at one extreme) high-level diplomatic correspondence couched in French indistinguishable from central Parisian, and (at the other end of the spectrum) strictly local documents drawn up by men with a limited and purely functional grasp of an essentially foreign language. Such variation is of course endemic to most languages, and there is no reason to suppose that it could have been absent from Anglo-Norman, whether on its arrival in England in 1066 or on its demise, several hundred years later.

Rothwell, W. 1991. The missing link in English etymology: Anglo-French. *Medium Aevum*, 60: 173–96.
—— 1994. The trilingual England of Geoffrey Chaucer. *Studies in the Age of Chaucer*, 16: 45–67.
—— et al. (eds) 1977–92. *Anglo-Norman Dictionary*. London.
Trotter, D. A. 1994. L'anglo-français au Pays de Galles: une enquête préliminaire. *Revue de linguistique romane*, 59: 461–88.

D. A. TROTTER

Anglo-Saxon (see under *English*)

Arabic

A **Semitic language* now spoken over much of the Middle East and throughout North Africa from Egypt to Morocco. Arabic can count as a European language by virtue (a) of the fact that the Arabs occupied extensive parts of southern Europe, in some cases for lengthy periods, during the Middle Ages, (b) of the existence of a long-standing Arabic-speaking community in Cyprus (see *Cypriot Arabic), and (c) of the recent settlement of large numbers of Arabic speakers in western Europe, particularly France (see *Community languages (France)).

Within less than 80 years of the death of Mohammed in AD 632, the Arabs or Saracens had taken control of northern Africa as far as Morocco. In 711 an army of Arabs and Berbers landed at Gibraltar and within seven years had subdued most of the Iberian Peninsula with the exception of a small area in the north. They crossed the Pyrenees in or about 718–720 and occupied much of southern France, reaching Poitiers where, in 732, they were defeated by a Frankish Christian army and were turned back. They remained in occupation of much of the south of the Gaul until 759 when they lost to the Franks their last stronghold north of the Pyrenees, Narbonne.

The Christian Reconquest of the Iberian Peninsula which began in Asturias in the 8th c. was to take over 700 years before it was complete. Meanwhile, extensive tracts of the Peninsula remained under Arab domination and the Kingdom of Granada, the last remaining Arab-held territory stretching from Gibraltar to about half-way between Almería and Cartagena, survived from 1275 to 1492.

Although Arabic was the language of administration and culture in the Arabic-dominated parts of Iberia, the *Romance speech of the area remained as a spoken vernacular (see *Mozarabic) but, not surprisingly, given the lengthy period of Arab rule, it absorbed some hundreds of Arabic words, numbers of which (quoted here first in their Spanish form) have come down into modern *Spanish, *Catalan and **Portuguese** (many of them retaining the Arabic definite article, *al*, either in the form *al-* or reduced to *a-*), e.g. *aceite* (Port. *azeite*) 'olive oil', *alcoba* (Cat., Port. *alcova*) 'bedroom', *aldea* (also Cat.; Port. *aldeia*) 'village', *algodón* (Port. *algodão*) 'cotton', *arroz* (also Port.; Cat. *arròs)* 'rice', *azul* (also Port.) 'blue', *berenjena* (Cat. *albergínia*, Port. *berinjela*) 'aubergine', *halagar* (Cat. *afalagar*) 'to flatter' (Port. *afagar* 'to stroke'), *tarea* (Port. *tarefa*) 'task', *taza* (Cat. *tassa*, Port. *taça*) 'cup', *zumo* (Port. *sumo*) 'fruit juice'.

Another important area of Saracen penetration into Europe was in the central Mediterranean. At various times from the 8th to the 10th centuries, there were raids on or short-term occupations of parts of Corsica, Sardinia and the Italian mainland, but, apart from Malta, where the *Maltese language (derived from Arabic) is well alive, the main sphere of Arab domination was Sicily which was invaded in 827 and remained largely or totally under Arab control until the island was conquered by the Normans (1031–91). It is for this reason that borrowings from Arabic are more wide-spread in Sicilian than in the dialects of mainland southern Italy, e.g. *abbraciu* 'coarse cloth', *burnia* 'earthenware jar', *dzágara* 'orange blossom', *fastuka* 'pistachio', *karkoccula* 'artichoke', *rábbatu* 'suburb'.

Agius, D. A. 1996. *Siculo Arabic*. London.
Corriente, F. 1992. *Árabe andalusí y lenguas románicas* ('Andalusian Arabic and Romance Languages').
    Madrid.

Kiesler, R. 1994. *Kleines vergleichendes Wörterbuch der Arabismen im Iberoromanischen und Italienischen* ('Short Comparative Dictionary of Arabisms in Ibero-Romance and Italian'). Tübingen.
Varvaro, A. 1981. La Sicilia musulmana. In Id., *Lingua e storia in Sicilia*, Palermo, vol. 1, 80–124.

GLANVILLE PRICE

Arabic, Cypriot, see *Cypriot Arabic*

Aragonese (see under *Spanish*)

Aramaic

Aramaic (also known as 'Chaldaic') is a north-west *Semitic language. It was spoken in many varieties and written in many scripts in the Near East in antiquity, where it was the lingua franca for centuries, starting in the 6th c. BC. Around that time, it began to replace *Hebrew as the vernacular language of the Jews. It was later to be the language of the first Christians, and was the language of Christ. Among the best-known varieties are Syriac, Mandaic and Nabataean.

Various forms of Jewish Aramaic were brought to Europe around a millennium ago and became rooted in both major European Jewish culture areas: Sefarad (in the Iberian Peninsula, and, after the expulsions of the 1490s, in Holland, Greece, Turkey and other exile centres), and Ashkenaz (in the Germanic-speaking lands of central Europe, later extending to the Slavonic and Baltic regions of eastern Europe).

The biblical narrative describing Abraham, the first Jew, as a migrant from Ur of the Chaldees who resettled in Canaan (Genesis 11.31) has undoubtedly contributed to the permanent mystique of Aramaic among Jews.

Aramaic is the language of many of the sacred texts which were brought to Europe from the Near East and were widely studied throughout European Jewish history. These include small sections of the Old Testament (in Daniel and Ezra), most of the Babylonian and Jerusalem Talmuds, much of the Kabbalah, and a number of prayers, including the kaddish prayer for the dead which is one of the most emotive in the Jewish canon.

Although not spoken, Aramaic (like Hebrew), was read, studied, recited and uttered in these various contexts. In addition, it has remained a vibrant and highly creative written language for select genres, capable of producing masterpieces. This is quite remarkable, bearing in mind that it was the more esoteric and much less well known of the two sacred languages, both of which participated in internal Jewish trilingualism with the Jewish vernacular language (Judezmo or *Judeo-Spanish in Sefarad, *Yiddish in Ashkenaz). In Yiddish, one of the names for Aramaic is *Targum-loshn* (literally 'translation language', the usage deriving from the Targum, the classic Aramaic translation of the Hebrew Bible), which is also used humorously in the sense of 'unintelligible language' (cf. 'it's Greek to me'). The usage illustrates the status of Aramaic as a language for the most learned members of the community.

Aramaic held pride of place in new works of Kabbalah or Jewish mysticism. In fact, the central work of kabbalistic literature, the *Zohar* ('Book of Splendour'), was apparently written in Spain in the late 13th c. (and attributed to an ancient mystic). Kabbalistic Aramaic boasts a wealth of terminology that cannot properly be translated into Western languages.

Aramaic was also the preferred language of Talmudic commentary. For example, the best-known Bible and Talmud commentator Rashi (1040–1105), born in France and active in Germany, wrote his commentary to the Bible in Hebrew, and to the Talmud in Aramaic. Aramaic treatises on Kabbalah and Talmud continue to be written to this day by rabbinic scholars in many countries, especially in traditional Hasidic communities.

Aramaic hymns (many of them kabbalistic) are popular as adjuncts to the canonical Sabbath prayers, and on various festivals throughout the year. The Haggadah, which is nearly all in Hebrew, is recited on the first two nights of the most beloved Jewish festival, Passover. It begins with an evocative Aramaic piece on the welcoming of poor guests, and ends with a happy Aramaic song, 'Chad gadyo' ('One Kid'), which first appears in Prague in the 16th c. Scholars believe it to be a translation from Yiddish, illustrating the multiplicity of interrelationships between Aramaic and the other Jewish languages of Europe.

Katz, D. 1985. Hebrew, Aramaic and the rise of Yiddish. In Fishman, J.A. (ed.), *Readings in the Sociology of Jewish Languages*, Leiden, 85–103.

DOVID KATZ

Arbëresh (Arbresh)

A term applied to the *Albanian-speaking communities in Greece and Italy and their language. See also *Arvanite.

Famiglietti, M. 1983. Le comunità italo-albanesi ('The Albanian-Italian communities'). In Freddi, G. (ed.), *L'Italia plurilingue*, Bergamo, 212–28.

Archi (see under *Caucasian languages. IV. North-East Caucasian family*)

Armenian

An *Indo-European language of the *satem* group which includes principally the *Indic, *Slavonic, *Baltic and *Iranian languages. The problem of the precise relationship of Armenian to other Indo-European dialects forms an important field of study both for Armenian and for Western linguists. Armenian is spoken in the Republic of Armenia and by communities in Iran as well as by substantial diaspora communities in the Middle East, Europe and America.

Origins

In his enumeration of the great army of the Persian king Xerxes (519–465 BC), the Greek historian Herodotus includes the Armenians who he informs us were 'Phrygian colonists'. This statement, coupled with the linguistic position of Armenian within the Indo-European family, suggests that the Armenians, like the Phrygians, emigrated from the Balkans into Asia Minor. More recently the real

'Urheimat' of the Proto-Indo-Europeans has been sought in Eastern Anatolia, south of the Caucasus, where modern Turkey, Iraq and Syria meet. This thesis directly affects the Armenians since, on this basis, they would no longer be considered immigrants into their historical homeland but rather would be indigenous to the area they currently inhabit. The name 'Armenia' (*Armeniya*, cf. Greek *Armenioi*, Latin *Armenii* 'Armenians') itself occurs in inscriptions as early as about 600 BC. Furthermore, the name *Hayasa*, found in Hittite records from the Late Bronze Age, recalls that of *Hay*, which was the name the Armenians gave to themselves, to this day calling their homeland *Hayastan* and their language *Hayeren*.

Alphabet

The Armenian alphabet (see fig.1), like the Gothic and the *Cyrillic, was created for religious and cultural purposes. Christian preaching reached Armenia towards the end of the 3rd c., from Caesarea in Cappadocia and Edessa (Urfa) in Mesopotamia. By 314, Christianity had become the state religion of the Armenians. The alphabet was invented in 406 by a learned cleric, Mesrop Maštoc', who created an alphabet of 36 letters which was original and distinctive and completely expressed the phonetic peculiarities of Armenian and has served the language through all stages of its history. Additional letters (the last two in fig. 1) were introduced to render the foreign sound [f] (11th c.) and the diphthong [aw] (12th c.) (later simplified to [o]). The distinctive features of the alphabet are (i) that it is written from left to right; (ii) that it is completely phonetically based: every sound has its own distinctive letter and each letter represents only one sound; and (iii) that each letter, whether written at the beginning, in the middle, or at the end of a word, has one invariable form.

The versatility of the Armenian alphabet is evidenced by the fact that in the corpus of Armenian manuscripts there is a large number of *Arabic, Syriac (see under *Assyrian), *Turkish, *Tatar and Kipchak (see under *Tatar) texts written in Armenian characters.

Early and medieval literature

Although Armenian historians never refer to literature written in the national language before the Mesropian period, some scholars have unreservedly accepted the existence of such a literature and of a cultivated language. There is extant from the 5th c. an extensive original, translated and interpretative literature which displays advanced grammatical forms and rich vocabulary and style. Neither the works of Eznik, Koriwn, Ełišē, Movsēs Xorenac'i, dating from this period, nor the translation of the Bible (AD 413) can be considered as characteristic of the elementary stages of a written language. If the beginnings of Armenian literature were really in the 5th c., it would not have been possible for the literary language to possess such a rich vocabulary, to express with extreme accuracy the niceties of the texts translated, or for the literature to commence on such a high thematic note. This classical idiom (*grabar* 'the written word') was the principal literary medium from the 5th to as late as the 19th c., although from the 12th c. onwards some works, including law-codes, fables and poetry, were written in a language (known as *Mijin hayeren* 'Middle Armenian')

Capital	Small	Transliteration	Phonetic value	Fig. 1 The Armenian
Ա	ա	a	[a]	*alphabet* The transliteration given is that of the Hübschmann–Meillet–Benveniste system (other systems also exist). The phonetic values given are those of eastern Armenian, with those of western Armenian in parentheses where they differ markedly from those of eastern Armenian. For the values of the characters of the International Phonetic Alphabet, see pp. xvi–xvii.
Բ	բ	b	[b(p)]	
Գ	գ	g	[g(k)]	
Դ	դ	d	[d(t)]	
Ե	ե	e	[ɛ, jɛ]	
Զ	զ	z	[z]	
Է	է	ē	[e]	
Ը	ը	ə	[ə]	
Թ	թ	t'	[tʰ]	
Ժ	ժ	ž	[ʒ]	
Ի	ի	i	[i]	
Լ	լ	l	[l]	
Խ	խ	x	[x]	
Ծ	ծ	c	[ts(dz)]	
Կ	կ	k	[k(g)]	
Հ	հ	h	[h]	
Ձ	ձ	j	[dz(ts)]	
Ղ	ղ	ł	[ɣ]	
Ճ	ճ	č	[tʃ(dʒ)]	
Մ	մ	m	[m]	
Յ	յ	y	[j]	
Ն	ն	n	[n]	
Շ	շ	š	[ʃ]	
Ո	ո	o	[o, vo]	
Չ	չ	č'	[tʃʰ]	
Պ	պ	p	[p(b)]	
Ջ	ջ	ǰ	[dʒ(tʃ)]	
Ռ	ռ	ṙ	[rr]	
Ս	ս	s	[s]	
Վ	վ	v	[v]	
Տ	տ	t	[t(d)]	
Ր	ր	r	[r]	
Ց	ց	c'	[tsʰ]	
ւ	ւ	w	[v, w]	
Փ	փ	p'	[pʰ]	
Ք	ք	k'	[kʰ]	
Օ	օ	ō	[o]	
Ֆ	ֆ	f	[f]	

that was closer to the spoken vernaculars (e.g. Nersēs Šnorhali (1102–73), Mxit'ar Goš (1140–1213), Vardan Arewelc'i (1200–71)).

The collapse of the Cilician Armenian kingdom in AD 1375, the division of Armenia between Persia and Turkey, and incessant emigration brought about the decline of Middle Armenian and its evolution into Modern Armenian. Factors such as the growth of national liberation movements, increasing trade and economic contacts between different parts of the country and with other peoples, the establishment of cultural centres in the Armenian dispersion, the development of printing in Armenian (Venice, 1512) and of a popular press (Madras, 1794), and the founding of the Mekhitharist Armenian Catholic Congregation in Venice (1717), hastened the need to forge a new literary language. Middle Armenian had gone out of use and Classical Armenian, though still used as the language of literature and the church, was quite incomprehensible to the majority of Armenians and so could not serve as a means of communication.

Modern Armenian

Academician Ĵahukyan suggests that the historical development of Modern Armenian falls into three periods: (a) Early *Ašxarhabar*, from the early 17th to the middle of the 19th c.; (b) two-branch *Ašxarhabar*, from the middle of the 19th c. to 1920; (c) contemporary Armenian, from the establishment of the Soviet Socialist Republic to the present day.

Hovhannēs Holov, in his Armenian grammar (Constantinople, 1674), distinguishes three 'Armenian' varieties, Classical, Colloquial (*vulgaris*) (by which he meant the dialects), and Civil (*civilis*) which represented a fusion of the other two. Modern Armenian began to develop on the basis of a splitting of Civil Armenian on two different dialectal bases (see below, 'Dialects'). The language of J. J. Schröder's *Thesaurus linguae armenicae* (Amsterdam, 1711), based on the Ararat dialect and *um*-branch dialects (see below), emerged as Eastern Armenian. Only 16 years later, in 1727, Mxit'ar Sebastac'i, in his introduction to the grammar of Armenian *ašxarhabar*, elaborated a modern form of Western Armenian on the basis of *ke*-branch dialects (see below).

Dialects

Though dialectal phonemes do not occur in 5th-c. Armenian, many dialectal features that are not attested in *grabar* (see above, 'Early and medieval literature') – diphthongization of [e], monophthongization of [aw] – can be shown to date from the very early period. The fall of the Cilician Armenian state in 1375 and the partition of Armenia between Persia and Turkey were the historical conditions for the decline of Middle Armenian, leading to the formation of dialects in the 15th and 16th centuries. Armenian linguists accept that the dialectal bases of literary two-branch *Ašxarhabar* ('Civil' or 'Secular' Armenian) are two of the great dialects. The dialectal basis of literary Eastern Armenian is the Ararat dialect, while that of literary Western Armenian is the Polis (Constantinople) dialect.

Armenian has over 60 dialects. These were classified by Arsēn Aytĕnian

(1825–1902) into four categories based on geographical-territorial distribution: (1) Van (SE Turkey), Mesopotamia, and adjacent regions; (2) Constantinople and Asia Minor; (3) Western Poland, Transylvania; (4) eastern provinces, Astrakhan, Persia, Russia, India. H. Ačaṙyan (1876–1953), in his *Classification des dialectes arméniens* (Paris, 1909), employing a stylistico-grammatical system, identifies three categories: (1) the *um*-branch, where the present tense is formed by the particle *um, am, im,* a characteristic of eastern dialects, those of Erevan, Tiflis, Agulis, Julfa, and later of literary Eastern Armenian; (2) the *kě/ku*-branch, where the present tense is formed by the particle *kě, ku, ge, ga, gi, go, gu,* and the perfect is formed by *ēr,* which are characteristic features of western dialects, those of Karin, Van, Tigranakert, Cilicia, Syria, Constantinople, the Crimea, and later of literary Western Armenian; (3) the *el*-branch, where adverbs ending in *-el, -il, -al* participate in the formation of the present tense, as in the dialects of Maraš, Khoy and Ardvin. The 100-feature system elaborated by G. Ĵahukyan is the most comprehensive for the study of Armenian dialects since its application gives a better idea of the relationship of the two literary variants of *Ašxarhabar* not only with *grabar,* Middle Armenian and the dialects, but also to each other.

The Armenian dispersion

The origins of the Armenian dispersion go back to the fall of the Bagratid kingdom in AD 1045. The first emigration from Armenia enabled Armenians to establish a new kingdom in Cilicia (1080–1375). From here, Armenians crossed the Black Sea to found colonies in the Crimea, Russia, Poland, Romania and Moldavia. The fall of Constantinople to the Ottoman Turks in 1453 was followed by a fresh carve-up of Armenia between Ottoman Turkey and Safavid Persia. In 1604, Shah Abbas the Great of Persia deported large numbers of Armenians, mostly from the plain of Ararat, to his capital at Isfahan. There they founded a colony at New Julfa and spread thence into India, Singapore, Java and Australia.

Armenian emigration into Europe began following the massacres of 1894. The Armenian population today numbers 386,000 in western Europe, some 1,610,000 in the USA, and around 40,000 in Canada.

Following the massacres and deportations of 1915, a sizeable Armenian diaspora was created in the Middle East. Some 60,000 Armenians remain in modern Turkey, mostly in Istanbul. The Armenian community in Iran provides the Iranians with an unbroken cultural link with their Aryan past. During the First World War 250,000 Armenians took refuge in Syria (which then included the Lebanon), Palestine, Egypt and Iraq. The Armenian community in Lebanon numbered 160,000 before the civil war of 1975.

Present situation

Eastern Armenian is now the official language of the Republic of Armenia (population 3,500,000) and is also used by the Armenian communities in Iran while the Western variety predominates in the diaspora in the Middle East, Europe and America. The bond between the Armenians in the homeland and the dispersion is the common linguistic identity forged by the use of *Ašxarhabar*, the focal point of 'ingathering' of the world's Armenians.

Andesian, S. and Hovanessian, M. 1988. L'arménien: langue rescapée d'un génocide. In Vermes, G. (ed.), *Vingt-cinq communautés linguistiques de la France*, Paris, vol. 2, 60–84.

Clackson, J. 1994. *The Linguistic Relationship between Armenian and Greek*. Oxford.

Diakonoff, I. M. 1984. *The Prehistory of the Armenian People*, translated from the Russian by L. Jennings with revisions by the author. New York.

Greppin, J. A. C. 1975. An overview of Armenian linguistics. *Journal of Armenian Studies*, 1: 54–64.

—— and Kachaturian, A. A. 1986. *A Handbook of Armenian Dialectology*. New York.

Jahukyan, G. 1964. *Hayoc' lezvi zargac'man p'ulerě* ('The Stages in the Development of the Armenian Language'). Erevan.

—— 1972. *Hay barbařagitut'yan neracut'yun* ('Introduction to Armenian Dialectology'). Erevan.

—— 1980. On the position of Armenian in the Indo-European languages. In Greppin, J. A. C. (ed.), *First International Conference on Armenian Linguistics Proceedings*, New York, 3–16.

—— 1987. *Hayoc' lezvi patmut'yun: naxagrayin žamanakašr'jan* ('A History of the Armenian Language: The Pre-written Stage'). Erevan.

Meillet, A. 1936. *Esquisse d'une grammaire comparée de l'arménien classique*. 2nd edn. Vienna.

VREJ NERSES NERSESSIAN

Aromanian

Aromanian, otherwise known as Macedo-Romanian or Vla(c)h, is a dialect of *Romanian but sometimes considered as a distinct language, spoken by scattered communities in Greece, Albania, Bulgaria, and parts of the former Yugoslavia, and by émigré communities in North and South America and Australia. Estimates of numbers of speakers vary from 300,000 to 600,000. The earliest text is an inscription of 1731 on an icon. We also have *inter alia* from the 18th c., and in the Greek alphabet, a Liturgy, a collection of religious translations, and some bilingual (with Greek) or multilingual glossaries; later writing (collections of folklore, some original texts, translations) is in the Latin alphabet; the principal poet is George Murnu (1868–1957).

Capidan, T. 1932. *Aromânii. Dialectul aromân* ('The Aromanians. The Aromanian dialect'). Bucharest.

Caragiu-Marioţeanu, M. 1972. La romanité sud-danubienne: l'aroumain et le mégléno-roumain. *La Linguistique*, 8: 105-22.

Kramer, J. 1989. Aromunisch. In Holtus, G., Metzeltin, M. and Schmitt, C. (eds), *Lexikon der Romanistischen Linguistik*, Tübingen, vol. 3, 423–35.

Saramandu, N. 1984. Aromână ('Aromanian'). In Rusu, V. (ed.), *Tratat de dialectologie românească* ('Treatise on Romanian Dialectology'), Craiova, 423–76.

GLANVILLE PRICE

Artificial languages

Artificial languages merit mention in this encyclopedia for the reason that, of the hundreds of schemes (most of them having only an ephemeral existence) for a 'universal language', 'auxiliary language' or 'international language' put forward from the mid-17th c. onwards, the few that have had more than strictly limited success all derive to some extent, particularly in respect of their vocabulary, from European natural languages.

The first such scheme that for a while seemed to have great promise was Volapük, launched by a German priest, Johann Martin Schleyer, in 1880. Though its morphology was totally invented, the grammatical categories (cases, tenses, moods, voices, etc.) with which it operated were typically *Indo-European. Its vocabulary was drawn largely from English with some contribution from German, French, Italian and Spanish, but the words were so drastically modified as to be frequently unrecognizable. Although Volapük met with considerable world-wide success in its initial stages, its popularity began to wane after about 20 years and by the outbreak of the First World War it was in a state of terminal decline.

The most celebrated and most successful artificial language, Esperanto, was the invention of Ludwig Zamenhof (1859–1917). Like Volapük, Esperanto is undeniably Indo-European-based, both in its lexicon which derives largely (and much more transparently so than in the case of Volapük) from Latin or *Romance roots, supplemented by others from such languages as English, German, Greek, Russian, and in the grammatical categories with which it operates.

After its first appearance in a booklet by Zamenhof published in Russian in 1887, Esperanto quickly made great headway in very many countries (the booklet was published in English in New York under the title *An Attempt towards an International Language* as early as 1889). It survived splits within the ranks of its supporters and two world wars and is now the only artificial language to enjoy a substantial measure of support. However, although it has been used as a working language at international conferences of one kind or another, it has never been adopted on a large scale as an auxiliary international language. Estimates of the number of speakers vary so wildly, ranging from some tens of thousands to several millions, as not to be worth quoting. As a written medium it has served effectively for a wide range of purposes (including literary translation and scientific articles) and books and pamphlets published in Esperanto can by now be numbered in their thousands. The 'governing body' of the Esperanto movement is the Universal Esperanto Association based in Amsterdam.

Among later proposals, including 40 or more derived directly or indirectly from Esperanto, we mention only the following:

(1) *Idiom Neutral* (1902), an offshoot of Volapük;
(2) *Latino sine flexione* ('Latin without inflection') (1904), devised by an Italian mathematician, Giuseppe Peano, who later renamed it 'Interlingua' (not to be confused with (6) below);
(3) *Ido*, a derivative of Esperanto launched in 1907 and still enjoying a limited measure of support;
(4) *Novial* (1928), the invention (but derived to some extent from Ido) of the Danish linguist Otto Jespersen;
(5) *Interglossa* (1943), proposed by the biologist Lancelot Hogben, as 'an attempt to apply semantic principles to language design'; Interglossa is a flexionless language whose vocabulary draws much more extensively than other schemes on Greek roots

that are internationally current in scientific and technical terminology; much modified by W. Ashby and R. Clark as *Glosa* (1981);

(6) *Interlingua*, a primarily Romance-based language launched in 1951 under the auspices of the International Auxiliary Language Association (founded 1924).

Cresswell, J. and Hartley, J. 1987. *[Teach Yourself] Esperanto*, revised by J. H. Sullivan. London.
Large, A. 1985. *The Artificial Language Movement*. Oxford.

GLANVILLE PRICE

Arvanite

A term applied to the **Albanian*-speaking communities of northern Greece and their language. Given the intolerant attitude of the Greek state towards all its linguistic minorities, Arvanite has no official status or other public recognition whatsoever. See also **Arbëresh*.

Aryan languages

An obsolete term that has been used as an equivalent both for **'Indo-European languages'* and for 'Indo-Iranian languages' and which should therefore (and quite apart from its possible associations with the misuse of the term 'Aryan' in Nazi Germany) be avoided.

Assyrian

The Assyrians (also known as Syrians and, disparagingly in Tsarist Russia, as Ayssorians) refer to themselves as Aturai, Surai, or Kaldai (? = 'Chaldeans'). They are descended from the Aramaeans (see **Aramaic*) and speak a **Semitic language* which derives from the dialect of classical Aramaic universally known as Syriac but which has developed markedly from other languages of the family (having developed vowel-harmony, conjugated tense-mood paradigms and a wide use of analytic forms). Over one million speakers are spread over Iran, Iraq, Syria, Turkey, the former USSR and the USA. At the time of the last Soviet Census (1989) there were 26,289 living in the Soviet Union, of whom 6,183 lived in Armenia and 5,286 in Georgia. In Georgia alone, where the language was actually taught for a time, at least during the Soviet period, no fewer than five dialects are attested, including that of Urmia which became the basis of the literary language formed in the 1840s. The Assyrians are Christians (Jacobite, Nestorian, Catholic, Orthodox).

B. GEORGE HEWITT

Asturian (see under *Spanish*)

Auregnais, see *Alderney French*

Avar (see under *Caucasian languages. IV. North-East Caucasian family*)

Azerbaijani, see *Azeri*

Azeri

A member of the Oghuz (south-western) group of *Turkic languages, spoken by 83% of the population of 7 million of the Republic of Azerbaijan. In Iran, it is the spoken language of the province of East Azerbaijan and most of the provinces of West Azerbaijan and Zanjan.

Designations

In pre-modern works in Azeri, the language is referred to as 'Turkish' (*turki*). In the late 19th c., to distinguish it from Ottoman *Turkish, it was called 'Azeri' or 'Azerbaijani Turkish'. In some Russian sources it was referred as the language or dialect of the Caucasian Tatars. In the mid-1930s the name was changed by the Soviet regime (the Azerbaijani Soviet Socialist Republic) to 'Azerbaijani', to avoid the designations 'Turk' and 'Turkish' for the people and language.

Early texts and the period up to the eighteenth century

The earliest Azeri texts date from the 14th c.; their language is that of contemporary Anatolian Turkish (Old Ottoman) texts. In the 15th and 16th centuries, as a result of political and cultural polarization, Azeri underwent the influence of Central Asian Turkic literary works, grammatically, lexically, and to some extent orthographically. These are the main characteristics that mark off the Azeri of this period from the unitary literary language that was by then current in the Ottoman domain. It was in the course of the 17th and 18th centuries that Azeri became uniform by shedding the parallel grammatical and lexical forms current in the previous two centuries.

Nineteenth and twentieth centuries

After the submission of Northern Azerbaijan to Russian rule, as a consequence of the treaties of 1813 and 1828 which established the Russo-Persian border, the country underwent radical cultural and social changes. The appearance of M. F. Akhundov's plays (1850 onwards) and Zardabi's weekly *Ekinchi* (the first Azerbaijani newspaper, established in 1870), based on vernacular usage, laid the foundations of modern Azeri literary prose. However, besides this relatively simple idiom there existed a contrasting tendency making use of Ottoman Turkish as a literary language. A section of Azeri authors chose to write in the elaborate Ottoman which was adopted by the literary journal *Fuyuzat* but which was far beyond the comprehension even of most educated Azerbaijanis.

It must be noted that until the 19th c. Azerbaijan was essentially part of Persia and literate Azerbaijanis were bilingual in Azeri and Persian. Their literary production consisted predominantly of poetry – prose works, in the form of translations of Persian religious and hagiographic texts, were comparatively few. The poetry of the period consists on the one hand of classical poetry (lyrical and narrative) in quantitative metre, modelled on Persian poetic works, and, on the other hand, of indigenous Turkic stanzaic verses in syllabic metre in a simpler language destined for and enjoyed by the majority of the people.

The contemporary uniform written language is based on that of cultured men of letters working and writing in the capital, Baku, who adopted supradialectal norms and eschewed the Ottomanisms of the late 19th and early 20th centuries.

Scripts

Until 1929, Azeri was written in the Arabic-Persian script. A modified Latin script was in use between 1929 and 1939 but in 1940 a form of the *Cyrillic alphabet was introduced; this underwent a number of changes leading to the acceptance of a much more satisfactory form in 1958. After the collapse of the Soviet Union the Latin-based alphabet was introduced, largely as a symbol of newly established national independence.

Dialects

In Azerbaijan itself, Azeri dialects and subdialects fall into four geographical groups: (i) an eastern group (dialects of Kuba, Baku and Shemakha, and the subdialects of Mughan and Lenkoran); (ii) a western group (dialects of Kazakh, Karabagh, and Ganja, and the Ayrum subdialect); (iii) a northern group (the Nukha dialect and the Zakatala–Kakh subdialect); and (iv) a southern group (dialects of Nakhichevan and Ordubad). These dialects, although mutually intelligible, differ from one another and from the literary (standard) language in a number of phonetic and grammatical features.

Foreign influences

Like the languages of all Islamic Turkic peoples, Azeri has a significant proportion of *Arabic and Persian words (it was almost always through Persian that Arabic words entered these languages), and numerous Persian calques. In both written and spoken Azeri, Arabic coordinating conjunctions and plural endings and Persian conjunctions (notably the subordinating conjunction *ki* 'that'), adverbs and particles are frequent. Azeri has also received a number of Mongolian words via Central Asian Turkic. From the beginning of the 19th c., as a result of direct contact with Russia, a large number of words from Russian and other European languages, particularly technical terms, found their way into Azeri in their Russian forms, a process that was intensified under Soviet rule.

Present situation

After the dissolution of the Transcaucasian Federation (1922–36), modern Azeri became the official language of the Azerbaijani Soviet Socialist Republic and, during the Soviet period, was used alongside Russian for all functions (i.e. in the legal system, education, the mass media and public life in general). It is now the sole official language of the Republic of Azerbaijan.

Before 1917, Azeri was the lingua franca of the whole of Transcaucasia (except for some parts of Georgia) and of south Daghestan. Between 1923 and 1928, Azeri replaced Arabic as the school language in Daghestan.

In Persia, except in Persian Azerbaijan for a short period during the rule of the Democratic Party (1945–6), Azeri has never enjoyed official status and, during most of the Pahlavi period (1924–79), its use in a written form was actively discouraged and, indeed, banned. After the establishment of the Islamic Republic of Iran in 1979, the new Constitution brought some relaxation with regard to its use in the press and on the radio, but it has not become the language of instruction at any level of education.

Azizbekov, Kh. A. 1969. *Азербайджанско–русский словарь* ('Azerbaijani–Russian Dictionary'). Baku.

Caferoğlu, A. and Doerfer, G. 1959. Das Aserbeidschanische ('Azerbaijani'). In Deny, J. et al. (eds), *Philologiae Turcicae Fundamenta*, Wiesbaden, vol. 1, 289–307.

Hajiyev, T. 1976–87. *Azärbayjan ädäbi dili tarikhi* ('A History of the Literary Language of Azerbaijan'), 2 vols. Baku.

TOURKHAN GANDJEÏ

B

Bable
A term widely used with reference to the Asturian dialect of *Spanish.

Bačka (see under *Ruthenian*)

Bagvalal (see under *Caucasian languages. IV. North-East Caucasian family*)

Balkar (see under *Karachay-Balkar*)

Baltic languages
A branch of the *Indo-European languages, with two subgroups, eastern and western. *Latvian and *Lithuanian belong to the eastern subgroup, together with the extinct languages or dialects *Curonian, *Selian and *Zemgalian, while western Baltic is represented by extinct Old *Prussian and perhaps by extinct *Yatvingian.

Baltic-Finnic languages
A subdivision of the *Finno-Ugrian branch of the *Uralic languages, including *Estonian, *Finnish, *Ingrian, *Karelian, *Livonian, *Veps and *Votic, all of them spoken around the Gulf of Finland. Ludian and Olonets, which have sometimes been taken as individual languages, are here counted as Karelian dialects. It is likely that *Sámi also belongs to this group although its origin is uncertain. Finnish, Ingrian and Karelian constitute a northern Baltic-Finnic group, with Veps clearly an offspring of Karelian. Livonian is closely related to Estonian and together they form

the southern group. Votic forms a link between the northern and the southern languages.

Laanest, A. 1982. *Einführung in die ostseefinnischen Sprachen* ('Introduction to the Baltic-Finnic Languages'). Hamburg.
Viitso, T. -R. 1985. Kriterien zur Klassifizierung der Dialekte der ostseefinnischen Sprachen ('Criteria for the classification of the Baltic-Finnic languages'). In Veenker, W. (ed.) *Dialectologia Uralica: Materialien des ersten internationalen Symposions zur Dialektologie der uralischen Sprachen*, Wiesbaden, 89–97.

WOLFGANG GRELLER

Bambara (see under *Community languages (France)*)

Bashkir

A member of the Volga-Kama group of the Kipchak or NW *Turkic languages, its closest relative being the *Tatar language of Kazan. Bashkir is spoken mainly in the Bashkir Republic (capital, Ufa) (Russian Federation), on the western bank of the Ural river where it changes direction to the west. Some 32% of the Bashkirs live in adjacent districts outside the Republic. Of the 1.5 million speakers in 1989, some 72% gave Bashkir as their mother-tongue or first language. No dialectal survey of Bashkir has yet been undertaken but, especially in its eastern dialects, it has undergone strong phonetic influences from *Kazakh.

Only since 1920 has Bashkir been a written language. Earlier poets and novelists used the Tatar language or, before that, *Chaghatay, an Islamic literary language used by the Turkic peoples of European Russia from the 15th to the 19th c. It has been suggested that national differences between Bashkirs and Tatars were created artificially for political reasons in order to undermine a Volga Muslim unity, since the Bashkir language, except for minor phonetic differences, is virtually indistinguishable from Tatar. For the emerging Bashkir literary language, the Latin alphabet was used from 1929 until 1939, when it was replaced by an adaptation of the *Cyrillic alphabet. Among Bashkir writers are M. Osmani, Sa'id Myras and T. Yabani. In their novels, dramas and poems, Bashkir writers deal with heroic and nostalgic themes from the Bashkir past.

Battal-Taymas, A. 1963. Die Literatur der Baschkiren. In *Handbuch der Orientalistik*, vol. 5, *Turkologie*, Leiden–Cologne, 439–41.
Benzing, J. 1959. Das Baschkirische. In Deny, J. et al. (eds), *Philologiae Turcicae Fundamenta*, Wiesbaden, 421–34.

WOLFGANG GRELLER

Basic English

Basic English, an auxiliary language designed between 1926 and 1930 by C. K. Ogden (1889–1957), differs from *artificial languages in that it represents a lexically and, to some extent, syntactically simplified form of a natural language, *English. 'Basic', in this context, not only bears its conventional meaning but was used by Ogden as an acronym for 'British American Scientific International Commercial'.

Basic English has a core vocabulary of 850 words, to which are to be added numerals and the names of the days of the week and the months and a limited number of 'international words' (*coffee, hotel, radio, sport, university*, etc.). This list can be supplemented by lists of technical terms for special purposes (scientific discourse, biblical translation, etc.).

Basic English attracted widespread attention after Ogden published his first book on the language in 1930 and even more so after Winston Churchill took a keen interest in it and in 1943 had a committee set up to explore its possibilities as a future international language. While undoubtedly proving relatively easy to understand, Basic English suffered from the great disadvantage that, with its limited vocabulary, the active use of it involved a great deal of often inadequate or cumbersome paraphrase ('to buy', for example, could be rendered by 'to give money for'). Interest in the language has declined considerably since the 1960s and it is probably now of little more than historical significance.

Ogden, C. K. 1930. *Basic English*. London.
——— 1932. *The ABC of Basic English*. London.
McArthur, T. 1992. Basic English. In Id. (ed.), *The Oxford Companion to the English Language*, Oxford, 107–9.
Richards, I. A. 1943. *Basic English and Its Uses*. London.

GLANVILLE PRICE

Basque

Basque (*euskara*) is a non-*Indo-European language of uncertain origin. Various hypotheses have been put forward regarding its relationship with other language groups. Whilst some scholars concentrate on Basque's relation to *Iberian in pre-Roman Spain and see also a link with North African languages (Berber and Eastern Hamitic languages), others highlight certain similarities between Basque and *Caucasian languages. No hypothesis has been substantiated with conclusive evidence. Today the language is spoken, with varying degrees of intensity, in Euskal Herria, an area straddling the Pyrenees and comprising seven provinces, three of which (Soule, Labourd and Basse-Navarre) constitute the French Basque Country (Iparralde); the Basque Autonomous Community (Euskadi – provinces of Alava, Guipúzcoa and Vizcaya) and the Autonomous Community of Navarre constitute the Spanish Basque Country (Hegoalde).

Earliest attestations

The earliest written record of the language is found in an 11th-c. charter recording the donating of the monastery of Ollazabal (Guipúzcoa) by García Azenáriz and his wife to San Juan de la Peña (Collins 1990: 194–5); the charter includes Latin formulae, but details of the boundaries are given in Basque. Some traces of Basque are to be found in the *Glosas Emilianenses* of the monastery of San Millán de la Cogolla (probably 11th c.), and a 12th-c. pilgrims' guide to Santiago de Compostela, attributed to Aimeric Picaud, includes a small Basque vocabulary. The first work written entirely in Basque, *Linguae Vasconum Primitiae*, a collection of poetry by the priest Mosén Bernart Dechepare, was published in Bordeaux in 1545.

Emergence of a literary standard

The main Basque literary dialects (*guipuzcoano*, *vizcaíno* and *labortano*) (see below, 'Dialects') had already undergone some degree of standardization before the establishing of one unified dialect became one of the prime preoccupations of *Euskaltzaindia* (Academy of the Basque Language, founded 1919). Following heated debate concerning the most suitable path to standardization, the foundations for *euskara batua* were laid in 1968; this official standard norm bears the closest resemblance to *guipuzcoano*, although some features of *labortano* are also to be detected. The establishing of the norm and the promotion of its use have led to some animated discussion, not least amongst speakers of *vizcaíno*, who feel that their dialect has been overlooked. *Euskara batua*, or *batua*, represents an attempt to eliminate dialectal variants and streamline, amongst other features, the complex verbal system, at the same time as expanding the parameters of the language to accommodate new lexical items and new concepts associated with the spheres from which Basque was excluded before achieving the status of co-official language.

Importance as a literary medium

Basque possesses a rich popular literature, primarily oral, which includes a number of legends featuring mythical and fantastical creatures. A significant place is occupied by verse and, with it, music (elegies; erotic, burlesque and satirical songs). The *bersolari*, excelling in the art of improvising verses on a range of topics (religious, profane, political), still occupies a prominent position in popular culture. Dechepare's *Linguae Vasconum Primitiae*, written in the *labortano* dialect (on dialects, see below, 'Dialects'), marked the beginning of a written literary tradition in Basque, which has been somewhat limited in output and, up to the 19th c., mostly confined to religious topics. Characteristics of the *labortano* dialect, together with elements of the *suletino* dialect, also feature in the translation of the New Testament and Calvinist catechism by Joanes de Leizarraga (d. *c*.1600). *Suletino*, which flourished in the field of popular theatre, did not enjoy the same influence in written literature, and works in the dialect received a modest reception. Manuel de Larramendi secured considerable prestige for *guipuzcoano* in the 18th c., although his main works were written in Castilian (*El imposible vencido*, 1729 – the first Basque grammar; and *Diccionario Trilingüe del Castellano, Bascuence y Latín*, 1745). Writers in *guipuzcoano* include Father Agustín Cardaberaz (1703–70) and Father Sebastián Mendiburu (1708–82), both authors of religious works. Juan Ignacio de Iztueta (1767–1845), known for his secular writing, provides in *Guipuzcoaco dantza gogoangarrien condaira* (1824) a description of the dances and geography of Guipúzcoa. The literary tradition of *vizcaíno* was consolidated towards the end of the 18th c. and the beginning of the 19th c. with the work of Juan Antonio Moguel y Urquiza (1745–1804) and Pedro Antonio de Añibarro (1748–1830). Moguel, primarily an author of sacred works, gives in *Peru Abarka* (not published until 1881) a description of rural life in Vizcaya in the last years of the 18th c. Towards the end of the 19th c. and the beginning of the 20th c., literary production began to cover a wider spectrum (including the translation into Basque of non-religious works). A leading figure of this period is Resurrección María de Azkue (1864–1951), founder of the literary journals *Euskalzale* and *Ibaizabal*, and author of several linguistic studies of Basque (also first director of the Basque Language Academy and proponent of *Gipuzkera Osotua*, a Basque standard norm based on *guipuzcoano*). Literary production, hampered in the years following the Civil War of 1936–9, was subsequently revived by writers of lyric poems, including Salvador Michelena and Jaime de Querexeta. Children's literature and pedagogical material now represent an expanding field.

Geographical spread and recession

It is generally accepted that the territories where Basque is currently spoken (see map 19) represent a small proportion of the area where the language was once used. Toponomy provides the clearest evidence of Basque presence over a wide expanse of the Iberian Peninsula before Romanization. It has been suggested (Tovar 1959: 93) that some 3,000 years ago Basque, or a language very similar to it, was spoken as far west as the valleys of Santander and Asturias. The northern frontier of the Basque-speaking territory has remained fixed at Bayonne since the 12th c. The disappearance of Basque from the Central Pyrenees and the plains of Navarre seems to have been brought about by Romanization; considerable Latin influence can be detected in the lexicon (*abere* 'animal' < *habere; errota* 'mill' < *rota; errege* 'king' < *rege; atxeter* 'doctor' < *archiater*). The fragmentation of the Roman Empire from the 3rd c. is considered by some to have contributed to the preservation of Basque: the absence of large towns gave Latin little opportunity to flourish, and Basque even experienced some expansion. The spread of Basque in La Rioja, Burgos and Soria has been interpreted (Lapesa 1986: 31–2) as a result of repopulation by Basque-speakers between the 9th and 11th centuries. From the 11th c. the language lost its hold in the southern plains exposed to Moorish attack (although in the 13th c. it was spoken in the valley of Ojacastro, Logroño), and the expansion of Basque-speaking territories in the mid- and late Middle Ages was short-lived. The pilgrim routes to Santiago de Compostela increased exposure to foreign influences; Basque was displaced by Latin, and subsequently by *Romance. As the latter became the favoured language in ecclesiastical contexts and amongst the nobility, Basque came to be associated with the peasantry; the second half of the 18th c. saw considerable erosion in Alava, and to a lesser degree in Navarre. In the coastal provinces, the only areas of bilingualism were the major towns of Bilbao, San Sebastián and Bayonne, although industrialization and improved communications soon brought Castilian to smaller communities. Since the mid-1980s there has been an attempt to revive, maintain and propagate the language in the Spanish Basque provinces and to implement the linguistic normalization laws in force since the early 1980s.

Dialects

Several attempts have been made to classify the numerous dialects, subdialects and local varieties of Basque, and opinions differ regarding their number. The culmination of Louis-Lucien Bonaparte's research, carried out during five trips through various parts of Euskal Herria between 1856 and 1869, was the dialectological map, *Carte des Sept Provinces Basques montrant la délimitation actuelle de l'Euskara et sa division en dialectes, sous-dialectes et variétés* (1863; published London 1866). Here he refers to three dialectal groups: *vizcaíno* (Group 1); *guipuzcoano, labortano, alto-navarro septentrional, alto-navarro meridional* (Group 2); *suletino, bajo-navarro oriental, bajo-navarro occidental* (Group 3), 25 subdialects and 50 varieties. Subsequent modifications and reappraisals have led to the redefining of certain varieties as separate dialects and to the regrouping of others.

Present vitality

Official Census figures for 1991 record the following numbers of speakers aged two years and above claiming fluency in Basque: Basque Autonomous Community: 543,617 (26,28%); Navarre: 52,023 (10.34%). No official census figures are available for Basque-speakers in France; estimates based on the results of one sociolinguistic survey carried out in 1991 amongst speakers aged 16 years and above (Intxausti 1992: 30) would suggest a total of 85,302 speakers (34.22%). According to information relating to the late 1950s/early 1960s, Basque-speakers in the Americas totalled 125,000.

Official status

The legal status of Basque varies considerably between territories. In the Basque Autonomous Community, Basque has had co-official status alongside Castilian (i.e. Spanish) since the approval of the Statute of Autonomy of 1979. The Law of Linguistic Normalization of 1982 consolidates Basque's position as co-official language in education, administration and the media. Provisions in the education system range from the teaching of Basque as a second language in an otherwise Castilian-medium school to the teaching of Basque and the use of the language as a medium for the teaching of other subjects. Every citizen is guaranteed the right to use either language when dealing verbally or in writing with public bodies. There is one Basque television channel broadcasting exclusively in Basque (ETB1), and one public (national) radio station (Euskadi Irratia) that broadcasts exclusively in Basque. A number of private radio stations use varying amounts of Basque. One daily newspaper, *Euskaldunon Egunkaria* (est. 1990), is currently available. In Navarre, the Ley de Reintegración y Amejoramiento del Régimen Foral of 1982 declares that Castilian is the official language of the Community, although Basque enjoys co-official status in the Basque-speaking areas. In the French state, no official recognition is given to Basque, and use of the language relies on the initiative of local individuals or associations.

Aulestia, G. 1989. *Basque–English Dictionary*. Reno, NV.
—— and White, L. 1990. *English–Basque Dictionary*. Reno, NV.

Collins, R. 1990. *The Basques*, 2nd edn. Oxford.

Euskaltzaindia (Academy of the Basque Language) 1977. *El libro blanco del euskera*. Madrid.

Intxausti, J. 1992. *Euskera, la lengua de los vascos* ('Basque, the Language of the Basques'). San Sebastián.

King, A. R. 1994. *The Basque Language: A Practical Introduction*. Reno, NV.

Lapesa, R. 1986. *Historia de la lengua española*, 9th edn. Madrid.

Michelena, L. 1988. *Historia de la literatura vasca*. San Sebastián.

Tovar, A. 1959. *El euskera y sus parientes* ('Basque and Its Relations'). Madrid.

Trask, R. L. 1997. *The History of Basque*. London.

Zubiri, I. 1994. *Gramática didáctica del euskera*. Bilbao.

CATRIN REDKNAP

Basque–Icelandic pidgin

The existence of a basically ***Basque–*Icelandic *pidgin**, but which also incorporates English, ***Romance** and other (possibly Dutch) elements, is revealed by a few sentences included in one of three 17th-c. Basque–Icelandic word-lists. It was used in contacts between Basque whalers in Icelandic waters and Icelanders.

Bakker, P. 1987. A. Basque nautical pidgin. *Journal of Pidgin and Creole Languages*, 2: 1–30.

Bats(bi) (see under *Caucasian languages. III. North Central Caucasian family*)

Belarusian

Formerly known as B(y)elorussian, White Russian or White Ruthenian, Belarusian (the preferred spelling since Belarus declared independence in 1991) belongs to the eastern branch of the ***Slavonic languages**. It is an official language of Belarus.

Origins and dialects

The Slavonic dialects that formed the basis of what was to become Belarusian were spoken by tribes known to early chroniclers as the Dregovichi, Radimichi and Krivichi, who began to settle in the area bounded by the rivers Pripiat' in the south (flowing west to east, eventually joining the Dnepr), Dvina in the north (flowing east to west into the Baltic), and the Dnepr itself in the west (flowing roughly north–south towards the Black Sea). Linguistic and archaeological evidence attests to the presence of a small ***Baltic**-speaking population already living in the region. Some linguists explain certain dialect features, especially in the north-west of Belarus, as the result of absorption by the Slavs of these Balts. This process is still continuing: there are pockets of ***Lithuanian** speech inside Belarus, and Belarusian long ago established itself within the frontiers of modern Lithuania. The Belarusian dialects of today range from the north-eastern group to the south-western; the dialects of the centre are usually said to form the basis of the modern literary language. One special dialect, in the extreme south-western Palessie region (the marshlands of the river Pripiat'), shares certain features with ***Ukrainian**. There have been sporadic attempts since the late 1980s to raise it to the status of a literary language called 'Polissian' – it has been used in a few issues of a newspaper called *Zbudinne* ('Awakening').

Early history and the medieval period

The most powerful city in early medieval Belarus was Polatsk; by the 11th c. it exerted control over the river Dvina as far as the Baltic. The population expansion into the predominantly Lettish region undoubtedly formed the basis of the Belarusian presence in present-day Latvia. Unfortunately the early historical chronicles of Polatsk were, it is believed, destroyed in a fire in the 18th c.

The earliest surviving text that clearly exhibits features of Belarusian is the 1229 treaty between Mstislav Davidovich of Smolensk (now in Russia, but certainly founded by the Krivichi), Riga and Gotland. By the 15th c. we find increasing use being made of what can only be described as an early form of Belarusian and Ukrainian – which some scholars prefer to call Ruthenian – as the official language of administration of the Grand Duchy of Lithuania. Although without doubt the Grand Duchy was ruled by Lithuanian-speakers (in the modern sense) in the initial period after it was created in the middle of the 13th c., its expansion by a mixed process of dynastic marriages and conquest soon led to its becoming a predominantly Slav state.

The post-medieval period

This written language attained its greatest period in the 16th c., when it was used by Francis Skaryna (*c.*1485–*c.*1551) as the basis of his translations of many books of the Bible (published in Prague and Vilnius (Belorusian, Vilnia; Polish, Wilno)) and, more particularly, his discursive prefaces to each book. This form of Belarusian was used for the intense religious polemics of the time, as well as for the three versions of the law codes of the Grand Duchy of Lithuania (1529, 1566, 1588). *Polish influence, in grammar as well as lexis, is particularly noticeable after the 1569 Union of Lublin. In 1696 Polish was declared the sole language for the administration of the Polish–Lithuanian Commonwealth. The educated classes of society turned to Polish language and Polish Catholic culture. Belarusian disappeared almost totally from literary usage, except for comic effect in the works of certain Polish playwrights.

The revival of the language in the 19th c. is in some respects due to the partitions of the Polish Commonwealth. All the Belarusian lands now formed part of the Russian Empire. Both Russian and Polish scholars, for primarily political reasons, began to investigate the mainly peasant population of the newly acquired lands, with the aim of demonstrating that the people there were 'Russian' or 'Polish'. In the course of these investigations a wealth of folklore was revealed, and the existence of a clearly separate language demonstrated. The most important works of this period are the dictionary of Ivan Nosovich (1788–1877) and the studies of Belarusian language and literature by Efim Karskii (1861–1931). Individual writers began to use Belarusian as a literary means of expression – including a parody of the *Aeneid*, called *Taras na Parnasie* ('Taras on Parnassus'), but as yet without any attempt to formulate a single system of spelling and grammar.

Scripts

Until the 17th c. the only script used for Belarusian was ***Cyrillic**. The Latin script
was introduced in the 19th c. in a modified form of Polish orthography. The first
newspaper in the language, *Nasha Niva* ('Our Cornfield'), which began to appear in
1906, was published for several years in two versions, Latin script and Cyrillic script,
reflecting the division of Belarusians into Catholics and Orthodox. Occasional use of
the Arabic script was made by Belarusian Tatars for glosses on the Koran. The only
script in official use in the Soviet period and now in independent Belarus is the
Cyrillic. The Latin script continued to be used by Belarusian Catholics in Poland
between the wars and in the post-1945 emigration.

The twentieth century

The first grammars of Belarusian, by the linguist Branislau Tarashkevich and the
German Slavist Rudolf Abicht, came out in 1918. Tarashkevich consciously chose
his recommended literary norms from a variety of dialects, with the aim of producing
a literary language that was distinct from Polish and Russian. His grammar set the
standard both for the official language of the Byelorussian Soviet Socialist Republic
(BSSR) in the 1920s, and for the large number of Belarusians in eastern Poland. The
first bilingual dictionaries appeared in this period, and terminological commissions
were given the task of drawing up word-lists necessary for using Belarusian in all
areas of state administration, including the armed forces, and science.

The emergence of Belarusian as a fully fledged language used in all areas of human
activity came to an abrupt halt with the onset of Stalinism at the beginning of the
1930s. The grammar and spelling norms of the Tarashkevich grammar were altered
by decree in 1933 to bring them closer to Russian. Active use of Belarusian was likely
to attract accusations of 'bourgeois nationalism' and the inevitable consequences.

After 1945 the pace of Russification quickened, so that by the 1970s there were
almost no schools, and certainly no higher educational establishments, in which
classes were conducted in Belarusian. Parents were given the right to withdraw their
children from what were supposed to be compulsory Belarusian language classes, and
apparently made abundant use of that right. The Byelorussian Soviet Socialist
Republic was virtually the only 'national' (i.e. non-Russian) republic in the USSR in
which such a situation had been allowed to arise. Literary Belarusian was confined
almost exclusively to literature, linguistics and, to an extent clearly prescribed by the
authorities, history. No use was made of it in any area of state administration.

The post-war years saw the emergence of active Belarusian communities in the
USA, Canada and western Europe. Belarusians in eastern Poland were given permission to organize cultural institutions in 1956. The only department of Belarusian
language and literature anywhere in the world outside the BSSR itself was established in the same year in Warsaw University.

The years of *perabudova* 'reconstruction' that began in 1985 saw the beginning of
protest against the neglected status of Belarusian in the Republic where Belarusians
were supposedly in the majority. Belarusians in Lithuania and Latvia also became

more active. This process culminated in the Byelorussian Soviet Socialist Republic with the formation of a Belarusian Language Society and the passing, on 26 January 1990, of a law on languages. Article 2 of this law made Belarusian the sole official language. A decree of the Supreme Soviet, passed on the same day, provided three years for Belarusian to become the language of science, the mass media, signboards, names of organizations, place-names and personal names, three to five years for all civil servants to acquire a knowledge of the language, five years for it to become the language of the service sector and pre-school facilities, and ten years for it to become the sole means of communication in law and all forms of education.

A certain amount of progress was made in the years that the law was in operation. The publication of a wide range of specialist dictionaries and encyclopedias gave the lie to those who maintain that Belarusian is a 'peasant dialect' unsuited for scholarly uses. However, all the advances are now being undone as a result of the referendum held on 14 May 1995, in which 53.5% of the electorate voted to give Russian equal status with Belarusian. Formal equality is likely to lead to the disappearance of Belarusian. It is not necessary to look far to find the reason. The oft-quoted figure from the census returns of 1979, viz. that 85.5% of Belarusians in the BSSR regard Belarusian as their native language, is in fact misleading. It implies strength, whereas in fact there is weakness. Very few of those Belarusians would be able to draw a precise distinction between Belarusian and Russian. The Belarusian that they claim as their native language is likely to be for domestic use only, and not in its standard literary form. Literary Belarusian is now mainly used as the means of communication of nationally conscious urban intellectuals. Belarusian, unlike *Slovak for example, has probably arrived too late on the scene to be promoted to the ranks of 'high-culture' languages.

Dingley, J. 1989a. Ukrainian and Belorussian – a testing ground. In Kirkwood, M. (ed.), *Language Planning in the Soviet Union*, Basingstoke, 174–88.
—— 1989b. The Byelorussian language – creation and reform. In Fodor, I. and Hagege, C. (eds), *Language Reform. History and Future*, Hamburg, vol. 4, 141–61.
Mayo, P. 1976. *A Grammar of Byelorussian*. Sheffield.
—— 1993. Belorussian. In Comrie, B. and Corbett, G. G. (eds), *The Slavonic Languages*, London and New York, 887–946.
Pashkievich, V. 1974–8. *Fundamental Byelorussian*, 2 vols. Toronto.

JIM DINGLEY

Belgium

Belgium has three official languages, **Dutch**, **French** and **German**, and four officially designated linguistic areas, as follows (see map 1):

(1) in the northern part of the country, Flanders, the official language is Dutch;
(2) in most of the southern part, Wallonia, the official language is French;
(3) in two small areas of eastern Wallonia, centred on the towns of Eupen and Sankt-Vith (St-Vith), the official language is German;
(4) the Brussels region is officially bilingual (Dutch and French).

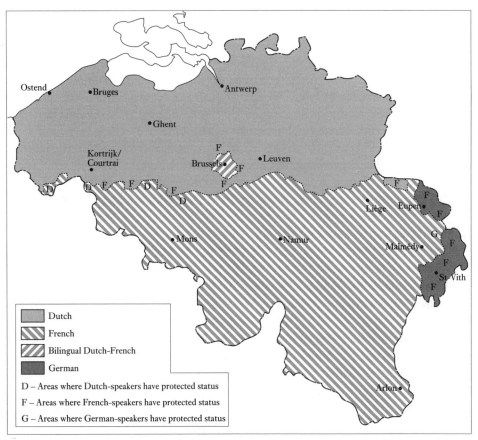

Map 1   Officially designated linguistic areas in Belgium

In addition, speakers of a national language other than the official language of the area where they reside enjoy a protected status in the fields of administration and education, as follows:

(1) Dutch-speakers in Wallonia, in four areas in the west (indicated by D on the map), in and around the towns of (from west to east) Comines (Komen), Mouscron (Moeskroen), Flobecq (Vloesberg) and Enghien (Edingen);

(2) French-speakers in Flanders in (i) the district of 's Gravenvoeren (les Fourons) in the east; (ii) in three areas to the north, east and south of Brussels; (iii) in three areas further west, in and around the towns of (from west to east) Spierre (Espierres), Ronse (Renaix) and Bever (Bievène); these are indicated by F on the map;

(3) French-speakers in the whole of the officially German-speaking areas;

(4) German-speakers in an area (indicated by G on the map), centred on Malmédy, contiguous to the two officially German-speaking areas.

On the non-standard French dialects of Belgium see under ***Picard** and ***Walloon**. The teaching of these dialects and of the Germanic ***Luxemburgish** dialect of the Arlon area in the south-east of Belgium is authorized under a decree of 1990 (see under *Walloon).

GLANVILLE PRICE

Belorussian, see *Belarusian*

Bengali (see under *Community languages (Britain)*)

Berber (see under *Community languages (France)*)

Bezht'a (see under *Caucasian languages. IV. North-East Caucasian family*)

Bokmål (see under *Norwegian*)

Bosnian

The term 'Bosnian' is the official name of the variant of *Serbo-Croat used in the Federation of Bosnia and Hercegovina. It is not accepted in the Bosnian Serb Republic.

The evolution of the political situation in the Republic of Bosnia-Hercegovina will undoubtedly have an effect on the language spoken in the various regions. Before the civil war of the early 1990s, language usage there varied from the use of the Croatian variant to the Serbian variant through all possible shades in between. The Serbo-Croat used in Bosnia is in fact an intervariant type, basically *ijekavian* (see *Serbo-Croat, 'Dialects') with numerous lexical doublets which vary in strength of opposition from very pronounced to very weak, depending on region and ethnic composition. Whereas some variant forms are more common or typical than others, e.g. eastern *ko* not western *tko* 'who', western *mrkva* not eastern *šagarepa* 'carrot', in other cases alternative forms are used equally frequently, e.g. *kino, bioskop* 'cinema'. Since, in practice, Bosnian is the language spoken by Muslim Bosnians as a means of differentiating themselves from both Serbs and Croats, it is characterized by the incorporation of increasing numbers of words of *Turkish, *Arabic and Persian origin into the everyday language.

Although a Bosnian dictionary has been published in America (Uzicanin 1995), the Bosnian variant is very hard to codify. Before the outbreak of the war, there were attempts by linguists and others to codify and recommend a 'collective usage', but these attempts were all unsuccessful. The language is written in both the Latin and (by Serbs) the *Cyrillic alphabet.

Herrity, P. 1982. The problem of lexical variants in the standard language in Bosnia-Hercegovina. *Die Welt der Slaven*, 27: 77–89.
Isaković, A. 1992. *Rječnik karakteristične leksike u bosanskome jeziku* ('Dictionary of the Characteristic Lexicon of the Bosnian Language'). Sarajevo. (Reprinted, Wuppertal, 1993.)
Uzicanin, N. 1995. *Bosnian–English English–Bosnian Dictionary*. New York.

PETER HERRITY

Botlikh (see under *Caucasian languages. IV. North-East Caucasian family*)

Breton

A member of the ***Brittonic** subgroup of the ***Celtic languages**. Breton is far closer to ***Cornish** than to ***Welsh**, but the genetic relationship with Welsh is still fairly apparent (though, contrary to a widespread belief in both countries, not to the extent of easy mutual comprehension). Breton is spoken in the department of Finistère and the adjacent western halves of the departments of Côtes-d'Armor and Morbihan in Brittany in western France. The Breton name *brez(h)oneg* preserves a traditional name (lost in the sister languages Cornish and Welsh) to which the learned term 'Brittonic' corresponds.

Origins

The term 'Brittonic' cannot be passed over in silence here, for it implies a purely British origin for Breton. Though this became the orthodox view after it was proclaimed by Joseph Loth in 1883, it is now far from universally accepted. The uncommon alternative 'Gallo-Brittonic' would be more suitable as it allows for a non-insular strand in the make-up of Breton and draws attention to the particularly close relationship between Brittonic and ***Gaulish** which is now widely accepted.

There is universal agreement that the linguistic distinctiveness of Brittany is due to a large-scale immigration of Britons from SW Britain from the 5th to the 7th centuries AD. In the absence of clear contemporary documentation, our knowledge of this period is based almost entirely on hagiographic and toponymic evidence which, besides the problems inherent in such sources, only takes us back to the 9th c. Loth assumed that Gaul had been completely Romanized by the 5th c. and that Breton was imported lock, stock and barrel from Britain – a hypothesis fitting in well with the nationalistic climate in France at the time, which considered France to be a natural, eternal truth. This hypothesis was first seriously challenged by Falc'hun (1963), for whom Gaulish substratum influence of variable intensity seemed a possible explanation of the rather marked dialectal variations within Breton. Fleuriot (1980) asserted even more strongly the survival of Gaulish up to the period of the incoming of the Britons, though disagreeing with Falc'hun on matters of important detail. Falc'hun believed the SE dialects to be the most Gaulish, Fleuriot the NW dialects, though both are unduly specific in their claims. Jackson (1967) backs his rejection of the theory of the survival of Gaulish with assertion rather than demonstration and many Breton nationalists fiercely condemn a theory which makes Bretons basically Gauls 'just like the French'. Documented Gaulish is both geographically and chronologically too remote from the invasions of the Britons to make any hypothesis definitive.

The scenario would appear to have been a considerable military and civilian migration of a Christian, 'Brittonic'-speaking people, who considered themselves Roman, encouraged by the authorities in the first place as a defensive strategy for a crumbling Roman empire. They probably found a rural population substantial numbers of whom still spoke a continental variety of their own language, still familiar to anyone involved at that time in continuing cross-Channel contacts. There is reason to suppose that the successful establishment of the insular variety was favoured by this survival. It can be further surmised that this dialect had enjoyed a higher social status in its less Romanized homeland, a status reinforced by its function as the language of the new aristocracy.

History

The small Breton kingdoms established in western Brittany had become difficult to contain by the 8th c. and there was an eastward surge in 850, under Salomon, which extended Breton power deep into Romance territory and led to the permanent incorporation in their domains of the large and thoroughly Romanized cities of Rennes and Nantes and their hinterlands. This made Brittany a biethnic unit politically dominated by its richer, **Romance**-speaking portion, whether it was a largely – and in the 15th c. increasingly – independent duchy or, from 1532, a semi-autonomous province. The French Revolution or, more specifically, the Jacobin constitution of 1793, although proclaiming linguistic uniformity (and hence the elimination of Breton) as one of its conscious objectives, brought no immediate change in the status of Breton. Although it can be presumed to have been the oral medium of the ruling class at least up to the 9th c., there is no clear evidence that Breton was ever used in an official capacity. Breton ceased to be the language of the Dukes by the early 12th c., well before union with France, and this long-standing lack of institutional status has been a major contributory factor in its superficially sudden decline.

Early attestations

Old Breton (800–1100) is attested only in glosses and onomastic material. This is relatively abundant, running to about 4,000 lexical items, but entirely fragmentary in nature, with morphological and syntactic data distinctly restricted. The language shares a very high proportion of its forms with Old Welsh, many forms being identified as Breton on solely palaeographical grounds. This is partly because the two languages had not yet diverged very far, and partly because they shared a common orthographical tradition based on British ecclesiastical adaptation of Latin conventions to the vernacular.

Middle Breton

Onomastic material provides almost the only evidence for the first 300 years of the Middle Breton period (1100–1400). From 1450 the language is quite substantially recorded, printed material, the first in any Celtic language, beginning with the *Catholicon*, a Breton–French–Latin dictionary printed in 1499 (the manuscript dates from *c*.1464). There are 23,000 lines of verse and 150 pages of prose, the latter consisting of translations strongly marked in idiom and syntax by French and Latin. The contrast with Old Breton is to some extent superficial since the predominantly French spelling conventions do not necessarily imply radical phonetic change. A more profound innovation is the massive presence of French loan-words. The language is fairly uniform but it is not certain whether this reflects a widely current standard or simply the common geographic origins of the texts in the wealthy Morlaix district.

Modern Breton

Modern Breton is traditionally said to begin in 1659 with the Jesuit Maunoir's elimination of mute consonants and his indication of initial consonant mutations, bringing spelling into line with the spoken practice of Léon in the north-west. This is the period in which more localized norms appear in the south-east (1631) and the north-east (18th c.). The term 'Modern Breton' is, however, often restricted to the period following the reforms of either Le Gonidec (1807) or Vallée (1908), or even the realization of 'total unification' in 1941. This last orthography, used in about 70% of publications, is associated with the strongly normative attitudes of Roparz Hemon who favoured adhesion to a lexically puristic variety of the NW dialect of Léon.

Breton as a literary medium

There is no extant Old Breton literature although the *matière de Bretagne*, i.e. literature (mainly Arthurian) containing themes of British and/or Breton provenance, is taken by some as pointing to a 'lost' literature. Against this may be noted the complete absence of Breton texts, despite the preservation of a substantial number of Latin manuscripts of Breton provenance. Middle Breton literature, much of it dramatic, is dominated by religious themes and associated with the activities of the mendicant orders. The distinctive versification, with its systematic use of internal rhymes, implies the presence of trained practitioners, though its complexity does not approach that of Welsh *cynghanedd* with which it is frequently compared.

Devotional literature predominated until the evaporation, after the Second World War, of a traditional popular readership, which was never a majority. Paradoxically, writing in Breton is more abundant and varied than ever, producing a personal, cultivated literature for an intellectual public. Some degree of particularism is the common stimulus, for there is no longer a public which can only be reached through the medium of Breton; indeed, for many writers and readers it is an acquired language, sometimes very obviously so. The briefer genres are the most widely cultivated and there are writers of skill and talent.

Spatial and statistical aspects

For the medieval period, the eastern boundary (see map 2) of Breton is derived from place-name evidence: the 9th-c. boundary is represented by the divide between -é (in territory already Romanized) and -ac (in territory not yet Romanized) as reflexes of the Gaulish suffix Latinized as -acum; the 12th-c. boundary encloses a zone in which Breton elements are found interspersed with French elements which became current in the 11th and 12th centuries. Later boundaries are based on more specific data, Bertrand d'Argentré's map of 1588 and later surveys, notably those of Sébillot (1886) and Panier (1942).

No statistics exist for numbers of Breton-speakers but there are a number of global estimates, not all of them strictly comparable: 1500 – 430,000; 1808 – 967,000; 1905

– 1,400,000; 1962 – 686,000; 1991 – 250,000. In 1905, monoglots were estimated at 60% of the total Breton-speaking population, while the percentage in rural areas would have been substantially higher whereas the towns had the only notable concentrations of monoglot French-speakers. The ports of Brest and Lorient, planned in the 17th c., have been particularly active agents in the propagation of French.

From the 14th to the 20th c. the geographical situation was dominated by a very gradual westward movement of the linguistic divide. Schooling generalized the knowledge of French from the late 19th c. and, by the 1960s, even in the most resistant areas, between Carhaix and Lannion, Breton-speaking parents were bringing up

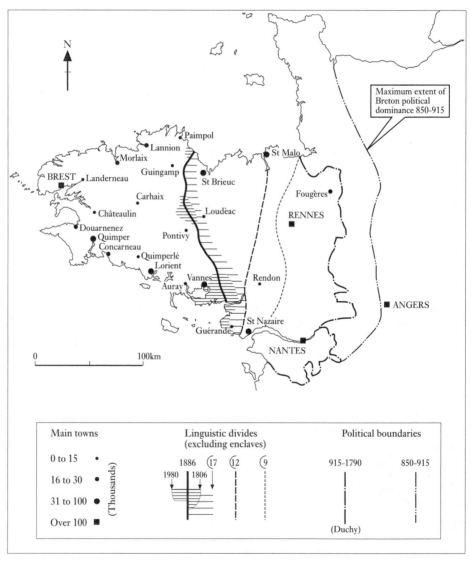

Map 2   Linguistic and political boundaries in Brittany

their children in French. By the 1990s it was common to find parishes where over 90% of the population aged over 60 were Breton-speaking but where the children were almost totally ignorant of the language. All observers report Breton as being most resistant in the most rural situations, with women showing a greater readiness than men to abandon it – despite the fact that the last generations of monoglots were overwhelmingly women. Substantial influxes of monoglot French have only locally been a major factor.

Dialects

Traditionally, the dialects have been identified with the four ancient bishoprics of Tréguier (NE), Léon (NW), Quimper (SW and centre) and Vannes (SE), the last sometimes being considered as a separate language and remaining outside any attempts at overall unification until 1941. Dialectal variety is more usefully schematized as having two contrasting poles in Léon and Vannes, separated by a broad transitional zone running SW–NE which developed around Carhaix, which had been the hub of the Roman road network.

Breton in education, the church and the media

The complete absence of Breton from any publications of an official nature (with the exception of the first years of the Revolution) was reinforced by its complete exclusion, with the general connivance of the population, from the school system set up in the 1880s. The *loi Deixonne* of 1951 opened the doors grudgingly for the teaching of Breton (together with *Basque, *Catalan and *Occitan) and there has since been some expansion, though only 5% of the school population is affected. A small number of state schools have been designated bilingual while a voluntary organization, Diwan, runs – now with some official recognition – bilingual schools catering for some 1,500 pupils.

The 19th-c. Catholic Church continued to use Breton, fiercely resisting the imposition of French in the catechism in 1903. After 1918, French progressed steadily as the language of the catechism, to displace Breton completely by 1950. Regular Breton sermons survived here and there into the 1960s but have since become very occasional events. The directive of the Second Vatican Council in 1966 to use the vernacular in the mass came too late and Breton is used regularly only for a handful of mainly urban activist worshippers.

Popular monthlies – generally Bretonist, that is to say, showing some degree of conscious particularism, since 1920 – ceased publication by 1945. Breton broadcasts, started during the Second World War, were resumed in 1947 at the rate (lower than during the war) of 30 minutes a week and were aimed initially at an elderly audience. There has since been a gradual, modest expansion to some 15 hours a week, locally supplemented by private stations. Television transmits 90 minutes a week in Breton.

Recent developments

The recent history of Breton has been one of generalized collapse within its traditional territory, brought about by the convergent pressures of a number of different factors: the exclusively French education system (not generally perceived as oppressive), the upheavals of two world wars, and, not least, drastic rural depopulation and the disappearance of a largely self-sufficient peasant economy. There has, of course, been a particularist reaction, initially antiquarian in origin and more institutional than linguistic in nature. Its activities and attitudes have often been counterproductive, 19th-c. regionalism having close associations with an anti-republican church and landed gentry, 20th-c. nationalism an influential fascist wing whose attitude during the German occupation was perceived as collaborationist.

Against a background of decline, Breton-language activities have expanded in the fields of publishing and education, though the numbers of those involved are small. The attitude of the general public and of the authorities at all levels has probably never been as favourable as at the present time but seems nevertheless willing to be satisfied with a purely symbolic recognition.

Balcou, J. and Le Gallo, Y. 1985. *Histoire littéraire et culturelle de la Bretagne*, 3 vols. Paris and Geneva.
Falc'hun, F. 1963. *Histoire de la langue bretonne d'après la géographie linguistique*. Paris.
Favereau, F. 1992. *Dictionnaire du breton contemporain*. Morlaix.
Fleuriot, L. 1980. *Les Origines de la Bretagne*. Paris.
Hemon, R. 1975. *Historical Morphology and Syntax of Breton*. Dublin.
Humphreys, H. Ll. 1992. The Breton language. In Price, G. (ed.), *The Celtic Connection*, Gerrards Cross, 245–75.
—— 1993. The Breton language: its present position and historical background. In Ball, M. J. (ed.), *The Celtic Languages*, London, 606–43.
Jackson, K. H. 1967. *A Historical Phonology of Breton*. Dublin.
Piette, J. R. F. 1973. *French Loanwords in Middle Breton*. Cardiff.
Trépos, P. 1960. *Grammaire bretonne*. Rennes.

HUMPHREY LLOYD HUMPHREYS

British, see *Brittonic languages*

British Sign Language (see under *Sign languages*)

Brittonic languages

One of the two surviving branches (the other being the ***Gaelic languages**) of the ***Celtic languages**, represented by ***Welsh**, ***Cornish** and ***Breton**. The terms 'Brythonic' and 'British' are also used.

Before the coming of the English, most or all of Britain south of the Forth–Clyde valley, and perhaps also north of it (see ***Pictish**), was occupied by Brittonic-speaking peoples. Brittonic elements survive in place-names in many parts of England, e.g. the six rivers *Avon* (= Welsh *afon* 'river'), or *Lytchett* (Dorset) and the first element in *Lichfield* (*Liccidfeld* in the 8th c.), both from earlier *Letoceto* (corresponding to Welsh *llwyd* 'grey' + *coed* 'wood').

With the arrival and westward expansion of the Angles and Saxons from the 5th c. onwards, British was ousted from most of the lowland zone of the island and confined to northern and western parts. In the late 5th and early 6th centuries, the continued westward thrust of the English split the Brittonic-speaking territory into three separate areas, corresponding approximately to (i) southern Scotland and the extreme north and north-west of England, where Brittonic survived into the early Middle Ages as *Cumbric, (ii) a central area including but more extensive than present-day Wales, and (iii) the south-west, which by the 12th c. was probably confined to Cornwall.

Jackson, K. 1953. *Language and History in Early Britain. A Chronological Survey of the Brittonic Languages, 1st to 12th c. AD* Edinburgh.
Rivet, A. L. F. and Smith, C. 1979. *The Place-Names of Roman Britain*. London.

GLANVILLE PRICE

Bruttian (see under *Oscan*)

Brythonic languages, see *Brittonic languages*

Budukh (see under *Caucasian languages. IV. North-East Caucasian family*)

Bulgarian

A member, together with *Slovene, *Serbo-Croat and *Macedonian, of the southern subgroup of the *Slavonic languages. Bulgarian is spoken mainly in Bulgaria, where it is the official language, but dialects are spoken elsewhere in the Balkans, including parts of the former Yugoslavia and Greece, and in Romania and parts of the former Soviet Union.

Origins

The name 'Bulgarian' derives from that of the Bulgar tribes who settled in the eastern Balkans in the 7th c. AD and, in union with the Slavs who had inhabited the area since the previous century, founded a state in AD 681. The predominant view of the language of the Bulgars, on the basis of inscriptions and a list of the names of the Bulgar khans in Slavonic, is that it was probably *Turkic, though the extant words and names appear to be Perso-Iranian. Soon after the union of the Bulgars with the Slavs, they adopted Slavonic speech. Few words from the original Bulgar language survive, the most important being the name 'Bulgar(ian)' itself.

History

The history of the Bulgarian language reaches back to the second half of the 9th c. when, after the adoption of Christianity, a Slavonic literary language, based on a spoken Bulgarian dialect of southern Macedonia and written in a Slavonic alphabet (see below, 'Orthography and standardization'), was created for ecclesiastical purposes. Known variously as 'Old *Church Slavonic', 'Old Slavonic', 'Old Bulgarian', and even 'Old Macedonian', this was the first Bulgarian literary language and the official church and state language of the first Bulgarian kingdom. It remained the literary language of Bulgaria until the Ottoman conquest in 1396, although, during the period of the Byzantine domination of Bulgaria from 1018 to 1187, ***Greek** became the administrative language; widespread destruction of Slavonic service-books and local and unofficial Hellenization took place. Literary writing in Bulgarian during this period was mainly restricted to the copying of service-books and older works. Linguistically, the 13th and the first half of the 14th c. were characterized by much variation in the linguistic norms adopted by the different literary centres. In particular, the reforms effected in the late 14th c. by the Tărnovo school (see under 'Orthography and standardization') with a view to restoring the 'classical' Old Bulgarian norm led to a long-lasting fossilization of the literary language and deepened the gap between it and the vernaculars. After the Ottoman conquest, Bulgarian continued to be written and was taught in the monasteries where the literary tradition was maintained.

The gradual evolution of the grammatical structure from synthetic to analytic, which was basically complete by the end of the 15th c. and has made of Bulgarian by far the most analytic of the Slavonic languages, underlies the division of the history of the language into three periods: Old Bulgarian (9th–11th centuries); Middle Bulgarian (12th–14th centuries); and New or Modern Bulgarian (15th c. onwards).

Up to 1878, when Bulgaria regained its independence from the Ottoman Empire, the administrative language was ***Turkish**, and the language of the service of the Bulgarian Orthodox Church, which until it gained its autonomy in 1870 was under the authority of the Patriarchate of Constantinople, was Greek. The schools also taught in Greek (the first secular Bulgarian school was founded in 1835).

By the mid-18th c. two basic literary forms of Bulgarian had developed, differing in structure and function. The archaic form, used mainly in ecclesiastical writing, continues the Old Bulgarian tradition and is influenced by the norms of Old Bulgarian and of Russian Church Slavonic; it differs greatly from the spoken language. The *damaskini* or 'damascenes' (see below), collections translated or adapted into Bulgarian in the 17th and 18th centuries, supply evidence for the development of a simplified form of the literary language which is also found in annals and in marginal notes. The linguistic norm of modern Bulgarian was not firmly established, however, before the late 19th c.

Earliest attestations

Funerary inscriptions (in ***Cyrillic** script) are known dating from the 10th c. (the earliest from 943). The earliest manuscripts are in Glagolitic script (see ***Cyrillic and Glagolitic Scripts**) and include, for example, the 10th-c. *Codices Zographenses, Marianus* and *Assemanianus*; a collection of homilies known as the *Codex Clozianus*; and the 11th-c. *Psalterium sinaiticum* ('Sinai Psalter') and *Euchologium siniaiticum*. Early Cyrillic manuscripts include the 11th-c. liturgical books *Savina kniga* ('Book of Sava'), *Codex supraliensis* and the *Apostle of Enina*.

Bulgarian as a literary language

In the 9th to the 11th centuries a rich literary tradition, predominantly religious in character, flourished under royal patronage and two influential literary schools were established at Ohrid and Preslav in the 10th c. During this period, often called the 'Golden Age' of Old Bulgarian literary culture, a number of translations from Greek were produced, including translations of the Old and New Testaments, liturgical, devotional and encyclopedic works, and treatises. Most notable among the translations are John the Exarch's versions of St John Damascene's *Exposition of the True Faith* and of St Basil the Great's *Hexaemeron*, and a collection of selected sermons of St John Chrysostom which also contains original Bulgarian works. Secular works include, for example, a geographical work by Cosmas Indicopleustes and the *Physiologos*. A particularly rich current is formed by apocryphal works, including Old and New Testament pseudepigrapha, legends, chronicles, books of divination, prayers, etc.; apocrypha such as the *Book of Enoch*, the *Apocalypse of Abraham* and the *Ladder of Jacob* survive only in Old Bulgarian translations. Original work dating from this period includes Clement of Ohrid's hymnographic compositions, sermons and eulogies, Chernorizets Hrabă's *Essay on the Slav Alphabet* (*c*.893), Constantine of Preslav's *Acrostic Prayer* (*c*.894) and his hymnographic works, Cosmas the Priest's *Treatise against the Bogomils* (*c*.969–72), and Jeremiah the Priest's *Legend of the Root-Tree* (10th c.).

The Byzantine domination during the 11th and 12th centuries brought about a stagnation of literary life though some original works, mainly anonymous, were produced such as the *Popular Life of St John of Rila*, the *Salonica Legend* and the *Bulgarian Apocryphal Chronicle*. In the 13th and 14th centuries the centre of literary life was the capital, Tărnovo. The influence of its literary school spread beyond Bulgaria and, after 1393, its traditions were preserved in Serbia and Russia. During this period numerous translations of religious, philosophical, historical and literary works were produced together with original works including hagiographical and hymnographical literature, eulogies, treatises and apocryphal works. The Orthodox mystical doctrine of Hesychasm had an enormous impact on the leading writers of the Tărnovo school and, under Hesychast influence, perceptions of language and style changed and resulted in the creation of new linguistic and stylistic principles.

The Ottoman conquest led to at least two centuries of stagnation but did not totally interrupt the literary tradition. Literary activities were resumed in the 16th c. in the form of translations and compilations of modern Greek religious and edifying texts known as *damaskini* (after the 16th-c. Greek author Damascene Studite whose collection *Thesauros* was translated into Bulgarian in the late 16th c. and became the model for a whole genre). More than 190 *damaskini* are preserved.

The first Bulgarian printed book, the *Chasoslovets*, a collection of prayers, eulogies, lives of religious writers and apocrypha, was produced in 1566 by the printer Yakov Kraikov of Sofia in Venice; during the next six years, he printed four other religious books including a Psalter and Missal. The first printed book whose language has modern features is *Abagar* (Rome, 1651), printed by Filip Stanislavov, the Roman Catholic bishop of Nikopol, which takes its title from the main place in the collection, a short New Testament apocryphon about Abagar, king of Edessa; it has the form of a scroll designed to serve as an amulet; the script is similar to Bosnian Cyrillic.

The first literary works in modern Bulgarian date from the 19th c. when literature was dominated by national ideals. Such writers as Lyuben Karavelov, Hristo Botev and Ivan Vazov were the most influential in forming the modern literary language and in the developing of modern genres. In the 1890s there began the 'Europeanization' of Bulgarian literature which developed modernist and individualist trends. This brought about a rapid evolution of the poetic language in particular. Some of the best modern works of Bulgarian literature date from the 1910s to the 1930s.

Orthography and standardization

It is uncertain whether the Glagolitic or the Cyrillic script (see ***Cyrillic and Glagolitic scripts**) was the first to be used though the earliest extant texts (manuscripts and inscriptions) are in Glagolitic; the two scripts were in parallel use until the 12th c. when Cyrillic replaced Glagolitic completely in Bulgaria. Two varieties of Cyrillic, Old Bulgarian and Church Slavonic, were in use in Bulgaria up to the 19th c., the latter having been diffused from the 17th c. onwards through the medium of religious books written in Russia in the Russian version of Church Slavonic. For example, Pětăr Beron, the first author to write consistently in the spoken language, and Ivan Bogorov, the author of one of the first Bulgarian grammars (1844), use simplified versions of the Church Slavonic alphabet.

In the 19th c. the question of orthography was further complicated by the need to take decisions concerning the representation of various sounds, and by the 1870s a state of complete orthographical chaos had been reached. Some grammarians advocated a system of only 24 letters, others one of 38 (modern Bulgarian uses 30). It was only in 1892 that an orthographical commission was set up, and the first official orthography (which followed proposals made by Marin Drinov in 1870) was sanctioned by the Ministry of Education in 1899. Since the orthographical reform of 1945, when two characters not used in Russian were dropped, the Bulgarian form of the Cyrillic alphabet is identical with the Russian version except for the different values of the characters щ ([ʃt] in Bulgarian, [ʃtʃ] or [ʃʃ] in Russian) and ъ ([ə] in Bulgarian, silent in Russian) and the fact that it does not include the Russian characters э, ё, and ы.

On the use of the Latin alphabet for Bulgarian dialects in the Banat in the 19th c., see under 'Dialects' below.

The earliest attempt at codifying the language was made in the second half of the 14th c. (1371–93) by Evtimii of Tărnovo and the literary school he established there. They carried out a linguistic reform with the apparent aim of eliminating variability (which they interpreted as 'heretical corruptions of the sacred books') and unifying the literary language in accordance with strict and rigidly conservative grammatical and orthographical principles derived from the 'classical' Old Bulgarian norm. The result of this was an archaization of morphology, syntax, lexis and literary style.

In the debates about the language question in the 1820s–40s it was discussed whether the modern literary language should be based on the language of the Tărnovo school combined with that of 17th- and 18th-c. Russian Church Slavonic printed texts, and three schools of thought emerged. A pro-Church Slavonic school represented the ideological climate of 18th- and 19th-c. Europe and regarded the modern stages of the language as decayed variants of an earlier 'pure', 'classical' state. Support for Old Bulgarian was motivated by revivalist ideas of the glorious past of Bulgaria and a return to a Golden Age. Supporters of 'New Bulgarian' argued that the literary language should be based on contemporary vernaculars; the main objection raised to this was the fact that the vernaculars used a definite article which was considered by opponents to be a 'barbaric feature' that excluded Bulgarian from the family of the Slavonic languages.

More than 25 grammars (the earliest being Neofit of Rila's *Bolgarska gramatika* of 1835) were published between 1835 and 1878 but, since they represented the different schools of thought, linguistic chaos continued and it is difficult to speak of codification. The ideas of the New Bulgarian school prevailed in the 1850s but it was not until 1899 that the language was officially codified by the Ministry of Education.

Dialects

On a simplified basis, dialects can be divided into eastern and western and further subdivided as follows:

(1) eastern Bulgarian: Moesian (the NE region bordered by the Black Sea, the Danube and the eastern end of the Stara Planina mountain range); Balkan (the region of the Stara Planina); and 'Rupski' (Thrace, the Strandzha and Rhodope mountains, and parts of the Pirin mountain in the south-west);

(2) western Bulgarian: northern and southern.

The modern literary language is based mainly on the NE dialects with a few western Bulgarian elements. The most archaic dialects are the SE ones in the Rhodope mountains.

There is no sharp division between the dialects of western Bulgaria and those of Serbia and of the former Yugoslav Republic of Macedonia. The Macedonian language is structurally similar to Bulgarian and has, indeed, been regarded by some (including some non-Bulgarian scholars) as a dialect of Bulgarian.

The dialects of Bulgarian-speaking communities (descended from immigrants who left Ottoman-ruled Bulgaria in the mid-18th to mid-19th centuries and estimated to number now some 300,000) in parts of the former Soviet Union (Bessarabia, Tavria, the Odessa and Kirovgrad regions of Ukraine) vary but derive mainly from eastern dialects that preserve a number of archaic features.

Bulgarian communities in the Banat are descended from Roman Catholic refugees who settled there in 1738–41 after fleeing from Bulgaria. Their numbers (estimated in the mid-1960s at about 17,500 in Romania and 5,000 in Serbia) are constantly dwindling. In the course of their history, they have undergone linguistic influence from ***Serbo-Croat**, ***Hungarian** and ***Romanian**. A 19th-c. revival of sorts led to the introduction of Bulgarian in place of Croatian in schools and attempts at creating a literature in Bulgarian (a number of textbooks, translations and newspapers were published), using an orthography based on the Croatian and Hungarian versions of the Latin alphabet. In the 1930s a new attempt at resisting linguistic assimilation was made which resulted in writing and publishing in the local dialect (a basically eastern Bulgarian dialect which preserves archaic features). This is the only Bulgarian dialect for which the status of a separate literary language has been sought.

Contact with other languages

As a result of historical circumstances, Greek and Turkish constitute the main sources of lexical influence on Bulgarian. Although there are fewer Greek than Turkish loan-words, it is Greek that has been regarded as the main threat to Bulgarian, especially in the 18th and 19th centuries when there were deliberate attempts at Hellenization.

Bulgarian has been exposed to Greek influence throughout most of its existence and over long periods Greek was the language of the church liturgy and of the schools. Old Bulgarian borrowed from Greek many words in the field of religious concepts and ecclesiastical life (e.g. *igumen* 'abbot', *pop* 'priest') and formed calques based on Greek compound words. Greek nouns were borrowed in such areas as administration, military matters, education, family and social relationships, customs, commerce, nature, wild animals, parts of buildings and roads, household items and clothes, and the Slavonic names for the months were replaced by their Graeco-Roman equivalents. Verbs, too, were borrowed as well as a number of conjunctions and particles (e.g. *ala* 'and, however', *oti* 'why', *nimà* 'really? is it possible?', *mìgar* 'is it really so?').

Turkisms are the most numerous foreign elements in Bulgarian and can be found in practically every sphere of life, e.g. *pazár* 'market', *kùla* 'tower', *pervàz* 'window-sill', *kilìm* 'rug', *tèndzera* 'saucepan', *badzhàk* 'thigh', *chorbà* 'soup', *lalè* 'tulip', *gàrga* 'crow', *kanarà* 'crag, rock', *tavàn* 'ceiling', *yavàsh* 'slowly', *tamàn* 'precisely', *demèk* 'in other words', *aslă* 'precisely so'. Many attempts at purging the language of its Turkisms have been made and Turkisms were consistently replaced by Russian and Church Slavonic equivalents, with the result that parallel words often exist for one and the same object or concept. However, Turkisms play a great stylistic role in Bulgarian as expressive means and, though their use was severely restricted especially after 1944, they form an integral part of colloquial speech. The contact with Turkish has been so profound that not only the lexicon but the phonetics and intonation of the language have been affected.

Russian constitutes another major influence on Bulgarian, principally in the lexis but also in morphology. Through the Russian version of Church Slavonic and the fact that in the 19th c. many Bulgarian literary figures were educated in Russia, Russian contributed greatly to the formation of modern Bulgarian, even though in the 19th c. Russian influence was combated by the Bulgarianization of Russian words. Its impact grew after Bulgaria achieved independence in 1878. In addition to words borrowed from Russian itself, much international terminology has also passed into Bulgarian via the medium of Russian. The Sovietization of Bulgaria after 1944 introduced a great number of typically Soviet words, especially in such fields as work, military matters and education.

Bulgarian has also acquired words from other languages with which it has been in contact. At an early period, Balkan Latin gave such words as *kòmka* 'Holy Communion' < *communicare, kum* 'godfather' < *compater, tsar* 'king' < *Caesar*. More recent borrowings include, from German, *kartòf* 'potato', *kèlner* 'waiter', etc.; from French, *byuro* 'desk, office', *nyuàns* 'nuance', *shantàzh* 'blackmail', etc.; from Italian, *mandzha* 'dish, meal', etc.; and from English a massive influx of words in such fields as technology, culture, music, sport, etc., e.g. *kompyùtăr* 'computer', *chip* 'chip', *flopi disk* 'floppy disk', *trilă* 'thriller', *sekyuriti* 'security', *bodigard* 'bodyguard', *fitnes* 'fitness', *gol* 'goal'. Romanianisms were typical of the writings of Bulgarian émigrés during the 19th-c. Bulgarian Revival but nowadays borrowings from Romanian are found mainly in dialects bordering on the Danube, though some internationalisms survive in the literary language in a form that reflects a Romanian origin, e.g. *broshùra* 'leaflet', *krìza* 'crisis'.

Present situation

Bulgarian is the official language of Bulgaria and is used in the legal, governmental and educational systems and in the media, and its status is protected by a language law. There are nearly 9 million speakers in Bulgaria itself and small communities in Bessarabia (Moldavia) and other parts of the former Soviet Union, Romania, Serbia and Greece (see above under 'Dialects'). It is also spoken by immigrant groups in Israel, western Europe, the USA and Canada but no figures are available for the numbers of native speakers world-wide.

Atanasova, T. et al. 1988. *Bulgarian–English Dictionary*, 3rd revised edn. Sofia.

Atanasova, T., Harlakova, I. and Rankova, M. 1987–8. *English–Bulgarian Dictionary*, 2 vols. Sofia.

Bernstein, S. B., Hewko, E. B. and Zelenina, E. I. 1958. *Атлас болгарских говоров Советского Союза* ('Atlas of the Bulgarian Dialects of the Soviet Union'). Moscow.

Gyllin, R. 1991. *The Genesis of the Modern Bulgarian Literary Language*. Uppsala.

Henninger, T. 1987. *Balkanische Lexik im Schrifttum der bulgarischen Wiedergeburt* ('Balkan Lexicon in the Writings of the Bulgarian Revival'). Neuried.

—— 1995. *Animal Names in Bulgarian. Balkan versus Slavonic in the Nineteenth Century*. Prague.

Mirchev, K. 1978. *Историческа граматика на българския език* ('A Historical Grammar of the Bulgarian Language'). Sofia.

Scatton, E. A. 1984. *A Reference Grammar of Modern Bulgarian*. Columbus, OH.

SONIA I. KANIKOVA

Burgundian

The Burgundians were a Germanic people speaking an East **Germanic language*. After suffering a crushing defeat at the hands of the Huns in AD 437 in which they are said to have lost 20,000 men, those of them that remained were settled by the Romans in Savoy and the neighbouring part of Switzerland. They later took over also a substantial area of east central France. This Burgundian-occupied territory corresponds, if only approximately, to the **Francoprovençal*-speaking area and it has been argued, but is not universally accepted, that the linguistic identity of this area, such as it is, can be attributed to the influence of a Burgundian substratum. It is possible, but not certain, that some specifically Francoprovençal words, e.g. *brogî* 'to ponder', *budda* 'cowshed', were borrowed from the East Germanic language of the Burgundians.

Byelorussian, see *Belarusian*

C

Cambodian (see under *Community languages (France)*)

Campanian (see under *Oscan*)

Camunic

A language of unknown affiliation, attested in some 70 inscriptions found in the Valcamonica, an Alpine valley in the province of Brescia in NW Italy. Only a few have been found outside the Valcamonica. As most of the inscriptions are carved on rocks in the Valcamonica, they can be found *in situ*, e.g. in the Parco nazionale delle iscrizioni rupestri at Naquane, while rich documentation as well as information on the archaeological background can be obtained at the Centro camuno di studi pre-istorici at Capodiponte.

The alphabet of the inscriptions is a modified *Etruscan alphabet, the so-called Sondrio alphabet. The inscriptions date back to the second half of the first millennium BC. Since they are very short, little can be said about their contents. As for the character of the language documented by them, it is possible but not certain that Camunic is related to Etruscan and *Raetic.

Nevertheless, one can justifiably speak of a Camunic language. The Valcamonica still continues the name of the tribe of the Camunni, who are mentioned several times by Greek and Roman historians as inhabitants of that area. Thus, there can be no doubt that the Valcamonica inscriptions are texts in the language of the Camunni.

Mancini, A. 1981. *Le iscrizioni della Valcamonica* ('The Valcamonica Inscriptions'). Urbino.
Prosdocimi, A. L. 1965. Per una edizione delle iscrizioni della Val Camonica ('Towards an edition of the Val Camonica inscriptions'). *Studi Etruschi*, 33: 575–99.

STEFAN SCHUMACHER

Carian

The Carians are known mainly as a people living in Classical times in SW Asia Minor, but it appears from Greek sources that they had previously formed a pre-Hellenic population in some of the Aegean islands and part of the Greek mainland. A few Carian inscriptions in an alphabetic script from Asia Minor have not been definitively interpreted but, taken together with the evidence of a small number of glosses in Greek texts and of place-names, lead to the conclusion that the language was probably ***Indo-European**.

Georgiev, V. I. 1966. Cario. In Id., *Introduzione alla storia delle lingue indeuropee*, Rome, 237–43.

Cassubian

Cassubian or Kashubian (*kašëbskô mova*), a member of the ***Lechitic** subgroup of the West ***Slavonic languages**, is spoken in northern Poland (see map 18). The dialect of the west Cassubians, who were Lutherans and sometimes applied the adjective *słowińsczi* 'Slovincian' to their speech (though it has never been argued that it was anything more than a Cassubian dialect), became extinct in the mid-20th-c. Today all Cassubians are Catholics.

The earliest written record dates from 1402, but all texts from before the 19th c. are in a kind of ***Polish** mixed with Cassubian features, not in true Cassubian. This hybrid was used among the Slovincians until about 1730 for formal (mainly religious) purposes and in the Lutheran devotional books (16th and 17th centuries) which constitute the earliest Cassubian printed texts. The church language of the Catholic Cassubians was always (until very recently) standard Polish. No alphabet other than the Latin has ever been used to write Cassubian and the spelling systems (of which there have been several) are all broadly based on Polish with a few additional diacritics. As a result of centuries of contact with German (mainly Low German), the proportion of German loan-words is somewhat higher here than in most other parts of Poland (estimated at 5%, compared with 3% elsewhere). Syntax too has been influenced by German. The effect of Polish interference is elusive, but the difference between Polish and Cassubian would probably be even greater were it not for the centuries of Polish influence. There are vestiges of an Old ***Prussian** substratum. Toponymical evidence shows that the Cassubian speech-area once reached as far west as the River Parsęta (Ger. Persante). It gradually receded eastwards in the face of German expansion, but even at the beginning of the 20th c. Cassubian (Slovincian) was still spoken nearly 37 miles (60 km) west of the nearest point where it is spoken today.

The first writer of true Cassubian was Florian Ceynowa (1817–81), whose works included a grammar of Cassubian written in Cassubian. Literature consists mainly of verse and short prose works, but there is one novel and there have been several periodicals. A Cassubian translation of the New Testament was published in 1993.

Cassubian is today spoken to the west, north-west and south-west of Gdańsk, in an elongated band of territory stretching from the Baltic coast to a point about 120 km inland (see map 18). Although it has no official standing and may be perceived as a Polish dialect, its individuality is such that it is widely regarded as a separate language. Poles from other regions have difficulty in understanding it and it is used colloquially by all social strata, including intellectuals. There are no official figures, but the number of speakers is sometimes put as high as 150,000. Despite its uncertain status, Cassubian has attained a modest presence in a few schools and at the University of Gdańsk. There are fortnightly television programmes and weekly radio broadcasts. The recent practice in several churches of celebrating mass in Cassubian is a significant innovation.

Stone, G. 1993. Cassubian. In Comrie, B. and Corbett, G. G. (eds), *The Slavonic Languages*, London and New York, 759–94.

GERALD STONE

Castilian, see *Spanish*

Catalan

A member of the ***Romance** family of languages, spoken in the eastern part of Spain (including the Balearic Islands) (see map 19), in the French *département* of Pyrénées-Orientales, in Andorra, and in the port of Alghero in Sardinia.

External history

The earliest attestations of Catalan in a form distinct from its parent language, Latin, are certain proper names occurring in Latin documents from the early 9th c. AD, produced in the foothills of the eastern Pyrenees. A fragment of a translation of the *Forum Iudicum*, the Visigothic law code, is dated to the first half of the 12th c. The first substantial text is a collection of sermons, or perhaps rather notes for sermons, known as the *Homilies d'Organyà*, from the late 12th c. Until well into the 14th c., the majority of texts from the then Catalan-speaking regions continue to be in Latin, though, in the case of notarial documents in particular, this was sometimes little more than vernacular disguised by conventional Latin orthography and inflection.

As with other Romance languages, the writing conventions of Catalan have developed from those of Latin adopting some regional peculiarities. There are also a very few Judeo-Catalan manuscripts of the 15th c. which are written in ***Hebrew** letters: these include some wedding songs in verse. If Catalan was ever written in Arabic script (as Spanish was), no texts have survived.

Catalan is a variety of Latin that developed originally on a small territory on either side of the Pyrenees. This territory, the *Marca Hispanica*, was not subject to Arab rule for any substantial period, and formed a redoubt from which the 'reconquest' of lands further south was organized from the 8th c. onwards. It seems likely that the Romance that was spoken in the northernmost areas which did fall under Arab control was very similar to the Romance of the *Marca Hispanica*. The 'reconquest' of Girona (785), of Vic and Cardona (798) and of Barcelona (801) will thus not have been accompanied by significant language shift, whether or not there were movements of population. Subsequent expansion southwards did involve substantial population movements, with Catalan speakers from *Catalunya Vella* 'Old Catalonia' – the area under Christian control at the beginning of the 9th c. – replacing or dominating speakers of other languages. In *Catalunya Nova* 'New Catalonia' – the area between the Llobregat and the Ebro south and south-west of *Catalunya Vella* – there had been speakers both of Arabic and of an Al-Andalus Romance (***Mozarabic**) variety significantly different from Catalan, in unknown proportions. As the Christian expansion progressed: Cervera (1050), Tarragona (1116), Tortosa (1148), Lleida and Fraga (1149), political authority came increasingly under the counts of Barcelona until in 1162 Alfons I, count of Barcelona, became also King of Aragon. In 1151 a treaty between the kings of Aragon and Castile carved up the future conquest of territories still under Arab control, so that Valencia would fall to the crown of Aragon, while lands further west would be attached to Castile. The kingdom of Valencia was captured in the 1230s and was populated by speakers from various parts of Catalonia and Aragon, though a numerous subordinate population of Arabic-speaking *moriscos*, as they were called, remained until their expulsion in 1609. The Balearic Islands were conquered between 1229 and 1287, and resettled by speakers largely from eastern Catalonia. Sicily was also captured for the house of Barcelona (1282) as was Sardinia (1323–27); Catalan was widely used as an official language in Sicily until the 15th c. and in Sardinia until the 17th. Only the port of Alghero in Sardinia was subject to Catalan resettlement, and has remained Catalan-speaking to the present day. The original expansion southwards of Catalan following the 'reconquest' extended as far as Murcia and Cartagena, though the kingdom of Murcia became Spanish-speaking during the 15th c. Within the kingdom of Valencia the region of Oriola (Sp. Orihuela) was Catalan-speaking until the 17th c.; language shift appears to have followed Spanish settlement in the region after the expulsion of the *moriscos*.

Catalan in literature

Catalan began to be extensively used in prose, as an official and literary language, in the second half of the 13th c., in the various law codes (including the *Llibre de Consolat de Mar* which became the basis of international maritime law), and in the religious and philosophical works of Ramon Llull (1232–1315). Prose literature, including history – the four Great Chronicles – and translations from Latin and Italian, developed in the 14th c. and reached a peak in the first half of the 15th c. with masterpieces of extended fiction: the anonymous *Curial e Güelfa*, and Joanot Martorell's *Tirant lo Blanch*. The language was essentially that of the royal chancellery, dialectally fairly neutral, and influenced in style by Latin and Italian models. There was relatively little orthographic variation, so it is appropriate to speak of a standard literary language at this period. Until the 15th c., poetry was written in ***Occitan**; writers such as Guillem de Berguedà and Cerverí de Girona contribute a significant part of the troubadour corpus in more or less standard Occitan. This tradition was maintained in serious verse, although the Occitan veneer was increasingly superficial and inaccurate, despite the treatises composed to correct it, until the major poets of the 15th c., such as Auziàs March (1397–1459) and Jaume Roig (1402?–78), cast off the alien disguise. From the 16th c. until the literary and cultural revival (the *Renaixença*) of the 19th c., Catalan literature was in decline. Though works in many genres continued to be written and printed, none achieved much prestige or, apparently, wide circulation. It is only since the 1970s that some of the texts of this period have come to be re-evaluated. (Medieval Catalan literature was widely esteemed in its own time, and often translated, into e.g. Spanish, Latin or Italian.)

The *Renaixença* began as a literary and cultural revival, parallel to other movements in 19th-c. Europe. During most of the 19th c. only verse and popular theatre were significant, but as cultural renewal developed into political nationalism, in Catalonia at least, towards the end of the century, the other genres, including fiction, translations and journalism, came to take their place alongside. In the 20th c. there has been an abundance of literary works of all kinds, from all parts of the Catalan territories, though publication and circulation of work in Catalan was very seriously restricted under the Franco dictatorship, especially between 1939 and about 1960. Little modern Catalan literature has been translated into English, but rather more has been translated into other languages, particularly Spanish.

Standardization

As we have mentioned, a unified literary Catalan koine had become well established by the 15th c. With the subsequent cultural decline, awareness of the conventions of this koine, and of the linguistic and cultural unity of the Catalan territories it reflected, was gradually dissipated, so that, by 1800 or so, writers had in mind only a regionally limited audience for works in a local idiom. One of the goals of the *Renaixença* was the restoration or reconstruction of a Catalan standard language. The standardization movement crystallized in the work of Pompeu Fabra (1868–1948), whose orthographic norms (1913), grammar (1918) and dictionary (1932) were immediately adopted by official institutions in Catalonia, and quickly became accepted elsewhere. The bases of Fabra's standard were the medieval koine, current educated usage in Catalonia, particularly in Barcelona, contemporary dialects, and the removal of 'barbarisms'. Fabra's intention was that the standard should be open to development, and to further incorporation of non-Barcelona usage, but the circumstances of the Civil War and the Franco period had the effect of turning Fabra's works into an orthodoxy, deviation from which was regarded as unpatriotic. It is only since the 1980s that the Institut d'Estudis Catalans and associated institutions have regained the authority to expand and modernize standard Catalan, introducing recommendations for terminology, for spoken usage in the mass media, and for regional 'parastandards'. In fact, in addition to the Barcelona-based norm which is used throughout Catalonia and to some extent elsewhere, *de facto* standards for Valencian and Balearic (see below, 'Dialects') had already grown up, largely through publishers. These 'parastandards' differ from the Barcelona norm only in retaining some regional differences of vocabulary and morphology which were part of the literary tradition. The differences are comparable to those between British and American English; one may easily read a page of text before coming on a feature which marks it as of one regional standard variety rather than another. In recent years some writers and publishers in Catalonia have argued for, and practised, modifications of the standard language reflecting more popular usage, especially that of Barcelona, in vocabulary and syntax. The vehemence of the polemic surrounding these 'deviations' is out of proportion to the rather modest scope of the innovations proposed. A potentially much more serious trend since the 1980s has been one associated with the claim that Valencian is not just a regional variety of Catalan but a separate language. This has led to the development by the Reial Academia de Cultura Valenciana of a different orthography, grammar and vocabulary, reflecting more closely (but by no means entirely consistently) the popular speech of Valencia; this alternative standard has won some official backing, for example in the city government of Valencia, but has generally been opposed by educational institutions, publishers, and most creative writers in Catalan.

Dialects

Though there are significant dialect differences in Catalan, the dialects are to a high degree mutually intelligible. They are conventionally divided into two groups, on the basis of differences in phonology as well as in some features of verb morphology; there are some interesting lexical differences, too. The Eastern Dialect Group includes Northern Catalan or *rossellonès* (in French Catalonia), Central Catalan (in the eastern part of Catalonia), Balearic, and *alguerès* (in Alghero). The Western Group consists of NW Catalan (western and southern Catalonia and eastern Aragon) and Valencian. For the most part the boundaries between Catalan and neighbouring languages are quite sharp, but the dialect of the valley of Capcir is transitional between Catalan and Occitan, and the dialects of Alta Ribagorça in the Aragonese Pyrenees are transitional between Catalan and Aragonese.

Contact with other languages

No part of the Catalan territories has ever experienced universal monolingualism, though multilingualism has often been widespread only among the literate classes (universal in the second half of the 20th c.). In the area where Catalan originated, there is evidence that at least four languages had been spoken before Romanization: **Celtiberian, another Indo-European language called *'Sorothaptic' by the Catalan scholar J. Coromines, *Iberian and *Basque. (A Basque-like language probably continued to be spoken in Ribagorça, Pallars, Andorra and part of Cerdanya until the 10th c.) The imprint of these languages on Catalan is largely on toponymy, though a handful of other words may be attributable to each of these substrates. The Latin of the Visigothic and Frankish kingdoms, of which the original Catalan area was a part, was marked by the incorporation of ***Germanic** vocabulary, and, especially in Catalonia, by a Germanization of place and personal names which have remained in use until the present day. The repopulation of *Catalunya Nova* brought Catalan into contact with Al-Andalus Romance with significant influence in onomastics and certain items of general vocabulary. In the same region, and to a greater extent in Valencia and the Balearics, Catalan was in contact with, and gradually supplanted, ***Arabic** – an Arabic itself containing Al-Andalus Romance elements. The Arabic contribution to Catalan vocabulary is notable in many fields, and is comparable in proportion to the Arabic element in ***Spanish** and ***Portuguese**. Examples are: *de gairell* 'obliquely', *gatzara* 'uproar', *gerra* 'jug', *racó* 'corner', *rajola* 'floor tile', *rambla* 'intermittent watercourse, avenue'.

The political union of Catalonia with Aragon, and the settlement of the kingdom of Valencia jointly by Catalans and Aragonese-speakers, initiated the linguistic contact of Catalan with the Romance varieties further west. The phonological and morphological characteristics of the dialect of the city of Valencia and its environs probably reflect a strong Aragonese substratum/adstratum from an early period. The chancellery of the kingdom of Aragon was trilingual, using Latin, Catalan and Aragonese as occasion required. By the 15th c. Aragonese was itself, except in its more extreme forms in the High Aragonese valleys, giving way to Castilian. In 15th-c. Valencia the court was already bilingual, and after the merger of the Aragonese and Castilian crowns, in 1479, Spanish (Castilian) gradually increased in prestige throughout the Catalan territories, with the urban and literate classes becoming bilingual. From the 16th c. Catalan came increasingly under Spanish influence, in vocabulary, syntax, pronunciation and orthography, as a result of the social and cultural prestige of Castile.

Since the Second World War most of the Catalan-speaking territories have experienced substantial immigration of non-Catalan speakers. In France these have been people of European origin resettled from Algeria and retired people from various parts of France. In Catalonia and Valencia the population almost doubled between 1950 and 1975 as people from less developed southern Spain sought employment in manufacturing and service industries. Mallorca and Eivissa (Ibiza) have attracted a work-force from many parts of Spain, feeding the tourist industry. Many immigrants have wished to acquire Catalan, or at least have wished their children to do so, as an aid to integration, but until the late 1970s there were few opportunities to realize this. These large Spanish-speaking communities have added to the institutional and cultural pressures in favour of the use of Spanish in the Catalan territories.

In 1659 Philip IV ceded the northern part of Catalonia (essentially the modern *département* of Pyrénées-Orientales) to the French crown. From that point North Catalonia became subject to the linguistic unification policies of the French state; French became the official language in 1700, and has had a marked influence on the vocabulary of North Catalan, and in recent times on its phonology as well. Menorca was under British rule during most of the 18th c., and there is a handful of Menorcan Anglicisms of vocabulary dating to that period. The dialect of Alghero is, not surprisingly, heavily influenced by Sardinian and even more by Italian, in all components of the language.

Present situation

The territories where Catalan is natively spoken are:

(1) The Principality of Andorra
(2) In France: almost all of the *département* of Pyrénées-Orientales
(3) In Spain:
     Catalonia (under the autonomous government, the *Generalitat*, of Catalonia), except for the Gascon-speaking Val d'Aran;
     the eastern fringe of Aragon;
     most of the *Comunitat Valenciana*, excepting some regions in the west and south

which have been Aragonese/Spanish-speaking since the reconquest, or at least
since the 18th c.;
El Carxe, a small area of Murcia, settled in the 19th c.;
the Balearic Islands: Mallorca and Menorca (Balearic *stricto sensu*), Eivissa (Ibiza)
and Formentera (strictly *Illes Pitiüses*)
(4) In Italy: the port of Alghero in Sardinia.

A conservative estimate of the number of native speakers of Catalan is about 6.5
million (based on the 1991 census in Catalonia, Valencia and the Balearics, with estimates for the remaining territories). Within Spain a further 3 million claim to
understand Catalan; partly as a result of the incorporation of Catalan into the education system, there are within Spain increasing numbers of second-language
speakers.

The status, situation and prospects of the Catalan language are significantly
different in each of the territories enumerated above, though each of those in Spain
shares, in some way, the consequences of Catalan's having been for centuries an
oppressed 'minority' language. We have already mentioned the cultural decline and
loss of prestige affecting Catalan from the 16th c. onwards. The defeat of the Catalans
in the war of the Spanish Succession initiated a series of measures extending
throughout the 18th and 19th centuries, imposing the use of Spanish in public life,
for example, in accounts, in preaching, in the theatre, in the criminal courts, in education, in legal documents, in the civil registers, on the telephone. In the 20th c. these
measures were mostly repeated, and supplemented by the imposition of Spanish in
catechism, by prohibition of the teaching of Catalan, and by sanctions against persons
refusing to use Spanish. The Second Republic (1931–9) to a large extent removed
these restrictions, but Franco's victory in the Spanish Civil War was followed in 1940
by a total ban on the public use of Catalan. This ban was subject to a series of relax-
ations from the 1950s onwards, allowing (subject to censorship applied generally in
Spain) the publication of increasing numbers of Catalan books from the 1960s,
though Catalan remained excluded from nearly all public institutions until Spain's
adoption of a democratic constitution in 1978.

That constitution enjoins respect for and protection of Spain's 'other' languages,
and opened the way for statutes of autonomy in the various regions. In the early 1980s
Catalonia, Valencia and the Balearics obtained their respective statutes of autonomy,
involving co-officiality for Spanish and Catalan. All of these statutes promote
'language normalization', the goal of which is universal bilingualism without
diglossia. In Catalonia the expressed aim of the Generalitat goes much further than
this: to make the 'local language' the normal medium of public life, with Spanish
having a secondary role as an auxiliary language, or a home language for its native
speakers. In Valencia and the Balearics, the *de facto* policy has been to promote effective knowledge of Catalan and to enhance its status, while largely preserving a
diglossic relationship between Spanish and Catalan.

In Catalonia, Catalan is co-official and its knowledge and use are actively promoted
by the autonomous government and by local government. Teaching of Catalan is

obligatory in all schools, and primary and secondary education through the medium of Catalan now reaches about 60% of the population; the provision includes, since 1993, some Catalan immersion programmes in Spanish-speaking suburbs. There are two Catalan language TV stations, with wide audiences, and numerous radio stations. Catalan is still clearly in a minority position in the periodical press, in advertising, in cinema/video, and in the administration of justice, but a gradual advance is noted here too.

In the Aragon fringe, Catalan has no official status, though the Aragonese autonomy statute speaks of protection and support of minority languages. In the villages in question there are many cultural associations promoting Catalan (not necessarily by that name), and in many cases the local administration supports Catalan teaching in schools. Radio and TV from Catalonia are accessible, of course. Language shift (except through emigration) is minimal.

The language situation in the Community of Valencia is extremely complex, politically, culturally and geographically. Catalan has been strongest in the countryside and among the urban working classes. The language policy of the Generalitat Valenciana, responding to popular pressure, has largely concentrated on education, and Catalan is available in around 80% of state schools. A shortage of teachers prevents advance here. Teaching through Catalan is available in a minority of schools. A Valencian state TV station broadcasts bilingually. Catalan is quite prominent in cultural life; it is present in administration and in commerce, and there is evidence of popular demand for, and expectation of, a greater use of Catalan.

Though the Balearic Islands Council passed a 'linguistic normalization' law in 1986, little has been done to put it into effect. Spoken Catalan is predominant except in Palma and in Eivissa (Ibiza), where immigration is highest, and where there is recent evidence of some intergenerational language shift to Spanish. Catalan has some place in local radio, including 'pirate' stations, and Catalan TV stations from the mainland have a wide following. The local press outside Palma is largely Catalan. In schools, Catalan as a subject is widely available, responding to pressure from parents and from local administrations (though in Eivissa 20% of pupils do not receive the prescribed hours of Catalan teaching). In 1990–1 17% of pupils had Catalan as their medium of education, in whole or in part; this trend is strongest in Menorca. In advertising and commerce Spanish predominates, but with Catalan increasing its role somewhat.

In Andorra, Catalan has always been the sole official language, though until recently secondary education was provided by the French and Spanish states, in their standard, monolingual, model. Spanish-speaking immigrants account for almost 40% of the population of about 50,000. Spanish and French are widely used in commerce, but Catalan predominates in other areas of public life. In 1993 Andorra adopted a new constitution, and the government has been pursuing an active 'Andorranization' policy, involving Catalan-medium education.

The status and position of Catalan in North Catalonia is closely parallel to that of the other traditional minority languages in France. Language shift was all but universal after the Second World War, so that most native speakers are over 50 years old. Catalan has at best an occasional, decorative, role in public life. In primary schools, some 30% study Catalan (as a 'foreign' language), and some 15% in secondary schools.

In Alghero, in 1987, it was estimated that about 58% of the population of 37,000 understood *alguerès*. However, intergenerational language shift to Italian is proceeding apace. Stimulated in part by Catalan revival further west, a certain pro-Catalan cultural movement can be observed, evident in local associations and local TV and radio. The language has no official role in the education system.

Carulla, M. 1990. *La lengua catalana en la actualidad*. Barcelona.

Ferrando, A. and Nicolás, M. 1993. *Panorama d'història de la llengua*. Valencia.

International Journal of the Sociology of Language, 47. 1984. Catalan sociolinguistics.

Oliva, S. and Buxton, A. 1983. *Diccionari anglès–català*. Barcelona.

—— 1986. *Diccionari català–anglès*. Barcelona.

[Various authors] 1991. Katalanisch. In Holtus, G., Metzeltin, M. and Schmitt, C. (eds), *Lexikon der Romanistischen Linguistik*, Tübingen, vol. 5.2, 127–310 (11 articles, 7 in Spanish, 1 in French, 1 in Italian, 2 in German).

Webber, J. and Strubell i Trueta, M. 1991. *The Catalan Language: Progress towards Normalisation*. Sheffield.

Wheeler, M., Yates, A. and Dols, N. 1999. *Catalan: a Comprehensive Grammar*. London.

MAX W. WHEELER

Caucasian languages

I General

The Caucasian languages constitute a group consisting of at least three language families indigenous to the Caucasus and spoken both north and south of the main chain (see map 3). The relevant speech communities are currently divided between the Russian Federation, Azerbaijan, Georgia and the disputed territory of Abkhazia. The group comprises roughly 40 languages, which, with the exception of Georgian, have either acquired a written form only within relatively recent history or remain unwritten.

The 10th-c. Arab geographer, al-Mas'udi, aptly named the Caucasus 'the mountain of tongues', and already at the start of the modern era the Greek geographer, Strabo, had written of Dioskurias, today's Abkhazian capital Aqw'a (known as Sukhum to non-Abkhazians): 'Seventy tribes gather there [. . .]. They all have a different language by reason of their living scattered about and separately because of their wilfulness and wildness [. . .]. They are all Caucasians.' Flanking the main Caucasus chain, which boasts Europe's highest peak, Elbrus, and runs for some 500 miles between the Black and Caspian Seas to form what many regard as the natural boundary between Europe and Asia, the various administrative divisions of the North Caucasus, which presently lie within the Russian Federation, and the newly recognized Transcaucasian republics of Georgia and Azerbaijan are home to speakers of a number of languages in addition to those peoples who are deemed to be the

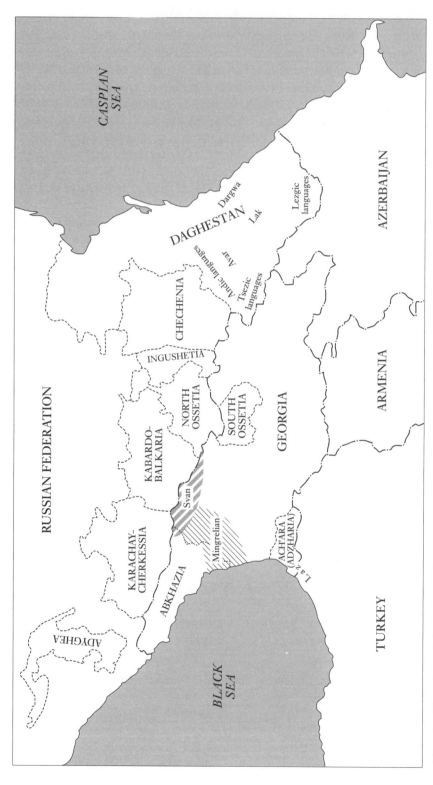

Map 3   Georgia and the northern Caucasus

autochthonous denizens of this region. It is only the languages of these latter which are referred to by the term 'Caucasian languages' – synonyms such as 'Japhetic languages', introduced by the eccentric Georgian-Scot Nikolai Marr, or 'Ibero-Caucasian languages', which is often used in the Caucasus itself, should be avoided.

Apart from Georgian, it was only in the 19th c. that sporadic attempts were made to introduce alphabets for some of these tongues, and during the Soviet period 11 were selected to hold the status of 'literary languages', possessing their own alphabets and enjoying rights in publishing, broadcasting and, to a greater or (more typically) lesser extent, education. The literary languages of Daghestan in the NE Caucasus (as well as Georgian) serve(d) more peoples than just the relevant eponymous ethnic group, and from *c*.1930 it became the norm within the USSR for one's ethnicity to be determined by which local literary standard one employed. This meant that all subsequent Soviet censuses were inaccurate in terms both of the actual size of some ethnic groups and of the picture of the first and second language-knowledge of the peoples affected by this artificial categorization. All native Caucasians living on formerly Soviet territory and educated during the Soviet period may be assumed to have command of Russian in addition to any other local language(s), and the influence of Russian, particularly in the semantic fields of science and civil administration, has been widespread and far-reaching. Centuries-old multilingualism has led to a great deal of mutual borrowing between neighbours. Traditionally, subordinate clauses (i.e. sequences containing conjunction and a finite verb with its arguments) have not been typical of North Caucasian languages; where we find these constructions developed or developing today, it is tempting to assume the influence of some neighbouring, non-North Caucasian language, but it is often impossible to be precise about the source of such influence (Indo-European, Turkic, South Caucasian).

Pioneering collections of folk tales and songs with musical notation, as well as ethnographic descriptions, for Caucasian languages can be found in the monumental series *Sbornik materialov dlja opisanija mestnostei i plemen Kavkaza* (henceforth abbreviated as *SMOMPK*) ('Collection of Materials for the Description of the Places and Peoples of the Caucasus'), which was produced in St Petersburg between 1883 and 1915. For some of the languages of Daghestan no dictionaries exist (at least in published form), and for many the only bilingual dictionaries (whether adequate or not) are with Russian as the second language.

Caucasian languages form three (possibly four) language families: **South Caucasian** (or **Kartvelian**), **North-West Caucasian**, **North Central Caucasian** (or **(Vei)Nakh**), and **North-East Caucasian** (or **Daghestanian**). These last two are clearly related, so that many prefer to deal with them as one family styled Nakh-Daghestanian. Some claim that all the northern languages are genetically related, but the incorporation of the three members of the North-West Caucasian group as joint descendants of a single proto-North Caucasian parent must be regarded as still awaiting final proof. It is, however, indisputable that the four Kartvelian languages have no genetic affiliation with their northern neighbours. Various attempts have been made to connect a number of languages (such as the extinct Anatolian Hurrian or the Iberian isolate ***Basque**) with this or that Caucasian family, but again no such hypothesis can be judged proven.

II The North-West Caucasian family

The family consists of **Abkhaz-Abaza, Circassian (Cherkess)** and **Ubykh**. The traditional homeland of these people was the (north-)east Black Sea coast and its hinterland, stretching at one time from the River Kuban (and possibly the Don) in the north down to Mingrelia (or even Guria) in today's Georgia. The Circassian tribes were the most northerly and numerous, abutting the Iranian-speaking Ossetians at the eastern fringe of their range, the Turkic-speaking Karachay-Balkars in the mountains to the south (after the appearance of this group in the wake of the Golden Horde) and the Ubykhs (native term [tʷaχə́] (an acute accent on a vowel indicates stress); the language is called [tʷaχə́ bza] or just [ʃəbzá] 'our language') around Sochi on the coast itself, whilst to the south of the Ubykhs lived the Abkhazians, who in turn were neighbours to the Kartvelian Mingrelians and Svans; the first wave of Abazinians migrated out of Abkhazia over the Klukhor Pass to the North Caucasus in the 14th c. to settle around today's Karachaevsk in what was to become Karachay-Cherkessia. This demographic picture suffered severe distortion when Tsarist Russia finally conquered the whole North Caucasus in 1864. Most of the Circassians and Abkhazians plus the entire Ubykh nation (along with, or followed over the years by, representatives of many other peoples from the North Caucasus) migrated to Ottoman lands, where today they form a diaspora-community of between 2 and 4 millions, concentrated in Turkey (with offshoots now resident in Germany and Holland) but actually stretching from Kosovo to Jordan. Subsequent decades saw large influxes of Slavs and, in the south, Kartvelians and Armenians on to historically North-West Caucasian territory.

Various attempts have been made to identify these peoples with some opaque ethnic terms employed by Greek authors as early as 500 BC, but it seems reasonably safe to link the Apsilians (Pliny the Elder's *gens Absilae* of the 1st c.) with the Abkhazians, whose own ethnonym is *Aps+wa* (collective plural *Aps+w[a]+aa*; the language is called [ápswa bəzʃʷa] or [ápsʃʷa]) and Arrian's *abasgoi* a century later with the Abazinians, who call themselves *Abaza* – the *sanigai*, whom Arrian locates to the north of the *abasgoi* apparently in the neighbourhood of today's Sukhum, are possibly to be identified with the one-time northern Abkhazian Sadz tribe, called in Abkhaz *A-sádz-kʷa*. Perhaps the earliest reference to North-West Caucasian languages comes in the *Libellus de notitia orbis* of Johannes de Galonifontibus of 1404, who, when speaking of 'Zikia or Circassia', states: 'They have their own language and writing [*sic*].' He adds: 'Beyond these is Abkhazia [. . .]. They have their own language.' And the medieval Georgian chronicles explain the sobriquet 'Lasha' of their sovereign Giorgi (1213–22) as 'meaning "enlightenment" in the language of the Apsars', when in Abkhaz we have [á-laṣa] 'clear' and [a-laṣára] 'light'. However, the first concrete examples of the languages are found in the word- and phrase-lists of the half-Abkhazian Turkish traveller of the 1640s, Evliya Çelebi, who quotes Circassian, Abkhaz (called 'Abaza') and Ubykh (called 'Sadsha-Abaza') examples (Gippert 1992). Circassian (Kabardian) was one of the languages included in the word-lists compiled by Johann Anton Güldenstädt during his 1770–3 travels in the Caucasus for the St Petersburg Academy, described in two volumes published in 1787 and 1791.

Dialects

Within **Abkhazia** two dialects are spoken: the northern, phonetically more complex (with 67 consonantal phonemes) Bzyp, and the southern Abzhui (or Abzhywa), which has 58 consonantal phonemes. Abaza is normally described as having two dialects of its own, namely T'ap'anta and Ashkharywa, though linguistically speaking it is more accurate to think in terms of a single Abkhaz–Abaza dialect continuum with Abzhywa at one extremity and T'ap'anta at the other; it has been suggested that Ashkarywa occupies a transitional position between T'ap'anta and the Sadz dialect, which today survives only in Turkey.

The **Circassian** dialects divide into a western and an eastern group. The former, usually referred to as Adyghe (N.B. *all* Circassians call themselves [ádəγe] and their language [ádəγe bze]), consists of: Bzhedukh (the most complex in terms of consonantal phonemes with 66), Shapsugh, Temirgoy and Abadzekh (Abzakh), of which the last predominated in pre-1864 Caucasia and is perhaps the most widespread of the diaspora dialects, though today only a single village, Shovgenovskij, remains in the Caucasus. East Circassian, commonly known as Kabardian, has two dialects: Kabardian (proper; phonologically the simplest of the whole North-West Caucasian family with 45 consonantal phonemes in its literary form) and Bes(le)ney.

Ubykh (with 83, possibly 84, consonantal phonemes, if one includes three that appear only in loans) was already in terminal decline when it became the object of philological investigation, making it impossible to detect any dialectal distinctions; it effectively became extinct in October 1992 with the death of the last fully competent native speaker, Tevfik Esenç. In their native environment it seems the Ubykhs were all bilingual in either (? Sadz) Abkhaz or Circassian; in their adopted homeland the Ubykhs' universal Caucasian language (whether in addition to Ubykh or exclusively so) has been Circassian, and this has been argued to represent a quite distinct variety of Circassian (Smeets 1988).

Study and writing

Abkhaz: Apart from an unpublished early 19th-c. Abkhaz–Russian dictionary reported to survive in a Tbilisi archive, serious study of Abkhaz, if one excludes a brief description by G. Rosen in the 1840s, began in the 1860s with the work of the pioneer investigator of North Caucasian languages, the Russian soldier-linguist Baron P. K. Uslar, whose monograph on Abkhaz first appeared in lithographic form in 1863 and was the first of the seven grammars he was to produce in a decade – see also A. Schiefner's *Ausführlicher Bericht über des Generals Baron Peter von Uslar Abchasische Studien* of 1863. The alphabet Uslar devised was based on

*Cyrillic and consisted of 55 characters, which did not quite manage to distinguish all the phonemes of the Bzyp dialect he was describing. Various adaptations were introduced until A. Ch'och'ua's version was adopted in 1909 to last for 20 years, in which medium the Gospels (1912) and Ch'och'ua's own school-primer (1920) were published. Marr employed his idiosyncratic 'Analytical Alphabet' of 75 characters for his *Abkhaz–Russian Dictionary* (1926), but, though based on the Roman alphabet, this was too complicated for general use. As a result a new Roman-based script was devised by N. Jakovlev, and this 'Unified Abkhaz Alphabet' was introduced in 1928 as part of the USSR's 'Latinization' drive for the so-called 'Young Written Languages'. It was at about this time that the literary standard shifted from Bzyp to Abzhui, which was not only less complex in its sound-system but represented the dialect of most of the main writers of the day. When these Roman-based scripts were generally abolished in favour of Cyrillic-based systems in 1936–8, Abkhaz (like the Ossetic in Georgia's province of South Ossetia) had to adopt a Georgian-based script as part of (Georgian) Stalin and (Mingrelian) Beria's policy of Georgianizing Abkhazia (and South Ossetia). This script continued until the deaths of Stalin and Beria in 1953, though in fact little was published since from the mid-1940s Abkhazian schools were replaced by Georgian schools and publishing was banned. The literary status of the language was subsequently restored with a new, Cyrillic-based script, which was devised by a committee; it utilizes no fewer than 14 non-Cyrillic characters (some borrowed from Uslar's system) and is inconsistent in its marking of some phonological features. Despite these drawbacks, this alphabet is still in use, though suggestions have been made that it should be replaced by a Roman-based variant that would be especially attractive to Turkish Abkhazians and thus serve as a universal form of written communication among Abkhazians both at home and abroad if it used the phonetic values of the Roman characters well established for Turkish itself; in Turkey, Abkhaz is neither taught nor written and, like other such languages there, is gradually being lost as young people migrate from village to town or abroad for economic reasons. The establishment of a writing system that would be easy to learn and type on Turkish typewriters, especially if it could provide a written medium for all the varieties of North-West Caucasian still extant in Turkey, could provide just the focus these languages need if they are to survive.

Though merely a divergent dialect of Abkhaz, the T'ap'anta variant of Abaza was awarded literary status and provided with a Roman-based alphabet in 1932; the Abazinians, after all, live geographically isolated from the bulk of the Abkhazians. In 1938 this yielded to the Cyrillic-based script that still functions today. It resembles the other North Caucasian scripts in employing only one character not found in the modern Cyrillic alphabet, namely the old Cyrillic capital <I>; it thus differs considerably from the post-1953 Abkhaz script.

Circassian: For Circassian the Kabardian Shora Nogma (1801–44) devised a Cyrillic-based alphabet for his dictionary and grammar of his native dialect (published in two volumes in Nal'chik in 1956 and 1959). Later, Arabic was tried for both eastern and western Circassian, as in L. Loewe's *A Dictionary of the Circassian Language* (published in 1854 by the British Philological Society), though a Roman transcription is also given. The early Soviets established two literary standards for Circassian, selecting the Temirgoy and Kabardian dialects for the western and eastern varieties respectively. Kabardian devised a form of Roman to replace Arabic in 1924 and shifted to Cyrillic in 1936, whereas Adyghe replaced Arabic with Roman in 1928 and moved to Cyrillic in 1938. Whether as part of a policy of *Divide et impera!* or for the less sinister reason that different scholars were charged with the separate tasks, the two Circassian scripts do look as though they were designed to split rather than unite this single speech community: the sound [qʷ] is represented in Kabardian by the tesseragraph <кхьу> but in Adyghe by the trigraph <кьу>, whilst the sound [ʃ] is represented in Kabardian by <ш> and in Adyghe by <щ>; in Adyghe the character <ш> has the value [ʂ], whilst in Kabardian the character <щ> has the value [ɕ]. Discussions are currently taking place about the possibility of redesigning a Roman-based alphabet for Adyghe at least. Amongst the diaspora it seems to be only in the two Shapsugh villages found in Israel that Circassian is taught on a regular basis. The distinguished Russian Caucasologist, N. Jakovlev, wrote grammars of both literary Kabardian (1948) and (in association with D. Ashkhamaf) literary Adyghe (1941) – his grammar of Abkhaz remains unpublished.

Ubykh: The only linguist to have an opportunity to investigate Ubykh before the exodus was Uslar, whose observations are incorporated as a separate essay in his monograph on Abkhaz. In exile the Ubykhs were visited by the Dane Benediksten, whose notes were never published, the German Adolf Dirr, who wrote sketches of *all* the Caucasian languages in his time, the Hungarian Julius von Mészáros, and most significantly the late Georges Dumézil, whose voluminous work on North-West Caucasian languages began in the 1920s and to whom we owe most of the Ubykh material in existence (especially in collaboration with Tevfik Esenç from the 1950s). Hans Vogt and Georges Charachidzé have also contributed to the study of this language.

Numbers of speakers

Abkhaz: According to the last Soviet census of 1989, some 102,938 Abkhazians lived in the USSR, of whom 95,853 resided in Georgia, the majority of 93,267 within the then Abkhazian Autonomous Soviet Socialist Republic itself, where they represented 17.8% of the population; the demography of Abkhazia was radically altered as a result of the war sparked by the Georgian invasion on 14 August 1992 and the Abkhazian victory 14 months later, which presented the republic with a *de facto* but uncertain independence that still obtains at the time of writing. Those Abkhazians who lived in mixed communities with Mingrelians tended to speak Mingrelian also, whilst those who were educated in the 1940s could be expected to know Georgian. There were 33,801 Soviet Abazinians, of whom 27,475 formed 6.5% of the population of the then Karachay-Cherkess Autonomous Region (capital Cherkessk); Abazinians in the Caucasus tend to speak Kabardian also.

Circassian: There were 124,941 Soviet West Circassians, of whom 95,439 formed 22% of the population of the then Adyghe Autonomous Region (capital Maykop), most of the rest living in the neighbouring Krasnodar District, including 10,000 Shapsughs around Tuapse on the Black Sea. East Circassians living in Karachay-Cherkessia were in Soviet terminology known as Cherkess, and there were 52,356 on Soviet territory, of whom 40,230 constituted 9.6% of the population of this region, whilst the rest were called Kabardians, the total USSR population of whom numbered 394,651; of these 363,351 made up 48.2% of the population of the then Kabardino-Balkar Autonomous Soviet Socialist Republic (capital Nal'chik).

Influence of other languages

Iranian (?**Ossetic**) and *****Turkish** influence is present throughout the family, whilst four different strata of Kartvelianisms in Abkhaz-Abaza are detectable: (1) those found even in T'ap'anta Abaza; (2) those extending to Ashkharywa but absent from T'ap'anta; (3) those attested among the diaspora but absent from the Abaza dialects in the North Caucasus today; (4) those that infiltrated with the increasing Kartvelian presence in Abkhazia following the loss of much of the native population. Ubykh borrowed from both its sisters.

III The North Central Caucasian ((Vei)Nakh) family

This family comprises **Chechen, Ingush** and **Bats(bi)**, the non-geographic designations for the group deriving from their common lexicon for '(Our) People' – the occasionally heard synonym 'Kist' languages' should be avoided. Most commentators talk of a level of mutual intelligibility between Chechen and Ingush dialects, but no such link exists between either and Bats, thanks to the physical separation of this last from the Chechen-Ingush speech community, which lies in the east of the North Central Caucasus between North Ossetia and Daghestan, the Ingush being the buffer between Ossetes and Chechens. The Bats seem originally to have resided in a handful of villages in the northern Georgian province of Tusheti (from which comes their Georgian name of *Ts'ova-Tush*), but they began to migrate to lowland Georgia early in the 19th c. and now live compactly in the single village of Zemo Alvani in the eastern Georgian province of K'akheti(a), numbering at most 5,000. Some Chechens live in Daghestan and eastern Georgia, and both Ingush and Chechens can be found on former Ottoman territory (especially Jordan) or in Central Asia, where the entire Chechen and Ingush nations were deported in 1944 by Stalin on the trumped-up charge of collaboration with the invading Nazis (who never actually reached this part of the North Caucasus), their eponymous regions being renamed and distributed among neighbouring administrative units, as may be seen on all Soviet maps produced between then and their official permission to return home in 1957, when the territorial names were re-established (albeit with certain boundary changes). At the start of the great Caucasian War in 1817 many Ingush were resettled in lowland areas around Nazran, which was eventually to become their 20th-c. capital, though the most intensive period of their resettlement from mountain areas occurred between 1830 and 1860.

Names

The Chechens call themselves *Nwokhchuo* (plural *Nwokhchi:*) and their language *Nwokhchi:^{n} mot:*, the term 'Chechen' deriving from the name of the first Chechen village encountered by Russians in their imperial drive to conquer the Caucasus. Of parallel origin is the term 'Ingush', for these people have the self-designation *Ghalghaj*, and the language is *Ghalghaj mot:*. A male Bats calls himself *Batsav* (plural *Batsbi*) and his language *Batsb-ur mot:*.

Dialects

Neither Ingush nor Bats is differentiated dialectally, whilst Chechen comprises Lowland Chechen (the base of the literary language) plus, according to the adjectival forms given in Russian sources: Cheberlojskij, Sharojskij, Shatojsko-Itumkalinskij, Galanchzhojskij, Akkinskij (the form spoken by Chechens around Khasavyurt in Daghestan, otherwise known as the Aukhov Chechens) and the Mountain dialect consisting of the subdialects Khildikharojskij and Majstinskij, which subforms are spoken by those Chechens who migrated to eastern Georgia between the 17th c. and the late 19th c., though in Georgian sources those mountain-Chechens who neigh-bour the northern Georgian Khevsur, Pshav and Tush tribes are known as 'Kist's'. Correspondingly, Georgians refer to a 'Kist' dialect, and the (Soviet) Georgian Encyclopaedia maintains that Chechens living in eastern Georgia speak in the home a mixed Kist'–Georgian patois.

Earliest attestations and scholarly interest

Reference to the Chechens as 'Nakhchamatyan' is found in an Armenian source of the 7th c. The neighbouring Kumyks call them 'Michigish' (from the River Michik), and it is under the title 'Mizdschegische Mundarten' that Güldenstädt presents the first attested examples for all three languages of the family in the 1770s. Bats was the first of the group to become the object of linguistic attention when A. Schiefner published his *Versuch über die Thusch-Sprache* in 1856. The first scholarly study of Chechen was made by Uslar, whose grammar appeared in 1888 as the second in his series of seven monographs. Jakovlev published a comprehensive study of the syntax in 1941, but his separate treatment of morphology, though completed in 1939, was published only in 1959. The first grammar of Ingush was by the native Z. Mal'sagov and published in Russian in Vladikavkaz in 1925.

Written forms

In the words of one local linguist, A. Magomedov, writing in 1974: 'The results of Tsarist politics in the Caucasus created conditions which excluded any possibility of raising the question of a joint Chechen–Ingush written language from the very first days of the establishment of Soviet power.' Consequently, two literary languages were created: for Chechen the Lowland dialect was selected as the standard, and an

Arabic-based script was tried between 1920 and 1924, which gave way to a Roman system from 1925 to 1937, which in turn yielded in 1938 to a typically North Caucasian Cyrillic-based alphabet, which however was not fully phonemic in so far as it failed to differentiate all the vocalic oppositions. A new Roman script was introduced in 1993 after the collapse of the USSR and General Dzhokhar Dudaev's declaration of independence. The Roman alphabet was used as the basis for the first Ingush script as early as 1923, but in 1938 this was superseded by Cyrillic. Bats has never been officially written; the 1984 *Ts'ova–Tush–Georgian–Russian Dictionary* by Davit and Nik'o Kadagidze quotes Bats entries in both the Georgian script and a Roman-based transcription.

Numbers of speakers

In 1989 the Soviet Chechen population amounted to 958,309, whilst that of the Ingush was 237,577 – in 1944 it seems that about 400,000 Chechens and 100,000 Ingush suffered deportation, losing up to half these numbers in the process. Of the 1989 totals some 734,501 Chechens and 163,711 Ingush together constituted 70.7% of their then joint Chechen–Ingush Autonomous Soviet Socialist Republic within the Russian Federation. At the beginning of Soviet power in the North Caucasus Chechenia and Ingush(et)ia were part of a larger Mountain Autonomous Soviet Socialist Republic. From this various regions gradually split off, including Chechenia in 1922 and Ingush(et)ia in 1924, both becoming separate Autonomous Regions. They were united in 1934, again as an Autonomous Region with the capital in the oil-town of Groznyj (originally built at the start of the 19th-c. Caucasian War as a fortress and given its Russian name meaning 'menacing, threatening, terrible' to instil appropriate alarm in the natives – in vain), but the territory's status was raised to that of an Autonomous Republic in 1936. This remained the case after the Chechens and Ingush were allowed (but not assisted) to return home after their Central Asian exile in 1957, except that a portion of Ingush land, the Prigorodnyj Raion, was left in North Ossetian control. After General Dudaev announced he was exercising his right under the Soviet constitution to take Chechenia out of the Russian Federation, the Ingush were persuaded again to split off from the Chechens. Fighting between Ossetes and Ingush in 1992 caused many deaths and a flight of refugees. The stand-off between President Yeltsin and Dudaev came to a head on 11 December 1994 when the Russian airforce began bombing Groznyj. The subsequent campaign killed up to 40,000 (mainly civilians) and caused huge numbers of refugees to flee into both Ingush(et)ia and Daghestan. During the years of exile the Chechens and Ingush made certain that their language(s), religion (a conservative form of Islam that was introduced in Chechenia from the 16th c., though the Ingush were only converted as late as the 19th c.) and culture survived, although they were permitted no facilities for doing so, as a continuing sign of resistance to the Russians which had begun with the defensive campaigns of the Chechen Sheikh Mansur in the 1780s.

Influence of other languages

Arabic, Iranian (especially Ossetic), Turkish and Georgian influences are detectable in all three of the languages in this family. Bats, however, has been subjected to particularly heavy Georgian influence; all Bats speak Georgian, are educated in it, and use it as their first literary language. The future of Bats must be reckoned especially bleak.

IV The North-East Caucasian (Daghestanian) family

Not only is the multilingualism in the uniquely cosmopolitan republic of Daghestan often of staggering proportions but, because of local conditions (with many languages spoken in remote mountain regions in perhaps only a handful of villages), it regularly happens that inhabitants of the highest areas additionally speak the language of those residing below them and so on down to the plains. Dirr states how his informant for Archi, Mohamed Mohamedlin Lo, also spoke Lak, Avar, Aghul (as well as Turkic Kumyk, Arabic and Russian). Census data do not exist for many of the smaller language-groups, as the speakers categorize themselves according to which local language they learn at school and thus use as their primary literary language (e.g. 'Avars' include the speakers of all the Andic and Tsezic languages). It is sometimes even the case that a local ethnonym for a particular speech community does not exist, speakers identifying themselves, when asked to be precise, as natives of this or that *aul* 'village'.

Daghestanian languages, some of which are spoken only outside the Daghestan republic (principally in Azerbaijan), fall into three main subgroups:

(1) The **Avaro-Ando-Tsezic(Didoic)** subgroup, which is especially rich in lateral consonants, consists of:
Avaric: **Avar**
Andic: **Andi, Botlikh, Ghodoberi, K'arat'a, Akhvakh, Bagvalal, T'indi, Ch'amalal**
Tsezic: **Tsez** (Dido), **Khvarshi, Hinukh, Bezht'a** (K'ap'uch'a), **Hunzib** (some treat these last two as co-dialects).
(2) The **Lako-Dargic** subgroup consists of:
Lakic: **Lak**
Dargic: **Dargwa** (Dargin) – the language vs. dialect status of the K'ubachi, Chiragh and Megeb varieties is disputed.
(3) The **Lezgic** subgroup consists of:
Lezgi(an), Tabasaran, Rutul (Mukhad), **Ts'akhur, Aghul, Udi, Archi, Budukh, Khinalugh, Kryts'.**

Territorial spread

Although today North-East Caucasian speakers are found in the capital of Daghestan, Makhachkala, and the non-mountainous region to its north, their ancestral distribution in their original mountain areas is roughly as follows: in the heights to the east of Chechenia live the Andic speakers, with Andi the northernmost, T'indi the southernmost; Ghodoberi, Botlikh and K'arat'a lie to the south of Andi moving west to east, whilst to their south in a parallel spread lie Ch'amalal, Bagvalal and Akhvakh. Avar runs from east of the Andic subgroup in the northern mountains down towards central Daghestan. Bounded by Andic, Avar and the Georgian provinces of Tusheti (in NE Georgia) and K'akheti (in eastern Georgia), into which their range slightly extends, lie the Tsezic group, Tsez abutting Tusheti and divided from T'indi by Khvarshi; to the south of Tsez lies Hinukh, to the south of which Bezht'a is in turn spoken; Hunzib is squeezed between Avar and each of its immediate sisters. The east of central Daghestan is the home of the Dargic group (K'ubachi being spoken only in its eponymous *aul* in the south-east), but the coastal strip down to the Lezgian speech community is settled by (Turkic) Kumyks (see *Kumyk) with some (Iranian) Tats (see *Tat) towards the south of the range. Between Dargic and Avar lies Lak, with Archi split off from its sister Lezgic tongues in a pocket between Avar and Lak. Southern Daghestan and northern Azerbaijan is the home of the Lezgic group, with the Lezgian speech community actually straddling the now international Russo-Azerbaijani border. Lezgian is cut off from Lak–Dargwa by Tabasaran in the east, Aghul in the centre (though with a pocket of Lak speakers in between them) and Rutul to the west, to the west of which in its turn lies Ts'akhur; Rutul, Ts'akhur and (to the west) Avar all extend into Azerbaijan. Budukh, Khinalugh and Kryts', whose genetic affiliation to the Lezgic group has been doubted by some, are spoken only in northern Azerbaijan, whilst Udi is spoken in two villages of Azerbaijan (Vartashen and Nidzh) and in one (Okt'omberi, formerly Zinobiani) in eastern Georgia – it has been suggested that Udi is the descendant of the 'lost' Caucasian Albanian, which was the third major Transcaucasian language (alongside Georgian and Armenian) in the first millennium of our era with (like them) its own alphabet.

Dialects, names, and numbers of speakers

Avaric: The Avars are the largest of the peoples with a 1989 pan-Soviet total (inflated as explained above) of 604,202. Mystery surrounds the origin of this ethnonym. They are certainly not related to the Turkic-speaking Avars, who reached Europe in the Middle Ages. They refer to themselves as [maʕarul tʃi] 'Mountain Person' and call their language similarly [maʕarul mats:']. The Georgians call them [xundz-eb-i]. The language is rich in dialects and subdialects. The main divisions are: northern Khundzakh vs southern Ants'ukh and Ch'ar vs intermediate Batlukh – a mixed form of Avar that served in pre-Russian days as a north Daghestanian koine was known as [bol mats:'] 'People's Language'.

Andic: When Ilia Tsertsvadze wrote his Andi grammar in Georgian in 1965, he numbered the speakers at up to 9,000; a male Andi calls himself [q'vann-av], whereas a woman will be [q'vann-aj], and the language is [q'vann-ab mits:'i] – the more familiar designation derives from the Avar ethnonym, which is also true of the other Andic languages. There is an upper and a lower group of dialects. The upper consists of the varieties found in Andi, Ghaghatl, Rik'van, Chankho and Zilo, whilst the more homogeneous lower dialect incorporates the speech of Munib and Kvankhidatl. There are a few, but rigidly observed, distinctions between the speech of men and women. In 1973 P. Saidova numbered Ghodoberi speakers at above 2,500. They call themselves [ɣibdidi] and their language [ɣibdikɬ: mits:i] (their Avar designation is [ɣodoberisel]). Spoken in the two *auls* of Ghodoberi and Zibirkhali, local differences are mainly limited to the Ghodoberi palatalization of Zibirkhali velars. In 1963 T'ogo Gudava in his Georgian grammar numbered Botlikh speakers at no more than 3,000. They call their language [bujxadɬi mits:i]. The language is spoken in the two *auls* of Botlikh and Miarsu, the native term in the former village being [bujxe], whilst in the latter it is [kilu]. The two forms of the language are very close, with the speech of Miarsu holding an intermediate position between Botlikh proper and Ghodoberi. In his 1971 Georgian monograph, Gudava numbered the speakers of the six *auls* that constitute the Bagvalal speech community at up to 4,000. Bagvalal is extremely close to T'indi. Native speakers have no self-designation in their language, taking the term *Bagvalal* from Avar; sometimes they refer to their language after the name of the largest *aul*, K'vanada. The speech of each of the six *auls* has its own characteristics. In her 1971 Russian monograph, Z. Magomedbekova numbered the speakers of K'arat'a at around 6,000, distributed among ten *auls*, each of which has its own linguistic peculiarities, although there are two main dialects: K'arat'a proper and (in the Russian adjectival form) *Tokitinskij*. The native term for the language is [k:irkɬ:i mats:'i], which is to be understood as 'the language of (the *aul*) K:'ira', whose Avar designation is [k:'arat'a]. In her Russian grammar of 1967, Magomedbekova numbered Akhvakh speakers at around 5,000, living in nine *auls*. An Akhvakh male calls himself [aʃwado], and his language is [aʃwakɬ:i mits:i], whilst the Avars call them [ʕaẋwalal] ([ẋ] indicates palatalized [x]). There is a basic north(-west) vs south(-east) dialectal division, the northern group being more uniform than the southern with its three subdivisions. For the 1966 4th volume in the series *Jazyki Narodov SSSR* ('Languages of the Peoples of the USSR'), which covered all the Caucasian languages, Gudava numbered the speakers of T'indi at about 5,000, living in five *auls*, of which the largest is called in the local language Idari, though the Avars name it T'indi. The language is designated after the local name of the main *aul* (viz. [idarab mits:i]), whilst native speakers call themselves after the name of their particular *aul*. There are no real dialectal divisions. T'indi, Bagvalal and Ch'amalal form an especially close subgroup within Andic. In the same 1966 volume, Magomedbekova numbered the speakers of Ch'amalal at around 4,000, distributed among nine *auls*. The language is known locally as [tʃ'amalaldub mits:']. It may be divided into the two dialects of Gakvari and Gigatl (after their Russian titles).

Tsezic: In his comparative 1963 Russian monograph on Dido (the Georgian term for Tsez, which latter is the speakers' self-designation) and its cognates (Hinukh and Khvarshi), Davit Imnaishvili pointed out that the tribal terms *Diduri* and *Diduroi* appear in the works of the 1st-c. Pliny the Elder and of the 2nd-c. Ptolemy. He numbered the Tsez speakers at the time at about 7,000 (which figure, however, seems merely to have been repeated from the 1926 first pan-Soviet census, quoted by E. Bokarëv in his 1959 book on the Tsezic tongues), as against 200 Hinukhs (the same number apparently as in 1926) and 2,000 (double the 1926 total) speakers of Khvarshi, which latter is sharply divided into Khvarshi proper and Inkhokari, the dialect of the majority of speakers. The differences between the Tsezic subgroup of languages are in general greater than those differentiating the Andic subgroup. In 1966 Bokarëv (*Jazyki Narodov SSSR,IV*) gave the number of Hunzib speakers as 600 (again identical to the 1926 census figure). For Bezht'a, E. Bokarëv and G. Madieva gave the number of speakers as 2,500 (yet again a mysterious repetition of the 1926 census data), divided into the three clearly demarcated dialects of Bezht'a proper (over 1,500 speakers), Tljadal (*c.*500 speakers), and Khochar-Khota (*c.*300 speakers). The most recent figures available (van den Berg 1995) are: Tsez 14,000; Bezht'a 7,000; Hunzib 2,000; Khvarshi 1,500; Hinukh 500.

Lakic: In 1989 there were 118,386 Laks in the USSR. Their self-designation is *Lak*, and the following dialectal divisions have been proposed: Kumukh, Vitskhin, Bartkhin, Arakul, Shadnin, Vikhlin, Pervocovkrin, Kajalinsko-Mashchikhin, and Vachi-Kulin.

Dargic: In 1989 some 365,797 Dargwas lived in the USSR. They call themselves [dargan] and their language [dargan mez]. In his 1985 Russian monograph entitled *Darginskij i Megebskij Jazyki* 'The Dargwa and Megeb Languages', S. Khajdakov sets out the dialects according to the schema:

Darwa root-language

Khajdak branch	*Aqush branch*
Khajdak	Aqush
Chiragh	Gubden
Ts'udaqar	Huraq
K'ubachi	Dibgash–Megeb
Tant	Kichigamri

A native of K'ubachi calls himself [ʕuːɣbugan].

Lezgic: The 1989 pan-Soviet total of Lezgians was 466,833. The native designation is *Lezgi*, whilst the language is called [lezgi tʃ'al]. There are no great dialectal divisions, though the three groups of Kjure, Akhtseh and Quba have been proposed. According to the 1989 census the total of Soviet Tabasarans was 98,448. Their self-designation is *Tabasaran*, and they call their language [tabasaran tʃ'al]. There are two main dialects, a northern (retaining, for example, a two-way class-system) and a southern (where grammatical class-marking has disappeared). The 1989 Soviet census included three other Lezgic-speaking peoples: there were 20,672 Rutuls, 20,055 Ts'akhurs (though I. Ibragimov's 1990 Russian monograph speaks of 30,000) and 19,936 Aghuls. The Rutul dialects are Mukhad, Mukhrek-Ikhrek and Borch. A rutul calls himself [məxaʃura] and his language [məxanid tʃ'al]. The Ts'akhur dialects are Ts'akhur proper, Mishlesh, Mikik and Gilmits'. A Ts'akhur calls himself [jəqʰi] and his language [ts'äxna miz] (where the diaeresis marks pharyngalization). For Aghul one can perhaps distinguish the two dialects of Aghul proper and Kosh. An Aghul calls himself [aɣul ʃuj] and his language [aɣul tʃ'al]. There are about 1,000 speakers of Archi, who live in a single *aul* of the same name. A male speaker calls himself [arʃiʃt:uv], a female [arʃiʃt:ur], and the language is [arʃat:en tʃ'at]. Thanks to the four-volume (Russian) grammar and dictionary by A. Kibrik (1977), this language is one of the best described of any in Daghestan. In the penultimate Soviet census of 1979 it seems that there were 6,863 Udis, of whom 89.9% declared Udi to be their native language. Classical Greek knew the ethnonym Οὐίτιοι and Armenian had [utəkʰ]. They call themselves Udi. The speech varieties of the villages Vartashen and Nidzh differ greatly, whilst the Udi of the one Georgian village is close to Vartashen. About 1,000 Budukhs live in the one *aul* of the same name in northern Azerbaijan, where they call themselves [budad] and their language [budanu mez]. Some 8,000 speakers of Kryts' live in about five *auls* in northern Azerbaijan, where the language divides into four dialects: Kryts' proper, Dzhek, Khaput and Alyk. The speakers call themselves [ɢrəts'ar] and their language [ɢrəts'ä mez] ([ä] indicates a very open [a]). About 2,000 Khinalughs live in the one *aul* of the same name in northern Azerbaijan. They themselves call this village *Ketsh* and from it come both their self-designation of [ketʃ xalx] 'the Ketsh folk' and their term for the language, namely [ketʃ/kätʃ mits'].

Literary varieties

For most of the Soviet period, the Daghestanian literary languages were Avar, Lak, Lezgian, Dargwa and Tabasaran. Arabic was used for some literature in Avar, Lak and Dargwa from the 19th c., and in the 1920s some textbooks and a Dargwa paper were printed using it, but in the main these literary languages were provided with Roman-based orthographies only in 1928, being then wrenched into Cyrillic in 1938. For Tabasaran, however, the Roman script was created only in 1932. The Avar dialect chosen as the basis for the literary language was the northern Khundzakh, just as this same dialect had underlain the earlier *Bol mats:'*. For literary Lak the Kumukh dialect was selected. Literary Dargwa is based on Aqush. For Tabasaran the southern dialect (without class distinctions) became the literary standard, whilst for Lezgian the type of Kjure known as Gjune (from the former name of the district where it is spoken) was chosen. In addition to these established literary languages, the attempts to create similar literatures for Ts'akhur, Aghul, Rutul and Udi in the early 1930s (i.e. during the so-called Latinization drive) failed. A version of the Gospels in Udi had in fact been printed in *SMOMPK* (see above, I, 'General') in 1893, and in 1934 an alphabet-reader of Vartashen by F. Dzheiranishvili appeared. Interestingly the Ts'akhurs, Aghuls and Rutuls are attempting to re-establish a writing system for their languages today, and there has been talk of creating an alphabet for Tsez.

Earliest attestations and scholarly interest

Güldenstädt provides the first citations for some of the Daghestanian languages in his 1770s collection. He omits entirely any reference to the Lezgic subgroup (along with North-West Caucasian Ubykh and South Caucasian Laz), and quotes three dialectal forms of Avar (Ants'ukh, Ch'ar and Khundzakh) alongside Dido as forming a single language-group. Under the rubric *Sprachen der Kasikumüken, Andi und Akuscha* he illustrated respectively Lak (Q'azi-q'umukh), Andi and (the Aqush dialect of) Dargwa (clearly Andi is misplaced both linguistically and territorially). In addition to his work on Bats and Abkhaz, Anton Schiefner contributed a 54-page work on Avar (*Versuch über das Awarische*) in 1862 (his *Awarische Texte* followed in 1873) and a 110-page description in 1863 on Udi (*Versuch über die Sprache der Uden*). But it was Uslar who produced full grammars of the following five major Daghestanian languages: Avar (1889), Lak (1890), Dargwa, which he called *Xjurkilinskij* (1892), Lezgian, which he called *Kjurinskij* (1896), and Tabasaran (1979). The dates refer to the publication of the printed versions, for all the monographs were completed in the 1860s–early 1870s. His description of Tabasaran, however, remained incomplete, and the manuscript disappeared, to be rediscovered in the 1940s. It was photographically reproduced to mark the anniversary of the author's death. Material for the remaining languages of Daghestan received their first citation in Roderich von Erckert's *Die Sprachen des kaukasischen Stammes* (1895). Dirr then published sketches of Udi, Tabasaran, Andi, Aghul, Archi, Rutul and Ts'akhur in various fascicles of *SMOMPK* between 1903 and 1913.

Influence of other languages

Islam came early (viz. 8th–9th c.) to at least parts of Daghestan, which was an acknowledged centre of learning for Arabic and Islam until this was suppressed by the Russians. In addition to Arabic and the Avar *Bol mats:*', *Azeri traditionally served as a Daghestanian lingua franca, especially in the south, where it is still known by Daghestanis both in northern Azerbaijan and in southern Daghestan – in the early Soviet period, in order to break the reliance on Arabic, Turkic *Kumyk was encouraged in the north of the autonomous republic. After 135 years of Russian rule (including 70 years of communist isolation), virtually all Daghestanis have a good knowledge of Russian in addition to whatever other language(s) they may speak. It is, thus, quite natural to find widespread influence on all the indigenous languages of the region from Arabic, Turkic (Azeri or Kumyk) and Russian (in addition to the influence of the major local tongues on the smaller ones).

V The South Caucasian (Kartvelian) family

This family consists of Georgian (treated separately under **VI** below by virtue of its unique position as the only Caucasian language with a centuries-old literary tradition), **Svan**, **Mingrelian (Megrelian)** and **Laz (Ch'an)**. Svan is the most archaic, whilst the most recent division is that between Mingrelian and Laz. Indeed, these are the only two members of the family between which there is any mutual intelligibility, and for this reason some (particularly in the Caucasus) prefer to view them as dialects of the so-called Zan language. Svan is spoken in the remote mountainous region of NW Georgia, abutting Georgian to the south-east, Mingrelian to the south-west and Abkhaz to the west; the Lower and Upper Bal dialects of Upper Svaneti(a) nestle in the upper reaches of the Ingur river, whilst the Lashkh and Lent'ekh (possibly also Cholur) dialects of Lower Svaneti(a) are heard in the upper reaches of the Tskhenists'q'ali river. The traditional locale of Mingrelian extended from the Tskhenists'q'ali in the east to roughly the Ingur in the north-west and down to the province of Guria (south of the port of Poti, the ancient Phasis) in the south, though over the last century it has been yielding to Georgian in the east of its range whilst gaining ground to the disadvantage of Abkhaz in the north-west. There are at least the two dialects of Zugdidian (from the old capital, Zugdidi) in the west and Senak'ian in the east. Though pockets of Laz-speakers are found along the Black Sea coast in both Abkhazia and Georgia's province of Ach'ara (Adzharia), the main homeland of Lazistan runs from the Georgian–Turkish border at Sarpi along Turkey's coastline almost up to Rize. Laz has the three main dialects of Khopa, Vitse-Arkabe and Atina.

Svans call themselves *Shwan-är (Mu-shwän,* in the Upper Bal singular form) and their language *Lushnu nin;* the native Mingrelian ethnonym is *Margal-i* (though the Svans call them *Zan-är*), whilst that of the Laz is *Laz-i*; the native terms for the last two languages are respectively *Margal-ur-i nina* and *Laz-ur-i nena.* Among the various tribal names found in the ancient authors for those residing in the poorly defined geographical area known as Colchis, which in the 1st c. seems to have run roughly from Pitsunda in N. Abkhazia to Trebizond, we read, in Strabo for instance, of the *Soanes*, who are placed more or less in the area still occupied by the Svans, and of the *Sannoi* (otherwise referred to as *Tzan(n)oi)* above Trebizond; other authors know a people called *Makrones.* The kingdom of Lazica in the region of Colchis was well known to writers in the middle of the first millennium of the Christian era. It has been proposed that an uninterrupted Laz–Mingrelian speech community will have extended along the Black Sea coast until the arrival of Georgian-speakers in their flight from the Arabs, who appeared in central Georgia in the mid-7th c., split them by creating the Georgian-speaking provinces we call today Guria and Ach'ara.

Earliest attestations, scholarly interest, and the written varieties

Johannes de Galonifontibus noted in 1404 that moving eastwards from Abkhazia 'in the direction of Georgia, lies the country called Mingrelia [. . .]. The people have their own language.' As with Abkhaz, perhaps the first attestation of the language itself is found in the examples of it quoted by Evliya Çelebi from the 1640s. Both Mingrelian and Svan figure in the vocabulary lists of Güldenstädt (1770s). Laz was the first of the unwritten Kartvelian languages to attract scholarly attention, in a 38-page description published in 1844 by the German Georg Rosen, who devoted 40 pages out of a total of 84 in a later work (1846) dealing mainly with Ossetic to observations on Mingrelian, Svan and Abkhaz. In 1880 the Georgian Aleksandre Tsagareli produced two volumes of 'Mingrelian Studies' (in Russian) with some texts, including sections of the Gospels, written in the Georgian script, which can easily accommodate Mingrelian with the addition of just two extra characters and (especially for Senak'ian) the palatal glide character that was used in Old Georgian. The grammar of Mingrelian with chrestomathy (using the adapted Georgian script) and Mingrelian–Russian lexicon published by the Georgian Ioseb Q'ipshidze in 1914 (republished in Tbilisi in 1995) made Mingrelian at that time perhaps the most impressively described of all the Caucasian languages. This work was, in fact, closely modelled on a Laz grammar (number 2 in the Russian series 'Materials on Japhetic Linguistics') published in 1910 by Marr, who also employed the Georgian script to render the Laz. In 1864 there had been published in Tbilisi a so-called *Lushnu Anban*, which is the Svan for 'Svan Alphabet'. Uslar is believed to have been the author, and his monograph on Abkhaz actually closes with an 18-page essay on Svan. The *Anban* contains in three columns Svan–Georgian–Russian equivalents of words, phrases and sections from the Gospels. The script devised for the Svan data was Cyrillic-based, as was that used in I. Nizharadze's *Russian–Svan Dictionary* (1910). In fact, the Georgian script can be easily adapted for the rendition of Svan: in addition to two Old Georgian characters no longer needed for Modern Georgian plus the same character used to represent the neutral vowel of Mingrelian, one may also need (depending on the dialect) the diaeresis to mark umlaut and the macron for vowel length. Indeed, this is how Svan material has been reproduced in those occasional specialist works published in post-Tsarist Georgia for the benefit of professional folklorists and linguists. In general, such was the only type of work in these languages to be approved for publication within Soviet Georgia, where one need only mention the failure to print Svan–Georgian and Mingrelian–Georgian dictionaries over the years as a sign of the lack of support these minority Kartvelian tongues have enjoyed among the speakers of the prestige Kartvelian tongue.

No serious attempt seems ever to have been made to accord literary status to Svan, though some regional papers from at least 1988 have displayed a readiness to print the occasional folklore text. The same is not true for Mingrelian, for contemporary accounts are available in Georgian sources of a move to introduce a Mingrelian liturgy along with biblical material in Mingrelian in the 1880s. The script is reported to have been based on Cyrillic, presumably identical to the one employed in the 100-page *Mingrel'skaja Azbuka* 'Mingrelian Alphabet' published in Tbilisi in 1899. The project failed, both ecclesiastically and linguistically. The question of literary status for Mingrelian arose again in the 1920s when the early Soviets were creating literary standards for a range of previously unwritten languages. The case in favour of Mingrelian acquiring such status was advanced by Isak' Zhvania, the most important Mingrelian politician in the years before Beria arrogated this title, but this was vigorously opposed by such Mingrelian intellectuals as K'onst'ant'ine Gamsakhurdia (father of the later post-Soviet president and one of the most distinguished writers of *Georgian* prose), who stressed the same (questionable) arguments that have been made since the 1880s to the present day, namely that this would mean Mingrelians being cut off from Georgian culture and could lead to the political dismemberment of the Georgian state. Although Mingrelian ultimately failed to achieve literary status, a few communist treatises were produced in it, and, as part of the campaign to spread the new ideology amongst the peasantry around Zugdidi, 1 March 1930 saw the first edition of what became in 1932 a daily newspaper in Mingrelian, using the same adapted form of Georgian that Tsagareli had introduced in the 1880s. This *Q'azaq'ishi Gazeti* ('Peasant's Paper') was replaced on 1 January 1936 by the half-Mingrelian, half-Georgian *K'omunari* ('Man of the Commune'). From 22 July 1938 Zugdidi became served by the wholly Georgian *Mebrjoli* ('Warrior') – the Abkhazian authorities introduced an Abkhaz–Russian–Mingrelian paper *Gal* for the Mingrelian residents of their southernmost Gal province in June 1995. More surprising was the fact that from 1927 to 1938 the negligible numbers of Laz (no more than 2,000) enjoyed a cultural autonomy which saw them develop a Roman-based alphabet, a short-lived daily newspaper in 1929, and even a five-class school with teaching in Laz, for which a 1st-year primer *Alboni* was published in 1935 in Sukhum. Not only did the Soviet Laz lose this privilege; they were later (in mid-1949) to suffer the fate of some other Caucasian peoples (including the Meskhians and Hemshinli, or Muslim Armenians, from Georgia) in being deported to eastern parts of the USSR. Although such endeavours even in 1995 are not entirely free from risk, there are moves to establish a writing system for native speakers of Laz in Turkey. The 1991 publication *Nana-nena* ('Mother Tongue') is a primer utilizing both Roman- and Georgian-based scripts on facing pages throughout.

Numbers of speakers

There are no figures for the numbers of Kartvelians living in Turkey, though significant numbers of both Laz and Georgians reside there, many finding themselves on the Turkish side of the border when the frontiers were redrawn after the First World War. Equally for Georgia the numbers are unknown, for the simple reason that since *c.*1930 all Mingrelians, Svans and Laz resident there have been classified for census purposes as 'Georgians', Georgian being (for all Svans and most Mingrelians, who will have attended Georgian rather than Russian schools) their language of tuition and thus their principal literary language, many Mingrelians and some Svans no longer learning their respective native tongues. For the first all-Soviet census of 1926 this artificially imposed ethnicity had yet to be introduced, and that year 242,990 declared Mingrelian nationality, with a further 40,000 stating Mingrelian to be their native tongue, whilst 13,218 styled themselves Svans. Unofficially one hears in Georgia figures of approximately 50,000 for the Svans and between a half and one million for the Mingrelians. The artificiality of 'Georgian' ethnicity for the Mingrelians (and, by extension, the Svans) is confirmed by the fact that amongst Turkish Kartvelians the Laz (and those Mingrelians living there) consider themselves to be quite distinct peoples from their (Imerkhevian) Georgian neighbours. We may take this to have been the pre-Stalinist state of self-awareness within Georgia too. In defence of the post-1930 view one hears such arguments as that Georgian was always spoken by Mingrelians and Svans, and that the only devotional or literary language the Mingrelians and Svans ever had was Georgian. Whilst Kartvelians may always have worshipped in Georgian, a more credible assumption to be drawn from this fact would be that no greater knowledge of this language will have existed amongst Orthodox Kartvelian peasants, who most certainly will have had no need of any literary language, than did knowledge of Latin among the Catholic peasantry of most of medieval Europe. As for a centuries-old bilingualism in Georgian, there is the specific testimony of the (Ushgulian) Svan Bessarion Nizharadze, who in a 15-page grammatical sketch of his native tongue in 1913 under the Georgian pseudonym *Tavisupali Svani* 'The Free Svan' in vol. 2 of *Jveli Sakartvelo* 'Old Georgia', claims that most Svans at the end of the 19th c. had no understanding of Georgian, whilst the necessity of using Mingrelian for propaganda purposes in the regional capital's daily paper as late as the early 1930s casts grave doubt on the validity of the assertion of long-standing bilingualism for Mingrelia also. In the fragmented state in which Georgia finds itself at the time of writing, the question of the distinctiveness of (especially) Mingrelian remains an extremely sensitive topic, as it is feared that emphasizing the linguistic differences between Mingrelian and Georgian might be the first step towards political separatism.

Influence of other languages

All three of the non-literary Kartvelian languages, especially Mingrelian, show the influence of Georgian itself. Abkhaz influence is detectable in Mingrelian and has even been suggested for both Laz and Svan, though one more often reads of Circassian influence on the latter – publication by the Linguistics Institute in Tbilisi of the long-delayed Svan–Georgian dictionary will help to clarify this situation. One of the ways in which Laz differs from Mingrelian is the level of Greek and Turkish penetration it has undergone, aspects of its syntax exhibiting particularly interesting parallels with Turkish.

VI Georgian

Georgian is the most widely spoken of the South Caucasian (Kartvelian) family of the Caucasian languages. It is the main language of (the one-time Soviet republic of) Georgia. A Georgian calls himself *kartv-el-i* (hence the designation 'Kartvelian' for the language family as a whole or as a generic term for any of the four ethnic groups speaking one of these languages), his language *kart-ul-i ena*, and his country *sa-kartv-el-o* (literally 'place designated for the Kartvels') – the term 'Georgia' (cf. Russian 'Gruzija', Turkish 'Gürcüstan') has nothing to do with the country's patron saint (St George) but seems to derive (via the Persian rendition of the consonant-complex *vr-*) from the Old Armenian genitive *vr-ac^h* 'of the Georgians' (cf. nominative plural *vir-k^h* 'Georgians' and Graeco-Roman *Iberia/Iveria*, deriving from *i vir-s* 'to/among the Georgians').

Dialects

In west Georgia, Gurian (south of Mingrelian) and Ach'aran/Adzharian (between Gurian and Laz) lie along the Black Sea coast, whilst inland they abut Imeretian. To the north of Imeretian lie the NW dialects of Lechkhumian (east of Mingrelian and south of Svan) and, to its east, Rach'an (between Svan and the Ossetic of South Ossetia). Of the northern dialects (east of South Ossetia), Mokhevian approaches the southern slopes of the main chain, whilst Mtiuletian (or Mtiulur-Gudamaq'rulian) is its southern neighbour. Of the NE dialects Khevsurian is found east of Mokhevian, whilst to its south lies Pshav(ian), and, to the north-east of Pshavian, Tush is isolated in the mountains bordering Chechenia and Daghestan – since Georgians usually call the North Central Caucasian language Bats *Ts'ova Tush*, as Tusheti was their original home, the term *Chaghma Tush* is used to refer to the relevant Georgian dialect. K'akh(et)ian forms the eastern dialect, whilst Kartlian is spoken in the large central region and is the basis of the modern literary language – Kartli incorporates the capital Tbilisi, etymologized as 'place of warm springs' from earlier T'pilisi (source of the older designation Tiflis), the root of which is viewed as a borrowing from Indo-European *tep-* 'warm' (cf. English 'tepid'). The south(-west)ern dialects are Dzhavakhian to the SW of Kartlian and, to its west, Meskhian (south of Imeretian and east of Ach'aran). Outside Georgia the following dialects are found: Ingiloan (in the Zakatala region of Azerbaijan abutting K'akh(et)ian); the obsolescent Qizlar-Mozdokian (spoken in the north central Caucasus by descendants of those who fled there from eastern Georgia in the 18th c.); Imerkhevian (spoken in those historical Kartvelian lands that lie today in eastern Turkey – these were centred in what was known as the region of T'ao, which, together with its neighbour K'lardzheti, formed the hearth of Georgian culture during the Old Georgian period); Fereydanian (the dialect that has been preserved with some interesting linguistic peculiarities by the descendants of an east Georgian community transplanted to Fereydan in Iran by Shah Abbas in the 17th c.).

Earliest attestations

Both Plato and Aristotle mention 'Iberians' (Greek *Íberes*), but it is not clear whether reference is to the Georgians or the inhabitants of the Iberian Peninsula. It is only from the 1st c. that there is indisputable evidence in the sources for the classical world's eastern Iberians – the much older term 'Colchians' undoubtedly referred indiscriminately to the ancestors of both the Laz–Mingrelians and the Abkhazians, both of which groups may be presumed to have occupied the Black Sea's eastern littoral at that time. The earliest Georgian inscription was discovered in the 1950s when the remains of a Georgian church were being excavated in the Judaean desert near Bethlehem and is dated to *c.*430; on Georgian soil the oldest inscription (from 494) is found on the little church at Bolnisi, 60 km south of Tbilisi.

History of the scripts

The official adoption of Christianity as the state religion of Georgia is dated to the 330s, and the script, written from left to right, is assumed to have been created some time later in the 4th c. to help disseminate Christian literature. Modern Georgian employs 33 characters, though originally there were 38. There have been three alphabets. The first, attested from the 5th to the 9th c., consisted of rounded characters

	Transliteration	*Phonetic value*
ა	a	[a]
ბ	b	[b]
გ	g	[g]
დ	d	[d]
ე	e	[ɛ]
ვ	v	[v]
ზ	z	[z]
ჱ	ē	[ɛ(j)]
თ	t	[t]
ი	i	[i]
კ	k̇	[k']
ლ	l	[l]
მ	m	[m]
ნ	n	[n]
ჲ	y	[j]
ო	o	[o]
პ	ṗ	[p']
ჟ	ž	[ʒ]
რ	r	[r]
ს	s	[s]
ტ	ṭ	[t']
ჳ	wi	[wi]
უ	u	[u]
ფ	p	[p]
ქ	k	[k]
ღ	ǧ	[ɣ]
ყ	q̇	[q']
შ	š	[ʃ]
ჩ	č	[tʃ]
ც	c	[ts]
ძ	j	[dz]
წ	ç	[ts']
ჭ	č̣	[tʃ']
ხ	x	[x]
ჴ	q	[q]
ჯ	ǰ	[dʒ]
ჰ	h	[h]
ჵ	ō	[o(w)]

Fig. 2 The Georgian mxedruli alphabet For the values of the characters of the International Phonetic Alphabet, see pp. xvi–xvii. ['] after the symbol for a consonant indicates an ejective consonant.

and is styled *mrg(v)lovani* 'rounded' (an alternative name is *asomtavruli* 'majuscule'). From this there developed the second script, *k'utxovani* 'angular' (or *nusxuri* 'minuscule'), which bears a strong visual resemblance to the angular characters that have always been employed for Armenian (see fig. 1); this is first attested in the testament appended to the (oldest dated) manuscript, known as the Sinai Polycephalon of 864, and continued to be used in most manuscripts written in the 10th–11th centuries; in these manuscripts one often finds characters from the oldest script employed as capitals (hence the alternative designations of the first two scripts). In the 11th c. there was a further development back to rounded characters, producing the so-called *mxedruli* 'military' script still used today (see fig. 2). However, the Georgian Church continued to use the majuscule–minuscule combination of the earlier scripts, which are thus jointly designated *xucuri* 'ecclesiastical' to distinguish them from the secular usage reserved for the successor. The earliest manuscripts and inscriptions are referred to as *xanmet'i* 'with extra *x*' or *haemet'i* 'with extra h' depending on which of these letters is used to mark third-person indirect objects and second-person subjects within the verb; it is unclear whether this particular distinction was of a diachronic or a dialectal nature.

Literature

It is customary to make the following (somewhat arbitrary) divisions: Old Georgian (5th–11th centuries); Medieval Georgian (12th–18th centuries); Modern Georgian (post-18th c.). Old Georgian is characterized by religious writings, original as well as translated. The first extant native work is Iak'ob Tsurt'aveli's *Martyrdom of St Shushanik*, which purports to have been written between 476 and 483, though the oldest surviving manuscript is much more recent. The oldest dated manuscript of the Gospels is the Adysh Manuscript (897). Georgia's 'Golden Age' coincided with the reign of Queen Tamar (1184–1213), and it was at this time that the national epic poem 'The Man in the Panther's Skin' was composed by Shota Rust(a)veli. Little was written in (? survived from) the centuries of Tatar–Mongol–Khorazmian depredations (13th–15th centuries).

Scholarly interest

The earliest known work to deal with grammatical issues in Georgian was a short treatise on the article written in the 11th–12th c., possibly by either Eprem Mtsire or Arsen Iq'altoeli. It was discovered in 1984 in a collection of texts (MS 6) from the Georgian Iveron Monastery on Mt Athos and published in Tbilisi in 1990. The first native dictionary, which remains a source of valuable information, appeared in 1716, composed by the greatest man of letters of his day in Georgia, Sulkhan Saba Orbeliani (1685–1725), whilst the first native grammar came from the pen of Zurab Shanshovani in 1737, to be followed in 1753 and 1767 by versions of a more comprehensive treatment, which today has no practical value, by the patriarch, Ant'on I (1720–88). Ak'ak'i Shanidze (1887–1987) laid the foundations for modern Georgian scientific investigation both in Georgia and abroad (thanks to his tutelage of the Norwegian Kartvelologist, Hans Vogt (1903–86)). An 8-volume 'Explanatory

Dictionary of the Georgian Language' was produced between 1950 and 1964 by the Georgian Academy. However, it was Italian Theatine missionaries who made the first studies of Georgian in the 17th c.: the *Alphabetum Ibericum, sive Georgianum, cum Oratione Dominicali [. . .]* 'The Iberian, or Georgian, Alphabet, with the Lord's Prayer [and other prayers]' and S. Paolini's *Georgian–Italian Dictionary* were the first printed works in Georgian, published in Rome by the Fide Press (the first printing press in Georgia itself was established by King Vakht'ang VI in 1709–12, where the first printed book was an edition of the Gospels, Rust(a)veli's epic gaining its first printing in 1712 – this beautiful edition was reproduced in facsimile in both 1937 and 1975), which also published the first Georgian grammar, by Maggio, in 1643. Facsimiles of these three historic works were published in a single volume in Tbilisi in 1983.

Numbers of speakers

The number of Georgian speakers outside Georgia (particularly beyond the frontiers of the former USSR) is not known. According to the last Soviet census (1989), there were 3,983,115 'Georgians' living within the Soviet Union, of whom 3,787,393 resided in Georgia itself, where they constituted 70.1% of the population. However, this figure conceals the deliberate ethnic obfuscation which, as explained above, can be traced to *c.*1930, when all Kartvelians (and even the North Central Bats people) living within the USSR were officially designated as 'Georgians' – previously, Mingrelian, Svan and Bats had existed as distinct ethnic categories. Estimates would suggest a maximum figure of 3 million Georgians proper living in Georgia in 1989.

Influence of other languages

All of the imperial powers that have been active in the Caucasus, the intersection of Europe and Asia, have left linguistic traces in Georgian. Of the Graeco-Roman, Persian, Arabic, Turkish and Russian elements, the Persian and Russian are the most thorough-going. The closeness of the two Orthodox Christian cultures of Transcaucasia has also seen the infiltration of Armenian elements into Georgian. North Caucasian elements are not unknown (e.g. *muxa(j)* 'oak' from Nakh-Daghestanian).

Aronson, H. I. 1990. *Georgian: A Reading Grammar*, 2nd edn. Chicago.
Gvarjaladze, Th. and I. 1979. *Georgian–English Dictionary*. Tbilisi.
Hewitt, B. G. 1995a. *Georgian – A Learner's Grammar*. London.
—— 1995b. *Georgian: A Structural Reference Grammar*. Amsterdam.
—— 1996. *A Georgian Reader*. London.
Rayfield, D. 1994. *The Literature of Georgia: A History*. Oxford.
Tschenkéli, K. 1958. *Einführung in die georgische Sprache* ('Introduction to the Georgian Language'), 2 vols. Zurich.
—— et al. 1965–74. *Georgisch–Deutsches Wörterbuch* ('Georgian–German Dictionary'), 3 vols. Zurich.
Vogt, H. 1971. *Grammaire de la langue géorgienne*. Oslo.

VII General bibliography

Charachidzé, G. 1981. *Grammaire de la langue avar (langue du Caucase Nord-Est)*. Paris.

Chikobava, A. 1965. *iberiul-k'avk'asiur enata shesc'avlis ist'oria* ('History of the Study of the Ibero-Caucasian Languages'). Tbilisi.

Dumézil, G. 1967. *Documents anatoliens sur les langages et les traditions du Caucase*, vol.4, *Récits lazes (dialecte d'Arhavi)*. Paris.

—— 1975. *Le verbe oubykh. Étude descriptive et comparative* (en collaboration avec Tevfik Esenç). Paris.

——, Esenç, T. and Charachidzé, G. (forthcoming). *Dictionnaire de la langue oubykh*. Paris. (Replaces Vogt, H. 1963, same title.)

Feurstein, W. 1992. Mingrelisch, Lazisch, Swanisch. Alte Sprachen und Kulturen der Kolchis vor dem baldigen Untergang ('Mingrelian, Laz, and Svan. Ancient languages and cultures of Colchis in the face of imminent extinction'). In Hewitt, G. (ed.), *Caucasian Perspectives*, Unterschleissheim (Munich), 285–328.

Gippert, J. 1992. The Caucasian language material in Evliya Çelebi's 'Travel Book'. In Hewitt, G. (ed.) *Caucasian Perspectives*, Unterschleissheim (Munich), 8–62.

Harris, A. C. (ed.) 1991. *The Indigenous Languages of the Caucasus*, vol.1, *Kartvelian Languages*. New York.

—— and Smeets, R. (eds) (forthcoming). *The Indigenous Languages of the Caucasus: The Languages and Their Speakers*. Edinburgh.

Haspelmath, M. 1993. *A Grammar of Lezgian*. Berlin.

Hewitt, B. G. (in collaboration with Z. K. Khiba) 1989a. *Abkhaz*. London. (First published 1979, Amsterdam.)

—— (ed.) 1989b. *The Indigenous Languages of the Caucasus*, vol.2, *North West Caucasus*. New York.

—— 1995. Yet a third consideration of *Völker, Sprachen und Kulturen des südlichen Kaukasus*. *Central Asian Survey*, 14.2: 285–310.

Job, M. (ed.) (forthcoming). *The Indigenous Languages of the Caucasus*, vol. 3, *The North East Caucasian Languages*, part 1. New York.

Klimov, G. 1994. *Einführung in die kaukasische Sprachwissenschaft* ('Introduction to Caucasian Linguistics'), translated from the Russian original (1986) by Jost Gippert. Hamburg.

Kuipers, A. H. 1960. *Phoneme and Morpheme in Kabardian*. The Hague.

—— 1975. *A Dictionary of Proto-Circassian Roots*. Leuven.

Lucassen, W. (forthcoming). *Abkhaz–English Dictionary*.

Moor, M. 1985. *Studien zum lezgischen Verb* ('Studies in the Lezgi Verb'). Wiesbaden.

Palmaitis, L. and Gudjedjiani, C. 1985. *Svan–English Dictionary* (edited with a Preface and Index by B. G. Hewitt). New York.

Paris, C. and Batouka, N. 1987–92. *Dictionnaire abzakh (tcherkesse occidental) – Phrases et textes illustratifs*, vol. 2, parts 1–3. Paris.

—— (forthcoming). *Dictionnaire abzakh (tcherkesse occidental)*, vol. 1. Paris.

Schulze, W. 1983. *Die Sprache der Uden in Nord–Azerbajdzhan* ('The Language of the Udi in Northern Azerbaijan'). Wiesbaden.

Smeets, R. 1984. *Studies in West Circassian Phonology and Morphology*. Leiden.

—— 1988. On Ubykh Circassian. In Thordarson, F. (ed.), *Studia Caucasologica*, vol. 1, Oslo, 275–97.

—— (ed.) 1994. *The Indigenous Languages of the Caucasus*, vol. 3, *The North East Caucasian Languages*, part 2. New York.

van den Berg, H. 1995. *A Grammar of Hunzib*. Unterschleissheim (Munich).

Wixman, R. 1980. *Language Aspects of Ethnic Patterns and Processes in the North Caucasus*. Chicago.

B. GEORGE HEWITT

Celtiberian

Celtiberian is the name given to the long-extinct ***Celtic language** attested by a number of inscriptions from NE Spain, south of the Ebro and NE of Madrid. According to Classical Latin sources, this area was inhabited by the *Celtiberi*. Celtic was undoubtedly spoken outside this area too, since Roman sources employ the term *Celtici* for all Celtic tribes of Hispania other than Celtiberians. The scanty information we possess concerning the language(s) of these Celtici does not allow us to assess their linguistic relationship to Celtiberian. The term *Hispano-Celtic* refers to the remains of all Celtic languages in the Iberian Peninsula. There is no evidence that Celtiberian is more closely cognate with ***Gaulish** than with the Insular Celtic languages.

Archaeological evidence indicates that the Celtiberians may already have been present in Spain in the 8th c. BC. Their culture was influenced by the Iberians, from whom they learnt the art of writing (see ***Iberian**). Between 197 and 133 BC, the Celtiberians waged three wars with the Romans. After the fall of their main stronghold, Numantia, in 133 BC, they were finally subdued. Their territory formed part of the Roman province of *Hispania Citerior*.

The Celtiberian texts date from approximately the early 2nd c. BC to perhaps the 1st c. AD. The earlier texts are written in the Iberian script, which is ill-suited to represent the Celtiberian speech sounds. In a number of late texts the Latin alphabet is employed. In so far as the inscriptions contain words other than names, they are very difficult to interpret: our knowledge of Celtiberian vocabulary is extremely limited. Nevertheless, the texts provide us with important information concerning the grammar. Many inscriptions contain a stereotyped onomastic formula, such as can be found on the gravestone of Ibiza: '*Tirtanos* of the kin of the *Abolus*, son of *Letondu*, from *Kontrebia Belaiska*.'

A large number of coins are inscribed with the Celtiberian name of the city or the inhabitants of the city where the coin was issued.

About 20 inscribed *tesserae hospitales* have been found, which are small plaques of bronze used as a symbol of a pact between two parties, usually between an individual and a community, with which the bearer could probably claim hospitality on his travels. Most inscriptions are brief, the tessera of Luzaga being an exception (24 words).

The spectacular bronze plaque found at Botorrita (near Zaragoza) and first published in 1971 contains more than 200 words. Although the interpretation is still far from clear, it seems to be an official legal document dealing with the use and abuse of a particular terrain. New excavations at Botorrita in the early 1990s have yielded an even longer Celtiberian inscription.

Finally, the 17 rock inscriptions of Peñalba de Villastar may be mentioned, which are written in Latin script.

De Hoz, J. 1988. Hispano-Celtic and Celtiberian. In MacLennan, G. W. (ed.), *Proceedings of the First North American Congress of Celtic Studies (Ottawa 1986)*, Ottawa, 191–207.

Lejeune, M. 1955. *Celtiberica* (in French). Salamanca.

Tovar, A. 1961. *The Ancient Languages of Spain and Portugal.* New York.
Untermann, J. 1975– . *Monumenta Linguarum Hispanicarum* (in German). Wiesbaden.

PETER SCHRIJVER

Celtic languages

A branch of the ***Indo-European** family of languages, once widely spoken not only in western mainland Europe (including the Iberian Peninsula and present-day France and Italy) but through much of central and south-eastern Europe and as far as Asia Minor, but now restricted to the western fringes of France and of the British Isles.

The extant Celtic languages fall into two groups:

(1) the ***Brittonic** (also termed Brythonic or British) languages, ***Breton** (but see also below) and ***Welsh**; to this group also belong ***Cornish**, which died out at the end of the 18th c., long-extinct ***Cumbric**, and probably ***Pictish** (see below);
(2) the ***Gaelic** or Goidelic languages, ***Irish** and ***Scottish Gaelic**, together with ***Manx**, the last native speaker of which died in 1974.

These two groups together are sometimes referred to as 'Insular Celtic', as distinct from the extinct 'Continental Celtic' languages of mainland Europe, the only ones of which anything much is known being ***Celtiberian**, ***Gaulish** and ***Lepontic**.

Though now located on the mainland of the Continent, Breton can legitimately be considered as an 'insular' Celtic language on the grounds that it was reintroduced to the mainland by immigrants from south-western Britain in the 5th to the 7th centuries AD. The formerly widely held assumption that, by that time, Gaulish had completely died out and that the incoming Britons found a population speaking only a ***Romance** speech has recently been challenged and it is argued by some scholars, though by no means universally accepted, that some of the dialectal variations within Breton can be attributed to the survival in the areas in question of Gaulish-speakers whose language influenced that of the newcomers to which it was perhaps closely related (see below).

Pictish was certainly a 'P-Celtic' language (on this term, see below) and probably Brittonic, though it has been argued (but on limited evidence) that it would be better classified as a distinct member, beside Brittonic and Gaulish, of a Gallo-Brittonic subgroup.

If, apart from the precise status of Breton and the problem of Pictish, the classification of the Brittonic and Gaelic languages presents no great difficulty, the relationship of the Continental Celtic languages to one another and to the Insular Celtic languages is highly uncertain. It is claimed by some scholars, but again not accepted by all, that Gaulish was so closely related to Brittonic that the two could perhaps be considered to be dialects of one and the same language, and Lepontic was probably a close relative. The position of Celtiberian is much more obscure; it has been argued, but not conclusively demonstrated, that it was closer to Gaelic than to Brittonic and Gaulish.

The terms 'P-Celtic' and 'Q-Celtic' that have been, and in some quarters still are, used with reference to the Brittonic and Gaelic languages respectively, call for some comment. They relate to the fact that Indo-European [kʷ] became [p] in Brittonic but, in Gaelic, at first remained as [kʷ] (a phoneme represented in the *Ogam script by a character conventionally transcribed as <q>) and then became [k] (written <c>). We therefore have, for example, Welsh, Cornish *pen*, Breton *penn* 'head' beside Irish, Scottish Gaelic *ceann*, Manx *kione*, and Welsh *pedwar*, Cornish *peswar*, Breton *pevar* 'four' beside Irish *ceathair*, Scottish Gaelic *ceithir*, Manx *kiare*. But it is unsatisfactory to base such a classification on just one feature and one, at that, that is not particularly striking. The change [kʷ] > [p] is not uncommon in languages: it occurs, at least in certain circumstances, in for example *Greek (cf. Greek *hippos* with Latin *equus* 'horse'), in *Oscan and *Umbrian (languages closely related to Latin), and, within the Romance field, in *Romanian (e.g. *patru* 'four' < Latin *quattuor*, *iapă* 'mare' < Latin *equa*). Furthermore, the criterion is of no great use when applied to Continental Celtic: briefly, Gaulish is partly but not totally a P-language, Lepontic seems from the limited evidence available to be a P-language, while Celtiberian is a Q-language.

The earliest known attestations of any form of Celtic are inscriptions and coin-legends some of which may go back to the 6th c. BC.

Ball, M. J. (ed.) 1993. *The Celtic Languages*. London.
Lewis, H. and Pedersen, H. 1989. *A Concise Comparative Celtic Grammar*, 3rd edn. Göttingen.
MacAulay, D. (ed.) 1992. *The Celtic Languages*. London.
Russell, P. 1995. *An Introduction to the Celtic Languages*. London.

GLANVILLE PRICE

Chaghatay

An extinct eastern *Turkic language spoken in central Asia that was also used as a literary lingua franca, written in the Arabic alphabet, by various Turkic-speaking Islamic peoples in European Russia from the 15th to the 19th c. (see under *Bashkir, *Kazakh, *Tatar).

WOLFGANG GRELLER

Chaldaic, see *Aramaic*

Ch'amalal (see under *Caucasian languages. IV. North-East Caucasian family*)

Ch'an (see *Laz* under *Caucasian languages. V. South Caucasian family*)

Channel Islands French

The indigenous forms of French spoken in the Channel Islands are dialects not of standard *French but of Norman French and are closely related in pronunciation, structure and lexicon to the dialects (in so far as they remain) of the mainland of Normandy.

The Duchy of Normandy came into being in 911 when the French king ceded to the Vikings who had settled there an area around the lower reaches of the river Seine. In the course of the next quarter of a century, the Normans, who within perhaps no more than three generations were to abandon their *Norse speech for French, extended their territory westwards and took possession of the islands in 933. When, after the Norman Conquest of 1066, the Dukes of Normandy also became Kings of England, the islands remained part of their Norman, not of their English, domains. They were separated administratively from mainland Normandy in 1204 when the French king, Philippe Auguste, conquered the rest of the duchy and this separation was duly recognized in 1304 when England formally ceded Normandy, with the specific exception of the Channel Islands, to France. Though possessions of the British Crown, the islands have never formed part of England (or, indeed, of the United Kingdom which is, however, responsible for them in matters of defence and foreign relations) but consist of the two largely self-governing bailiwicks of Guernsey and Jersey.

One important medieval French writer, Wace (c.1100–75), the author of two lengthy historical poems, hailed from Jersey. Thereafter, there is no evidence of any literary use of the various insular dialects until the 19th c.

For the later history of French in the Channel Islands, see *Alderney French, *Guernsey French, *Jersey French and *Sark French.

Le Maistre, F. 1947. Le normand dans les Îles Anglo-Normandes. *Le Français moderne*, 17: 211–18.
Price, G. 1984. French in the Channel Islands. In Id., *The Languages of Britain*, London, 207–16.
Spence, N. C. W. 1984. Channel Island French. In Trudgill, P. (ed.), *Language in the British Isles*, Cambridge, 345–51.

GLANVILLE PRICE

Chechen (see under *Caucasian languages. III. North Central Caucasian family*)

Cheremis, see *Mari*

Cherkess (see *Circassian* under *Caucasian languages. II. North-West Caucasian family*)

Chinese (see under *Community languages (Britain; France; Netherlands)*)

Chiragh (see under *Dargwa* under *Caucasian languages. IV. North-East Caucasian family*)

Church Slavonic
Church Slavonic is a *Slavonic literary language which was originally based on the South Slavonic dialects of Bulgaria and Macedonia, with an admixture of West Slavonic linguistic elements. In its Russified modern form it is used for liturgical

purposes by Slav members of the Eastern Orthodox Church and by Roman Catholic Slavs who follow the Eastern rite (sometimes referred to as Uniats).

The earliest form of the language is termed Old Church Slavonic. It is attested in a handful of 10th-c. inscriptions in the south-east Balkans and a small number of manuscripts, mostly from the same area, which are generally ascribed to the late 10th or the 11th c. and constitute the earliest extensive record of a Slavonic language. These attestations appear in two alphabetic writing systems (see ***Cyrillic and Glagolitic scripts** and fig. 5): Glagolitic, generally thought to be the creation of St Cyril (827–69), survived longest among the Catholics of Croatia and Dalmatia but has now fallen out of ordinary use; Cyrillic, based partly on Glagolitic, partly on Greek, is in use to this day. Both alphabets were used in the earliest Church Slavonic printed books: the Glagolitic Missal of 1483 (possibly printed in Venice) and five Cyrillic liturgical books printed in Kraków in 1491.

Church Slavonic evolved in the first place as a vehicle for translating scriptural, liturgical and theological texts from Greek, and the principle of maximal fidelity which underlay the translations led to a Greek influence on vocabulary, word-formation and syntax which tended to increase with time as translations were revised to mirror their sources more closely. However, Church Slavonic was also used among the Orthodox Slavs from the late 9th to the late 17th c. as a literary language in which original works, especially but not exclusively those of religious content, were composed. During this period a number of regional varieties developed, such as the Church Slavonic of Bulgaria (used up to the 16th c. also by the Orthodox Romanians), Croatia, Russia and Serbia, whose pronunciation (and so orthography) and grammatical forms reflected to some extent the linguistic peculiarities of the local Slavonic vernaculars.

From the 17th c. the character and function of Church Slavonic changed in two ways. Firstly, a grammatical codification of the language was effected in the Ukraine and adopted with some modification in Russia. As Russia assumed a leading role in maintaining Eastern Orthodoxy, the church books revised and printed there came to be generally used and regarded as authoritative among all the Orthodox Slavs, including those of the Balkans, and thus Russian Church Slavonic superseded earlier local Church Slavonic norms. Secondly, the development of national literary languages for secular purposes in the 18th and especially the 19th c. led to a reduction in the use of Church Slavonic, which lost its wider literary functions and survived only in the strictly religious sphere. Even there it shows signs of retreat before the increasing use of the modern Slavonic languages, for instance in translations of Scripture.

It is difficult to estimate the number of people who use Church Slavonic as a liturgical language today, and still harder to gauge their knowledge of it, which is normally passive and restricted. On the one hand, the diaspora from eastern Europe during the late 19th and the 20th c. has spread people of Slavonic origin around the whole world. On the other hand, both the secularizing pressures at work in eastern Europe and the tendency for the offspring of émigrés to adopt the languages of their new countries have led to a reduction in familiarity with Church Slavonic. The rough estimate of 80,000,000 users of Church Slavonic, which is based on the approximate numbers of membership for the relevant parts of the Christian Church at the beginning of the 1990s, may well be wide of the mark.

D'yachenko, G. 1899. *Полный церковно-славянский словарь* ('Complete Church Slavonic Dictionary'), 2 vols. Moscow.

[Gamanovich], Ieromonakh Alipii 1964, *Грамматика церковно-славянскаго языка* ('Grammar of Church Slavonic'). Jordanville, NY.

Huntley, D. 1993. Old Church Slavonic. In Comrie, B. and Corbett, G. G. (eds), *The Slavonic Languages*, London and New York, 125–87.

Jagić, V. 1913. *Entstehungsgeschichte der kirchenslavischen Sprache* ('Genesis of Church Slavonic'). Berlin.

Kurz, J. et al. (eds) 1996– . *Slovník jazyka staroslověnského. Lexikon linguae palaeoslovenicae* ('Old Church Slavonic Dictionary'), 4 vols. Prague.

Picchio, R. 1980. Church Slavonic. In Schenker, A. M. and Stankiewicz, E. (eds), *The Slavic Literary Languages*, New Haven, CT, 1–33.

Plähn, J. 1978. *Der Gebrauch des modernen russischen Kirchenslavisch in der russischen Kirche* ('The Use of Modern Russian Church Slavonic in the Russian Church'). Hamburg.

Roberson, R. G. 1990. *The Eastern Christian Churches. A Brief Survey*, 3rd edn. Rome.

Schenker, A. M. 1995. *The Dawn of Slavic. An Introduction to Slavic Philology*. London and New Haven, CT.

Tolstoi, N. I. 1988. *История и структура славянских литературных языков* ('The History and Structure of the Slavonic Literary Languages'). Moscow.

Vaillant, A. 1964. *Manuel du vieux slave*. Paris.

Večerka, R. 1989– . *Altkirchenslavische (altbulgarische) Syntax* ('Old Church Slavonic (Old Bulgarian) Syntax'), 4 vols. Freiburg im Breisgau.

C. M. MACROBERT

Chuvash

Chuvash, the only living representative of the Hunno–Bolgaric group of the ***Turkic languages**, is spoken mainly in the Chuvash Republic (capital Cheboksary) (Russian Federation), south of the Volga. The Chuvash-speaking area also extends into the Ul'yanovsk district and into the Tatar Republic. Other groups of speakers are found in the Bashkir Republic and elsewhere in the Volga region, while small contingents live in the Urals and western Siberia. The total number of speakers in all these areas was given in 1989 as 1,842,346.

Chuvash is the most divergent of the Turkic languages, forming a subdivision of its own. This situation has been attributed by some to an early split between Chuvash and Common Turkic while others claim that the divergence is due to strong Mongolian influence. The view that Chuvash is a Turkicized ***Finno-Ugrian language** is no longer held. There are only minor dialectal differences between (i) upper Chuvash and (ii) lower Chuvash (these terms reflect their position along the Volga).

If Chuvash is indeed the only continuer of the ***Hunnic** language, their migratory history is reflected in Chinese and European sources (cf. Chinese *Hiung Nu*, Greek *Hounnoi*, Latin *Hunni*), though this view has been criticized and the Hunnic linguistic evidence is too scarce for conclusions to be drawn. Be that as it may, there is no doubt about the Volga-Bolgar origin of Chuvash to which the linguistic remains of the Khazar language are also believed to belong. There are indications that the clearly Turkic language of the Volga-Bolgars, as revealed in its early (11th–14th c.) attestations in the Arabic alphabet, is continued in modern Chuvash. The political realm of the Volga-Bolgars was destroyed by the Mongol conquest in 1236. The name 'Chuvash' is first recorded in 1551. After a gap of some 400 years, Chuvash became a written language again in the 18th c., using the Russian alphabet until 1874 when, after several earlier attempts at reform, a more adequate variation of *Cyrillic script was introduced.

Benzing, J. 1959. (a) Das Hunnische, Donaubolgarische und Wolgabolgarische (Sprachreste) ('Hunnic, Danube-Bolgar and Volga-Bolgar (linguistic remains)'); (b) Das Tschuwaschische ('Chuvash'). In Deny, J. et al. (eds), *Philologiae Turcicae Fundamenta*, Wiesbaden, 685–95, 695–753.

WOLFGANG GRELLER

Cimbrian

The Cimbri were a tribe originating in Jutland, where their name is recalled in that of the Himmerland region. In the late 2nd c. BC they migrated southwards and west-wards, crossing in or about 110 BC into Gaul, and then, *c*. 105 BC, into Spain whence they were expelled by the Celtiberians. Returning through Gaul and southern Germany, they crossed the Alps into Italy and in 101 BC were virtually annhilated by the Romans at a battle in the Po valley, possibly near Vercelli (between Turin and Milan). Nothing remains of their language but, despite claims sometimes made that they were Celts, there is little doubt that they were a *Germanic-speaking people.

The term 'Cimbrian' has also been applied to the now mainly extinct Germanic dialects of parts of Alpine north-eastern Italy, on the mistaken assumption that they derived from the speech of the ancient Cimbri. In reality, they were south Bavarian dialects of *German introduced into the area in the 12th c., the only surviving remnant of which is the speech of a few hundred inhabitants of the village of Luserna (province of Trento) where it was introduced from Lavarone in the 15th c.

Cimmerian

The Cimmerians were a prehistoric people (mentioned by Homer) who dwelt for some centuries in eastern Ukraine (including the Crimea) and the northern Caucasus until they were driven out by the Scythians in the 8th c. BC. There is no direct evidence in the form of inscriptions, etc. for their language, which was probably *Indo-European and possibly a branch of Thracian (see under *Daco-Thracian) or *Iranian, and from which the *Baltic and *Slavonic languages are believed to have borrowed a number of words (e.g., to give them in their Russian form, *svobodnii* 'free', *testo* 'dough').

Circassian (see under *Caucasian languages. II. North-West Caucasian family*)

Community languages

In addition to indigenous languages, many languages that are not in the strictest sense of the word 'European' but have been brought to Europe in the relatively recent past are spoken by substantial communities in a wide range of European countries. Most are associated with groups who have come as workers to meet the needs of an expanding economy, though some have come as refugees. Many are associated with peoples linked to the host community by a colonial past. The term 'community languages' is now widely used in preference to the term 'immigrant languages' (French *langues immigrées*) to differentiate the languages of these more recent arrivals from the older mother tongues.

Given the impossibility of covering every such language in every relevant country in Europe, we shall devote attention mainly to the United Kingdom which has the greatest variety of community languages and the greatest number of speakers thereof of any country in Europe. Briefer entries are also provided on two other states, France and the Netherlands, where there are large numbers of speakers of community languages other than those that are among the ones most widely spoken in Britain. (See also *Greenlandic.)

Community languages (Britain)

The extent of linguistic diversity in the United Kingdom is particularly striking (Alladina and Edwards 1991). A language census undertaken by the Inner London Education Authority in the late 1980s recorded 172 different languages spoken in the schools of the capital. The presence of a wide range of non-European languages in the UK is not, of course, a new phenomenon. The first Africans arrived in Britain in Elizabethan times; there is evidence of a Bengali-speaking community in the East End of London as early as 1873; the Chinese also came to Britain as seamen in the 19th c.

The 15-year period between 1955 and 1970, however, marked an unprecedented growth in both the numbers of speakers of other languages and the range of languages spoken. Post-war industrial expansion created an urgent need for labour. Indigenous workers were reluctant to accept jobs with low pay or anti-social hours, and major employers such as the National Health Service and London Transport actively recruited labour in New Commonwealth countries such as India, Pakistan and the former British West Indies.

Progressively more stringent legislation enacted through the 1960s meant that, by the early 1970s, immigration had reduced to a trickle. Since that time, new arrivals have been limited to dependants rejoining members of their family already settled in the UK, or to political refugees such as the Ugandan Asians, Sri Lankan Tamils, Vietnamese, Somalis and Bosnians.

For present purposes, discussion will be limited to the larger and more established minority language communities in the UK: Bengali, Gujarati, Panjabi, Urdu and Chinese. However, it is important, at the outset, to discuss a range of issues which affect all linguistic minorities.

Some common concerns

It is impossible to estimate the size of linguistic minority communities with any degree of accuracy. Census data report those born outside the UK, but do not account for their British-born children and grandchildren; nor do they include information on community languages. Attempts to estimate the size of communities from alternative sources, such as ethnic names in telephone directories or electoral registers, are no more likely to produce accurate results. Names often offer important clues to religious and national affiliation, but links with language are more tenuous. Mohammed Arif, for instance, could be a Pakistani Muslim who speaks Panjabi or Urdu, or a Bengali-speaking Bangladeshi.

In contrast, our information on patterns of language maintenance and shift is rather more reliable, thanks, in the main, to the Linguistic Minorities Project (LMP) (1985) which investigated language use in 11 different communities in several English cities. Although there has been a marked shift from community languages to English in second and subsequent generations, most minority communities are making vigorous efforts to transmit their language and culture through classes organized by overseas embassies and religious and community groups. Many thousands of children study their community languages as part of the curriculum; far more attend classes in the evening and at weekends. To take just one example, classes in 18 different languages were being offered in the early 1980s to over 8,500 children in just three local education authorities (Bradford, Coventry and Haringey) (LMP 1985).

Mainstream English-speaking society is also showing a greater awareness of the needs of linguistic minorities. Pressure from various groups has ensured that libraries in areas of important settlement are well stocked with books in community languages and that public health and other information is translated into the appropriate languages. A growing range of children's literature in other languages is found in schools: both single language books, imported from the country of origin, and dual-language books with text in English and the minority language. Growing numbers of children are taking public examinations in community languages.

Bengali

Bengali belongs to the ***Indic** branch of the ***Indo-Iranian** subgroup of the ***Indo-European** language family. Although its roots lie in Prakrit, the modern variety of the classical language Sanskrit, it has existed as an autonomous language for ten centuries or more.

Bengali is the medium of a rich oral culture and a long and important written literature embracing writers such as Rabindranath Tagore, who won the Nobel Prize for Literature in 1913. Like some 200 other Indian and Southeast Asian scripts, the Bengali writing system (see fig. 3) developed from Brahmi, widely used as early as the 3rd c. BC, via the Devanagari script associated with Sanskrit. It runs from left to right with the words hanging from the line, rather than resting on it as in the Latin and other European scripts. It is a syllabic writing system; all consonants are

Bengali

সিলিয়ার ভীষণ রাগ হলো।

Gujarati

પરંતુ હિપોપૉટેમસ્ની એક વાત ચિત્તાને હેરાન કરતી.

Panjabi

ਮੇਰੇ ਮਾਤਾ ਜੀ ਨਾਸ਼ਤਾ ਲਿਆ ਰਹੇ ਹਨ ।

Urdu

پھر عمران کو ایک مشکل پیش آئی۔ وہ بولا میری مدد کرو !

Chinese

出門時，蓋爾穿上短上衣。

Fig. 3 Examples of scripts used for community languages in Britain

perceived as containing an inherent short *a*, the most commonly occurring vowel in Indian languages. It also contains a large number of conjuncts made up of two or more characters, but often looking very different from the original components.

Today Bengali is associated mainly with the geographical areas of West Bengal and Bangladesh. The current situation, however, is the product of a highly complex history. After partition in 1947, West Bengal remained a part of India with Bengali as the official state language. Muslim East Bengal became East Pakistan, adopting Urdu (see below) as the official language. The Bengali language was an important focus of the independence movement and when, after a bitter civil war, East Pakistan achieved independence in 1971, as Bangladesh, it became the official language.

The Bengali community in the UK consists of a small, mainly Hindu community from Indian West Bengal and a much larger Muslim Bangladeshi community, most of whom come from the Sylhet region which has long-standing ties with the UK through the jute, tea and shipping industries. West Bengalis speak varieties close to the standard language; most Bangladeshis speak Sylheti as their home language but will have received their education through the medium of standard Bengali if they went to school in Bangladesh. Children attending community language classes in the UK will also learn standard Bengali.

Sylheti has no written tradition and is not accorded language status in Bangladesh. There is, however, considerable controversy over whether it should be considered as a language in its own right or as a dialect of Bengali. It has been suggested, for instance, that the differences between Sylheti and Bengali are greater than those between Bengali and Assamese, yet Assamese is recognized as an autonomous language. It seems reasonable to suppose that the reasons for classifying Sylheti as a dialect are more socio-political than linguistic.

The Bengali speech community in the UK is concentrated in the London Boroughs of Tower Hamlets and Camden, though smaller settlements are also to be found in cities such as Coventry and Bradford. Many Bangladeshi children attend Qur'anic classes in Arabic, as well as community language classes in Bengali, several times a week after school.

Gujarati

Gujarati, like Bengali, belongs to the *Indic branch of the *Indo-Iranian subgroup of the *Indo-European language family. A rich literary tradition dates back to the 10th c. AD. The Gujarati writing system (see fig. 3), like Bengali, developed from Brahmi, via the Devanagari script used for Sanskrit and Hindi. It is a syllabic system, running from left to right and hanging from – rather than resting on – the line, but without the continuous horizontal line running along the top which is associated with Hindi and Panjabi. It also has a large number of conjunct characters which often look quite different from the component parts.

Some members of the Gujarati speech community use Kachchi as the language of the home. Kachchi is a variety closely related to Sindhi and may have developed from earlier varieties of Sindhi and Gujarati. However, because Gujarati is the language of state government and education, Kachchi has traditionally been considered a dialect of Gujarati rather than an autonomous language, a position to which most Kachchi speakers in the UK also subscribe.

Gujarati speakers form the second largest south Asian community in the UK and are believed to number in excess of 300,000. They are scattered throughout the country with particular concentrations in Greater London and the Midlands. Approximately 30% of Gujaratis came direct from India; the rest arrived via East Africa where they had moved at the beginning of the 20th c. to work as farmers and traders. Differences between the Gujarati of Indian and East African speakers are most striking in the area of vocabulary: many Swahili words such as *jugu* ('peanuts') and *maramoja* ('quick') have been adopted by East African Gujaratis. Three-quarters of the Gujarati community are Hindu; the rest are Muslims whose home language is either Gujarati or Kachchi, but who have varying degrees of loyalty to Urdu and Qur'anic Arabic.

Many of the 500 or so organizations in the UK which form the National Federation of Gujarati Organizations promote cultural events which, in turn, encourage the use of Gujarati. Of particular note are the activities of the Gujarati Literary Academy which has developed a syllabus and textbooks for five graded examinations for young people living in countries where English is the dominant language; it also organizes conferences on literature and language.

Panjabi

Panjabi, like Gujarati and Bengali, belongs to the ***Indic** branch of the ***Indo-Iranian** subgroup of the ***Indo-European** language family. It is the language of a rich folk tradition, as well as the medium of a rich literary tradition dating back to the 15th c. Because it is the language of the holy book, the Guru Granth Sahib, it is treated with understandable respect by Sikhs. It is written in a script (see fig. 3) called Gurmukhi (meaning 'proceeding from the mouth of the guru'), devised by the second of the ten great founders of Sikhism. Gurmukhi is a syllabic system which reduced the 52 letters of the Devanagari script used for Hindi to 35, and added a further five characters from Persian. It is characterized by an almost continuous horizontal line running along the top. Like most other Indian languages, it runs from left to right and hangs from – rather than rests on – the line.

Panjabi-speakers came originally from the Panjab – or 'land of five rivers' – and form three extremely heterogeneous communities. The same geographical area was traditionally occupied by Hindus, Sikhs and Muslims. However, following partition in 1947, the Panjab was divided between India and Pakistan. It is estimated that 70% of Panjabi-speakers are currently resident in Pakistan; the remaining 30% live in India. Panjabi-speakers in Pakistan look to Urdu as the language of religion and high culture. The Hindu majority in the south of the region look in turn to Hindi. The new state of Harayana was formed in 1966 and most Hindus are concentrated in this area. Of all the groups which occupy the Panjab, the Sikhs owe their main loyalty to Panjabi.

Sikhs form the largest of the south Asian communities in the UK and are estimated to number at least 400,000. The most important areas of settlement are London, the West Midlands and the northern cities of Leeds and Bradford. Most came direct from India; some, however, arrived via Asian communities settled in East Africa since the early 20th c. Like other East African Asians, their vocabulary shows the influence of Swahili.

The Sikh temple or *gurdwara* forms the centre of religious, social and community life. Weddings, funerals and religious festivals such as Baisakhi, the New Year celebration in April and Diwali, the festival of lights which marks the onset of winter, are conducted in Panjabi. Community classes for British-born children are also usually based at the *gurdwara* and aim to teach Panjabi language and literature, as well as Sikh studies.

Urdu

Urdu, like all the other major south Asian languages spoken in the UK, belongs to the *Indic branch of the *Indo-Iranian subgroup of the *Indo-European language family. It was originally spoken in the Hindi region of India, together with Avadhi, Brijbhasha and Kari Boli. During the 16th c. large areas of India fell under the rule of Muslims whose language and culture were predominantly Persian. While the structure of Urdu remained essentially Indian, the vocabulary was greatly influenced by Persian. Urdu spread all over India through administrative structures, army encampments and bazaars. The word 'Urdu' comes from the Farsi *Zaban-e-Urdu-e-mu'alla* ('language of camp and court'), a gloss which gives important clues to its history.

The linguistic status of Urdu has been the subject of fierce debate. Some writers argue that spoken Hindi and Urdu should be treated as the same language; others argue that differences not only in lexical choice but in word order and script demand that they be treated separately.

Urdu is written in the Nastaliq script (see fig. 3), a consonantal system in which the vowels are indicated with diacritics above or below the letters. Characters change according to their position in the word – initial, medial, final or isolated – and run from right to left. Nastaliq is based on the Farsi writing system and differs in small but important respects from the Naskh script used for Arabic.

Perso-Arabic scripts pose particular challenges for word-processing (Multilingual Resources for Children Project 1995). Good programs offer 'contextual analysis' which automatically supply the correct character variant. Less sophisticated programs require the operator to search through levels of shift on the keyboard for the correct variant. The level of resolution achieved by cheaper programs also poses problems. Many people feel that it is better to write a language with an impressive calligraphic tradition like Urdu by hand, rather than to produce an imperfect word-processed version.

Urdu is spoken as a first or second language by over 30 million Muslims in India. Following partition in 1947, it became the official language of Pakistan where it is the mother tongue of some 5 million, and is used as a second language by a further 40 million speakers. The Urdu speech community is spread throughout the UK, with important settlements in London and the south, the Midlands and the north of England. Urdu speakers are estimated to comprise, for instance, 10% of the population of Bradford. They include a small number of native speakers from India and Pakistan, as well as Gujarati Muslims who use the language for religious purposes. By far the largest group, however, is made up of Muslim speakers of Panjabi from the Mirpur district of Azad Kashmir in Pakistan, who use Urdu as the language of religion and high culture.

Chinese

The main *fanyan* or regional varieties of Chinese spoken in the UK are Cantonese (or Yue), Mandarin (or Putonghua) and Hokkien (or Fukien). All belong to the Sinitic branch of the Sino-Tibetan language family. Although these varieties are mutually unintelligible, they share a common writing system built around thousands of logographs which have no relation to the spoken word. It has been estimated, for example, that you need to know between 4,000 and 7,000 characters to read a Chinese newspaper. In the People's Republic of China, attempts have been made to promote Mandarin through simplified characters using fewer strokes. The Chinese abroad, however, have preferred to maintain the traditional writing system (see fig. 3).

Traditionally, characters started at the top right-hand corner of the page and made their way from top to bottom. Sometimes – as in newspapers – writing from left to right is interchanged with the traditional directionality, even within the space of the same page. Characters are written in relation to a notional square. Children are taught how to write the various kinds of strokes – lines, sweeps, angles and hooks – and the basic sequence (left to right, top to bottom). They practise characters over and over until they are perfect. If a single stroke is forgotten or misplaced, the meaning may be changed completely, so attention to detail is essential.

Literacy is a high-status activity within the Chinese community. Books are held in high esteem and parents believe that children must prove themselves worthy through hard work. Children are given books as a reward after they have successfully learned to read rather than as an incentive to persuade them to read.

The Chinese form the third largest ethnic minority community in the UK. The largest group comes from Hong Kong. Following the requisition of land from farmers for development purposes and an influx of refugees from the People's Republic during the Cultural Revolution, unemployment became a serious problem and many people, especially those with limited formal education, sought work in the growing catering business in the UK. More recently, in anticipation of the return of Hong Kong to China in 1997, new arrivals came increasingly from professional backgrounds. About 70% of Hong Kong Chinese speak Cantonese which also serves as a lingua franca.

Other ethnic Chinese in the UK include a refugee community of approximately 25,000 from Vietnam, speaking Cantonese, Putonghua, Hokkien, Chiuchow, Hakka and Hainanese, but using Cantonese as the lingua franca; and small numbers of professional Chinese from Singapore and Malaysia, mainly Putonghua speakers who came to the UK as students. Approximately half of the Chinese population of the UK live in London, although there are also significant settlements in Manchester, Liverpool, Birmingham and Glasgow.

Alladina, S. and Edwards, V. (eds) 1991. *Multilingualism in the British Isles*, 2 vols. London.
Linguistic Minorities Project 1985. *The Other Languages of England*. London.
Multilingual Resources for Children Project 1995. *Building Bridges: Multilingual Resources for Children*. Clevedon.

VIV EDWARDS

Community languages (France)

The situation of community languages in France is far less well documented than that of such languages in Britain. The data presented here are drawn mainly from the contributions to Vermes (1988).

Arabic

For a variety of political and economic reasons, there has been substantial immigration of Arabic-speakers into France from the three Maghreb states (Morocco, Algeria, Tunisia) particularly since the 1950s. Their numbers are estimated by Jerab (in Vermes 1988) at some 2 million. In consequence of an agreement with the Maghreb states, the teaching of Arabic in schools (which in practice means primary schools), and within the normal timetable, has been authorized since 1975, but the fact that the language taught is classical Arabic and not the spoken vernaculars is a discouraging factor. There is also a limited amount of broadcasting in classical Arabic on Radio-France International and in both classical and vernacular Arabic on certain local radio stations.

Berber

The term 'Berber' relates to a group of dialects or languages spoken by large populations (estimates range from 8 to 12 million) in North Africa, principally in Algeria and Morocco, in both of which countries Berber lacks any official recognition, and to some extent in Mauritania, Niger, Mali and elsewhere. Migration of both Berber- and Arabic-speakers to France from Algeria began in the 19th c.; that from Morocco dates mainly from the post-Second World War period. Numbers of Berber-speakers in France are estimated by Chaker (in Vermes 1988), allowing for a wide margin of error, at over half a million.

West African languages

In the 1960s and 1970s, large numbers of speakers of West African languages arrived in France, principally but not solely from the former French colonies of Mauritania, Mali, Senegal, Guinea and Côte d'Ivoire, and settled mainly in the Paris area where their numbers are estimated at about 100,000. Platiel (in Vermes 1988) itemizes as the principal ethnic groups represented (and, by implication, languages spoken, among a multiplicity of others), in decreasing order of numerical importance, Soninke, Fula, Bambara, Malinka, Soso, Wolof and Dyula. Of these, Fula (otherwise known as Fulani or Peul) and Wolof are members of the northern group of the West Atlantic language family, while Bambara, Dyula (Jula), Malinka (sometimes considered as three dialects of the same language), Soninke and Soso (Susu) are members of the NW group of Mande (Mende, Mandingo) languages.

South-west Asian languages

Speakers of the national languages of the independent states of Vietnam, Cambodia and Laos, i.e. the former French Indo-China, arrived in France in substantial numbers after the establishment in 1975 of communist regimes in the whole of Vietnam and in Laos and of the Khmer Rouge regime in Cambodia. It appears from Simon-Barouh's wide-ranging survey (in Vermes 1988) that there were in France in 1987 some 32,000 Vietnamese, some 48,000 Cambodians (a significant but unquantifiable proportion of whom, however, would have had as their first language not

Khmer (Cambodian) but Chinese (see below)), some 25,000 speakers of Lao and perhaps 8,000 speakers of Hmong, a language with no standard written form and spoken mainly in China though the Hmong speakers in France are from Laos. Vietnamese and Khmer belong to different branches of the Mon-Khmer language family, Lao to the Daic family, and Hmong to the Miao family.

Chinese
Chinese-speakers in France, who for the most part have settled in Paris, fall broadly speaking into two groups. There are first some thousands of those (or their descendants) who, largely for economic reasons, migrated to France at various times from the period of the First World War onwards. A numerically much more important group consists of those, amounting probably to over 40,000, who have arrived since 1975 as refugees from the states of former Indo-China (see above).

Creoles
French-based *creoles are widely spoken (a) in the Caribbean area, including the overseas *départements* of Guadeloupe, Martinique and French Guyana together with Haiti and the former British colonies of Dominica, Grenada, St Lucia and Trinidad, and (b) in various Indian Ocean islands, including not only the overseas *département* of Réunion but Mauritius (and its dependency, Rodrigues Island) and the Seychelles. Large-scale immigration to France from the overseas *départements* dates from the 1960s and early 1970s. The number of immigrants from the overseas *départements* in general, of whom the great majority can be assumed to be creole-speakers, was estimated by Tessonneau (in Vermes 1988) at over 300,000, to whom should be added an unspecified number of refugees from Haiti.

Vermes, G. (ed.) 1988. *Vingt-cinq communautés linguistiques de la France*, vol. 2, *Les Langues immigrées*. Paris. (S. Platiel, 'Les langues d'Afrique Noire en France', 9–30; N. Jerab, 'L'arabe des maghrébins', 31–59; I. Simon-Barouh, 'Les langues de l'Asie du Sud-Est. Le vietnamien. Le kmer. Le lao. Le hmong', 85–131; J. P. Hassoun, 'Le chinois', 132–44; S. Chaker, 'Le berbère', 145–64; A. Tessonneau, 'Le Créole en métropole', 165–93.)

GLANVILLE PRICE

Community languages (Netherlands)
The recent colonial past has meant that a number of non-indigenous languages are spoken in the Netherlands.

Malay is spoken by an estimated 40,000 Moluccans. The Dutch colonial army recruited most of its soldiers in the Moluccas in the Indonesian archipelago and, upon Indonesian independence in 1949, these soldiers and their families were evacuated to the Netherlands because of hostility towards them from other Indonesians. After an initial period of relative isolation, the Moluccan people in the Netherlands are slowly integrating into Dutch society, with the result that there is a lower degree of proficiency in Malay among the younger generation.

There are approximately 200,000 Surinamese in the Netherlands. Their linguistic background is closely tied up with the linguistic situation in Surinam, where, apart from Surinamese Dutch and Amerindian languages (with very few speakers), the major native languages are the English-based ***creole Sranan** (spoken by the creole population), the Hakka dialect of Chinese (spoken by the Chinese population), Javanese, and Hindi (known as Sarnami). Immigrants from these last three speech communities arrived in Surinam as plantation workers after the abolition of slavery in 1863. All three languages have developed local varieties in Surinam. Sranan, Sarnami, Javanese and Surinamese Dutch have the largest numbers of speakers in the Netherlands, although not much research has been carried out into the exact numbers and into the maintenance or decline of these languages.

Papiamentu, a Spanish- and Portuguese-based creole, is the native language of some 70,000 immigrants from the Dutch West Indies (Aruba, Bonaire and Curaçao).

Recent decades have also seen the establishment in the Netherlands of sizeable communities of 'guest workers' and their families from Turkey (*c*.150,000) with Turkish or Kurdish as their native languages, and from North Africa (*c*.100,000) with Arabic or Berber as their languages.

Extra, G. and Verhoeven, L. (eds) 1993. *Community Languages in the Netherlands*. Amsterdam.

ROEL VISMANS

Continental Celtic

Continental Celtic (as opposed to Insular Celtic) is the collective term for all ***Celtic languages** that were spoken on the European Continent in the Iron Age. All Continental Celtic languages probably became extinct at some time in the early centuries AD. Three different languages can be identified: ***Celtiberian** (Spain), ***Lepontic** (northern Italy) and ***Gaulish** (France, northern Italy). There is archaeological and, more to the point, scanty onomastic evidence that Celtic-speaking peoples were once more widespread. Leaving aside the British Isles, there are indications that, at some time after 500 BC, speakers of Celtic lived in present-day Spain and Portugal, France, Belgium, the southern parts of the Netherlands and Germany, southern Poland, Switzerland, Austria, Northern Italy, Bohemia, Hungary, northern Croatia and Serbia, the Balkans, northern Greece. In Asia Minor they were known as the Galatians.

The dichotomy of Insular vs Continental Celtic does not imply a genetic dichotomy. The linguistic differences between Celtiberian and Gaulish are so considerable that the assumption of a particularly close genetic relation between the two is unwarranted. The ***Brittonic languages** of Insular Celtic are traditionally regarded as being genetically closest to the Continental Celtic language Gaulish. This notion has recently come under heavy attack, however: important arguments have been raised for a closer connection between Brittonic and ***Irish**.

Eska, J. F. and Evans, D. E. 1993. Continental Celtic. In Ball, M. J. (ed.), *The Celtic Languages*, London, 26–63.
Evans, D. E. 1979. The labyrinth of Continental Celtic. *Proceedings of the British Academy*, 65: 497–538.

Schmidt, K. -H. 1978–80. On the Celtic languages of Continental Europe. *Bulletin of the Board of Celtic Studies*, 28: 189–205.

PETER SCHRIJVER

Cornish

A member of the ***Brittonic** subgroup of the ***Celtic languages**, Cornish is closely related to ***Breton** and more distantly to ***Welsh**. Cornish as a spoken vernacular had disappeared by the end of the 18th c., though there is some evidence to suggest the survival of fragments of popular knowledge of the language into the late 19th and perhaps even early 20th centuries, while individual words have survived into the contemporary Cornish dialect of English. A small but persistent revivalist movement has emerged in the 20th c.

The Old Cornish period

Old Cornish emerged as a result of the separation of SW Britain from other Celtic areas by the Saxon advance in the late 6th c. AD. Place-name evidence suggests that by the late 7th c. the Saxon advance (and with it the English language) had intruded into the far north-east of Cornwall. Meanwhile, in response to a complex series of events that is still imperfectly understood (but included pressure from both the Saxon advance and Irish colonization), a flow of emigrants from SW Britain to the Armorican peninsula ensured the development of close linguistic and cultural ties between Cornwall and Brittany in the early medieval period. In 926 the Athelstan settlement, which established the River Tamar as the border between Cornwall and Wessex, provided a political stability which allowed the survival of Cornwall as a territory and the Cornish (with their language) as a separate people.

The earliest written survivals from Old Cornish are glosses dating from the late 9th and 10th centuries. The first 19 are written on the text *Smaragdus's Commentary on Donatus*, while three later glosses appear on the manuscript *Oxoniensis Posterior*. More significant are the *Bodmin Gospels*, in which are recorded in Old Cornish the names and details of slaves freed in Bodmin between the mid-10th and mid-11th centuries. Also important is the *Old Cornish Vocabulary*, a late 11th- or early 12th-c. Latin–Cornish translation (containing some 961 words) of a Latin–English dictionary. The first full sentence in Cornish to have survived is from the Old Cornish period, occurring in a story recounting the foundation in 1265 of the church of St Thomas at Glasney (Penryn) in which is fulfilled an ancient Cornish punning prophecy: 'In Polsethow ywhylyr anethow'. *Anethow* has two meanings, so the translation is 'In Polsethow shall be seen dwellings' or 'marvels'.

The Middle Cornish period

The first evidence of Middle Cornish is a 41-line piece of poetry written before 1400 on a charter relating to the parish of St Stephen-in-Brannel. The substantial survivals of the Middle Cornish period, however, are the miracle plays. These are expressions of a wider medieval European literary and religious genre, but they have a peculiarly

Cornish flavour and together form a substantial corpus of material. The earliest is the *Ordinalia*, dating from the latter part of the 14th c. and probably written at Glasney College, Penryn, the home of medieval Cornish scholarship. Composed of three separate parts (*Origo Mundi* 'The Origin of the World', *Passio Christi* 'The Passion of Christ', and *Resurrectio Domini* 'The Resurrection of the Lord'), the *Ordinalia* were designed to be performed over three days in the traditional Cornish outdoor amphitheatre or *plen an gwarry* ('playing place').

Related to the *Ordinalia* is *Pascon Agan Arluth* ('Passion of Our Lord', often referred to as the 'Passion Poem'), written at about the same time in the same syllabic (rather than rhythmic) manner, apparently borrowing some 23 lines from the *Ordinalia*. Also echoing the *Ordinalia* is *Greans an Bys* ('The Creation of the World'), although the manuscript that has survived dates from a much later period, having been copied out in 1611 by one William Jordan of Helston. Despite the passage of several centuries, Jordan's version is constructed in a manner that closely follows *Origo Mundi*.

More original in content and composition is *Beunans Meriasek* ('The Life of St Meriasek'), the only complete saint's play to have survived in the whole of Britain. Although focused on the district of Camborne and celebrating a saint with a cult in Cornwall and Brittany, *Beunans Meriasek* is a standard late *vita*, composed in the wider tradition of European miracle drama, asserting the fundamental tenets of medieval Catholic Christendom.

The retreat of Cornish

Conventional wisdom suggests that the language was in retreat throughout the Old Cornish and ensuing Middle Cornish periods, continually losing ground as English spread ever westwards from the Tamar. By 1500, it has been argued, Cornish had been pushed back as far as the Fowey–Camel line in mid-Cornwall. However, more recent work on place-name and other evidence suggests a more complex process. It is now hypothesized that after the Norman Conquest the Cornish language enjoyed a resurgence, 're-Celticizing' the eastern parts of Cornwall so that Cornish may have been spoken as far east as the Tamar until perhaps as late as the Reformation. Certainly, there were bilingual Cornish/English speakers in St Ewe in mid-Cornwall as late as 1595.

The overtly Catholic nature of *Beunans Meriasek* (see above) meant that its performance did not survive the Reformation. In other respects the Reformation also posed a challenge to the Cornish language, representing as it did a further intrusion into Cornwall by the Tudor State. The Cornish Prayer Book Rebellion of 1549 was in part a reaction against the introduction of English into church services. The failure to translate the Bible and Prayer Book into Cornish was a major disability, as were the suppression of Glasney College by Henry VIII and the weakening of ties between Cornwall and Brittany after the Reformation. However, during the brief return to Catholicism in the reign of Mary Tudor, the 12 homilies of Edmund Bonner, Bishop of London, were translated into Cornish by one John Tregear. The *Tregear Homilies*, as they are known, show how the Cornish language had further developed by the mid–16th c., moving from its Middle to Late period.

In 1602 Richard Carew, in his *Survey of Cornwall*, indicated that the Cornish language had become limited to the western districts and that there were few who could not also speak English. The upheavals of the Civil War put further pressure on the language, as did the rapid socio-economic change precipitated by Cornwall's early experience of industrialization in the 18th c. It has been estimated that there were perhaps as many as 22,000 Cornish speakers in 1600 (at the language's peak, *c.*1300, there were possibly 38,000 speakers), declining to about 5,000 in 1700 and with very few left by 1750. Dolly Pentreath, the Mousehole fishwife who died in 1777, is popularly supposed to have been the 'last speaker of Cornish' but she was certainly survived by others with at least some native knowledge of the language. For example, one John Tremethack (who died in 1852 aged 87) was reported to have taught Cornish to his daughter, a Mrs Kelynack of Newlyn who was still alive in 1875, and John Davey of Zennor (who died in 1891) was supposed to have conversed on various subjects and sung in Cornish.

Despite this decline, the Late Cornish period was marked by considerable activity. William Scawen in his *Antiquities Cornu-Britannick* (*c.*1680) noted the reasons for the decline and indicated that the language was by then spoken only on the Lizard and Penwith (Land's End) peninsulas. At about the same time a group of scholars led by John Keigwin emerged in the Penzance area to study and foster Cornish. They busied themselves translating biblical passages and collecting proverbs, colloquial sayings and popular songs. In 1700 John Boson, one member of the group, published his *Nebbaz Gerriau dro tho Carnoack* ('A few words about Cornish'). Another, William Gwavas, collected a number of Cornish manuscripts and carried on a correspondence entirely in Cornish with Boson. In contrast to the verse and register of the medieval miracle plays, much of the surviving material from the Late period is prose and often colloquial. Also significant is the fact that Edward Lhuyd, the Celtic scholar, visited Cornwall in about 1700 to investigate and record the language. His *Archaeologia Britannica* is thus the only guide to the pronunciation of Cornish compiled while the language was still a living vernacular.

Revivalist movements

Although Cornish opinion in the 19th c. generally welcomed the demise of Cornish, considering that the language would have been an inconvenient impediment in a rapidly industrializing society, there was antiquarian interest in its remains. By the early 20th c. this had been transformed into a revivalist enthusiasm, driven by the model of the wider 'Celtic Revival' and given relevance in Cornwall by a desire to look back over the debris of a by now rapidly de-industrializing society to a time when Cornwall was 'more Celtic'. Henry Jenner's *Handbook of the Cornish Language* (1904) was an early milestone in the revival but the full-scale reconstruction of Cornish was undertaken in the inter-war period by Robert Morton Nance. Basing his work principally on the texts of the medieval miracle plays, Nance termed his synthesis 'Unified' Cornish. However, although 'Unified' was readily embraced by enthusiasts in Cornwall, Celtic scholars were on the whole sceptical of Nance's methodology. Moreover, Nance's ideological commitment to recreating a *medieval* language was to lead, in the years after 1945, to an increasing unease in Cornwall itself, as was the apparent inconsistency of 'Middle Cornish' spelling and 'Late Cornish' pronunciation inherent in Nance's system.

A Cornish Language Board was set-up in 1968 to manage the revival of Cornish but in the subsequent period serious rifts appeared in the language movement in Cornwall. Nance's view that the contemporary pronunciation of English in Penwith reflected that of Late Cornish was challenged increasingly, adding to academic objections to his work, and a handful of concerned activists in Cornwall began to construct what was to become a post-Nancean agenda.

One outcome was Ken George's *The Pronunciation and Spelling of Revived Cornish* (1986) which reinforced the medieval focus of the revived language but also attempted to match George's estimation of Cornish phonology as it had been in about 1500 to a newly devised 'phonemic' orthography. This new system was known as 'Kernewek Kemmyn' ('Common Cornish'). Although adopted by the Cornish Language Board, its introduction was resisted by defenders of 'Unified', not least by Nicholas Williams (1995, 1997) who furnished an array of academic objections to George's work and sought instead to 'modernize' 'Unified' by incorporating within it consideration of the *Tregear Homilies* (which had been unavailable to Nance) and dropping the archaisms inherited from the *Ordinalia*.

At the same time others were drawn to the work of Richard Gendell (1991a, 1991b, 1992, 1997) which, building on the efforts of Lhuyd and Jenner, sought to construct 'Modern Cornish' ('Kernuack') from Late Cornish material. For those critical of the medievalist predilections of Nance and the early revivalists, the emphasis on Cornish as it was more recently spoken was attractive, as was Gendall's insistence that he was reliant solely on textual examples without recourse to 'invention'. Gendall also insisted that the contemporary pronunciation of English in Penwith was, after all, a guide to the sounds of Late Cornish because (he said) it closely matched that recorded by Lhuyd.

A Cornish Language Council was formed to promote 'Modern Cornish' and by the mid-1990s, with still perhaps only 50 really fluent speakers of any type of revived Cornish, the competing organizations supporting the three variants ('Unified', 'Kemmyn' and 'Modern') each had their own members, funds, publications and evening classes. But although this fragmentation was viewed with dismay by some observers, the willingness of Cornish revivalists to move beyond the Nancean synthesis and to engage in vigorous debate about both the shortcomings and the future of the revived language was perhaps evidence of a new maturity in the quest for 'authenticity'.

Ellis, P. B. (n.d.) *The Story of the Cornish Language*. Truro.
Fudge, C. 1982. *The Life of Cornish*. Redruth.
Gendall, R. M. M. 1991a. *A Student's Grammar of Modern Cornish*. Menheniot.
—— 1991b.*A Student's Dictionary of Modern Cornish*, Part 1: English–Cornish. Menheniot.
—— 1992. *An Curnoack Hethow: Cornish Today*. Menheniot.
—— 1997. *A Practical Dictionary of Modern Cornish*, Part 1, *Cornish–English*. Menheniot.

George, K. 1986a. How many people spoke Cornish traditionally? *Cornish Studies*, 14: 67–70.

—— 1986b. *The Pronunciation and Spelling of Revived Cornish*. Torpoint.

Jenner, H. 1904. *A Handbook of the Cornish Language*. London.

Lewis, H. 1946. *Llawlyfr Cernyweg Canol* ('A Handbook of Middle Cornish') (in Welsh). Cardiff.

Padel, O. J. 1985. *Cornish Place-Name Elements*. Nottingham.

—— 1988. *A Popular Dictionary of Cornish Place-Names*. Penzance.

Payton, P. (forthcoming). The ideology of language revival in contemporary Cornwall. In Black, R., Gillies, W. and O'Maolalaigh, R. (eds), *Celtic Connections*. Edinburgh.

—— and Deacon, B. 1993. The ideology of language revival. In Payton, P. (ed.), *Cornwall Since the War: The Contemporary History of a European Region*, Redruth, 271–90.

Pool, P. A. S. 1975. *The Death of Cornish*. Penzance.

Wakelin, M. F. 1975. *Language and History in Cornwall*. Leicester.

Weatherhill, C. 1995. *Cornish Place Names and Language*. Wilmslow.

Williams, N. J. A. 1995. *Cornish Today*. Sutton Coldfield.

—— 1997. *Clappya Kernowek: An Introduction to Unified Cornish Revised*. Portreath.

PHILIP PAYTON

Corsican

A member of the south central group of the dialects of *Italy, Corsican is spoken in the island of Corsica and, under the name of Gallurese, in the Gallura district in the north of the neighbouring island of Sardinia.

History

Until quite recently, for socio-historical and socio-cultural reasons, Corsican was not written: the first attestations of it go back only to the 19th c. At first, Italian (i.e. Tuscan) served (except in so far as these functions were fulfilled by Latin) as the official and prestige language and as the language of the law, of administration and of religion, not only during the period of Pisan domination (10th–12th centuries) but also during the period of Genoese domination (13th–17th centuries). French later took over, though not immediately upon the acquisition of the island by France from Genoa in 1768: it was not until the mid-19th c. that French really took over and has made constant progress since. Corsican has therefore functioned as a vernacular, at first in relation to Italian (constituting the everyday spoken variant of written Tuscan) and later in relation to French. It is in the context of this relation to French that one must see both, on the one hand, the decline of Corsican in everyday use and, on the other, its acquisition of the status of a written language, with the emergence of a specifically Corsican literature, and current claims for its recognition as an official language. At the same time, and in spite of some hesitations, there has come into use a more or less stable written norm, based mainly on that of Italian, but being differentiated from it by a few symbolic features.

Though the Corsican of the north of the island and that of the south are closer to central (or indeed northern) and southern dialects of mainland Italy respectively, there are no marked dialectal divisions. One can, however, largely on historical grounds, distinguish between a conservative southern variety (Corso-Gallurese) and a more or less heavily Tuscanized central and northern variety, with, between them, in the valley of the river Taravo, a band of local speech varieties presenting a few minor but historically significant features.

The Latinization of Corsica dates from the period following the First Punic War (3rd c. BC). Little is known about the earlier linguistic situation: a few terms remaining in place-names, such as *cala, calanca, cucca*, and also *corse-* 'steep terrain' (the reputed etymon of the name of the island), have been attributed to a 'Mediterranean' substratum, together with a few words including *talavellu* or *tarabucciu* 'daffodil', *caracutu* 'holly'. It is possible, but not certain, that an important phonetic feature of southern Corsican dialects, a retroflex or cacuminal consonant usually written as *-dd-* (e.g. *cavaddu* 'horse', corresponding to Italian *cavallo*) which links Corsican with Sardinian and Sicilian, also goes back to a pre-Latin substratum.

For several centuries from the Roman period onwards, Corsica and Sardinia were united, politically and linguistically, but, from the 8th c., a distinctive Corsican speech variety began to emerge. Whereas Sardinia developed to some extent in isolation and later looked towards Spain, Corsica was open to Italian and more especially Tuscan influences which are felt throughout the island, though more strongly in the north than in the south. This is seen both in the lexicon (in, for example, such words as *ava(le)* 'now', *zitellu* 'child', *veculu* 'cradle', corresponding to Italian *ora, bambino, culla*) and in the grammar (in, for example, the use of an enclitic possessive, *babbitu* 'your dad', *mammata* 'your mum', for Italian *tuo babbo, tua mamma*, and in features of the morphology of the verb) – all of these correspond to forms that occur in mainland Italy.

The influence (which may, however, be underestimated) of a Genoese adstratum is usually considered to be limited to a few words referring to the domains of urban life, fashion and food, e.g. *baina* 'slate', *carrega* 'chair', *carbusgiu* 'cabbage', *sciogna* 'pillow-case', *spighjetti* 'spectacles'.

The influence of French is of a quite different order since it is tending to lead to outright substitution. What began with the introduction of French words for new concepts (e.g. *vittura* 'car', corresponding to French *voiture*, for Italian *macchina*) has become the wholesale adoption of Gallicisms in place of authentic Corsican words that are being forgotten. Consequently, there is a noticeable inversion of roles: French which, at the beginning of the century, was a 'Sunday best' language, learned at school, is now the mother tongue of all the younger generations, albeit with a regional colouring, evolving a familiar register and becoming a genuine vernacular. At the same time, Corsican, in line with cultural revival movements that have grown up in the latter part of the 20th c., is acquiring a renewed vitality and a broadening of its spheres of use and is tending more and more to become a language of everyday use.

Present situation

Given the lack of official census figures, the number of Corsican-speakers can only be estimated. There are probably from 120,000 to 150,000 in Corsica itself with as many again outside the island, mainly in mainland France. Generally, with the exception of a number of Italians from Sardinia or from mainland Italy, outsiders who take up residence on the island do not acquire the language.

A law of 1951 (the *loi Deixonne*) laying down the conditions in which regional languages could be taught in French schools specified only *Basque, *Breton, *Catalan and *Occitan and so made no provision for Corsican. The first attempts to teach Corsican date from 1968 but it was not until 1974 that the provisions of the 1951 act were extended to apply to Corsican. Under the act, three hours per week are to be devoted to the relevant regional language where the demand for it exists, but on a strictly voluntary basis on the part both of teachers and of parents (in the sense that children cannot be obliged to attend such classes). Consequently, provision of classes is patchy. A complete course in Corsican language and literature is offered at the University of Corsica at Corte, a programme for recruiting people to teach the language at secondary level exists, and the provision of teaching materials is subsidized by the local government authority.

As elsewhere in France, the only official language is French and demands at the present time for the recognition of Corsican as an official language come up against the refusal of France to sign the European Charter on Minority Languages. In the Roman Catholic Church, although Corsican translations of the liturgy and the New Testament exist, services in Corsican are rare; if families so request, hymns may be sung in Corsican at marriages and funerals, but the text of the service and the sermon are always in French. After 20 years of campaigning, road signs which were previously in a French or Tuscanized form are gradually becoming bilingual. There is also an increasing use of Corsican in some other aspects of public or private life (shops, streets, names of localities, the use of Corsican Christian names).

In the media, the local editions of daily papers published in the south of mainland France (*Nice-Matin* and the Marseilles-based *Provençal*) accord a minimum of space to Corsican and there is some limited provision for the language in two local political weeklies. Of the radio stations transmitting in Corsican, the most popular is the state radio; regional television provides a daily six-minute news bulletin and one 30-minute programme per week, and there are plans to increase the output in Corsican.

Dalbera-Stefanaggi, M.-J. 1978. *Langue corse: une approche linguistique*. Paris.
——— 1991. *Unité et diversité des parlers corses*. Alessandria.
——— 1997. Corsica. In Maiden, M. and Parry, M. (eds), *The Dialects of Italy*, London, 303–10.
Loi Corvetto, I. and Nesi, A. 1993. *La Sardegna e la Corsica*. Turin.
Marchetti, P. 1974. *Le corse sans peine*. Chennevières-sur-Marne.
U Muntese 1985. *Dizziunariu corsu–francese/Dictionnaire corse–français*, 4 vols. Levie.
Thiers, J. 1988. Le corse. L'insularité d'une langue. In G. Vermes (ed.), *Vingt-cinq communautés linguistiques de la France*, vol. 1, *Langues régionales et langues non territorialisées*, Paris, 150–68.
[Various authors] 1988. Korsisch. In Holtus, G., Metzeltin, M. and Schmitt, C. (eds), *Lexikon der Romanistischen Linguistik*, Tübingen, vol. 4, 799–835 (4 articles, 2 in French, 1 in Italian, 1 in German).

MARIE-JOSÉ DALBERA-STEFANAGGI AND GEORGES MORACCHINI

Creoles

Creoles derive typically from *pidgin languages but, whereas a pidgin is an accessory language and no one's first language, 'a creole arises when a pidgin becomes the mother tongue of a speech community. The simple structure that characterized the pidgin is carried over into the creole but since a creole, as a mother tongue, must be capable of expressing the whole range of human experience, the lexicon is expanded and frequently a more elaborate system evolves' (Todd 1990: 2–3).

Pidgins and creoles are widely referred to as 'English-based', 'French-based', etc., but the terms 'Afro-English', 'Afro-French', etc., which avoid conveying a Eurocentric view of the languages in question, are also used with reference to creoles (though not to pidgins). The classification of pidgins and creoles poses intractable problems but, in a widely quoted survey, Hancock (1977) itemizes 127 (some of them now extinct), of which 35 are English-based, 15 French-based, 14 Portuguese-based, 7 Spanish-based, 18 are based on other European languages (for an example, see **Russenorsk**), while the remainder are based on non-European languages (mainly Amerindian, African or Asian).

Pidgins and creoles are found especially, but not exclusively (see Hancock 1977 and maps in Holm 1989, vol. 2), in the Caribbean area (including Louisiana and the Guyanas), West Africa, the Indian Ocean islands, and the islands of the SW Pacific area.

The most widely spoken creoles (as distinct from pidgins) are probably the French-based creoles of the Caribbean area (including Louisiana and French Guyana) (see below and also under **Community Languages (France)**). English-based creoles are spoken mainly in the Caribbean area, in West Africa, and in the SW Pacific area. The term 'Patwa' (= *patois*) is used with reference to both French-based and English-based creoles while the former are also termed 'Kwéyòl' (= *créole*). Spanish-based creoles occur in the Caribbean and the Philippines, and Portuguese-based in West Africa. Though the Dutch-based creoles of Guyana are nearly extinct, a derivative of a creolized form of Dutch flourishes in South Africa as Afrikaans (see under **Dutch**).

There are in Britain communities of speakers both of English-based and of French-based creoles. Over half a million West Indians emigrated to Britain between 1955 and 1971, but no reliable estimates exist for the numbers of speakers of English-based creoles and views differ within the West Indian community itself as to the opportuneness of introducing Patwa into the school curriculum. Kwéyòl-speakers in Britain (mainly in London), immigrants from the former British colonies of Dominica and St Lucia where French-based creoles are in use, are estimated to number some 15,000. Nwenmely (1995) finds that the shift from Kwéyòl to English was largely completed within 20 years but that, since the early 1980s, there have been determined attempts to assert the community's identity through the provision of language and literacy classes (the language is as yet only partly standardized) in schools.

Chaudenson, R. 1979. *Les Créoles français*. Paris.
Dalphinis, M. 1986. French creoles in the Caribbean and Britain. In Sutcliffe, D. and Wong, A. (eds), *The Language of Black Experience*, Oxford, 168–91.
—— 1991. The Afro-English speech community. In Alladina, S. and Edwards, V. (eds),

Multilingualism in the British Isles, vol. 2, *Africa, the Middle East and Asia*, London, 42–56.

Hancock, I. F. 1977. Repertory of pidgin and creole languages. In Valdman, A. (ed.), *Pidgin and Creole Linguistics*, Bloomington, IN, 362–91.

Holm, J. 1989. *Pidgin and Creole Languages*, 2 vols. Cambridge.

Nwenmely, H. 1991. The Kwéyòl speech community. In Alladina and Edwards (see Dalphinis 1991), 57–68.

—— 1995. *Language Reclamation: French Creole Language Teaching in the UK and the Caribbean*. Clevedon.

Sebba, M. 1986. London Jamaican and Black London English. In Sutcliffe and Wong (see Dalphinis 1986), 149–67.

Todd, L. 1990. *Pidgins and Creoles*, 2nd edn. London.

Valdman, A. (ed.) 1977. *Pidgin and Creole Linguistics*. Bloomington, IN.

GLANVILLE PRICE

Cretan pictographic script

In the first half of the second millennium BC, and somewhat earlier than the *Linear A script, there came into use in the Minoan civilization in Crete what is usually referred to as pictographic script (sometimes, but less accurately, referred to as a hieroglyphic script) which is found on such objects as seals, clay tablets, vases, etc. This script remains completely undeciphered and one can do no more than speculate as to the language it represents, which may have been the unknown pre-Greek language of the Minoans.

Crimchak, see *Karaim*

Crimean Gothic

Crimean Gothic is a fragmentary member of the East Germanic subgroup of the *Germanic languages. Evidence was recorded in a personal letter dated 1562 from the Imperial Ambassador at the Ottoman Porte, the Flemish nobleman Oghier Ghislain de Busbecq, telling of an encounter with two representatives of a people of Germanic appearance and customs (the letter is edited and translated by Stearns 1978). Busbecq listed some hundred separate linguistic forms in all, consisting of words and phrases, 18 cardinal numbers and the first three lines of a song. This corpus is too meagre to draw safe conclusions regarding the more detailed affiliation of the language, but opinion tends to the view that it is not a direct descendant of Wulfila's (Visi-)Gothic, but a late remnant of the Ostrogothic speech of the part of the tribe which remained in the Crimea (see *Gothic).

The corpus is problematic in so far as the linguistic competence of the informants is uncertain, because of interference from Greek; the interpretation of Busbecq's spelling conventions is difficult, as he uses Flemish and German orthographic conventions; and the letter comes down to us in a copy, whose relationship to the lost original letter is unclear. However, Crimean Gothic is valuable for Germanic philology, as it supplements our knowledge of Gothic in important ways. On the one hand, it contains a number of words not attested in the rest of the corpus, e.g. *ada* 'egg', *ael* 'stone', *apel* 'apple', *atochta* 'bad', *bars* 'beard', the etymologies of some of which are less than clear. On the other hand, it sheds light on possible diachronic developments in Gothic itself.

Stearns (1978, 1989), a summary of which appears in Robinson (1992), represents the most complete discussion of the language, but the majority of words are represented in Lehmann (1986) and also listed in Tollenaere and Jones (1976). Mossé's bibliography covers Crimean Gothic, but must be supplemented by more current reference works.

Lehmann, W. P. 1986. *A Gothic Etymological Dictionary*. Leiden.
Mossé, F. 1950. Bibliographia Gotica. *Mediaeval Studies*, 12: 237–324. (Supplements 15: 169–83 (1953); 19: 174–96 (1957); 29: 327–43 (1967); 36: 199–214 (1974).)
Robinson, O. W. 1992. Crimean Gothic. In Id., *Old English and Its Closest Relatives*, London, 50–1.
Stearns, MacD., Jr 1978. *Crimean Gothic: Analysis and Etymology of the Corpus*. Saratoga, CA.
—— 1989. Das Krimgotische ('Crimean Gothic'). In Beck, H. (ed.), *Germanische Rest- und Trümmersprachen* ('Fragments and Remains of Extinct Germanic Languages'), Berlin, 175–94.
Tollenaere, F. de and Jones, R. L. 1976. *Word-Indices and Word-Lists to the Gothic Bible and Minor Fragments*. Leiden.

JONATHAN WEST

Crimean Tatar

Crimean Tatar is generally considered to belong to the Ponto-Caspian group of the Kipchak or NW *Turkic languages*. It has sometimes been linked to the southern Turkic or Oghuz group but this may simply be due to its having come under continuous Ottoman influence. Its closest linguistic relatives are the languages of the Kumyks and the North Caucasian Turks (see *Karachay-Balkar*). The language is not directly related to those of the Kazan Tatars (see *Tatar*) or of the Nogay Tatars (see *Nogay*).

The break-up of the realm of the Golden Horde in the 15th c. gave rise to several independent khanates, among them that of the Crimean Tatars (1430–1783), which in 1475 became an Ottoman protectorate. The region came under Russian control at the end of the 18th c. Crimean Tatar has never achieved literary status.

Crimean Tatar is now spoken in the northern steppe part of the Crimea and in the towns of Simferopol', Feodosiya and Kerch'. During the Second World War, large numbers of speakers of the language were deported to Siberia and Central Asia and remained there in spite of the re-establishment of their homelands in 1957. Speakers in Ukraine in 1989 numbered 271,715. A group of some 20,000 Crimean Tatars live in the Romanian Dobruja in the southern part of the Constanţa district where their ancestors settled in the 18th c.

Doerfer, G. 1959. Das Krimtatarische. In Deny, J. et al. (eds), *Philologiae Turcicae Fundamenta*, Wiesbaden, 369–90.
Sheeby, A. 1973. *The Crimean Tatars, Volga Germans and Meshketians. Soviet Treatment of some National Minorities*. London.

WOLFGANG GRELLER

Croatian (see under *Serbo-Croat*)

Cuman (see under *Tatar*)

Cumbric

An extinct member of the ***Brittonic** branch of the ***Celtic languages**, and therefore related to ***Welsh**.

It is likely that, by the 7th c., the westward advance of the Angles had driven a
wedge between the territory of the northern Brittonic-speakers and that of their
Welsh kinsmen further south. In due course, the northern area came to consist of the
three kingdoms of Gododdin (between the Forth and the Tyne, with its capital at
Edinburgh), Strathclyde (covering much of SW Scotland, with its capital at
Dumbarton), and Rheged (corresponding roughly to modern Cumbria and possibly
extending into Scotland, with its capital perhaps at Carlisle).

Gododdin had fallen to the Angles by the mid-7th c. and it is not known how long
Brittonic speech survived there though elements remain in place-names: *Lanark*, for
example, corresponds to Welsh *llannerch* 'glade' and *Ecclefechan* to Welsh *eglwys
fechan* 'little church'.

The two western kingdoms survived somewhat longer, the subject of incursions,
occupations and rivalries between Angles, Scots, and incomers from Ireland of mixed
Irish and Viking origin. Although the name 'Cumbria' now refers only to the English
part of the area, there is historical justification for using it with reference to the whole
area, i.e. including the former kingdom of Strathclyde, and 'Cumbric' for the
Brittonic speech thereof. Strathclyde was incorporated in the kingdom of Scotland
in the 10th c. but here, too, numerous Brittonic place-names remain, e.g. *Ochiltree*
(cf. Welsh *uchel* 'high', *tref* 'township'). Our only direct evidence for Cumbric, other
than that of place-names, is also from this area, in the shape of three words incorporated in a Latin (11th c.?) legal text (e.g. *galnes* corresponding to Middle Welsh *galanas*
'blood-fine').

The fate of the language in modern Cumbria is even more obscure. Kenneth
Jackson's view that it had almost or entirely died out there but was reintroduced from
Strathclyde in the 10th c. has been widely accepted. However, Phythian-Adams
(1996) now argues that, at least in parts of the area, Celtic speech survived the Anglian
occupation and may have lasted even as late as the 12th c. However that may be, here
too there is place-name evidence for Cumbric, e.g. *Penrith* (corresponding to Welsh
pen 'end' + *rhyd* 'ford', so: 'the end of the ford'), *Carrock (Fell)* (cf. Welsh *carreg*
'rock').

Jackson, K. 1955. The Britons in Southern Scotland. *Antiquity*, 29: 77–88.
—— 1963. Angles and Britons in Northumbria and Cumbria. In Id., *Angles and Britons*, Cardiff, 60–84.
Nicolaisen, W. F. H. 1964. Celts and Anglo-Saxons in the Scottish border counties. *Scottish Studies*, 8:
    141–71.
Phythian-Adams, C. 1996. Britons: survival or revival? In Id., *Land of the Cumbrians. A Study in British
    Provincial Origins, AD 400–1120*, Aldershot, 77–87.
Price, G. 1984. Cumbric. In Id., *The Languages of Britain*, London, 146–57.

GLANVILLE PRICE

Curonian

An extinct *Baltic language or dialect spoken in parts of Latvia and Lithuania and which may have been transitional between *Latvian and *Lithuanian. No written records remain. It probably died out in the 16th c.

Cypriot Arabic

An *Arabic vernacular spoken by the inhabitants of the village of Kormakiti some 30 kilometres west of Kyrenia, in the Turkish military zone of Cyprus. Kormakiti is one of four Cypriot villages populated by Maronite (Lebanese Catholic) immigrants, but it is the only one to have preserved the Arabic spoken by the immigrants when they settled on the island. The date and circumstances of the settlement are open to surmise, but it is thought to have taken place around the 12th c. AD.

At the time of the Turkish invasion in July 1974, the Maronite inhabitants of Kormakiti numbered about 1,200 and were bilingual in Cypriot Arabic and Cypriot Greek. Five years later, the number was reduced to about 500 (mainly the old and the retired), the rest having left the village to settle for the most part in the chief urban centres of the southern Greek-controlled area: Nicosia (Greek zone), Larnaka and Limassol. Even before 1974, Kormakiti Arabic appeared to have been losing ground before Cypriot Greek. Its speakers were coping with a complex linguistic situation: Kormakiti Arabic, local Cypriot Greek, the Cypriot Greek koine, Demotic Greek, Puristic Greek and Turkish. The status of the dialect is low, owing to its isolation from mainstream Arabic and to the fact that, as in the case of the majority of Arabic vernaculars, it is not written. The 1974 invasion and the resulting effective division of the island have greatly hastened the process and virtually ensured its ultimate demise.

The linguistic appearance of the dialect is similar to that of other Arabic colloquials spoken in areas peripheral to the main core of Arab countries (e.g. Anatolian Arabic, *Maltese). It features some conservative traits but is characterized chiefly by innovations which are largely the result of a prolonged bilingual situation but which often develop in directions already adumbrated by the 'core' vernaculars spoken in Arab countries.

Borg, A. 1995. *Cypriot Arabic* (Abhandlungen für die Kunde des Morgenlandes, vol. xlvii-4). Stuttgart.
Newton, B. 1964. An Arabic–Greek dialect. *Word*, 20.3 (Supplement): 43–52.

JOSEPH CREMONA

Cypriot scripts

A small number of Bronze Age inscriptions from Cyprus, mainly from Enkomi in the east of the island, are in an undeciphered script, containing over 80 characters, that has been termed 'Cypro-Minoan' since it seems to have affinities with Minoan Cretan *Linear A. It may have been acquired by the Cypriots via contacts with Cretans at Ugarit in Syria. The earliest of these inscriptions probably dates from *c.*1500 BC, others from about the 12th c. BC. As they are at present undeciphered, the language in which they are written is unknown.

From the 7th to about the 3rd c. BC, we have in Cyprus inscriptions in a syllabic script (referred to as the 'classical Cypriot' script), containing some 55 characters, that is apparently related to the Cretan *Linear A and *Linear B scripts and may derive more directly from the Cypro-Minoan script (see above). Decipherment was made possible thanks to the existence of inscriptions having a text in this syllabic script together with another in either *Phoenician or *Greek. Most of the inscriptions in the syllabic script proved to be in Greek, but others are in an unknown language which has been termed 'Eteo-Cypriot' and which may or may not be the same as that of the earlier undeciphered Cypro-Minoan inscriptions.

Cypro-Minoan Script (see under *Cypriot scripts*)

Cyrillic and Glagolitic scripts
The oldest Slav alphabets are Cyrillic (see figs. 4 and 5) (after St Cyril) and Glagolitic (see fig. 5) (from *glagól* 'word, speech'), a variant of which was used until recently in a few places on the northern Dalmatian littoral and islands, while Cyrillic is current among Orthodox Slavs (and was used in Romania up to the 19th c.). There are no Glagolitic manuscripts from the East Slavonic area, but occasional Glagolitic letters and annotations are found in Cyrillic manuscripts. Glagolitic may have reached Kiev from Moravia in the late 9th or early 10th centuries. Cyrillic reached the East Slavonic area in the 10th c., before the conversion of 988–9.

Consensus gives temporal priority to Glagolitic, since (i) Glagolitic texts are in an older form of the language, both grammatically and lexically, than those in Cyrillic, (ii) palimpsests containing alphabets show Cyrillic imposed on Glagolitic, (iii) unlike Cyrillic, the numerical value of Glagolitic characters harmonizes with their alphabetical sequence (e.g. Cyrillic <б> [b] has no numerical value). The two alphabets differ in the shape and number of their letters, Cyrillic characters, unlike Glagolitic, being Greek in style, but both represent adequately the many sounds of *Slavonic languages.

In the 9th c., Glagolitic received papal sanction and was introduced into Moravia, whence it disappeared in due course, however, following the Pope's proscription of the Slavonic liturgy of the Roman Catholic Church. However, it was retained in Bulgaria and Croatia and spread along the Dalmatian coast south into Montenegro and west into Istria, and was also used by the Catholics of the western Balkan peninsula, but has now fallen out of ordinary use even there.

However, Cyrillic, being closer to the Greek alphabet, was more appropriate than Glagolitic to render Byzantine Christian literature, and by the 11th c. was extensively used. It derives from Bulgaria, where it was devised to represent the phonemes of the Macedonian Slavonic of Thessalonica (Slavonic Solun'), which was used by Cyril and Methodius (see below) for their scriptural and liturgical translations from Greek.

Cyrillic symbolized a literature, mainly ecclesiastical, that was imported into Rus' in the 10th c., together with the rudiments of Christian doctrine. Since the Slavonic languages were rich in sounds, however, and the Greek alphabet was incapable of coping with a Slavonic phonematic system (Byzantine had no equivalent for [b, g, ʒ,

(a) The Russian alphabet

(b) Additional characters not (or no longer) used in Russian

	Transliteration	*Phonetic value*
Аа	a	[a]
Бб	b	[b]
Вв	v	[v]
Гг	g (Bel, Uk h)	[g] (Bel, Uk [h])
Дд	d	[d]
Ее	e	[jɛ] (Uk [ɛ])
Ёё	ë	[jo]
Жж	zh, ž	[ʒ]
Зз	z	[z]
Ии	i	[i] (Uk [ɨ])
Йй	ĭ, j	[j]
Кк	k	[k]
Лл	l	[l]
Мм	m	[m]
Нн	n	[n]
Оо	o	[o]
Пп	p	[p]
Рр	r	[r]
Сс	s	[s]
Тт	t	[t]
Уу	u	[u]
Фф	f	[f]
Хх	kh, h/ch (Mac, Ser h)	[x] (Mac, Ser [h])
Цц	ts, c	[ts]
Чч	ch, č	[tʃ]
Шш	sh, š	[ʃ]
Щщ	shch, šč (Bul sht, št)	[ʃʃ] or [ʃtʃ] (Bul [ʃt])
Ъъ	" (Bul ă)	(silent) (Bul [ə])
Ыы	ȳ, y	[ɨ]
Ьь	'	(indicates palatalization)
Ээ	è, é, ė	[ɛ]
Юю	yu, ju	[ju]
Яя	ya, ja	[ja]

	Transliteration	*Phonetic value*
Ѓѓ	ǵ	Mac [gʲ]
Гг	g	Uk [g]
Ђђ	đ	Ser [dʲ]
Єє	e/ie, je	Uk [jɛ]
Ѕѕ	dz	Mac [dz]
Іі	i	Bel, Uk [i]
Її	yi/ï, ji	Uk [ji]
Јј	j	Mac, Ser [j]
Љљ	lj	Mac, Ser [ʎ]
Њњ	nj	Mac, Ser [ɲ]
Ћћ	ć	Ser [tʃʲ]
Ќќ	ǩ	Mac [kʲ]
Ўў	w, ŭ	Bel [ʊ]
Џџ	dž	Mac, Ser [dʒ]

ts, ʃ, tʃ] or the nasal vowels [ɔ̃] and [ɛ̃]), Cyrillic initially contained no fewer than 43 letters, comprising 24 from Greek and a further 19 representing sounds unknown in Greek and based on Glagolitic or Hebrew or specially devised. (Glagolitic consisted of 40 letters, outwardly very dissimilar from the Greek and Cyrillic scripts.)

Of the two brothers, Greeks from Thessalonica, apostles to the southern Slavs and the first translators of service books from Greek into Slav, St Cyril (*c.*827–69, known as Constantine the Philosopher before becoming a monk in 869, since he had been a professor of philosophy at the patriarchal school in Constantinople) was skilled in Slavonic, Greek, Latin, Hebrew and Arabic. In 863, following Prince Rostislav's request for missionaries, Cyril and his brother Methodius (*c.*825–84) were sent from Constantinople by the Emperor Mikhail III and Patriarch Photius to the principalities of Great Moravia (the territory of modern Slovakia) to preach Christianity in Slavonic, and it was then (some say, earlier) that Cyril is thought to have created the alphabet (either Glagolitic or Cyrillic), basing it on the Greek uncial script of the 9th c.

The Cyrillic alphabet has undergone considerable changes with the passage of time. Thus, the archaic uncials of 11th-c. Cyrillic made way for semi-uncials in the 14th c., with smaller letters and thinner strokes, and these in the 16th c. for a ligatured cursive script, used mainly for diplomatic and legal documents, uncials and semi-uncials being retained for religious texts.

Varieties of Cyrillic became the national scripts of the Bulgarians, Serbs, Russians, Belorussians and Ukrainians, and the modern Cyrillic alphabets have been modified from the original, mainly by the loss of superfluous letters. *Serbo-Croat is written in Cyrillic by the Orthodox Serbs and in the Latin alphabet by the Roman Catholic Croats. The alphabet was also adapted to many non-Slavonic languages in the Soviet period (*Finno-Ugric, Turco-*Tatar, *Iranian and *Caucasian, and *Moldavian, i.e. the Romanian of Moldavia (Moldova)).

TERENCE WADE

Fig. 4 The modern Cyrillic alphabet. Various systems exist for the transliteration of Cyrillic. The forms given here are those that are the most widely used. For the values of the characters of the International Phonetic Alphabet, see pp. xvi–xvii. The phonetic values given in (a) are the principal ones valid for Russian but it should be noted that, as in the case of many languages using the Latin alphabet, the characters may in certain contexts have different phonetic values. We also give the major differences that characterize other *Slavonic languages (Bel = *Belarusian, Bul = *Bulgarian, Mac = *Macedonian, Ser = Serbian (see under *Serbo-Croat), Uk = *Ukrainian). Note, however, that the characters of the Russian alphabet do not necessarily all occur in all other Slavonic languages that use Cyrillic. Characters that occur in other Slavonic languages but not (or no longer) in Russian are listed in (b). No account is taken of adaptations of Cyrillic script for non-Slavonic languages (principally *Caucasian, *Finno-Ugrian and *Turkic languages).

Glagolitic (Old Church Slavonic forms)	Glagolitic (Croatian forms)	Cyrillic (Old Church Slavonic forms)	Transliteration (for Old Church Slavonic)	Phonetic value
Ⰰﾐ	ⰰ	а	a	[a]
Ⰱ	Ⰱ	б	b	[b]
Ⰲﾐ	ⰲ	в	v	[v]
Ⰳﾐ	ⰳ	г	g	[g]
Ⰴﾐ	ⰴ	д	d	[d]
Ⰵ	ⰵ	є	e	[e]
Ⰶﾐ	ⰶ	ж	ž	[ʒ]
Ⱇﾐ	ⰷ	ѕ, ꙃ	dz	[dz]
Ⰸﾐ	ⰸ	з	z	[z]
Ⰹ/Ⱅ	ⰹ/ⰺ	ї	i	[i]
Ⰻﾐ	ⰻ	и	i	[i]
Ⰼﾐ	ⰼ		ǵ	[gʲ]
Ⰽﾐ	ⰽ	к	k	[k]
Ⰾﾐ	ⰾ	л	l	[l]
Ⰿﾐ	ⰿ	м	m	[m]
Ⱀﾐ	ⱀ	н	n	[n]
Ⱁﾐ	ⱁ	о	o	[o]
Ⱂﾐ	ⱂ	п	p	[p]
Ⱃﾐ	ⱃ	р	r	[r]
Ⱄﾐ	ⱄ	с	s	[s]
Ⱅﾐ	ⱅ	т	t	[t]
Ⱆﾐ	ⱆ	оу, ꙋ	u	[u]
Ⱇﾐ	ⱇ	ф	f	[f]
Ⱈﾐ	ⱈ	х	x, kh	[x]
Ⱉﾐ	ⱉ	ѡ	o, ω	[o]
Ⱊﾐ	ⱋ	щ	št	[ʃt]
Ⱋﾐ	ⱌ	ц	c	[ts]
Ⱌﾐ	ⱍ	ч	č	[tʃ]
ⱎ	ⱎ	ш	š	[ʃ]
Ⱏ/ⱏ	ⱏ	ъ	ŭ	[ʊ]
ⰟⰉ/ⰟⰊ		ы	y	[ɨ]
Ⱐﾐ	Ⰺ	ь	ĭ	[ɪ]
Ⱑﾐ	Ⰰ	ѣ	ě	[æ]
Ⱓﾐ	Ⱓ	ю	ju	[ju]
		ꙗ	ja	[ja]
		ѥ	je	[jɛ]
ⱔ		ѧ	ę	[ẽ]
ⱗ		ѩ	ję	[jẽ]
ⱙ		ѫ	ǫ	[õ]
ⱚ		ѭ	jǫ	[jõ]
		ѯ	ks	[ks]
		ѱ	ps	[ps]
ⱛ	ⱛ	ѳ	f	[f]
ⱜ	ⱜ	ѵ	u	[i, v]

Czech

A member, with ***Slovak**, ***Polish** and ***Sorbian**, of the western subgroup of the ***Slavonic languages**. It is spoken preeminently in the Czech Republic where it has the status of official language.

Earliest attestations

The earliest attestations, in the form of isolated words (often names), glosses and insertions in Latin manuscripts, date from the 10th c. Longer consecutive texts appear from the mid-13th c., with one isolated complete sentence from the early 13th c., added to the Latin deed founding the Leitmeritz (Litoměřice) chapter in 1057. The maturity of early Czech is ascribed in part to the indirect effect of ***Church Slavonic** as the first literary language used on Czech soil. The oldest recorded literary work is a four-verse hymn, from the second half of the 13th c., included in a Latin codex. The text of its opening verse (version A below) may serve not only to illustrate the orthography of the period but also, through its transcription according to modern orthographic conventions (B) and a modern rendering (C) to show how little (in some respects) Czech has changed over the centuries:

A. *[Z]louo do zveta ztworene / v boſtui zhowano, / ieſ pro Euino zreſſenie / na zuet pozlano.*

B. *Slovo do světa stvořenie / v božství schováno, / jež pro Evino shřěšenie / na svět posláno.*

C. *Slovo do světa stvoření / [bylo] v božství schováno, / jež pro Evino shřešení / [bylo] na svět posláno.*

Translation: 'Before the Creation of the world, the Word / was concealed in the Divinity, / (and) because of Eve's sinning / it was sent down to the world.'

Czech as a literary language

The 'classical' period of Old Czech literature is the 14th and 15th centuries, which produced a wealth of legends of the saints, chivalrous verse (the Czech *Alexandreid*), chronicles (the 'Dalimil' chronicle), vernacular, not to say ribald, religious plays (the Easter *Mastičkář* 'The Unguentarius'), courtly love lyrics, religious and secular 'fables' (such as those of the Hradec MS), the first work whose authorship is known (Smil Flaška z Pardubic's *Nová rada* 'New Council', a kind of 'Parliament of the Animals'), legal texts (Ondřej z Dubé's *Práva zemská česká* 'Law of the Land of Bohemia') and early translations of some of the Gospels (all 14th c.), and, in the

Fig. 5 The Glagolitic and Old Church Slavonic Cyrillic alphabets. For the values of the characters of the International Phonetic Alphabet, see pp. xvi–xvii.

15th c., more chronicles (*Kronika trojanská* 'Trojan Chronicle', *c.*1468, the first Czech printed book), major classics such as the works of the religious reformer Jan Hus (John Huss) and the theological and philosophical writings of Petr Chelčický, political pamphlets (the verse disputation *Hádání Prahy s Kutnou Horou* 'Disputation of Prague with Kutná Hora'), early short stories (*Valter a Grizelda*) and a great deal else besides. These are the beginnings of a long and continuous literary tradition of over 600 years. The common Czech perception is that after 1620, when the Bohemian Estates were finally defeated by the Habsburgs at the Battle of the White Mountain (a hill just east of Prague), the language and literature went into decline. However, if more Protestant writing shifted eastward to the more hospitable (Upper) Hungary, there was still a measure of Catholic literature in Czech ('Jesuit Czech'), and from the late 18th c. the modern literature, gradually evolving further in all genres, has gone from strength to strength. Literary works have, however, often been in direct response to prevailing political conditions and relatively few writers have achieved lasting recognition abroad through translation, despite the relatively large body of translations in absolute terms.

The modern standard language

The language as currently codified is largely attributable to the linguists-philologists of the National Revival. The first modern descriptive grammar, from which many later ones descend directly, is that by Josef Dobrovský (1753–1829), *Ausführliches Lehrgebäude der Böhmischen Sprache* ('Detailed System of the Bohemian Language') (1809; 2nd revised edition 1819). (Dobrovský is otherwise remembered as the father of Slavonic studies.) Apart from having little faith in the language's revivability (his grammar was written in the German with which he himself was more at home), Dobrovský included in his revised standard many features that were obsolescent or obsolete; they had been present, however, in some form or other, in the 16th and 17th centuries, seen as the Golden Age that preceded the language's perceived decline (degeneration). The other important 19th-c. name is that of Josef Jungmann (1773–1847), remembered both for his *Slovesnost* ('Literature', 1820), in which he sought to demonstrate, theoretically and practically, partly through translations, that Czech could be used for any genre or style, and for his great five-volume *Slovník česko-německý* ('Czech–German Dictionary', 1835–9), essentially the only serviceable dictionary of Czech for the next 120 years.

Of no small significance in the external history of Czech is the emergence in the 1920s of the Prague Linguistic Circle, which laid the foundations of one of the major modern approaches to linguistic analysis and description (though not directed solely to Czech as such).

Orthography

The oldest, 'primitive', orthography was ill-suited to Czech (see the hymn above), and was early replaced by versions of a system based on digraphs, but with limited attempts to reflect, for example, syllable length. The modern orthography uses the Latin alphabet with three diacritics: the *háček* 'hook' <ˇ> (but N.B. lower case <d'>

and <t'> corresponding to capital <Ď> and <Ť>); the *čárka* 'stroke', like an acute accent, to denote a long syllable; and a *kroužek* 'circle' <°>, which is used over long <u> in certain morphemically conditioned syllables. Credit for the introduction of diacritics, though not quite in the form used today, is accorded to the 14th–15th-c. religious reformer Jan Hus. The spelling system in use from the 16th to the 19th centuries (used also in the first Czech 'grammar', published in Náměšt' in 1533) differed from the current standard in the use of individual letters, their replacements being gradually introduced during the first half of the 19th c., when <au> was replaced by <ou>; < ſ> by <s>; < ſſ> by <š>; <g> by <j>; <ǧ> by <g> (rare, since [g] is a non-native sound); <j> by <í>; <cy/sy/zy> by <ci/si/zi>. The orthography is broadly phonemic, but with two letters <i, y> for [i], distributed according to historical or etymological principles. The year 1994 saw the most recent proposal for a revision of the orthography, going beyond that proposed by the Institute for the Czech Language in Prague, to simplify the distribution of <y> and <i>, and also <s> and <z>. It is the function of that Institute (a department of the Czech Academy of Sciences) to offer guidance on all linguistic innovations, which it does largely through the journal *Naše řeč* ('Our Language'), and to describe the evolving norm in usage, stylistics etc. through the pages of *Slovo a slovesnost* ('Word and Literature'), originally the organ of Prague Linguistic Circle, and monographic publications. Authoritative dictionaries have also usually been under the Academy imprint, but since 1989 some activities have been privatized, with many new, reputable, reference or encyclopedic publications now being issued by Encyklopedický dům.

Dialects

The Czech dialects divide broadly into (i) a Bohemian group, with not very striking dialects on the fringe surrounding Central Bohemian; and (ii) a variety of conspicuously distinct dialects in Moravia (Haná, Valašsko, Slovácko); that of Slovácko in the south-east is joined by a few isoglosses to Slovak, those in the north, in southern (Moravian) Silesia, having various shared features with Polish. The most important (social) dialect is undoubtedly that variously known as Common Czech or Common Colloquial Czech, which is in essence the everyday spoken language as it has developed in Central Bohemia, Prague in particular, unrestrained by linguists. Between it and the standard language there is a tension brought about by the 400-year gap between them; the grammarians of the National Revival (early 19th c.), codifying the new standard language, had taken as their model the 'richer', 'purer', 'undegraded' language of the 16th c. The standard language has itself evolved, even absorbing (being 'allowed' to absorb) some more upwardly mobile features of Common Czech. There have been some local aspirations (1830s, 1860s, 1990s) to see an alternative Moravian standard alongside the existing, theoretically Bohemian, standard, but these have gained little support.

Contact with other languages

The Czechs have throughout time lived adjacent to, mingled with or been surrounded by German-speaking populations; Prague and the second city, Brno, were largely German cities up to the 19th c. This has left its mark on the language in the shape of waves of loan-words for items brought in by the Germans, not all of which have been obliterated by the bouts of purism that have occasionally intervened against the natural processes of linguistic development through contact. Many Czech idioms and established metaphors have developed in parallel to German, and in the 19th c. in particular Czech showed a tendency to put the verb in clause-final position. Common Czech shows a marked tendency to use an excess of deictic pronouns in noun phrases, sometimes ascribed to unconscious imitation – rooted in the past – of the German definite article. Isolated other signs of German influence perhaps include the occasional postpositioning of certain prepositions such as *kvůli* or *navzdory*: *Petrovi kvůli* 'for Peter's sake', *jemu navzdory* 'despite him'.

During and after the National Revival, when terminologies were being actively created for Czech, much borrowing and adaptation from other Slavonic languages, especially Polish and Russian, helped to supply some of the gaps; such borrowed items sat quite easily in the receiving language. Later lexical intrusions from other sources include a number of Sovietisms, transliterated or calqued, but now obsolete, and Anglicisms, most strongly in sport (early 20th c.) and computer technology and business (late 20th c.), often mediated via German. Czech has been hospitable to a predictable range of cultural items from French and/or Italian, and a typical spread of internationalisms of Greek or Latin origin. Neighbouring Slovak, an official language of equal standing with Czech in former Czechoslovakia, has contributed relatively little, but a handful of lexical items are recognized as of Slovak origin. On the grammatical front the spread in some styles of participial phrases replacing relative clauses is sometimes ascribed to the influence of Russian.

Geography and demography

Czech in Europe is almost confined to the Czech Republic (*c.* 10 million speakers), though, as a survival from the once united Czechoslovakia, about half a million Czechs find themselves in Slovakia, through work, marriage, etc. Elsewhere, from waves of migration largely within the old Austrian Empire, scattered Czech communities are to be found in Poland, Croatia, Austria and Ukraine (Volynia, from where many have returned to the Czech Republic since 1989); 19th-c. Vienna had a sizeable Czech population, now largely assimilated. Further afield, there are Czech immigrant populations in Texas, Nebraska, Iowa (19th-c. economic migrants), Chicago, Toronto (largely 20th-c. political migrants) and elsewhere, with more diffuse immigrant groups throughout western Europe, the Americas and Australia. Of the North American populations only some seek actively to sustain the language, though with decreasing success. It is difficult to assess just how many *native* speakers of Czech there are world-wide: probably not more than 11 to 12 million.

Official status

As the Czech Republic's official language, standard Czech as a written language is used throughout the legal, government and education systems; few people adhere to all the norms of the standard language in everyday discourse, in which they use variously refined and locally varying versions of Common (Colloquial) Czech. Czech has no status as an international language (in contrast to its wide use as such in medieval times, even as far away as Constantinople), but Slovak law permits the use of Czech in defined circumstances (e.g. in the courts where a defendant is Czech); this is in recognition of the mutual intelligibility of the two languages and the tradition of their equal status in former Czechoslovakia.

Auty, R. 1980. Czech. In Schenker, A. M. and Stankiewicz, E. (eds), *The Slavic Literary Languages: Formation and Development*, New Haven, CT, 163–83, 271–4 (bibliography).

Čermák, F. 1987. Relations of spoken and written Czech. *Wiener Slawisticher Almanach*, 20: 133–50.

Čermák, F., Holub, J. et al. 1993. *Czech: A Multi-Level Course for Advanced Learners* (2 vols). London, Prague, Brno.

Chloupek, J., Nekvapil, J. et al. 1987. *Reader in Czech Sociolinguistics*. Amsterdam, Philadelphia, Prague.

Eckert, E. (ed.) 1993. *Varieties of Czech: Studies in Czech Sociolinguistics*. Amsterdam and Atlanta.

Pynsent, R. 1979. *Czech Prose and Verse: A Selection with an Introductory Essay*. London.

—— 1994. *Questions of Identity. Czech and Slovak Ideas of Nationality and Personality*. Budapest, London, New York.

Short, D. 1993. Czech Republic and Slovak Republic: language situation. In Asher, R. E. (ed.), *The Encyclopedia of Language and Linguistics*, Oxford, vol.2, 804–5.

—— 1993. Czech. In Comrie, B. and Corbett, G. G. (eds), *The Slavonic Languages*, London, 455–532.

—— 1996. *Essays in Czech and Slovak Language and Literature*. London.

Townsend, C. E. 1990. *A Grammar of Spoken Prague Czech*. Columbus, OH.

D. SHORT

D

Dacian (see under *Daco-Thracian*)

Daco-Getic (see under *Daco-Thracian*)

Daco-Moesian (see under *Daco-Thracian*)

Daco-Romance (see under *Romance languages*)

Daco-Thracian

The term 'Daco-Thracian' refers to the ***Indo-European language** or languages of peoples collectively referred to by Classical writers as 'Thracians' and who, from at least the 7th c. BC, occupied much of SE Europe from eastern Hungary to the Black Sea south of the Danube and to the Aegean Sea. Their territory included eastern Serbia, much of present-day Romania, the whole of Bulgaria, the Aegean coast from the Axios river to the Bosporus, and the northern Aegean islands of Thasos, Samothrace and Lemnos. The Thracians also crossed into NW Anatolia.

Other terms used with reference to some of the 'Thracian' peoples include Dacians (Latin *Daci*, Greek *Dakoi*), Moesi (Greek *Moisoi*) and Getae (Greek *Getai*). It is not clear how far these terms denote distinct tribes or groups or whether their undoubtedly related forms of speech are best regarded as dialects of one and the same language or as separate languages, or, in either case, how many varieties can be identified. Views among specialists are sharply divided and it seems advisable to leave the matter open.

While recognizing that, on one interpretation, Dacian is a variety of Thracian, we shall, for the sake of convenience, adopt the generic term 'Daco-Thracian', and, following widespread practice, reserve the term 'Dacian' for the language or dialect spoken north of the Danube, in present-day Romania and eastern Hungary, and 'Thracian' for the variety spoken south of the Danube. Further complications are caused by the terms 'Getic' and 'Moesian'. Though attempts have been made to distinguish between Dacian and Getic, there seems no compelling reason to disregard the view of the Greek geographer Strabo (*c.*64 BC–AD 21 (?)) that the Daci and the Getae, Thracian tribes dwelling north of the Danube (the Daci in the west of the area and the Getae further east), were one and the same people and spoke the same language; Romanian scholars in particular have tended to refer to this language as Daco-Getic. Another variety that has sometimes been recognized is that of Moesian (or Mysian) for the language of an intermediate area immediately to the south of the Danube in Serbia, Bulgaria and the Romanian Dobruja, while this and the dialects north of the Danube have been grouped together as Daco-Moesian.

It is likely that Thracian survived in isolated areas, such as the Rhodope mountains of southern Bulgaria, until the 6th c. AD and possibly a little longer.

No lengthy texts in Daco-Thracian exist. The Latin poet Ovid tells us that he composed a book (of poems) in Getic during his exile at Tomis (modern Constanţa) on the Black Sea at the beginning of the 1st c. AD (*Getico scripsi libellum sermone* 'I have written a book in the Getic language'), but these have not come down to us. Surviving evidence for the language is limited to very brief and imperfectly understood inscriptions, glosses in Greek and Latin writers, and proper names occurring in Greek or Latin texts or inscriptions. Of the five known inscriptions claimed as Thracian or Dacian (one on a tombstone, the others on rings or pots), four are in Greek script and from Bulgaria, and are therefore Thracian in the narrow sense of the word as defined above, and one is in Latin script and from Romania, and so Dacian. Thracian is represented by about 40 glosses from various sources, giving us such words as *bria* 'town', *skalme* 'knife, sword', while the main source of Dacian glosses is a list of 57 names of medicinal plants given in a treatise by a 1st-c. AD physician Dioscorides. Some 1,500 relevant names of localities, rivers, mountains, individuals, divinities, tribes, are known from the Thracian area, as compared with fewer than 200 from the Dacian area, but such are the uncertainties surrounding their interpretation that they provide us with only some 200 understood lexical items and a few suffixes.

It is generally agreed that some ***Romanian** words of otherwise unknown etymology are probably of Dacian origin, but estimates of the numbers of such words range from about 30, which is almost certainly too low, to over a thousand, which is far too high. More plausible estimates range from about 60 to about three times that number. Romanian words for which a Dacian origin is widely accepted include *balaur* 'dragon', *brânză* 'cheese', *mal* 'bank, shore', *strugure* 'bunch of grapes'.

Crossland, R. A. 1982. Linguistic problems of the Balkan area in late prehistoric and early classical periods [. . .]. II, Thracians and associated peoples. In Boardman, J. et al. (eds), *The Cambridge Ancient History*, 2nd edn, Cambridge, vol. 3, part 1, 836–9.
Detschew, D. 1976. *Die thrakischen Sprachreste* ('The Linguistic Remains of Thracian'), 2nd edn. Vienna.
Georgiev, V. I. 1983. Thrakisch und Dakisch ('Thracian and Dacian'). In Temporini, H. and Haase, W. (eds), *Aufstieg und Niedergang der römischen Welt* ('Rise and Fall of the Roman World'), II, Berlin and New York, vol. 29, part 2, 1148–94; Thrakische und dakische namenkunde ('Thracian and Dacian Onomastics'), ibid., 1195–1213.
Polomé, E. G. 1982. Balkan languages [. . .]. II, Thracian and Daco-Moesian. In Boardman et al. (see Crossland 1982), 876–88.

GLANVILLE PRICE

Daghestanian languages (see under *Caucasian languages. IV. North-East Caucasian family*)

Dalmatian

An extinct ***Romance language** formerly spoken on the Croatian islands of Krk, Cres and Rab and, further south, along the Adriatic coast of Croatia, at least in the towns of Zadar, Trogir, Split and Dubrovnik and possibly elsewhere, and in Kotor in Montenegro.

References to the existence of the language occur from the 10th c. onwards and it has been estimated that it may at one time have been spoken by up to 50,000 people. Apart from a few words borrowed by the Croatian (see under ***Serbo-Croat**) dialects of the region, little or nothing is known of most varieties of Dalmatian. We do, however, have more substantial evidence for two varieties, representing a southern and a northern dialect respectively and separated in time by over 500 years.

The southern variety, often termed 'Ragusan' from the Italian name, Ragusa, of Dubrovnik, is known from a few brief texts, foremost among them two letters dated 1325 and 1397 respectively, and a handful of other medieval texts the language of which, however, is not pure Dalmatian but heavily influenced by the Italian dialect of Venice. These texts are all given by Bartoli (1906, vol. 1, cols 261–66), together with four words of Dalmatian (*pen* 'bread', *teta* 'father', *chesa* 'house', *fachir* 'to do') quoted by an Italian, Filippo Diversi, who had been the headmaster of a school in Dubrovnik in the 1430s, and a few words and phrases from other sources. The fact that the Senate of the city state of Ragusa decided in 1472 that, henceforward, its debates were to be conducted solely in *lingua veteri ragusea* ('the old Ragusan language') and that the use of Slavonic (*lingua sclava*), i.e. Croatian, was forbidden seems to indicate not only that the language was still alive but that it was felt to be under threat. It seems likely that, in Dubrovnik and neighbouring towns where it may have survived up until that time, it died out some time in the 16th c.

The northern dialect of Dalmatian, usually known as 'Vegliote', from the Italian name, Veglia, of the island of Krk in the northern Adriatic off the east coast of the Istrian peninsula, is relatively well documented. The last speaker of Vegliote, and therefore of Dalmatian, Antonio Udina Burbur, a labourer, was killed aged 77 on 10 June 1898, in an explosion on a road-building site he was working on. His language had, however, been studied, principally by an Italian scholar, Matteo Giulio Bartoli, who had visited him in 1897. Bartoli took down from Burbur's lips several thousand words (accounts of his own life and the life of his people, anecdotes, songs, lists of words and phrases, etc.) and reproduced them with an Italian translation in his book (1906) together with a wealth of information on all that was known about the history of the language and an account of its phonology, grammar and lexicon.

Bartoli, M. G. 1906. *Das Dalmatische*, 2 vols. Vienna.
Doria, M. 1989. Dalmatisch/Dalmatico (in Italian). In Holtus, G., Metzeltin, M. and Schmitt, C. (eds), *Lexikon der Romanistischen Linguistik*, Tübingen, vol. 3, 522–36.

GLANVILLE PRICE

Danish

A member of the northern or *Scandinavian subgroup of the *Germanic languages. In addition to being the sole language of mainland Denmark, Danish is the second official language (together with *Faroese and *Greenlandic respectively) in the Faroe Islands and Greenland.

History

The history of the Danish language can divided into the following periods:

    Old Danish: 800–1100
    Middle Danish: 1100–1525
    Early Modern Danish: 1525–1700
    Modern Danish: 1700–present day

The first of these periods is also dealt with under the entry for Old *Norse (where it is argued that a sensible date to set for the end of Old Norse, and therefore the gradual emergence of Danish as a distinct language, is when the inflectional system of the Scandinavian languages began to show signs of simplification; in the case of Danish, this began to happen in the 12th c.).

Old Danish

Throughout this period, there are no native manuscripts, and therefore the main sources for our knowledge about the language are: foreign accounts which either deal with or make reference to Denmark and things Danish and which provide information on place- and personal names; the Danish linguistic expansion abroad which left a not inconsiderable legacy in the form of loan-words in other languages; place-names datable to this period; and runic inscriptions datable to this period.

The most significant foreign texts are the Old English poems *Wīdsīð* and *Beowulf*, which contain Anglicized forms of Scandinavian place-names; King Alfred the Great's translation of Orosius's *History of the World*, which includes two travel accounts relating to Scandinavia by Wulfstan and Othere; and Adam of Bremen's report on Scandinavia in *Gesta Hammaburgiensis Ecclesiae Pontificum*.

In those areas which were either settled by or came into contact with Danish Vikings, especially the Danelaw and to a lesser extent Normandy, we find many traces of Danish; in east England there are hundreds of place-names ending in *-by*, *-thorpe*, *-gate* and *-toft*, and many terms in English relating to government as well as basic words are loans from Scandinavian, e.g. *law, bylaw, riding, give, take, hit, die, sky* and *they*; and in the Norman dialect of *French, some 300 items of Scandinavian origin, many of them relating to maritime matters, have been identified, some of which have passed into standard French, e.g. *tillac* 'deck' from *þilja*.

Danish place-names from this period, especially those which are composites including a personal name, provide not only linguistic information but also an indication of the economic and social activity in this time (e.g. the establishment of agricultural communities).

Danish runic writing (see *Runes) experienced a considerable revival in this period; the shorter, 16-symbol 'younger futhark' was now in use. There are 412 Danish inscriptions, 240 of which are on stones, and their subject-matter is generally along the lines of 'X raised this monument after Y, his son, who [. . .]'. The use of runes continued in Denmark until about 1350, and the runic evidence therefore is carried over into the next period of the Danish language.

The spread of Christianity to Denmark, which can be viewed as having been finally completed in the 11th c., meant that in this period Danish received its first major influx of foreign loans. These derived largely from Greek and Latin, via Old English, Old *Frisian or Old Saxon (the languages spoken by the missionaries), and relate to the religious sphere, e.g. *kirke* 'church', *kristen* 'Christian', *biskop* 'bishop', *præst* 'priest', *påske* 'Easter', *pinse* 'Whitsuntide'.

Middle Danish

By the beginning of the Middle Danish period, the Viking Age was at an end, and Denmark had emerged as a separate Scandinavian nation, geographically, politically and linguistically. To the south, the country's border was formed by the River Ejder and Levenså; and to the east, Skåne, Blekinge and Halland (now all part of southern Sweden) were still within the Danish kingdom. There were some conquests further to the south, but these had not resulted in any colonial or linguistic expansion. Indeed, from the 12th c. there began a German colonization of the largely uninhabited region immediately to the north of the River Ejder, and by the beginning of the 1200s this area was largely peopled by West Germanic speakers.

In the years around 1100, monasteries began to be established, and one consequence of this was that, through both the clergy and the religious community, links with the rest of Europe began to be forged as a result of pilgrimages, study trips abroad, etc. Outside spiritual circles, foreigners began to arrive and become resident in Danish towns; these were merchants and traders from the Hanseatic towns and others, and in their wake followed many German craftsmen. Additionally, foreign nobility had begun to move to Denmark; some acclimatized linguistically, whereas others retained their Low German tongue and thereby contributed to the use of *Plattdeutsch* in Denmark, which for part of this period at least was prevalent as a lingua franca in the country. This growth in trade, coupled with the increasing foreign presence, meant that for the first time in its hitherto short history, Danish, in town and trading circles at least, was exposed to considerable foreign (especially Low German) influence. This was not, however, the case with the rural communities, which for perhaps the first time were experiencing a period of relative calm and quiet – and isolation – from the economic advances taking place around them, and as a result the isolation of the country dweller in various parts of the country set the preconditions for the development of Danish dialects.

Foreign sources for our knowledge of Danish at this time become less important, since there was a rapid growth in domestic writing. This took two forms: writing in runes, and writing in the Latin alphabet. Runes continued to be used for the first half of this period, but the information they can provide about the language is limited. Much more important are the sources written in the Latin alphabet. We do not know precisely when and where this new alphabet began to be used in Denmark, but this is perhaps not of great importance, since many of the early writings were in Latin. More important are those texts which were written in Danish. The oldest such texts written in Danish are legal documents, medical tracts and religious literature, and of these the legal texts are the most significant for our knowledge of the Danish language at this time. None of the extant legal texts in the form we have them is older than 1300, though we do know that some of them were originally written down prior to this date (e.g. the so-called *Jyske Lov* ('Jutlandic Law') from 1241).

From the 14th c. legends and chronicles also started to be written down in Danish, though many of these were translations, principally from Latin. The language that was used in them reflects local dialectal usage, in that a standard language was still not in existence at that time. However, it is possible even at this early stage to trace a certain dominance of the Zealandic form of the language in the late Middle Ages, since Zealand had already become the administrative, ecclesiastical and commercial centre of Denmark, through the increasing importance of the towns of Roskilde and Copenhagen, both of which lie on the eastern side of the island. Indeed, a Zealandic so-called 'Chancery Style', inspired by both German and Latin, was already developing at this time.

During the Middle Ages, Danish conquests temporarily expanded the kingdom both to the south and to the east, to include some of the Baltic areas of present-day Germany and Poland, together with Estonia, and to the north, where Norway came under the Danish Crown in 1380 and became part of the 'Dual Monarchy' (until 1814). For a brief period, Sweden too was a member of this Nordic Union.

Syntactically, Danish word order became standardized during this period: the finite verb, which hitherto had often occurred in clause-final position, especially in subordinate clauses, increasingly became attached to the subject. At the same time, the vocabulary was extended by over 1,500 loan-words, the vast majority coming from Low German owing to the extensive trade links (and sometimes wars) with the Hanseatic League. Even loan-words of Latin origin were nearly all introduced via the medium of Low German.

Early Modern Danish

The 16th c. saw the beginning of the orthographical standardization of Danish. There were two important events which contributed to this: first, the introduction of printing in 1482; and second, the Lutheran Reformation of 1536. With the Reformation, Danish of necessity replaced Latin as the main ecclesiastical language; the first Danish Bible translation (Christian III's Bible) was published in 1550, and this had great importance for the language, in that for the first time we find a consistent orthography and a style which could be considered as being 'pure', and which used 'plain' Danish as opposed to either 'Latinisms' or 'Germanisms'. From this time we are fortunate to have preserved a work entitled *Visitatsbogen* ('The Book of Visitations') (*c.*1543–4) by Peder Palladius; not originally intended for publication, this is a selection of sermons and talks aimed at introducing the new Lutheran faith to some 390 churches in Zealand, and consequently it was written in an everyday language and style specifically intended both to appeal to and be accessible to lay congregations; it has frequently been described as a written 'tape-recording' of the common language of the day.

From the 17th c. we begin to find much more literature being written in Danish. There was a pressing political need not only to promote the new religion of the day, but also to provide a canon of new hymns and prayers in Danish, and to this end Thomas Kingo (1634–1703) was engaged by the Crown to compile and write a Danish hymnal. The end result, *Den forordnede ny Kirke-Salmebog* ('The Ordained New Church Hymnal') (1699), represents some of the finest achievements of Danish baroque poetry, and Kingo, together with other poets such as Anders Bording (1619–77), a leading writer of pastoral and occasional poetry, served finally to establish Danish as a viable poetic medium. Around this time we also find a selection of dramas being written in Danish as opposed to Latin – the so-called *Skoledramaer* ('school dramas'), which were never intended for publication but were penned by schoolmasters for their pupils to perform for both their and their audiences' general moral instruction and edification, together with collections, either private or in book form, of medieval Danish ballads. One further work which deserves mention here is Leonora Christine's *Jammersminde* ('Memory of Woe') (1663–85), which the authoress wrote while imprisoned in the notorious *Blåtårn* ('Blue Tower') in Copenhagen on suspicion of treason against the state. Although not strictly speaking literature, this is a 'secret' diary in which she professes her innocence; from a linguistic point of view, it provides us with a marvellous record of the language not only of the nobility, but also of a broad cross-section of the community as a whole, faithfully reproducing as it does many aspects of the common speech of the day.

In this period, we find a wealth of loan-words coming into the language, especially from (High) German, French and Latin, but also from a wide variety of other languages. One particularly important area in this respect was the military, which adopted much German together with some French terminology. Many seafaring terms were also being actively borrowed from Low German and Dutch.

The sphere of Danish linguistic influence in the outside world, however, began to contract in the 17th c. with the loss of Skåne, Halland and Blekinge to Sweden.

Modern Danish

At the start of this period, German and French were still the dominant linguistic influences on Danish; these were the prestige languages of both the Court and the nobility. The Danish royal family was of German stock, and several kings had German as their mother tongue; and French was generally regarded as the language of culture.

Nevertheless, the 18th c. was the age that saw the final establishment of Danish as a literary medium. Its first major author was Ludvig Holberg (1684–1754); born in Bergen, Norway, he became a professor at Copenhagen University who, outside his academic production, also wrote popular comedies (not dissimilar to Molière's) and other literary works in both poetry and prose. Although in his comedies he frequently lampoons those who chose to make use of foreign (especially French and Latin) words and phrases in their speech, he at times makes considerable use of words from these languages himself in his more philosophical works, for example in his *Epistler* ('Epistles') and *Moralske Tanker* ('Moral Thoughts').

The middle of the 18th c. (from approximately 1745 onwards) saw the rise of a strong purist movement as a reaction to this linguistic trend of Holberg and others. There was a concerted and conscious effort on the part of its proponents to rid Danish of what was viewed as being unhealthy foreign influences. A leading figure of this movement was Jens Schielderup Sneedorff (1724–64), who was against the influence that French and Latin had exerted on Danish and who wanted to see Danish words formed much more on the model of German. The purist movement spawned several decades of lively linguistic debate, and succeeded in some instances in ousting foreign words, and in others in producing new concurrent forms which served to enrich and enhance the Danish language.

The beginning of the 19th c. saw the advent of Romanticism in Danish cultural and literary life. At the outset, there were three main exponents of this new movement: Schack Staffeldt (1769–1826), Adam Oehlenschläger (1779–1850) and N. F. S. Grundtvig (1783–1872). Both Staffeldt and Oehlenschläger tended to look towards their German counterparts and models with regard to their linguistic expression, with Oehlenschläger also making some use of the language found in the Danish medieval ballads; Grundtvig on the other hand turned towards Old Norse in his (largely unsuccessful) attempts to renew and revitalize the Danish language. German continued to retain its strong influence on Danish for much of the century.

In 1814, at the end of the Napoleonic Wars, Denmark was forced to cede Norway to Sweden under the terms of the Treaty of Kiel, but it still retained its sovereignty over the old Norwegian 'tax lands' of the Faroe Islands, Iceland and Greenland. In 1864, Denmark lost Slesvig-Holsten (Schleswig-Holstein) to Germany, though

North Slesvig was returned in 1920 following a referendum in the two Duchies. In 1944 Iceland gained independence from Denmark, and subsequently both the Faroe Islands and Greenland were granted home rule status while still remaining part of the Kingdom of Denmark.

It was not until about 1870 that the influence of English (both British and American) began seriously to be felt in the Danish language. But once it had begun, the domination of German rapidly diminished, and English loan-words rapidly, and particularly after the Second World War, proliferated in numerous areas of the Danish language, such as sport, technology, music, business, fashion, etc. Today, the influence of English on Danish vocabulary is far-reaching. Most English loan-words have retained their original spelling, yet they nevertheless fall into two distinct groups: those that can easily be matched with Danish pronunciation, and which consequently have assumed Danish inflections and are felt to be Danish, e.g. *bar, bus, droppe, film, slum, smart, teste*; and those which deviate from the basic orthographical and phonetic structures of Danish and are therefore still felt to be loan-words, e.g. *free lance, image, playboy, show*. A third group comprises those words which are loan translations, e.g. *frynsegoder* ('fringe benefits'), *hjernevask* ('brain-wash'), *sameksistens* ('co-existence').

By 1800 the orthography of Danish had by and large been standardized, although spelling debates and reforms (for example <aa> versus <å>, the latter form finally being legalized in the middle of the 20th c.) continued until well into the 20th c., the last major reform taking place in 1948. Modern Standard Danish (*rigsdansk*) is largely based on the language of the upper classes in and around Copenhagen.

Dialects and regional languages

The dialects that are to be found in Denmark are traditionally divided into three broad groups: *jysk* (Jutlandic), *ømål* (insular Danish, spoken on the islands of Funen, Zealand and the smaller islands to the south) and *bornholmsk* (spoken on the island of Bornholm to the south of Sweden). The places where dialects are still most prevalent are North Jutland, South Jutland, West Jutland and Bornholm, especially in the smaller towns and villages. Some 3,000,000 Danes speak what are now commonly termed *regionalsprog* ('regional languages'), which are regarded as kinds of 'watered-down' dialectal usages of the language. They have arisen because of the increased social interaction and mobility of the population, especially during the 20th c. These 'regional languages' have retained certain characteristics of the local dialects from which they are derived, but can also be viewed as simply being regional variants of the standard Danish language. A striking feature of Danish pronunciation is the glottal stop (*stød*), the use of which varies from region to region; its presence (or absence) is also used by linguists to distinguish dialectal variants.

Present situation

Today, Danish is the native language of the 5,200,000 Danish inhabitants of Denmark and is one of the official languages of the European Union, which Denmark joined along with Great Britain and the Republic of Ireland in 1973. In

North Slesvig there is a German-speaking minority, while in South Schleswig a Danish-speaking minority is still to be found. In the Faroe Islands and Greenland, Danish is the second official language and is taught as the first foreign language in schools.

In 1955, the body called *Dansk Sprognævn* ('Danish Language Council') was established. Its brief was and still is to monitor the development of Danish, by collecting and registering new words and expressions, and to provide advice on the spelling and pronunciation of foreign words and names. It is now the highest authority on the modern Danish language, and as well as regularly publishing information booklets on current trends in Danish it also periodically updates the official dictionary of Danish spelling (*Retskrivningsordbogen*).

Allan, R., Holmes, P. and Lundskær-Nielsen, T. 1995. *Danish: A Comprehensive Grammar*. London and New York.

Brink, L. and Lund, J. 1975. *Dansk Rigsmål* ('Danish Standard Language'), 2 vols. Copenhagen.

Haberland, H. 1994. Danish. In König, E. and van der Auwera, J. (eds), *The Germanic Languages*, London and New York, 313–48.

Hansen, Aa. 1967. *Moderne dansk* ('Modern Danish'), 3 vols. Copenhagen.

Haugen, E. 1976. *The Scandinavian Languages: An Introduction to Their History*. London.

Jacobsen, H. G. and Skyum-Nielsen, P. 1996. *Dansk sprog. En grundbog* ('Danish Language. A Primer'). Århus.

Lund, J. 1982. *Sprog og sprogbrug i dag* ('Language and Usage Today'). Copenhagen.

Nielsen, B. Kj. 1991. *Engelsk–Dansk Ordbog* ('English–Danish Dictionary'), 4th edn. Copenhagen.

Petersen, P. R. 1984 *Nye ord i dansk 1955–75* ('New Words in Danish 1955–75'). Copenhagen.

Politikens Nudansk Ordbog ('Politiken's Dictionary of Present-Day Danish'), 16th edn. 1996. Copenhagen.

Retskrivningsordbogen ('Orthographic Dictionary'), 2nd end. 1996. Copenhagen.

Skautrup, P. 1944–70. *Det danske sprogs historie* ('The History of the Danish Language'), 5 vols. Copenhagen.

Sørensen, K. 1973. *Engelske lån i dansk* ('English Loans in Danish'). Copenhagen.

—— 1995. *Engelsk i dansk – er det et must?* ('English in Danish – Is It a Must?'). Copenhagen.

Vikør, L. S. 1993. *The Nordic Languages. Their Status and Interrelations*. Oslo.

Vinterberg, H. and Bodelsen, C. A. 1990. *Dansk–Engelsk Ordbog* ('Danish–English Dictionary'), 3rd edn by V. Hj. Pedersen. Copenhagen.

ROBIN ALLAN

Danubian Bulgarian
A term that has been applied to the language of a *Turkic-speaking people who crossed the Danube into what is now Bulgaria in AD 679. It is known only from a few odd words and probably became extinct in the 9th c. (see *Bulgarian, 'Origins').

Dargwa (Dargin) (see under *Caucasian languages. IV. North-East Caucasian family*)

Dido (see *Tsez* under *Caucasian languages. IV. North-East Caucasian family*)

Dolomitic Ladin (see under *Italy. III. Northern Italy*)

Dutch

A West *Germanic language whose closest relatives are Low and High *German, spoken to the east of the Dutch language area. Flemish in its strictest sense refers to a group of dialects of Dutch spoken in the Belgian provinces of East and West Flanders and in the southernmost area of the province of Zeeland in the Netherlands (Zeeuws-Vlaanderen). In a wider sense, the name 'Flemish' is given informally to the regional form of standardized Dutch as it is spoken in northern Belgium.

The name 'Dutch'

The source of the English term 'Dutch', as of German *deutsch* 'German', is Latin *theodiscus* (the word *Teutonic* is related) 'the language of the people', as opposed to the language of the Church, i.e. Latin. In the early Germanic dialects *theodiscus* became *diets* (now used with an often romantic connotation to refer to older forms of Dutch), *duuts, duits* (the modern Dutch word for 'German'), *deutsch*. It is not until the 16th c. that a differentiation in nomenclature begins to emerge and references are made to *Nederduytsch* 'Low German' and *Nederlandsch* 'Netherlandish', i.e. 'Dutch'. The present Dutch word for 'Dutch', *Nederlands*, became firmly established in the course of the 19th c., but by that time the word 'Dutch' had already taken root in English.

Origins and early history

The Rhine was established early on as the northern border of the Roman Empire. Initially it also formed the border between Celtic tribes to the south (known collectively as 'Belgae') and Germanic tribes to the north (most notably the Frisians who ranged between the mouths of the rivers Rhine and Ems). The Romans eventually left the defence of their northern frontier to Germanic tribes who were invited to come and live south of the Rhine. In the course of the 3rd and 4th centuries a group of such tribes, collectively known as 'Franks', settled south of the Rhine. However, with the disintegration of the Empire in the 5th c., the Franks started to dominate the region and eventually a united Frankish force under Clovis, the founder of the Merovingian dynasty, conquered Gaul as far south as the Loire. When the Carolingian dynasty took over the rule of the Franks in the 9th c., a period of further expansion started. Among those conquered by Charlemagne were the Frisians and Saxons who lived to the north of the Franks in what are roughly the present-day Dutch provinces of Friesland, Groningen, Drenthe and Overijssel (the river IJssel, a branch of the Rhine, is generally seen as the border between Saxons and Franks and, in the present-day linguistic situation, between Frankish and Saxon dialects of Dutch).

The Germanic-speaking Franks were instrumental in establishing the language border between *Romance and Germanic in its present position. Whereas during the Roman Empire Romance speech moved north towards the Rhine, the centuries following the collapse of the Empire saw a gradual southward Germanization extending possibly as far as the Loire. This was followed in turn by a Romance push north in the 7th and 8th centuries. The northern border between Romance and

Germanic eventually settled on a line running east from Étaples. This border has changed little except in the west where, under political pressure, it was pushed further north beyond Dunkirk in the course of the following centuries. The political border between the Belgian province of West Flanders and France now corresponds to the linguistic border in the south-west of the Dutch-speaking area, apart from the continuing presence of a small minority of speakers of a Germanic (West Flemish) dialect in the present French department of Pas-de-Calais. This area is known as French Flanders (*Frans-Vlaanderen* or the *Westhoek*).

Earliest attestations

The oldest written remains of Dutch date from the 10th and 11th centuries. The Frankish dialects of that time are commonly referred to as Low Franconian. Low Franconian was spoken in the Lower Rhine valley and the south of the present-day Dutch language area: Flanders, Brabant, Limburg, southern Holland and Utrecht. Low German (Saxon) dialects were spoken to the east of this region, *Frisian to the north. Although very little is known of the language, two branches of Low Franconian are commonly distinguished, West and East Low Franconian.

The best-known remnant of West Low Franconian is a three-line section from what is assumed to be a love poem written by a Flemish scribe trying out his pen *c*.1100, known as the *probatio pennae*:

Hebban olla vogala nestas hagunnan	All the birds have begun their nests
hinase hic enda thu	except me and you
uuat unbidan uue nu	what are we waiting for

One further remnant is a transcription, also *c*.1100, of an originally East Low Franconian text, a version of the Song of Songs by the Abbot of Edersburg, Williram.

If West Low Franconian is the percursor of the dialects of Flanders and Holland, East Low Franconian can be seen as having that role for the dialects of Limburg and the Rhineland. The best-known remnant of East Low Franconian is the 10th-c. *Wachtendock Codex*, named after the last known keeper of the original manuscript (now lost).

Middle Dutch

The troubadour Hendrik van Veldeke (second half of the 12th c.) is claimed by both Middle Dutch and Middle German literary history as their first known poet. This is quite appropriate: medieval poetry is written in the local dialect, not in a standard language, and Veldeke came from the area around Maastricht in Limburg, where the local dialect is still very close to the German dialects just across the border. Middle Dutch dialects can be divided into three groups: the dialects of Holland, Zeeland and Flanders (coastal dialects), the south-east (Brabant and Limburg), and the north-east (originally Low German dialects which begin to show more and more similarities with Dutch in the Middle Ages).

In the 13th c. the dialects of Flanders and Brabant gained prominence through the development of the urban patriciate of cities like Bruges, Ghent and Ypres. As well as literary texts (e.g. the works of Jacob van Maerlant and the anonymous fable *Van den Vos Reinaerde* in Flanders, the mystic Hadewych in Brabant) from *c.*1250, more and more non-literary texts were written in the vernacular (as opposed to Latin). This phenomenon spread from Flanders northwards. Literary production continued to increase in the 14th and 15th centuries not only in Flanders, Brabant and Limburg, but also increasingly in Holland.

Middle Dutch spelling reflects local variation and is more 'phonetic' than that of modern Dutch. Contracted forms, e.g. those in which verb and subject are written as one word, are very common: *segghic* > *segghe ic* 'say I'. The influence of French through (literary) fashion is noticeable in the vocabulary: names for food (*fazant* 'pheasant', *taart* 'tart') and household goods (*tapijt* 'carpet' < *tapis*) as well as ethical vocabulary (*spijt* 'regret' < *despit*). A morphological phenomenon is the affixation of French endings on Dutch stems, e.g. the nominal suffix -*age* on the verbal stem *vrij-*: *vrijage* 'love affair'.

The use of the vernacular in civic texts may have been a first impulse towards standardization. Two important developments, the political unification of the Low Countries and the invention of the printing press, ensured that by the end of the Middle Ages a standardized form of Dutch was emerging. For the Dukes of Burgundy, especially Philip the Good (1396–1467), expansion was a way of life. By the middle of the 15th c., Holland, Zeeland, Flanders, Artois, Hainaut, Brabant, Limburg, Luxembourg and Gelre (now Gelderland) were under Burgundian control, and the bishoprics of Utrecht and Liège were under Burgundian influence. Although French was the language of their administration, the Burgundians allowed the use of the vernacular. Moreover, the centre of gravity moved towards the Low Countries, especially when Burgundy itself was lost to the king of France in 1477 and the court moved permanently to Brussels. The standardization of the written language also allowed the market for the printed word to grow.

The sixteenth century onwards

Mary of Burgundy married into the imperial Habsburg family. Her grandson Charles V (born 1500) united in one person the Lordship of the Netherlands, the Kingdom of Spain, and the (German) Holy Roman Empire. Charles consolidated his hold on the Netherlands and modernized the administration. In 1548 his possessions in the Low Countries were united in the 'Burgundian Circle' consisting of the present-day Benelux countries plus the Burgundian possessions in the north of France. This, together with the increasing output of the printing industry, the Reformation and the humanist tradition, allowed the standardization of Dutch to intensify in the course of the 16th c. The cultural and commercial centre moved to Antwerp.

A decisive moment for the history of the Low Countries and the Dutch language came in the 1560s. In 1555 Philip II succeeded his father Charles V as Lord of the Netherlands and King of Spain. Dissatisfaction with his policies for the Low Countries (increasing centralization, heavy taxation, an uncompromising anti-Reformation stance) led to a popular revolt, first in the southern provinces (Flanders and Brabant) and later in the northern provinces. Philip's generals managed to suppress the revolt in the south, but not in the north, which resulted in a division by 1585 between the independent Northern Netherlands (also known as the United Provinces or the Dutch Republic) and the Spanish Southern Netherlands. Many southerners, mainly well-to-do merchants and intellectuals who supported the Reformation, were forced to flee to the north.

Between 1585 and the beginning of the 19th c., the history of the Dutch language is that of two communities: the independent Protestant Republic and the occupied Catholic Southern Netherlands. In the north the standard language developed steadily under the pressure of national unification and an increasingly assertive Calvinist church. In the south, on the other hand, the language of national adminis-tration (and of the Catholic Church too) remained French which on a local level gained more and more prestige. The Dutch dialects in the south reverted, therefore, to what they were in the Middle Ages: a local means of communication without national importance.

In the time of the Republic, the basis for the standard was the dialect of the most influential province, Holland. However, Holland gained this influential position partly because of the influx of prestigious refugees (mainly Brabançons) from the south who brought with them a wealth of commercial contacts as well as an intellec-tual elite. Their southern influence on the standard language is well documented. The main (but not the only) features of this are lexical: many formal words in present-day standard (northern) Dutch are colloquial words in southern dialects, e.g.:

north	south	
vaak	*dikwijls*	'often'
al	*reeds*	'already'
gooien	*werpen*	'throw'
huilen	*wenen*	'cry'

The 17th c. is known as the Dutch Golden Age. While the war with Spain continued until 1648 (mainly fought in the Southern Netherlands), the Dutch built up a large commercial enterprise. Amsterdam became the staple market of Europe, the East India Company (1602) and West India Company (1621) were the main European carriers to and from the new colonies, and the Dutch were the only Europeans with a trading settlement in Japan. In cultural terms, too, the Republic flourished; witness the abundance of Dutch art from the period. The works of Joost van den Vondel, P. C. Hooft, G. A. Bredero and C. Huygens (to name a few) show that in literature, too, the Dutch produced masterpieces. This intellectual activity has left its mark on the language in several ways. The most important linguistic enterprise of the century was the translation of the Bible. The *Statenbijbel* (1637) is a monumental work completed in 18 years by a committee in which the various regions were represented. This regional variation is reflected in the translation, e.g. in the adoption of the Saxon third-person reflexive *zich* (as opposed to *hem*, *haar*) which has found its way into the standard language. The influence of the *Statenbijbel* has been enormous because of the strong Calvinist tradition and a higher level of literacy than elsewhere in Europe: every Protestant family owned a bible which was read every day. Numerous expressions from this translation have entered the language in the course of the centuries.

The influence of French on the Dutch language became quite strong in terms of vocabulary in the course of the 18th c. through social pressures (e.g. *visite* for *bezoek* 'visit', *feliciteren* for *gelukwensen* 'to congratulate').

In the early Republic pride in the Dutch language also led to the introduction of many newly coined words for concepts expressed by Latinisms in other languages. The scientist Simon Stevin was at the forefront in this and introduced words like *driehoek* ('triangle'), *hoogtelijn* ('altitude') and *zwaartelijn* ('median') into the science of *wiskunde* ('mathematics'). But in other fields, too, new Dutch words were introduced, e.g., in linguistics, *werkwoord* ('work word' = 'verb'), *zefstandig naamwoord* ('independent name word' = 'noun'), *bijvoeglijk naamwoord* ('additive name word' = 'adjective'), *onderwerp* ('subject') and *(lijdend) voorwerp* ('(direct) object').

The Republic's policies towards other religions meant that it was relatively easy for Jewish refugees to settle in Amsterdam. Ladino (***Judeo-Spanish**), the language of the Sephardim, has hardly served as a source for borrowing, whereas ***Yiddish**, the language of the much poorer Ashkenazim, has made a considerable contribution to the Dutch (especially colloquial) vocabulary.

The colonial exploits of the Dutch gave the language a number of words from exotic languages, especially Malay, the lingua franca in the Dutch East Indies.

Many languages have borrowed Dutch words from the seafaring and shipping vocabulary (e.g. English *dock, buoy, yacht, freight, keelhaul*).

Standardization

It was the Napoleonic fervour for regulation that eventually led to the establishment of the first official Dutch spelling in 1804 (devised by Siegenbeek) and the publication of an official grammar in 1805 when the Netherlands were under French rule (1795–1815). The Siegenbeek spelling was adopted in the south too, and later the spelling of De Vries and Te Winkel (1863) was introduced in both the Netherlands and Belgium.

Both the Netherlands and Belgium (and, since the 1993 federal Belgian constitution, Flanders) have ceded linguistic sovereignty to a bi-national body, the Dutch Language Union, established under the terms of the Dutch Language Union Treaty (1982). The Union is empowered to look after the Dutch language on behalf of the Dutch and Flemish authorities, including the determination of an official spelling and grammar and also its promotion abroad. Dutch spelling has been subject to a number of minor changes since the De Vries–Te Winkel spelling of 1863, but it is the topic of vigorous debate highlighting the need for regulation. The latest spelling change was introduced in September 1996 (see *Woordenlijst van de Nederlandse Taal* in the bibliography). In terms of grammar and vocabulary the Union is less prescriptive. It has made resources available for the production of an authoritative grammar (*Algemene Nederlandse Spraakkunst*: Haeseryn et al., 1997) and the completion of the *Woordenboek der Nederlandsche Taal* (started by De Vries and Te Winkel in 1882).

Dutch in Belgium

After the defeat of Napoleon, the Northern and Southern Netherlands were united for the first time for 230 years as the United Kingdom of the Netherlands. Although this ended in the Belgian uprising of 1830 and the independence of Belgium in 1831, the foundations for standardization of the Dutch language in the south were probably laid in this short period. The Kingdom of the Belgians was governed by a French-speaking elite that also dominated the Dutch-speaking part of the country for the simple reason that in order to get on one had to speak French. It is for that reason, too, that in the course of the 19th c. Brussels rapidly changed from a largely Dutch-speaking city to one where the vast majority spoke French.

Dutch was recognized as a 'national language' in Belgium in 1831 and as an 'official language' in 1898, but it took a hundred years from Belgian independence before Dutch was fully recognized as having equal status to French in the courts, in administration and in education. The University of Ghent became the first Dutch-language university in Belgium in 1932. In 1963 Belgium was officially divided into four language areas: Dutch, French, German, and bilingual (Dutch–French) Brussels (see map 1).

The standardization of Dutch in Belgium came about after long discussions as to whether Flemish should adopt the existing northern standard (the view of the 'integrationists') or create a new southern one (that of the 'particularists'). The integrationists eventually won the argument, partly because of the close cooperation between Dutch and Flemish linguists from an early stage. This integrationist strategy was enshrined in various post-war bilateral agreements, culminating in the Dutch Language Union Treaty of 1982 (see above under 'Standardization'). Despite this high degree of linguistic integration, the Flemings (and the Dutch) are conscious of the differences between northern and southern Dutch. With their confidence growing in other respects too (Flanders has become economically superior to Wallonia), it seems unlikely that Flemish will adopt the northern norm completely. This attitude is strengthened by a perceived indifference in the Netherlands to the whole issue of linguistic integration.

Present situation

Dutch is spoken in the Netherlands and Flanders by approximately 15 million and 6 million speakers respectively. Brussels is officially bilingual, although its actual linguistic make-up is extremely complex. There are only a few thousand speakers of Dutch dialects in French Flanders. Dialect differences are still very strong, particularly in Flanders where many people speak the local dialect alongside standard Dutch in a diglossic situation. But also in the eastern, southern and northern provinces of the Netherlands there are still many dialect speakers. Dutch dialects still show a division between east and west (as in Middle Dutch) with western dialects showing ***Ingvaeonic** characteristics and eastern dialects Saxon traits. In addition, a number of urban dialects have emerged as the size and importance of towns and cities has grown. (See also ***Frisian** for the position of that language in the Netherlands).

As well as being the official language of the Netherlands and one of the official languages in Belgium, Dutch is one of the official languages of the European Union.

Dutch is also the official language of the former Dutch colony of Surinam in South America, of Aruba, Bonaire and Curaçao in the Leeward Islands, and St Maarten (which is half French), St Eustatius and Saba in the Windward Islands. However, Papiamentu, a Portuguese-based creole, is the native language of most people on the Dutch Leeward Islands, and English on the Dutch Windward Islands. The linguistic situation in Surinam is more complex, owing to a number of waves of (often enforced) migration from Africa, the Dutch East Indies (especially Java) and India. A local variety of Dutch (Surinamese-Dutch) is taking root and has found its way back to the Netherlands by way of Surinamese immigrants.

Dutch-based *pidgins and *creoles

The establishment of New Amsterdam (now New York) in America gave rise to simplified versions of Dutch (Jersey and Mohawk Dutch) which survived into the 18th c. Dutch has also been the basis for a number of creoles and pidgins, most of them now extinct. *Negerhollands* was spoken in the Virgin Islands until the early 20th c. and 'Negro Dutch' in New York. Berbice, named after a river in Guyana, is virtually extinct. Petjok, which arose in the barracks of the Dutch East Indian army, is a creole based partly on Dutch (especially in its vocabulary) and partly on Malay. It was taken back to the Netherlands after Indonesian independence.

Afrikaans

Afrikaans is the best-known descendant of Dutch. It arose in the Cape Colony after the Dutch East India Company founded a settlement there in 1652. Afrikaans developed in the following years under the influence of local languages and other (Portuguese- and Malay-based) pidgins. The creolized forms of Dutch spoken in the Cape Colony 150 years later were the basis for a new language which developed in the course of the 19th c. as a reaction to the imposition of English. A second language movement arose after the Boer Wars, in which Afrikaans eventually became a standardized code. Today it is the native language of approximately 6 million people, half of them non-white.

Brachin, P. 1985. *The Dutch Language. A Survey*. Cheltenham.

Donaldson, B. C. 1983. *Dutch. A Linguistic History of Holland and Belgium*. Leiden.

—— 1993. *A Grammar of Afrikaans*. Berlin.

—— 1997. *Dutch. A Comprehensive Grammar*, 2nd edn. London.

Geerts, G. and Heestermans, H. 1992. *Van Dale Groot Woordenboek der Nederlandse Taal* ('Van Dale Large Dictionary of the Dutch Language'), 12th edn. Utrecht.

Haeseryn, W. et al. 1997. *Algemene Nederlandse Spraakkunst* ('General Dutch Grammar'), 2nd edn. Groningen.

Instituut voor Nederlandse Lexicologie. 1882– . *Woordenboek der Nederlandsche Taal* ('Dictionary of the Dutch Language'). The Hague and Leiden.

—— 1995. *Woordenlijst van de Nederlandse Taal* ('Word-list of the Dutch Language'). The Hague and Antwerp.

Martin, W. and Top, G. A. J. 1984. *Van Dale Groot Woordenboek Engels–Nederlands* ('Van Dale Large Dictionary, English–Dutch'). Utrecht.

—— 1986. *Van Dale Groot Woordenboek Nederlands–Engels* ('Van Dale Large Dictionary, Dutch–English'). Utrecht.

Ponelis, F. 1993. *The Development of Afrikaans*. Frankfurt.

Robinson, O. W. 1992. Old Low Franconian. In Id., *Old English and Its Closest Relatives*, ch.8. London.

Vandeputte, O. et al. 1995. *Dutch. The Language of Twenty Million Dutch and Flemish People*. Rekkem.

Vries, J. W. de, et al. 1994. *Het Verhaal van een Taal. Negen Eeuwen Nederlands* ('The Story of a Language. Nine Centuries of Dutch'). Amsterdam.

ROEL VISMANS

Dyula (see under *Community languages (France)*)

E

East Italic

A purely geographical term applied by some scholars to the quite different languages of two groups of inscriptions found along and in the hinterland of the Adriatic coast of Italy and probably dating from the 6th to the 4th centuries BC (see ***North Picenian** and ***South Picenian**).

Pulgram, E. 1978. East Italic. In Id., *Italic, Latin, Italian: 600 BC to AD 1260*, Heidelberg, 73–7.

Whatmough, J. 1933. East Italic. In Conway, R. S., Whatmough, J. and Johnson, S. E., *The Prae-Italic Dialects of Italy*, London, vol. 2, 207–57.

Elymian

Elymian is the name of the extinct language of western Sicily (see map 10) (for ancient eastern Sicily, see ***Sicel**). Our sources are extremely scanty: (1) place-names and personal names; (2) a few coin legends, in Greek script, showing the name of the city issuing the coin (e.g. Segesta, Eryx) followed by a non-Greek suffix; (3) most importantly, about 170 fragments of pottery inscribed in Greek script, which have emerged from deposits in the sanctuary of Segesta.

The texts date from approximately the 6th to the 4th c. BC. Most of the pottery inscriptions are extremely short and fragmentary (one to three characters). The somewhat longer texts seem to contain the name of a dedicant in the dative case, sometimes followed by 'I am'. The only complete inscription, on the Montedoro vase (found in a necropolis 15 km SW of Palermo), contains a similar message, which may be tentatively translated as 'I [the pot] am [a gift] for/by Ata Tuka' (?). The language would seem to be ***Indo-European**, but its closer affinities (with ***Italic**, according to Lejeune) are a matter of conjecture.

Lejeune, M. 1970. Notes de linguistique italique. XXV. Observations sur l'épigraphie élyme. *Revue des études latines*, 47 (1969): 133–83.

PETER SCHRIJVER

Emilian-Romagnol (see under *Italy. III. Northern Italy*)

Engadinese (see under *Romansh*)

English
A member of the West Germanic group of the ***Germanic languages**, its closest relative being ***Frisian**. Historically, the following periods are identified: Old English (or Anglo-Saxon) (up to *c.*1100), Middle English (1100–1500), Modern English (1500 to the present). The last of these is sometimes further subdivided into early Modern English (1500–1700), later Modern English (1700–1900) and Present English (20th c.), but it is perhaps better to treat the period as a whole and use Present English for the most recent state of the language. In Europe, its spread is mainly confined to the British Isles (including the Channel Islands), in some parts of which it is spoken alongside indigenous languages (***Welsh**, ***Scottish Gaelic**, ***Irish**, ***Channel Islands French**, and some would add ***Scots**) or recently arrived ***community languages**; it is also the dominant language in the British colony of Gibraltar and is an official language (with ***Maltese**) in Malta. World-wide, it is estimated to be the first language of some 377 million speakers.

Old English

Origins and the early period. 'Old English' is the term now normally used for the earliest period of the English language, as distinct from 'Anglo-Saxon', the older term, now used of the people, their history and archaeology. The origins of the language lie with the Germanic tribes living along the North Sea coast of the Continent, in modern terms from southern Denmark to Holland. Small groups from these tribes were employed by the Romans in defending the eastern and southern coasts of Britain during the last years of Roman rule in the province, but the main infiltrations were in the period following the departure of the Roman legions in the early 5th c.

The period between about 500 and 600 was one of gradual penetration of Britain by groups of Germanic settlers. There seems never to have been a large-scale invasion, rather groups of raiders and settlers, sometimes reaching far inland via the large rivers, like Thames and Trent, established settlements next to or in place of the local Celtic inhabitants. By the early 7th c. there were what could be called Anglo-Saxon kingdoms side by side with Celtic ones, in the north, for example, the English *Deira* besides the Celtic *Elmet*. Wales and Cornwall and the more northerly parts of Scotland were not penetrated by the new settlers.

Celtic and the Germanic languages of the early settlers would have been mutually unintelligible. The diplomatic contact between neighbouring kingdoms was no doubt carried out through interpreters and it is difficult to see a general need for either group to learn the language of the other. There is no way of knowing what kind of everyday contact there was between the ordinary Germanic settlers and their Celtic neighbours but place-name evidence suggests that co-existence was at least as common as the fire and sword described by the early chroniclers. Early place-names with *Walh* meaning 'Briton' rather than 'slave', e.g. Walton, Walcot, and with *Cumbre* meaning 'British' (cf. Welsh *Cymro* 'Welshman', *Cymru* 'Wales'), e.g. Cumberland, Comberbatch, suggest recognition by Germanic-speakers of continuing Celtic settlement, less certainly suggested by the purely Celtic topographical names, e.g. Thames, Severn, Calder, Avon. There are still very few certain Celtic borrowings into English of the period, but it is likely that on a local, and perhaps temporary, level there were far more.

Besides language, the other great difference between Celts and Anglo-Saxons lay in their beliefs. The Celts had been converted to Christianity whilst still under Roman rule and had an organized church. The Anglo-Saxons were still pagan. The conversion of the Anglo-Saxons began in the 6th c. and was largely complete (though not always lasting) by the end of the 8th c.

Scripts. Christianity meant not only a new religion but also a new language and access to a new means of recording events and ideas. The Anglo-Saxons, like their north Germanic neighbours, used *runes. What survives suggests, however, that both before and after the coming of Christianity runes were used for commemoration, to express ownership, empowering (of weapons, in particular) and, perhaps in all cases, decoration rather than communication. Though it is possible that messages cut in wood formed an everyday practical use for runes, no unequivocal evidence has survived from England. A very few, very brief inscriptions survive from the pagan Anglo-Saxon period, cut on bone or impressed on pottery, but the majority are later. Even these are not numerous or on the whole very long. The Ruthwell cross (Dumfriesshire) inscription, with 290 existing runes and at least a further 100 lost through the 17th-c. breaking up of the cross, is the longest.

The frequency of writing Latin after the coming of Christianity and the relatively easy adaptation of its alphabet for the writing of English no doubt made it inevitable that Roman rather than runic letter forms would become the norm. Though primarily used for cutting in stone, bone or clay, and therefore straight-sided, runes could have been adapted, but with a highly developed series of alphabets derived from Roman capital and cursive already in existence there was little need to do so. The only additions to the Roman alphabet were the runic letters <Þ> (*wynn*) for [w] and <þ> (*thorn*) for [θ] or [ð], and the adapted <d>, <ð> (*eth*), used side by side with <þ>. It should not be imagined that adoption was immediate and uniform. In the early stages experiments were clearly made. There are early examples of <th> rather than <þ>, and <u> or <uu> is used sporadically throughout the period side by side with <Þ>.

Dialects. As runic inscriptions and written vernacular texts make clear, there were a number of dialects in Anglo-Saxon England, possibly as a result of the differing regions of the Continent from which the early settlers came but as likely from differences which developed after settlement in widely separated areas of England. Broad differences existed between Anglian in the midlands and north, West Saxon in the south and Kentish in the south-east, but there are also variations within these areas, particularly Mercian and Northumbrian within Anglian. Since early records are few, most of the evidence for dialect variations, as for all linguistic features, comes from the 8th c. and later. By the 10th c. West Saxon, because of the political dominance of the West Saxon kings, had become widespread throughout England as an administrative language and had also achieved something of the status of a standardizing literary language into which earlier works were copied. Before that happened, however, the relative stability of the Anglo-Saxon kingdoms was to be broken.

Scandinavian and other influences. From the late 8th c. onwards Scandinavian marauders subjected the east and south coasts of England to a series of raids culminating in the mid-9th c. in larger-scale invasions. After a series of defeats the English eventually rallied under Alfred, king of the West Saxons, and a settlement was made dividing England into the Danelaw, under Scandinavian control, north and east of a line roughly drawn from London to Chester, and Wessex, under English control, to the south and west. There are two major differences between this settlement and the earlier Germanic one of Celtic Britain: first, the relationship between English and the Scandinavian languages was close as they were branches of earlier Germanic, and secondly, whereas the Celts gradually lost control of eastern, central and southern Britain, the Scandinavians for a time ruled the northern and eastern parts of England which they had overrun, and then later (11th c) gained control for a time of the whole of England. As with the earlier Germanic settlement, however, it was once again a matter of Christian inhabitants and pagan invaders. Little is known of the early linguistic interaction but the Scandinavian settlement left a varied and lasting residue of Scandinavian words and forms of every grammatical category, as well as influencing the forms and meanings of some English words. Largely due no doubt to the dominance of West Saxon in the 10th c., these words and forms do not appear in texts in any number until after the end of the Old English period. (Nouns: *bracken* (1300), *keel* (1398), *law* (1000), *leg* (1300), *sky* (1289), *window* (1225); adjectives: *awkward* (1425), *flat* (1330), *ill* (1200); verbs: *call* (1225), *die* (1175), *drown* (1325), *get* (1200), *hit* (1075), *lift* (1200), *raise* (1200), *scrape* (1225), *take* (1100), *want* (1200); prepositions: *fro* (1200), *till* (800); pronouns: *they, them, their* (1200). Dates given are of the earliest recorded uses according to *MED* or *OED*.)

The Scandinavian languages were not the only sources of new words. A number of Latin borrowings of a largely non-Christian kind existed early in the Germanic languages either brought from the Continent or taken over from Latin-speaking Celts in Britain. From the time of the arrival of the Christian missionaries with new concepts and a language carrying the prestige of the new religion, words were taken into English from Latin but, since the Germanic process of creating new words from within the language was still dominant at that time, new borrowings existed side by side with numerous new creations, largely loan-formations or loan-translations, in the area of the new religion. Probably from contact while still on the Continent are: *street* (OE *strǣt*), *mile* (OE *mil*), *mint*, from Lat. *moneta* 'coin' (OE *mynet*), *silk* (OE *sioluc*); from British–Latin contacts: *strap* (OE *stropp*), *pail* (OE *pǣʒel*), *pot* (OE *pott*), *cat* (OE *catt(e))*, *cock* (OE *cocc*); later borrowings and new creations: *abbot* (OE *abbod*), *mass* (OE *mæsse*), *alms* (OE *ælmesse*); OE *Þrowung* = Lat. *Passio* 'Passion', OE (*leornung-*)*cniht* = Lat. *discipulus* 'disciple', OE *mildheortnesse* = Lat. *misericordia* 'mercy'; OE *Þrynnes* = Lat. *Trinitas* 'Trinity'.

By the time of the Norman Conquest of 1066 the process had already begun whereby English gradually lost almost all of the inflectional system which had marked distinctions between classes of nouns, verbs and adjectives as well as gender, case, tense and number. No doubt interaction between two distinct but similar Germanic languages had some effect through the stressing of stem rather than inflection, but the main cause is likely to have been the tendency of English stress to fall on the first syllable thereby leaving inflections weakly stressed or not stressed at all.

Old English literature. The Old English period traditionally ends with the Conquest though nothing like so sharp a break actually existed. At the time of the conquest, English possessed a flourishing literature – poetry: secular, heroic (e.g. *Beowulf*) and elegiac (e.g. *The Wife's Lament, The Ruin*), and religious (e.g. *Dream of the Rood, Judith*); prose: saints' lives (by, for example, Ælfric), the *Anglo-Saxon Chronicle*, homilies (e.g. *Blickling Homilies*), scientific works (e.g. Byrhtferth's *Enchiridion*). Though Latin remained the primary language of learning and religion, English through translation and original composition had achieved a position of considerable prestige. It was also the common administrative language, used for law codes as well as charters, grants of land and wills.

Middle English

French influences. The Norman Conquest marks a considerable change in the linguistic context of English, its first effect being to move English from its position of administrative prestige as second only to Latin. In origin the Norman invaders were Scandinavian but they had adopted the language of the land they had conquered and consequently introduced a further language, Norman French or *Anglo-Norman, into England. There had been contact between Anglo-Saxon England and France before the Conquest – such as to leave a small inheritance of loan-words (e.g. *castle, tower, bacon, proud*) – but the major influence of Norman French on English comes in the period of social dominance in the late 11th and 12th centuries. Norman-French-speakers fairly quickly took over the dominant positions in secular and religious affairs thus creating after a while a prestige language of religious and social life and administration.

This new linguistic invasion differed markedly from its predecessors. Once again mutually unintelligible languages had come together but this time with one as a socially dominant partner which had to be learnt and understood in some form by at least some of the members of the other language community. As a result, the two languages remained functioning separately, in different parts of the community, each influencing the other.

Norman French in England gradually developed its own form of the language, Anglo-Norman, and its own literature. The loss of Normandy in 1204 did not mean the loss of English possessions in France and there is a continuing French influence, from Anglo-Norman within the country and its sphere of influence, and from Central French, especially that of Paris, abroad – no longer influence through invasion but through cultural desirability.

By the middle of the 14th c. Anglo-Norman was giving way to English as the language of administration. Signs of this are the Statutes of Pleading, which made English rather than French the language of the law-courts, and the opening of Parliament in English, both in 1362. French as a teaching medium in schools also appears to have been giving way to English at this time, and the 14th c. sees the burgeoning of literature in English: chronicles, romances, lyrics, poetry of every kind. As a literary medium French was almost entirely superseded in England by the end of the 14th c., but by that time English was a vastly different language from the one it had been at the time of the Conquest. The most notable legacy of French (both Anglo-Norman and Central French) was in the vocabulary, and words were introduced in every area of human activity and ultimately penetrated every level of society, often producing French/English pairs which have later become differentiated in meaning, e.g. *mutton/sheep, royal/kingly*; or Anglo-Norman/Central French pairs e.g. *warden/guardian, cattle/chattel, catch/chase*. The spelling system also had been much affected: <ch, qu, sh, z> were all French innovations.

Dialects and the standard. The fact that English was not subject to the standardizing influences and needs of areas like administration during the period before the 14th c. meant that dialectal differences, already present in the Old English period and heightened by the Scandinavian settlement in the north and east, established themselves in written form. Five generally distinctive areas are usually distinguished: Northern, East Midland, West Midland, Southern and Kentish, and in addition, by the end of the period, Scottish. No one of these carried greater prestige than another and all produced a considerable number of literary texts, but with the development of London as a metropolitan centre a particular form of English began to develop which, though based on East Midland forms, was also affected by speakers from other areas of England.

By the 14th c. the earlier establishment of the Chancery at Westminster showed signs of producing an inclination towards a 'correct' form of the language for administrative use. The end of the 15th c. saw the introduction of printing into England and Caxton, the first printer, expressed concern about varieties of English and the need to find appropriately acceptable and lasting forms of words for the language. This cluster of influences contributed to the growth of a standard written English, though it is unlikely that the feeling of this as a 'correct' form at first spread far outside London, or even isolated groups within London.

Middle English literature. Despite the social prestige of Anglo–Norman in the early part of the period, English retained a place in literature – not only sermons and religious instruction (in the case of a work like *Ancrene Wisse (A Guide for Anchoresses)* of high literary as well as didactic value) but also secular and religious history and legend in works like Laȝamon's *Brut* and the *Cursor Mundi*. By the end of the period English was again the dominant literary language represented in particular in the work of Geoffrey Chaucer, William Langland and the anonymous author of the poems of the *Gawain/Pearl* manuscript in the later 14th c. The 15th c., though not perhaps matching the earlier period in quality, established English in a new and expanding range of literary work, so that with the advent of printing at the end of the century it was English as much as Latin works that were published.

Modern English

Despite the wide variety of developments affecting the English language in the 15th c., geographically it remained a language confined almost to the boundaries that contained it at the end of the Anglo-Saxon period. The only extensions were of a small kind in Ireland, Wales and Cornwall. The 16th c. began the outward expansion of English. It also saw further extensions in the range of the vernacular, largely through translation, into areas of scholarship once entirely Latin. The Reformation established English as the language of religion and the Renaissance helped to create a new self-consciousness in English literary and linguistic endeavour in its attempts to match the achievement of Latin.

Early foreign contacts and the English overseas. At first, rather than exporting the English language, trade, and later simply travel, brought English-speakers into contact with a variety of new languages, and with familiar ones in a new context, resulting in varied and extensive borrowing. At the same time there was extended contact with other languages through printed works of every kind. Borrowings from Spanish came about to a great extent as a result of trading in the New World – new situations and new names for new objects – and there was not just borrowing of Spanish words but also of words from the indigenous languages of the New World through the medium of Spanish. Some recorded early borrowings were: *sherris* (later *sherry*) 1540, *primero* (the card game) 1533, *tornado* 1556, *alligator* (*al lagarto* = 'the lizard') 1568, *armadillo* 1577, *mosquito* (= 'little fly') 1583; and from native languages: *canoe* (Sp. from Haitian) 1555, *maize* (Sp. from Cuban) 1585, *banana* 1597. Examples of later borrowings are: *vanilla* 1662, *avocado* 1697, *barbecue* 1697 – the latter two from native languages. The same is true to a more limited extent of Portuguese in Africa and Asia. From Portuguese were, for example: *flamingo* 1565, *molasses* 1582, *madeira* 1595, *caste* 1613, *dodo* 1628; *yam* (? African word) 1588, *assagai* (Port. from Arabic from Berber) 1625, *macaw* 1668, *mandarin* (Port. from Malay) 1589, *pagoda* (Port. from an Indian language) 1634. There was a continued borrowing of words from French, and, on a smaller scale, from Dutch. From French: *trophy* 1513, *pioneer* 1523, *viceroy* 1524, *genteel* 1599, *rendezvous* 1591, *machine* 1549 (a Scottish use), *hautboy* 1575, *promenade* n. 1567, v. 1588, *moustache*

1585; and later: *fanfare* 1605 (a Scottish use), *stockade* 1614 (from Spanish), *unique* 1602, *ballet* 1667, *burlesque* (from Italian) n. 1667, *tableau* (at first = 'picture, graphic description') 1699, *champagne* (wine) 1664, *compote* 1693 (earlier borrowed as *compost* 1420). From Dutch: *luck* 1500, *isinglass* 1545, *cambric* 1530, *splice* 1524–5, *yacht* 1557, *wagon* 1523, *uproar* 1526; and later: *etch* 1634, *landscape* 1603, *rant* 1602, *stoker* 1660, *keelhaul* 1666, *duffle* 1677. These borrowings clearly reflect opportunities for contact, but often they also reflect the importance of certain languages in various areas of expertise or fashion: music, the visual arts, warfare, seafaring, cookery.

Later in the 16th c. Italian words began to appear. A few had existed already in Middle English but the vast majority date from the 17th c. and later, partly as a result of Italian dominance in many areas, artistic and domestic, partly as a result of the growing importance of the grand tour. Many have remained specific to Italian circumstances, the country and its way of life, but many began as specific but later became generalized. Some have retained their original form, and to an extent pronunciation, many have become wholly Anglicized: of the 16th c. are: *nuncio, podesta, doge, duomo, piazza, madonna, strappado, duello, macaroni, parmesan, artichoke, cupola, madrigal, stanza*; of the 17th c: *capriccio, vermicelli, recitative, cameo, model, miniature, intrigue, gazette, bulletin, opera, volcano*. Dating of word borrowing is always difficult since the first recorded use is all there is to go by and words borrowed orally rather than in written form can exist for some time without record. This was true of Scandinavian in the late Old English period and Norman French in the early Middle English, and it is true again of borrowings from other European languages in the early modern period. The main difference lies in the volume and variety of English literature and the new interest in language.

Though Latin retained its position as the primary learned language, every kind of literature was now produced in English from printed ephemera like broadside ballads to philosophic and scientific treatises. The growth of learned writing in English, often translation from Classical originals, meant that everyday (and exotic) words were entering English not only from the living languages of Europe and the wider world but also from the Classical languages. This 'foreign contact' was entirely a paper one. Often with the intention of improving the language, its 'beauty' (as they saw it) or its range, large numbers of learned words were borrowed from Latin. This was largely a literary matter, but so extreme did the borrowing of Latin words become that a body of opinion arose condemning the overuse of these 'inkhorn terms', as they were abusively called, words born of the inkpot not the human mind.

Many of the borrowings survive and no longer seem outlandish, eg. *conscious, reciprocal, defunct, spurious, inflate* (v.), *strenuous*, many hardly survived their first appearance (except in dictionaries of 'hard words'), e.g. *obstupefact, furibund, oblatrant, magnificate*. All the words quoted here, Ben Jonson holds up to ridicule in his play *The Poetaster* (1602). The later borrowings from the Classical languages, Latin and Greek, or in some cases words created on Classical models, were largely scientific. Latin had from its first appearance in England been a source of technical words of all kinds because it was the language of all learning. It was the expansion of science (in its modern meaning) and the taking-over of the area by English that produced the new influx of borrowings or creations, e.g. from Latin in the 17th c.: *specimen, spectrum, formula, stamen, nebula, antenna, momentum*. Another area in which the influence of Latin was felt was in the (sometimes quite erroneous) remodelling of the spelling of words on the lines of their supposed originals, e.g. *doute* from French, respelt *doubt* because of Latin *dubitum*.

Early language study. The condemnation of 'inkhorn terms' is a sign of another characteristic of 16th-c. England, an interest for the first time in the language for itself, or for the sake of improving and regulating it. One of the first weaknesses of the language to catch attention was orthography, where the mismatch between spelling and pronunciation was apparent. Those who considered that spelling should reflect pronunciation were drawn into the first systematic investigations of the pronunciation of English as well as into an examination of English spelling practices. John Harte's *Orthographie* (printed 1569) was one of the earliest and most remarkable of these, providing a new orthography as well as an analysis of English spelling and pronunciation. In the course of the 17th c., phonetics became an independent study, partly at least because of the concern with teaching English to foreigners. Christopher Cooper late in the century, gives a remarkably full account of English pronunciation (*English Teacher*, 1687). The early attempts at radical spelling reform, however, having failed to gain general acceptance, gave way to regularization of traditional spellings, something which printers had been doing since the late 16th c. By the beginning of the 18th c., spelling was by and large fixed in its present form.

Early attention was also given to lexicography. Latin–English glossaries of a limited kind had existed since the Old English period. Somewhat fuller vocabularies were produced in the 15th c. (*Promptorium Parvulorum c.* 1440 and *Catholicon Anglicum* 1487) and in a similar form continued into the 16th c. It was not until the later 16th c. that there was a call for an English dictionary (Bullokar 1580, Mulcaster 1582). In the same century a number of bilingual dictionaries appeared: French–English (Palsgrave 1530), Italian–English (Thomas 1567, Florio 1598), Spanish–English (Percyvall 1591). Springing partly from the influx of new words and partly from the new self-awareness in language matters, the first English dictionary appeared in 1604, Robert Cawdrey's *A Table Alphabeticall, conteyning and teaching the true writing, and understanding of hard vsuall English wordes*. As its title suggests, it is little more than an alphabetically ordered glossary. It was followed in 1616 by John Bullokar's *English Expositor*. A series of dictionaries appeared during the 17th c. and early 18th c. The number of words is continuously expanded, often by the inclusion of what would now be considered encyclopedic or gazetteer information, and matters such as etymology, and register were touched on sporadically and inadequately. Elisha Coles's *An English Dictionary* (1676) includes large numbers of regional and archaic words. It was not until the early 18th c. that something like a comprehensive dictionary as opposed to a dictionary mainly concerned with explaining unusual words was produced.

A systematic treatment was also given to grammar, starting with William

Bullokar's *Bref Grammar* (1586). Grammar is treated along with pronunciation in a number of works of the early 17th c. culminating in John Wallis's *Grammatica Linguæ Anglicanæ* (1653), which attempts to take the description of English grammar out of the Latin mould. Wallis demonstrates the influence of antiquarianism by including a history of the language.

Interest in language also extended to areas like slang and thieves' cant and in the 17th c. to dialect vocabulary and idiom. This very broad interest, however, was over-shadowed by the growing desire amongst scholars to establish and retain a 'true' form of the language.

Literature from Reformation to Restoration. The 16th c. and early 17th c. was a period of unprecedented literary activity, beginning with the new translations of the Bible early in the 16th c. (Coverdale, Tyndale), expanding into areas of religious debate and extensive translations of the Classics (Plutarch, Pliny, Euclid) and contemporary European languages (Ariosto, Montaigne), and achieving an exceptional richness in original writing in prose, poetry and drama (Bacon, Nashe; Spenser, Sidney; Marlowe, Shakespeare, Jonson, Webster). One of the most important linguistic results of the activities of the playwrights was that, because of the remarkable range of language registers represented, for the first time the full variety of English speech was reflected in literature. As the 17th c. progressed drama took a second place to poetry (Milton, Dryden), and even to a still-developing prose writing (Bunyan, Hobbes, Milton, Dryden), though it revived to some extent after the reopening of the theatres at the Restoration.

Later developments in language study. The 17th c. had seen the growth of interest in an academy as a means of refining the language and fixing it in a true and permanent form. The existence of the Italian (1582) and French (1635) academies provided a stimulus and Dryden and later Swift, among others, advocated some form of academy. The Royal Society (1662) might have served the purpose but in the end turned its back on language study, which thus remained uninstitutionalized.

The desire for improving the language and preventing change went hand-in-hand with a desire for standardization and regularization. Though some advocated the importance of current usage as a guide, the apparently uncontrolled variety of this was uninviting to most writers of the time. Instead appeals were made to logic, etymology and analogy (the 'genius of the language') to provide authoritative guid-ance as to what should be considered 'correct'. It should be said that the notion of a 'correct' form of the language was a desirable one for those who had to teach and those who wanted to learn the language.

One of the most remarkable achievements in the systematic study of the language at the time was Samuel Johnson's *A Dictionary of the English Language* (1755). Johnson's *Dictionary* demonstrates the settling of lexicographical practice very largely into what is that of later historical dictionaries. Johnson improves on his predecessors in his definitions, which are on the whole fuller and more analytic, in his coverage, where he reduces the encyclopedic content and expands the number of ordinary words, and by his inclusion of quotations to illustrate the use of words. His work dominated the dictionary-making of the 18th c. and as a basis for other dictionaries lasted well into the 19th c. Thomas Sheridan (1780) and John Walker (1791) used Johnson's as the basis for their definitions but expanded and improved the information on pronunciation in their Pronouncing Dictionaries. Dictionaries continued to appear throughout the 19th c. but until the advent of the *New English Dictionary* there were no major developments in England. In America the work of Noah Webster not only resulted in an important dictionary (1828) but also established the different system of spelling for American English.

Concern with establishing a standard in grammatical usage led to the prescriptive grammars of Robert Lowth (1762) and most influentially Lindley Murray (1794). These undoubtedly had a standardizing effect on many elements of the written language, which in some cases lasted until the 20th c.

The historical study of the language had begun in the 16th c. through the investigation of Old and Middle English texts for evidence of the antiquity of the English church as an independent institution. A dictionary of Old English had been published in 1659 and in 1689 the great grammar of George Hickes appeared. Despite these early beginnings the study did not move forward until the late 18th c., with Sir William Jones's work on Sanskrit, and the 19th c. through the activities of continental scholars, for example Rasmus Rask in Denmark and the brothers Grimm in Germany. The extensive re-examination of manuscripts and the publication of texts to which this gave rise joined with the movement for creating a new dictionary on historical principles proposed by the Philological Society in 1858. The Early English Text Society was founded in 1864 at least partly to provide texts for the new dictionary.

English overseas. Most important for later developments in the spread of English world-wide was the setting up of English colonies on the eastern seaboard of North America from Virginia in the south to New England in the north in the early 17th c. In 1783, with the conclusion of the War of American Independence, the United States of America became a separate state which developed its own pronunciations, spellings and traditions of English. At present nearly two-thirds of the world's English-speakers are American. Also in the 16th c. a rather shifting series of island and mainland colonies was developing in the Caribbean, soon to be populated predominantly by black African slaves. These ex-colonies also developed their own Englishes which in turn were brought back to Britain with the immigration of the 1950s and later. Developments on the other side of the world were a feature of the late 18th c. (1788 Botany Bay, the first penal settlement in Australia; gradual settlement in New Zealand from the 1790s). South Africa is largely a 19th-c. development and West African colonies also mainly developed in the 19th c., though contact had existed from early in the 16th c. The British presence in East Africa is late 19th-c. and 20th-c. Regular contact with the Indian sub-continent dates from 1612 (trading station at Surat) and grew in importance during the 18th c.

English remained the first language in the USA, Australia, New Zealand and parts of Canada. In other ex-colonies it has usually retained a place in some form: as the official language, in general use in administration and education, as a second language, sometimes without any official status. In a number of countries a *creole based on English has developed.

The expanding vocabulary. The vocabulary continued to grow during the 18th and 19th centuries through ordinary contact with its European neighbours and to a growing extent through colonial contact with languages in the rest of the world. A wide variety of words have been borrowed from Europe: 18th c. from Italian: *alfresco, casino, semolina, crescendo, fracas, firm* (sb.), *lotto*; 19th c. *graffiti* (originally an art term), *salami* (originally plural), *gorgonzola, spaghetti, cadenza, fiasco, studio, scenaria*; 18th c. from Portuguese: *veranda, ayah* (from Indian vernacular); 18th c. from Dutch: *gin, caboose, mangle*; 19th c. *spook, waffle, boss* (all three probably via USA); 18th c. from Spanish: *stevedore* (via USA), *quadrille, cigar.*

Contact with a new environment in Australia and New Zealand and with aboriginal languages in Australia and the Maori language in New Zealand led to a number of new creations and borrowings: *kangaroo* 1770, *boomerang* 1827, *corroboree* 1793, *coolibah* 1887 (all aboriginal in origin); *kiwi* 1835, *moa* 1842, *taboo* 1777 (Maori except for the last which is recorded from Tonga; Maori 'tapu'). Contact with the languages of the Indian sub-continent grew during the 18th and 19th centuries. From the 17th c. come *guru* 1613, *pundit* 1672, *chintz* 1614, *dungaree* 1696 (*dungarees* = 'trousers' 1891), *mongoose* 1698, *kedgeree* 1625, *bungalow* 1676; from 18th c. and 19th c.: *sari* 1785, *mynah* 1769, *chit* 1785, *jungle* 1776, *thug* 1810, *puttee* 1800, *pyjamas* 1886, *panda* 1835, *deodar* 1842, *chupatty* 1810, *dinghy* 1810, *gymkhana* 1861. Through the retention of Canada, contact was not lost with the American Indian languages: *pemmican* 1801, *toboggan* (through French) 1829, *tepee* 1872 (American-Indian borrowings); *kayak* 1757, *igloo* 1856 (Inuit borrowings).

Besides the continuing influence of other European languages the period also saw a large increase in technical vocabulary, either direct from Latin and Greek, formed on the model of Classical words, or created through the use of Latin or Greek elements (affixes or stems); 18th c. from Latin: *nucleus, inertia, auditorium, deficit, habitat*; 19th c.: *dementia, pupa, incunabula, sanatorium, aquarium, bacillus*; 18th c. formed with Greek stems and/or affixes: *chronometer* 1735; 19th c.: *anthropoid*, adj. 1837, *archaeopteryx* 1859, *bronchitis* 1836, *biochemistry* 1881, *eucalyptus* 1809, *geophysics* 1889, *heliotropism* 1854. Most of the examples given have entered the main word-stock of the language, but there are many technical words that remain in restricted use.

English continues to accept and to use words from other languages, not only in the technical and scientific sphere but in all areas of human activity. Some examples of borrowings in the 20th c. are: *conga* (American Spanish) 1935, *cosmonaut* (Greek elements) 1959, *courgette* (French) 1931, *diabolo* (Italian) 1907, *dirndl* (German dialect) 1937, *espresso* (Italian) 1945, *fascist* (Italian) 1921, *gopak* (Russian) 1929, *kibbutz* (Hebrew) 1931, *numbat* (Australian Aborigine) 1923, *shashlik* (Russian/Turkish) 1925, *shubunkin* (Japanese) 1917. Words are also borrowed from other Englishes, especially American: *kitchenette* 1910, *klaxon* 1910, *stooge* 1913. The creation of words from the native word-stock, from adopted elements from other languages (e.g. Greek *homo-*, *micro-*) and from trade names and initials is almost certainly the major source of new words: *email* (not yet in OED), *escapologist* 1926, *sellotape* 1949, *sexism* 1968, *see-through* 1950, *metalanguage* 1935, *microwave* 1935, *videotape* 1953, *windsurfer* 1969, *aerosol* 1923 (present usual meaning, 1944), *ahistorical* 1957.

Present situation of English

English in the late 20th c. has developed into a wide range of more and less closely related 'Englishes'. This combined with the economic dominance of the USA has turned English into a world language. By far the largest number of speakers are in the USA (*c*.221 million), with Britain next with *c*.56 million. The other countries make up the remaining 100 million (Crystal 1995: 109). English is also learnt as a second language by possibly a further 98 million people. Besides this there are a large number of speakers of creoles and pidgins with English as a base.

The world-wide use of English and the diversity of its origins and early developments mean that there are considerable differences between the various Englishes. Between the two largest of these, American and British English, the differences are, however, small. By and large, grammar is the same; there are numerous semantic differences but not such as seriously to inhibit communication; and the differences in spelling, though immediately obvious, are not significant.

If 'standard' implies a generally recognized and accepted form of the language in grammar, vocabulary, spelling and pronunciation, then a standard British English does not exist. A 'standard' is required for teaching purposes and even there there has been debate about what form it should take. It is safe only to say that British English spelling has achieved and maintained standardization, that a standard grammar is broadly accepted for writing, that there is a common word-stock which constitutes a 'standard' vocabulary, though the borders could not be rigidly defined, and that there is no single 'standard' pronunciation. RP or Received Pronunciation (a form abstracted from SE English speech) seemed 50 years ago to be on the way to becoming an accepted pronunciation for British English. Now its primary use is for comparative purposes in linguistic analysis and for using as a form in teaching foreign, and to a very limited extent, native learners. It has become a variety of English amongst many but still retains some social prestige. Regional dialects generally survive though some of the variety has disappeared (see map 4). Regional accents are now a common feature of broadcasting.

English remains a major literary language. Not only British and American English but a large number of other Englishes have made a major contribution in the 20th c., sometimes side by side with writings in native languages, sometimes at odds with them. Novels, plays and poetry are all represented.

English is estimated to be the first language of 377 million speakers world-wide. Britain itself is now home not only to speakers of British English, Irish, Scots, Scottish Gaelic, Welsh and Channel Islands French but also to those speaking

Map 4   Traditional English dialect areas. From Peter Trudgill, *The Dialects of England* (Oxford, Blackwell, 1990).

varieties of world English and languages from the Indian sub-continent and else-where. What effect this will have on British English in the future remains to be seen.

Aarsleff, H. 1983. *The Study of Language in England, 1780–1860*. Minneapolis and London.

Barber, C. 1997. *Early Modern English*, new edn. Edinburgh.

Baugh, A. C. and Cable, T. 1978. *A History of the English Language*, 3rd edn. London and New York.

Blake, N. (ed.) 1992. *The Cambridge History of the English Language*, vol. 2, *1066–1476*. Cambridge.

Burchfield, R. (ed.) 1994. *The Cambridge History of the English Language*, vol. 5, *English in Britain and Overseas: Origins and Development*. Cambridge.

Crystal, D. 1995. *The Cambridge Encyclopedia of the English Language*. Cambridge.

Gelling, M. 1978. *Signposts to the Past: Place-Names and the History of England*. London.

Hogg, R. M. 1992. *The Cambridge History of the English Language*, vol. 1, *The Beginnings to 1066*. Cambridge.

Jones, R. F. 1953. *The Triumph of the English Language*. Stanford.

Kurath, H. et al. (eds) 1952– . *Middle English Dictionary (MED)*. Ann Arbor.

McArthur, T. (ed.) 1992. *The Oxford Companion to the English Language*. Oxford.

Milroy, J. and Milroy, L. 1991. *Authority in Language*, 2nd edn. London.

Oxford English Dictionary (OED), 1989, 2nd edn. 20 vols. Oxford.

Quirk, R., Greenbaum, S., Leech, G. and Svartvik, J. 1972. *A Grammar of Contemporary English*. London and New York.

Scragg, D. G. 1974. *A History of English Spelling*. Manchester and New York.

Serjeantson, M. S. 1935. *A History of Foreign Words in English*. London.

Sheard, J. A. 1954. *The Words We Use*. London.

Trudgill, P. 1990. *The Dialects of English*. Oxford.

PETER MEREDITH

Erse

An obsolescent term, derived from medieval *Scots *Er(i)sche* 'Irish', used in the past with reference to *Scottish Gaelic. It is now occasionally used (though better avoided) with reference to *Irish.

Erza (see under *Mordvinian*)

Eskimo, see *Greenlandic*

Eskuara, see *Basque*

Esperanto (see under *Artificial languages*)

Estonian

Estonian (*eesti keel*) is, with *Finnish, a member of the *Baltic-Finnic subgroup of the *Finno-Ugrian languages and is more distantly related to *Hungarian. It is spoken mainly in the Republic of Estonia where it is the official language.

External history

Dialects akin to those of Modern Estonian have been spoken in the Estonian region for at least 2,000 years following the gradual differentiation of the Baltic-Finnic proto-language into Finnish, **Karelian**, *Veps, *Votic, Estonian and *Livonian. The earliest documented sources of Estonian are personal and place-names, words and phrases in 13th-c. Latin chronicles. Printed evidence of Estonian dates from the Reformation in the 16th c. The earliest known example of a continuous Estonian text (though now lost) appeared in 1525 in a quadrilingual publication of the mass. The earliest surviving text, a bilingual catechism, was published in Wittenberg in 1535. A German-language grammar of Estonian appeared in 1632 and translations were published of the New Testament in 1686 (in the Tartu dialect) and 1715 (in the Tallinn dialect) and of the whole Bible in 1739. The first grammar of Estonian, based on the Northern dialect, *Anführung zu der Esthnischen Sprach* ('Introduction to the Estonian Language'), was published by Pastor H. Stahl in 1637. A grammar based on the Southern dialect in 1648, Pastor J. Gutslaff's *Observationes Grammaticae circa Linguam Esthonicam*, also contains the rudiments of a German–Latin–Estonian dictionary. The script was adapted from the Roman alphabet with additions based on German (i.e.<ä, ö, ü>). A new grapheme, <õ>, was introduced in the 19th c. In addition to the Roman consonants, Modern Estonian also uses <š> and <ž>.

The early history of Estonian before the differentiation of the Baltic-Finnic languages is similar to that of Finnish. In addition to the influence of Ancient Balt and Old *Germanic dialects, the lexis of Estonian was also influenced by Old *Latvian. During the present millennium, until the acquisition of independence in the 20th c., the Estonians have been ruled by a succession of outsiders. In the 11th c. a large part of the region came into the possession of Kiev. In 1347, after more than two centuries of bitter fighting with the Teutonic Knights and the Danes, the whole of the present area finally came under Baltic German rule. In the 17th c. Estonia became part of Sweden until ceded to Russia in 1721. Estonia became independent in 1918 but was occupied by Soviet forces in 1940 and only recovered its independence in 1991. From a linguistic and cultural point of view, the principal influence has been Baltic German. German became and remained the language of the elites (i.e. of government, administration, education and culture) for some 500 years, while most Estonian-speakers lived in conditions of serfdom. The Baltic German influence is especially noticeable in the lexis. Where the lexis of modern Finnish, for example, has drawn heavily on Swedish, Estonian has drawn on German.

The literary language

Until the 19th c., two literary versions of the language were in use: the Tallinn and Tartu variants. Those who wrote in Estonian were for the most part pastors whose first language was German and whose command of Estonian was often far from perfect. It was only early in the 19th c., with the emergence of writers for whom Estonian was the first language, that an accepted codification began to emerge. Based on the Tallinn variant, it was adopted by exponents of the national movement and by the turn of the century had become the normative form. As the language innovators worked to transform Estonian into a national language, they drew heavily on the experience of the Finns both in their approach to neologization and in direct borrowing and adaptation of lexical items already coined for Finnish.

The use of Estonian as a literary medium took root early in the 19th c. It found its first expression in poetry. A major factor in consolidating the position of Estonian as a literary medium was the publication by F. R. Kreutzwald in 1861 of the Estonian national epic, *Kalevipoeg* ('Son of Kalev'), a work which drew on traditional stories and was cast in the trochaic tetrameters of traditional Estonian oral poetry. The Estonian national movement subsequently grew in strength and the language was institutionalized as part of the fabric of a new national culture through, for example, its use in education, administration, business and the arts. By the beginning of the 20th c. a new generation of writers had emerged. While their work reflected the specific national concerns of the Estonians, it was cast in the genres and forms of the Western literature of the day.

Dialects

Estonian has two main dialect groups: Northern and Southern. The boundary between the two dialects follows the Emajõgi river west from Lake Peipus to Lake Võrts, thence further west as far as the town of Viljandi. The parishes of Paistu and Halliste mark the western boundary between the two groups. The Northern dialects are further divided into Eastern, Middle and Western dialects. The distinguishing features between the dialects arise from extensive and detailed systematic phonological variation. A special group within the Southern dialects comprises the Setu Estonians of SE Estonia who also inhabit adjacent areas of Russia. As they are members of the Russian Orthodox Church (other parts of Estonia have traditionally been Lutheran), the Setu dialect has acquired numerous Russian cultural features including loan-words.

Present situation

Estonian is spoken by some 963,000 speakers in the Republic of Estonia. Though few in number, Estonian-speakers are also located in the Estonian border regions with Latvia and Russia. Small groups of Estonian-speakers, the descendants of 19th-c. exiles, still live in central Russia and Siberia. The largest outflow of Estonians from Estonia proper arose from political emigration to Sweden (*c*.60,000) and North America (*c*.5,000) during the Second World War. Smaller groups of refugees settled in western Europe.

Estonian has been the official language of Estonia since its declaration of independence in 1918. Although the use of Estonian was restricted during the Soviet period, it remained the language of much of education, culture and internal administration. Estonians were, however, obliged to study Russian at school and to use it in specific situations. The large flow of Russian enterprises and workers into Estonia during the Soviet occupation, with their concentration in particular areas, threatened to undermine the position of Estonian in the long term. With the re-establishment of independence, this trend has been halted. Moreover, since a command of the Estonian language is now a required qualification for citizenship, growing numbers of Russians and Ukrainians permanently resident in Estonia have started to learn Estonian.

Collinder, B. 1957. Estonian. In Id., *Survey of the Uralic Languages*, Stockholm, 133–79.

Hajdu, P. 1975. The Estonians, In Id., *Finno-Ugrian Languages and Peoples* (transl. G. F. Cushing), London, 192–8.

Laakso, J. (ed.) 1991. Virolaiset ('The Estonians'). In Id., *Uralilaiset kansat* ('The Uralic Peoples'), Helsinki, 84–115.

Raun, A. and Saareste, A. 1965. *Introduction to Estonian Linguistics*. Wiesbaden.

Suhonen, S. 1995. Viron kieli ('The Estonian language'). In Zetterberg, S. (ed.), *Viro: historia, kansa, kulttuuri* ('Estonia: History, People, Culture'). Helsinki, 196–225.

MICHAEL BRANCH

Eteo-Cretan, see *Minoan*

Eteo-Cypriot (see under *Cypriot scripts*)

Etruscan

Although, as we shall see, still presenting innumerable and, in the present state of our knowledge, perhaps insuperable problems, Etruscan is the one and only non-*Indo-European language dating from classical times of which we have more than fragmentary knowledge.

The area of ancient Etruria, in NW central Italy, from which the surviving evidence stems, stretches from Faesule in the north (modern Fiesole), just north of the river Arno, as far south as the Tiber, the southernmost Etruscan cities being Caere (modern Cerveteri) and Veii (Veio, some ten miles NW of Rome) (see map 10).

Surviving evidence for Etruscan is deceptively abundant. We have, from the 7th to the 1st centuries BC, some 13,000 inscriptions, but the vast majority of these are from tomb paintings or on small artefacts (vases, urns, mirrors, gems, coins, dice, etc.) of clay, stone, bronze, lead, ivory and other materials, and are highly repetitive, consisting in many cases only of personal names and/or formulaic expressions (e.g. *eca suthi* 'this is the grave'). One of particular importance is a bronze model of a sheep liver (now in the museum of Piacenza, near where it was found), used for purposes of divination and giving (in many cases more than once) 21 names of divinities.

Few of the inscriptions are much longer. Three important exceptions are: (i) a terracotta tile from Capua (now in the Staatliche Museen Berlin), dating from the 5th or 4th c. BC and including some 300 words; (ii) a stone cippus or pillar from Perugia (now at the museum in the city), dating from the 2nd or 1st c. BC and containing 130 words; and (iii) a pair of tablets found at Pyrgi (the former harbour of Caere and modern Santa Severa) containing over 50 words (for more on this, see below).

The longest known piece of Etruscan, however, is something of a curiosity, consisting as it does of a text of some 1,200 words in all (including repetitions – there are about 500 different words) discovered on the linen wrappings of a mummy that was apparently acquired in Egypt in the mid-19th c. and is now in the National Museum at Zagreb. Although it is only partially intelligible, it is now agreed that,

Transcription/ phonetic value	Seventh century south Etruscan (Caere)	Seventh century north Etruscan	Hellenistic south Etruscan	Hellenistic north Etruscan
a	𐌀	𐌀	𐌀	𐌀
c (k)	𐌂		𐌂	𐌂
e	𐌄	𐌄	𐌄	𐌄
v	𐌅	𐌅	𐌅	𐌅
z	𐌆	𐌆	𐌆	𐌆
h	𐌇	𐌇	𐌇	𐌇 ⊘
θ (th)	⊗ ⊕	⊕ ○	○	○
i	𐌉	𐌉	𐌉	𐌉
k	𐌊	𐌊		𐌊
l		𐌋	𐌋	𐌋
m	𐌌	𐌌	𐌌	𐌌 Λ
n	𐌍	𐌍	𐌍	𐌍
p	𐌐	𐌐	𐌐	𐌐
q	𐌒			
ś		𐌑		𐌑
r	𐌓 ᗡ	𐌓	𐌓	ᗡ 𐌓
s	𐌔	𐌔	𐌔	𐌔
s̀	𐌔		𐌔	
t	𐌕	𐌕	𐌕	𐌕
u	𐌖 V Y	V	V	V
φ (ph)	𐌘	𐌘	𐌘	𐌘
χ (kh)	𐌙	𐌙	↓	↓
ṡ	+			
f			8	8

before being cut up to make the wrappings or bandages, it consisted of a ritual text prescribing the ceremonies to be carried out on various occasions in a religious calendar. How it found its way to Egypt is not known.

With the exception of about 30 late inscriptions in the Roman alphabet, all the Etruscan material is in a script which derives from the Greek alphabet and is written from right to left (see fig. 6). The full alphabet (known as the 'model alphabet'), in the form in which it is written out (apparently for decorative purposes) on various artefacts, consists of 26 characters, but four of these are not used in the actual inscriptions or on the mummy wrappings. The Romans derived most of the characters of their own alphabet from the Etruscan script, which is also the source of the scripts used for other early languages of Italy such as ***Oscan**, ***Umbrian**, ***Venetic** and ***Raetic**.

Thanks to the work of a number of scholars over the last century, a fair amount is now known about the language, but much still remains to be elucidated. Such bilingual (Etruscan and Latin) texts as there are are few and of limited value, consisting mainly of proper names and formulae. Some further enlightenment was provided by the discovery at Pyrgi in 1964 of three gold tablets, two inscribed in Etruscan and one with a parallel but not identical text (a dedication to a goddess) in Punic (see ***Phoenician**). A few Etruscan words, with meanings, are known to us through having been quoted in Greek or Latin texts.

Well over 200 words can be understood with reasonable certainty (e.g. *ais* 'god', *puia* 'wife', *tur-* 'to give', and certain of the numerals, including those up to 'six', *thu, zal, ci, śa, mach, huth*), together with a number of place-names. A certain amount is also known about the grammar, in particular certain features of the morphology of nouns, pronouns and verbs. A few Latin words are of Etruscan origin, e.g. *atrium* 'entrance-hall of a house', *histrio* 'actor', *stilus* 'writing-implement'.

While no Etruscan literature has come down to us, having presumably been written on perishable materials, the chance survival of the Zagreb mummy wrappings is an indication that the language was used for more than inscriptional purposes. Latin and Greek sources refer to the existence of sacred books in Etruscan and there are no *a priori* reasons why a secular literature too should not have existed; indeed, the 1st-c. BC Roman writer, Varro, mentions one Volnius, of whom no more is known, *qui tragoedias Truscas scripsit* 'who wrote tragedies in Etruscan'.

The language may have died out by the beginning of the Christian era, but it has been suggested (Bonfante 1983: 47) that it may have continued 'to be read and used by priests as a sacred language', perhaps until the early 5th c., since, in 408, Etruscan priests used Etruscan prayers and incantations in a vain attempt to defend Rome against Alaric the Goth.

*Raetic, known from a number of inscriptions from northern Italy (but far fewer than we have for Etruscan), seems to have been related to Etruscan. Another language

Fig. 6 Forms of the Etruscan alphabet. From G. Barker and T. Rasmussen, *The Etruscans* (Oxford, Blackwell, 1998).

related to Etruscan, but for which there is far less evidence even than there is for Raetic, is known to have been spoken on the Aegean island of Lemnos (see ***Lemnian**). Otherwise, though wholly unsuccessful attempts have been made to establish connections with ***Basque**, Etruscan has no known relatives.

Bonfante, G. and Bonfante, L. 1983. *The Etruscan Language*. Manchester.
Bonfante, L. 1990. *Etruscan*. London. (Also in Hooker, J. T. (ed.), *Reading the Past: Ancient Writing from Cuneiform to the Alphabet*, London, 1990, 321–78.)
Pallottino, M. 1968. *Testimonia linguae etruscae*, 2nd edn. Florence.
—— 1975. The Etruscan language. In Id., *The Etruscans*, revised edn, London, 187–234.
Pfiffig, A. J. 1969. *Die etruskische Sprache* ('The Etruscan Language'). Graz.

GLANVILLE PRICE

European, Old, see *Old European*

Euskara (Euskera), see *Basque*

F

Faliscan

The Faliscans occupied an area north of Rome between Monte Climino and the Tiber (see map 10). Their main city, Falerii Veteres (on the site of which Città Castellana, some 40 km north of Rome, now stands), was destroyed by Rome in 241 BC. Faliscan was an ***Italic language** closely related to ***Latin** – cf. Faliscan *foied vino pipafo, cra carefo*, Latin *hodie vinum bibam, cras carebo* 'today I shall drink wine, tomorrow I shall do without'. Indeed, it has sometimes been claimed that it was a dialect of Latin, but that is an extreme view. Faliscan is known from well over 200 inscriptions, most of them dating from the 4th and 3rd centuries BC, in an alphabet similar to but not identical with that of Latin, a few of them running to several words but the majority of them very brief (often consisting of no more than a name or a fragment of a word or words). The main collection of inscriptions is to be found in the Villa Giulia museum in Rome.

Giacomelli, G. 1963. *La lingua falisca*. Florence.
—— 1978. Il falisco. In Prosdocimi, A. L. (ed.) *Popoli e civiltà dell'Italia antica*, vol.4, *Lingue e dialetti*, Rome, 505–42.

Faroese

A member of the North Germanic subgroup of the ***Germanic languages**, spoken only in the Faroe Islands.

Origins

Faroese is descended from Old *Norse, the language of the settlers who early in the 9th c. took possession of the then virtually uninhabited Faroe Islands (a few Irish hermits seem to have arrived before the Norsemen). Judging by the form of Faroese during its recorded history, the bulk of the settlers must have originated in western Norway.

The medieval period

For whatever reason, the Norse settlers in Faroe do not appear to have developed a written culture of any significance. Only a handful of runic inscriptions (see *Runes) have been discovered, difficult to date, but possibly spanning the period *c.*1000–1500. Roman-alphabet writings emanating from or pertaining to the islands in the pre-Reformation period (i.e. prior to *c.*1540) are also few and far between, and it is often hard to determine the linguistic affiliations of the scribes. The oldest of these documents (all are legal or diplomatic in nature) are from the second half of the 13th c., but the majority are or seem to be from the 15th.

The post-medieval period

The language of the Reformation in Faroe was *Danish. This came about for two main reasons. First, it is unlikely that any native written medium existed into which the relevant literature could have been translated (or anyone capable of doing the work even had there been a strong tradition of writing). Second, Denmark had assumed effective control of Faroe after its absorption of Norway in the century or so following the establishment of the Union of Kalmar in 1397 (Faroe seems to have become tributary to Norway about 1035). From the Reformation till the 19th c., the written medium of the islands continued to be Danish. The only glimpses we get of Faroese in the early post-Reformation period come from (a) Faroisms in copies of medieval documents made by Faroese scribes (approximately 16th c.), (b) a few fragmentary 17th-c. ballad recordings, (c) occasional Faroisms in Danish writings (16th and 17th centuries). In effect, the native speech of the islands – whatever its status before the Reformation – had by the end of the 16th c. become little more than a language of work and the home. Public, religious and legal affairs were all conducted in Danish (bar the occasional use of medieval Norwegian law manuscripts or copies thereof).

We thus have only the scantiest knowledge of linguistic development in Faroe from the time of the settlement until the first attempts late in the 18th c. to write down oral texts in the native language. A few of the features that characterize modern Faroese can be traced in such medieval and early post-Reformation sources as exist, but beyond that the shape of the language at different stages of its development can only be inferred through internal and external reconstruction.

It was in 1781 that a young Faroeman named Jens Christian Svabo was given a royal warrant to travel to his native islands (from Denmark) and compile a report on their economic state. His interests did not only lie in economic development, however. As early as the 1770s he had begun work on a Faroese–Danish–Latin dictionary, and he used some of the roughly 15 months he spent in Faroe to increase his stock of words and to amass a collection of ballads. In order to record all this material, Svabo devised an orthography for Faroese which is both remarkably consistent and – if account is taken of his Danish spelling habits – orthophonic. Svabo's principal motivation was concern that the Faroese language should not pass into oblivion unrecorded. He regarded its contemporary state with distaste, contrasting an apparently already heavily Danicized Faroese unfavourably with Old Norse. It is not wholly clear what future he thought the language had, but he recommended his native islanders to adopt Danish instead (a) because it was a more perfect language, and (b) because it was desirable that all the citizens of a realm should speak the same tongue.

Ultimately, Svabo's efforts probably helped to achieve the reverse of what he had recommended. Although the Faroese lacked a written literature in the Middle Ages, they developed a strong oral tradition, which, it has been argued, helped in some measure to preserve the language from even greater depredations than those that were felt to have afflicted it in the late 18th c. Svabo's ballad manuscripts were not published until the 1930s (the dictionary only 1966–70) and were largely ignored by his contemporaries, but the early 19th c. saw the awakening of a fresh interest in the Faroese ballad. New collectors appeared, some of whom sought advice from Svabo (who died as late as 1824), and his work came to greater prominence in the learned world. The first printed book in Faroese, H. C. Lyngbye's *Færøiske Qvæder om Sigurd Fofnersbane og hans Æt* ('Faroese Ballads about Sigurd the Dragon-Slayer and His Lineage'), was an edited collection of ballads about the legendary Germanic hero, Sigurd the dragon-slayer. It appeared in 1822, and the 1840s and 1850s saw the publication of further ballads and other oral material. It is hard to estimate how great an influence the availability of these works in printed form had on attitudes to Faroese. Interest in collecting oral material and making it available to a wide public, not least outside Faroe, was inspired by the National Romantic climate of the times, but it is clear that knowledge of the existence of such literary wealth, and its exploitation as a linguistic resource, were of considerable importance for the advancement of the language in the years to come.

The most prominent publisher of Faroese oral literature in the 19th c. was V. U. Hammershaimb. Partly arising out of his editorial labours and partly because of concerns about the position of Faroese after the introduction of compulsory schooling in the 1840s (whereby Danish was assumed to be the mother tongue), Hammershaimb began to devise a standard orthography for his native language. In its initial form it appeared for the first time in 1846. Over the next half century it was gradually refined, but as early as 1854 it had achieved something close to the final shape. Hammershaimb's orthography was based on a mixture of Old Norse and ***Icelandic** (in effect on etymological principles), which meant that the gap between the spoken and the written language was considerable. In favour of his creation it has been argued that it enabled speakers of other Scandinavian languages to read Faroese more easily and that it united the many divergent phonological systems of Faroese in a common written form. Despite attempts in the late 19th c. to make it more ortho-phonic, Hammershaimb's orthography has persisted to the present day and is now universally used and accepted.

The second half of the 19th c. saw the beginnings of modern Faroese literature. A number of patriotic poems were composed, and several plays. Despite the establish-ment of a written norm, however, little of this was published at the time. In the 1890s, the earliest Faroese-language newspapers were launched, but it was not until 1909 that the first Faroese novel appeared.

Dialects and the problem of standardization

Since the 18th c. at least, Faroese has exhibited considerable linguistic variation. A number of major dialect boundaries have been drawn, but it is also claimed that each village has its own recognizable form of speech. Most of the variation appears to be on the phonological level, although morphological, lexical and syntactic differences are also found. There is no problem of mutual comprehensibility, however: each speaker uses his/her own variant of the language and is well understood. Because of the position of Danish as the official language of the islands in earlier times, no stan-dard form of Faroese has developed. Whether this will happen in the future is as yet unclear. Since 1958 a language institute (subsequently language committee) has been at work overseeing the development of Faroese, but the activities of this body have been geared more towards purifying the language of Danish and other foreign elements than considering the possible shape of a future standard.

Present situation

The struggle to establish Faroese as an official language in the islands, and one that could function as satisfactorily as Danish in all walks of life, has been long and diffi-cult. Only in 1938 was Faroese granted equal status with Danish in schools, and it was 1939 before general permission was given for the use of Faroese in church services. The Home Rule Act of 1948 established Faroese as the principal language of the islands, but even today Danish is used for some purposes in the administra-tion and the legal system. Improvements in the official status of Faroese have by no means solved all the problems. The smallness of the population (some 48,000) means that production of written materials of all types (including schoolbooks) proceeds slowly, and that there is insufficient money and talent to sustain the full range of modern mass media. Faroe publishes an impressive number of books relative to the population, but the majority of books sold in the islands are nevertheless Danish. There are several Faroese newspapers, but magazines are overwhelmingly imported from Denmark. In 1957 Faroe established its own broadcasting service, which uses Faroese exclusively, and in the 1980s television made an appearance, although most of the programmes are imports, often Danish. In spite of these problems, Faroese is the language predominantly used in Faroe today, in virtually every sphere of life.

Because there is little mutual comprehensibility between the two languages, all Faroese adults acquire a command of Danish, though proficiency varies consider-ably. This allows Danes living in Faroe to continue to use their mother tongue, and most speak and write Danish only, although they will often understand both spoken and written Faroese.

Barnes, M. P., with Weyhe, E. 1994. Faroese. In König, E. and van der Auwera, J. (eds), *The Germanic Languages,* London, 190–218.

Djupedal, R. 1964. Litt om framvoksteren av det færøyske skriftmålet ('Something about the development of the Faroese written language'). In Hellevik, A. and Lundeby, E. (eds), *Skriftspråk i utvikling,* Oslo, 144–86.

Hagström, B. 1984. Language contact in the Faroes. In Ureland, P. S. and Clarkson, I. (eds), *Scandinavian Language Contacts,* Cambridge, 171–89.

Lockwood, W. B. 1977. *An Introduction to Modern Faroese,* 3rd printing. Tórshavn.

Werner, O. 1964. Die Erforschung der färingischen Sprache ('The study of the Faroese language'). *Orbis,* 13: 481–544.

—— 1965. Nachtrag zu: Die Erforschung der färingischen Sprache ('Addendum to: The study of the Faroese language'). *Orbis,* 14: 75–87.

MICHAEL P. BARNES

Finnish

Finnish (*suomen kieli*) is spoken principally in the Republic of Finland. It is, with ***Estonian**, a member of the ***Baltic-Finnic** subgroup of the ***Finno-Ugrian** languages and is more distantly related to ***Hungarian**.

External history

Comparison with other Baltic-Finnic languages (i.e. Estonian, ***Karelian**, ***Veps**, ***Votic**, ***Livonian**) shows that dialects akin to those of Modern Finnish have been spoken in southern and central Finland for at least the last two millennia. The interrelationship of Finnish with other languages goes back several millennia before the ancestors of the Finns had become linguistically fully differentiated from other speakers of the Baltic-Finnic languages in the NE Baltic region. Common to all the Baltic-Finnic languages are phonological, morphological and lexical features, indicating contacts with speakers of Ancient Balt languages and various strata of Old ***Germanic**. Earlier theories localizing such contacts to specific regions and periods (i.e. first Balt, then Germanic) are now discounted. The prevailing view is that such contacts probably occurred concurrently over several millennia before the Christian era throughout the Baltic-Finnic region. Lexical evidence is easier to identify than phonological and morphological influence. Nevertheless some scholars argue that certain distinctive features of the morphophonemics of the Baltic-Finnic languages derive from adjustments which occurred in the speech of Ancient Balt and Germanic speakers, as they adopted Baltic-Finnic dialects, and which were subsequently absorbed by native speakers.

Borrowings in Finnish and other Baltic-Finnic languages from Ancient Balt amount to at least a hundred. They brought to the lexis terms referring to nature and the environment, technology, buildings, subsistence, society and culture; e.g. *meri* 'sea', *heinä* 'grass, hay', *halla* 'summer frost', *hanhi* 'goose', *hirvi* 'elk'; *kirves* 'axe', *terva* 'tar'; *karsina* 'animal pen', *aitta* 'shed'; *ansa* 'trap', *lohi* 'salmon', *villa* 'wool', *siemen* 'seed'; *heimo* 'clan', *morsian* 'daughter-in-law', *sisar* 'sister', *talkoot* 'bee, group-labour'; *kantele* 'stringed musical instrument', *virsi* 'poem, song', *perkele* 'devil'.

The number of Early ***Indo-European** and Old Germanic loans in the Baltic-Finnic languages is larger and may amount to several thousand as new etymological techniques reveal further evidence of language contacts. Finnish absorbed Germanic loans both before and after its differentiation into a separate group of dialects spoken on the northern side of the Gulf of Finland, although population mobility makes it difficult to separate these two phases linguistically. It is only early in the first millennium AD that a distinction can be made between loans of Old Germanic origin and Old Scandinavian loans entering Finland from Sweden. Well-attested Germanic loans can be found in almost every sector of human activity: nature and environment, buildings, clothing, household, travel, fishing, animal husbandry, arable farming, technology and use of metals, measurement and time, society, and belief systems: e.g. *kari* 'reef', *ranta* 'shore', *kaisla* 'reed', *varjo* 'shade, shadow', *mato* 'worm, snake', *kana* 'hen', *nauris* 'turnip'; *ahjo* 'forge', *kammio* 'chamber', *lattia* 'floor', *porras* 'step'; *hame* 'skirt', *paita* 'shirt, shift', *sauma* 'seam', *vaate* 'item of clothing'; *leipä*, 'bread, loaf', *taikina* 'dough', *kattila* 'pan', *kehto* 'cradle', *pöytä* 'table', *saippua* 'soap'; *laiva* 'ship', *satula* 'saddle'; *merta* 'fish trap', *siima* 'fishing line'; *laidun* 'pasture', *lammas* 'sheep', *nauta* 'cattle', *juusto* 'cheese'; *akana* 'chaff', *aura* 'plough', *humala* 'hops', *mallas* 'malt', *multa* 'soil', *pelto* 'field', *ruis* 'rye'; *kaira* 'drill, bore', *keihäs* 'spear', *kello* 'bell', *miekka* 'sword', *rengas* 'ring', *saha* 'saw', *kulta* 'gold', *rauta* 'iron'; *arki* 'weekday', *viikko* 'week', *raha* 'money'; *hallita* 'to rule', *joulu* 'Christmas', *juhla* 'festival', *kuningas* 'king', *murha* 'murder', *tuomita* 'to judge', *kauppa* 'trade'; *taika* 'magic', *siunata* 'to bless', *vainaja* 'the deceased'.

During the last 2,000 years, outside influences on Finnish have come from three directions. In the first millennium AD, various forms of Old ***Norse** and ***Swedish** extended the lexis in the range of human activities outlined above. Since the 13th c., when Finland became part of Sweden, until the 19th c., Swedish was the principal source of new vocabulary, also serving as the medium for borrowings from other European languages. With the Reformation, Swedish became the principal language of education and administration in Sweden-Finland. In Finland, however, Finnish was also used alongside Swedish by the Church and Finns had the right to use Finnish in their legal affairs. This situation had two outcomes of linguistic significance. One was the predominance of Swedish as the main lexical influence. The other was that the semantics and style of written Finnish began to mirror those of Swedish. Thus despite the structural differences between Swedish and Finnish, the modern languages are relatively close to each other in terms of *Sprachbund* criteria.

Two other sources of influence should also be taken into account. One is Old ***Slavonic**, in the first half of the first millennium AD, and later, Old ***Russian**. Examples of lexis from these sources are: *risti* 'cross', *pakana* 'heathen', *pappi* 'priest', *raamattu* 'Bible'; *sukkula* 'shuttle', *värttinä* 'distaff'; *saapas* 'boot', *viitta* 'cloak'; *ikkuna* 'window', *pätsi* 'furnace', *veräjä* 'gate'; *ahrain* 'fish-spear', *katiska* 'fish-trap'; *papu* 'bean', *sirppi* 'sickle'; *lusikka* 'spoon', *piirakka* 'pasty'; *määrä* 'amount', *tavara* 'stuff'. Russian borrowings as such found their way into Finnish in relatively small numbers in the 19th and 20th centuries partly through phonological adaptation and partly through adoption of words of Russian origin which had been absorbed earlier in the East Finnish dialects and Karelian. The other source of lexis is ***Sámi** which has contributed a number of items relating to the specific environmental conditions of the far North; e.g. *suopunki* 'lasso', *seita* 'religious site', *tokka* 'herd', *tunturi* 'fell'.

The literary language

Documentary evidence survives from the late Middle Ages in the form of personal and place-names, words and phrases embedded in Latin-language tax, property and court records. The shaping of a written language began during the Reformation (1523–1640). The principal architect was Mikael Agricola, Bishop of Turku, who published a Finnish ABC book (*ABCkiria*), *c.*1542, followed in 1544 by a catechism (*Katkismus*) and a prayer book (*Rucouskiria*); his translation of the New Testament was published in 1548. The first translation of the complete Bible appeared in 1642. Agricola adapted the Roman script for Finnish, with certain additions borrowed from Swedish (i.e. <ä, ö, y>). Present-day Finnish has 13 consonants: <d, g, h, j, k, l, m, n, p, r, s, t, v>, and eight vowels: <a, ä, e, i, o, ö, u, y>. Either as survivals of older grapheme forms or to accommodate new loans, the following consonants also occur in Modern Finnish: <b, c, f, q, š, w>.

The literary language shaped by Agricola in the 16th c was based mainly on the SW Finnish dialects. This variant was further formalized in the 17th c. through the publication of Finnish grammars (the first to appear was Bishop E. Petraeus's *Linguae Finnicae brevis institutio* in 1649) and dictionaries (cf. H. Florinus's *Nomenclatura rerum brevissima Latino–Sveco–Finnonica*, 1678). It remained the basis of the normative register until the early 19th c. when Finnish nationalists began to transform Finnish into a national language alongside Swedish. Controversy about the comparative suitability of the SW, Savo and Karelian dialects as the basis of the national language lasted until the middle of the 19th c. when a standard language was adopted which was based on the old literary form while incorporating features from other dialects. Parity with Swedish was officially granted in 1863. At the same time, a conscious shift was made towards generating new lexis through neologization rather than phonological adaptation. Mechanisms were later put in place to advise officially on language usage and development. Today responsibility for this rests with the government-funded Kielitoimisto (Language Office) in Helsinki.

Finnish has served as a medium of secular literature alongside Swedish since the 17th c. Throughout the 17th and 18th centuries literary output was small, consisting for the most part of poetry, frequently cast in the trochaic tetrameters of traditional Finnish-Karelian oral poetry (the so-called *Kalevala* metre). In the 19th c. the collection of this traditional poetry became a patriotic mission leading to the publication in 1835 and 1849 of the first and second editions of E. Lönnrot's *Kalevala* ('Land of Kaleva') based on epic poetry and in 1840–1 of his *Kanteletar* ('Spirit of the *kantele*') based on lyric poetry. Translations of the *Kalevala* brought Finnish international recognition as a language of literature. Encouraged by the Finnish Literature Society (founded 1831), Finnish writers began to develop a tradition of prose writing about national themes which found its first significant expression in A. Kivi's *Seitsemän veljestä* (1871, 'Seven brothers'). Since the 1880s the genres, forms and themes of Finnish literature have reflected mainstream Western writing.

Dialects

Finnish dialects are characterized as western and eastern with the dividing line running historically from the Hamina area on the SE coast in a line north-west to the Kemi region. The Finnish spoken in Finnish Lapland represents a western dialect. In more recent times the two main eastern dialects, Savo and SE Finnish, have spread further west with the Savo dialects forming a wedge between the western dialects, i.e. the SW, Häme and southern Ostrobothnian dialects in the south and the remaining Ostrobothnian dialects in the north. The dialects are distinguished by phonological, morphological and lexical features. In general the western dialects are more conservative, retaining features which no longer occur in Standard Finnish; corresponding features in the eastern dialects have developed new and often multiple variants which are similarly absent from Standard Finnish, e.g.

Standard	Western	Eastern	
paidan	*paiðan, pairan, pailan*	*paian*	'shirt' (genitive)
lahden	*lahðen, lahren, lahlen*	*lahen*	'bay' (genitive)
teeri	*teeri*	*tetri*	'black grouse'
tuoda	*tuoda*	*tuua, tuuvva*	'to bring'

The adaptation by Standard Finnish of dialect variation in the lexis is less exclusive. Both forms are often adopted but with one becoming more specific in usage. The Standard Finnish words for 'summer' and 'evening' illustrate this phenomenon. East Finnish *kesä* is the form adopted for Standard Finnish; West Finnish *suvi* can be used to evoke a poetic sense of 'summer'. Similarly, while the East Finnish *ilta* is the Standard Finnish for 'evening', West Finnish *ehtoo* is used poetically or figuratively (cf. English *eve*). East Finnish *härkä* has become standard for 'ox', while its West Finnish equivalent, *sonni*, has become Standard Finnish for 'bull'.

Present situation

After acquiring official language status in 1863, Finnish had become by the 1920s the language used by all groups of the population, including a majority of Finland's elites, in all sectors of public and private life. Although Swedish continues to be spoken as the other national language, equal with Finnish, its use is declining as speakers of Finland-Swedish increasingly adopt Finnish as their language of habitual usage for reasons of intermarriage and social and employment mobility. A similar process is occurring among the speakers of the Sámi dialects in Northern Finland.

At the end of the 20th c. Finnish is spoken as the mother tongue by some 4.9 million people in Finland. Other speakers of Finnish as first language live in Russia (some 15,000 Ingrians in the St Petersburg oblast and the Petrozavodsk district of the Karelian Republic) and in Sweden. In Northern Sweden and Norway, some 30,000

Finnish speakers inhabit border areas with Finland; until the 19th c. Finnish was still spoken in several communities in Värmland by the descendants of 16th and 17th-c. immigrants from Savo. More recently, in the 1960s and 1970s, Sweden has seen an economic immigration of some 300,000 Finns to industrial and mining communities in various parts of Sweden. Finnish settlement in North America amounting to some 400,000 dates from the 1880s; a hybrid of English and Finnish ('Finglish') is still spoken by some older people. Through the efforts of recent immigrants and with the support of the Finnish government, some revival has occurred in North America of the use of Finnish as a second language. A similar process is also occurring among Finnish economic immigrants in Australia and New Zealand, numbering some 18,000. In 1994, with the accession of Finland to the European Union, Finnish became one of the Union's official languages.

Branch, M. 1987. Finnish. In Comrie, B. (ed.), *The World's Major Languages*, London and Sydney, 593–617.

Collinder, B. 1957. Finnish. In Id., *Survey of the Uralic Languages*, Stockholm, 1–131.

Hajdu, P. 1975. The Finns, In Id., *Finno-Ugrian Languages and Peoples* (transl. G. F. Cushing), London, 177–92.

Hakulinen, L. 1961. *The Structure and Development of the Finnish Language* (transl. J. Atkinson). Bloomington, IN.

Laakso, J. (ed.) 1991. Itämerensuomalaiset – sukukielemme ja niiden puhujat ('The Baltic Finns – our related languages and their speakers'). In Id., *Uralilaiset kansat* ('The Uralic Peoples'), Helsinki, 49–83.

MICHAEL BRANCH

Finno-Ugrian languages

One of the two branches, the other being *Samoyedic, of the *Uralic languages. With the exception of the Hungarians on the Carpathian plains and some small groups in western Siberia, the Finno-Ugrian peoples live mainly in the north and north-east of Europe. The Finno-Ugrian languages can be classified as follows: (i) *Baltic-Finnic, consisting of *Finnish, *Estonian, *Karelian, *Veps, *Ingrian, *Livonian and *Votic; (ii) Lapp or *Sámi, which is problematic in its classification but is closely related to the Baltic-Finnic languages; (iii) Volga-Finnic, i.e. *Mordvin(ian) and *Mari; (iv) the Permic group, i.e. *Komi and *Udmurt; and (v) the *Ugric languages, i.e. *Hungarian and its Siberian relatives, Vogul (Mansi) and Ostyak (Hanti). It is only since 1920 that many of the lesser languages have developed standard written forms.

Branch, M. 1993. The Finno-Ugrian peoples. In Honko, L., Timonen, S. and Branch, M. (eds). *The Great Bear: A Thematic Anthology of Oral Poetry in the Finno-Ugrian Languages*, Helsinki, 25–41.

WOLFGANG GRELLER

Flemish (see under *Dutch*)

Franco-Icelandic pidgin

In his article on 'Scandinavian languages' in the 1911 edition of the *Encyclopaedia Britannica* (vol. XXIV, p. 293), A. Noreen writes: 'As a matter of curiosity it may be noted that on the western and eastern coasts [of Iceland] traces are found of a French-Icelandic language, which arose from the long sojourn of French fishermen there.' One wonders whether this was not perhaps the same as the ***Basque–Icelandic pidgin** language known to have been used in Iceland.

Francoprovençal

The ***Romance** dialects of western Switzerland, adjoining parts of central eastern France, and the extreme north-west of Italy (the Val d'Aosta) (see map 6). The notion of a Francoprovençal language distinct from French is not accepted by all scholars (see below, 'The notion and geographical limits of Francoprovençal').

The notion and geographical limits of Francoprovençal

Whereas the ***Gallo-Romance** area had been conventionally divided into a northern area (i.e. that of ***French**) and a southern area (i.e. that of ***Occitan**, or, as it was then more usually termed, 'Provençal'), an Italian scholar, Ascoli, in 1873 published an important article arguing that the dialects of the east central area were sufficiently different from either of these to constitute a distinct linguistic variety to which he applied the term 'Franco-Provençal'. The spelling 'Franco-Provençal' (in French, *franco-provençal*) is still used, but the form 'Francoprovençal' (*francoprovençal*), without a hyphen, has also been adopted in order to avoid the implication that the dialects in question represent a mixture of French and Provençal.

The limits of the Francoprovençal area cannot be defined with great precision as they depend on the specific linguistic (and, in particular, phonetic) criteria one adopts. Broadly speaking, however, it corresponds to the following areas:

   (a) *la Suisse romande*, i.e. the western and officially French-speaking part of Switzerland, taking in the cantons of Geneva, Vaud, Neuchâtel, Jura, much of Fribourg and Valais, and a small part of Berne (see map 20);
   (b) in France, parts of the regions of Franche-Comté and Rhône-Alpes, extending well to the west of Lyons and taking in part or all of the *départements* of Doubs, Jura, Loire, Rhône, Ain, Isère, Savoie, and Haute-Savoie, and, in the south of Burgundy, part of Saône-et-Loire;
   (c) in the extreme NW of Italy, the Val d'Aosta region, i.e. the Val d'Aosta itself (including a part of the valley that lies within the Turin region) and its tributary valley; it is probably here that Francoprovençal is best maintained; there is also a dwindling Francoprovençal community, dating from a 13th- or early 14th-c. colonization, at Faeto and Celle San Vito in the Foggia region of SE Italy.

Nowhere is Francoprovençal anything more than a patois, mainly limited to rural areas; the urban and cultivated language, where it is not Italian, in all three countries is French.

It must also be added that not all specialists accept the existence of any such language as Francoprovençal. Hall (1949), for example, characterizes

Francoprovençal as 'simply the central eastern portion of [an] immense transitional area between Northern French and the rest of the Romance-speaking world'.

Origins

Whereas the north of France, i.e. the French-speaking area, corresponds more or less to that part of Roman Gaul that was occupied from the 5th c. AD onwards by the Franks, the Francoprovençal area corresponds broadly to that occupied by a different Germanic tribe, the Burgundians. It has been suggested that this difference in the linguistic superstratum is at the root of some of the phonetic and lexical differences between the two areas, but this theory, though not implausible, cannot be proved and is not accepted by all scholars.

Francoprovençal as a written language

Though no standard form of the language has ever emerged, there has been a long if meagre tradition of writing in the language. An early 12th-c. fragment of 105 lines of a poem on Alexander the Great and a mid-12th-c. epic of 10,002 lines, *Girart de Roussillon*, have been claimed for Francoprovençal, but this cannot be taken as proved, though the language of the former certainly contains Francoprovençal features; the editor of the authoritative edition of the Girart poem considers rather that its language reveals a mixture of French and Occitan forms. From the 13th c. we have a translation (in the patois of Grenoble) of the Latin *Summa* of the legal code of Justinian, a variety of legal documents (mainly from Lyons and Fribourg), and two works of devotion (an account of a vision and a life of Saint Beatrix of Ornacieux) by Marguerite d'Oingt (d. 1310 or 1311), in the Lyonnais patois.

A consciously dialectal literature in Francoprovençal came into being in the 16th c. and the earliest printed texts, both from Lyons, are a Christmas carol (1530) and a collection of 22 carols and other songs (1555). There has been continuous, if somewhat intermittent, literary activity since that period, in both Switzerland and France, in various genres (satirical works, poetry, plays, journalism, etc.). One of its most recent productions is an edition (1994), under the title *Kan la téra tsantè* ('When the earth sang'), of the complete works (poems, short stories, sketches, essays, etc.) of Joseph Yerly (1896–1961) who wrote in the patois of Gruyères (canton of Fribourg).

Chenal (1986) is the only complete grammar of any variety of Francoprovençal.

Present situation

The language is characterized by marked dialectal fragmentation, even within the relatively close confines of the Val d'Aosta. There are no official figures for the number of speakers of Francoprovençal. Tuaillon (1988), while warning that there is inevitably a wide margin of error, estimates that there could be some 60,000 in France and 70,000 in Italy. No estimates for Switzerland appear to be available from any source. It can be assumed that all speakers in France and Switzerland are bilingual with French while in Italy the language is up against competition not only from both French and Italian but also from Piedmontese (see under *Italy, III. Northern Italy).

Francoprovençal has no official recognition in any of the three countries in which it is spoken. While certain regional languages in Italy, such as Dolomitic Ladin (see ***Italy**, III. Northern Italy), German, Slovene and Sardinian, have a recognized status in the educational system, the only language other than Italian recognized in schools in the Val d'Aosta is French.

Aebischer, P. 1950. *Chrestomathie franco-provençale. Recueil de textes franco-provençaux*. Berne.

Chenal, A. 1986. *Le franco-provençal valdôtain*. Aosta.

Duraffour, A. 1969. *Glossaire des patois francoprovençaux*. Paris.

Hall, R. A. 1949. The linguistic position of Franco-Provençal. *Language*, 25: 1–14.

Jochnowitz, G. 1973. *Dialect Boundaries and the Question of Franco-Provençal*. The Hague.

Martin, J. -B. 1990. Frankoprovenzalisch/Francoprovençal (in French). In Holtus, G., Metzeltin, M. and Schmitt, C. (eds), *Lexikon der Romanistischen Linguistik*, Tübingen, vol. 1, 671–85.

Sala, M. and Reinheimer, S. 1967–8. Bibliographie francoprovençale. *Revue de linguistique romane*, 31: 383–429, 32: 199–234.

Tuaillon, G. 1988. Le franco-provençal. Langue oubliée. In Vermes, G. (ed.), *Vingt-cinq communautés linguistiques de la France*, Paris, vol. 1, 188–207.

GLANVILLE PRICE

Frankish

The Franks were a Germanic people, speaking a West ***Germanic language**, one branch of whom, the Salian Franks, began occupying northern Gaul in the late 5th c. AD. By 536 they controlled most of what is now France though it seems probable that the mass of the ***Romance**-speaking population remained and that the Franks were never numerically dominant. After, doubtless, a lengthy period of bilingualism their descendants abandoned their Germanic speech in favour of the ***Gallo-Romance** speech of the bulk of the population. A substantial number of Frankish words were, however, adopted into the Romance speech of the area, especially into that of northern Gaul: the total of such words that passed into French has been estimated at over 200 of which, however, many have since gone out of use or now exist only in dialects. Examples of words of Frankish origin that remain in standard French are *cruche* 'pitcher', *danser* 'to dance', *écharpe* 'scarf', *épervier* 'sparrow-hawk', *gant* 'glove', *hache* 'axe', *houx* 'holly', *honte* 'shame', *marais* 'marsh', *trêve* 'truce'.

The term 'Frankish' has also been used, but is better avoided, with reference to Franconian dialects of modern ***German**.

French

A member of the ***Gallo-Romance** branch of the ***Romance languages**, spoken (in Europe) in France (see map 6), southern Belgium (Wallonia) (see map 1), western Switzerland (see map 20), Luxembourg, Monaco, the Val d'Aosta in Italy, and the Channel Islands.

Origins and earliest attestations

French is the form taken by ***Latin** and the later form thereof, Gallo-Romance, in the northern part of the Roman province of Gaul (north of a line running approximately from the mouth of the Garonne, passing between Poitiers to the north and Limoges to the south and around the northern edge of the Massif central, and thence eastward to the Jura mountains). On the basis of the different forms for 'yes', namely *oïl* (which later became *oui*) in the north and *oc* in the south, the northern language (i.e. French) and the southern language (i.e. **Occitan**) came to be known respectively as *langue d'oïl*, which is still sometimes used as a semi-technical term to designate the ensemble of French, as opposed to Occitan, dialects, and *langue d'oc*, which remains as a non-technical equivalent of 'Occitan'.

Since the medieval period French has become the major spoken language of the whole of France, largely but not totally superseding both other Romance varieties (Occitan, **Gascon**, **Francoprovençal**, **Catalan**, **Corsican**) and non-Romance languages (**Breton**, **Basque**, **German** in Alsace and Lorraine, **Dutch** (Flemish) in the extreme north), and the only official language for the whole of France.

The linguistic situation in what is now France in the early centuries of the Christian era is discussed under Gallo-Romance. Opinions differ as to the period at which the language of the northern part of the area can properly be termed 'French', but there are good reasons for reserving this term for the language of the period from about the year 900. One brief document (127 words in all) has come down to us from a little before that date, so from what one might term the 'proto-French period'. It consists of the text of two oaths sworn by a grandson of Charlemagne, Louis, and the army of his brother Charles (the oaths sworn by Charles and by Louis's army are in German) when they formed an alliance at Strasbourg in 842, against their brother Lothair. But the version of the 'Strasbourg Oaths' that we have is found only in one manuscript, dating from about the year 1000; it presents a number of problems of interpretation, and we have no means of establishing how closely it corresponds to what was actually spoken. The evidential value of the oaths is therefore slight.

The earliest known text in what is indisputably French, and, indeed, the earliest literary text in any Romance language, is a 29-line poem, in an extreme northern dialect of French, on the martyrdom of St Eulalia composed around 880 and preserved in a manuscript of not much later, now at the Bibliothèque municipale at Valenciennes. From the 10th c. we have some notes for a sermon on Jonah, two more religious poems (756 lines in all) and then, in a number of 11th-c. manuscripts, a poem of 625 lines on the life of St Alexis.

Periodization

The following is a widely accepted periodization of the French language:

(1) Old French: up to *c.*1300
(2) Middle French: 14th and 15th centuries
(3) The Renaissance period: 16th c. (considered by some as part of the Middle French period)
(4) Modern French: from the 17th c. to the present day.

At all periods, French has been one of the major literary languages of Europe and, indeed, of the world. Among the hundreds of Old French texts are a number of epic poems (foremost among them the *Song of Roland*, extant in a 12th-c. version but certainly going back at least to the late 11th c.), courtly romances (including those of Chrétien de Troyes, fl. 1160–85), the fables and lays of Marie de France (second half of the 12th c.), versions of the Tristan legend, the 13th-c. *Romance of the Rose* by Guillaume de Lorris and Jean de Meung, various saints' lives and other religious material, plays (both religious and secular), the verse tales of Reynard the Fox, and, in prose, the chronicle of the Fourth Crusade by Villehardouin (*c*.1150–*c*.1216) and the Life of St Louis by Joinville (1225–after 1309).

Literature in Middle French is abundant but this is not one of the most brilliant periods of French literature; among texts that deserve to be mentioned, however, in even the briefest survey of writing in French are the massive chronicle of the Hundred Years' War by Froissart (1337–1404 or later), the lyric poems of François Villon (mid-15th c.), the cycle of 'mystery plays' by Arnoul Gréban, generally known as the *Mystère de la Passion* (first performed *c*.1450), and the *Mémoires* of Commynes (1447–1511).

Post-medieval literature

At every period from the 16th c. onwards, France has produced writers who would figure in any survey of world literature. The following list could easily be multiplied:

16th c.: Rabelais (d. 1553), Ronsard (1524–85), Montaigne (1533–92);
17th c.: Descartes (1596–1650), Pierre Corneille (1606–84), La Fontaine (1621–95), Molière (1622–73), Pascal (1623–62), Racine (1639–99);
18th c.: Montesquieu (1689–1755), Voltaire (1694–1778), Rousseau (1712–78), Beaumarchais (1732–99);
19th c.: Balzac (1799–1850), Hugo (1802–85), Baudelaire (1821–67), Flaubert (1821–80), Verlaine (1844–96);
20th c.: Gide (1869–1951), Proust (1871–1922), Valéry (1871–1945), Sartre (1905–80), Anouilh (1910–87), Camus (1912–60).

Standardization

Many old French texts are written, if not in pure dialect, at least in a French heavily marked by dialectal features (see below, 'Dialects'). However, the dialect of the Île-de-France, to which the term *français* originally applied but which is now referred to as *francien* (see below, 'Dialects'), gradually came to enjoy special prestige. Paris had been since the 10th c. the chief seat of the monarchy, the principal educational establishments (including the University, founded in 1253) and courts of law were there, and the Abbey of St Denis to the north of Paris was the ecclesiastical centre of the kingdom. By the end of the 13th c., the use in writing of dialects other than *francien* had been largely (though not entirely) discontinued. The issue was settled by the end of the 14th c., and the coming of printing (the first press was set up in Paris in 1470 and the first book in French published in 1476), which ensured that all published work in French was in *francien*, merely reflected and consolidated an already existing state of affairs.

A few medieval treatises on the French language, designed in most cases for English learners, are known but it was not until the Renaissance that the French language became an object of serious study. The first grammar of French was in fact published in England, again for the use of English-speaking learners of French and, despite its French title, is written in English. This was Palsgrave's *Esclarcissement de la langue françoyse* ('Explanation of the French Language'), London, 1530. The following year there appeared the first French grammar to be published in France (but written in Latin), namely the *In linguam gallicam isagωge* ('Introduction to the French Language') by Jacobus Sylvius (the Latinized version of the author's real name, Jacques Dubois). Grammars written in French were to follow, the first being Louis Meigret's *Tretté de la grammere françoeze* of 1550. The earliest dictionaries of French (other than some medieval French–Latin glossaries) date from much the same period. Robert Estienne published a Latin–French dictionary, *Dictionarium Latino-Gallicum*, in 1538, and a reverse presentation of much the same material in the form of a French–Latin dictionary, *Dictionaire françois–latin*, in 1540.

The Renaissance period also saw growing concern to widen the scope of writing in French and enable it to be used for purposes that had hitherto been largely or wholly the preserve of Latin. The first translations of the Bible appeared (a Roman Catholic one by Lefèvre d'Étaples, 1523–30, and a Protestant one by Olivetan, 1535); the first theological work was Calvin's French translation (1541) of his *Institution de la religion chrétienne* (first published in Latin in 1536). This was soon to be followed by a surgical treatise by Ambroise Paré in 1545 and, later in the century, by works in French in such fields as, among others, mathematics, astronomy, medicine and geography. In 1549 Du Bellay's *Deffence et illustration de la langue françoyse,* which can be regarded as the manifesto of the school of poets known as the Pléiade (chief among them being Ronsard), urged the claims of French as a medium for all purposes. This burgeoning activity inevitably led to the need to supplement the vocabulary of the French language by drawing on the resources of the classical and other modern languages (see below 'Contact with other languages') and creating new words by composition and derivation. The word-stock of the language was, in consequence, substantially enriched in the course of the 16th c.

Linguistic activity in the 17th c. was characterized primarily by the desire to bring the by now perhaps over-exuberant vocabulary under control, by selection and careful definition of words, and to codify the grammar. In the early part of the century, François de Malherbe, who occupied from 1605 the role of court poet, exercised considerable influence on the vocabulary, grammar and style of his contemporaries (particularly his younger contemporaries), taking the line that the literary language should not admit words that would not be intelligible to all and proscribing the use in literature of archaisms, neologisms, learned borrowings, provincialisms and technical terms. He also pronounced on matters of morphology and syntax. Malherbe's activity, says the distinguished historian of the French language, Ferdinand Brunot, 'ouvre le règne de la grammaire, règne qui a été, en France, plus tyrannique et plus long qu'en aucun pays' ('opens the reign of grammar, a reign that has been, in France, more tyrannical and longer than in any [other] country'). Discussion of points of language and style was to become a favourite activity at the literary *salons* that flourished in Court circles in the mid-17th c. and from these *salons* and this activity emerged, to quote only two outstanding developments, the Académie française and Vaugelas. The Academy was founded in 1635 and, in its Statutes (1637), was charged with regulating and purifying the language and rendering it capable of dealing with 'the arts and the sciences'. It was to produce a dictionary and a grammar (on these, see below), and also works on poetics and rhetoric, neither of which has ever appeared. Vaugelas was one of the founder members of the Academy and worked on its dictionary. In 1647 he published his influential volume, *Remarques sur la langue françoise* ('Observations on the French Language'), a series of commentaries on points of pronunciation, orthography, morphology and, above all, vocabulary and syntax, about which there was uncertainty or debate in cultivated circles (the *salons*) or on the part of writers. He saw his role not as laying down the law but as that of an observer and arbiter of 'good usage', which he defined as 'the way of speaking of the soundest sections of the Court, in conformity with the way of writing of the best authors of the time'. In general, he avoids the excesses of artificiality or doctrinaire purism that characterized some of his contemporaries, and many of his recommendations on matters of vocabulary and syntax, which were much studied, discussed and often acted upon by writers of the time, constituted a significant contribution to the fixing of literary usage.

The first edition of the Academy's dictionary appeared in 1694, the eighth in 1932–5, and the first fascicle of the ninth edition in 1986. These latest editions, however, have never enjoyed the prestige of various other dictionaries, in particular Émile Littré's *Dictionnaire de la langue française*, 1863–72, Paul Robert's *Dictionnaire alphabétique et analogique de la langue française*, 7 vols, 1951–70 (2nd edn, 9 vols, 1985–6), and the *Trésor de la langue française* (first editor, Paul Imbs), 16 vols, 1971–94.

Numerous grammars, written from different theoretical standpoints and of greatly uneven value, have appeared in the course of recent centuries. It is curious, however, given the great attention paid to the language not only in the French educational system but in cultured circles generally, that no acceptable officially sponsored grammar has ever been written. The most authoritative and influential is probably Maurice Grevisse's *Le Bon Usage*, first published in Belgium in 1936 and now in its thirteenth edition (1993), substantially revised by André Goosse. One of the tasks set the Académie française in its Statutes of 1637 had in fact been to compose a grammar, but this took nearly three centuries and the resulting *Grammaire de l'Académie française* (1932) attracted well-founded criticism from such sources as the foremost contemporary authority on the French language, Ferdinand Brunot, and is not regarded as in any way authoritative.

Orthography

French has always been written in the Latin alphabet. However, from the outset this proved inadequate in some respects for a language that had developed sounds that had not existed in Latin. Furthermore, though pronunciation has changed very considerably since the Old French period, the orthography has evolved relatively little and still, in many respects, reflects that of seven or eight hundred years ago. The position is aggravated by the fact that thousands of Latin and other words have been borrowed with little or no orthographic adaptation. In consequence, the mismatch between pronunciation and orthography is even greater in French than in English. After a long history (going back to the 16th c.) of attempted reforms, some (though few) of which have been adopted, proposals in the 20th c. (most recently in 1992) for the introduction of even modest and thoroughly sensible modifications have encountered great resistance and have failed.

Dialects

In French, as in other languages, it is not in general possible to establish clear geographical boundaries between dialects (see map 6). That major regional differences existed in the Middle Ages is beyond dispute but, on the ground, they tended to shade into one another. In so far as the dialects have not disappeared in the face of a more or less common Paris-based spoken tongue, that is still the case.

For our knowledge of medieval dialects, we are dependent on the evidence of texts written in these dialects, or rather, since it is unlikely that any of our existing texts are written in pure dialect, texts whose language is coloured to a greater or lesser degree by the dialect of the author and/or of the copyist of a particular manuscript. These include both literary texts and also a considerable number of legal documents. On the basis of these, we can identify as the major dialectal areas in the Old French period the Île-de-France, i.e. the area surrounding Paris (see below), Normandy, Picardy, the Walloon area, Lorraine, and the south-west of the *langue d'oïl* area (Poitou, Saintonge, Anjou). These are generally referred to by means of the adjective applied to the areas (in most but not all cases, provinces) to which they broadly correspond, i.e. *normand, picard, wallon, lorrain, champenois*. The adjective corresponding to 'France', a term that originally related only to the Île-de-France, is of course *français*, but since this has come to refer to the language as a whole, it is no longer appropriate with reference to the specific dialect of the Île-de-France. Consequently, in works on French dialectology, the term *francien*, which dates only from the late 19th c., has been adopted.

French had come into use in legal documents (although Latin was still to predominate for centuries to come) as early as the 13th c., and, whereas at first such documents in the provinces reflected at least to some extent the language of their area, by the end of the century *francien* was widely used in areas other than the Île-de-France and soon came to predominate. The last major writer to show much influence of non-*francien* features in his French was Froissart, in the 14th c., and he too largely abandoned them as time went by.

The main dialects or dialectal groupings identifiable in the modern period can be considered to be the following (though other classifications are possible): (i) a central group including, together with the dialects of the Île-de-France, those of Champagne to the north-east and the Orléanais to the south-west; (ii) Norman; (iii) Picard; (iv) Walloon; (v) Lorrain; (vi) a south-eastern group (i.e., south-eastern within the *langue d'oïl* area, not of course within France as a whole) covering the Franche-Comté and northern Burgundy; (vii) a southern group covering the Bourbonnais and the Berry; (viii) a western area covering Touraine, Maine, Anjou, western Normandy, and the Gallo area, i.e. eastern (non-Breton-speaking) Brittany; and (ix) a south-western area, covering Poitou, Aunis, Saintonge and the Angoumois. Though the status of 'language' is sometimes claimed for some of these varieties, it is only ***Walloon** and perhaps ***Picard** to which it can be applied with much plausibility.

Though all mainstream French literature for the last 500 years has been written in the national language, a certain amount of writing in dialect (verse, plays, some prose) has been produced, particularly from the 18th c. onwards. Though much of this is in totally non-standardized orthographies, widely accepted standardized orthographies have been devised for Walloon, Picard and Gallo and are used both for literary purposes and in scholarly works on the dialects in question.

As compared with the situation in England, the modern French dialects are well documented. We have, on the one hand, a considerable number of dialectal glossaries, dictionaries and monographs, of greatly varying quality (ranging from serious and competent linguistic studies to amateurish and virtually worthless publications) and, on the other, invaluable linguistic atlases. The first of these (and the world's first major linguistic atlas) was the *Atlas linguistique de la France* by J. Gilliéron (the director of the project) and E. Edmont (the field-worker, who cycled round France and contiguous French-speaking areas, finding informants and eliciting their responses to a detailed linguistic questionnaire). The result is a collection of 1,920 maps (some of them, however, covering only southern areas) plotting for 639 localities the renderings provided by Edmont's informants for words and phrases designed to illustrate lexical, phonetic, morphological and, in a very few cases, syntactical features of the local dialect. The atlas covers the whole of Romance-speaking France and so includes data for the Occitan- and Franco-provençal-speaking areas, and the small Catalan-speaking area in and around Perpignan, so only approximately half of the material relates specifically to French. Though the information provided by the atlas is now a century old (Edmont carried out his field-work in the years 1897–1901), it is still an invaluable research tool, having been elaborated as it was at a time when the dialects were considerably more flourishing than they are today. It is, therefore, supplemented rather than replaced by the regional linguistic and ethnographical atlases proceeding from an initiative launched by Albert Dauzat in 1939 and that have been appearing since 1950 (many but not all of them are now complete in two or more volumes). The *langue d'oïl* area is covered by those for the Île-de-France and the Orléanais, Normandy, Picardy, Lorraine, Champagne and Brie, Franche-Comté, Burgundy, central France (*le Centre*), the West (Poitou, Aunis, Saintonge, Angoumois), and Romance-speaking

Brittany, Anjou and Maine. The Walloon area is excluded from this series of atlases as it is already covered by its own linguistic atlas, Jean Haust's *Atlas linguistique de la Wallonie* which started publication in 1953.

Contact with other languages

French retains a number of words (perhaps 50 or 60 in the standard language but possibly three times as many when one counts those that survive only in dialects) borrowed from ***Gaulish** during the Gallo-Romance period. The great majority of these relate to agricultural and rural concepts, e.g. *boue* 'mud', *claie* 'hurdle', *soc* 'ploughshare', which are cognate with Welsh *baw*, *clwyd*, *swch* which have the same meanings, and *mouton* 'sheep', *pièce* 'piece, etc.', *trogne* '(substandard for) face', related to Welsh *mollt* 'wether', *peth* 'thing', *trwyn* 'nose'.

The Frankish occupation of northern Gaul from the 5th c. onwards resulted in the importation into the Romance speech of the area of a considerable number of Germanic words, many of them to do with military or administrative matters (e.g., to give them in their modern form, *blesser* 'to wound', *fourbir* 'to burnish', *heaume* 'helmet', *sénéchal* 'seneschal', *trêve* 'truce'), with agriculture and the countryside (the Franks were not a nation of town-dwellers) (e.g. *blé* 'wheat', *bois* 'wood', *gerbe* 'sheaf', *haie* 'hedge', *houx* 'holly', *mésange* 'tit', *troène* 'privet'), with social customs, items of clothing, etc. (e.g. *cruche* 'jug', *danser* 'to dance', *fauteuil* 'armchair' (earlier 'folding stool'), *feutre* 'felt', *gant* 'glove', *poche* 'pocket', *rôtir* 'to roast') or with emotions or personal characteristics (e.g. *haïr* 'to hate', *honte* 'shame', *laid* 'ugly' (but earlier 'disagreeable'), *orgueil* 'pride', *rang* 'rank').

The incursions of another Germanic-speaking people, the Vikings or 'Northmen' that began in or about the early 9th c., led eventually to permanent settlement when, in 911, the French king Charles the Simple ceded to them a tract of land around the estuary of the Seine that was in due course to lead to the creation of the Duchy of Normandy whose name derives from that of the new occupiers. Many place-names in the area (e.g. *Caudebec* 'cold stream') are patently of Norman origin as are a few words relating mainly, and not surprisingly, to seafaring matters, e.g. *crique* 'creek', *étambot* 'sternpost', *tillac* 'deck', *vague* 'wave'.

Throughout the Old and Middle French periods, a steady trickle, but little more than a trickle, of words entered the language from living foreign languages such as English (e.g. names for points of the compass, *nord, sud, est, ouest*) and Arabic (e.g. *coton* 'cotton', *gazelle, jupe* 'skirt'). By far the main source of new acquisitions, however, was Latin, particularly in the 14th and 15th centuries when the Latinisms borrowed (the great majority of which are still in the language) can be numbered in hundreds. To quote (in their modern spelling) only a handful of examples, from the 13th c. we have *austérité, excessif, politique, possibilité*, and, from the Middle French period, *absent, acte, applaudir, assister, classe, délicat, divorce, famille, final, fragile, information, poème, primitif, satisfaire*. This process of drawing on Latin for, in particular, abstract and technical terminology has continued throughout the centuries.

From the Renaissance onwards, French has borrowed words from many languages but the two principal such sources have been Italian and English. A series of military campaigns in Italy between 1494 and 1525 brought France into contact with the Italian Renaissance and led to the arrival in France of Italian architects, painters, musicians and writers. Italian words (a number of which had already come into French in the 14th and 15th centuries, e.g. *alarme, banque, banquet, brigand, camp, médaille*) now flooded into the French language and, though many were only ephemeral borrowings, many have remained, particularly in the fields of military and artistic terminology, e.g. *alerte, appartement, architecte, attaquer, bataillon, escorte, infanterie, réussir, risque, arcade, ballet, balcon, concert, façade, grotesque, modèle, sonnet, sérénade*, but also others, including *artisan, briller, manquer, récolte, saucisson*.

17th-c. borrowings from English include *flanelle, pamphlet, paquebot* 'liner' (from *packet-boat*), *rhum* 'rum'. Growing interest in later centuries in English customs and political institutions and practice and the technological developments of the Industrial Revolution gave rise to further borrowings, e.g., in the 18th c., *budget, club, congrès, jury, pudding, vote*, and, in the 19th, *bifteck* 'steak' (from *beefsteak*), *chèque, football, rail, sandwich, sport, ticket*. The influence of English in the 20th c., and, particularly in the second half of the century, of American English has been as great on French as on very many other languages, but, whereas other languages have often absorbed these recent Anglicisms (as indeed could also have been the case with French), some intellectual circles in France have reacted with exaggerated fears for the future of the French language. This has led not only to the setting up of bodies to draw up lists of French terms for use in technical, commercial, administrative and other fields but to the passing of laws (in particular the *loi Bas–Lauriol*, named as is usual practice in France, after the members responsible for steering it through parliament, of 1975 and, most recently, the *loi Toubon* of 1994) designed *inter alia* to ban or restrict the use of foreign words (which, in practice, means Anglicisms) in contracts, advertising, etc.

Official status

France. As we have seen, in the course of the 16th c. French gradually took over a wide range of functions from Latin. The use of French instead of Latin for various purposes was specified in three royal edicts of 1490, 1510 and 1535, but these all clearly allowed the use of regional languages. Finally, in an ordinance issued in 1539 (usually known as the Ordonnance de Villers-Cotterêts), King François I decreed that, thenceforward, all records of legal proceedings and judgements in the courts at all levels and all contracts, wills, and other legal instruments deriving therefrom were to be in French. While this was designed to ensure the use of French rather than Latin for the purposes specified, it is not clear whether the intention was now also to proscribe the use of regional languages and dialects, but in practice, from a very early stage, French alone was used. Curiously, however, it was not until 1992 that a clause was introduced into the constitution of the French Republic specifying that the official language of the Republic is French.

Elsewhere in Europe. In Belgium, French is the official language in the southern part of the country (Wallonia), consisting mainly of the provinces of Hainaut, Namur,

Luxembourg, Liège, and the southern portion of Brabant, while the capital, Brussels, is officially bilingual (French and Dutch). In the Grand Duchy of Luxembourg, where ***Luxemburgish** is officially designated as the 'national language', French is (together with German) an official language and is the language of legislation. In Switzerland, French is one of four official languages (the others being German, Italian and ***Romansh**). It is the official language of the Principality of Monaco. In the Channel Islands, French still enjoys marginal official status but, in practice, its use is strictly limited (see ***Channel Islands French**).

Outside Europe. French is an official language in all French-governed territories (i.e. French Guyana and numerous islands in the Western Hemisphere, the Indian Ocean and the Pacific), whatever their precise constitutional relationship to France. In Canada, French has been an official language throughout the federation since 1969; in the Province of Quebec it is (except for federal matters) the only official language. French is also an official language in Haiti (where the vernacular is a French creole), Mauritius (with English), Madagascar (with Malagasy), the Comoros, the Seychelles (with Creole and English), and, in Africa, in Benin, Burkina, Burundi (with Kirundi), Cameroon (with English), Central African Republic, Chad (with Arabic), Congo (Brazzaville), Congo (Kinshasha), Djibouti, Gabon, Guinea, Ivory Coast, Mali, Mauritania, Niger, Rwanda (with Kinyarwanda), Senegal, and Togo.

International organizations. French is an official language of the United Nations, of the European Union, and of the Organization of African Unity.

Numbers of speakers

While no linguistic data are provided by official censuses of France, it can safely be assumed that French is spoken (in most cases as a first language) by virtually the total population of over 57 million. It is the first language of some 4 million (40% of the total population) in Belgium and about 1.3 million (19%) in Switzerland. French is also spoken by some 80,000 in the Val d'Aosta in Italy and by probably over 20,000 in the Principality of Monaco (total population, 27,000). We have, therefore, a total of over 62 million speakers in Europe, to which one can add the great majority of the native population of Luxembourg (some 275,000), where French is universally understood and used though the first language is in most cases Luxemburgish.

The main population of native-speakers of French outside Europe is in Canada (over 6 million, of whom over 5 million are resident in Quebec). There are substantial numbers of French-speakers in Louisiana and in French-administered territories scattered throughout the world, though in both cases accurate figures for those who speak French as distinct from a French-based creole (see below) are not available. There are also significant numbers of French-speakers (for most of whom, however, it is a second language) in those African republics where it is an official language, in the Maghreb states (Morocco, Algeria, Tunisia), and in Madagascar. When one takes account of these and also of those Europeans and others for whom it is not a native language but who have a good command of French, a recent estimate (Rossillon 1995: 124) of nearly 90 million speakers of French is probably not an exaggeration.

French *creoles

French-based creoles are spoken in three main areas: (i) Louisiana; (ii) the Caribbean area (Haiti; the French 'overseas departments' of Guadeloupe, Martinique and, on the South American mainland, French Guyana; the former British colonies, now independent, of Dominica, Grenada, St Lucia and Trinidad); (iii) in the Indian Ocean islands of Réunion (a French 'overseas department') and former British colonies, now independent, of Mauritius and the Seychelles (in the latter, Creole is an official language, together with French and English).

Ager, D. 1990. *Sociolinguistics and Contemporary French*. Cambridge.
Ayres-Bennett, W. 1996. *A History of the French Language through Texts*. London.
Battye, A. and Hintze, M. -A. 1992. *The French Language Today*. London.
Brunot, F. 1905–53. *Histoire de la langue française des origines à 1900*, 13 vols. Paris.
Chaurand, J. 1972. *Introduction à la dialectologie française*. Paris.
Corréard, M. -H. and Grundy, V. 1994. *The Oxford–Hachette French Dictionary*. Oxford.
France, P. (ed.) 1995. *The New Oxford Companion to Literature in French*. Oxford.
Grevisse, M. 1993. *Le Bon Usage*, 13th edn recast by André Goosse. Paris and Louvain-la-Neuve.
Holtus, G., Metzeltin, M. and Schmitt, C. (eds) 1990. *Lexikon der Romanistischen Linguistik*, vol. 5.1, *Französisch/ Le français*. Tübingen (61 articles, 29 in French, 32 in German).
Imbs, P. (ed.) 1971–94. *Trésor de la langue française*, 16 vols. Paris.
Lodge, R. A. 1993. *French: From Dialect to Standard*. London.
Offord, M. 1990. *Varieties of Contemporary French*. London.
Posner, R. 1997. *Linguistic Change in French*. Oxford.
Price, G. 1971. *The French Language, Present and Past*. London.
—— 1993. *L. S. R. Byrne and E. L. Churchill's A Comprehensive French Grammar*, 4th edn. Oxford.
Rickard, P. 1989. *A History of the French Language*, 2nd edn. London.
Rossillon, P. (ed.) 1995. *Atlas de la langue française*, Paris.
Sanders, C. (ed.) 1993. *French Today. Language in its Social Context*. Cambridge.

GLANVILLE PRICE

Frentanian (see under *Oscan*)

Frisian

Frisian belongs, together with *English**, to the North Sea subgroup of the West *Germanic languages**. Its natural habitat stretches from Holland to Denmark along the North Sea coast where the Frisians have survived as a seagoing and trading nation for 2,000 years, along the periphery of a succession of more powerful states.

The three varieties of Frisian

There are today three distinct, and not mutually intelligible, varieties of Frisian (see map 5): (i) West Frisian (in Frisian, Frysk), in the province of Friesland (Fryslân), including the islands of Terschelling (Skylge) and Schiermonnikoog

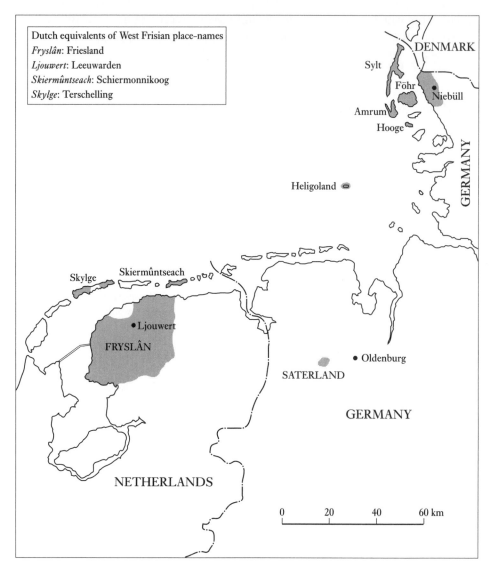

Dutch equivalents of West Frisian place-names
Fryslân: Friesland
Ljouwert: Leeuwarden
Skiermûntseach: Schiermonnikoog
Skylge: Terschelling

Map 5   The Frisian-speaking areas

(Skiermûntseach), in the Netherlands, with some 400,000 speakers; (ii) East Frisian (sometimes referred to as Saterlandic), around the villages of Ramsloh, Strücklingen and Scharrel in Saterland, near Oldenburg in Lower Saxony, in NW Germany (about 1,000 speakers); and (iii) North Frisian (Frasch), on the islands of Sylt (Söl), Föhr (Feer), Amrum (Omram), Hooge and Heligoland (Deät Lun) and part of the west coast of Schleswig-Holstein in northern Germany, south of the Danish border (9,000 speakers).

Periodization

The history of Frisian is usually divided into three periods; (i) Old Frisian, up to 1500; (ii) Middle Frisian, from 1500 to 1800; (iii) Modern Frisian, from 1800 to the present.

Old Frisian

During the Roman period, as we know from the works of Pliny, Tacitus and Ptolemy, *Frisia Magna* extended from the Rhine to the Weser. Of the language of that period, nothing remains other than a few problematic runic inscriptions (see ***Runes**).

Throughout the Middle Ages, Frisian trade flourished across the *Mare Frisicum* and traces of extensive contact with the Anglo-Saxon (see under ***English**) and ***Scandinavian languages** can be found in the Frisian language today. From the 7th c. onwards, the Frisians began to settle on the Danish islands, moving later on to the coast of Schleswig, which in due course led to the separate development of North Frisian. From the year 695, when Willebrord became the first bishop of the Frisians in Utrecht, they were Christianized and were subsequently incorporated into the Carolingian empire. Frisian law and liberty were codified in 802 in Charlemagne's *Lex Frisionum*. In Alfrid's Life of Liudger (9th c.), the blind bard Bernlef is mentioned but of the oral literature of his days nothing has survived.

The main body of Old Frisian texts is preserved in a number of manuscript codices in Latin script, dating from the 13th to the 16th centuries and containing legal documents such as statutes, charters, letters and contracts. The language of these documents has some characteristic literary features (rhythm, alliteration, metaphor) and they also contain interesting non-legal material such as sagas, riddles and a fragment of a psalm translation.

From the 13th c. onwards there was steady geographical, social and functional decline of Frisian, under pressure from its continental neighbours, the emerging ***German** and ***Dutch** languages. In Germany, East Frisian was largely ousted by Low German in the 15th c. In the Netherlands, where Frisian, Saxon and Frankish elements merged into what eventually became the Dutch language, the West Frisian language area was gradually reduced to the present-day province of Friesland, which was incorporated into the Habsburg Empire in 1524. In the domain of public administration this led to the complete replacement of Frisian by Dutch; the last official document in Frisian dates from 1573.

Middle Frisian

In the Middle Frisian period (1500–1800), the East and North Frisian dialects survived as spoken vernaculars while Low German continued to expand. The West Frisians joined the Dutch Republic and were faced, in the 17th c., with the rise of Holland and Amsterdam as the new economic, political, cultural and linguistic centre of gravity. Along with intense cultivation and promotion of the Dutch language, this generated in Holland a persistent tradition of ridicule aimed at Frisian and Frisian-speakers. Within the federal Dutch Republic, however, Friesland retained its sovereignty. It had its own centre of culture and government in the capital, Leeuwarden (Ljouwert), and a centre of learning, from 1585 to 1811, in the University of Franeker (Frjentsjer).

The linguistic situation in Friesland from the late 16th c. onwards was one of functional and social diglossia. Dutch was the language of law, of public administration, and of the upper strata of society. In the towns, we find the early beginnings of a Dutch–Frisian creole, the so-called *Stedsk* or 'Town Frisian', which is really a Dutch dialect with a Frisian substrate. Dutch also became the language of the Church, especially after the promulgation of the Dutch State Bible of 1637. At the same time, West Frisian continued to be in daily use as the spoken vernacular of the common people in the countryside, which was protected by its geographical isolation.

An important development in this period is the coming of age of West Frisian literature. The central figure is the Renaissance poet Gysbert Japicx (1603–66), who adapted the models of his contemporaries in Dutch Golden Age literature and set out to emulate their efforts at language cultivation. His *Fryske Rymlerije* ('Frisian Poetry') (1668) demonstrated that Frisian could very well be used for literary and cultural expression, and constitutes the high point of Middle Frisian literature. Japicx's work established a clear supradialectal literary standard for West Frisian and has been an inspiration for all subsequent revivals of Frisian literature in the 19th and 20th centuries.

In the 18th c. Frisian literature went into decline. Intellectuals like the Frisian noblemen Willem and Onno Zwier van Haren became leading authors in Dutch, starting a long line of authors from Friesland who have made major contributions to Dutch literature in later centuries. In 1795 the old federal structure of the Dutch Republic gave way to a new unitary state, which put an end to Frisian sovereignty. From then on, Dutch was strongly promoted as the national standard language.

Modern Frisian (East and North Frisian)

In the Modern Frisian period, the East Frisians in Saxony were incorporated into Prussia in 1815, followed in 1866, after three wars over Schleswig-Holstein, by the North Frisians. For both, the main trend since then has been a shift from speaking Frisian first to Low German and then to High German. As a result, East Frisian, which died out on the German islands at the beginning of the 20th c., is now on the verge of extinction in Saterland. In North Friesland, the shift to German has been exacerbated by a range of social factors: the lack of a written standard, with North Frisian divided into ten different, mutually unintelligible dialects; its general lack of prestige and its absence from the mass media and the schools; the need to emigrate in search of employment; the large influx of non-Frisian-speakers, which has made German the dominant lingua franca; the complex patterns of multilingualism involving North Frisian, Danish, Jutish and Low German in linguistic competition with High German, the national standard language. While some poetry in North Frisian exists, notably the work of Jääns Mungard (1886–1944), one has to turn to a 19th-c. German novel, Theodor Storm's *Der Schimmelreiter* ('The Ghost Rider') (1888), for a literary account of North Frisian life in former times. Since 1964, the

North Frisian Institute in Bredstedt (Bräist) has been active in developing language courses, compiling dictionaries and describing dialects. But all in all, North Frisian, while still taught in about 30 schools, may well like East Frisian disappear within a generation.

Modern Frisian (West Frisian)

In the Netherlands, the modern development of West Frisian has taken a different course. Since 1814 Friesland has been a province of the Kingdom of the Netherlands and Dutch therefore was – and is – the dominant official language of administration, the law, the Church and education. It is also the dominant language in the upper strata of society. Within this basic political setting, however, the West Frisian language has managed more or less to hold its own. In this respect, it has greatly benefited from the activities of the Frisian Movement.

In the early 19th c. the Frisian Movement was part of the wider Germanic revival, inspired by Romanticism, after the Napoleonic era. Following Herder and the Grimm brothers, the *Selskip foar Fryske Tael en Skriftekennisse* ('Society for Frisian Language and Literature'), founded in 1844, advocated the use of Frisian in the theatre, song and literature, and in education. To this end, it took many important initiatives, such as the production of a grammar, an orthography, a dictionary, and a scholarly journal in Frisian. Throughout the 19th c. Frisian literature and popular culture flourished, with a succession of leading writers, in particular the Halbertsma brothers, Waling Dykstra, and Piter Jelles Troelstra. The classic work of this literature is the collection of poems and stories in the Halbertsmas' *Rimen en Teltsjes* ('Rhymes and Tales') (1871). There is a strong romantic impulse, too, in the famous hoax of *Thet Oera Linda Bok* ('The Oera Linda Book') (1872), a mythical account of Frisian origins in Atlantis, claiming that the ancient civilizations of Greece, India and the Incas all descended from the Frisians.

At the end of the 19th c. the world economic and agrarian crisis led to a mass exodus. Many Frisians emigrated to the USA, many found employment in Amsterdam or in the Dutch colonial empire in the East Indies (now Indonesia). The poet and politician Troelstra left Friesland to become leader, from 1897 until 1925, of the new national Labour Party in the Dutch parliament.

In Friesland, the early 20th c. brought the Young Frisian Movement of 1915, led by Douwe Kalma. The renewed efforts for cultural, linguistic and political rights for the Frisians achieved a number of successes: in 1928 the Centre for Frisian Language Learning, AFUK, was founded, in 1933 the New Testament was translated into Frisian, in 1937 Frisian was recognized as an optional school subject, and in 1938 the *Fryske Akademy* was founded in Leeuwarden as a centre for research into Frisian language, culture, history, law and folklore.

During the Second World War, the Nazi occupiers managed to seduce a few Frisian nationalists with promises of Frisian autonomy, but on the whole the Frisian movement steered clear of these delusions. After the war, it took the Frisian language riots of 1951 to restart the process of recognition that had begun earlier in the century. This has led to a gradual recognition of Frisian in education (1955), the courts (1956), the churches (in the 1970s), and in government and administration (1986). Frisian is now the second official language in the Netherlands (1970). In these various domains, official recognition is followed up by an active language policy, prepared with the help of advice from the Frisian Language Board, established in 1984. Frisian language courses and teaching materials are produced; there is a new official orthography (1980); the Fryske Akademy is publishing an 18-volume scholarly dictionary of the language and regularly carries out sociolinguistic research into the changing situation of Frisian in the province. In 1992 Frisian was recognized as an official minority language in the EU and the Fryske Akademy is actively involved in the EU Mercator-Education network.

The 20th c. has brought a lively production of literature in Frisian: novels, short stories, poetry, literary criticism, essays, children's books, and translations of Shakespeare, Shelley and Lewis Carroll, together with recordings of oral literature. Since 1969, one has been able to ring *Operaesje Fers* ('Operation Verse') and listen to a Frisian poem on the telephone. Today about 100 books in Frisian are published each year, which is quite high given the size of the Frisian-speaking community. A leading figure in post-war literature was the poet, critic and novelist Anne Wadman (1919–97) whose bilingual last novel *De frou yn'e flesse* ('The Woman in the Bottle') (1988) tells the story of a Dutch boy who falls in love with his teacher of Frisian, thus thematizing the eroticism of learning Frisian in contemporary society.

In the field of Frisian culture, new initiatives are being taken to strengthen the Frisian profile. Early in 1995, Leeuwarden presented itself as the cultural capital of the Frisians, with the production of the first Frisian opera, *Rixt*. Recent years have seen the success of two full-length Frisian films, *The Dream* (1987) and *The Lighthouse* (1994), both made by Pieter Verhoeff. In many parts of the province, local theatre groups are keeping alive the tradition of Frisian popular theatre. And on the Internet we find the *Digitale Regio Fryslân* (at http://utopia.knoware.nl/users/fryslan/frysk/index.htm).

Present situation

In stark contrast to these developments in Frisian culture, literature and language policy, a number of sweeping demographic and socio-economic changes that have taken place since the war cannot fail to have an impact on the situation of the language. Modern transport and communications have ended the traditional geographical isolation of the province. There is a continuing large influx of Dutch-speakers, now amounting to 25% of the population of the province, both in the towns and in the traditionally Frisian-speaking countryside. About one and a half million tourists per year visit the province. In the growing number of linguistically mixed marriages, parents increasingly give up using Frisian with the children and turn instead to the more prestigious Dutch. In any case, Frisian is mostly a spoken language and, although there is a written standard, only 10% of Frisians can write Frisian. The media offer little help: Frisian TV is in financial difficulties and the two provincial newspapers only carry one page each per week in Frisian.

As a result of all these factors, there is now a situation of unequal and unstable bilingualism in a linguistically heterogeneous and increasingly Dutch-dominated society. While native speakers of Frisian still constitute the majority of the population, many of them expect a further shift to Dutch in the near future. Dutch words and constructions are seeping into Frisian. Some Frisians are abandoning their mother tongue altogether while in the towns Frisian is giving way to an urban Dutch dialect with some Frisian features.

The clash between this ongoing Dutchification of Frisian society and, on the other hand, the cultural developments and policies outlined above has generated in recent years a lively debate on how to meet these challenges to the future of the Frisian language. After all, what good is it to give official recognition to Frisian in education when one in eight schools can opt out and most schools spend only one hour per week on Frisian? Rather than fighting for recognition of Frisian in formal and institutional domains, should not the Frisians invest more in their own community, in Frisian nursery education, in positive action to stimulate the intergenerational transmission of their language in the family, the village, the neighbourhood? The key question that emerges is how to counter the ongoing language shift. What initiatives can be taken and what is the most effective action to enhance Frisian language, literature and culture when the Frisian-speaking community that is its breeding-ground is being eroded by the combined forces of modernization, urbanization, immigration, tourism, market forces and the ever-increasing centralization of the Netherlands? Will Frisian language and culture be able to survive and adapt to these changing circumstances?

These are crucial questions. On the positive side we note that there is still today, after four centuries of bilingualism and increasing domination of Dutch, a solid core of 300,000 native speakers of Frisian. This clearly testifies to the tenacity of language as a long-term factor in history which seems no less important than long-term trends in material culture, and it provides a basis for the revitalizing and refocusing of Frisian language policy. It will be interesting to see how the Frisian Movement meets these challenges in the next century.

Bremmer, R. H. et al. (eds) 1990. *Aspects of Old Frisian Philology*. Amsterdam.

Breuker, Ph. H. et al. 1996. *Orientation in Frisian Studies*. Leeuwarden and Amsterdam.

—— and Salverda, R. (eds) 1994. *The Frisians. Language, Literature, Cultural History* (= *Dutch Crossing*, 18.2). London.

Feitsma, A. 1989. A history of the Frisian linguistic norm. In Fodor. I. and Hagège, C. (eds), *Language Reform: History and Future*, Hamburg, vol. 4, 247–72.

Fishman, J. A. 1991. The cases of Basque and Frisian. In Id., *Reversing Language Shift*, Clevedon, 149–86.

Gorter, D. (ed.) 1987. The sociology of Frisian (= *International Journal of the Sociology of Language*, 64).

—— et al. (eds.) 1988. *Language in Friesland*. Leeuwarden.

—— and Jonkman, R. J. 1995. *Taal yn Fryslân: op 'e nÿ besjoen* ('Language in Friesland Revisited'). Ljouwert.

Hoekstra, J. and Tiersma, P. M. 1994. Frisian. In König, E. and van der Auwera, J. (eds), *The Germanic Languages*, London, 505–31.

Markey, T. L. 1981. *Frisian*. The Hague.

Tiersma, P. M. 1985. *Frisian Reference Grammar*. Dordrecht.

Visser, W. 1985. *Frysk Wurdboek. Nederlânsk–Frysk* ('Frisian Dictionary. Dutch–Frisian). Drachten and Ljouwert.

Walker, A. G. H. 1980. North Frisia and linguistics. *Nottingham Linguistic Survey*, 4, no. 1: 1–30.

——— 1990. Frisian. In Russ, C. (ed.), *The Dialects of Modern German*, London, 1–30.

Ytsma, J. and De Jong, S. 1993. Frisian. In Extra, G. and Verhoeven, L. (eds), *Community Languages in the Netherlands*, Amsterdam, 29–49.

Zantema, J. W. 1984. *Frysk Wurdboek. Frysk–Nederlânsk* ('Frisian Dictionary. Frisian–Dutch'). Drachten and Ljouwert.

REINIER SALVERDA

Friulian (see under *Italy. III. Northern Italy*)

Fula (Fulani) (see under *Community languages (France)*)

G

Gaelic languages

One of the two surviving branches (the other being the ***Brittonic languages**) of the ***Celtic languages**, represented by ***Irish**, ***Scottish Gaelic** and ***Manx** (the last native speaker of which died in 1974). The term 'Goidelic languages' is also used.

Gaelic, Scottish, see *Scottish Gaelic*

Gagauz

A member of the Oghuz or southern branch of the ***Turkic languages**, Gagauz is sometimes thought to be of pre-Ottoman origin but the general view now is that it is basically a dialect of Ottoman ***Turkish** and that the supposed connections with the NW Turks are not substantial or that they came about because of the proximity of ***Tatar** and ***Nogay**. Gagauz is therefore to be seen as a Turkish dialect which achieved an exceptional linguistic and cultural position as a result of having come under far-reaching Slavonic influence, especially in its syntactic structure. The earlier view that Gagauz originated from the Pechenegs, whose name appears in Old Russian, Byzantine and Armenian sources and who spread across SE Europe in the 11th c., is now in doubt.

The Gagauz originally lived exclusively in Bulgaria and it was only in the 18th and 19th centuries that they migrated northwards to Bessarabia. They now live primarily in the southern part of the Republic of Moldavia (Moldova) and in SW Ukraine in the Izmail district. These areas included 197,768 Gagauz-speakers in 1989. There are also estimated to be some 7,000 speakers in scattered settlements in the Deli Orman district of NE Bulgaria and a further 4,000 in Macedonia. Some speakers are also thought to survive in the Romanian Dobruja. The Gagauz adopted Orthodox Christianity and for this reason are often called Christian Turks. It is not clear whether the Gagauz of SE Macedonia are defined linguistically on the basis of their dialect or because of their Christian religion.

Doerfer, G. 1959. Das Gagausische. In Deny, J. et al. (eds), *Philologiae Turcicae Fundamenta*, Wiesbaden, 260–72.
Yasemee, F. 1993. The Turkic peoples of Bulgaria. In Bainbridge, M. (ed.), *The Turkic Peoples of the World*, New York, 41–53.

WOLFGANG GRELLER

Galician

Galician (*galego*, and sometimes referred to in English as 'Gallego') is a member of the *Ibero-Romance subgroup of the *Romance languages and closely related to *Portuguese. It is spoken in the autonomous region of Galicia in NW Spain (see map 19), where it is an official language alongside Spanish.

Origins and early history

Galician may be considered the direct descendant of the Latin of the region. Portuguese is the other member of the Galician–Portuguese language group, representing the official language of the state of Portugal, having its origins in the county of Oporto and spreading south during the Reconquest. There is a dialect continuum between Galician and Portuguese, extending from the south of the provinces of Pontevedra and Ourense to at least the river Douro.

In the years immediately following the independence of the fledgeling Portuguese state from the kingdom of Leon-Castile in 1139, the county of Galicia to the north presumably experienced little linguistic change. However, the southward progress of the Reconquest in both Leon-Castile and the new kingdom of Portugal during the 12th and subsequent centuries inevitably brought a shift in the centre of gravity in the Peninsula. Galicia's geographical isolation from Leon-Castile, which may be held to have contributed to its relative freedom from the worst ravages of the Arab conquest and subsequent predations, now turned it into something of a backwater, with Portugal to the south and difficult mountains to the east. It is generally held that the local Galician nobility's failure to back the winning side in the civil war of the late 14th c. led to its wholesale replacement by outcomers, and that this, combined with a tendency to appoint non-Galician bishops, contributed to the growing influence of Castilian on the Galician of the documents produced in this century and the next.

The resolution of another political crisis at the end of the 15th c. began what are known in Galician circles as the Dark Ages (*os séculos escuros*). The Catholic monarchs subdued the fractious petty nobility, exporting them to fight in Granada and Italy, and Castilianized the Church and the law, with the result that by the second decade of the 16th c. Galician had disappeared completely from written sources, not to reappear in any significant form until the 19th-c. revival. There is the odd poem of circumstance in the 17th c., and the observations of enlightened clergymen in the 18th, but nothing else.

Nineteenth and twentieth centuries

The 19th-c. revival (*Rexurdimento*) followed a familiar pan-European pattern, having its roots in the Romantic discovery of a mythical Celtic past. In Galicia it had the side-effect of reawakening interest in the language (whose differences from Castilian were thought to be due to Celtic substrate influences – though the only clear evidence of this is to be found in toponyms), and the first text entirely in Galician ever to be printed was Rosalía de Castro's *Cantares gallegos* in 1863. There was subsequently a gradual increase in production in Galician, culminating in the cultural output of the *Nós* movement of the 1920s and 1930s and the political activities of the contemporaneous *Irmandades da fala* ('Brotherhoods of the language'); this spectrum of regionalist/autonomist activity generally had the installation of Galician in all domains as one of the planks in its platform.

The Franco revolt and subsequent victory in the Civil War (1936–9) put a stop to all regional aspirations, including those of Galicia, despite Franco's Galician origin. Galician, together with *Basque and *Catalan, was not permitted in any official sphere; but, presumably because the regime did not imagine that such elite interests would move the people to revolt, literary works were allowed to be published in all three languages.

Gradually, as the grip of the regime loosened, Galician started to gain ground, until, just before the death of the dictator in 1975, a chair of Galician and an Institute of the Galician Language (*Instituto da Lingua Galega*) were created in the region's only University at Santiago de Compostela, and a number of publishing houses were producing material in the language. After the transition to democracy, Galicia was declared a 'historical autonomy' in the Spanish federal state, and legislation was enacted, along similar lines to that in the Basque Country and Catalonia, to give Galician equal status with Castilian in the territory of the Galician Autonomous Region. Galician became a subject in the school curriculum in the region (though at this stage there was no attempt, officially at least, to teach other subjects through the medium of Galician), and citizens had the right to use it in their dealings with agencies of the regional government. The normalization of Galician in the media since Franco is represented by a television station broadcasting exclusively in Galician, a number of local and regional radio stations using only Galician or a Castilian/Galician mix, and various levels of installation of the language in the periodical/newspaper area, including a daily newspaper entirely in Galician.

The situation with regard to the spoken language is strikingly different. The power relations which Castilianized the upper layers of society did not have the same effect on the peasantry, with the result that Galician was the first language for the majority of the population until the middle of the 20th c. Galicia was in the same relationship to the rest of Spain for much of the 19th c. and the early part of the 20th as Ireland was to Great Britain: it was a primarily agricultural region which had hardly been touched by the Industrial Revolution, whose administrators and clergymen were despatched from Madrid, and whose aristocracy looked to the court there as the centre of fashion and manners. Bright young men sought their careers outside the province, and the Church ensured that, at least in theory, the priests were trained in the language of Empire. The poor emigrated in vast numbers throughout this period, in another Irish parallel, first to Latin America until the Second World War, then to Europe. In the post-Franco period, emigration has slowed to a trickle, and one has the impression that Galicians are now faced with the difficult task of ensuring that their own land provides a home for most of its people.

Orthography

Since the 19th-c. revival the orthography of Galician had been a matter of individual preference, though there was a more or less agreed norm used by the publishing house Galaxia. Inevitably, since this had been built up over the years, there were many inconsistencies and it was therefore necessary to standardize the orthography. This was finally achieved in 1982 in the form of norms agreed by the Royal Galician Academy and the *Instituto da Lingua Galega*, which followed the trend of the previous hundred years in adopting a basically Castilian system while expurgating from the lexicon all manner of hyper-Galicianist, Portuguesist and Castilian detritus. The resulting norms have not been uncontroversial, despite (or, more probably, because of) being accepted by the regional government and its many agencies, and there is still a sector which advocates orthographies with varying degrees of Portuguese-style solution.

Geographical extent and dialects

The language is spoken in the political region of Galicia, and in addition in a strip to the east of Galicia's borders with Asturias, Leon and Zamora. As to dialectology, Fernández Rei's detailed analysis is generally accepted, whereby Galician is divided into three main areas, north to south: Coastal, Central and Eastern. The principal differences between Standard Peninsular Portuguese and Galician are: the absence in Galician of voiced sibilants, e.g. *casa*, Gal. [kasa], Port. [kaza] 'house'; Gal. *pracer* [praθer], Port. *prazer* [prazer] 'pleasure'; Gal. *xenro* [ʃenro], Port. *genro* [ʒenro] 'son-in-law'; the lack in Galician of those Portuguese nasal vowels that result from the loss of intervocalic [n], e.g. (from *germanum*) Gal. *irmao* or *irmán*, Port. *irmão* 'brother'; the fact that Galician is largely stress-timed, in contrast to syllable-timed Portuguese; and certain differences in verb morphology, e.g. Gal. *dixo*, Port. *disse* '(he, she) said' (from Latin *dixit*).

Present situation

Although the pressures on Galician from Castilian have grown steadily stronger as the weakening Franco regime and its successor democracy have moved inexorably towards parity with the rest of Europe, all the surveys show that Galicians still claim a very high level of competence in Galician: more than 90% understand it, and around 60% actively speak it. Research has shown that the relationship to Castilian has changed significantly since the establishment of democracy and the achievement of official status for the language, moving from a situation in which Castilian was perceived as the 'High' variety to Galician's 'Low', to one in which a 'High' Galician exists alongside a 'High' Castilian, and in which there are either two 'Low' varieties, one Castilian, the other Galician, both suffering heavy interference from the other, or one 'Low' Galician, heavily contaminated by Castilian bombardment in the media.

Alvarez Blanco, R., Monteagudo, H. and Regueira, L. X. 1993. *Gramática galega*, 4th edn. Vigo.

Ares Vázquez, M. do C. et al. 1990. *Diccionario Xerais da Lingua* ('The Xerais Dictionary of the [Galician] Language'), 3rd edn. Vigo.

Fernández Rei, F. 1990. *Dialectoloxía da lingua galega*. Vigo.

Maia, C. de Azevedo 1986. *História do galego-portugués*. Coimbra.

Monteagudo, H. and Santamarina, A. 1993. Galician and Castilian in contact: historical, social, and linguistic aspects. In Posner, R. and Green, J. N. (eds), *Trends in Romance Linguistics and Philology*, Berlin, vol. 5, 117–73.

Normas ortográficas e morfolóxicas do idioma galego 1995. 12th edn. Vigo.

[Various authors] 1994. Galegisch. In Holtus, G., Metzeltin, M. and Schmitt, C. (eds), *Lexikon der Romanistischen Linguistik*, vol. 6.2, *Galegisch, Portugiesisch*, Tübingen, 1–129 (8 articles, 7 in Galician, 1 in German.)

DAVID MACKENZIE

Gallego, see *Galician*

Gallo-Romance languages

A subgroup of the *Romance languages whose territory coincides broadly with that of modern France and consisting of *French, *Francoprovençal and *Occitan (including *Gascon, which can however be considered as a distinct language) (see map 6).

The Romans moved into the south of what is now France in the 2nd c. BC and, after a four-year campaign (125–121 BC) against the Ligurians and the Gauls, founded their first province in the area, the Provincia Narbonensis extending from Toulouse to the Alps. The rest of Gaul, as far as the Rhine and the present-day Low Countries, was conquered by Caesar in the Gallic War of 58–51 BC.

Northern Gaul was occupied by the Germanic-speaking Franks in the 5th c. Whereas the *Frankish language remained in the extreme north-east of the area, where one dialect of it survives as *Dutch and another as the *German dialects of the Rhineland (including Alsace and parts of Lorraine), over the greater part of the area the invaders, who had probably remained a minority, albeit a ruling minority, after doubtless a lengthy period of bilingualism abandoned their Germanic speech and adopted the Romance speech of the majority of the population which was to evolve into French. The Gallo-Romance of an area of central eastern France was to become Francoprovençal while that of the south evolved into the various Occitan dialects.

Though the concept of Gallo-Romance is widely accepted, the similarities

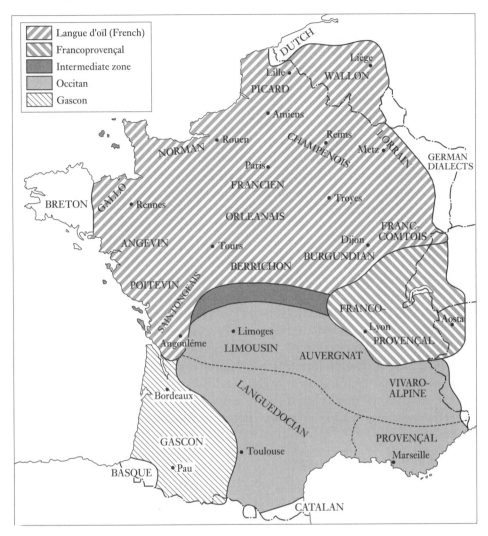

Map 6   The Gallo-Romance area. Inhabitants of those parts of France where languages other than French are spoken are in general either bilingual or else speak French only.

between the southernmost member of the group, Occitan, and of its neighbour to the south, ***Catalan**, which is generally classified as one of the ***Ibero-Romance languages**, are such that some scholars argue that it is unsatisfactory to separate the two in this way. A good case can be made out for regarding the Occitan–Catalan area as the central zone of a continuum stretching from the French-speaking area in the north-east to the Spanish- and Portuguese-speaking area in the south-west.

GLANVILLE PRICE

Gascon

Gascon, sometimes considered to be a dialect of ***Occitan**, is the variety of ***Gallo-Romance** spoken mainly in SW France (perhaps by the descendants of Aquitanians, whom Julius Caesar distinguished from the Gauls) (see map 6).

Earliest attestations

Although Gasconisms sporadically appear in 11th-c. Latin legal texts and arguably in the Occitan lyrics of the troubadour Marcabru (active 1130–49), they first achieve high density in three vernacular charters written between 1179 and 1186 in the Comminges region (Montsaunès, near Saliès-du-Salat, Haute-Garonne) and in ten lines of a multilingual poem (a *descort*) composed by the Provençal troubadour Raimbaut de Vaqueiras probably in the late 12th c.

Codification

The artificial written Gascon used in medieval administrative records (see above) betrays influence of Occitan, Low Latin and, eventually, French. The first Gascon literary writer to eschew Occitan was Pey de Garros of Lectoure, whose translations of the Psalms (1565) and *Poesias gasconas* (1567) reflect almost exclusively his native central dialect. Yet even today Gascon and Bearnese orthography is not fully standardized (for Bearnese, see below, 'Geographical spread and dialects'); neither the system (to some extent phonetically based) proposed by the Escole Gastoû Febus between 1900 and 1906 and used by Palay in his dictionary (1991, 1st edn 1932–4) nor the more etymologically based system proposed in 1952 by the Institut d'Estudis Occitans and generally adopted in Morà's concise dictionary (1994) has been universally adopted.

Gascon as a literary medium

In the decades following Garros's publications, Gascon baroque poets and, in Protestant Béarn, translators of biblical and Calvinist texts were prolific. Verdié's comic satires, Bladé's prose folk-tales and, in Béarn, Navarrot's political songs and Lalanne's short stories are highlights of a 19th-c. literary renaissance continued in the 20th c. with Palay, Casebone, Camelat, Manciet, P. Bec and Sabalòt among others.

Geographical spread and dialects

Geographically, Gascon occupies an approximate triangle bounded by the Atlantic, the Pyrenees (minus the northern Pays Basque but extending into the Val d'Aran in Catalonia), and the rivers Dordogne (as far as Libourne), Garonne and Ariège. Between the Dordogne and the Garonne, the parishes of La Petite-Gavacherie have, since 1456, formed a pocket of French immigration from Saintonge and Poitou. Gascon isoglosses have, it seems, hardly moved since the late 15th c.

Occasional dialectalisms in medieval Gascon notarial records suggest that there were already several regional varieties, the most distinctive being those geographically furthest from Languedocian, namely Bearnese and the *parlar negre* ('obscure idiom') of the Landes. Other dialects occur in the Médoc, Bazadais, Albret, Lomagne, Comminges, Couserans, Val d'Aran and Armagnac.

Interrelationship with other languages

Gascon differs from Occitan by its greater affinity with ***Ibero-Romance** and in the greater influence exercised on its vocabulary by ***Basque**, which it must have largely displaced in some areas by the early Middle Ages. With Ibero-Romance, Gascon shares a wide range of lexis and some phonological features: Latin *f* > [h], e.g. *filium* 'son' > *hilh* (cf. Castilian *hijo*); loss of intervocalic *-n-*, e.g. *luna* 'moon' > *lua* (as in Portuguese); reduction of *mb* > [m], *nd* > [n], e.g. Celtic *cumba* 'valley' > *coma* (as in Catalan), *vendere* 'to sell' > *béne* (cf. northern Catalan *venre*); preservation of [kw] and [gw] as in Ibero-Romance, e.g. *quando* 'when' > *quan* [kwan] (cf. Castilian *cuándo*, Portuguese *quando*), Germanic *wardon* > *guardar* [gwa . . .] 'to watch, guard'.

Aquitanian or Old Basque lexical borrowings include terms designating plants, animals, landscape, husbandry, climate and social life. The absence of Saracen settlement in the region meant that Gascon vocabulary and place-names show no direct borrowings from Arabic (cf. ***Occitan**).

Numbers of speakers

With Béarn, Gascony covers all or part of nine *départements*, today numbering about 3,106,000 inhabitants. There are no accurate surveys or reliable unofficial estimates of how many have some knowledge of Gascon or use it daily. However, a 1994 survey of 1,000 interviewees in 53 Bearnese-speaking localities in the Pyrénées-Atlantiques indicated that 41.3% of the local population understood Bearnese and that 26.2% could speak it (14% with fluency), although only 11% did so daily. In the Val d'Aran in 1986, of a total population of 5,299 only 6.8% knew no Gascon; an estimated 3,100 (58.5%) spoke it regularly.

Role and official status

In Béarn, Gascon was used in parliamentary decrees until the province was annexed by France in 1620, and it survived in customary laws (*Fors*) and governmental debates until 1789. Today, despite United Nations and European Community moves to protect minority languages, in France (unlike the Val d'Aran) little official status is accorded to Henri IV de Navarre's first language, which Montaigne valued and Du Bartas occasionally used. Nevertheless, following the *loi Deixonne* (1951 – see ***Occitan**, 'Role and official status') and subsequent modest reforms due to pressure from the Institut d'Estudis Occitans, Gascon is taught, albeit sometimes only nominally, in local state primary and secondary schools and studied at French universities. The first teachers' training certificates (CAPES) in Gascon were awarded in 1992; and more recently, François Bayrou, the Bearnese-speaking French Minister for Education, moved to support Gascon and Occitan in education and the media (see ***Occitan**). The language is broadcast, if sometimes intermittently, from local radio stations and occasionally on regional TV from Toulouse. At least four regional newspapers print occasional Gascon items, and several young singers and bands produce recordings of popular and folk songs in Gascon. An approved Gascon Roman Catholic liturgy appeared in 1973, followed by a commercially available recording of a Gascon mass celebrated by the Archbishop of Auch on 31 August 1980 at the abbey of Flaran (Gers).

Baldinger, K. 1958. La position du gascon entre la Galloromania et l'Ibéroromania. *Revue de linguistique romane*, 22:241–92.

Birabent, J. -P. and Salles-Loustau, J. 1989. *Memento grammatical du gascon*. Pau.

Grosclaude, M. 1977. *Lo Gascon lèu e plan* ('Good Gascon by the Rapid Method') (with two audio-cassettes). Paris.

Kristol, A. M. and Wüest, J. Th. 1985. *Drin de tot. Travaux de sociolinguistique et de dialectologie béarnaises*. Bern.

Morà, P. 1994. *Diccionari occitan–francés segon los parlars de Gasconha* ('Occitan–French Dictionary Based on the Dialects of Gascony'). Gradignan.

Palay, S. 1991. *Dictionnaire du béarnais et du gascon modernes*, 3rd edn (1st edn, 1932–4). Paris.

Rohlfs, G. 1977. *Le Gascon: études de philologie pyrénéenne*, 3rd edn. Tübingen.

Séguy, J. et al. 1954–86. *Atlas linguistique et ethnographique de la Gascogne*, 6 vols. Paris.

P. V. DAVIES

Gaulish

An extinct member of the *Celtic branch of *Indo-European. Its exact position within the Celtic family tree is a much-debated issue (see *Continental Celtic). The surviving documents may be dated approximately to between the late 3rd c. BC and the 4th c. AD. Most texts cannot be accurately dated. There are indications of dialect differences.

Gaulish inscriptions have been found throughout present-day France – except notably in Aquitaine (see *Basque) – and in northern Italy. It is possible that the Gaulish language was spoken further north (Belgium, southern part of the Netherlands) and east (southern Germany, Switzerland). The spread of the Gaulish language is generally believed to be connected with the spread of the Iron Age La Tène culture (5th c. BC onwards).

Our knowledge of Gaulish derives from a number of sources: the few Gaulish loan-words in *French; Gaulish words, personal and tribal names and toponyms, in Greek and Latin sources; most importantly, the hundreds of Gaulish inscriptions. Many inscriptions consist of only a few words (often names) in stereotyped phrases; many are fragmentary.

The six inscriptions from northern Italy are written in the 'Lugano alphabet' (see *Lepontic). Two of the three monumental inscriptions on stone are bilingual, Gaulish–Latin: the funerary inscription from Todi (Umbria) and the Vercelli dedication (eastern Piedmont). The inscriptions seem to date from a time when the political and linguistic influence of Rome was already strong in northern Italy (late 3rd c. BC or later).

Gaulish inscriptions in Greek script are found mainly in the Rhône delta. They date from the end of the 3rd c. BC to the beginning of the 1st c. AD. The use of Greek script originated in the Greek colony of Massilia (Marseille). About 70 inscriptions on stone (funerary inscriptions and dedications) have been found. There are approximately 220 inscriptions on pottery (mostly brief fragments).

Gaulish inscriptions in Latin script, which date from the period after the conquest of Gaul by Caesar (52 BC), have been found mainly in the centre of present-day France. There are approximately 15 brief inscriptions (funerary and dedicatory monuments) on stone. Extensive fragments of a calendar, dating back to the 2nd c. AD, have been found at Coligny (Ain). The ancient centres of pottery industry at La Graufesenque, Lezoux and Banassac have yielded numerous potters' stamps and accounts, containing mainly names of potters, a few technical terms, and numerals, partly in Gaulish and partly in Latin. Other important documents are spindle-whorls containing brief erotic messages (mainly around Autun); a number of short inscriptions on pottery; and the magic charms for the curing of illnesses in Marcellus of Bordeaux (4th–5th c. AD).

Between 1970 and 1985 three longer inscriptions in Latin cursive script were found. The fragmentary Lezoux Plate (around 50 words) may contain a list of moral maxims. The small lead tablet of Chamalières (over 50 words; early 1st c. AD) and an inscription, also on lead, from l'Hospitalet-du-Larzac (approximately 200 words; *c.* AD 100) contain magic imprecations. The interpretation of these texts presents numerous difficulties.

Duval, P. -M. (ed.) 1985– . *Recueil des inscriptions gauloises*, 3 vols (2 more planned). Paris.
Lambert, P. -Y. 1994. *La langue gauloise*. Paris.
Meid, W. 1992. *Gaulish Inscriptions*. Budapest.

PETER SCHRIJVER

Genoese (see *Ligurian (Genoese)* under *Italy. III. Northern Italy*)

Georgian (see under *Caucasian languages. VI. Georgian*)

German

A member of the West Germanic (WGmc) subgroup of the ***Germanic languages** and most closely related to ***Dutch**, ***English**, ***Frisian** and ***Yiddish**. In Europe, it is spoken by over 100 million people and is the national language in Germany, Austria and Liechtenstein, a co-national language in Switzerland (with French, Italian and Romansh) and Luxembourg, and an indigenous minority language in France, Belgium, Holland, Denmark, Italy, Poland, the Czech Republic, Slovakia, Hungary, Romania and other countries of eastern Europe.

Documentary evidence and periodization

If we neglect some 25 early runic inscriptions (see ***Runes**) dating from the 6th and 7th centuries, which can be regarded as reflecting a very early form of German, the earliest manuscript documents may be assigned to the second half of the 8th c. This earliest period in the history of German (Old High German, abbreviated OHG, *c.*750 to *c.*1050) is characterized by the dominant position of Latin as the normal written medium. After a hiatus in the documentation of German in the mid-11th c., German sources increase markedly in number and scope. The Middle High German (abbreviated MHG, *c*.1050–*c*.1350) and Early New High (or Early Modern) German (abbreviated ENHG, *c*.1350–*c*.1750) periods are characterized by the gradual replacement of Latin and the emergence, in the later period, of the modern standard. The modern language is conventionally termed New High (or Modern) German. Germany pioneered the technique of printing from movable type, first in Latin (Gutenberg's 42-line Bible, 1452–6) and then in German (Ulrich Boner's *Edelstein* and Johannes von Tepl's *Ackermann aus Böhmen*, both 1461), although the absolute number of German titles did not exceed those in Latin until well into the 17th c. The German equivalent of *Books in Print (Verzeichnis lieferbarer Bücher*, VLB) now lists between 60,000 and 70,000 new titles annually.

German as a literary language

German has a rich and varied literature from the early Middle Ages onwards, to which it is impossible to do justice in this limited space. Literary and linguistic developments often go hand-in-hand and inclusion in this account implies an important linguistic contribution. It must always be borne in mind with regard to the history of literature and language alike that attempts to group and periodize the evidence can do no more than point to interesting connections. It is also important to recognize that German-speaking peoples, while retaining their regional character, have always been united by a common language and culture which has transcended political arrangements.

The beginnings of German literature were fostered by the Christianization of the German tribes and the adoption of Latin. A few fragments of Germanic epic survive (notably *Hildebrandslied* 'The Lay of Hildebrand'), but these are insignificant beside examples of the genre in Old English and Icelandic, and most German writing in the OHG period consists of translations and adaptations of Latin texts. Of the products of Irish and Anglo-Saxon as well as Frankish-Roman monastic foundations, the work of the Isidore school, which rendered a series of difficult Latin texts into idiomatic German prose, and of Notker III of St Gallen, who found successful translations for many Latin concepts, are particularly noteworthy. There is also a German literature in Latin, e.g. Roswitha of Gandersheim (*c*.935–after 973), Ekkehart I of St Gallen (died 973). The subsequent history of German literature down to the modern period may be characterized as a slow emancipation from the dominant position of Latin as the standard literary language and the use of German in an increasing number of text-types and genres (first verse, then drama and prose).

After a lacuna in the German literary tradition in the mid-11th c., the early MHG period is characterized by a new beginning and noteworthy linguistic production in the Austrian monastic foundations of the south-east. The texts are mostly religious in character: Frau Ava, the authoress of a life of Christ (*c*.1120), is the first poetess in the German language. The 12th c. saw the growth of more secular genres, a development reflected in the Latin sources too (*Carmina Burana*, 13th c.). The first secular epic in rhyming couplets was written on the basis of a French text (Alberich de

Besançon) by a monk, Pfaffe Lamprecht (*c*.1140), who a little later translated the French *Chanson de Roland*. French also furnished the model for the first prose tale (*Lanzelet*, *c*.1220). The major German monuments of the high Middle Ages – the so-called 'classical' MHG period – are lyric and epic poetry, the products of courtly society with important lexical influence from France and the Low Countries, but they should not be seen simply as the German reworking of French originals. The lyric poems of Der von Kürenberg (*fl. c*.1170–5), probably the earliest of the *Minnesänger* ('Singers of Courtly Love'), and 140 others including Walther von der Vogelweide (*c*.1170–*c*.1230), are preserved in the sumptuous *Manessische Liederhandschrift*, now in the University Library in Heidelberg. The courtly epics of Hartmann von Aue (1160/70 to after 1210), Wolfram von Eschenbach (*c*.1170–*c*.1220) and Gottfried von Straßburg (died *c*.1210) drew on the tales of King Arthur and the Matter of Britain which inspired medieval French writers. The major surviving heroic epic is an anonymous reworking of the cycle of sagas surrounding the figure of Dietrich von Bern (i.e. Theoderic [the Great] of Verona – see *Gothic), the *Nibelungenlied*.

The period of the late Middle Ages, characterized by increasing urbanization and the social upheavals typified by the effects of the Black Death, is often seen as one of degeneration and decay, but it witnessed the beginnings of the drama as a German genre (Easter and Christmas plays developed from antiphonal chants) and also the growth of prose and an increasingly urban readership. For example, the translation of Aquinas's *Summa Theologica* (after 1270) brought a key scholastic text to German readers; the prose versions of courtly romances bear witness to the increasing market for German-language material to be read. The mystics of the 14th c., e.g. the Dominican Meister Eckhart (1260–1327/8), Johannes Tauler (*c*.1300–61) and Heinrich Seuse (1293–1366), put German on an equal footing with Latin for the first time, and enriched the language especially in the area of word-formation (abstract derivations in *-ung*, *-heit*, *-schaft*, etc.). They and others – e.g. Claus Cranc's translation of the Prophets (*c*.1350), the first prose translation of a biblical text in German – may be seen as preparing the ground for the reformers of the 16th c., most notably Martin Luther (1483–1546), who dominates the output of the Reformation period, but also figures such as Martin Bucer (1491–1551) and Johann Eberlin von Günzberg (*c*.1470–1531), probably the greatest German stylist of the period after Luther himself.

In common with other Renaissance vernaculars, the problem for literary German in the 16th c. was primarily one of vocabulary: as the prestige (inter)national literary medium, Latin offered an immediate model and source of new words. Humanist writers such as Jakob Wimpfeling (1450–1528) continued to translate Latin, Greek and other works into German, partly as a means of refining the language. Some wrote original works in German, even Johannes Reuchlin (1455–1522), the most celebrated Hebrew scholar of his day. Yet others published works in both languages: for example, Johannes Aventinus (Turmaier) (1477–1534) translated his own *Annales ducum Boiariae* ('Annals of the Dukes of Bavaria', 1521) into German between 1522 and 1533. The most successful textbook of the age, Sebastian Münster's (1488–1552)

Cosmographia ('Description of the World', Basle, 1500) was a compilation of largely translated sources. The immensely popular moral satire Sebastian Brant's (1457–1521) *Narrenschiff* ('Ship of Fools') of 1494 was one of the few works to be written first in German. Translations fostered indigenous production, which admittedly drew inspiration from classical sources, Arthurian romances and the like. Martin Luther's most influential work is also a translation – the last edition of his Bible translation which he corrected himself appeared in 1545 – and this, his catechism and other theological writings accounted for a considerable proportion of German printed books in the early 16th c. His influence on other literary production of the period is plain, whether this was broadly supportive as in the plays, prose dialogues and lyric poetry of Hans Sachs (1494–1576) or gave voice to dissent as in the satires of Thomas Murner (1475–1537). Two representatives of the SW German Reformation, Jörg Wickram (*c.*1500–62) and Johann Fischart (1546–90), provide the most significant examples of the new genre of the prose novel. Indeed, German was used in almost every area of literary activity: to use R. E. Keller's terms, the functional bilingualism of the Middle Ages had given way to a bilingualism of the educated.

The position of German declined in the 17th c., largely due to the effects of the Counter-Reformation. Education in both the Catholic south and the Protestant north returned to the use of Latin. Indeed, Latin remained the language of learning in the 17th and first half of the 18th c., while French became the language of society and German held its position as the language of literature. When the philosopher Christian Thomasius (1655–1728) announced a lecture course in German at Leipzig in 1687, he was persuaded to resign and move to the new university of Halle. By 1711, most Halle professors were lecturing in German, including Christian Wolff (1679–1754), whose pupils were appointed to almost all the chairs of philosophy in Protestant Germany, and who did more than anyone else to establish a system of mathematical and philosophical terminology in German. Leibniz (1646–1714), the greatest German thinker of the age, wrote mainly in either Latin or French, but encouraged his contemporaries to use German, reflecting the aspirations of many intellectuals. The excellence of their 'ancient, original and heroic language' (*Uhralte Haubt- und Heldensprache*) – original because it was held by contemporaries to be directly descended from the post-Babel confusion – was trumpeted in the ten eulogies of Justus Georgius Schottelius's (1612–76) influential *Ausführliche Arbeit von der Teutschen HaubtSprache* ('Complete Description of the Original German Language', Brunswick, 1663). Schottel and his contemporaries cultivated German in language societies, the earliest of which, the *Fruchtbringende Gesellschaft* ('fructifying society') (founded 1617 and modelled on the Florentine Accademia della Crusca, founded 1582), aimed to preserve the High German language and to cultivate the best pronunciation and the purest forms in writing and poetry. Its membership included eminent aristocrats such as its patron Prince Ludwig von Anhalt-Köthen (whose residence at Halle the author of *The High Dutch Minerva*, the first known grammar of German written in English, called 'the very Athens of the most refined Wits and language'), and many of the leading writers of the age such as Andreas Gryphius

(1616–64) and Martin Opitz (1597–1639). One writer who does not appear to have been associated with the *Sprachgesellschaften* was Johann Jakob Christoffel von Grimmelhausen (1621/2–76), whose novels of the colourful Thirty Years War characters Simplicissimus, Springinsfeld and Courage have probably best stood the test of time.

The language problem of the 17th c., as expressed by Martin Opitz in his theoretical *Buch von der Deutschen Poeterey* ('Book concerning German poetry', Breslau, 1624), concerned firstly the question of the norm versus regional forms of the language, and secondly the purity of the language in the face of Latin, French, Spanish and other foreign loans, although it should be noted that the thrust of the book concerns the application of the rules of rhetoric in German. Leibniz demanded three qualities of a language: *Reichthum* ('richness', i.e. self-sufficiency in vocabulary), *Reinigkeit* ('purity', i.e. perspicuity and regularity) and *Glanz* ('elegance', i.e. of style). In the hands of writers of the next century such as Friedrich Gottlob Klopstock (1724–1803), Gotthold Ephraim Lessing (1729–81), Christoph Martin Wieland (1733–1815), Johann Wolfgang von Goethe (1749–1832) and Johann Christoph Friedrich Schiller (1759–1805), this ideal was undoubtedly achieved. Schottel had already recognized the supraregional nature of *Hochdeutsch* ('High German') and affords some priority to 'Meißnisch' (the educated usage of Leipzig, Merseburg, Dresden and Wittenberg, but not the rural dialects), a view which is essentially repeated by Johann Christoph Gottsched (1700–66) in his *Deutsche Sprachkunst nach den Mustern der besten Schriftsteller des vorigen und itzigen Jahrhunderts* ('A German Grammar Based on the works of the Authorities of both this and the previous Century') (Leipzig, 1748) and by Johann Christoph Adelung (1732–1806) in his *Umständliches Lehrgebäude der Deutschen Sprache* ('A Comprehensive Grammar of the German Language') (1782), whose works became widely used and were declared obligatory in the schools of nearly all German regions. It is perhaps also significant that many major writers of the period lived and worked in the East Central German area, and also the philosophers Thomasius and Wolff. Adelung's dictionary (see above) was the first comprehensive, scholarly dictionary of German and was used as a reference work by eminent literary figures such as Goethe and Schiller.

Goethe's influence in particular was so pervasive that much of 19th-c. German literature can be seen as an imitation of, extension of, or reaction to his work. Certainly, 19th-c. writers were equipped with a language of great expressive power which gradually became common currency among educated people and has remained a standard throughout the 20th c. The following are generally reckoned to be among the most significant in their respective periods, but the lists could easily be augmented:

Romanticism: Ernst Theodor Amadeus Hoffman (1776–1833), Heinrich von Kleist (1777–1811), Novalis [Friedrich von Hardenberg] (1772–1801), August Wilhelm Schlegel (1767–1845), Friedrich Schlegel (1772–1829), Ludwig Tieck (1773–1853);

Biedermeier (conservatives of the period 1820–1850): Franz Grillparzer (1791–1872), Nikolaus Lenau (1802–50), Eduard Mörike (1804–75), Annette von Droste-Hülshoff (1797–1848);

Junges Deutschland ('Young Germany') (liberal reformers of the period from 1830 until the 1848 Revolution): Georg Büchner (1813–37), Heinrich Heine (1797–1856), Friedrich Hebbel (1813–63);

Realism: Theodor Fontane (1819–98), Wilhelm Raabe (1851–1910), Gottfried Keller (1819–90), Theodor Storm (1817–88), Adalbert Stifter (1805–68);

Naturalism and its critics: Stefan George (1868–1933), Gerhart Hauptmann (1862–1946), Hermann Hesse (1877–1962), Hugo von Hofmannsthal (1874–1929), Christian Morgenstern (1871–1914), Rainer Maria Rilke (1875–1926), Stefan Zweig (1881–1942);

Since 1900: Bert(olt) Brecht (1898–1956), Franz Kafka (1895–1924), Heinrich Mann (1871–1950), Thomas Mann (1875–1955), Robert Musil (1880–1942).

Notable writers of the post-1945 era include: Heinrich Böll (1917–85), Friedrich Dürrenmatt (1921–), Max Frisch (1922–), Günter Grass (1927–), Uwe Johnson (1934–), Christa Wolf (1929–).

It is difficult to assess the output of the 19th and 20th centuries in terms of the effect it has had on the language, but it is tempting to say that the decisive influences on German in the modern period are no longer primarily literary, at least in the narrow sense. Figures from the mid-1980s suggest that some 10 million newspapers and over 12 million magazines were published every day in West Germany alone. In addition, the pervasive influence of English in written, visual and spoken media cannot be overlooked. The advent of television, especially the explosion of satellite channels, has presented the German-speaking viewing public with such a wide selection of largely excellently dubbed and original English-language programmes that it is bound to have an effect on the position of the literary language.

The emergence of the standard language

At the beginning of the ENHG period, writing in German was still relatively unusual: the function of the standard written language was exercised by Latin. German texts of the period may be characterized, in terms of orthography, grammar and lexis, as idiosyncratic, regional and non-standardized. In these regional languages, called *lantsprâchen* by contemporary MHG writers, the influence of spoken forms of the language can be readily inferred. The subsequent standardization process involved the emergence of a supraregional, written norm, largely independent of the spoken language. Indeed, the emergence of new colloquial varieties (*Umgangssprachen*), which encroach on the traditional dialects during the modern period, especially in urban areas, is largely due to the influence of the written language.

The emergence of the standard written language itself (*neuhochdeutsche Schriftsprache*) proceeded in two stages. The first was one of largely unconscious convergence, especially in texts intended to be read in other areas of Germany. In this process, the beginnings of which can be traced back to the end of the MHG period (*c*.1350), the opening decades of the 16th c. with the spread of the Reformation, the growth in book production and the reading public, the development of the towns and secular educational establishments, can be seen as particularly significant. We now know that all regional variants of German participated in the process and that the importance of East Central German and of Martin Luther have probably been overemphasized in the past. The second stage involved conscious standardization on the part of grammarians and lexicographers. Grammatical standardization began somewhat earlier (16th c.) than the restriction of regional lexical items, a range of which are still acceptable for some concepts (e.g. northern *Sonnabend*, southern *Samstag* 'Saturday'). Opinions differ as to when the standardization process as a whole was largely complete; 1650, a date much advanced in the literature, is almost certainly too early, as regional written forms are still evident, but the need for a written standard was recognized by that time (Schottel's *Ausführliche Arbeit*, 1663, see above). It is, however, more probable that a significant degree of standardization was achieved in the work of Johann Christoph Gottsched (*Deutsche Sprachkunst*, 1748, see above) and Johann Christoph Adelung (*Versuch eines vollständigen grammatisch-kritischen Wörterbuches der Hochdeutschen Mundart, mit beständiger Vergleichung der übrigen Mundarten, besonders aber der Oberdeutschen*: 'Prolegomena to a complete grammatical-critical dictionary of the High German dialect, with comprehensive comparison with the other dialects, but especially with Upper German', Leipzig, 1774–86, of which six editions were published up to 1818, the majority in Vienna).

Spelling reform was a concern of the 17th and 18th centuries, but the proposals of radical reformers such as Philipp von Zesen and Klopstock were rejected in favour of a more evolutionary approach, which, although it was broadly speaking based on phonetic principles, was tempered by considerations of etymology (e.g. NHG *Rad* [raːt] 'wheel', genitive *Rades* vs *Rat* [raːt] 'advice', genitive *Rates*), economy (e.g. unnecessary double consonants were expunged, so *unndt* became *und* 'and'), tradition (e.g. word-initial <v> was retained for [f] beside initial <f>) and clarity (e.g. NHG *Waise* 'orphan' vs *Weise* 'way', both [vaɪzə]). Again, it was Adelung's *Vollständige Anweisung zur deutschen Orthographie* ('Complete Handbook of German Orthography') (1788) which provided the spelling for the literary language of the 19th c. Philipp von Zesen was probably the most notable of a number of language reformers who introduced German words beside foreign loans. Some have survived (e.g. *Hochschule*, literally 'high-school', beside *Universität*, both meaning 'university'), but others never passed into general use. Further inconsistencies in the emerging standard were removed during the 19th c. Konrad Duden (1829–1911) published the first edition of his *Orthographisches Wörterbuch der deutschen Sprache* ('Orthographical Dictionary of the German Language') in 1880: the seventh edition (1902) incorporates the agreement of the Berlin conference on orthography (1901), and the latest modern edition (20th edn, 1991) is still regarded as the standard reference work. It is important to stress that the standardization process took place in the written medium: there is still no standard spoken German, except in so far as the written language is 'translated' into spoken form. Theodor Siebs's *Deutsche Bühnenaussprache* ('Pronunciation of the German Stage') has not been adopted by most speakers and the spoken language exhibits a broad spectrum of supraregionally accepted but diatopically restricted regional features.

Scripts

Apart from the few runic inscriptions, German has always been written in variants of the Latin alphabet. The earliest German was written in Anglo-Saxon (Insular) script or Early Caroline minuscule, which gradually gave way to the type known as Gothic. This in turn tended to be replaced by Roman script from the 15th c. onwards, although German *Kurrentschrift* (Gothic script) which had developed from the Gothic cursive continued to be taught in schools well into the 20th c., and books printed in Gothic type were common before the Second World War.

Geographical spread

In the pre-literary period, there is evidence for a southward movement of proto-German-speakers from the area on and around the Danish peninsula into areas of modern France and southern Germany where a variety of *Continental Celtic was spoken. Classical authors cannot always distinguish between Germans and Gauls. The period of the Great Migrations (*Völkerwanderung*) is traditionally said to begin with the destruction of the Ostrogothic kingdom in southern Russia (see *Gothic) by the Huns around the year AD 375. By the beginning of the literary period (8th c.) a Frankish kingdom had developed, the eastern portion of which, roughly from present-day Alsace and Lorraine to the Elbe, formed the nucleus of the medieval German-speaking area. During the Middle Ages the western border to France remained relatively stable, but German speakers gradually colonized what is now eastern Germany and then large portions of eastern Europe (*Ostkolonisation*). Before the Second World War, German-speaking enclaves were to be found as far east as the Baltic states and the Black Sea, but Germany's military defeat in 1945 resulted in large-scale transportation of native speakers to the west (or, in the case of the Volga Germans, to Siberia). During the 19th c. substantial numbers of German-speakers emigrated to North and South America, Algeria, Israel, Australia and New Zealand, Hawaii, and the then German colonies in Africa, such as present-day Tanzania and Namibia, where German is now either extinct or under threat from the major local languages.

Dialects

German dialects (see map 7) are conventionally divided, using the reflexes of the Second Sound Shift (see below) as a criterion, into a northern type (Low German, abbreviated LG), a southern type (Upper German, abbreviated UG) and a central type (Central German, abbreviated CG). The terms 'Upper' and 'Low' German reflect the predominant topography of these areas, the flat North German plain contrasting with the South German uplands. The major divisions (UG–CG–LG) also correlate broadly with distinctive realizations of the diminutive suffix, NHG

Map 7 German dialects. (i) The part of Switzerland indicated as German-speaking includes the bilingual Romansh-speaking areas (see maps 14 and 20). (ii) Areas of Belgium, France and Italy where a substantial proportion of the population is German-speaking are shaded. (iii) German-speaking areas to the east of Germany and Austria are not shown. (iv) For Frisian-speaking areas in north-western Germany, see map 5. (v) For the Sorbian-speaking area in eastern Germany, see map 18.

-chen or *-lein*, but it is usual to subdivide these dialect groupings further, using a variety of criteria.

The LG diminutive suffix is *-ken* [kən]. Roughly speaking, West LG is spoken in Schleswig-Holstein, Niedersachsen, the Lower Rhine area, Westphalia and Eastphalia, and is marked by a unitary plural ending *-(e)t: wi, gi, se maakt* (NHG *wir machen, ihr macht, sie machen*) 'we, you, they do'. The unitary plural ending in East LG, which is spoken in the rest of northern Germany up to the River Oder, is *-(e)n: wi, gi, se maaken*.

The CG form of the diminutive suffix is *-chen*, realized as [ʃə(n)]. West CG is spoken in the Rhineland, Rheinland-Pfalz, the Saarland, Hessen and the German-speaking areas of Lorraine, and is marked by the retention of initial [p] in words such as [pɛnɪŋ] NHG *Pfennig* 'penny'; in this position, the East CG dialects of Thuringia and Upper Saxony typically have initial [f], e.g. [fɛnɪʃ]. The term *Plattdeutsch*, or *Platt*, is sometimes used to indicate LG, but is used by speakers of CG as well to indicate their own dialects.

The UG diminutive suffixes contain [l]. West UG – diminutive suffix [li] – comprises Alemannic (the dialects of Switzerland, Alsace, Vorarlberg, most of Baden-Württemberg) and Swabian. East UG – diminutive suffix [ə(l)] – comprises the dialects of Bavaria and Austria, which linguists group together under the heading of Bavarian. UG has, in addition to western and eastern varieties, a northern variety spoken in northern Bavaria and adjacent parts of Baden-Württemberg. The urban centres here are Nuremberg, Regensburg and Würzburg, and the diminutive suffix is [la], [lɛ], [lɪ].

The major distinguishing criterion between the dialects is the incidence of the Second or High German Sound Shift. Broadly speaking, this involves, in the UG dialects, the shifting of WGmc voiceless stops [p, t, k] to (originally double) fricatives [ff, ss, xx] medially and finally after vowels and to homorganic affricates [pf, ts, kx] initially, after liquids and nasals, and in gemination. LG shows no trace of this change (except via borrowing from CG and UG), essentially retaining the consonant system of WGmc. CG can be seen as a 'half-way house', shifting some consonants and not others:

LG	WCG	ECG	UG	NHG
[piːp] 'pipe'	[paɪf]	[faɪfə]	[pfaɪf(ə)]	*Pfeife*
[maːkən] 'to do'	[maxə]	[maxə]	[maxən]	*machen*
[kɪnt] 'child'	[kɪnt]	[kɪnt]	[kɪnt]/[kxɪnt]	*kind*
[dat] 'that'	[dat]/[das]	[das]	[das]	*das*
[tiːn] 'ten'	[tseːn]	[tseːn]	[tseːn]	*zehn*

The southernmost dialects of UG retain initial [kx]; ECG shows initial [f]. Another criterion used to differentiate German dialects involves the reflexes of the NHG diphthongization (MHG [iː, uː, yː] > NGH [aɪ, aʊ, ɔy], which, broadly speaking, affected EUG and CG and Swabian, but not the rest of WUG and LG: Bavarian, CG, Swabian [haʊs, hɔʊs] vs Swiss and LG [huːs], NHG *Haus*.

In German studies, a distinction is usually recognized between the standard language (*Hochdeutsch / High German*, the written, supraregional norm), the dialects (the indigenous forms of local speech furthest removed from the standard) and collo-quial language (German *Umgangssprache*, the idiom of everyday speech). Colloquial German is a comparatively recent variety, having developed principally in new urban areas under the influence of the emerging standard language (see above). The most conservative dialect speakers are therefore located in rural communities and statis-tics suggest that they are relatively more numerous in the south. All spoken German is regional to a greater or lesser extent, and speakers use varieties of colloquial German closer to the dialects or closer to the standard according to a number of factors (informal vs formal; private vs public). The former are informally designated *Dialekt / Mundart / Platt* (dialect) and the latter *Hochdeutsch* (High German), although this designation belongs properly only to the written language. It should also be noted that, unlike English regional speech, the German equivalent is not socially stigmatized as a general rule. Flexibility in usage and control of colloquial varieties depend on factors such as the level of education or the distance a speaker travels to work, some speakers being able to switch according to situation. However, speakers' own distinctions between 'dialect' and 'High German' do not always corre-spond to objective criteria.

Swiss German

In German-speaking Switzerland, Swiss German (*Schwyzertüütsch*) regularly alter-nates with an Alemannic variety of colloquial German close to the written standard to produce a situation of diglossia (similarly in Luxembourg). Swiss German is a term used to cover many local varieties. The dialects of Zurich (*Züritüütsch*) and Berne (*Bärndütsch*) are probably numerically the most important, but the southern Highest Alemannic dialects (*Höchstalemannisch*) are noteworthy because of their conser-vatism (e.g. retention of inflected predicative adjectives; preservation of distinct weak verb classes, etc.). Dialect is the normal medium of oral communication among Swiss except in formal contexts, although it appears that there has been some movement in favour of the regional varieties in recent years. For example, formal lectures, sermons, the main news on radio and television would almost always use High German; face-to-face discussions, local news and sports reporting would be more likely to make use of dialect.

Interrelationship with other languages

In terms of loan-words, the major influence on German in the historical period has been Latin. It was the source of prehistoric cultural loans also attested in other WGmc languages (*Wein* 'wine' < *vinum*; *Pfeil* 'arrow' < *pilum*); ecclesiastical loans in the OHG period (*Klause* '[monk's] cell' < *clusa*; *Tinte* 'ink' < *tincta*); didactic, reli-gious and scholarly loans in the MHG period (*Dekret* 'decree' < *decretum*; *Pulver* 'powder' < *pulvis -eris*; *Einigkeit* 'unity', a loan-translation of *unitas*); ecclesiastical, scholarly, philological, legal, scientific, mathematical and artistic terms in the ENHG period (*Kapitel* 'chapter' < *capitellum*; *Talar* 'gown' < *[vestimenta] talaria*; *Vokal* 'vowel' < *vocalis*; *Klausel* 'clause' < *clausula*; *Horizont* 'horizon' < *horizon, -ontis*;

Quadrat 'square' < *quadratum; Tragödie* 'tragedy' < *tragœdia*), to name but a few of the major categories. The modern language has also borrowed freely from Latin: e.g. *Bazillus* 'microbe, germ' < *bacillus; Konjunktur* 'economic situation' < *conjuncturus; Podium* 'stage' < *podium* and many more. Indeed, any Latin or Greek word is a potential source, especially for learned and scientific loans. (Greek words are usually reckoned to be imported via Latin.) Latin may have influenced the syntax of German in the ENHG period and was possibly also instrumental in increasing the number and complexity of compound types.

French is another important source of loan-words, sometimes acting as a vehicle for words from other languages, first during the MHG period (*Admiral* 'admiral' < OF *amiral* 'oriental commander or prince', cf. Arabic *emir; Fasan* 'pheasant' < OF *faisan; fehlen* 'to miss' < OF *faillir; Panzer* 'armour' < OF *pancier; Pinsel* 'paintbrush' < OF *pincel; Ingwer* 'ginger' < OF *gingibre*), carrying on throughout the ENHG period, reaching a peak in the 17th and 18th centuries and continuing down to the present day (e.g. *abonnieren* 'to subscribe to [a journal]'; *Adresse* 'address'; *Appetit* 'appetite'; *Bordell* 'brothel'; *Armee* 'army'; *Bagage* 'baggage'; *Parkett* 'parquet'; *Kompliment* 'compliment'; *liberal* 'liberal'; *Parfüm* 'perfume'). Italian loans appeared due to commercial and cultural relations in the ENHG period (e.g. *brutto* 'gross'; *Dattel* 'date'; *Konto* 'account'; *netto* 'net'; *Schachtel* 'box'; *Spargel* 'asparagus') and later due to Italian artistic and culinary influence (e.g. *Adagio, Dilettant, Spaghetti, Torte*).

English influence became significant only in the 20th c., although it began in the late MHG period (e.g. *Boot* 'boat') and in the 19th c. supplied words (either as borrowings or loan-translations) in the fields of literature (e.g. *popular song* > *Volkslied; blank verse* > *Blankvers*), science (*horse power* > *Pferdekraft; steam engine* > *Dampfmaschine*), politics (*coalition* > *Koalition; opposition* > *Opposition*) and commerce (e.g. *bank note* > *Banknote; Manchester* > *Manchester(hosen)* 'corduroy'). Modern loans are legion and it remains to be seen how many of them will be retained for how long. Particularly receptive areas of vocabulary include sport (*Caddie, fit*), entertainment (*die Band, Party*), social life (*Hobby, sexy*), commerce (*Boykott, Discounting*), politics (*Interview, Votum* 'vote'), science (*Computer, Transistor*), fashion (*Jeans, Slip* 'knickers') and food (*Keks* 'biscuit' < *cakes; Sandwich*). Surprisingly, the influence of German on English is not as marginal as was once thought: a recent study (Pfeffer and Cannon 1995) lists over 6,000 loan-words.

Present situation

There are commonly reckoned to be some 110 million speakers of German around the world, but it should be noted that figures from different countries are often not comparable and are therefore unreliable indicators in their raw form. German has sole official language status in the present Federal Republic of Germany, incorporating the old German Democratic Republic (77,981,000), in the Federal Republic of Austria (7,605,000) and in the Principality of Liechtenstein (28,000). In Switzerland (4,141,000) it is a co-official language with French, Italian and *Romansh, and with French and *Luxemburgish in Luxembourg (372,000). In

France (1,200,000) a variety of Upper German is spoken in Alsace, especially by older speakers, and Lorraine, although here the language is under particular threat from French. In Belgium, where German is a recognized regional official language (see ***Belgium**), there are Franconian dialect-speakers in Eupen, St Vith and Montzen and speakers of Luxemburgish around Arel/Arlon (66,000). The German-speakers in Denmark (North Schleswig) (22,000) typically use a Danish dialect at home. The area of the Netherlands around Maastricht retains German dialect-speakers (*Limburgisch*) who use Dutch as their official language (no figures available). In Italy, the South Tirol is the home of a significant minority (280,000, some 65%) of German-speakers. In addition, some 13,000 ***Rhaeto-Romance**-speakers of Northern Italy use German as one of their official languages. These figures are taken from Ammon (1991), the most extensive recently published survey, and Althaus et al. (1980), comparison of which reveals growth at the centre (Germany, Austria and Switzerland) and attrition in the enclaves and around the periphery, especially in those areas where German lacks official status.

This is apparent in eastern Europe, where large areas had been settled by German-speakers during the Middle Ages and from where the vast majority were resettled after the Second World War. Of the areas bordering the present German-speaking area, Poland (1937 *c*.10.4 million, 1989 1.1 million), Hungary (1930 *c*.0.7 million, 1989 0.22 million) and former Czechoslovakia (1937 *c*.3.2 million, 1989 32,000) accounted for most, although significant minorities existed elsewhere: the former republic of Yugoslavia (1939 0.6 million, 1980 *c*.20,000); Romania (1930 *c*.0.8 million, 1980 0.2 million). The 300 speakers in Bulgaria were resettled in 1943. The former Soviet Union is something of an exception to the trend of attrition: in 1969, some 1.2 million recorded their language as German; Ammon's most recent figures indicate just over 1.1 million German-speakers.

Outside Europe, decline is obvious everywhere. A survey in 1970 estimated that just over 6 million spoke German as children in the USA. However, the number who use the language daily must have been much smaller then and is probably considerably smaller now. Ammon's figures indicate 1.6 million. Canadian census returns indicate 0.56 million speakers in 1971 and *c*.0.45 million ten years later. Latin America has a number of more or less stable minorities, with over 2 million estimated speakers, about three-quarters of them in Brazil. German has official status in Namibia beside English and Afrikaans and is therefore used more widely than in the relatively small German community (*c*.20,000); some 41,000 German-speakers live in neighbouring South Africa. About 109,000 recent German-speaking immigrants live in Australia, numerically dwarfing the 19th-c. settlements. Finally, some 96,000 German native speakers live in Israel. All these communities are suffering competition and attrition from local languages, although German churches and media, and the cultural agency the Goethe Institut, sometimes provide a beneficial focus for German language and culture.

Because of Germany's economic position in the world (the language is ranked anywhere from sixth to tenth numerically, but must be ranked third after English and Japanese on the basis of the disposable income of its speakers), German is widely taught as a second language in schools. In Europe (see Sturm 1987) this is recognized most clearly in Finland, where, in 1982, 78% of secondary school children were taught the language (compared to 56% in Iceland, 48.5% in Norway, 46.4% in Sweden, 35% in the Netherlands, 13.6% in Belgium, 5.7% in Ireland and only 2% in the UK).

Althaus, H. P., Henne, H. and Wiegand, H. W. 1980. *Lexikon der germanistischen Linguistik* ('Dictionary of German Linguistics'). Tübingen.

Ammon, U. 1991. *Die internationale Stellung der deutschen Sprache* ('The International Position of the German Language'). Berlin and New York.

Barbour, S. and Stevenson, P. 1990. *Variation in German. A Critical Approach to German Sociolinguistics*. Cambridge.

Blackall, E. A. 1959. *The Emergence of German as a Literary Language*. Cambridge.

Clyne, M. 1995. *The German Language in a Changing Europe*. Cambridge.

Durrell, M. 1991. *Hammer's German Grammar and Usage*. London.

—— 1992. *Using German. A Guide to Contemporary Usage*. Cambridge.

Frenzl, H. A. and Frenzl, E. 1953. *Daten deutscher Dichtung. Chronologischer Abriß der deutschen Literaturgeschichte* ('Dates in German Literature. A Chronological Survey of German Literature'). Cologne.

Garland, H. and Garland, M. 1976. *The Oxford Companion to German Literature*. Oxford.

Keller, R. E. 1978. *The German Language*. London.

König, W. 1978. *dtv-Atlas zur deutschen Sprache* ('dtv Atlas of the German Language'). Munich.

Pfeffer, J. A. and Cannon, G. 1995. *German Loanwords in English. An Historical Dictionary*. Cambridge.

Russ, C. V. J. 1990. *The Dialects of Modern German*. London.

—— 1994. *The German Language Today*. London and New York.

Schlosser, H. D. 1990. *dtv-Atlas zur deutschen Literatur* ('dtv Atlas of German Literature'), 4th edn. Munich.

Scholze-Stubenrecht, W. and Sykes, J. B. (eds) 1994. *The Oxford–Duden German Dictionary*. Oxford.

Sonderegger, S. 1974. *Althochdeutsche Sprache und Literatur* ('Old High German Language and Literature'). Berlin.

Stevenson, P. (ed.) 1995. *The German Language and the Real World. Sociolinguistic, Cultural and Pragmatic Perspectives on Contemporary German*. Oxford.

Sturm, D. (ed.) 1987. *Deutsch als Fremdsprache weltweit. Situation und Tendenzen* ('German as a Foreign Language World-wide. Situation and Trends'). Munich.

Wells, C. J. 1987. *German. A Linguistic History to 1945*. Oxford.

Wolff, G. 1994. *Deutsche Sprachgeschichte* ('History of the German Language'), 3rd edn. Munich.

JONATHAN WEST

Germanic languages

Classification

'Germanic' designates a group of *Indo-European** languages, conventionally divided into three subgroups: North Germanic (the *Scandinavian languages**) comprises *Icelandic**, *Faroese**, *Norwegian** (West Norse), *Swedish** and *Danish** (East Norse); West Germanic comprises *English**, *Frisian**, *German**, *Yiddish**, *Dutch** and Afrikaans; East Germanic is represented principally by *Gothic**. Opinion now tends to the view that West Germanic and North Germanic share sufficient common innovations to warrant the reconstruction of a stage of common development, usually termed NW Germanic. However, some scholars prefer to see East Germanic and North Germanic as being particularly closely related (the so-called Gotho-Nordic theory). Tacitus's early division of the West Germanic tribes into Erminones (Elbe Germans), Istvaeones (Weser-Rhine Germans) and Ingvaeones (North Sea Germans) (see ***Ingvaeonic languages**) bears some relationship to linguistic reality. The North Sea Germanic languages share a striking series of features, e.g. unitary plural in verbs, loss of nasals before fricatives (English *five* = German *fünf*), 3rd person pronoun with *h-* (English *he* = German *er*) and pronouns without final *-r* (English *we* = German *wir*).

Contacts with other language groups

A significant proportion of the Common Germanic vocabulary, particularly concerning seafaring (e.g. *mast, keel, storm, ebb*), animal husbandry and hunting (e.g. *calf, horse, lamb, bear*), social life (e.g. *thing* 'assembly', *folk, king, thief*) and warfare (e.g. *sword, helmet, bow*), is not Indo-European, nor can it be explained by borrowing from neighbouring peoples. These words may point to a non-Indo-European substratum in north-west Europe. The Germanic peoples had early contact with proto-Finns, who borrowed a number of Germanic words – e.g. Finn. *kuningas* < Gmc **kuningaz* (English *king*), Finn. *patja* 'quilt' < **badjan* (English *bed*); Finn. *pelto* 'field' < **felþan* (English *field*); Finn. *ahjo* 'chimney, forge' < Gmc **asjô* (New High German *Esse* 'chimney'); Finn. *kaunis* 'beautiful' < Gmc **skauniz* (German *schön*) – probably reflecting important cultural loans. This points to a period of close contact probably in southern Scandinavia, the presumed Germanic homeland, in prehistoric times. Loans from ***Continental Celtic** indicate early contacts to the south: German *Amt* 'office' is ultimately derived from a ***Gaulish** word *ambactos* (known indirectly through Classical sources) meaning 'servant', and other words reflecting social organizations such as words for 'oath' (cf. Old Irish *óeth*), 'hostage' (German *Geisel*, cf. Old Irish *gíall*) and 'realm' (German *Reich*, cf. Old Irish *ríge*) suggest cultural dominance of Celtic-speaking peoples in La Tène Europe (5th c. BC onwards). This tends to be confirmed by technological loans such as the words for 'iron' (cf. Welsh *haearn*), 'lead' (cf. Middle Irish *luaide*), 'wagon' (English *car*, cf. Gaulish *carros*), 'soft cheese' (German *Zieger*), 'breast armour' (German *Brünne*, cf. Old Irish *bruinne* 'breast'). The loans from Latin in the Common Germanic period are already significant, mostly to do with trade and luxury goods (e.g. *wine* from Latin *vinum*), although it is often difficult to establish the relative chronology of many early loans.

Linguistic evidence for Germanic life and culture

Comparative linguistics, supplemented by archaeological and some textual evidence from Classical sources, allows us to make limited deductions about Germanic life and culture. For example, as the reconstructed kinship terms centre around the word for 'father', it is likely that the Indo-European tradition of patriarchal social organization was continued. Social organization was based on the extended family (Gothic *þiuda* 'people' = Old Irish *túath* 'tribe' = Lithuanian *tautà* 'people, nation'). In common with other Indo-European groups, the way of life was probably initially semi-nomadic and wealth was measured in livestock (English *fee* = German *Vieh* 'cattle'), but increasing use of iron allowed more intensive and settled agriculture (words for 'rye', 'wheat', 'bean', 'flax' are all Common Germanic).

Sources of information

As Germanic is a reconstructed language, many of the reference works deal with the Germanic languages as a whole. A readable account in English is Robinson (1992), which also contains bibliographies for each of the languages and a useful general bibliography at the end. Markey et al. (1977) contains an extensive bibliography up to 1976. The best dictionary is still Falk and Torp (1979) and the most readable grammar still Prokosch (1939), which is usefully supplemented by Kufner and van Coetsem (1972).

Falk, H. and Torp, A. 1979. *Wortschatz der germanischen Spracheinheit* ('Lexicon of the Germanic Linguistic Unity') (reprint of the 4th edn of 1909). Göttingen.

Kufner, H. L. and van Coetsem, F. (eds) 1972. *Toward a Grammar of Proto-Germanic*. Tübingen.

Markey, T. L., Kyes, R. L. and Roberge, P. T. 1977. *Germanic and Its Dialects: A Grammar of Proto-Germanic*, vol. 3, *Bibliography and Indices*. Amsterdam.

Meillet, A. 1970. *General Characteristics of the Germanic Languages* (transl. W. P. Dismukes). Coral Gables, FL.

Prokosch, E. 1939. *A Comparative Germanic Grammar*. Philadelphia.

Robinson, O. W. 1992. *Old English and Its Closest Relatives*. London.

Streitberg, W. 1943. *Urgermanische Grammatik. Einführung in das vergleichende Studium der altgermanischen Dialekte* ('Proto-Germanic Grammar. Introduction to the Comparative Study of the Old Germanic Dialects'). Heidelberg.

JONATHAN WEST

Getic (see under *Daco-Thracian*)

Ghodoberi (see under *Caucasian languages. IV. North-East Caucasian family*)

Ginukh (see *Hinukh* under *Caucasian languages. IV. North-East Caucasian family*)

Glosa (see under *Artificial languages*)

Goidelic languages, see *Gaelic languages*

Gothic

Gothic is the only member of the East Germanic subgroup of the ***Germanic languages** for which significant textual evidence survives. Other East Germanic dialects were probably spoken by the Vandals, Burgundians, Gepids, Rugians and Herulians. Gothic is of crucial importance for Germanic philology in providing the oldest large corpus of text in a Germanic language.

Salient linguistic features

Gothic retains archaic features (such as an inflected present passive and a dual number in verbs and pronouns), but also shows significant innovations. These include levelling of consonant alternations in the strong verb paradigm and loss of the instrumental case, both these features being preserved in West Germanic. Apparent archaisms, such as the fourth class of weak verbs, may in fact be innovations, and other archaisms, such as the retention of full vowels in unstressed syllables and the use of reduplication to mark the past tense, are shared by West Germanic languages. In relative terms, therefore, Old High German could be regarded as more archaic.

Areas where spoken

The account of the 6th-c. Gothic historian Jordanes, according to which the Goths migrated from Scandinavia (*ex Scandza insula*) to *Gothiscandza* (probably the area around the mouth of the Vistula) in the early 1st century BC, is generally accepted as being substantially correct. During the 2nd c. AD, they migrated again to the area north of the Black Sea (see ***Crimean Gothic**). From this time on, we can trace the movements of the Ostrogoths and the Visigoths separately.

The Ostrogoths remained in the area between Dniester and Dnieper; the Visigoths were largely absorbed into the Eastern Roman Empire, especially after the invasions (from AD 375) of a non-Germanic tribe, the Huns, and were the first to adopt (Arian) Christianity. However, under Alaric, they pushed westwards, sacking Rome in AD 410, and, after Alaric's sudden death, established a Gothic kingdom in southern France and northern Spain, where they have left traces in loan-words (e.g. *guerre/guerra* 'war') and personal names (e.g. *Rodrigo, Alfonso, Fernando*). In 451 they fought at the battle of the 'Catalaunian Plains', which stemmed the advance of the Huns and their allies, among which were Ostrogoths.

A large proportion of the Ostrogoths were assimilated by the Huns, whose leader is even known to us by a Gothic name, *Att-ila* 'little father'. This close association explains the importance of Attila in later Germanic heroic literature (Icelandic *Atli*, Middle High German *Etzel*). After the collapse of the Hunnish empire (455), the Ostrogoths settled in the Roman province of Pannonia (eastern Austria, Styria, Krajina and NW Hungary). Under Theodoric, who had been brought up as a hostage at the Eastern Roman court in Constantinople, they plundered the Balkans, at that time part of the Eastern Roman Empire. Meanwhile, the Germanic chieftain Odoacer had supplanted the last Western Emperor (the boy Romulus Augustulus, 475–6). The Eastern Emperor Zeno named Theodoric *magister militum* and *patricius* of Italy in 488 and authorized him to invade Italy, probably hoping to get rid of Theodoric and neutralize Odoacer. After the three-year siege of Ravenna (490–3, the *Rabenschlacht* of medieval German saga), Odoacer was murdered by Theodoric, who then ruled Italy until his death in 526. The Gothic kingdom survived in northern Italy until the mid-6th c.

Texts

Gothic is known principally from the Visigothic translation of the Bible ascribed to the Arian bishop Ulfilas (*c*.311–83, probably **Wulf-ila* 'little wolf'). This is one of the oldest witnesses to the Syriac tradition (the Greek 'original' is in fact reconstructed from the Gothic). The surviving manuscripts of his translation (mostly of portions of the New Testament) were largely written during the 6th c. in northern Italy, and are therefore Ostrogothic: the largest and most superbly appointed, the *Codex Argenteus* ('The Silver Codex'), has been in the University Library in Uppsala since the Thirty Years War (1618–48). The MSS are written in a special Gothic alphabet, derived mainly from 4th-c. Greek uncial, but with Latin and runic accretions (see ***Runes**).

Bennett (1960) contains an edition of the *Skeireins*, a commentary on the Gospel of John. Other short texts include part of an ecclesiastical calendar, parts of two bills of sale, two Gothic alphabets and a few sentences with Latin transliteration and a Gothic fragment in a Latin epigram, apart from onomastic material in Classical sources and a few runic inscriptions from the 3rd c.

Sources of information

There is a facsimile of the Codex Argenteus (1927), but the standard edition of the Gothic Bible, which also contains the minor fragments and a comprehensive glossary, is still Streitberg (1919), often reprinted. A separate dictionary is now available (Köbler 1989), and linguistic work is facilitated by Tollenaere and Jones's (1976) complete concordance to Streitberg (1919). Feist's etymological dictionary (1939) has now been recast by Lehmann (1986) and contains invaluable bibliographical references. Mossé's bibliography of Gothic studies (1950) has not been updated for a number of years, but much of the important material is noted or reviewed in issues of the bibliographical journal *Germanistik*. Scardigli (1973) is probably the most informative background work on history, language and culture, including Classical sources. Marchand's short survey (1970) of the language also contains information on the location and contents of the manuscripts.

Bennett, W. H. 1960. *The Gothic Commentary on the Gospel of John*. New York.

Codex Argenteus 1927. *Codex Argenteus Upsaliensis Iussu Senatus Universitatis phototypice editus* ('The Silver Codex of Uppsala published in facsimile by order of the Senate of the University'). Uppsala.

Feist, S. 1939. *Vergleichendes Wörterbuch der gotischen Sprache* ('Comparative Dictionary of the Gothic Language'), 3rd edn. Leiden.

Köbler, G. 1989. *Gotisches Wörterbuch* ('Gothic Dictionary'). Leiden.

Lehmann, W. P. 1986. *A Gothic Etymological Dictionary*. Leiden.

Marchand, J. W. 1970. Gotisch. In Schmitt, L. E. (ed.), *Kurzer Grundriß der germanischen Philologie bis 1500* ('Short Survey of Germanic Philology to 1500'), Berlin, 94–122.

Mossé, F. 1950. Bibliographia Gotica. *Mediaeval Studies*, 12: 237–324. (Supplements 15: 169–83 (1953); 19: 174–96 (1957); 29: 327–43 (1967); 36: 199–214 (1974).)

Scardigli, P. 1973. *Die Goten. Sprache und Kultur* ('The Goths. Language and Culture'). Munich.

Schwarz, E. 1956. *Germanische Stammeskunde* ('The Germanic Tribes'). Heidelberg.

Streitberg, W. 1919. *Die gotische Bibel* ('The Gothic Bible'). 2nd edn. Heidelberg.

Tollenaere, F. de and Jones, R. L. 1976. *Word-Indices and Word-Lists to the Gothic Bible and Minor Fragments*. Leiden.

JONATHAN WEST

Gothic, Crimean, see *Crimean Gothic*

Greek

Greek constitutes a branch of the *Indo-European family of languages in its own right, though it probably once formed a fairly close subgroup with *Indo-Iranian and *Armenian within Indo-European. Within Europe, it is spoken today principally in Greece and Cyprus, though there are also Greek communities in Germany and the United Kingdom.

Origins and earliest attestations

Greek is now widely believed to be the product of contact between the indigenous populations of the Balkan peninsula and Indo-European invaders beginning around 2000 BC. It has the longest continuous recorded history of any European language, with the earliest documents, corpora of clay tablets written in the *Linear B syllabary, dating from the second half of the second millennium BC. The surviving texts record details of the economic activity of the Mycenaean civilization of southern Greece and Crete (so-called after Mycenae, one of its principal centres in the Peloponnese).

After the collapse of the Mycenaean world around 1200 BC, writing disappeared for several centuries and we enter the Greek Dark Age. During the late 9th or early 8th c., writing was reintroduced through an adaptation of the *Phoenician alphabet in which redundant consonant signs were redeployed to represent vowel sounds (the Latin alphabet was borrowed from Greek colonies in southern Italy; for the Greek alphabet, see fig. 7). The earliest surviving alphabetic inscriptions are scratched on pottery and can be dated to the latter part of the 8th c., but thereafter the body of material increases steadily, and large collections of 'official' inscriptions on stone and bronze are available from most parts of the Greek world from around the 5th c. BC onwards.

Dialects in the classical period

The political fragmentation of Greece at this time meant that local dialects were employed by each city for official purposes, and we therefore have a rich store of information about the dialectology of ancient Greek (see map 8). The breakdown of the Mycenaean civilization had forced massive emigration during the Dark Age, and colonies were established throughout the Aegean, along the coasts of Asia Minor and the Black Sea, in north Africa, in Sicily and southern Italy (Magna Graecia), and as far west as Marseilles. These colonies originally spoke the dialects of their mother cities, but though these inevitably began to evolve independently, an acute sense of Greek cultural identity, backed up by trade and travel, ensured that the various dialects remained mutually comprehensible.

Greek letter (name)	Ancient pronunciation (5th–4th c. BC)	Modern pronunciation
Αα (alpha)	[a, aː]	[a]
Ββ (beta)	[b]	[v]
Γγ (gamma)	[g]	[ɣ, j]
Δδ (delta)	[d]	[ð]
Εε (epsilon)	[e]	[e]
Ζζ (zeta)	[zd]	[z]
Ηη (eta)	[ɛː]	[i]
Θθ (theta)	[tʰ]	[θ]
Ιι (iota)	[i, iː]	[i, j]
Κκ (kappa)	[k]	[k]
Λλ (lambda)	[l]	[l]
Μμ (mu)	[m]	[m]
Νν (nu)	[n]	[n]
Ξξ (xi)	[ks]	[ks]
Οο (omikron)	[o]	[o]
Ππ (pi)	[p]	[p]
Ρρ (rho)	[r]	[r]
Σσ/ς (sigma)	[s]	[s]
Ττ (tau)	[t]	[t]
Υυ (upsilon)	[y, yː]	[i]
Φφ (phi)	[pʰ]	[f]
Χχ (chi)	[kʰ]	[x, ç]
Ψψ (psi)	[ps]	[ps]
Ωω (omega)	[oː]	[o]

Fig. 7 The Greek alphabet. For the values of the characters of the International Phonetic Alphabet, see pp. xvi–xvii.

The dialects of the classical period (5th–4th centuries BC) are standardly divided into East Greek and West Greek subgroups. The former comprises, on the one hand, Attic (the dialect of Athens and Attica) and the closely related Ionic (the dialects of the central and northern Aegean and much of the Asia Minor coast), and, on the other, Arcadian (spoken in the central Peloponnese) together with Cypriot; the latter

Map 8   The Greek dialects in the classical period. After John Chadwick, 'The Greek dialects and Greek pre-history', *Greece & Rome*, 2nd series, vol. 3 (1956), by permission of Oxford University Press.

group comprises Peloponnesian Doric (spoken in the rest of the Peloponnese and its colonies, including many southern Aegean islands and much of Magna Graecia) and North-West Greek. The Aeolic dialects (spoken in Thessaly, Boeotia, and the island of Lesbos plus adjacent territory in Asia Minor) seem to have been originally of West Greek type with an early East Greek admixture (perhaps forming a 'bridge' between the major groups), and to have evolved a distinctive identity in early post-Mycenaean times.

The much earlier Mycenaean dialect of the Linear B tablets, however, already has an 'East Greek' character, and it is clear that varieties of this type were once widespread in southern Greece as far north as Boeotia, with 'West Greek' confined largely to areas north and west of the Mycenaean heartlands. It seems, then, that much of the later diversification and the redistribution into the later East–West division was due to Dark Age migration. Thus Attic–Ionic, as well as Aeolic, seems to be an essentially post-Mycenaean development, as is the distinction between a northern (North-West Greek) and a southern (Peloponnesian Doric) branch of West Greek. Arcadian represents a residue of Mycenaean speech after the arrival of West Greek speakers from the north, while Cypriot (the only classical dialect written with a syllabary, related to Linear B) is the dialect of early colonists.

The earliest literature

The earliest Greek literature has a clearly dialectal quality reflecting the speech of the regions where its various genres were first developed or where they received their definitive form. For example, Homer's epic poems the *Iliad* and the *Odyssey* represent the culmination of a tradition of oral poetry which flourished in Ionia towards the end of the Dark Age (mid-8th c. BC), and the dialect used is fundamentally Ionic. The tradition, however, almost certainly originated in the Mycenaean period, and there is also evidence for a parallel Aeolic tradition from which phraseology was borrowed and Ionicized as far as the product was compatible with epic metre. Thus the language of the poems is in fact an amalgam of Ionic with archaisms and Aeolicisms, preserved because of their metrical utility in the development of rhythmically defined formula systems essential to the task of oral composition and performance.

The enormous prestige of these poems influenced the Greek conception of 'poetic' diction ever after, and all other genres display some degree of epic influence in the distancing of their language from that of everyday discourse through the incorporation of archaism and unusual vocabulary, the elaboration of a characteristic phraseology, and the avoidance of linguistic parochialism. The language of choral lyric, for example, displays a number of epicisms and Aeolicisms in combination with a generalized (but non-localizable) Doric that reflects the crucial Dorian role in the development of the genre; and even 5th-c. Athenian tragedy (the dramas of Aeschylus, Sophocles and Euripides) employs a characteristically archaic/foreign vocabulary alongside a stylized Attic, with its choral lyrics continuing to show a strong, if highly conventionalized, Doric component. In short, the language of nearly all early Greek poetry was in some degree archaizing, artificial and genre-specific.

During the 6th c. BC the writing of literary prose began, once again in Ionia, in a development associated with the beginnings of the period of intellectual ferment that ushered in the classical era. A form of literary Ionic soon evolved, significantly different from the official varieties known from inscriptions, as the vehicle for the new disciplines of science, philosophy and historiography. Again, such was the prestige of this early work, that, for a time at least, later practitioners, regardless of their native speech, naturally employed this variety for their compositions.

The emergence and evolution of a standard language

During the course of the 5th c. BC, Athens, through its efforts to repulse Persian aggression, became a major imperial power and soon emerged as the primary cultural focus of the Greek world. Though composed in Attic, its earliest prose literature (e.g. the history of Thucydides) shows marked Ionic influence in deference to the Ionian tradition, and elements of this Ionicized Attic soon began to appear even in official inscriptions. By the 4th c. BC, the unique cultural prestige of Athens in fields such as rhetoric (e.g. Isocrates) and philosophy (Plato and Aristotle) was such that literary Attic inevitably became the norm for all serious writing throughout the Greek world.

This evolution of Attic towards standard-language status was supported at another level by the fact that the Athenian empire consisted very largely of Ionic-speaking cities, so that Athenian government and routine dialect contact led to the progressive (top-down) disappearance of Ionic as a distinct group and the emergence of an international form of administrative Attic ('Great Attic') that displayed considerable Ionic influence in morphology, syntax and vocabulary. As the 'business' language of the middle and upper classes, spoken and written, this variety, closely related to literary Attic and aided by its associations with high culture, soon expanded beyond the confines of the empire.

The crucial step in the emergence of (Great) Attic as the standard language of the Greek world, however, was its adoption as a prestigious symbol of Hellenic identity by the court of the rapidly expanding Macedonian kingdom in the 5th c. BC. As Macedonia came to control first the Greek cities and then, as a result of the campaigns of Alexander the Great against the Persians in the second half of the 4th c. BC, vast territories ranging from Egypt to the borders of India, Attic was imposed as the official administrative language throughout the Macedonian empire, with the masterpieces of Athenian literature forming the centrepiece of the higher education system. This 'Hellenistic' Greek world soon split into a number of hereditary monarchies based in Macedonia, Egypt, Syria and Asia Minor.

The immediate result of these developments was diglossia in 'old Greece', the local dialects being used for day-to-day communication and local affairs, and the Koine or 'common dialect' (i.e. administrative Attic) for other purposes, with classical literary Attic impinging on upper-class usage through the education system. Inevitably we start to find interference phenomena in dialect inscriptions, and eventually the ancient dialects, subject to ever greater Koine penetration, declined to the status of spoken patois, finally dying out altogether as not only the written Koine but also its spoken varieties (with regional accents and local differences) became the natural medium of expression. The spoken dialects of modern Greek descend ultimately from local forms of the Koine, though substrate elements (mainly lexical and phonological) still reflect ancient dialect phenomena in some rural areas. The major exception is the rapidly declining spoken dialect of the south-eastern Peloponnese (*Tsakonian), which, as a result of its geographical and later political isolation, underwent less thoroughgoing Koineization and preserved a distinctively Doric character.

In the 'new' Greek world Hellenization was initially confined largely to the cities which were founded by the conquerors and populated by colonists from the old Greek world. But since the Graeco-Macedonian aristocracies employed the standard Koine for all official purposes and promoted an education system based on a study of classical (mainly Attic) literature, the original mixture of old dialects imported by the mass of the population evolved quickly into new spoken varieties of the Koine.

Bilingualism also became routine in many areas as the native population sought integration and employment and standard written Koine was widely learned (together with literary classical Attic if individuals received a higher education) alongside local spoken varieties (ranging from educated standard to regional vernacular according to the level of contact). In this way Greek eventually became the lingua franca of the Hellenistic East.

Although study of the classical past was central to Hellenistic culture as a means of providing a unifying 'heritage' for its disparate lands, this was also a period of radical innovation in science and philosophy. The written Koine, suitably adapted, was generally felt to be an appropriate medium for such writing, even if poets found it 'sterile' and reverted to literary dialects modelled on those of the classical masters. As time went on, however, the elite became conscious of a gap opening up between the literary Attic of the canon and the Koine, which, even in its higher registers, was beginning to reflect developments in the spoken language. Important sources of evidence for the Koine include administrative inscriptions, the Septuagint (a translation of the Old Testament for the Jewish population of Alexandria), and Egyptian papyri ranging from official documents to private letters and fragments of 'popular' literature. Henceforth the language of the more belletristic prose genres (e.g. Polybius's history, 2nd c. BC), became more conservative and so began to detach itself stylistically and grammatically from even educated writing of a technical or official character.

During the latter part of the 1st c. BC this trend culminated in the Atticist movement, which sought to restore the language of educated prose writing and declamation to its classical 'purity' by the careful emulation of the best classical authors. Though in part a reaction to the earlier revival of a peculiarly florid rhetorical style known as Asianism (after the region where it first flourished), the long-term impact of Atticism can best be understood in the context of the progressive encroachment of Rome into the Hellenistic world from the middle of the 2nd c. BC.

Unlike the west, where the Romans could present themselves as the bringers of civilization to barbarians, the Hellenistic world was already the locus of high culture. The Romans therefore drew a distinction between the ancient Greeks, who had invented the urban culture they so admired, and contemporary Greeks, who in their view had become decadent and so in need of the moral guidance which they alone were able to impose, having redefined this culture in terms of a universal framework of law, custom and ethical ideals. Increasingly, then, Roman imperialism was justified on the basis of values associated with a particular reconstruction of the Greek past.

Among the Greeks, unsurprisingly, alienation from a political system over which they had little control led to nostalgia for past glories and to the construction of a cultural world in which their own preoccupations were paramount and through which they felt able to make some impact on their Roman masters. By the 2nd c. AD., renewed prosperity and cultural self-confidence fuelled the emergence of an extraordinarily flamboyant expression of Hellenism known as the Second Sophistic. This symbol of the resilience of the Greek urban aristocracy, however much it represented a contemporary renaissance, was founded in a desire to reconnect with the classics through the restoration of ancient literary glory. This entailed the parallel revival of its linguistic vehicle, and Atticism flourished in educated circles as never before, encouraged both by Roman enthusiasm for the Greek past and the pride of the Greek aristocracy in a linguistic hallmark that distinguished it from the common herd. Literary Attic, already 600 years old, was now widely viewed as the 'correct' form of Greek, the Koine representing a degenerate variety, acceptable in its higher forms for practical purposes, but generally felt to have decayed through ignorance and neglect.

An Attic or Atticizing style (however imperfectly controlled) was now the aim of all writers of artistic prose, and even those who rejected extreme Atticism as pedantry, adopted a style that acknowledged elements of classical precedent. Henceforth the development of the written Koine in its highest registers was shaped by a continuous compromise between the fixed classical ideal and the evolution of the spoken language (itself inhibited, for the elite, by education). Thus the language of imperial and, with the advent of Christianity, ecclesiastical administration became steadily more 'remote' from ordinary speech, even though the Koine in its lowest registers (e.g. the private letters of people with minimal classical learning) naturally followed the evolution of the vernacular more closely. From now on evidence for the 'natural' development of Greek necessarily comes from subliterary documents in which Atticizing influence, whether through ignorance or design, is largely absent.

Christian Greek

Of particular interest here is the New Testament, composed in (or, in the case of some books, perhaps translated from Aramaic into) a range of low-to-middle-brow styles by men who in the main lacked a literary education. After the adoption of Christianity as the official religion of the Empire, we might have expected a shift in favour of the 'ordinary' Koine as the language of Holy Scripture, but the progressive conversion of the aristocracy led, during the 4th and 5th centuries, to doctrinal debates which were inevitably conducted within the broad intellectual framework of pagan Greek culture, a development which also imposed the Atticizing norm on educated Christian discourse. Thus, while elaborated 'literary' Greek was very largely rejected by the earliest Apostolic Fathers, later Patristic literature was routinely composed in a style heavily influenced by the classical learned language. Important figures include, for the earlier period, Clement of Alexandria (late 2nd–3rd c. AD) and Origen (AD 184–254), and later, Eusebius (260–339), Basil the Great (329–79), Gregory of Nazianzus (*c*.330–*c*.389), Gregory of Nyssa (*c*.335–*c*.394) and John Chrysostom (*c*.347–407).

Greek in the Roman Empire

Though the Hellenistic world had been fully incorporated into the Roman Empire by the end of the 1st c. BC, Greek remained the sole language of culture and education in the east, and the Romans were generally content also to employ the established language of administration for most practical purposes. Latin was therefore never a serious threat to Greek (despite its protracted use by, for example, the legal profession and the army), though Greek naturally absorbed many loan-words and the two languages do show some signs of convergence at other levels. The position of Greek was strengthened after the division of the Empire into western and eastern (Byzantine) parts at the end of the 4th c. AD, and with the final collapse of the Roman state in the west in the 5th c., Greek quickly superseded Latin in even its residual functions (though the inhabitants of the Byzantine Empire, with its capital at Constantinople, thought of themselves as 'Romans' throughout their long history).

Byzantine Greek

Byzantine territory, after the recovery of North Africa and Italy in the 6th c., was progressively whittled away by 'barbarian' invasion. Thus the crushing of Persia in the 7th c. was quickly followed by Arab assaults which deprived Constantinople of the Middle East and Egypt, while a contemporary Slavic invasion led to the loss of most of the Balkan peninsula. Between 850 and 1050, however, the Byzantines staged a remarkable recovery during which much lost territory was recovered and Orthodox Christianity, together with other facets of Byzantine culture, was carried to Moravia, Bulgaria and Russia (the *Cyrillic alphabet is an adaptation of the Greek invented by Byzantine missionaries). But things again changed for the worse when the Normans invaded southern Italy and the Seljuk Turks occupied eastern and central tracts of Asia Minor after their victory at Manzikert (north-east of Lake Van) in 1071. Still worse was to follow. The revival of the west and the growing power of the papacy led to the arrival of Crusaders, closely followed by Italian traders greedy for profit. Ill-feeling came to a head in 1204 when Constantinople was sacked by the Fourth Crusade and the bulk of its empire divided among the victors, most notably the Venetians. Although the capital and part of the Peloponnese were eventually restored to Byzantine rule, the empire never recovered militarily or economically. By the 15th c. Constantinople was virtually all that remained, and the Ottoman Turks, having already overrun much of eastern Europe, stormed the city in May 1453.

The early Byzantine period naturally saw a vast increase in the output of Christian literature, in particular church histories and saints' lives. While the first category employed the Attic style of traditional historiography, the second provided edifying tales for a more popular audience and used a middle-to-low register of the contemporary Koine, analogous to that of the gospels. After the disasters of the 7th c., literary output declined until the 9th-c. recovery, but a strong survivor from the earlier period was the chronicle, a genre motivated by a desire to unify the components of Byzantine culture through the assimilation of biblical and Graeco-Roman 'history' into a single chronological framework running from the Creation to the present. Written primarily as reference works, chronicles naturally employed the contemporary middle-brow Koine of routine administration. As stability and confidence returned, however, we also witness a series of classical 'revivals' in which an interest in ancient literary forms and a fresh commitment to Atticism reasserted themselves. Significant figures here include Phótios, the 9th-c. polymath and patriarch of Constantinople, and Micháil Psellós, the 11th-c. philosopher, historian and statesman.

Originally a conglomerate in which Greek was not even the sole language of culture (let alone the only spoken language), the Empire after the Seljuk invasions comprised territories where the majority were in fact Greek-speakers. This led accidentally to something approaching a 'Greek' national consciousness, and brought with it an important change of attitude towards language that permitted for the first time the cultivation of popular forms of Greek in literature aimed at an educated audience. Where 12th-c. Atticists (e.g. Anna Komniní, daughter of the emperor Aléxios I Komninós and author of a history of her father's times) sought a 'Greek' identity in the ancient past, others did so by experimenting with the language of popular oral poetry and the common language of the streets. One version of the 'epic' poem of Diyenís Akrítis, for example, represents a reworking of oral tales of derring-do from the old eastern frontiers (the language retains a characteristically oral 'mix' of old and new forms, or forms from different dialect areas, with different metrical values), while the poems of 'Poor Pródromos' (comic begging poetry addressed to the emperor) employ the same metre and a very similar language, but amusingly adapted to its new subject matter and milieu through the incorporation of contemporary phraseology and the parodic juxtaposition of popular and learned forms (a feature which must have characterized the formal speech and writing of many who had learned just enough classical Greek to become thoroughly confused). Such experimentation came to an end with the political disintegration of the end of the 12th c., and a 'vernacular' literary language only reappears with the verse romances of the 14th c. when, under the impact of western models, it finally became the accepted medium for fiction.

Greek in the period of Turkish domination

Creative writing quickly collapsed in the Ottoman Empire, and only traditional written forms of Greek survived, particularly the various registers of the administrative Koine through their use by the sole remaining Greek institution, the Orthodox Church. Written Greek reflecting the spoken norm again became the accidental product of ignorance, leaving only oral folk poetry (much of it extremely well crafted and deeply moving) to employ a vernacular style creatively. The spoken language naturally began to absorb many Turkish loans, and in isolated districts such as Cappadocia in central Anatolia began to adopt even phonological and grammatical phenomena. In areas outside the Ottoman Empire, however, the conventions of the centralized Byzantine state had already been lost with the advent of 'Latin' rule after 1204, and here the local forms of Greek not only underwent ***Romance**, particularly Italian, influence, but also acquired prestige of their own as official/literary media. In Venetian Crete in particular, dialect literature of exceptional quality began to emerge, with the remarkable 16th–17th-c. poetry of the Cretan renaissance occupying pride of place. Sadly, this too ended when Crete succumbed to the Turks in 1669.

The absence of a Greek state and the fact that the Renaissance could make only a limited impact on lands under diffuse and often short-lived western control severely inhibited the development of a standard form of modern Greek in the modern period. The Church and the Greek aristocracy clung to their ancient traditions, and such literary languages as did emerge were too 'local' to serve as national standards. The language question only became acute, however, during the 18th-c. Enlightenment when 'modern' thinking began to infiltrate Ottoman Greek lands, primarily through the influence of Italian and other western universities where many Greeks secured a higher education. By this time Greeks had also come to control much of the trade of the Ottoman empire with 'colonies' in Egypt, Russia and many western countries, while a number of aristocratic families effectively ran Ottoman foreign policy from Constantinople and ruled in the Danubian principalities of Wallachia and Moldavia (modern Romania), where western ideas also penetrated, via the Danube, from Vienna.

The quest for a modern standard language

All educated Greeks were in broad agreement that a standard written language was essential for the development of mass education and as a vehicle of culture and administration in any future Greek state. There was, however, no agreement as to the form such a language should take. The dispute was largely conducted, somewhat ironically, in a common rhetorical style which had evolved amongst the educated classes out of the archaizing, but not archaic, style of ordinary administration and had regularly admitted developments, particularly syntactic and lexical, from spoken Greek. Some advocated this as a basis for the evolution of a standard language, broadly in line with educated spoken usage, while others promoted the idea of its 'purification' in the direction of ancient Attic. Other groups, however, wished to build on the more archaic formal language of the aristocracy and church hierarchy, while others still, encouraged by western enthusiasm for ancient Greece and driven by sentiments akin to those that had fuelled the Second Sophistic, even planned the restoration of classical Attic. In contrast with all those who advocated some level of the traditional 'learned' language, a radical group, influenced by developments in the West, promoted the idea of a national language based on the living speech of the people.

As a background to subsequent developments, it will be useful at this point to present an outline history of Greece as it emerged from Ottoman tyranny. Growing national consciousness, dismay among intellectuals at Greek backwardness, and general frustration with Ottoman brutality and incompetence finally led to a war of independence and the establishment in 1833 of an autonomous Greek kingdom south of a line from Arta to Vólos. The subsequent history of Greece was dominated by economic weakness, political rivalry (between royalists and republicans, and later between right and left) and irredentism (most of the great centres of Greek population still lying outside the tiny kingdom). In the period before the First World War Greece expanded to something like its modern frontiers, but disaster struck in 1922 when, having sought to exploit the final collapse of the Ottoman Empire by launching a campaign deep into Asia Minor, the Greeks were decisively defeated. The result was an enforced exchange of populations which led to the final elimination of the Greek presence in Asia and an influx of one and a half million refugees. Further political instability led to military dictatorship, and, after the horrors of German occupation in the Second World War, to civil war between communists, who had led the resistance, and government forces backed by Britain and the USA. Political troubles continued after the communist defeat and finally resulted in another right-wing dictatorship (1967–74). The legacy of bitterness has only recently faded with the final abolition of the monarchy and Greek membership of the European Union (1981) which helped secure prosperity and democratic government. Mutual suspicion and hostility between Greece and Turkey remain, none the less, fuelled by territorial disputes in the Aegean and the unresolved Cyprus problem.

The establishment of the Greek state saw the *de facto* institutionalization of what was later known as *katharévousa* ('purifying' language), initially the contemporary educated written language, but subjected through most of the 19th c. to progressive 'purification' (i.e. antiquing). By the 1880s, poets and dramatists had rejected the increasingly sterile artificiality of *katharévousa* by writing in demotic (the language 'of the people'), and this encouraged the leaders of the demoticist movement to work for the abolition of *katharévousa* altogether. Though demotic was at last introduced into primary schools in 1913, it made little headway elsewhere, the real obstacle being the politicization of the language question, with demotic being associated by the establishment, quite unfairly, with the causes of the revolutionary left. Demotic was eventually put on an equal footing with *katharévousa* as a language of education in 1964, but the military dictatorship of 1967–74 immediately reversed the reform and the final adoption of 'Demotic' as the language of administration (1976) had to wait for the demise of this odious regime. Thereafter *katharévousa* was increasingly confined to the law, the army and the church, and today it has all but disappeared, thus bringing nearly 2,000 years of diglossia to an end and releasing Greeks at last from the burden of their linguistic past (albeit at the cost of rendering much earlier literature inaccessible). None the less, the relationship between modern Greek and the ancient language remains a hot educational and political potato, and creative writers still experiment with registers that reflect the complex history of their language.

The term 'demotic' is little used today, and 'common' or 'standard' modern Greek has largely replaced it. The reason is that the rather artificial polarization of the theoretical debate long disguised the fact that the institutionalization of *katharévousa* had had a marked impact on traditional spoken demotic. This was, of course, far from homogeneous in the early 19th c., given the geographical spread of the language, and it was a happy chance that the revolution centred on the Peloponnese, an area whose dialect lacked both the radical sound changes of northern varieties and the archaisms of Cretan or Cypriot, and which corresponded quite well with the traditional language of vernacular literature and the spoken usage of Constantinople. A new spoken Koine therefore quickly evolved in southern Greece, based on Peloponnesian, but influenced by the dialects of speakers who came to the new kingdom from all over the Greek-speaking world.

Nevertheless, those who promoted demotic as the basis for a national language at the end of the 19th c. had to face the fact that it lacked the grammatical uniformity and lexical range of a true 'standard', and so were obliged to systematize its grammar and enrich its vocabulary with coinages based on ancient roots recast in demotic form. The educated classes, however, brought up with *katharévousa*, largely rejected this 'artificiality', instinctively preferring internal borrowings from ancient Greek with minimal adaptation. Their spoken language therefore developed naturally as a mixture of demotic and *katharévousa*, and a written variety related to this mixture (though containing more *katharévousa*) came to be widely used in all but the most right-wing newspapers. Mid-20th-c. grammars of demotic based on a normalization of the usage of the folk songs and early demotic literature unaffected by *katharévousa* therefore represent an ideal which had already been superseded by events on the ground. By the early 20th c., the rural dialects of the uneducated (traditional demotic) stood in contrast with the mixed spoken/written usage of the educated urban classes. And as the spoken standard developed its own internal coherence and came gradually to be used, in a written form, in ever more fields once dominated by *katharévousa*, it naturally attracted still further characteristics of the old written language, some of which then passed in turn into educated spoken discourse. Though many conscientious demoticist writers continue to conform to the rules of their ideal, their language has in fact become an artificial 'literary' dialect. Today, therefore, both the local spoken varieties (which are in any case under pressure from universal education and the impact of radio and television) and written demotic are best seen as dialects subsumed under the umbrella of standard modern Greek, the contemporary form of the spoken and written language employed by the educated majority in the major urban centres.

Greek literature since the war of independence has been particularly rich and inventive, though none of any great merit has ever been produced in 'pure' *katharévousa*. Outstanding figures of international repute include Aléxandros Papadiamándis (1851–1911, who used a lively and accessible *katharévousa* in his short stories, but combined this with much demotic dialogue), the novelist Níkos Kazandzákis (1883–1957), and the poets Konstandínos Kaváfis (1863–1933), Yórgos Seféris (1900–71) and Odiséas Elítis (b.1911), the last two being Nobel laureates.

Present situation of the language

Greek is the sole official language of the Republic of Greece (*c*.10,000,000 speakers) and, with *Turkish, one of the official languages of the Republic of Cyprus (*c*.500,0000 speakers), and there are also large Greek-speaking communities in North America, Australia, Germany and the UK as a result of relatively recent emigration (some 2 to 3 million speakers). No accurate details are available for Greece since there has been no census including questions about language since 1951. At various periods in the past, however, Greek was spoken widely elsewhere in the Balkans, in Southern Italy and Sicily, in Turkey, the Middle East and North Africa, and in Ukraine and the Caucasus. Small numbers of speakers still survive in at least some of these regions (perhaps most notably southern Albania), but the 20th c. has seen a massive concentration of the Greek-speaking population through population exchanges (between Greece, Bulgaria and Serbia in 1913–19, and between Greece and Turkey in 1923) and repatriation (from the Soviet Union in 1919, and from Egypt under Nasser after 1952). Within Greece this, along with the German deportation and murder of the Ladino-speaking Jews (see *Judeo-Spanish) of Thessaloniki during the Second World War, has produced near-total linguistic homogeneity, though there are still a few speakers of *Macedonian Slav (in Macedonia), Vlach (see *Aromanian and *Megleno-Romanian) (in Macedonia and Epirus) and *Albanian (in Epirus, Attica, Boeotia and the Peloponnese), as well as large Turkish communities (*c*.100,000) in Thrace, these people having been permitted to stay under the terms of the 1923 exchange (as were the Greeks of Istanbul/Constantinople, though subsequent persecution has since forced the departure of virtually the whole Greek community).

Currently, standard modern Greek is used throughout the education system, in government, journalism and broadcasting, though traces of *katharévousa* persist in the legal profession, the army, and the Orthodox Church, where the Byzantine liturgy also remains in use alongside the original text of the New Testament. The principal spoken dialects can be divided into Peloponnesian-Heptanesian (the base for the modern standard), Northern, Old Athenian (which survives residually in Megara and central Euboea), Cretan-Cycladic and south-eastern subgroups, the last of which includes Cypriot as a rather aberrant member. Within Greece proper, these varieties are increasingly subject to the influence of the modern standard. Though the dialects of Cappadocia disappeared with the exchange of populations, Pontic dialects from the southern coast of the Black Sea are still spoken by the families of many refugees (though again subject to progressive assimilation) and small groups of Muslim speakers actually remain in the region of Trebizond. Very small numbers of Greek-speakers also survive in remote villages of Calabria and Otranto in southern Italy. The Italian and Asia Minor dialects, cut off from the mainstream for centuries, are naturally very different from the 'core' dialects, and could arguably be classified as separate languages. The special case of Tsakonian has already been discussed above (see under 'The emergence and evolution of a standard language').

Despite the widespread use of Greek as a lingua franca in Hellenistic, Roman, Byzantine and even Ottoman times (originally as a diplomatic language and latterly as the language of administration in the Danubian principalities), 19th-c. nationalism and 20th-c. population shifts have produced a situation in which it is no longer routinely learned as a second language in any non-Greek community. It is, however, one of the official languages of the European Union.

Blass, F. W. and Debrunner, A. 1961. *A Greek Grammar of the New Testament*, 6th edn, translated by Robert W. Funk. Chicago and London.

Browning, R. 1983. *Medieval and Modern Greek*, 2nd edn. Cambridge.

Holton, D. W., Mackridge, P. and Philippaki-Warburton, I. 1997. *Greek: A Comprehensive Grammar of the Modern Language*. London.

Horrocks, G. C. 1997. *Greek: A History of the Language and Its Speakers*. London.

Liddell, H. G., Scott. R., Jones, H. S. and McKenzie, R. 1940. *A Greek–English Lexicon*, 9th edn. Oxford.

Mackridge, P. 1985. *The Modern Greek Language*. Oxford.

Palmer, L. R. 1980. *The Greek Language*. London.

Schwyzer, E. 1939–71. *Griechische Grammatik* ('Greek Grammar') (4 vols: vol. 2 ed. A. Debrunner 1959; vols 3 and 4 by J. Georgacas 1953, and F. and S. Radt 1971). Munich.

Sihler, A. L. 1995. *A Comparative Grammar of Greek and Latin*. Oxford.

GEOFFREY HORROCKS

Greenlandic

West Greenlandic (Inuit, Eskimo) is spoken by a small group of bilingual Greenlanders more or less permanently resident in Denmark. They are spread throughout the country and so do not constitute a coherent population. No statistics are available as to their numbers and most of them have *Danish as their first language.

Guernesiais, see *Guernsey French*

Guernsey French (Guernesiais)

The variety of *Channel Islands French spoken on the island of Guernsey.

The Anglicization of Guernsey began in the 19th c. with the growth of trade and tourism, and was further encouraged in the latter part of the century by English-language education, but Guernesiais remained the language of most homes except in and around the capital, St Peter Port. Sjögren (1964: xiv–xviii) found in 1926 that few then knew the language in St Peter Port and the island's second town, St Sampson, and that it was seriously undermined in many rural areas, though it flourished in the south-west of the island and the northern parish of Câtel. As late as the 1930s, there were some who could not express themselves in English but the evacuation of most of the children in 1940 to England, where those who could speak Guernesiais largely lost their command of it, dealt the language a blow from which it has not recovered. In the post-war period, the decline has been aggravated by an influx of outsiders, either as residents or as tourists, and the Anglicizing influence of the mass media. No census figures are available for the number of speakers but they are unlikely to number more than five or six thousand, representing some 10% to 11% of the population, and very few under the age of 40 now speak it.

Guernesiais has been used in verse by the mid-19th-c. writer Georges Métivier (who also translated the Gospel according to St Matthew into Guernesiais, 1863) and others, and, in more recent times, for short plays and stories.

De Garis, M. 1982. *Dictiounnaire Angllais–Guernesiais*, revised edn. Chichester.

—— 1983. Guernesiais, a grammatical survey. *Société Guernesiaise: Report and Transactions*, 21: 319–53.

Sjögren, A. 1964 *Les Parlers bas-normands de l'île de Guernesey:* vol. 1, *Lexique français–guernesiais*. Paris.

GLANVILLE PRICE

Gujarati (see under *Community languages (Britain)*)

Gunzib (see *Hunzib* under *Caucasian languages. IV. North-East Caucasian family*)

Gypsy, see *Romani*

H

Hebrew

A NW *Semitic language, employed since biblical times by Jews. In Europe it has been primarily a medium of writing and recitation rather than a mother tongue. Today most European Jews (concentrated in Britain and France) learn to recite it phonically for occasional worship; a small minority can understand and perhaps express themselves in written and/or spoken Hebrew – the latter reintroduced early in the 20th c. and now the main language of some 4 million Israeli Jews.

Hebrew as a vernacular survived in Judaea until the 2nd c. From their initial dispersal around the Roman Empire in the 1st c., Hebrew was probably widely studied and recited by European Jews as the main language of scripture and liturgy, commonly known as *Leshon Qodesh* 'the Holy Tongue'. For other purposes, a variety of Judaized local languages were used. The large Jewish population of the Roman Empire has left little Hebrew behind. However, from the 10th–11th centuries onwards we have major manuscripts of sacred texts and many secular documents, indicating that Hebrew was not just a sacred tongue but the high-function language in a polyglossic system. Indeed, it has sometimes served as an oral Jewish lingua franca.

The use of Hebrew to study and recite Jewish sacred texts (notably the Bible, Prayer Book, Talmud and their later commentaries), taught intensively to the young, has continued down to the present day. In addition, the Hebrew alphabet and vocabulary were the subject of esoteric speculation and manipulation in some Jewish circles, notably in medieval central Europe, and subsequently among the Christian Kabbalists of the Renaissance, who inspired the trilingual (Latin–Greek–Hebrew) educational system of Tudor England and the Hebraic Puritan culture that was transported to the New World. Among Jews, some men and probably most women, with little access to schooling, simply learned to read without much understanding; and with the broad decline in Orthodox Judaism throughout Europe owing to modernization and the effects of Hitler and Stalin, only a small minority of European Jews today acquire a working understanding of Hebrew.

The productive use of Hebrew for writing emerged with a Hebrew school of liturgical poetry in 9th-c. Italy, and as the Jewish cultural focus moved from the Near

East to southern Europe, the next two centuries witnessed an explosion of Hebrew poetry – and, in Christendom, a burgeoning of Hebrew prose, philosophical, legal, historical, scientific and commercial. Faced by the prestige of medieval *Arabic, Jews under Islam did not feel confident about writing Hebrew prose. However, the courts of Jewish grandees serving the Muslim rulers of Andalusia produced a secular Hebrew poetry, modelled on the Arabic poetry of wine, women and patronage but linguistically a celebration of biblical Hebrew, in direct challenge to Qur'anic triumphalism. Thus began a 500-year so-called Iberian Golden Age of Hebrew creativity. Meanwhile, throughout Christendom, from Castile to Byzantium, Hebrew was *the* Jewish written language for both poetry and prose, and it was in no sense tied to biblical norms: the prose tended to follow the ongoing tradition of Rabbinic legalese and narrative or Middle Arabic in grammar and lexis, though inevitably influenced to an extent by the local vernaculars; the poetry, though largely liturgical, was often exuberantly innovative in its language, quite atypical of the stereotype of a frozen classical tongue. The Hebrew of law and mysticism was in fact a blend with Judeo-*Aramaic, a semi-hallowed language (related to Hebrew and sharing the same script) in which much of the Talmud and Kabbalah was couched. As the main vehicle for the transfer of scientific knowledge from the Arab world to Christendom, medieval Hebrew evolved a rich new vocabulary, with heavy calquing from Arabic as well as internal innovation. Until the late 19th c., however, Hebrew used very few direct European borrowings. By sheer intensive use, identifiable norms evolved for the various genres, but no explicit standards and no grammatical dialects – for all the prestige of the medium, no grammars of post-biblical usage were created until the 19th c., and only biblical grammar was studied, often for exegetical rather than prescriptive purposes. Naturally, European Hebrew, unlike spoken languages, never cut loose from its ancient forms; in all its stages and genres it is one language, and both religious and secular writers have tended to draw upon the classical phraseology open-endedly. In turn, the Jewish vernaculars took on a Hebrew colouring.

Pronunciation, by contrast, has varied sharply by region, almost to the point of mutually incomprehensible dialects – despite the use of a single Hebrew orthography across Europe since the 13th c. Indeed, despite ostensible regulations on recitation of scripture, many graphemic distinctions have long been ignored. Although the difference between Sephardi (Iberian, later Balkan) and Ashkenazi (central and eastern European) pronunciation is considered fundamental, major differences have existed for a few hundred years between, for example, German, Central Polish, Lithuanian Hebrew, under vernacular influence. Additionally, there are large variations on a scale of formality: the Hebrew of Torah recitation > of worship > as the odd phrase incorporated into the vernacular.

Though important post-medieval changes occurred (e.g. the expulsion of Iberian Jewry, the steady migration towards eastern Europe, the demise of Hebrew *belles-lettres* in central and eastern Europe), the broad picture persisted until the 19th c., when a succession of ruptures ensued in central and then in eastern Europe. Jews were encouraged to integrate and many abandoned their Jewish languages for all but religious purposes. Commercial Hebrew was effectively outlawed. For a time, a

	Name	Phonetic value
א	alef	[ʔ]
ב	beys	[b, v]
ג	gimel	[g]
ד	daled	[d]
ה	hey	[h, ʔ]
ו	vov	[v]
ז	zayen	[z]
ח	khes	[x]
ט	tes	[t]
י	yud	[j]
ך, כ	khaf	[k, x]
ל	lamed	[l]
ם, מ	mem	[m]
ן, נ	nun	[n]
ס	samekh	[s]
ע	ayen	[ʔ]
ף, פ	pey	[p, f]
ץ, צ	tsadi	[ts]
ק	kuf	[k]
ר	reysh	[ʁ]
ש	shin	[ʃ, s]
ת	tov	[t, s]

Fig. 8 The Hebrew alphabet. These are the names and phonetic values most typical of Hebrew in pre-Second World War European Jewish society. For the values of the characters of the International Phonetic Alphabet, see pp. xvi–xvii.

group of Hebraists (the *Maskilim*) promoted Hebrew as a classical tongue comparable to Latin – even writing novels in biblical style to prove it – or as a modern counterpart of literary German or Russian; in a bid to 'modernize' the Jewish masses, Hebrew newspapers and literary journals sprang up and popular science was translated. In response, traditionalist Hasidic Jews created a new Hebrew folk literature. But it was out of a realization that Hebrew among Westernizing Jews was doomed to go the same way as Latin that a handful of Zionists, led by Ben-Yehuda, set out in the 1880s to create a Hebrew-speaking society in the Holy Land. This was both revolution and continuity: they used traditional lexis and hundreds of new coinages, European Hebrew syntax, biblicized morphology, and a pointedly different pronunciation with Middle Eastern and biblicizing features. The runaway success of Zionism and of Native Hebrew, named *Ivrit* in contradistinction with the traditional *Leshon Qodesh*, in turn engendered a large-scale Hebrew-speaking school system in inter-war Poland. But hopes for the flowering of a modernized Hebrew-speaking society in eastern Europe were dashed by the Holocaust and by a Soviet state that committed linguacide against Hebrew for its purported 'reactionary clericalism'. Today, Hebrew in the Diaspora has retreated to the synagogue and the school, but not without further change: as a token of modernity and identification with the State of Israel, an Israeli pronunciation has been widely adopted for religious use.

Hebrew has always employed a Hebrew script (see fig. 8). For poetry and in sacred texts with strict recitational standards, diacritics are added to indicate vowels and other features. Otherwise, the script is predominantly consonantal.

Alcalay, R. 1965. *The Complete Hebrew–English English–Hebrew Dictionary*, 2 vols. Tel-Aviv.
Fishman, J. (ed.) 1985. *Readings in the Sociology of Jewish Languages*. Leiden.
Glinert, L. 1989. *The Grammar of Modern Hebrew*. Cambridge.
—— (ed.) 1993. *Hebrew in Ashkenaz: A Language in Exile*. New York.
Harshav, B. 1993. *Language in Time of Revolution*. Berkeley.

LEWIS GLINERT

Hindi (see under *Community languages (Netherlands)*)

Hinukh (see under *Caucasian languages. IV. North-East Caucasian family*)

Hirpinian (see under *Oscan*)

Hispano-Romance languages, see *Ibero-Romance languages*

Hmong (see under *Community languages (France)*)

Hungarian

Hungarian (Magyar) is a member of the Ugrian subgroup of the *Uralic languages. Other members of the Ugrian subgroup include Vogul (Manysi) and Ostyak (Hanti).

Today most Hungarian speakers (some 10 million) live in the Republic of Hungary. There are also large groups (about 3 million in all) in the neighbouring countries, i.e. Austria, Slovakia, Slovenia, Croatia, Serbia, Romania and Ukraine.

External history

As the common designation of the language family shows, the parent language or proto-Uralic is assumed to have been spoken in the region of the Ural mountains.

The ***Finno-Ugrian** period which followed is dated to 4000–2000 BC and is located between the rivers Volga and Kama and the Ural mountains. It is assumed that the separation and emergence of Hungarian took place about 1000–500 BC, perhaps as a result of the appearance of ***Turkic**-speaking groups.

The ethnonym 'Magyar' is first attested in the 9th–10th centuries in Muslim and Byzantine sources as a tribal designation. It appears as the generic name of all Magyar-speakers in the form *mogyeri* in a 12th-c. chronicle.

The periodization of the history of the language is:

  I.   Proto-Hungarian (Uralic period until 1000 BC)
 II.   Ancient Hungarian (1000 BC to AD 896)
III.   Old Hungarian (AD 896 to the 16th c.)
 IV.   Middle Hungarian (16th c. to the late 18th c.)
  V.   Modern Hungarian (late 18th c. to the present).

While the above periodization follows political and cultural events which played a part in the history of the language, another periodization, which takes the internal development of the language as its basis, is also possible. According to this, the Old Hungarian period came to a close in the mid-14th c., by which time a great many important phonological changes had been completed; the Middle Hungarian period falls between the mid-14th and late 16th centuries; and the modern period is dated from the emergence of the Hungarian literary language around the turn of the 17th c.

Earliest attestations

The first attestations of the Hungarian language are titles, tribal, personal and place-names and common nouns appearing in Arabic, Persian, Byzantine and western European sources dating from the 10th to the 12th centuries. Such fragments occur in greater numbers in foreign-language sources produced in Hungary from the 11th to the 15th centuries. One of the earliest in this group is the deed of gift of the nuns from the Veszprém valley, written in Greek and dating from before 1002, and the deed of endowment of the Monastery of Tihany from 1055, written in Latin. The latter contains numerous Hungarian words and suffixes and the fragment of a Hungarian sentence. Further fragments can be found in judicial documents, lists relating to taxation, and in medieval Latin chronicles and their marginal notes explaining foreign-language texts. Among the latter, particularly well known are the word-lists of Königsberg (14th c.) and of Beszterce (1380–1410).

The first written document containing continuous Hungarian is the Funeral Oration (*Halotti Beszéd*, c.1200), containing 190 words. Another early Hungarian text of similar importance for the history of the language is the Old Hungarian Mary Lament (*Ómagyar Mária Siralom*) from around 1300. It is a free artistic translation of a Latin hymn and therefore the first poetic document in the Hungarian language. The 15th and 16th centuries are sometimes called the 'period of codices'; a large number of Hungarian religious chronicles survives from this period. These works are primarily translations. The earliest, the so-called Jókai codex (1448), recounts the life and deeds of St Francis. The first Hungarian Bible translation, also known as the Hussite Bible after the religious affiliation of its authors, survived in three codices (the Codex of Vienna, the Apor Codex and the Codex of Munich, all written between 1450 and 1490). From the end of the 15th c., alongside the religious literature we find texts of a more secular nature, including letters and historical chronicles, medical books, calendars and love poetry. While all these texts survived in manuscript form, in the 16th c. we also have the first Hungarian printed books. The first printing office was actually set up in the 15th c. by András Hess in Buda, but the first books printed here were written in Latin. The first Hungarian printed books were produced in Kraków (the school books of János Sylvester in Latin and Hungarian, 1527; the Letters of Pál Zenth by Benedek Komjáti, 1533) and Vienna (Aesop's Fables, 1536, and the New Testament, 1536, both by Gábor Pesti). The first Hungarian-language book printed in Hungary was János Sylvester's translation of the New Testament, published in Sárvár in 1541.

The Reformation promoted religious teaching in Hungarian and, combined with the spread of humanism, created fertile ground for the promotion of Hungarian in all walks of life. While early authors produced works in their own local dialect, the first signs of the emergence of regional written norms appear in the late 16th c. The unification of these written idioms was accomplished over the 17th and 18th centuries. By the late 18th c., i.e. the age of Enlightenment, the number of literary norms was reduced to two, the western and the eastern. At the turn of the 19th c. we have the emergence of a unified literary idiom in the so-called Reform Period. This unification was greatly assisted by the language reform that was first promoted by the literati of the Enlightenment in their struggle against the widespread use and official status of German. To promote Hungarian became part of the nationalists' programme. The language reform created a situation in which the conservatives (*ortológus*) and modernists (*neológus*) confronted each other starkly. This fight ended with the victory of the modernists, and as a result a great number of words invented by the reformists have become integrated into modern Hungarian. The first important synthesis of the efforts of the language reformers was the epic poem 'The Flight of Zalán' (*Zalán futása*) by Mihály Vörösmarty in 1825. This was followed by the first efforts to standardize spelling (1832), but it was not until 1844 that the Hungarian language was given official status by a decree of Parliament. The first normative grammar and spelling, mainly the work of the poet Vörösmarty, were also the products of this period. In spite of attempts to Germanize immediately after the defeat of the 1848–9 Revolution and War of Independence, the second half of the 19th c. witnessed a revival of interest in the history of the language; it is in this period that J. Budenz (who was of German extraction) laid the foundations for research into the Finno-Ugrian origins of Hungarian.

Scripts

Apart from some of the early scattered materials in the foreign-language documents, all the above-mentioned materials were written in the Latin alphabet, but mention must be made of the scattered remains of the Old Hungarian runic alphabet (see

Runes), associated with the pre-Christian history of the Hungarians, traces of which must have survived well into the Middle Ages.

Dialects

The major Hungarian dialects include the Western group (spoken to the west of the Danube); the Northern group, including the Palóc dialects, which extends from the Nyitra–Szolnok–Kassa line towards the north; the Southern group, including dialects spoken in the south-eastern parts of Transdanubia, the Szeged region and the Great Hungarian Plain; and the Eastern group, covering the dialects spoken east of the Tisza–Körös line, around the southern course of the Körös, and the western and north-western Hungarian settlements in Romania.

Interrelationship with other languages

While Hungarian vocabulary has been heavily influenced by a number of other languages, it is generally accepted that about 80% of the modern written and spoken language is made up of Finno-Ugrian-type elements.

One of the earliest layers of loan-words in Hungarian is of **Iranian** origin. Within this, several sublayers can be distinguished, from the early stages of migration in the Ural region to contacts with Iranian groups who settled in Hungary during the 13th c.

While one must reckon with **Caucasian** influences upon Hungarian vocabulary during the period of migration, much greater influence has been exerted by Turkic languages. Three layers of Turkic loan-words can be distinguished: (a) loan-words dating from before the Conquest of the Carpathian Basin in the 10th c.; while some of these borrowings may have dated from before the migration away from the Uralic *Urheimat*, most of them date from the period of migration and reveal the influence of Common Turkic or **Chuvash**-type Turkic languages; this borrowed vocabulary consists of about 300 words, mostly related to animal husbandry, agriculture, accommodation, clothes and social life; (b) borrowings from Kipchak-type (see under **Tatar**) Turkic languages appeared in Hungarian in the 11th to the 14th centuries as a result of the immigration of Pecheneg and Cuman (see under **Tatar**) groups into the country; (c) the last layer is the result of the Ottoman conquest of parts of Hungary and dates from the 16th and 17th centuries; the majority of these borrowings have become obsolete and only about 30 are widely used in the modern language; it is also likely that some of these borrowings came into Hungarian via Southern **Slavonic** dialects.

The small group of Greek loan-words is the result of contacts with Byzantium which began before the arrival of Hungarians in the Carpathian Basin and continued well into the 12th c.

A considerable proportion of the loan-words in Hungarian are from Slavonic languages, and those in active use today total approximately 600. This vocabulary came into Hungarian at different times from various host languages: Old Russian, Southern and Western Slavonic dialects. These words relate to agriculture and animal husbandry, social, family and religious life, manufacturing, fishing, hunting, animal and plant names, and the names of some of the days, for example *kapál* 'to dig' < *kopát; apáca* 'nun' < Southern Slav *opatica; kereszt* 'cross' < Serbo-Croat *krst; ruha* 'dress' < *rucho; utca* 'street' < Slavonic *ulica*. Modern borrowings from Russian in the socialist period have also left their mark, e.g. *kolhoz* 'cooperative' < *kolhoz, kulak* 'rich peasant' < *kulak*.

German loan-words appeared in Hungarian as a result of several waves of immigrants, mainly urban, from the 12th and 13th centuries onwards. German influence increased during the 16th to the 18th centuries and continued into the 19th c., partly through renewed immigration and partly through the policies of the Habsburg administration. The German loan-words represent several German dialects and are far from homogeneous. A great deal of this vocabulary relates to food, clothes, military expressions, and to social and court culture, e.g. *polgár* 'burgher, citizen' < Middle High German *burgaere; pór* 'peasant' < Middle High German *bure*, German *Bauer; céh* 'guild' < Bavarian *Zech; copf* 'plait' < *Zopf; pucol* 'to clean' < *putzen*. In addition, German also acted as a mediator of western cultural words from other languages.

Borrowings from ***Romance languages** include four major groups. Approximately 2,000 words were borrowed from Latin, which was both the liturgical language of medieval Christian Hungary and an important carrier of secular culture. This vocabulary includes expressions relating to religion and religious organization, law, animal and plant names, the names of the months, e.g. *iskola* 'school' < *schola; ceruza* 'pencil' < *cerussa; juss* 'right, inheritance' < *jus; fülemüle* 'lark' < *philomela; petrezselyem* 'parsley' < *petrosillum; patika* 'pharmacy' < *apotheca*. In addition, a great many modern scientific and cultural expressions are also derived from Latin, e.g. *stilus* 'style' < *stylus; véna* 'vein' < *vena*.

Dynastic and cultural contacts resulted in some borrowings from French during the 12th and 13th centuries, while later borrowings came in via German mediation (particularly in the 18th and 19th centuries); *mécs* 'night-light' < Old French *meche*.

Italian loan-words came into Hungarian as a result of strong political contacts in early medieval times which, however, weakened in the 15th c., e.g. *mandula* 'almond' < *mandorla, mazsola* 'raisins' < *malvasia, piac* 'market-place' < *piazza*.

*Romanian influence is naturally more considerable in the Hungarian dialects of Transylvania. Examples of Romanian loan-words in Hungarian include *kaláka* 'voluntary communal work' < *clácă; cimbora* 'friend, pal' < *simbra*.

In addition, there is a large number of direct or indirect borrowings from modern European languages and international words derived from Latin and Greek.

Present situation

Hungarian today is the official language of the Hungarian Republic. It is spoken by approximately 10 million people in Hungary, over 3 million in adjacent regions, and about 1 million in western Europe, the USA and Canada. According to recent statistics published by Hungarian demographers, the number of Hungarians in 1990 in Austria (Burgenland) was 15,000, in Slovakia 765,000, in Slovenia (Muravidék) 10,000, in Serbia (Vajdaság) 400,000, in Romania (Erdély, i.e. Transylvania) 2,000,000, and in Ukraine (Kárpátalja) 200,000.

Abondolo, D. M. 1988. *Hungarian Inflectional Morphology*. Budapest.

—— 1990. Hungarian. In Comrie, B. (ed.), *The Major Languages of Eastern Europe*, London, 185–200.

Bárczi, G., Benkő, L. and Berrár, J. 1967. *A magyar nyelv története* ('A History of the Hungarian Language'). Budapest.

Benkő, L., Abaffy, E. and Rácz, E. (eds) 1991–2. *A magyar nyelv történeti nyelvtana* ('Historical Grammar of Hungarian'), vol. 1, *A korai ómagyar kor és előzményei* ('The Early Period of Old Hungarian and Its Antecedents'); vol.2, *A kései ómagyar kor. Morfematika* ('The Late Period of Old Hungarian. Morphematics'). Budapest.

Benkő, L. and Imre, S. (eds) 1972. *The Hungarian Language*. The Hague and Paris.

Benkő, L. et al. (eds) 1967–84. *A magyar nyelv történeti–etimológiai szótára* ('Historical–Etymological Dictionary of the Hungarian Language'), 4 vols. Budapest.

Horváth, J. 1986. *Focus in the Theory of Grammar and the Syntax of Hungarian*. Dordrecht.

Kiefer, F. (ed.) 1982. *Hungarian Linguistics*. Amsterdam and Philadelphia.

Országh, L. 1982. *A Comprehensive English–Hungarian Dictionary*, 2 vols. Budapest.

—— 1982. *Hungarian–English Dictionary*, 2 vols. Budapest.

ILDIKÓ BELLÉR-HANN

Hunnic

In the period of 80 years or so between the time when the Huns moved westwards into European Russia in or about AD 370 and the defeat of Attila in 451 at the battle of the 'Catalaunian Plains', an unidentified site in France, possibly near Troyes, after which they rapidly disappear from history, the Huns ravaged much of Europe. No linguistic trace of their passage through Europe appears to remain but, from the evidence of a few words and fragments from Chinese sources, it can be established that Hunnic was an early *Turkic language.

Thompson, E. A. 1996. *The Huns*, revised edn by P. Heather. Oxford.

Hunzib (see under *Caucasian languages. IV. North-East Caucasian family*)

I

Iatvingian, see *Yatvingian*

Iberian

A number of inscriptions from an extensive area of eastern Spain and dating from the 5th to the 1st centuries BC, most of them in the so-called 'Iberian script' in which most *Celtiberian inscriptions are written but a small number in Greek script, are in an unknown non-*Indo-European language that, for want of a better name, has been termed 'Iberian'. Attempts to establish a relationship with *Basque have so far proved unsuccessful.

Ibero-Romance languages

The SW group (also termed 'Hispano-Romance languages') of the ***Romance languages**, consisting of ***Portuguese**, ***Galician**, ***Spanish** and ***Catalan** (but see also ***Gallo-Romance languages**).

Icelandic

A member of the western branch of the ***Scandinavian** subgroup of the ***Germanic languages** and the official language of Iceland.

Origins and early texts

The settlement of Iceland by Scandinavians mainly from Norway in the late 9th c. is believed to have been complete by AD 930, the date of the founding of the Icelandic Commonwealth with the establishment of its Parliament, the *Alþingi*. Icelandic is thought to have begun its development as a language distinct from Norwegian in the 12th c., from the second half of which date the earliest preserved manuscripts. These mainly contain devotional and clerical literature translated or adapted from foreign sources, but also include a church inventory, a fragment of the Commonwealth law code (*Grágás*), and a treatise on calendrical computation. The earliest surviving manuscripts of the distinctively Icelandic prose literature known as sagas, which includes accounts of the lives of the kings of Norway, the lives of Icelandic bishops, and accounts of events of Icelandic history and prehistory, are from the 13th c. Preserved mainly as quotations in the sagas are the verses ostensibly on events of their poets' lifetimes that are known collectively as scaldic poetry, while from the late 13th c. dates the main manuscript of the 'Edda' poems, which deal with mythical and heroic subjects; both types of poetry may date originally from the 9th c.

While most of the extant medieval manuscripts are copies of lost exemplars, various original documents are preserved, of which a *necrologium* listing names of people from Iceland and dating probably from the 11th and 12th centuries may be taken as the oldest; and a number of runic inscriptions (see ***Runes**) survive from the 12th c. onwards.

Script

The script of the earliest manuscripts is the Carolingian minuscule, the form in which the Latin alphabet was introduced to Scandinavia in the wake of the conversion to Christianity, which was established in Iceland by a decree of the *Alþingi* in 999/1000. It is essentially the Roman alphabet that is in use today, with certain additions made in the medieval period as part of the process of adapting the Latin alphabet to the needs of Icelandic. These include the runic letter <þ>, borrowed from Old English and found in the oldest Icelandic manuscripts, and <ð>, borrowed from Old English by way of Norway and found in Icelandic manuscripts dating from the early 13th to the second half of the 14th c., but thereafter largely disappearing until the 18th and 19th centuries. The forms <þ> and <ð> are now used to indicate interdental fricatives, the former initially in a word or word stem, and the latter medially and terminally; their pronunciation may be voiced or unvoiced, depending on the context.

First grammars and dictionaries

Of great value for the study of the Old Icelandic sound system is the anonymous *First Grammatical Treatise*, written towards the middle of the 12th c. and preserved as the first and oldest of four grammatical treatises in a 14th-c. manuscript of the prose *Edda* of Snorri Sturluson (d.1241). The earliest printed grammar of Icelandic, Runólfur Jónsson's *Grammatica Islandica rudimenta*, dates from 1651. The earliest dictionary is the *Specimen lexici runici*, based on a glossary of Old Icelandic by Magnús Ólafsson of Laufás, in northern Iceland, and published in 1650. The first dictionary of the contemporary language is Guðmundur Andrésson's *Lexicon Islandicum*, published in 1683.

Printing

Printing was introduced to Iceland in the 16th c. The earliest Icelandic printed book, Oddur Gottskálksson's translation of the New Testament, was published in Roskilde, Denmark, in 1540, and the first complete Bible in Icelandic was published at the episcopal residence of Hólar, in northern Iceland, in 1584, under the editorship of Bishop Guðbrandur Þorláksson (1542–1627).

Modern literature

The tenacity of the metrical forms of the Edda poems is shown by the fact that an Eddaic metre was used for the Icelandic translation of Milton's *Paradise Lost* (by Jón Þorláksson, published in 1828). The alliteration characteristic of Eddaic and scaldic poetry, and also of the *rímur* (rhymed ballads, popular from the 14th c. onwards), is still used by some Icelandic poets. Of great importance for the interaction of the spoken and written language were the *Passíusálmar* ('Passion Hymns') by Hallgrímur Pétursson (*c*.1614–74) and the collection of prose sermons *Húspostilla* by Jón Vídalín (1666–1720), both frequently reprinted. The poet and naturalist Eggert Ólafsson (1726–68), who advocated a return to Old Icelandic spelling, may be mentioned as representative of those who sought to resist the ever-increasing influence of *Danish in the 18th c. (see below). The modern Icelandic novel effectively begins in the 19th c. with the work of Jón Thoroddsen (1818–68). The prose of the Golden Age of saga-writing (*c*.1230–80) can be read without great difficulty by modern Icelandic readers, and has posed for modern writers the problem of how to be innovative against the background of its influence. One writer who has engaged triumphantly with this problem – mainly as a novelist, though he has also written short stories, poems, plays and essays – is Halldór Laxness (1902–98), winner of the Nobel Prize for Literature in 1955. Younger Icelandic writers have meanwhile come to speak of the difficulty of writing 'in the shadow of Laxness', who has thus provided his contemporaries and successors with a standard comparable to that set by the sagas. Mention may also be made of the novelist, poet and playwright Thor Vilhjálmsson (1925–), winner of the Swedish Academy's Nordic Prize in 1992, and of the women writers Svava

Jakobsdóttir (1930–) and Steinunn Sigurðardóttir (1950–), both writers of fiction and plays and the latter also a poet.

Regional variation

Various factors have contributed to the relative freedom of Icelandic from dialect variation. These include a levelling of Scandinavian dialects among the earliest settlers, the fact that Icelandic has no substratum (since the country was virtually uninhabited before the settlement), the great distance of Iceland from countries where other languages are spoken, and the socially unifying influence of the *Alþingi* in the early period. Regional variation in pronunciation and vocabulary is today so slight that it would be misleading to speak of Icelandic dialects. Among pronunciation differences which might, however, be called dialectal are the presence in the north (as opposed to the absence elsewhere in Iceland) of an aspirated pronunciation of intervocalic [p, t, k] in such words as *tapa* ('to lose'), *láta* ('to let, allow') and *aka* ('to drive'); the tendency in the north towards a voiced pronunciation of [1, m, n, ð] before [p, t, k], with consequent aspirated pronunciation of the latter; and the tendency found in the south, and sporadically also in the west and east, towards what is popularly known as '*hv*- pronunciation' (as opposed to the now more widespread '*kv*- pronunciation') of *hv*-. Differences in vocabulary that might be described as dialectal may involve either the use of different words in the same sense, or the use of the same word in different senses, from one part of the country to another. As an example of the former, a tomcat is referred to as *högni* in the north of Iceland, *steggur* in the west, and *fress* in the south and east. As an example of the latter, the adjective *bjálfalegur* can be used in the meaning 'looking unwell' in the north, but elsewhere has the meaning 'stupid(-looking)'.

Loan-words and language purism

The conversion of Iceland to Christianity brought with it an influx of loan-words for ecclesiastical and educational concepts, many of them originally from Greek or Latin, but introduced into Icelandic by way of Germanic intermediaries, such as Old English and Old or Middle Low German. Examples are *kirkja* 'church', *messa* 'church service', *prestr* 'priest', *skóli* 'school' and *skrifa* 'to write'. The translating of chivalric literature during the period of saga-writing led to the introduction of such words as *riddari* 'knight' and *hæverskr* 'courteous' from Middle Low German, and in all probability *kurteiss* (also meaning 'courteous') from Old French. Iceland became subject to Norway in 1262–4, and later, when the Danish and Norwegian monarchies were united in 1380, to Denmark. From the 14th c. onwards, Icelandic and Norwegian became increasingly different, mainly as a result of changes in Norwegian. Icelandic loan-words from the turn of the 15th to the 16th c. reflect Low German influence, transmitted by trade and the presence of Low German books in Iceland from that time. Examples are *partur* 'part' (noun), *klókur* 'crafty' and *pína* 'to torment'. The Reformation in Iceland effectively took place in 1550, with the execution of its last Catholic bishop by the Danish authorities. German and Danish influence is especially evident in the vocabulary of the 16th-c. Icelandic translations of the Bible, much of which, in the light of subsequent purism, would look un-Icelandic to a modern reader; from this time also, however, date loan-words which have remained very much part of the language, e.g. *eyðileggja* 'to destroy' (cf. Danish *ødelægge*) and *kokkur* 'cook' (noun, cf. Danish *kok*, German *Koch*).

Danish influence on Icelandic became increasingly pronounced from the 16th c. onwards, affecting not only purely lexical matters: thanks to the social stratification introduced by the presence in Iceland of Danish officials, the forms *við* and *þið*, reflecting the Old Icelandic dual forms of the first and second person pronouns (meaning 'we two' and 'you two' respectively), were adopted as the plural forms of these pronouns (i.e. in the meanings 'we' and 'you', pl.), as a result of the increasing honorific use of what were originally their plural forms (*vér* and *þér*). This change appears to have spread from the south of Iceland over most of the country in the second half of the 17th c.

Language purism began in earnest in the Age of Enlightenment (1750–1830). Neologisms coined during that period and still in use include *gróðurhús* 'greenhouse' (literally 'growth-house') and *mannapi* 'anthropoid ape', both examples of compounds formed from already established words to denote new concepts. In the 19th c. the neologizing tendency became bound up with the struggle for national independence, eventually achieved with the proclamation of the Republic in 1944. Attributed to the Romantic poet Jónas Hallgrímsson (1807–45), an active proponent of this struggle and also a naturalist, are the compounds *aðdráttarafl* 'attractive force' and *dýrafræði* 'zoology'; from later in the 19th c. date the word *sími* (meaning originally 'cord') for 'telephone' and the compound *smásjá* 'microscope'. Among post-war neologisms may be mentioned *tölva* 'computer', formed from *tala* 'number' (noun), and *eyðni* 'AIDS', formed from *eyða* 'to destroy' (cf. *eyðileggja*), and echoing the pronunciation of the international expression.

Numbers of speakers

Apart from Iceland's present population of some 265,000 there are Icelandic speech communities in North America, where many Icelanders emigrated in the 19th and early 20th centuries. Census returns in 1930–1 showed 7,413 people of Icelandic descent in the USA and 19,382 in Canada; the corresponding figures for 1970–1 were 9,768 in the USA and 27,905 in Canada. In the 1931 Canadian census, about 82% of these listed Icelandic as their mother tongue; the corresponding figure for 1961 was about 28%. This decline is consistent with the decrease in the number of members of these communities who were actually born in Iceland; the proportion of these in Manitoba, which has the largest population of Icelandic descent in Canada, was about 30% in 1931 and about 5% in 1971.

Language policy

Four aspects of official language policy may finally be mentioned: the adoption in 1929 of a new statutory orthography, supplemented in 1974 by a virtual abolition of the letter <z>; the founding in 1965 of the Icelandic Language Committee (*Íslenzk málnefnd*, now spelt *Íslensk málnefnd*), entrusted with the making and collecting of *nýyrði* (neologisms) and with the task of 'guiding government agencies and the general public in matters of language on a scholarly basis'; the establishment in 1991 of the Personal Names Committee, 'for guidance in the giving of names'; and the Personal Names Act of 1996, exempting foreigners who take out Icelandic citizenship from the legal requirement, incumbent since 1925 on the great majority of Icelandic citizens, to follow the traditional name-giving practice of suffixing the forms *-son* ('son') or *-dóttir* ('daughter') to the genitive form of the father's (or, as has become increasingly popular in recent years, the mother's) Christian name, e.g. *Ólafur Guðmundsson, Ásdís Ólafsdóttir, Ingunn Ásdísardóttir.*

Benediktsson, H. 1961–2. Icelandic dialectology: methods and results. *Íslenzk tunga: Lingua Islandica*, 3: 72–113.

—— 1987. The Icelandic language. In Nordal, J. and Kristinsson, V. (eds), *Iceland 1986*, Reykjavík, 55–65.

Cleasby, R., Vigfusson, G. and Craigie, W. A. 1957. *An Icelandic–English Dictionary*, 2nd edn. Oxford.

Einarsson, S. 1949. *Icelandic: Grammar, Texts, Glossary*. Baltimore, MD.

Friðjónsson, J. 1978. *A Course in Modern Icelandic: Texts, Vocabulary, Grammar, Exercises, Translations*. Reykjavík.

Guðmundsson, H. 1977. Um ytri aðstæður íslenskrar málþróunar ('External factors concerning the history of Icelandic'). In Pétursson, E. G. and Kristjánsson, J. (eds), *Sjötíu ritgerðir helgaðar Jakobi Benediktssyni 20. júlí 1977*, 2 vols, Reykjavík, vol. 1, 314–25.

Halldórsson, H. (ed.) 1964. *Þættir um íslenzkt mál eftir nokkra íslenzka málfræðinga* ('Chapters on the Icelandic Language by Various Language Specialists from Iceland'). Reykjavík.

Hólmarsson, S., Sanders, C. and Tucker, J. 1989. *Íslensk–ensk orðabók: Concise Icelandic–English Dictionary*. Reykjavík.

Thráinsson, H. 1994. Icelandic, In König, E. and van der Auwera, J. (eds), *The Germanic Languages*, London, 142–89.

RORY MCTURK

Idiom Neutral (see under *Artificial languages*)

Ido (see under *Artificial languages*)

Illyrian (Ancient)

Before and during the Roman period, Illyrian tribes occupied an area to the east and north-east of the Adriatic, corresponding to much of the former Yugoslavia, except the east of Serbia and Macedonia, and to northern and central Albania. The term 'Illyrian' can therefore be properly applied to a little-known language spoken in the area at the time in question. There is no direct evidence for Illyrian now that a three-word inscription on a bronze ring found in Albania has been shown not to be Illyrian, as had been widely accepted, but probably Greek. Our sole source of information on the language, therefore, apart from four Illyrian words quoted by Greek or Latin authors (e.g. *sybinam appellant Illyri telum venabuli simile* 'sybina is what the Illyrians call a spear similar to a *venabulum* ["hunting spear"]'), consists of placenames and names of peoples and individuals given as Illyrian in Greek and Latin sources.

It is generally agreed, on the basis of principles of word-formation revealed in the onomastic evidence, that Illyrian was an ***Indo-European** language, though its position within the Indo-European family is controversial. ***Messapic** and ***Venetic**, once considered by some scholars to be varieties of Illyrian, are now usually reckoned to have been distinct languages, though Messapic (spoken in SE Italy) seems to have been closely related to Illyrian. There is some evidence that Illyrian may still have been spoken in parts of Bosnia when the Slavs overwhelmed the area in the 7th c. AD.

Given that ***Albanian**, a language with no close relatives, is spoken in a substantial part (the Kosovo area in southern Serbia as well as Albania) of the territory once occupied by Illyrian, it has often been suggested that Albanian is descended from Illyrian, but, in view of the fact that we know so little about Illyrian, this remains at best an unproven hypothesis with indeed some counter-evidence from what little we do know of Illyrian sound-developments.

Crossland, R. A. 1982. Linguistic problems of the Balkan area in late prehistoric and early classical periods [. . .]. III, The Illyrians. In Boardman, J. et al. (eds), *The Cambridge Ancient History*, 2nd edn, Cambridge, vol. 3, part 1, 839–43.

Polomé, E. G. 1966. The position of Illyrian and Venetic. In Birnbaum, H. and Puhvel, J. (eds), *Ancient Indo-European Dialects*, Berkeley and Los Angeles, 58–76.

—— 1982. Balkan languages [. . .]. I, Illyrian. In Boardman et al. 1982 (see Crossland 1982), 866–76.

Wilkes, J. 1992. *The Illyrians*. Oxford. (Illyrian language, 67–73; Illyrian names, 74–87.)

GLANVILLE PRICE

Illyrian (Modern) (see under (i) *Serbo-Croat*, 'Origins'; (ii) *Slovene*)

Immigrant languages, see *Community languages (Britain, France, Netherlands)*

Indic languages

One of the two subgroups (the other being the ***Iranian languages**) of the Indo-Iranian branch of the ***Indo-European** languages. The term 'Indo-Aryan languages' is also used. Indic languages included in this encyclopedia are Bengali, Gujarati, Panjabi and Urdu (all under ***Community languages (Britain)**), Hindi (under ***Community languages (Netherlands)**), and ***Romani**. Sanskrit, the language of the Vedas, the Hindu sacred texts, was an Indic language.

Masica, C. P. 1991. *The Indo-Aryan Languages*. Cambridge.

Indo-Aryan languages, see *Indic languages*

Indo-European languages

The Indo-European family of languages consists of all languages that demonstrably descend from one language, Proto-Indo-European. Proto-Indo-European is not an attested language but a language reconstructed on the basis of the attested

Indo-European languages by the intellectual efforts of generations of linguists. As insights into the structure of Proto-Indo-European deepened, so our picture of that language changed. Nowadays, in spite of numerous differences of opinion, often (but not exclusively) on minor matters, most scholars agree on most items of the sound structure and the nominal, pronominal and verbal inflexions of Proto-Indo-European. The amount of available knowledge about the intricate developments of the Indo-European languages from Proto-Indo-European up to their present state is enormous.

The notion that most European and a number of Asian languages show such striking similarities that they must be descended from a common ancestor language dates back to 1786, when Sir William Jones delivered his famous address to the Asiatic Society. In fact, a French priest, Cœurdoux, wrote down a similar theory in a letter dating from 1767, but this was not published until 1808. In the 19th c. the so-called 'comparative method' was developed, which enabled linguists to investigate systematically the relationships between the Indo-European languages and the structure of Proto-Indo-European.

The Indo-European languages can be divided into a number of branches, whose members show closer linguistic affinities with one another than with members of other branches. The main branches are the following: ***Celtic, *Italic** (whence ***Romance), *Germanic, *Baltic, *Slavonic, *Greek, *Albanian, *Armenian, *Indo-Iranian** (Sanskrit, Avestan and Old Persian are ancient representatives), Tocharian (1st millenium AD, in Chinese Turkestan) and Anatolian (2nd and 1st millennia BC, Asia Minor; the most important language is Hittite). Some of these branches show a number of remarkable agreements; hence one may speak of, say, Italo-Celtic and Balto-Slavonic. A number of extinct languages of which we have only a fragmentary knowledge belong to the Indo-European family but cannot be classified as belonging to one of the branches mentioned above: ***Lusitanian, *Venetic** (an Italic language?), ***Sicel, *Elymian, *Messapic, *Illyrian, *Daco-Thracian,** Old ***Macedonian, *Phrygian.** The branching of the Indo-European family reflects the way in which Proto-Indo-European split up into its various daughter languages.

The problem of the original homeland of the Indo-European languages, in other words the area where Proto-Indo-European was spoken, remains a bone of contention. Here the linguist and the archaeologist must cooperate. The linguist can solve only part of the problem, by using the method of 'linguistic palaeontology': if Proto-Indo-European had a word for a certain item, this item must have been known to the Proto-Indo-Europeans. If they had a word for 'horse', 'mountain', 'birch' (which they did), they must have known horses, mountains, birches, etc. In practice, the results of this method do not allow us to delimit strictly the area of the potential Indo-European homeland. A plausible theory identifies the Indo-Europeans with the *kurgan* cultures in southern Russia (5000–3000/2500 BC), in the area north of the Black Sea (Gimbutas 1973, Mallory 1989). In so far as this theory combines the linguistic with the archaeological evidence, it is vastly superior to the ideas of Renfrew (1987) and of Gamkrelidze and Ivanov (1985), who situate the Indo-

European homeland in Asia Minor. The migrations of speakers of Indo-European throughout Europe – irrespective of whether these were large-scale invasions or small-scale infiltrations – are often difficult to trace archaeologically (see Mallory 1989).

As a result of the reconstruction of many aspects of the Proto-Indo-European language, it has become possible to gain insights into Proto-Indo-European culture. In the poetry of some early Indo-European languages, a number of etymologically corresponding fixed phrases have been found, which point to the conclusion that there was a Proto-Indo-European poetic language, hence Proto-Indo-European poetry. The most famous of these correspondences is Greek *kléos áphthiton*: Vedic Sanskrit *ákṣitam śrávas* 'unperishable fame'. There have been interesting but ulti- mately unsuccessful attempts to reconstruct the metric structure of Proto-Indo-European verse.

The name of only one divinity can be traced back to Proto-Indo-European: Snaskrit *Dyáuṣ pitắ*, Greek *Zeús patḗr*, Latin *Iuppiter*. Words for 'sacred', 'worship', 'offer as a libation' can be reconstructed.

Indo-European society was patriarchal: the 'father' was 'head of the house' to his sons and their wives (at marriage, a woman left her own family and became a member of her husband's family). The kinship terminology can be reconstructed in detail. Words for 'people', 'king' and 'free man' are known.

A number of items belonging to agricultural terminology can be reconstructed, e.g. 'to sow', 'to plough', 'cultivated field', 'cow', 'ox', 'sheep', 'livestock (sheep and goats)', 'to milk', 'butter', 'cheese', 'wool', 'pig', 'dog'. An important role was played by the 'horse', and the Indo-Europeans may well owe their wide dispersion to their ability to tame this animal. Note also that there were words for 'to drive', 'wheel', 'axle-tree', which indicate that the Indo-Europeans drove in wagons. Examples of terms for domestic architecture are 'house', 'to construct, build', '(double) door', 'house-post'.

Scholars have wondered whether the Indo-European family is cognate with other language families, e.g. ***Uralic**, ***Semitic**, so that we could postulate an even more ancient ancestor family, which might then be labelled Indo-Uralic or Indo-Semitic. It is remarkable that Indo-European shares a small number of old words with Uralic. More importantly, there are a number of grammatical suffixes of similar form and meaning (e.g. accusative *-m*): these can hardly be explained as borrowings (gram- matical suffixes are hardly ever borrowed), hence they seem to go back to a common Indo-Uralic ancestor language. Attempts to connect Indo-European with other fami- lies have as yet been less successful.

Beekes, R. S. P. 1995. *Comparative Indo-European Linguistics*. Amsterdam.
Gamkrelidze, T. and Ivanov, V. 1985. The ancient Near East and the Indo-European question [and] the migration of tribes speaking Indo-European dialects. *Journal of Indo-European Linguistics*, 13: 3–91.
Gimbutas, M. 1973. The beginning of the Bronze Age in Europe and the Indo-Europeans: 3500–2500 BC. *Journal of Indo-European Studies*, 1: 163–214.
Lockwood, W. B. 1969. *Indo-European Philology*. London.

Mallory, J. P. 1989. *In Search of the Indo-Europeans*. London.
Renfrew, C. 1987. *Archaeology and Language: The Puzzle of Indo-European Origins*. London.

PETER SCHRIJVER

Indo-Germanic languages
An obsolete synonym, better avoided, for *'Indo-European languages'.

Indo-Iranian languages
A branch of the *Indo-European languages, with two subgroups, the *Indic languages and the *Iranian languages.

Indo-Uralic languages (see under *Indo-European languages*)

Ingrian
Ingrian (also known as Izhorian), spoken in Ingermanland west of St Petersburg, is a member of the *Baltic-Finnic branch of the *Finno-Ugrian languages. The Ingrians probably originated in the 17th c. from a mixture of former SW Karelians and settlers from Finland and, linguistically, Ingrian stands between *Finnish and *Karelian and is closely related to both. In the Soviet census of 1989, of the 820 persons who counted themselves as of Ingrian nationality, only 302 (37%) gave Ingrian as their mother tongue and the majority (52%) spoke only Russian. There was nevertheless an increase of 58 in the number of speakers since the previous census in 1979. The dialect of the village of Kukkosi plays a distinctive role in that the *Votic language spoken there has been strongly influenced by Ingrian. There has never been a literature of note in the Ingrian language and attempts in the 1930s to create a literary language, when a few textbooks in Ingrian for primary schools were published using the Latin alphabet, were soon abandoned.

Suhonen, S. 1985. Wotisch oder Ingrisch? ('Votic or Ingrian?'). In Veenker, W. (ed.), *Dialectologia Uralica. Materialien des ersten internationalen Symposions zur Dialektologie der uralischen Sprachen*, Wiesbaden, 139–49.

WOLFGANG GRELLER

Ingush (see under *Caucasian languages. III. North Central Caucasian family*)

Ingvaeonic languages
The term 'Ingvaeonic (Inguaeonic)' derives from the designation 'Ingvaeones' given by Tacitus, writing at the end of the 1st c. AD, to Germanic tribes occupying the coastal region of the modern Netherlands and Lower Saxony. It has been applied to the ensemble of the *Germanic languages and dialects of the region, notably western dialects of *Dutch, *Frisian, and north Saxon dialects of *German, together with the Old *English, that share a number of phonetic and some grammatical and lexical features.

Insular Celtic (see under *Celtic languages*)

Interglossa (see under *Artificial languages*)

Interlingua (see under *Artificial languages*)

Inuit, see *Greenlandic*

Iranian languages

One of the two subgroups (the other being the ***Indic languages**) of the Indo-Iranian branch of the ***Indo-European languages**. Iranian languages included in this encyclopedia are ***Alanic, *Kurdish, *Ossetic, *Talishi, *Tat** and ***Yassic**. Among other Iranian languages are Persian, Pashto, Tadzhik and Baluchi.

Irish

Irish belongs to the Goidelic or ***Gaelic** branch of the ***Celtic** family of languages. It is an official language in the Republic of Ireland.

Affinities and name

The earliest attested forms of Goidelic are found in Ireland, or in parts of Britain where migrants from Ireland are known to have settled, and in effect Goidelic is the Irish language. The divergence of this form of Celtic into the autonomous forms of Modern Irish, ***Scottish Gaelic** and ***Manx** is a recent development.

The word *Goidelic* derives from the Old Irish *Goídel* 'an Irish-speaking Celt'. In Old Irish the name for the language was *Goídelc*. *Goídel* and *Goídelc* were borrowed from British Celtic (see ***Brittonic languages**), their cognates in Modern ***Welsh** being *Gwyddel* and *Gwyddeleg*, during a prehistorical period of prolonged contact between Irish and British Celts. It has been proposed by the Indo-Europeanist E. P. Hamp that the Proto-British plural of *Gwyddel* was **wedēloi*, and that this may be assumed to be a close cognate of a form **wēdnioi*, a Proto-Irish precursor of Old Irish *Féni*, a designation by which the early Irish aristocracy knew themselves. Both forms would have originally meant 'woodsmen, hunters, warriors', an honorific type of appellation among Celtic peoples. The contemporary English word *Gaelic* derives from a modern Irish, or Scottish Gaelic, form of Old Irish *Goídelc*, Classical Modern Irish *Gaoidhealg*: Modern Irish *Gaeilge*, Scottish Gaelic *Gàidhlig*. The word *Gaelic*, as a term for the language, is generally regarded in Ireland as vaguely disparaging.

Social and political history

When Ireland's historical period begins, in the 5th c. AD, Irish is already established as the predominant vernacular. At least, there are no records of any other. In this early period, Ireland's population was establishing permanent settlements in western and northern Britain. As surviving inscriptions and later tradition testify, there were particularly extensive settlements in the area of South Wales and across the Severn estuary into Devon. These settlements were later absorbed in the consolidation of

Welsh lordships and by the Anglo-Saxon advance. In northern Britain, Irish-speaking supremacy expanded gradually from settlements on the coastal area of Argyll until it had by the 11th c. encompassed the whole of Scotland. By this period, *Norse settlements in the coastal regions and islands of Ireland and Scotland were being assimilated to Gaeldom and the Irish-speaking area had reached its greatest extent, but decline was soon to set in.

The Anglo-Normans began to settle in Scotland during the reign of Mael Coluim (1059–93), and initiated a process by which the Irish language had within three centuries receded to the Highlands in the north and to the Galloway region in the south-west. The Anglo-Norman intervention in Ireland began in 1169 and introduced a substantial settlement of *Anglo-Norman and English-speakers, mainly in urban centres. However, indigenous society regained its dominance and rural Ireland was by the end of the 14th c. almost universally Irish-speaking again, but the principal towns appear to have evolved towards a societal bilingualism in which English was the expected language in administrative and legal affairs. Irish thus never became the language of urban administration, and the Irish-speaking population never again achieved a full political autonomy.

On the other hand, during this period from the 13th c. to the 16th, powerful regional lordships emerged throughout the Gaelic world and provided an essential support for the Irish language and its institutions. Possibly the greatest of them was the Lordship of the Isles which, at the height of its power in the 15th c., included all of the Hebrides, the greater part of the Highland region, and much of Antrim in the north-east of Ireland, and undoubtedly played a decisive part in consolidating the Irish language and its institutions throughout the Highlands and Isles of Scotland. This lordship inevitably came into conflict with the Scottish Crown and was finally at an end by 1545 when its last ruler, Domhnall Dubh, died.

As the 16th c. progressed, the powerful Gaelic and Gaelicized lordships of Ireland were to suffer a similar fate: the earldoms of Desmond, Kildare, Tyrconnel, Tyrone, and the lordship of Fermanagh were all in turn destroyed. The 16th c. had brought a renewed drive to impose English rule on Ireland and, in the process, to destroy its cultural distinctiveness. The objective took some time to attain, but the suppressions and movements of population which took place during the reigns of the Tudors and Stuarts (1534–1610), the Cromwellian settlements (1654), the Williamite campaign (1681–91), and the subsequent Penal Law, did have the cumulative effect of eliminating the Irish-speaking aristocracy and their institutions. Throughout Ireland, an English-speaking 'ascendancy' was introduced and the mercantile and professional classes in urban areas quickly became English-speaking.

It has been reliably estimated that the population at the end of the 18th c. comprised 2 million Irish-speakers, one and a half million Irish–English bilinguals, and one and a half million English-speakers. Of these, the 2 million monolingual Irish-speakers included almost all of the most deprived rural poor and, though this class continued to increase rapidly in number, it was unprotected against economic disaster. From the end of the 18th c. it was repeatedly reduced by famine, epidemic and emigration, and was all but wiped out by the Great Famine of 1846–9 and its aftermath. According to the 1851 census of Ireland, the first to include a question on language, the total number of Irish-speakers had by then declined to 1,524,286, or just 25% of the population. And a precipitant shift to English was under way: the percentage of Irish speakers in the under-10 age-group was 12.6%, against 22.23% in the 10–19 age-group, and 24.91% in the 20–29 group. So it continued. By 1891, for the whole of Ireland, the percentage of Irish-speakers in the under-10 group had declined to 3.5%, and the language appeared to be on the point of extinction.

The Irish language fared better in the 20th c. than might have been predicted. First of all, the rate of language shift slowed as it encountered the densely populated, largely coastal, regions which were known as 'congested districts'. The impoverished communities which inhabited these districts were nearly autonomous in their subsistence economies, and had little contact with English. Broadly, they are the districts in which the contemporary *Gaeltacht* survives. Then, from the end of the 19th c., there was a vigorous language-restoration movement which provided one of the principal motivations for a renewed campaign for the political secession of Ireland from the United Kingdom. When the Irish Free State was established in 1922, Irish was designated the 'national language' in the constitution; its position in education was reinforced, and competence in it became obligatory for public-service employment. Although the position of Irish has remained weaker than many thought possible in a supportive State, there has been a continuing increase in the number of those who claim in censuses to be speakers.

As a result of the State's language policies, the population of active Irish-speakers has constantly been renewed through the induction of school-produced bilinguals; a degree of literacy in Irish has been disseminated throughout the community, thus allowing a wider use of Irish as an official and formal medium; there has been a reasonably high level of corpus planning and publication; and the function of Irish as a symbol of ethnic identity has been sustained through a century of sweeping economic and demographic change.

Records and varieties

The earliest extant records in Irish are in the script called ogham or *ogam, in which letters are represented as units of strokes and notches. While the scholarly consensus has for long been that ogham is a deliberate codification of the Roman alphabet, the fact that it is the medium for a well-defined orthography for Proto-Irish has until recently been less clearly recognized. This orthography differed from manuscript Old Irish in a number of ways, most notably in representing voiced stops [b, d, g] as B D G in positions where they were later represented by the letters <p, t, c>. Vestiges of such features of ogham orthography are sometimes found in the spelling of proper names in early Hiberno-Latin texts, and in the Irish glosses written by the *prima manus* in the *Codex Wirziburgensis* (see below). But the great bulk of early Irish manuscript writing is in a revised orthography, some of the ambiguities of which reflect a British pronunciation of Latin. This later orthography must therefore have evolved through the influence of the extensive British Christian missions which were undertaken in Ireland during the 5th and 6th centuries.

In the earliest manuscripts, Irish was written in the insular style of the contemporary minuscule script used throughout Europe. Irish scribal tradition adhered conservatively to this script and in time, as fashions changed elsewhere, it came to be associated exclusively with the writing of Irish. It continued to be used as the conventional script for Irish, in manuscript and in print, until the second half of the 20th c. For a number of reasons, mostly pragmatic, it was then officially discarded. It had been phased out of use in primary schools in the Republic of Ireland by 1964, and in secondary schools by 1970.

The earliest writing in Irish to have survived in a contemporary manuscript is the collection of annotations, or glosses, on the epistles of St Paul in the *Codex Wirziburgensis*, now preserved in the University library in Würzburg. A small number of the Würzburg glosses are in a distinct hand, the *prima manus*, and in an earlier form of Irish than the main body of glosses in the codex. These early glosses are thought to be not later than 700. The main body of Würzburg glosses belongs to the 8th century and follows the orthographic convention which was the norm in Old Irish.

Old Irish is the medium of a substantial literature. It includes lyrical and devotional verse, prose sagas, homilies, historical and legal tracts, and commentaries on biblical and Latin grammatical texts. In modern times, the Old Irish record has widely attracted the attention of linguists and literary scholars. Because Old Irish is the earliest variety of Celtic which is so fully attested, it provides significant evidence for the comparative reconstruction of Proto-*Indo-European. And its literature, though there is some disagreement on the extent to which it does, or does not, reflect an ancient pre-Christian tradition, is a distinctive and copious early medieval record which contains much of interest for literary scholarship.

Classical Old Irish, of the period 700–850, is known from the main body of Würzburg glosses and from other similar texts. It is highly uniform in its orthography, grammar and lexicon, but its greater uniformity in comparison with other Irish texts may in part be due to the chance survival in contemporary manuscripts of a relatively large and highly uniform body of writings, rather than to any particular uniformity in the literary language of the period.

In Ireland, few contemporary records of Old Irish have survived. The greater part of the early record has been preserved in manuscripts which were compiled in later centuries, generally from the 11th c. and after. The record preserved in such later sources has been subjected to considerable scribal intervention, deliberate and inadvertent, and almost all extant texts exhibit variation between earlier and later forms of language. It cannot always be determined whether the variation was introduced by later scribes, or was an intrinsic part of the text. Writers of Irish were, at all periods, tempted to archaize. It is nevertheless agreed that the extant record includes a corpus of texts which belong to the late 6th and 7th centuries and are in Archaic Old Irish. This corpus includes the *Amra Choluim Chille* (a lament for St Colmcille which is probably contemporary with his death in 597), archaic verse embedded in the genealogical records, and some law texts.

By the end of the 9th c. Old Irish was beginning to evolve to Middle Irish, the form of language broadly associated with the period 900–1150. Formally, Middle Irish is distinguished form Old Irish by a simplification of inflection, particularly in the verbal system. In the lexicon, contact with the Norse is beginning to be reflected in borrowings of terms connected with seafaring and trade. The period was one of political turmoil for the Gaelic world, but literary continuity was maintained, and extensive records are extant. They include the long sequence of cantos on biblical themes known as *Saltair na Rann* ('The Verse Psalter'), the historical poems of Flann Mainistrech (*c.* AD 1000–50), the large compilations in verse and prose of legends about famous places called *Dindshenchas*, adaptations of classical epics into the form of prose sagas, and a powerful satire on monks and literary men titled *Aislinge Meic Con Glinne* ('The Vision of Mac Con Glinne').

By the late 11th c. and early 12th, the Norse settlements had been absorbed culturally, but political strife was endemic. At various periods, for example, the Ó Briain dynasty of Thomond, one of the leading contenders for the kingship of Ireland and hegemony over the Gaelic world, gained control over the Norse kingdoms of Dublin, Man and the Hebrides. Such activity must have contributed to the full re-Gaelicization of these regions. More generally, it must have led to a levelling of regional variation in spoken Irish and created conditions favourable to the development of a new koine. At any rate, a comparative historical analysis of the modern spoken varieties of Irish and Scottish Gaelic reveals few features of divergence which can be traced further back than this period. The hypothesized late medieval vernacular, to which the modern spoken varieties are testimony, is sometimes called Common Gaelic.

Coincidentally, when this greater uniformity was being established in vernacular Irish, new monastic orders were being introduced from the Continent as part of an ecclesiastical reform, and the secular learning which had been maintained in the older Celtic foundations passed to an emerging class of hereditary lay scholars. These developments led to the emergence of a new literary norm, more consonant with the spoken Common Gaelic. This norm is known now as Classical Modern Irish. From the 13th c. to the 17th, the Early Modern Irish period, it was taught and used by the literary schools throughout Ireland, Gaelic Scotland and Man.

Verse compositions by professional poets are a substantial part of the literature of the period; they include encomiastic verse for patrons, but also devotional compositions and some personal poetry. Love poetry of the *amour courtois* genre enjoyed a vogue among the aristocracy. One of the great literary flowerings of the period was the extensive *Fenian* or *Ossianic* literature in prose and verse composed around the legendary Fionn Mac Cumhaill and his warrior band or *fian*, hence 'Fenian' and Irish *fianaíocht*/*fianaigheacht*; Fionn's son was Oisín, Anglicized 'Ossian', hence 'Ossianic'. This genre was later to become widely known through the purported translations of James Macpherson (1736–96), a native of Kingussie in the Scottish Highlands, and was a significant stimulus to the development of Romanticism.

Following the upheavals of the 17th c., and the destruction of native institutions of literacy and learning, the forms of written Irish became increasingly local, and the extant record to a substantial degree reflects the dialectal variation of the spoken language. Yet the literate were still familiar with the forms of Classical Modern Irish and strove to adhere to its conventions. This is the period of Post-Classical Modern Irish. Its literary record has survived in a manuscript tradition maintained in their spare time by artisans, farmers, priests, and schoolmasters. With the exception of one or two items such as Mícheál Coimín's *Laoi Oisín ar Thír na nÓg* ('Ossian's Song about the Land of Youth') (1750) and Brian Merriman's *Cúirt an Mheán Oíche* ('The Midnight Court') (1780), it has not attracted wider interest.

Spoken varieties and modern written norms

In the 20th c. Modern Irish survives in the first instance in its spoken varieties. These varieties are distinguished principally in their phonology, but also substantially in their morphology and lexicon. Differences of syntax are few, and on the whole varieties of Modern Irish are mutually intelligible.

As happens with dialectal variation everywhere, the regions of Irish which are differentiated by any one feature of phonological, morphological or lexical variation are seldom exactly conterminous with regions differentiated by any other such feature. But regional varieties of Modern Irish may be conveniently grouped, according to provincial boundaries (see map 9), into the dialects of:

(a) Munster, now spoken by scattered communities in the south and south-west of Ireland;

(b) Connacht, now spoken by communities in Co. Galway and Co. Mayo in the west of Ireland;

(c) Ulster, now spoken by communities in Co. Donegal in the north-west of Ireland.

From the end of the 19th c., as Modern Irish began to be redeveloped as a language of public affairs and high culture, the regional diversity of its spoken form was reflected, not only in works of creative literature, but in textbooks and public documents. It became necessary to define new norms for educational and official purposes. A new spelling norm was published in 1945 and, in revised form, in 1947; a new morphological norm was published in 1953 and, in revised form, in 1958. These spelling and morphological norms, the *Caighdeán*, are fully established in official publications. In literature, the more indigenous aspects of the tradition continue to attract the greatest international attention, as, for example, the oral lore which so copiously survived in Irish into modern times.

Present situation

Modern Irish is spoken as a minority language throughout Ireland. In the Constitution of Ireland (1937), Article 8.1 avers that 'the Irish language as the national language is the first official language'. The United Kingdom does not have a written constitution and none of its languages has a formally designated status, but in Northern Ireland the Irish language receives a much lower public recognition than, for example, the Welsh language does in Wales.

Of the population of the Republic of Ireland in 1991, the number of those aged 3 years or over who were returned in the national census as Irish-speaking came to

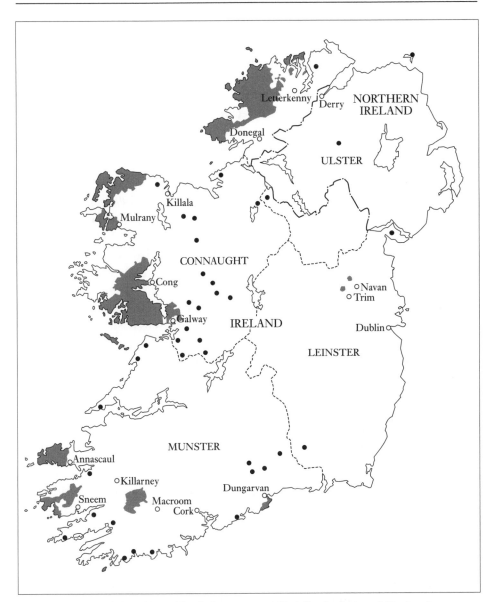

Map 9   The Irish language. Shaded areas are officially designated Gaeltacht areas. (.) indicates points outside the Gaeltacht covered by Heinrich Wagner's *Linguistic Atlas and Survey of Irish Dialects* (Dublin, Dublin Institute for Advanced Studies, 1958–69); the availability of informants reflects the geographical spread of Irish as a community language in the last decades of the 19th century.

1,095,830, or 32.5% of the total cohort. This figure does not distinguish different kinds of competence, nor between different degrees of commitment to use. However, taking the population of the State as a whole, the evidence from a variety of social surveys is that about 5% of the population has a high active competence in Irish, a further 10% or so has a good competence and regularly makes some use of the language, and another 20–30% are on a declining scale towards low passive competence. The 5% of the population which has a high active competence includes the traditional Irish-speaking communities of the *Gaeltacht*, the total population of which in 1991 was 82,268; of this total, 56,459 of those aged 3 or over were returned as Irish-speaking; this is significantly less than 2% of the total cohort for the State.

In Northern Ireland, a total of 142,003 were returned in the 1991 census as having an ability to speak Irish; 79,012 were returned as being able to speak, read and write the language. The figure of 142,003 represents approximately 10% of Northern Ireland's population but, as a proportion of the 'nationalist' community, is very similar to the proportion returned as Irish-speaking in the Republic of Ireland. So also, the northern figure includes a range of competences and commitments to use, and the more active end of the scale may be assumed to include Irish-speaking migrants from Donegal in the Republic of Ireland, natives of Irish-speaking households in Northern Ireland, and a number who have acquired a high competence in Irish as a second language. There are now no *Gaeltacht* areas within Northern Ireland.

Ford, P. A. and Williams, J. C. 1992. *The Irish Literary Tradition*. Cardiff.
Mac Eoin, G. 1993. Irish. In Ball, M. J. (ed.), *The Celtic Languages*, London, 101–44.
Ó Cuív, B. (ed.) 1969. *A View of the Irish Language*. Dublin.
Ó Dochartaigh, C. 1992. The Irish language. In MacAulay, D. (ed.), *The Celtic Languages*, Cambridge, 11–99.
Ó Murchú, M. 1985. *The Irish Language*. Dublin.
—— 1992. The Irish language. In Price, G. (ed.), *The Celtic Connection*, Gerrards Cross, 30–64.
—— 1993. Aspects of the societal status of Modern Irish. In Ball (1993) (see Mac Eoin), 471–90.
Thurneysen, R. 1946. *A Grammar of Old Irish*. Dublin.

MÁIRTÍN Ó MURCHÚ

Istro-Romanian

The moribund *Romanian dialect (sometimes considered to be a distinct language) of two small and separated areas in the Istrian peninsula in Croatia. Though no firmly established figures are available, numbers of speakers are usually estimated to be about 1,500 or less. There is no literary tradition, though a *Calendaru lu rumeri din Istrie* ('Calendar of the Romanians of Istria') was published in 1905 and collections of folk tales and poems have also appeared.

Dahmen, W. 1989. Istrorumänisch. In Holtus, G., Metzeltin, M. and Schmitt, C. (eds), *Lexikon der Romanistischen Linguistik*, Tübingen, vol. 3, 448–60.
Kovačec, A. 1971. *Descrierea istroromânei actuale* ('Description of Present-day Istro-Romanian'). Bucharest.
—— 1984. Istroromână. In Rusu, V. (ed.), *Tratat de dialectologie românească* ('Treatise on Romanian

Dialectology'), Craiova, 550–91.

Puşcariu, S., Bartoli, M., Belulovici, A. and Byhan, A. 1906–29. *Studii istroromâne*. Vol. 1, *Texte*; vol. 2, *Introducere, gramatică, caracterizarea dialectului istroromân* ('Introduction, Grammar, Characterization of the Istro-Romanian Dialect'); vol. 3, *Bibliografie critică*. Bucharest.

GLANVILLE PRICE

Italian (see under *Italy. II. Italian*)

Italic languages

A branch of the *Indo-European languages, with two main subdivisions: (a) *Latin and *Faliscan; and (b) the *Osco-Umbrian (sometimes termed *Sabellian) languages, consisting of *Oscan, *Umbrian and a number of central Italic languages, *Aequian, *Marrucinian, *Marsian, *Paelignian, *Pre-Samnitic, *Sabine, *South Picenian, *Vestinian and *Volscian, none of them known from more than a handful of inscriptions. It is a matter of debate whether the *Venetic language of NE Italy and the *Sicel or Siculan language of Sicily were or were not also Italic. (See map 10.)

Coleman, R. G. G. 1990. Latin and the Italic languages. In Comrie, B. (ed.), *The Major Languages of Western Europe*, London, 170–92.

Italo-Romance languages

A subgroup of the *Romance languages considered by many scholars to consist of two branches, Italian and Sardinian (see under *Italy, II. Italian, V. Sardinian). Other scholars do not accept this division into two branches and/or would also classify the *Rhaeto-Romance varieties (widely considered to be a separate Romance subgroup) under Italo-Romance.

Italy (Romance vernaculars)

I Introduction

The vexed problem of distinguishing between 'languages' and 'dialects' arises more acutely in relation to the Romance vernaculars of Italy than in any other context in contemporary Europe (see map 11).

That there is a standardized, national, literary language known as 'Italian' is beyond dispute. That language is discussed in Section II below. The problem arises in relation to the many regional vernaculars, some of which at least are considered by some to be languages and by others to be dialects. The relevance of dialectal writers for the history of Italian literature is well known and is especially true of the theatre: the most significant Italian playwrights have often used their native vernacular rather than standard Italian.

On the one hand, we have the case of varieties such as, say, Piedmontese, Lombard

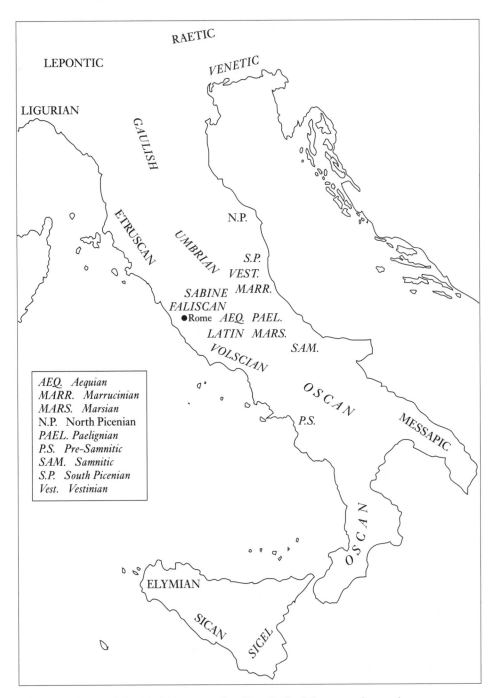

Map 10 *Italic and other languages of ancient Italy*. The map shows the approximate location of languages spoken in Italy in the last centuries BC. Names of Italic languages are printed in italics (N.B. the Italic nature of Sicel and Venetic is uncertain). Areas of Greek or Phoenician speech are not shown.

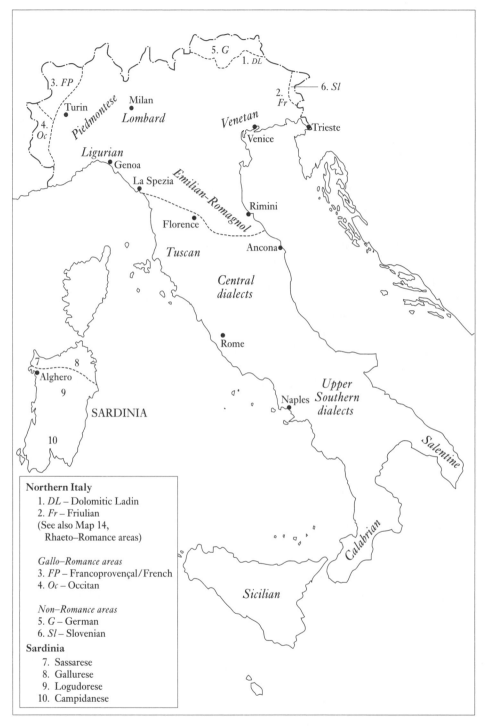

Map 11   Languages and dialects of modern Italy. Certain small linguistic 'islands'
(e.g. pockets of Germanic dialects in Piedmont and Veneto, Albanian- and Greek-
speaking villages in southern Italy, Occitan in Calabria, Catalan in Alghero) are not
shown.

and Sicilian, which some consider to be Italian dialects (though not dialects of Italian, i.e. they do not derive from the language commonly known as 'Italian' today – the distinction is an important one) while others would accord them the status of separate languages. This amounts in reality to little if anything more than a question of terminology, and we shall here treat separately the more important vernaculars in question without coming down on one side or the other in the 'language versus dialect' debate.

A different case is that of Dolomitic Ladin and Friulian which many scholars have traditionally grouped together with Swiss *Romansh under the heading of *Rhaeto-Romance (see map 14), while others, including the authors of the sections on Dolomitic Ladin and Friulian below, deny the validity of this grouping and equate them rather with northern *Italo-Romance varieties such as Piedmontese and Lombard. This is more than a question of terminology since, if the former view is accepted, this could imply that the three varieties in question once formed part of a now fragmented Rhaeto-Romance subgroup that can be distinguished from the Northern Italian subgroup.

Whatever the precise status of any of the varieties here considered, there is widespread agreement among specialists that there are valid grounds for dividing the Romance vernaculars of mainland Italy and Sicily into, on the one hand, a northern group (discussed in Section III below) and, on the other, a central and southern group (see Section IV below).

The status of Sardinian is different again since many, though not all, contemporary Romance linguists would consider it as a distinct branch (the other consisting of standard Italian and the other mainland and Sicilian vernaculars, together with *Corsican) of the Italo-Romance subgroup of the Romance languages. However, because, for the reasons outlined above, we are departing in the particular case of Italy from the method of classification generally followed in this encyclopedia and adopting a geographical arrangement, and since Sardinia is indisputably a part of Italy, there is no good cause not to include it as a final section (V) of this particular article.

The specific bibliographical references given at the end of each of the main sections should be supplemented by the more general ones listed at the end of the article.

The author of each section of what follows is indicated at the end of that section.

PAOLA BENINCÀ AND GLANVILLE PRICE

II Italian

A member of the Romance language group which derives from Latin, Italian is the official language of the Republic of Italy, of the Vatican City and of the Republic of San Marino. It is also one of the official languages of Switzerland and was an official language in Malta until 1934. Other Italian-speaking communities inside and outside Europe are described below.

Italian and the other languages and dialects of Italy

Italian, although almost universally understood in contemporary Italy, is not the first language of the majority of the population and its status as a national spoken language in the peninsula is of recent date. Approximately two-thirds of the population habitually use other forms of speech, and the last statistical survey (Doxa 1992: 89) still showed 11.3% claiming to speak only 'dialect' whether at home or to friends and colleagues at work (ISTAT 1989 gives 13.7% claiming to speak only or mainly dialect even with strangers). As recently as 1974 less than 50% of the population claimed they used Italian with any family member and today this remains true of the northeast and various southern regions. The language varieties used in such circumstances are usually those generally referred to as Italian 'dialects', e.g. Piedmontese, Sicilian. They may also be varieties of languages mainly spoken elsewhere, e.g. German in the Alto Adige, *Slovene on the NE border, *Occitan and *Francoprovençal on the NW border and pockets in southern Italy, where *Greek and *Albanian are also found, *Catalan in Sardinia. The intermediate status of 'minority' language accorded to these varieties within Italy is also nowadays shared by Sardinian, Friulian and Ladin. With respect to Tuscan, which evolved out of spoken Latin, to become the basis for the standard language, these three Romance varieties are parallel developments, as are the many other varieties into which Latin fragmented after the collapse of the Roman Empire. These last, the so-called Italian 'dialects', are thus historically speaking dialects of Latin not of Italian; their grammars can be as different from Italian as that of Spanish, for example, while the grounds for classifying them differently from Sardinian, Friulian and Ladin are principally socio-historical.

There are 15 main dialect groups in Italy (broadly corresponding to the geographical and administrative regions). A more satisfactory classification than the stark 'language'– 'dialect' dichotomy is proposed by Muljačić (1967) who distinguishes between H(igh), M(iddle) and L(ow) languages in a dynamic model that can accommodate changes in status. Italian functions as an H language (the most prestigious variety) in respect of all the other varieties spoken in Italy (it is the normal language of official transactions, politics, law, commerce, education, literature, the press, cinema, radio, television and written exchanges generally). The 'minority' languages and some of the 'dialect' koines are, in turn, H languages to less prestigious varieties and can be classed as M languages, used in some areas of public and literary activity (e.g. in the Veneto, a Venetan koine is H *vis-à-vis* local varieties; in Piedmont, a Turinese-based koine is H *vis-à-vis* the dialect of Mondovì or Biella). In some regions, e.g. Emilia Romagna, there is arguably no variety with sufficient prestige today to be considered an M language: Bolognese, for example, is today considered an L language, used mainly in the home and in very informal situations. (See Trumper 1993 for an overview of the present situation.)

External history

Italian evolved out of literary Tuscan, or more precisely, the vernacular of Florence (the epithet 'Italian' being first used by Leonardo da Vinci – see Muljačić 1997).

From a position of parity at the turn of the millennium among the hundreds of 'vernaculars' (regionally differentiated spoken varieties deriving from Latin, by then considered a separate language of learning), Florentine gradually gained in prestige throughout the peninsula. This was a consequence not of a centralizing, social and political hegemony of the sort that brought about linguistic cohesion in France and Spain (Italy remained politically divided until unification in 1861) but of a cultural pre-eminence in literature and the arts that from the Middle Ages inspired people from all corners of the peninsula to model themselves on Florentine masterpieces. The export of Florentine linguistic habits also owed much to the commercial success of medieval Florence and to the geographically central position of Tuscany, which rendered its speech transitional between northern and southern vernaculars. The fact that Tuscan had diverged less from Latin, the language of official and scholarly communication (a conservatism sometimes attributed to the structural distance between Latin and the Etruscan substrate), also made it a more acceptable common medium than some more radically divergent varieties.

In Italy the first unambiguously vernacular (rather than 'popular' Latin) attestations belong to the 10th c.; we must await the 12th c. for a Tuscan text (a Pisan naval account register), while the first Florentine text is a bankers' book dated 1211. The script used was the Roman alphabet adapted to cope with phonological developments such as consonant palatalization. From the late Middle Ages the vernacular began to encroach more and more on the domains of Latin (cultivated literature, statutes, chronicles and treatises) as communication was sought beyond the educated elite. At the close of the 15th c., however, Latin was still the medium used for serious works of scholarship and it remained for many centuries, especially during the Renaissance, an obvious model and a rich lexical source for vernacular writers. Another, increasingly influential, model was Tuscan: popular religious compositions and, later, chivalrous romances carried it outside Tuscany and already by the mid-14th c. Florentine had a body of cultivated literature unmatched elsewhere in the peninsula. The literary masterpieces of the writers known as the *Tre Corone* ('Three Crowns'), Dante Alighieri (1265–1321: *The Divine Comedy*), Francesco Petrarca (Petrarch) (1304–74: the *Canzoniere*) and Giovanni Boccaccio (1313–75: *The Decameron*) carried the Florentine-based language in which they were written far beyond the confines of Tuscany, in particular to northern courts such as that of the Visconti at Milan. In Florence, but also in Milan, Mantua and especially Venice, the appearance from the 1470s of vernacular literary texts in printed form helped to establish the prestige of Florentine: the printing of Petrarch's *Canzoniere* in 1470 and Boccaccio's *Decameron* in 1471 prepared the ground for Venice's virtual monopoly of vernacular printing in the 16th c.

Standardization and codification

Already for over a century a natural process of linguistic levelling had been operating in literary compositions and diplomatic exchanges between the many courts of Italy, the avoidance of the most idiosyncratic features of the various regional vernaculars often accompanying the adoption of a broadly Tuscan linguistic base. But it was not the 'language of the courtiers' (*lingua cortegiana*, as it was known in Renaissance discussions) or contemporary Tuscan that was to become the standard language of Italy. The *questione della lingua* (the 'question of the language', a debate as to which variety should be the language of literature) saw the triumph of a more strictly defined choice, not the outcome of a process of linguistic accommodation. Printing made more pressing the need for linguistic standardization and the most practical and efficient solution turned out to be that of the Venetian humanist, Pietro Bembo. Convinced of the classical principle that the language of literary composition should take the 'best' available model, in his *Prose della Volgar Lingua* (1525, 'Essays on the vernacular') Bembo advocated imitation of the Florentine used two centuries earlier by the *Tre Corone* (especially Petrarch for poetry and Boccaccio for prose). The first Italian grammar to appear in print was, however, that of Giovan Francesco Fortunio (*Regole della volgar lingua* 1516, 'Rules of the vernacular'), which also favoured this archaizing solution, albeit less rigorously. It also came to be adopted in numerous lexicographical reference works, the most important of which was the *Vocabolario* compiled by the Accademia della Crusca (first edition 1612), which became extremely influential in Italy and also abroad as a lexicographical model for other European languages. Here the linguistic canon was extended to include all 14th-c. production irrespective of literary quality.

The choice of a language belonging to a 'Golden Age' had the practical advantage of offering clear, easily accessible guidance, while not favouring excessively any one speech community (for Bembo there was little advantage to be gained from being Florentine, since the vernacular had evolved significantly since the 14th c.). It was only in Rome, due to the cosmopolitan nature of the papal city, and, to a lesser extent, in Naples, for cultural reasons, that Tuscan was known by appreciable sectors of the population. Nevertheless, this solution had the disadvantage of halting the natural development of the written language which over the next two centuries became more and more removed not only from the 'dialects' but also from the spoken Italian used mainly by the educated for interregional communication. It was not until the 19th c. that the impetus of social and political events, culminating in the unification of Italy in 1861, combined with the influence of a great writer, Alessandro Manzoni, to bring about a gradual modernization of the literary language and, slowly, the spread of Italian as a spoken national language (estimates of the proportion of the population able to speak Italian in 1861 range from 2.5% to 12.6%). Crucial to the dissemination of Italian were many social factors: the introduction of compulsory education, an increasing awareness of the importance of literacy for social advancement and careers, an awareness reinforced by massive emigration (between 1876 and 1970 almost 26,000,000 Italians emigrated), industrialization and accompanying urbanization. Urbanization, like military service and the First World War, brought together people from all regions, with mass migrations from the south to northern cities often forcing speakers to have recourse to a mutually intelligible common language. Finally, in the 20th c. the contribution of the mass media, radio, cinema and television, has been decisive. (For a comprehensive review of language debate in Italy since Unification and attitudes to dialect influence and foreign loan-words, especially French in the 19th c. and English in the 20th c., see Richardson (forthcoming).)

The prestige bestowed by the *Tre Corone* on Tuscan/Italian, further enhanced by Renaissance literary achievements, both artistic (e.g. Ludovico Ariosto's *Orlando Furioso* and Torquato Tasso's *Gerusalemme Liberata*) and scientific (e.g. Galileo), was crucial not only to linguistic standardization within Italy but also to the influence of Italian abroad. For several centuries from the Renaissance onwards some knowledge of Italian was considered essential for a cultured European and it has left its mark particularly on the vocabulary of music and the figurative arts.

Present situation

The adoption of Italian by increasing numbers of speakers of varying regional provenance and educational attainment has led to the development of numerous regional and social varieties, with varying levels of prestige, as well as to more flexible attitudes to what counts as acceptable Italian. Despite Manzoni's recommendation of a strict adherence to contemporary cultivated Florentine (exemplified in the final version of his famous novel, *I promessi sposi* 'The Betrothed' (1840), and in the dictionary *Novo vocabolario della lingua italiana secondo l'uso di Firenze* ('New dictionary of the Italian language according to Florentine usage'), 4 vols, 1870–97, compiled by E. Broglio and G. B. Giorgini in response to a report by Manzoni to the Ministry of Education) standard Italian has continued to evolve independently of it. Italian's tendency to preserve the structure of the traditional literary language, as indeed was foreseen by the linguist G. I. Ascoli, means that the language and literature of the great writers of 14th-c. Florence are accessible to modern readers. Since Unification Italian writers (e.g. Italo Svevo, Luigi Pirandello, Eugenio Montale, Italo Calvino, Umberto Eco) have continued to make major contributions to world literature and are widely translated.

Italian is used, with varying degrees of competence, by almost the entire population of $c.57$ million, at least for transactional purposes. It is an official language of Switzerland, which counts over 300,000 speakers in the cantons of Ticino and Graubünden, and of the European Union. 'Italian' communities outside Italy, however, may be indigenous populations whose mother tongue is frequently not Italian, e.g. Lombard in the Ticino, Ligurian in the principality of Monaco and in Nice (see Section III below, also *Corsican). Slovenia and Croatia have longstanding communities of Venetian origin in Istria and Dalmatia ($c.300,000$ people). In Malta, Italian established itself as the language of culture and administration, especially under the Knights (16th-18th c.). 19th-c. colonial expansion was responsible for the fact that Italian remains the second most important language in Eritrea, where it also spawned a true pidgin. Elsewhere Italian communities are the result of emigration: although Italian cannot compare with the spread of Spanish, Portuguese or French outside Europe, there are significant Italian minorities in the USA ($c.4,000,000$), in Argentina ($c.1,500,000$) and Brazil ($c.500,000$), favourite destinations before the First World War, and in Canada and Australia ($c.500,000$ each). Except for an educated minority, the speech of emigrant communities is usually their native dialect or a dialect koine which has developed in the host country and which is to a greater or lesser extent influenced by the local language. In Argentina a hybrid Spanish–Italian linguistic continuum goes by the name of *cocoliche*.

Bryce, J. et al. 1990. *Harrap's Italian Grammar*. London.

Clari, M. and Love, C. E. (eds) 1995. *Collins English–Italian Italian–English Dictionary*. London.

Galli De' Paratesi, N. 1982. Attitudes and standardisation trends in contemporary Italian: an enquiry. In Dittmar, N. and Schlieben-Lange, B. (eds), *Die Soziolinguistik in romanischsprachigen Ländern* ('Sociolinguistics in Romance-speaking Countries'), Tübingen, 237–48.

Lepschy, G. and Lepschy, A. L. 1988. *The Italian Language Today*, 2nd edn. London.

Maiden, M. 1995. *A Linguistic History of Italian*. London.

—— and Parry, M. (eds) 1997. *The Dialects of Italy*. London.

Marazzini, C. 1994. *La lingua italiana: profilo storico*. Bologna.

Migliorini, B. M. and Griffith, T. G. 1984. *The Italian Language*, revised edn. London.

Muljačić, Ž. 1997. The relationship between the dialects and the standard. In Maiden and Parry (see above), 498–505.

Renzi, L. et al. (eds) 1988–95. *Grande grammatica italiana di consultazione*, 3 vols. Bologna.

Richardson, B. (forthcoming). Questions of language. In Barański, Z. and West, R. (eds), *Cambridge Companion to Modern Italian Culture*. Cambridge.

Trumper, J. 1989. Observations on sociolinguistic behaviour in two Italian regions. *International Journal of the Sociology of Language*, 76: 31–62.

—— 1993. Italian and Italian dialects: an overview of recent studies. In Posner, R. and Green, J. R. (eds), *Trends in Romance Linguistics and Philology*, Berlin, vol. 5, 295–326.

Vincent, N. 1988. Italian. In Harris, M. and Vincent, N. (eds), *The Romance Languages*, London, 279–313.

MAIR PARRY

III Northern Italy

The reasons for identifying a northern Italian group are, on the one hand, strictly linguistic in that the vernaculars of northern Italy (including in some respects Florentine) share very important morphological and syntactic features. On the other hand, they have been linked since the Middle Ages by close economic and cultural ties and shared an early process in the direction of a subsequently aborted northern Italian koine. Identifiable groupings and subgroupings can be defined, despite subtle variations, on the basis of well-established linguistic characteristics and, in the case of subgroupings, of the fact that they developed around a major centre (such as Lombard around Milan) whose speech influenced the surrounding area, thereby bringing about a gradual levelling. On the other hand, within a single town or city we may find different varieties depending on district and on social stratum.

The northern vernaculars are here presented in an approximate geographical order, from west to east and from north to south.

PAOLA BENINCÀ

Piedmontese

Piedmontese is the indigenous vernacular of Piedmont, Italy's gateway to France and a region whose linguistic history reflects both the lack of a clearly defined political or cultural unity and the influence of two major European standard languages, one on either side. It was not until the 15th–16th centuries that a centralizing force emerged, as the Court of Savoy established its capital in Turin, by which time Tuscan literature was already circulating in Piedmont. French, the language of the Court, was also adopted by many writers, but written texts in Piedmontese, both literary and non-literary, exist from medieval times onwards and Piedmontese dominated the spoken medium until the 20th c. Religious texts appear first, with a rich collection of 12th-c. prose sermons, the *Sermoni subalpini*, traditionally but not uncontroversially the earliest text. In the 14th c. Piedmontese is attested in statutes, both religious and secular, and in model letters for translation into Latin in schools. Duke Emanuele Filiberto's edict of 1560 establishing the vernacular as the language of the law courts and of legal documents probably allowed for the oral use of Piedmontese, even if for official written documents a codified language, Italian (i.e. Tuscan), was preferred. A significant body of later literature exists in Piedmontese: a theatrical tradition goes back to the 16th-c. farces of Giovan Giorgio Alione of Asti; in poetry, the pungent satirical vein of Ignazio Isler (1702–88) acquired revolutionary fervour in the work of Edoardo Ignazio Calvo (1773–1804) and A. Brofferio (1802–66), while Pinìn Pacòt (1899–1964) gave new life to lyric poetry with the foundation of the *Companìa dij Brandé*; prose fiction, especially short stories, has appeared from the 19th c. onwards; there are also a number of monthly local or cultural publications.

The growth in the political and social pre-eminence of Turin led to its becoming the basis of a Piedmontese koine but, from the end of the 16th c., the use of Italian, supported by court patronage, became more and more widespread. Nevertheless, the achievement of independence in 1713 encouraged in some, such as M. Pipino whose *Gramatica piemontese* was published in 1783, the dream of a codified, official, national language. Codification of a Turin-based koine, begun by Pipino, has produced several grammars and dictionaries, in particular V. di Sant'Albino's *Gran dizionario piemontese–italiano* (Turin, 1859; reprinted Turin, 1964), and, more recently, the grammars of Aly-Belfàdel (1933) and of Brero and Bertodatti (1988) and Gribaudo's dictionary (1983). The orthography was standardized in 1930 by P. Pacòt and A. Viglongo.

Despite a French interlude during the Napoleonic regime, Italian remained the official language of Piedmont and in 1861 the Piedmontese-speaking King of Savoy became King of Italy. Given its lack of official or legal status, the use of Piedmontese in formal or semi-formal contexts is limited to notarial acts, optional use in local government, religious sermons and some church services (although it has no liturgical status). Some, mainly primary, schools provide basic (optional) instruction and there is some provision for Piedmontese on the radio, mainly on private local stations. The *Cà dë studi piemontèis* (a centre for Piedmontese studies) promotes Piedmontese culture and publishes academic studies. Calls (so far unsuccessful) are made annually by an international conference on Piedmontese language and literature for

Piedmontese to be recognized as a '(regional) language' by the Italian state.

Since the First World War, the mass immigration of southern workers (especially to Turin), educational and social pressures in favour of Italian, and the influence of the mass media, have drastically reduced the use of Piedmontese, particularly in towns and among the young, with almost all speakers being bilingual. ISTAT 1989 gives 23.4% of speakers using only or mainly Piedmontese in the family, 22.8% using both Piedmontese and Italian, but 53.2% using only or mainly Italian. Piedmontese-speaking descendants of immigrant communities are found in the USA, Canada, and especially Argentina.

Aly-Belfàdel, A. 1933. *Grammatica piemontese*. Noale.

Brero, C. and Bertodatti, R. 1988. *Grammatica della lingua piemontese*. Turin.

Gribaudo, G. 1983. *Ël neuv Gribaud. Dissionari piemontèis* ('The New Gribaud. Piedmontese Dictionary'). Turin.

Parry, M. M. 1994. Ël piemontèis, lenga d'Europa ('Piedmontese, a European language' [in English]). In Parry, M. M., Davies, W. V. and Temple, R. A. M. (eds), *The Changing Voices of Europe*, Cardiff, 173–92.

MAIR PARRY

Lombard

The Lombard dialects occupy the middle of the Po Valley and the corresponding section of the Alps. The dialects are highly differentiated, being partly based on the varieties of the larger towns which, in their turn, are more or less extensively influenced by that of Milan. Very roughly, two main areas can be distinguished, on linguistic and historical grounds: a western one, including Milan, Como and the Swiss canton of Ticino (where the dialect shades into Romansh), and an eastern one, including Bergamo, Brescia, and part of the provinces of Cremona and Mantua. The southern dialects show some Emilian features. The transitional dialects of the areas around Novara, in Piedmont, and Trento, in Trentino, are also fundamentally Lombard.

Some writers in Milanese are to be reckoned among the foremost names in Italian literature: Bonvesin de la Riva, born in Milan (?1240–1313), wrote many poems in a form of literary Milanese which is thought by some scholars to represent the first embryonic form of a later aborted 'northern Italian language'. Later, Carlo Maria Maggi of Milan (1630–99) used Milanese in burlesque poems and character comedies; Carlo Porta (1776–1821) wrote, in a realistic and dramatic vein, many poems which also count among the outstanding examples of Italian literature. The very complex language of an important 20th-c. Italian writer, Carlo Emilio Gadda, is tinged with Lombardisms, and among the most interesting of modern Italian poets is Delio Tessa of Milan (1886–1939) who used only Milanese, with very suggestive lyrical effects and gruesome humour. Some Milanese songs of the 1960s (e.g. *El purtava i scarp de tenis* 'He was wearing tennis shoes') became popular all over Italy.

The beginnings of the comparative study of the Lombard dialects can perhaps be traced to the translations of the ninth *novella* of the first *giornata* of Boccaccio's *Decameron* into Milanese and the dialect of Bergamo, included as examples of

Lombard in a 16th-c. collection by Lionardo Salviati, while B. Biondelli's *Saggio sui dialetti gallo-italici* ('Essay on the Gallo-Italic Dialects') (Milan, 1853) provides translations of the 'Parable of the Prodigal Son' in a number of Lombard varieties. The 19th c. also saw the appearance of important dictionaries by Pietro Monti of Como (1845), Antonio Tiraboschi of Bergamo (1873), and Francesco Cherubini of Milan (5 vols, 1835–56).

A Lombard koine developed later than the Venetan one and has always been more vague, mainly because the competing centres in the region were more numerous (Milan, Como, Bergamo, Brescia, Pavia, Mantua) and more influential.

While in the city of Milan itself the dialect is now very rarely spoken, it is still used in smaller centres and in the countryside and hill villages, and also in towns such as Como and Bergamo. It is well known, on the other hand, that in the past the situation was different – Manzoni, for example, had French and Milanese (not Italian) as his mother tongues. An abrupt change took place after the Second World War, and particularly in the 1960s, as a consequence of industrialization and massive immigration. The ISTAT survey of 1987–8 indicated that, of a total population of 8,200,000 over the age of 6 in the administrative region of Lombardy, 43.7% spoke dialect with the family (22.8% spoke only dialect). The proportion of those speaking dialect with strangers fell to 20%. More recent Doxa data are not comparable, showing a much higher figure than ISTAT for 1988 but a lower figure for 1991, which represents an increase in comparison with ISTAT but a decrease as compared with the preceding Doxa survey: very questionable results indeed.

Biondelli, B. 1853. *Saggio sui dialetti gallo-italici* ('Essay on the Gallo-Italic Dialects'). Milan.
Nicoli, F. 1983. *Grammatica milanese*. Busto Arsizio.
Sanga, G. 1984. *Dialettologia lombarda*. Pavia.

PAOLA BENINCÀ

Dolomitic Ladin

In the view of some scholars, the varieties in question here form part of a ***Rhaeto-Romance** subgroup of the Romance languages, the other members of which are Friulian (see below) and the ***Romansh** of Switzerland. In the view of others, including the present writer, the linguistic features that these 'Rhaeto-Romance' varieties have in common do not depend on a special common origin or history. Rather, we would argue that we are here dealing with peripheral dialects that have preserved conservative features which, at one time, were also present in other dialects of northern Italy but have been obliterated in the process of subsequent linguistic evolution.

The dialects in question are spoken in a few valleys in the Dolomites in an area that, with marginal variations, from 1363 to 1919 was ruled by Austria. They are divided between two regions and three administrative provinces, the Val Gardena and the Val Badia (Bolzano province) and the Val di Fassa (Trento province) in the Trentino–Alto Adige region, and Livinallongo and Ampezzo (with the adjacent Comelico) (Belluno province) in the Veneto region. There has never been a centre strong enough to produce any kind of common language. An attempt to devise a common form of Ladin is, however, at present under consideration, but the differences between the various dialects are such as to render the task a difficult one. No unified orthography has yet been devised.

While in the past writing in Ladin has been of little importance, more recently a number of poets have come to use their local varieties with interesting results.

There are in all some 30,000 speakers, virtually all of them bilingual with Italian (Trento and Belluno) or German (Bolzano) or trilingual with both. Both German and Italian are spoken in the communities and are taught in the schools; two hours a week are devoted to Ladin language and culture in the primary schools, where a good number of textbooks introducing the study of the language are available. Many good descriptive grammars, dictionaries and linguistic analyses of the language also exist (see the bibliography in Holtus et al. 1989, under '[Various authors]' below).

The most important dailies in the region, the German-language *Die Dolomiten* and the Italian-language *Alto Adige*, periodically include a page written in one variety or another of Ladin. Two excellent periodicals, *Mondo Ladino*, published by the Istitut Cultural Ladin (Fassa, Trento), mostly in Italian, and *Ladinia*, published by the Istitut Ladin (Val Badia, Bolzano), mostly in German, serve as a source of information on scholarly and artistic activities and political issues.

Elwert, T. W. 1943. *Die Mundart des Fassa-Tals* ('The Dialect of the Fassa Valley'). Heidelberg (reprinted 1972, Wiesbaden).
Haiman, J. and Benincà, P. 1992. *The Rhaeto-Romance Languages*. London.
Pellegrini, G. B. 1974. *Saggi sul ladino dolomitico e sul friulano* ('Essays on Dolomitic Ladin and Friulian'). Bari.
[Various authors]. 1989. Ladinisch. In Holtus, G., Metzeltin, M. and Schmitt, C. (eds), *Lexikon der Romanistischen Linguistik*, Tübingen, vol. 3, 646–763 (10 articles, 3 in Italian and 7 in German).

PAOLA BENINCÀ

Venetan

The region characterized by Venetan vernaculars includes the historical territory of the pre-Roman Venetic people; it occupies the NE part of the Po valley and the corresponding section of the Alps and their foothills, part of the coast, and the area surrounding the Venetian lagoon; its eastern boundary, separating it from Friuli, is formed by a small stream, the Livenza. The territory can be divided into two sub-areas on the basis of phonetic and grammatical features of the spoken dialects but the region as a whole shares a more or less strong dependence on a single centre which, from at least the 15th c., has been Venice. The northern area covers the provinces of Belluno and part of Treviso, with dialects shading into Ladin; the southern area has Padua as its historical centre and also includes Vicenza, Rovigo and part of Treviso (the dialect of Verona has a Lombard substratum but conforms in most respects to the south Venetan model).

Particular Venetan varieties (the so-called 'Colonial Venetian') are spoken outside the region proper in Friuli, Istria, and the city of Trieste, and can be attributed to the political dominance of Venice in this area from the Middle Ages and long-standing economic relations with that centre. A different case is that of the eastern Adriatic coast where, in Grado, Marano, and some localities in Istria, very ancient dialects of a Venetan type are spoken which developed in isolation and independently of Venetian influence. Many Venetan-speaking communities that have kept up their vernacular remain in Brazil, Argentina, Mexico, Australia and elsewhere.

A type of koine has evolved, which, though it was formed in and spread out from Venice, does not have the specific features of the dialect of Venice or, indeed, of any other centre, but represents, in essence, a kind of common denominator of all the dialects of the region. It is, moreover, characterized by considerable stability of final vowels, a feature that Venetan (and particularly the dialect of Padua) has in common with Florentine. Especial importance is probably to be attached to the role of Padua as a linguistic model, at least in the earliest centuries of this millennium, owing to the influence of the University of Padua which was founded in the early 13th c.

The earliest Venetan literary texts, dating from the 13th c. and hailing from Verona, are two poems by Giacomino, *De Gerusalem Celesti* ('On the Heavenly Jerusalem') and *De Babilonia Civitate Infernali* ('On Babylon, the Infernal City') that, because of the subject (a journey to the other world), are thought to have inspired Dante. Two highly significant texts are from Padua, translations from Latin into Paduan commissioned at the end of the 14th c. by Count Carraresi, the *signore* of the town: the *Bibbia Istoriata Padovana* and a pharmaceutical text, the *Libro agregà de Serapion* or *Erbario Carrarese*, originally composed in Arabic. Among important names in the history of Italian literature, especially in the field of theatre, who have written in Venetan are Angelo Beolco (il Ruzante) (?1496–1542), who wrote in the Paduan dialect a number of outstanding comedies, inspired by Classical models and transposed into the contemporary rural or urban context of the Paduan working class and which are still performed, and Carlo Goldoni (1707–93), who, in his plays that are even more widely known and still performed all over the world, used mainly the urban dialect of Venice but also, for some characters, other varieties such as Bergamasco. Eminent modern poets who have written in Venetan include Virgilio Giotti (1885–1957), who wrote in the 'Colonial Venetian' of Trieste, Biagio Marin (1891–1985), who used the dialect of Grado, and Andrea Zanzotto (b. 1921) who, while mainly writing in Italian, also makes sophisticated use of his native dialect, that of Pieve di Soligo (Treviso). Echoes of the dialect of Malo (Vicenza province) are to be found in the language of one of the most interesting contemporary Italian novelists, Luigi Meneghello. Venetan varieties are represented in Salviati's 16th-c. collection of translations of the ninth *novella* of the first *giornata* of Boccaccio's *Decameron* by Paduan, Venetian and Istrian.

The earliest dictionary of Paduan and Venetian is that of Gasparo Patriarchi (1775), which served as a basis for Giuseppe Boerio's *Dizionario Veneziano* of 1829 that is still in print in a revised version.

The dialect is still very widely used in conversation, and even in relatively formal situations, at all social levels; speakers in general have a command of two or three social registers, depending on the situation (the regional koine, possibly a provincial variety, and the local dialect). The koine, though not standardized, substitutes for

Italian in a variety of situations. According to the ISTAT survey (1987–8), 82.5% of the total Venetan population of 4,000,000 aged over 6 years speak dialect at least within the family (69% use dialect only) and 64.7% even with strangers (recent data collected by Doxa are unusable for our present purpose since those for Veneto are conflated with those for Trentino and Friuli).

Boerio, G. 1856. *Dizionario del dialetto veneziano*. Venice (reprinted 1993, Florence).
Pellegrini, G. B. 1977. *Studi di linguistica e filologia veneta*. Pisa.
Zamboni, A. 1974. *Veneto*. Pisa.

PAOLA BENINCÀ

Friulian

Friulian (considered by some scholars to be a Rhaeto-Romance language – see above under **I Introduction** and **Dolomitic Ladin**) is spoken in part of the Friuli-Venezia Giulia region in the extreme north-east of Italy, in an area bordering Slovenia to the east and Austria to the north and delimited by the coast on the south and the Venetan area on the west. Three sub-varieties can be identified, but the main linguistic features are shared by all: (i) central Friulian, the most widespread variety, spoken in an area that includes the capital, Udine; (ii) western Friulian, to the west of the Tagliamento river, the most innovative variety owing to close contact with Veneto; (iii) Carnic Friulian, the most conservative variety, spoken in the northern (Alpine) part of Friuli.

The earliest attestations of Friulian, dating from the 14th c., are exercises for translation into Latin, from the notarial school at Cividale. Also from Cividale, and dating from the end of the 14th c., are the earliest poetic texts, two ballads in the tradition of the Provençal courtly lyric. Literary use of the dialect developed mainly in the 16th c., when Udine became the main cultural centre and promoted its vernacular as the model for a literary language. The language of the principal Friulian poet, Ermes di Colloredo (1622–92), became the basis for a literary koine. 19th-c. texts, particularly almanacs, abound and were widespread among all strata of society; the most famous of these is the *Strolich furlan* ('Friulian Almanac') of Pietro Zorutti, a prolific and popular (if, in his time, overrated) poet. 20th-c. dialectal literature is more flourishing in Friuli than in other regions, in the form of almanacs, poems, plays, novels and short stories, and with writers meeting in groups such as the Academiuta of Casarsa and the Risultive group which were important in the 1940s.

Two attitudes towards the choice of a literary medium can be identified. On the one hand, writers of the Risultive group continue to use the traditional literary koine, based on the central Friulian of Udine; these include Giuseppe Marchetti (the founder of the group and the author of the first important Friulian grammar, 1952), Dino Virgili, Aurelio Cantoni, Alan Brusini, and Maria Forte. Others use their subregional or local varieties: Pier Paolo Pasolini, the important Italian writer and film-maker, was the first to choose the western variety of Casarsa, while Riccardo Castellani, Domenico Castellani, Novella Cantarutti and Amedeo Giacomini write in their own (also western) variety and Leonardo Zanier adopts the Carnic variety.

The above-mentioned literary koine is also generally used for official and other written purposes. Especially since 1963, when the Friuli-Venezia Giulia region achieved a degree of autonomy, there has been increasing use of Friulian in the mass media (newspapers, radio, TV) and for narrative works and essays, and there are proposals for the introduction of Friulian in the schools.

The increased use of the language has initiated a lively debate on the adoption of a unified orthography. That of the principal cultural body in the region, the Società Filologica Friulana, is widely used and has been adopted in the excellent dictionary *Nuovo Pirona*. A new unified orthography has been established within the framework of an important regional law of 1996 on the protection and promotion of Friulian.

Friulian is today spoken by over 700,000 people in its home region. Nearly all also know Italian, and in the urban centres and the western part of the area Venetan is also known. According to the 1988 ISTAT survey, Friulian is widely used not only within the family (55% use only Friulian while 18% alternate between Friulian and Italian) and with friends (46% and 28% respectively), but even with strangers (47% Italian only, 21.7% Friulian only, 30.2% both languages). Although one cannot properly speak of a common Friulian or of a Friulian spoken koine, the language is substantially homogeneous in its essential features and so there is no hindrance to intercommunication between speakers from different areas, using their respective native varieties. On the other hand, Friulian is used in a wide range of situations, which results in frequent code-switching and considerable interference (mostly lexical) from Italian. Furthermore, peripheral varieties (especially the more conservative Carnic variety) are liable to be influenced by the more widespread central (Udine) variety. Younger generations tend more and more to use Italian, but there is renewed interest in Friulian, at the expense of the so-called 'Colonial Venetian' (see above, under **Venetan**), a type of Venetian based on the language of the Republic of Venice that dominated Friuli from 1420 to 1797 and which until the mid-20th c. was considered a prestige dialect.

Outside Italy, Friulian-speaking communities in Romania, Australia, North America, South Africa and elsewhere number about 300,000 people.

Francescato, G. 1966. *Dialettologia friulana*. Udine.
Frau, G. 1984. *Friuli*. Pisa.
Gregor, D. B. 1975. *Friulian*. New York and Cambridge.
Haiman, J. and Benincà, P. 1992. *The Rhaeto-Romance Languages*. London.
Marchetti, G. 1952. *Lineamenti di grammatica friulana*. Udine.
Pirona, G. A., Carletti, E. and Corgnali, G. B. 1992. *Il Nuovo Pirona. Vocabolario friulano*, 2nd edn. Udine.
[Various authors] 1989. Friaulisch. In Holtus, G., Metzeltin, M. and Schmitt, C. (eds), *Lexikon der Romanistischen Linguistik*, Tübingen, vol. 3, 563–645 (8 articles in Italian).

LAURA VANELLI

Ligurian (Genoese)

Ligurian varieties extend beyond contemporary Liguria into Piedmont, Emilia, Tuscany and southern France (the Tende–Saorge area). The military and commercial prestige of Genoa from the Middle Ages onwards established its dialect as the basis of a regional koine standing in a diglossic relationship with the other main dialect groups of the area, western Ligurian and coastal Intemelian. The Genoese Republic's extensive maritime and commercial enterprises have left Ligurian communities in Monaco, Sardinia (Carloforte and Calasetta, to which localities they were transferred from their original settlement at Tabarka) and Corsica (Bonifacio), while links with Imperial Spain in the 16th and 17th centuries and 19th-c. mass emigration established South American communities (surviving in Argentina, Chile and Uruguay), with Ligurian contributing significantly to the River Plate Italo-Spanish linguistic continuum known as *cocoliche*.

Written Ligurian appears at the end of the 12th c. Genoese is contrasted with the more prestigious Provençal of the troubadours in Raimbaut de Vaqueiras's bilingual *tensó* (a debate in verse), and a Latin legal document contains the vernacular *dichiarazione di Paxia* (Savona, 1182) but the first major text, which had an enduring thematic ('national' pride) and formal influence on the development of Ligurian literature, is a late 13th-c. collection of verses by an anonymous native of Genoa. Religious lauds and prose follow and, although Latin continued to be used in the Genoese chancellery until the 18th c., the 15th c. saw increasing public and quasi-official use (in treaties, military reports, statutes) of a vernacular which was to a greater or lesser extent influenced by Tuscan or the northern koine. The end of the 16th c., however, marked a turning-point when the Senate rejected Paolo Foglietta's translation of his brother's Latin history of Genoa in favour of a Tuscan version. Foglietta's vigorous anti-Tuscan reaction and his widely acclaimed *Rime diverse in lingua genovese* ('Various Verses in the Genoese Language') of 1575 then assured the continuation of Genoese as an autonomous literary language, eminently suitable for public manifestations of Ligurian identity (though official correspondence was thenceforth in Italian). G. G. Cavalli's *Çitara zeneise* ('Genoese Zither') (1635) was hailed as a poetic masterpiece and the links between linguistic diversity, 'national' (i.e. Ligurian) identity and literary tradition became more insistent in the 18th c., as did the concern for linguistic normalization (orthographical rules, the publication of a Genoese–Italian dictionary, followed by several others in the 19th c., e.g. Casaccia's *Vocabolario* (1841–51, 1876)). However, as elsewhere in Italy, foreign domination (during the Napoleonic regime and later under the Kingdom of Savoy) fostered pro-unification sentiments, especially among the bourgeoisie, that were detrimental to the fortunes of Genoese. Within the city itself, two phonetically divergent varieties existed as a result of the conservatism of the Genoese aristocracy and, despite a literary revival in the late 19th c., the Genoese koine lacked the prestige of Italian. The 20th c. has also witnessed the written use of peripheral varieties.

The present status of Ligurian, despite signs of a reversal of the massive post-war rejection of 'dialect' in favour of Italian, is but a pale reflection of the one-time status of Genoese as a 'national' and quasi-official and literary language, and the future is uncertain. ISTAT 1989 shows a greater use of Italian at home and with friends and strangers in Liguria than in any other region except Tuscany. Doxa 1992, however, reveals far greater use of Ligurian (a reversal of the trend?), but, despite some cultural and educational activity, Ligurian has no official status.

Petracco Sicardi, G. 1980. 'Scripta' volgare e 'scripta' dialettale in Liguria. In Còveri, L., Petracco Sicardi, G. and Piastra, W. (eds), *Bibliografia dialettale ligure*, Genoa, 3–22.

——, Toso, F. and Cavallero, P. 1985–92. *Vocabolario delle parlate liguri*, 4 vols. Genoa.

Toso, F. 1994. Per una storia dell'identità linguistica ligure in età moderna. In Toso, F. and Piastra, W. *Bibliografia dialettale ligure. Aggiornamento 1979–1993*, Genoa, 5–43.

—— 1997. *Grammatica del genovese*. Genoa.

MAIR PARRY

Emilian-Romagnol

Emilian-Romagnol dialects are spoken in the Emilia-Romagna region and, in addition, Emilian-type dialects are found in southern Lombardy (in the provinces of Pavia, Voghera and Mantua) and in the Lunigiana district in Tuscany, while the Republic of San Marino and the entire province of Pesaro-Urbino in the Marche region are linguistically Romagnol. The Emilian-Romagnol varieties are subdivided as follows: (i) western Emilian varieties to the west of the Panaro river, in the provinces of Piacenza, Parma, Reggio Emilia and Modena; (ii) eastern Emilian varieties to the east of the Panaro, in the provinces of Ferrara and Bologna; (iii) Romagnol in the provinces of Ravenna, Rimini and Forlì, in San Marino, and in the northern Marche.

The existence of two different speech varieties within the city of Bologna is attested in Dante's *De vulgari eloquentia* (I.ix.4), that of the Strada Maggiore, corresponding to the historical centre of the city, and that of the Borgo San Felice, which at that time corresponded to the periphery of the city. The earliest written attestations of Emilian consist of sporadic non-literary texts, dating from the 13th and 14th centuries, in which dialectal characteristics are to some extent obscured by the use of a notarial, chancery type of language that avoids local linguistic features in favour of a type of northern koine based mainly on Venetan. A regional koine never developed. The earliest example of the real Emilian dialect is the Bolognese version included in Salviati's 16th-c. collection of translations of the ninth *novella* of the first *giornata* of Boccaccio's *Decameron*. Three centuries later, Biondelli included 22 Emilian-Romagnol versions in his collection of translations of the Parable of the Prodigal Son published in 1853. The first dialect dictionaries, mainly relating to urban varieties, also date from the 19th c.

The use of the dialect for literary purposes, though only on a limited scale, goes back to the 16th c. *Pulon Matt* ('Mad Paul'), an anonymous late-16th-c. burlesque epic in Romagnol, is worth particular mention. Giulio Cesare Croce wrote verses in Bolognese in the late 16th and early 17th centuries. There is a more varied and more interesting literary production from the 18th c., with in particular the *Rimedi per la sonn* (1703) of the Bolognese writer Lotto Lotti, and a number of plays, mainly comedies of a popular character. Some of the most important contemporary Italian poets, Aldo Spallicci, Nino Pedretti, Tonino Guerra, Tolmino Baldassari and Raffaello Baldini, write in Romagnol as well as in Italian.

The Emilian-Romagnol linguistic area is divided among a wide range of local varieties or patois that are relatively independent of one another, and urban varieties exert little influence on the language of surrounding areas. No regional or subregional koine exists or has ever existed. ISTAT data for the late 1980s show that, of a total population of some 4 million, more than half (53%) used exclusively or predominantly Italian within the family, while 23.5% alternated between Italian and dialect, and only 23.1% used habitually or only dialect. The exclusive or dominant use of dialect diminishes slightly, to 20.2% as the language used with friends, and plummets to 7.4% as the language used with strangers. These statistics show that the use of dialect is generally limited to the environment of the family or the peer group, while outside of these domains the language in general use is Italian. Italian and dialect are clearly separated in function and there is little code-switching and little linguistic interference between the two languages.

Coco, F. 1970. *Il dialetto di Bologna. Fonetica storica e analisi strutturale*. Bologna.
Gregor, D. B. 1972. *Romagnol: Language and Literature*. New York and Cambridge.
Neri, A. 1981. *Vocabolario del dialetto modenese*. Bologna.
Quondamatteo, G. 1982. *Dizionario romagnolo*, Rimini.
Schürr, F. 1974. *La voce della Romagna. Profilo linguistico letterario*. Ravenna.
Ungarelli, G. 1901. *Vocabolario del dialetto bolognese*. Bologna.

LAURA VANELLI

IV Central and southern Italy

The northern linguistic boundary of the area in question is marked by a line traditionally known as the 'La Spezia–Rimini Line', which in fact runs roughly from Carrara, along the northern boundary of modern Tuscany and through northern Marche, to Fano. This line corresponds approximately to the southern boundary of a new administrative territory established in the late 3rd c. AD by the Emperor Diocletian, and oriented no longer towards Rome but towards the new provincial capital of Milan, and with its major roads running no longer south–north but east–west. One effect of this change was the linguistic isolation of central and southern Italy from territories to the north, and perhaps also the reinforcement of linguistic differences already brought about by the geographical barrier of the Apennines. The subsequent politically fragmented history of the land to the south of this ancient boundary is reflected in a highly variegated modern linguistic picture. True, the Romance dialects of central and southern Italy have some distinctive common structural features, such as the conservation (shared with Sardinian) of the Latin opposition between long and short consonants, but there never was a language recognized as being distinctive of, and unique to, the whole of this territory. It is only in the 20th c. that standard Italian (i.e. Tuscan) has begun to be extensively spoken and written by the general populace.

Dialectologists usually recognize four major dialect areas in the centre and south of Italy, the last three of which are often grouped together, and distinguished from

Tuscan, as 'central southern' dialects: (i) Tuscan; (ii) 'central Italian', along a band of territory often known as the 'Rome–Ancona corridor'; (iii) 'upper southern' dialects, covering most of the remainder of mainland Italy; (iv) 'far southern' dialects, those of Salento and southern Calabria on the mainland and of Sicily.

It is possible that some dialect variations reflect the speech habits of the various peoples who adopted Latin in Roman times, but such 'substrate' influences are extremely difficult to demonstrate. Certain lexical items, e.g. *attrùfu* 'October' in parts of southern Campania and Basilicata, or *ghiefa* 'clod' around the Gulf of Otranto, reveal by their phonology an ***Oscan** origin. Whether the sound-change [nd] > [nn] continues the change [nd] > [nn] that was also characteristic of the ancient ***Osco-Umbrian** languages is difficult to determine. And there seems to be little substance to notions that the spirantization of voiceless stops (the so-called *gorgia toscana*) that is characteristic of much of modern Tuscan (e.g. [la hasa] for *la casa* 'house', [praθo] for *prato* 'meadow') has its origin in the consonantal aspiration characteristic of ancient ***Etruscan**, or that the supposed linguistic conservatism of Tuscany can be ascribed to the possibility that speakers of non-Indo-European Etruscan learned Latin more accurately than others who spoke ***Italic languages** closer to Latin.

If the linguistic divisions of central and southern Italy do not necessarily mirror substrate influences, they clearly do reflect older political and cultural boundaries, notably the medieval ones between the dominions of the Germanic-speaking Langobards (and later the Franks) on the one hand, and Byzantine dominions on the other. Thus, the Rome–Ancona corridor corresponds, along most of its length, to the 6th-c. corridor between Rome and Ravenna, which separated the Langobard Duchy of Tuscia from that of Spoleto, and later came to constitute the territory of the Papal States. The corridor also follows (again, very roughly) an earlier ethnic boundary between the ancient Etruscans and Gauls to the north and the Osco-Umbrians to the south. Sicily and the far south of the mainland were also a Byzantine possession (although from the 9th until the 11th c. much of Sicily was under Arab domination). The Duchy of Benevento contributed to reinforcing the southern boundary of that territory now occupied by 'upper southern' dialects, through the Langobards' defence of the frontiers of Latinity against Byzantine pressure from Basilicata and Puglia, and against Arab raids.

A factor that has made the linguistic picture yet more variegated is immigration, leading to the establishment in central and southern Italy of a number of non-native speech varieties, whose speakers (countable in tens of thousands) today virtually always also speak the surrounding indigenous dialects. From the 15th c., numbers of refugees from across the Adriatic entered southern Italy and there remain some 45 ***Albanian**-speaking villages scattered across southern Italy from Abruzzo to Sicily. There survive also three Croatian-speaking villages in Molise (for Croatian, see under ***Serbo-Croat**). From the 14th c., migrants of the Waldensian religion appear to have fled to Calabria from the sub-Alpine valleys of NW Italy, and a form of their speech survives in the ***Occitan**-based dialect of Guardia Piemontese (Calabria). The dialects of Faeto and Celle in Puglia have distinctively ***Gallo-Romance** (and, more specifically, **Francoprovençal) features, although the precise origins of these two speech communities remain problematic.

Probably the area most profoundly affected by immigration is Sicily. The theory that the original Romance speech of Sicily disappeared in the Middle Ages, with **Arabic** (introduced in the 9th c.) spoken in most of the island (where it has left a number of loan-words) and **Greek** in the east, and that Sicily was subsequently 're-Romanized' from the mainland, is no longer generally accepted. But it is clear that the arrival in the 11th c. of the Normans (from whose speech a number of terms entered Sicilian, such as *vuccèri* 'butcher') entailed a major influx, continuing into the 13th c., of populations from other parts of Italy, notably the north, the most tangible linguistic reflection of which is the presence of villages (Nicosia, Piazza Armerina, S. Fratello, Novara, Sperlinga, Aidone) speaking northern dialects broadly identifiable with the Monferrato area of northern Italy, but which is also detectable in a number of Gallo-Italian loans in Sicilian. Similar circumstances explain the presence of speech varieties with marked Gallo-Italian features in Picerno and Tito, near Potenza, and on the Gulf of Policastro. Greek is still spoken in nine villages in Salento south of Lecce, and in five localities in the Aspromonte area of Calabria. It appears to have survived until the 16th c. in Messina. It is now generally accepted that Greek was introduced under the Byzantines, rather than continuing (as has been suggested) the Greek of Classical antiquity, when eastern Sicily and the extremities of the mainland were Greek-speaking. At any rate, the once Greek-speaking area (including the whole of Sicily) now constitutes a separate subgroup of southern Italo-Romance characterized, for example, by raising the vowels [e] and [o] to [i] and [u] respectively (e.g. *tila* 'cloth', *suli* 'sun', corresponding to Latin and Italian *tela* [tela], *sole* [sole]), a feature that is also characteristic of the development of medieval Greek, and by lexical Grecisms such as [naka] 'cradle' from Greek *nakē* 'sheepskin'. A syntactic feature of post-Classical Greek that has affected the **Italo-Romance** of the far south (and also **Romanian** and other Balkan languages) is the non-use of the original infinitive form in subordinate clauses, of the type (Calabrian) *voliti mu veniti*, literally 'you want that you come', rather than 'you want to come' (as in Italian, *volete venire*). Greek also had an impact on writing: in monasteries in the far south the Greek alphabet continued to be used to write Romance texts, in some cases as late as the 16th c.

A later population movement with major linguistic consequences for Rome and its environs was the influx of non-Romans throughout the 15th c. (as a consequence of the return of the papacy to the city from Avignon in 1377) and particularly after the sack of Rome in 1527. The result was a gradual attenuation of markedly local features in favour of a speech variety (both in the city and in areas to the north and east under the influence of Rome) in which the increasingly prestigious Tuscan model played a major role.

Southern Italy was the cradle of the first uncontroversially Italo-Romance (rather than Latin) written texts, the so-called *Placiti cassinesi*, brief, formulaic, legal depositions written down between 960 and 963 and displaying distinctive southern Italian features (see Migliorini and Griffith 1984, Ch. 3, in the bibliography to Section II above, and Castellani 1973, in the General Bibliography below, for other early southern attestations of the vernacular, such as the Commodilla Inscription of Rome). Like many early Italo-Romance texts, these were drawn up in the Langobard domains, by scribes working in the Benedictine monasteries (pre-eminently that of Montecassino). Indeed, it was owing to Benedictine influence that some two-thirds of the vernacular texts produced in Italy between the 10th and the 13th centuries originated in the area between Lazio and Abruzzo, including not only legal documents but also religious and literary texts such as the *Ritmo su Sant'Alessio* or the late 11th-c. *Formula di confessione umbra*. From early 13th-c. Sicily, at the court of Frederick II, there emerged the profoundly influential 'Sicilian School' of poets. A form of Sicilian rapidly came to be used as a prestigious literary koine outside Sicily (many exponents of the Sicilian School were, however, from mainland Italy, not from Sicily), whose prestige was such as to have a major impact on nascent literary Tuscan (for example, on writers such as Guittone d'Arezzo). The influence of Sicilian declined rapidly after the mid-13th c., as Tuscan gained in prestige, with in particular immensely prestigious figures such as Dante, Boccaccio and Petrarch whose works rapidly became known throughout the peninsula. Indeed, the flourishing of central and southern vernaculars other than Tuscan as *written* varieties is largely confined to the Middle Ages. In some areas, writing in dialect seems to have emerged late and to have been short-lived, the earliest Sicilian vernacular texts dating from the 13th c. while the 15th c. was the most significant period for Calabria and Basilicata. With the appearance of Dante's *Divina Commedia*, Tuscan rapidly established itself as the prestigious written vernacular, a development often accompanied by an increasingly negative evaluation of the local dialects. In fact, a number of prestigious local written varieties had already emerged, notably Neapolitan, but under Angevin domination (1265–1442) the prestigious language in Naples was French, a fact which discouraged literary use of the vernacular.

As for Tuscan itself, the earliest texts reflect the rapid commercial and economic growth of Tuscany, beginning with Pisa and Lucca in the 11th and 12th centuries, with Florence becoming a major centre of commerce by the mid-14th c. The oldest surviving clearly Tuscan text is a Pisan naval account book (late 11th or early 12th c.); from 1211 we have a fragment of a Florentine bankers' book; from the mid-13th c. most Tuscan texts are from Florence, Siena and Arezzo, and indeed by 1375 eight-ninths of all Italian vernacular texts are in Tuscan. The first attested literary use of Tuscan is the *Ritmo Laurenziano* dating from the early 13th c. The economic and cultural rise of Tuscany was, significantly, accompanied by an explosion of literacy in the vernacular, even in rural communities. It is also possible that, in the latter half of the 13th c., the nature of urban Florentine was modified by large-scale movement of population from the countryside into the town.

In modern central and southern Italy, Tuscan-based standard Italian is universally accepted as the prestigious spoken and written language, and is almost universally understood. It is difficult to assess the numbers of speakers of central and southern dialects, particularly because passive knowledge of the dialects is frequently more extensive than active knowledge. The latter is best represented within the family. According to Còveri (1986) (see General Bibliography), in the early 1980s, in Abruzzo, Campania, Basilicata, Calabria and Puglia, between 50% and 60% of speakers reported that they still habitually used dialect in that context, a proportion that rises to over 70% in Sicily; the proportion was lower in Marche and Umbria (just under 40%) and lowest (for the whole of Italy) in Lazio (under 25%) and Tuscany (under 18%). Standard Italian is the sole variety now employed in official and formal uses.

Dialect speakers are widespread outside Italy, in the USA, Canada, South America, Australia, and elsewhere, as a consequence of emigration in the late 19th and 20th centuries. A Pugliese-speaking colony, introduced by migrants during the 19th c., survived into the 20th c. in the Crimea (see Šišmarëv 1978).

Bigalke, R. 1980. *Dizionario dialettale della Basilicata* ('Dialectal Dictionary of Basilicata'). Heidelberg.

Giammarco, E. 1968–90. *Dizionario abruzzese e molisano* ('Abruzzese and Molisano Dictionary'), 6 vols. Rome.

Loporcaro, M. 1988. *Grammatica storica del dialetto di Altamura* ('Historical Grammar of the Dialect of Altamura'). Pisa.

Pellegrini, G. 1989. *Ricerche sugli arabismi italiani con particolare riguardo alla Sicilia* ('Research into Italian Arabisms, with particular reference to Sicily'). Palermo.

Rohlfs, G. 1956–9. *Vocabolario dei dialetti salentini (Terra d'Otranto)* ('Dictionary of the Salentino Dialects (Terra d'Otranto)'). Munich.

—— 1977. *Nuovo dizionario dialettale della Calabria* ('New Dialect Dictionary of Calabria'). Ravenna.

—— 1984. *La Sicilia nei secoli. Profilo storico, etnico e linguistico* ('Sicily through the Centuries. A Historical, Ethnic and Linguistic Profile'). Palermo.

—— 1985. *Latinità ed ellenismo nel Mezzogiorno d'Italia. Studi e ricerche dalla Magna Grecia alla Grecia italiana* ('Latinity and Hellenism in Southern Italy. Studies and Researches from Magna Graecia to Italian Greece'). Catanzaro.

Šišmarëv, V. 1978. *La lingua dei pugliesi in Crimea (1930–1940)* ('The Language of the Pugliesi in the Crimea (1930–1940)'). Galatina.

Tropea, G. (ed.) 1985– . *Vocabolario siciliano* (founded by G. Piccitto). Palermo.

Varvaro, A. 1981. *Lingua e storia in Sicilia* ('Language and History in Sicily'), vol. 1. Palermo.

—— 1986. *Vocabolario etimologico siciliano*, vol. 1. Palermo.

MARTIN MAIDEN

V Sardinian

Sardinian, the language of the island of Sardinia, has a number of widely divergent dialects. The two main varieties are Logudorese in the north (other than the extreme north, see below) and Campidanese in the southern third of the island. Other important varieties are Nuorese (north-eastern central) and Arborense (western central). Gallurese, in the north-east, is a Corsican (and therefore Tuscan-based) importation while Sassarese, in the north-west, emerged as a lingua franca from the contact between Tuscan, Corsican, Genoese and Logudorese. The divergence between Logudorese and Campidanese is attributable principally to the early influence of Pisan brought to the south of the island by commercial settlers from the 11th c. onwards, and the later influence of ***Catalan** which also established itself more deeply there than in the north during the period of Aragonese rule (14th–15th centuries) (though Catalan is still spoken in the north-western town of Alghero). A consequence of the union of Aragon and Castile in the late 15th c. was the introduction into both varieties of further loan-words from Castilian (i.e. *Spanish), which however did not become the medium of official documents until the 17th c. In 1764, i.e. some time after Sardinia's integration into the Kingdom of Savoy in 1718, Castilian was replaced by Italian but it was only after the unification of Italy in 1861 that the official use of Italian, which had been a continuing presence owing to the prestige of Tuscan literature, increased significantly, while Catalan persisted in notarial usage.

Early vernacular texts, from the 11th c. onwards, are noteworthy for their number and length, and for the status (unusual within the Romance domain) accorded to Sardinian varieties which were used for official and legal purposes, e.g. the *Condaghes* (notarial acts recording donations) and the *Carta de Logu de Arborea* (an important 14th-c. collection of laws). Further testimony to a lack of familiarity with Latin brought about by centuries of Byzantine rule is provided by the existence of an 11th- or 12th-c. Campidanese text in Greek characters (though Latin orthography constituted the norm).

Though there is a strong popular oral tradition, the lack of literary works of sufficient stature, the marked dialectal differentiation, and the subordination of the Sardinian varieties to the diverse languages of foreign rulers, have meant that no standard language has yet emerged. However, a proposal put forward in the mid-1990s favours a dual norm based on the two main varieties, Logudorese and Campidanese.

Sardinian is spoken by 65–70% of the population of the island, i.e. by some 1,600,000 in all. However, though a stable diglossic situation held to the mid-1950s, now, as a consequence of far-reaching demographic changes (e.g. intensive immigration in industrial areas) and educational and social changes, Sardinian is yielding ground to Italian in domains it once controlled, such as in informal usage with family and friends and in the workplace. Data provided by ISTAT 1989 and Doxa 1992 show an exceptionally high proportion claiming to use Italian – e.g. 31.6% of Doxa respondents use only Italian with all members of the family and 54.4% claim to use only or mainly Italian outside the family (as contrasted with 14.1% and 27.1% respectively in Sicily).

Sardinian has no legal or official status. Calls (especially by the Sardinian Action Party) for linguistic autonomy and parity with Italian, which began in the 1970s, led to the recognition in 1981 by the regional council of equal status and the adoption of a policy of bilingualism. Although these decisions have yet to be ratified by the Italian state, some local authorities are already implementing them and Sardinian is taught in some schools. Much earlier, chairs of Sardinian were founded at the Universities of Cagliari (1954) and Sassari (1970). Sardinian is represented in the media in newspapers, both monolingual (e.g. *Sa Repubblica Sarda* 'The Sardinian Republic') and bilingual, and by some (mainly private) radio and television broadcasting. However, the codification of a norm is a serious problem that needs to be addressed urgently if language shift away from Sardinian is to be checked.

Blasco Ferrer, E. 1994a. *La lingua sarda contemporanea. Grammatica del logudorese e del campidanese* ('The Contemporary Sardinian Language. Grammar of Logudorese and Campidanese'). Cagliari.

—— 1994b. *Ello, Ellus. Grammatica della lingua sarda* ('Grammar of the Sardinian Language'). Nuoro.

Jones, M. A. 1993. *Sardinian Syntax*. London.

Loi Corvetto, I. 1993. *La Sardegna e la Corsica*. Turin.

Pittau, M. 1972. *Grammatica del sardo nuorese* ('Grammar of the Sardinian of Nuoro'). Bologna.

Rindler Schjerve, R. 1993. Sardinian: Italian. In Posner, R. and Green, J. R. (eds), *Trends in Romance Linguistics and Philology*, Berlin, vol. 5, 271–94.

Spano, G. 1975. *Vocabolario sardo-italiano e italiano–sardo*, 2 vols. Bologna. (Reprint of 1851–2 edn.)

[Various authors] 1988. Sardisch. In Holtus, G., Metzeltin, M. and Schmitt, C. (eds), *Lexikon der Romanistischen Linguistik*, Tübingen, vol. 4, 836–935 (6 articles, 5 in Italian, 1 in German).

Wagner, M. L. 1951. *La lingua sarda: Storia, spirito e forma*. Bern.

—— 1960–4. *Dizionario etimologico sardo*, 3 vols. Heidelberg.

MAIR PARRY

VI General bibliography

Brevini, F. (ed.) 1987. *Poeti dialettali del Novecento* ('Twentieth-century Dialect Poets'). Turin.

Bruni, F. 1992. *L'italiano nelle regioni* ('Italian in the Regions'). Turin.

Castellani, A. 1973. *I più antichi testi italiani* ('The Earliest Italian Texts'). Bologna.

Còveri, L. 1986. Chi parla dialetto in Italia? ('Who speaks dialect in Italy?'). *Italiano e oltre*, vol. 1, 198–202.

Devoto, G. and Giacomelli, G. 1972. *I dialetti delle regioni d'Italia* ('The Dialects of the Regions of Italy'). Florence.

Doxa 1992. Parlare in dialetto ('Speaking dialect'). *Bollettino della Doxa*, 46, nos 9–10: 77–92.

Holtus, G., Metzeltin, M. and Schmitt, C. (eds) 1988. *Lexikon der Romanistischen Linguistik*, vol. 4, *Italienisch, Korsisch, Sardisch*. Tübingen. (W. Forner, 'Ligurien' [in German], 453–69; T. Telmon, 'Piemonte', 469–85; O. Lurati, 'Lombardia e Ticino', 485–516; A. Zamboni, 'Veneto', 517–38; F. Ursini, 'Varietà venete in Friuli-Venezia Giulia' ('Venetan varieties in Friuli-Venezia Giulia'), 538–50; M. Metzeltin, 'Veneziano e italiano in Dalmazia' ('Venetian and Italian in Dalmatia'), 551–69; F. Foresti, 'Emilia e Romagna', 569–93; L. Gianelli, 'Toscana', 594–606; U. Vignuzzi, 'Marche, Umbria, Lazio', 606–42; M. Marinucci, 'Abruzzo e Molise', 643–52; E. Radtke, 'Kampanien, Kalabrien' [in German], 652–68; F. Fanciullo, 'Lucania', 669–88; P. Caratù, 'La Lucania meridionale' ('Southern Lucania'), 688–94; T. Stehl, 'Puglia e Salento', 695–716; A. Varvaro, 'Sicilia', 716–31.)

ISTAT (Istituto Centrale di Statistica) 1989. Lingua italiana e dialetto. *Notiziario ISTAT*, 4th series, 41 (Year X, no. 18): 1–12.

Maiden, M. 1995. *A Linguistic History of Italian*. London.

—— and Parry, M. (eds) 1997. *The Dialects of Italy*. London.

Papanti, G. 1875. *I parlari italiani in Certaldo* ('The Italian Dialects in Certaldo'). Livorno (reprinted 1985, Bologna).

Pellegrini, G. 1977. *Carta dei dialetti d'Italia* ('Map of the Dialects of Italy'). Pisa.

Rohlfs, G. 1966–9. *Grammatica storica della lingua italiana e dei suoi dialetti* ('A Historical Grammar of the Italian Language and its Dialects'), 3 vols ([1] *Fonetica* ('Phonetics'); [2] *Morfologia* ('Morphology'); [3] *Sintassi e formazione delle parole* ('Syntax and Word-formation')). Turin.

—— 1972. La struttura linguistica dell'Italia ('The linguistic structure of Italy'). In Id., *Studi e ricerche su lingua e dialetti d'Italia*, Florence, 1–15.

Sanga, G. (ed.) 1990. *Koiné in Italia dalle origini al Rinascimento* ('Koines in Italy from Early Times to the Renaissance'). Bergamo.

Serianni, L. and Trifone, P. (eds) 1994. *Storia della lingua italiana*, vol. 3, *Le altre lingue* ('History of the Italian Language', vol. 3, 'The Other Languages'). Turin.

Trumper, J. 1993. Italian and Italian dialects: an overview of recent studies. In Posner, R. and Green, J. R. (eds), *Trends in Romance Linguistics and Philology*, Berlin, vol. 5, 295–326.

PAOLA BENINCÀ, MARTIN MAIDEN, MAIR PARRY, LAURA VANELLI

Izhorian, see *Ingrian*

J

Jatvingian (Jotvingian), see *Yatvingian*

Javanese (see under *Community languages (Netherlands)*)

Jèrriais, see *Jersey French*

Jersey French (Jèrriais)

The variety of *Channel Islands French spoken on the island of Jersey. It is known locally as 'Jèrriais', 'Jersey French', 'Jersey Norman-French' or 'the Jersey language', and in French as 'jersiais'.

The Anglicization of Jersey began in the early 19th c. with, on the one hand, the bringing in of 2,000 English and Irish workers to work in the fisheries and, on the other, the settling in the island of numerous veterans of the Napoleonic wars. The process was hastened by the growth in contacts with England with the development of steamer services and the dominance of English in the fields of education and commerce. Such influences have grown steadily stronger throughout the 20th c. and, for all practical purposes, the island is now completely Anglicized though the presence of French (in forms ranging from Jersey French to standard French) is everywhere visible in the names of natural features, hamlets, roads and dwellings.

According to the 1989 census (the only time that a question on ability to speak 'Jersey-Norman French' has been included on the census form), it was spoken by 5,720 (6.9%) of the total resident population of 82,809. In only five (predominantly rural) parishes out of 12 was it spoken by up to 12% to 14% of the population, viz. St Ouen (with the highest proportion, 13.8%), St John, St Mary and Trinity, with 9.9% in St Peter. The great majority of speakers (89%) were aged 40 or over, with only 10% in the age group 15–39 and less than 1% in the group aged under 15. There are dialectal differences within the language, particularly between western and eastern forms.

Literature in Jersey French is more or less limited to two mid-19th-c. volumes of verse (one by A. Mourant and one anonymous) and two volumes (1973, 1976) of Jersey traditions and tales by George F. Le Feuvre. Other writing has included the quarterly bulletin (which lasted from 1952 to 1977) of the Assembliée d'Jèrriais and over 900 articles by Le Feuvre (who died in 1984) in the *Jersey Evening Post*. The basis of the language as now written is Le Maistre's monumental dictionary (Le Maistre 1966).

Birt, P. 1985. *Le Jèrriais pour tous: A Complete Course on the Jersey Language*. St Helier.
Don Balleine Trust 1979. *The Jersey Language* (five cassettes and accompanying booklet). St Helier.
Le Maistre, F. 1966. *Dictionnaire jersiais–français*. St Helier.
Liddicoat, A. 1994. *A Grammar of the Norman French of the Channel Islands. The Dialects of Jersey and Sark*. Berlin.
Spence, N. C. W. 1993. *A Brief History of Jèrriais*. St Lawrence, Jersey, Le Don Balleine.

GLANVILLE PRICE

Judeo-Spanish

Judeo-Spanish (also sometimes called *Judezmo*, or *Ladino*, but, by the Jews themselves, most frequently *español* 'Spanish') is the collective name given to those varieties of **Spanish* which emerged outside Spain, as a result of the expulsion of Jews in 1492 from the newly united kingdom of Castile and Aragon. Faced with a choice between conversion to Christianity and exile, many groups of Jews chose the latter. Some travelled to Portugal (from where they were expelled anew a few years later), others to the cities of North Africa and Northern Europe (especially Hamburg), or to Italy. However, the most fortunate were those who made their way to the Ottoman Empire, where they received a warm welcome and special privileges, and often attained positions of high social prestige. Communities of Sephardic (i.e. Spanish) Jews were established in cities throughout the territories which then comprised the Ottoman Empire, including Monastir, Sarajevo, Bucharest, Sofia, with particularly important centres in Salonika, Istanbul and Izmir.

Following the expulsion, contact between the Sephardic Jews and other speakers of Spanish was almost entirely lost, so that innovations which took place in post-15th-c. Peninsular Spanish could not spread to Judeo-Spanish, and vice versa. On the one hand, Judeo-Spanish retains features of late medieval Spanish, including features of pronunciation and vocabulary, which were lost or modified in Spain, while on the other it introduces features, again including some features of pronunciation, but most especially new items of vocabulary, which could not find their way to the Peninsula. These innovations include heavy borrowing of words from the languages with which Judeo-Spanish had come into contact, especially Greek and Turkish, but also other Balkan languages and Arabic. A further circumstance which helped to distance Judeo-Spanish from Peninsular and American Spanish was the fact that, from the 19th c., the education of the Sephardic Jews was carried out through the medium of French, as a result of the establishment of schools, in the cities concerned, by French-speaking members of the Alliance Israélite Universelle. In consequence, much of the vocabulary used by the Sephardim to express ideas pertaining to intellectual and sophisticated life was borrowed from French, and such borrowings often have unrelated counterparts in Peninsular Spanish. However, the fundamental structure of Judeo-Spanish remains similar to that of other varieties, and there is a reasonable degree of mutual comprehension among them.

Until the 19th c. there was an unbroken tradition of writing in Judeo-Spanish, in a form of Hebrew script (*rashi* characters), but at that stage writing began to be carried out in the Latin alphabet, using principles of sound–letter correspondences which were based upon French spelling practice. Books, periodicals and newspapers continued to be published in Judeo-Spanish until well into the 20th c., but this tradition has now all but dried up.

Spoken Judeo-Spanish disappeared earliest from Italy, later from Hamburg, and survived precariously into the 20th c. in North Africa, thereafter being used there only in certain songs. It flourished best in the Ottoman world, until the break-up of that empire and the growing nationalism of the Balkan states which emerged from it led to pressure towards linguistic conformity. The Second World War and its persecutions led to massive emigration and the virtual destruction of the Jewish communities in Turkey and the Balkans. Sephardic émigrés settled in Israel, in the USA (especially New York and Los Angeles), or in Spanish America, while an increasing trickle have found their way back to Spain.

Judeo-Spanish is today used only by the oldest members of Sephardic communities, and is not being passed on to younger generations. It seems likely that it will survive only a few decades more.

Entwistle, W. J. 1936. Jewish Spanish. In Id., *The Spanish Language, together with Portuguese, Catalan and Basque*, London, 177–83.
Harris, T. K. 1994. *Death of a Language: The History of Judeo-Spanish*. Newark, DE.

RALPH PENNY

Judezmo, see *Judeo-Spanish*

Jula (see under *Community languages (France)*)

K

Kabardian (see under *Circassian* under *Caucasian languages. II. North-West Caucasian family*)

Kachchi (see under *Community languages (Britain)*)

Kalmyk (Kalmuk)

A member of the Mongolian family of languages and the only member of that family spoken in Europe. It was brought in the 17th c. to a region north-west of the Caspian Sea to the west of the lower reaches of the Volga, in the present Kalmyk Republic (Russian Federation). The Kalmyks were deported *en masse* to Central Asia in 1943 but were allowed to return in the late 1950s. Estimates of the present number of speakers range from 125,000 to 150,000. Uniquely among the peoples of Europe, the Kalmyks are Buddhists. There is a literary form of the language and it is taught in schools.

Though a form of the Mongolian script (an alphabetic script written in vertical columns) was previously in use, the *Cyrillic alphabet (with additional characters) was imposed under Soviet rule in 1923 and, apart from a period in the 1930s when the Latin alphabet was adopted, has remained in use ever since.

K'ap'uch'a (see *Bezht'a* under *Caucasian languages. IV. North-East Caucasian family*)

Karachay-Balkar

Karachay and Balkar are usually considered as two dialects of the same language (sometimes referred to as Mountain Tatar) belonging to the Ponto-Caspian sub-division of the Kipchak or NW *Turkic family. Karachay and Balkar, now two separate written languages, had a common literary form up to 1941. They are spoken mainly in the Russian Federation to the north-west of the Caucasus mountains in the Karachay-Cherkess autonomous territory (where the main Karachay cultural centre is Klukhory (Karachaevsk)) and the Autonomous Kabardin-Balkar Republic; there are also some speakers in the Central Asian republics. Its closest relative is *Kumyk. Total numbers of speakers recorded in 1989 amounted to 155,936 for Karachay and 85,126 for Balkar.

While Karachay is more or less homogeneous, Balkar has four tribal subdivisions, corresponding to the rivers the communities in question live on, viz. (i) the Bakhsan dialect, (ii) the Chegem dialect, (iii) the Khulam-Bezinga dialect, and (iv) Balkar proper or the Cherek-Balkar dialect, the first two of which form the basis of the modern standard language. Karachay was the first of the two varieties to develop a written form and the first book, in Arabic script, was published in 1916. The modern language uses the *Cyrillic alphabet. The father of an independent Karachay-Balkar literature was Alilani Umar.

The ethnonym 'Karachay' is first mentioned in the report of a Russian envoy dating from 1649. At about the same time, the Balkars occur as 'Bolchary' in 17th-c. Russian annals. Both Karachays and Balkars were erroneously referred to as 'Ossetes' or 'Alans' by their Caucasian neighbours, which points to a strong political influence exercised by these peoples at one time. During the period 1944–6, the Karachay-Balkars were deported to Siberia and Central Asia and were not allowed to return to their homelands until 1957, though even then some of them remained in exile.

Pritsak, O. 1959. Das Karatschaische und Balkarische. In Deny, J. et al. (eds), *Philologiae Turcicae Fundamenta*, Wiesbaden, 340–69.

WOLFGANG GRELLER

Karaim

A member (also known as Crimchak) of the Ponto-Caspian group of the Kipchak or NW *Turkic languages. Of the entire Karaim population of 2,602 in Ukraine and Lithuania in 1989, only 503 were native speakers and 79% had no command of the language.

Before 1943, a small community of Western Karaim (or 'Polish Karaim') lived in Lithuania and western Ukraine, numbering approximately 650 in 1929; these communities are recorded since the 15th c. in the town of Troki (Trakai) and in Vilnius. Since the Second World War all traces of them have been lost. It is assumed that the language of the Lithuanian community was closer than that of the Karaim of SW Ukraine (who lived in the towns of Lutsk and Halich in the former Polish provinces of Volynia and Galicia) to that of the small communities of Eastern Karaim who lived in the Crimea, mainly in the urban area of Yevpatoriya; these no longer speak their language but have adopted *Crimean Tatar.

The original habitat of the Karaim was the southern Ukrainian and Crimean steppes. First records of the Kipchakian Karaites date back to the 12th c. It seems likely that some of them migrated westwards and northwards around the 14th c. to settle in Lithuania and the aforementioned parts of Ukraine. The Karaim are unique among the Turkic peoples in that they adopted Judaism, and their language is likewise unique in that it is the only Turkic language written in the *Hebrew alphabet. The oldest texts go back to the 16th c. Until the end of the 19th c., the use of the literary language was confined to religious texts. Since then, a modern western Karaim literature in orthographies based on those of Russian and Polish has emerged, consisting mainly of songs, ballads, dramas, etc. One of the better known writers is Shimage Firkovich (born 1897).

Pritsak, O. 1959. Das Karaimische. In Deny, J. et al. (eds), *Philologiae Turcicae Fundamenta*, Wiesbaden, 318–40.

WOLFGANG GRELLER

K'arat'a (see under *Caucasian languages. IV. North-East Caucasian family*)

Karelian

Karelian is, after *Finnish and *Estonian, the most widely spoken of the *Baltic-Finnic group of the *Finno-Ugrian languages. Of the 130,929 Karelians in Russia, according to the 1989 census, only about 50% spoke Karelian. After the Second World War some 300,000 Karelians emigrated to Finland where they were rapidly assimilated. A smaller southern group of Karelians, some 30,000 in all, have lived since the 17th c. to the north of the upper Volga close to Lake Rybinsk in the region of Tver' (Kalinin). There are four dialects: (i) northern or Archangel Karelian, north of Lake Onega; (ii) Olonets or Aunusian, north-east of Lake Ladoga; (iii) Ludian, east of the northern dialects, having some affinities with *Veps and sometimes considered a separate language; (iv) Tver' Karelian. (In Finland, the term 'Karelian' is usually applied to an eastern dialect of Finnish.)

The earliest references to the Karelians were made in the late 9th c. by a Norwegian traveller, Ottar of Halogaland, who called them 'Byarmians'. The oldest text in the language is a four-line prayer dating from the 13th c. From the 16th c. onwards writings increase, mainly official, religious or scholarly texts, but an independent Karelian literature never developed despite an attempt made in the 1930s when books and a journal were printed. Attempts are now being made in the Karelian Republic (Russian Federation) to revive the national language in schools.

Virtaranta, P. 1985. Kriterien zur Klassifizierung der Dialekte des Karelischen ('Criteria for the classification of the dialects of Karelian'). In Veenker, W. (ed.), *Dialectologia Uralica. Materialien des ersten internationalen Symposions zur Dialektologie der uralischen Sprachen*, Wiesbaden, 117–39.

WOLFGANG GRELLER

Kartvelian languages (see under *Caucasian languages. V. South Caucasian family*)

Kashubian, see *Cassubian*

Kazakh

Kazakh is, after *Turkish and Uzbek, the third most widespread of the *Turkic languages. It has been classified as belonging to what used to be called the Aralo-Caspian group but in more recent times has been termed the Central Turkic or Kipchak-Nogay group of the Kipchak or NW Turkic languages. Up to the 1920s, the term 'Kirgiz' was applied to Kazakh (Kazakh-Kirgiz) as well as to what is now known as Kirgiz (Kara-Kirgiz).

Kazakh is primarily a Central Asian language and is spoken in Europe only in the region between the lower Volga and the frontier of the Republic of Kazakhstan. The overall number of speakers, mainly in Kazakhstan, was given as over 8 million in 1989 but the number of speakers in the European part of its territory is unknown. Its closest relative in Europe is *Nogay.

The Kazakhs emerged during the 15th c. AD after the break-up of the realm of the Golden Horde and were united under a single rule in the early 16th c. Kazakh has been a written language since the second half of the 19th c. and has a notable modern literature. The founders of this modern literature were Abay Kunanbayoglu (1805–1906), Yusuf Küpeyoglu (1860–1931), Ahmed Baytursun (1873–1937) and Ali Khan Bükey Khan (1869–1932). Before an independent national Kazakh literature emerged, the Kazakhs contributed to the wider Islamic literature written in *Chaghatay, the Turkic lingua franca, until the end of the 19th c. The Arabic alphabet was in use up to 1930 when it was replaced by the Latin alphabet which itself gave way in 1940 to the Russian *Cyrillic alphabet.

Menges, K. H. 1959. Die aralo-kaspische Gruppe ('The Aralo-Caspian group'). In Deny, J. et al. (eds), *Philologiae Turcicae Fundamenta*, Wiesbaden, 434–89.

WOLFGANG GRELLER

Khinalug (see under *Caucasian languages. IV. North-East Caucasian family*)

Khmer (see under *Community languages (France)*)

Khvarshi (see under *Caucasian languages. IV. North-East Caucasian family*)

Kipchak (see under *Tatar*)

Kist' languages (see under *Caucasian languages. III. North Central Caucasian family*)

Komi

Komi (otherwise known as Zyrian or Ziryene) is a member of the Permic group of *Finno-Ugrian languages. The great majority of the Komi, numbered in 1989 at well over 300,000, live in the NE corner of Europe in the Komi Republic (capital, Syktyvkar) on the western slopes of the Ural mountains, while a southern group of over 150,000, the Komi-Permyaks, have their own National Region (capital, Kudymkar). There are also approximately 4,000 Komi further east on the river Yazva (a tributary of the Kama), and small communities on the Kola peninsula in NW Russia and, east of the Urals, near the town of Tyumen' in western Siberia.

Dialects and literary languages

The language falls into four dialects: (i) Komi proper, in the Komi Republic; (ii) northern Permyak, along the rivers Kosa and Kama; (iii) southern Permyak, around the river In'va and in Kudymkar; and (iv) eastern Permyak, along the river Yazva. Although the dialects are quite closely related, showing mainly phonetic differences, two separate standard languages have been created, Komi and Komi-Permyak, of which the former is the more widely used. An adaptation of the *Cyrillic alphabet is in use today. The Yazva Komi do not have their own literary language.

History

As early as the second half of the 14th c., a special alphabet for Komi was created by the Christian missionary Stephen of Perm (Styepan Hrap). This so-called 'abur' alphabet, a modification of Cyrillic and Greek characters, was in use from the earliest texts in the 14th c. until the 18th c. From the early period, several Old Permic glosses, liturgical texts, iconic legends and other fragments are extant. Komi therefore provides the second oldest texts (after *Hungarian) in any **Finno-Ugrian** language.

The forerunners of Komi and Komi-Permyak literature were mainly the same.

Ivan Kuratov (1839–75) is considered the first modern author. Also well known are the poet Mihail Lebedev (1877–1951) and the philologist and poet Vassily Lytkin (1895–1965). From the end of the 1920s, literature has also been published in Permyak in a literary language based on the Kudymkar dialect. Well-known authors in this dialect include Mihail Lihachov (1901–45) and Styepan Karavayev (1908–73).

Collinder, B. 1957. Ziryene. In Id., *Survey of the Uralic Languages*, Stockholm, 297–317.
Hausenberg, A. -R. 1985. Zur Einteilung der Dialekte des Syrjänischen ('The dialectal divisions of Zyrian'). In Veenker, W. (ed.), *Dialectologia Uralica. Materialien des ersten internationalen Symposions zur Dialektologie der uralischen Sprachen*, Wiesbaden, 219–21.
Rédei, K. 1978. *Chrestomathia Syrjaenica*. Budapest.
—— 1985. Kriterien zur Klassifizierung der Dialekte des Syrjänischen ('Criteria for the classification of the dialects of the Zyrian language'). In Veenker, W. (ed.), *Dialectologia Uralica* (see Hausenberg 1985), 221–31.

WOLFGANG GRELLER

Krevinian

An extinct and little-known ***Baltic-Finnic** language spoken in Latvia by descendants of Votes (see **Votic**) deported to Latvia from Ingermanland by the Teutonic Knights in the 15th c. and who, by the 19th c., had been completely assimilated. The term 'Krevinian' derives from the Latvian *Krews* 'Russian'.

WOLFGANG GRELLER

Kryts' (Kryz) (see under *Caucasian languages. IV. North-East Caucasian family*)

K'ubachi (see under *Dargwa* under *Caucasian languages. IV. North-East Caucasian family*)

Kuman (see *Cuman*, under *Tatar*)

Kumyk

A member of the Ponto-Caspian group of the Kipchakian or NW ***Turkic languages**, Kumyk is spoken in the NE part of the Caucasus mountains on the shores of the Caspian Sea in the south-west of the Daghestan Republic (Russian Federation). The main cultural centre is Makhachkala. Kumyk was until recently the lingua franca of the area and was also used by Chechens, Avars and other Caucasian peoples.

Kumyk is closely related to ***Karachay-Balkar**, which is also spoken in the Caucasus region. In its general phonetic and grammatical structure, Kumyk clearly belongs to the Kipchak languages although it has absorbed influences from the southern Oghuz Turks through the proximity of Azerbaijan and the cultural influence of the Ottoman empire. The language is subdivided into three major dialects: (i) the Khasav-Yurtic or northern dialect, which forms the basis of the modern standard language, in the villages around Makhachkala; (ii) the Buynak or central dialect in the town of Buynaksk and the surrounding villages with only minor differences from the northern dialect; (iii) the Khaydak or southern dialect, in the region of Derbent. The Khaydak dialect has even been taken by Caucasian neighbours of the Kumyks as an indication that the Kumyks constitute a different ethnic group of Mongolian origin but there is insufficient evidence of Mongolian elements in Khaydak to prove such a theory.

A few words in the Khaydak dialect are attested from the 17th c. but the first collection of Kumyk text material dates from 1814. No literary publications from the 19th c. are known. The standard language used the Latin alphabet from 1928 until 1938 when the *Cyrillic alphabet was introduced.

Benzing, J. 1959. Das Kumükische. In Deny, J. et al. (eds), *Philologiae Turcicae Fundamenta*, Wiesbaden, 391–407.

WOLFGANG GRELLER

Kurdish

A member of the *Iranian subgroup of the *Indo-European languages. Most estimates of overall numbers of speakers range from 7 or 8 million to 12 million (some put the figure much higher). The Kurdish-speaking heartland, or Kurdistan, lies mainly within Asia (Iran, Iraq, Turkey, Syria) but extends beyond the Araks river into western Armenia, where there may be as many as 50,000 Kurds. It is primarily on this basis that Kurdish can count as a European language. Outside Kurdistan there are, in Europe, substantial Kurdish communities in the other Caucasian republics of Georgia and, particularly, Azerbaijan, where they may number over 200,000, and in western Europe.

The northern or Kurmandji dialect spoken in Armenia (as also in Turkey and Syria) is now usually written in the Roman alphabet though some limited use of the *Armenian alphabet was made in Armenia after 1921 and, from 1946 to *c*.1990, the *Cyrillic alphabet was imposed in the Soviet Union. Other dialects are usually written in Arabic script. There are literary texts in Kurmandji from as early as the 17th c. but the present literary tradition dates from the late 19th c. and, given the various forms of repression to which the Kurds have been subject in various parts of Kurdistan at varying times, has flourished particularly among exiles in western Europe (see Kreyenbroek 1992).

Bedir Khan, Emir Djeladet and Lescot, R. 1970. *Grammaire kurde (dialecte kurmandji)*. Paris.
Kreyenbroek, P. G. 1992. On the Kurdish language. In Kreyenbroek, P. G. and Sperl, S. (eds), *The Kurds: A Contemporary Overview*, London, 68–83.
Pikkert, P. 1991. *A Basic Course in Modern Kurmandji*. Genk (Belgium).
Razgar, B. 1993. *Kurdish–English English–Kurdish Dictionary (Kurmancî)*. London.
Vanly, I. Ch. 1992. The Kurds in the Soviet Union. In Kreyenbroek and Sperl (eds) (see Kreyenbroek 1992), 193–218.

Kwéyòl (see under *Creoles*)

L

Ladin (Dolomitic) (see *Dolomitic Ladin* under *Italy. III. Northern Italy*)

Ladin (Engadinese) (see under *Romansh*)

Ladino, see *Judeo-Spanish*

Lak (see under *Caucasian languages. IV. North-East Caucasian family*)

Lallans (see under *Scots*)

Landsmål (see under *Norwegian*)

Langobardic
The Langobards were a Germanic people, speaking a West *Germanic language (an Old High German dialect), who, after settling for a while in the Hungarian plain, in AD 568 moved south-westwards into Italy. They established a kingdom that covered most of the north of present-day Italy (where their name is recalled in that of Lombardy) and extensive duchies elsewhere, in particular those of Spoleto and Benevento south of Rome. Their dominion lasted some two centuries until they were subdued by another Germanic people, the Franks, by which time they had probably long since abandoned their Germanic speech in favour of *Romance. A number of words of Langobardic origin remain in present-day dialects of Italy and in Italian, e.g. *guancia* 'cheek', *melma* 'slime', *nocca* 'knuckle', *schiena* 'back, ridge', *staffa* 'stirrup', *spaccare* 'to split', *taccola* 'jackdaw', *trogolo* 'trough'.

Langue des signes française (see under *Sign languages*)

Langue d'oc, see *Occitan*

Langue d'oïl
A term used with reference to the ensemble of the northern (i.e. *French) *Gallo-Romance dialects, as distinguished from the southern or *langue d'oc* (i.e. *Occitan) dialects. The terms *langue d'oïl* and *langue d'oc* are based on the words for 'yes' in the two languages, viz. Old French *oïl* (giving modern French *oui*) and Occitan *oc*.

Languedocian (see under *Occitan*)

Lao (see under *Community languages (France)*)

Lapp, see *Sámi*

Latgal(l)ian (see under *Latvian*)

Latin

The language of ancient Rome and surrounding communities and a member of the
*Italic subgroup of the ***Indo-European languages** (see map 10). Latin subsequently became the official language and common medium of communication of the
Roman empire and its successor states. In its written form Latin was preserved as the
common learned language of western Europe, and survives as such in a reduced range
of contexts to the present day. Its spoken forms evolved into the ***Romance
languages**.

Affiliation

The Italic family of languages includes Latin together with ***Oscan, *Umbrian** and
some less well attested dialects. There has been some debate about the exact relationship of Latin to the other Italic languages, but it is now generally held that the Italic
languages form a true subgroup within the Indo-European family.

Script

The alphabet was brought to Italy by Greek colonists in the 7th c. BC, and forms of
it were adapted to the writing of ***Etruscan** (see fig. 6) (a non-Indo-European
language) as well as Oscan, Umbrian and Latin. The Latin form of the alphabet is
attested from the 5th c. BC onwards. It appears that the Latin letter-forms and their
values owe something to a period of Etruscan influence, although the details are
uncertain. The Latin alphabet reached approximately its present capital form during
the period of the Roman Republic. Capitals were used for formal epigraphic
purposes, while cursive forms, of varying degrees of formality, developed for literary
and everyday use. In the late Roman Empire, a new form of script known as 'uncial'
developed out of Roman cursive as a formal book-hand. From this derived the
various local scripts of post-Roman Europe (one form of which survived until after
the Second World War as an official ***Irish** alphabet), and, later still, Carolingian
minuscule, the basis of modern lower-case letters.

   The Latin script is extensively used for very many European and also non-
European languages and is therefore one of the most enduring legacies of Roman
civilization to the modern world.

Early history

Records of Latin before the end of the 3rd c. BC are very sparse. Ancient Latium
covered approximately the southern half of the modern province of Lazio, but even
within this relatively small area there is evidence for dialectal variation; Latin communities such as Lanuvium or Praeneste had their own peculiarities of speech,
distinct from those of Rome. With the rise of Rome as a political centre, Roman
'urban' speech became accepted as standard and non-Roman features were stigmatized as 'rustic'. Latin shows traces of early mixture of dialects, with forms such as
popina 'cookshop' beside the expected Roman Latin *coquina* (Osco-Umbrian also

had *p* for original *q*). There was influence from ***Greek** in its Doric form, as spoken in southern Italy, giving such words as *machina* (modern 'machine'), and from Etruscan, to which we owe *histrio* 'actor' and *fenestra* 'window' among other items.

The beginning of the literary use of Latin is traditionally traced to the year 240 BC, when Livius Andronicus produced the first plays in Latin (based on Greek models); he also translated Homer's *Odyssey* into Latin, using the native Saturnian metre. The first complete literary texts extant today are the comedies of Plautus (from Umbria, beginning of 2nd c. BC), which exhibit a highly accomplished command of language in varied stylistic registers, and of Greek-based metre. Approximately contemporary with Plautus, the Southern Italian Q. Ennius (who was trilingual in Latin, Greek and Oscan) composed tragedies and gave Rome its first national epic, the *Annales*. The first major prose author was M. Porcius Cato (the Elder) in the first half of the 2nd c. BC. Only his technical treatise on agriculture survives complete; it gives an inadequate idea of his literary style. All these writers appeared archaic and rough-hewn to later generations, but in their time they were innovators. They established a relationship of what has been called 'creative imitation' between Latin and Greek, which persisted throughout antiquity. Roman originality was, however, apparent both in the treatment of the Greek genres and in the development of native forms, in particular satire.

The classical period

The literary language was progressively standardized during the 2nd and 1st centuries BC. There is evidence of debates on spelling, grammar and vocabulary among Roman men of letters at this period, for example in the satires of Lucilius at the end of the 2nd c. What we think of as standard Latin spelling was not entirely fixed until (at the earliest) the reign of Augustus; a spelling such as *deicere* for *dicere* occurs as late as *c*.20 BC. Archaic forms of the language were preserved or revived for legal and religious purposes, Roman law and religion being extremely conservative and attentive to literal detail; religious formulae were preserved long after they had ceased to be understood. A certain degree of archaism became a mark of poetic language. But in the 1st c. BC there was a clear movement of linguistic purism in Latin, which resisted archaisms, regionalisms and foreign borrowings; a prominent exponent of this tendency was Julius Caesar, according to whom unfamiliar words were to be avoided 'like rocks in the ocean'. The interrelation of Latin and Greek at this time is particularly complex: the acceptability of Greek loan-words varied from one literary genre, social context or semantic area to another, as well as according to the degree to which any particular borrowing had been naturalized in Latin usage. Many members of the Roman ruling class had some competence in Greek, and some may have been virtually bilingual.

At this time the Romans began to study rhetoric with Greek teachers and to make use of its techniques and styles in their native language. Pre-eminent among Roman orators was M. Tullius Cicero (106–43 BC), a native of Arpinum in southern Latium. The less formal registers of 1st-c. BC Latin can be seen in Cicero's correspondence and in some of the verses of his contemporary C. Valerius Catullus of Verona. Cicero also attempted successfully to naturalize Greek philosophy in Latin; a certain number of his lexical innovations modelled on Greek technical terms (such as *moralis* 'ethical', *beatitudo* 'well-being') gained universal currency, although he had too much respect for Latin to disfigure it with a large number of new coinages. A model for historical writing in the grand manner was provided a little later by Sallust (C. Sallustius Crispus, *c*.86–35 BC) and Livy (T. Livius, *c*.59 BC to AD 17, from Patavium (Padua)). Poetry, too, was increasingly refined on Greek models, culminating in the works of the Augustans Virgil (P. Vergilius Maro, 70–19 BC, from Mantua) and Horace (Q. Horatius Flaccus, 65–8 BC, from Venusia (Venosa) in southern Italy). The works of these authors became 'the classics' for succeeding generations, rivalling and eventually displacing Greek literature in the educational curriculum, and fixing the norms of classical Latin usage for ever afterwards; from then on, questions of correctness were typically resolved not by considering current usage but by appealing to the standard authors.

The Roman Empire

Meanwhile, Roman political, military and economic expansion carried the Latin language first to all parts of Italy, then into the rest of Europe west of the Rhine and south of the Danube, to much of North Africa, and in some measure to the East, although Greek remained the common language in what had been the Hellenistic world. In Italy and the western provinces, Latin eventually became the dominant spoken language, not so much because of any conscious policy of linguistic Romanization but merely because of the political power of Rome, the practical benefits of Roman citizenship, and the attractions of Graeco-Roman civilization. The other languages in peninsular Italy (Etruscan, Oscan, Umbrian, etc.) were dead or dying by the 1st c. BC; Greek retained a foothold in the south. In the northern region of Cisalpine Gaul, *Celtic and other languages also gave way to Latin; Cicero alludes to the pronounced regional colouring of the Latin of that area. In Gaul north of the Alps and in Spain, the local languages must have survived longer, although evidence is fragmentary, and no pre-Roman languages in this area have survived into modern times apart from the *Basque enclave north and south of the western Pyrenees. In Britain, the extent to which Latin was ever established as a common spoken language, even in the relatively Romanized south-east, is disputable. Its influence on insular Celtic speech is, however, undeniable; a significant proportion of the lexicon of modern *Welsh and the other *Brittonic languages derives from Latin words borrowed during the Imperial period (e.g. Welsh *aur* 'gold', *bresych* 'cabbage', *gwag* 'empty', *gwyrdd* 'green', *pechod* 'sin', *pont* 'bridge', from Latin *aurum, brassicae, vacuus, viridis, peccatum, pontem*). The *Germanic-speaking peoples also underwent Latin influence, first as enemies or neighbours of Rome, then as mercenary troops and settlers within the Empire, and eventually as conquerors and rulers of Roman territory. The modern Germanic languages show signs of an early stratum of Latin borrowings which dates back to the Roman Empire; to take English as an example, we may find in this category words such as *mile, pound, post, sack, silk*. The influence was reciprocal; the Romance languages (French most of all) absorbed substantial number of words from Germanic: obvious examples are the French colour-words, *bleu, blanc, brun, gris*. In North Africa ***Phoenician** or Punic (the ***Semitic language** of the Carthaginians) survived for some time alongside Latin, until both were displaced by ***Arabic** after the break-up of the Western Empire.

The consequences of this vast expansion for the Latin language itself were not immediately apparent. The system of literary and rhetorical education doubtless enforced a conservative linguistic standard among the ruling elite, an elite which was remarkably receptive to new arrivals from the provincial aristocracies; and the relatively good communications between different parts of the Roman world made for uniformity as long as the Empire functioned as a coherent political unit. Of the great Latin writers in the first two centuries of the Principate, a good number were from outside Italy; the Seneca family were of emigrant Italian stock in Spain, and the rhetorician Quintilian and the epigrammatist Martial were also of Spanish origin; the historian Tacitus was probably from southern Gaul, and the novelist Apuleius from near Carthage. Gaul and North Africa in particular were famous for their schools of Latin rhetoric. This was the so-called Silver Age of Latin literature, in which Latin writers were on the whole no longer mapping out new literary territory on Greek models, but measured themselves against their own Republican and Augustan classics, labouring more and more for startling effects of (as the case might be) brevity, wit, irony or horror, or (like Quintilian) rejecting the fashions of the age and promoting a Ciceronian classicism. The natural and colloquial tone hardly ever appears in the extant literature of this period, with one striking exception provided by Petronius's novel of low life, the *Satyricon* (reign of Nero).

The official Latin of the military and mercantile classes appears to have remained highly uniform; this is shown not only by inscriptions but also in such documents as the tablets from Vindolanda near Hadrian's Wall, which display few non-standard features. However, in the 1st and 2nd centuries AD, one begins to find written documents which deviate considerably from the norms of standard literary Latin: the Pompeian legal tablets (AD 37), the graffiti preserved at Pompeii and Herculaneum (before AD 79), the imitations of substandard speech in Petronius, the papyrus letters of Claudius Terentianus and others from Egypt (*c.* AD 120), etc. It is a striking fact about these texts that many of their deviations from standard written usage can be linked with changes that we know to have happened in Romance, and they can provide valuable evidence of an early date for these changes. Yet much care is needed in interpreting this evidence: to classify these texts (along with others of different dates and provenances) as examples of some more or less uniform entity called 'Vulgar Latin' is highly misleading. Account must be taken of the precise milieu in each case, and of the extent to which one may be dealing with (a) bad spelling representing standard pronunciation, where the standard written form is conservative and no longer represents spoken usage; (b) bad spelling representing non-standard pronunciation, in which case the question arises whether the non-standard features are determined regionally or socially or both; (c) mistakes made by writers who were not native speakers of Latin; (d) a literary imitation of non-standard usage, as in

Petronius; or finally (e) mere graphic errors that tell us nothing at all about the spoken language.

The later Empire

As time went on, the spoken Latin of the Roman Empire must clearly have diversified both regionally and socially, and the spoken varieties must have become more distant from the written standard. It is, however, extremely difficult to trace these changes with any completeness, owing to the prevailing uniformity of written Latin and the scattered nature of the evidence for deviations from it. Even the standard spoken Latin of the later Empire is very difficult to recover, although it is doubtless here that we must look for the origins of those non-Classical features that are common to all or most Romance languages, such as the new synthetic future formed from infinitive + *habere* (e.g. *cantare* + *habeo* 'I have to sing' > French (*je*) *chanterai*, Italian *canterò*, Spanish *cantaré*, etc., 'I shall sing'). This is normally excluded from writing but surfaces occasionally in Augustine and later writers. Around this time there also occurred phonetic changes such as the palatalization (or 'softening') of *c* [k] before front vowels, nearly universal in Romance (e.g. Latin *cera* [kera] 'wax' > French *cire* [s-], Portuguese *cera* [s-], Spanish *cera* [θ–, s–], Italian *cera* [tʃ-], Romanian *ceară* [tʃ-]).

The political disorder of the 3rd c. had apparently brought a temporary decline in Roman education and literary activity. After orderly government was restored, there was a revival of literature and of grammatical study. Attempts were made to reassert the norms of classical Latin against colloquial or regional usages which were viewed as corrupt, and the grammarians provide further evidence, so far imperfectly exploited, for the actual development of the language. Both pagan and Christian authors preserved the conventions of classical grammar and rhetoric in their writing, although among the Christians we can see the beginnings of a movement towards a style of writing nearer to contemporary spoken usage. But the Latin of the Christian writers also had peculiarities of its own, being heavily influenced by biblical phraseology modelled closely on Greek and Hebrew. From the linguist's point of view, a gem among late antique Christian writings is the so-called *Peregrinatio Aetheriae*, an account of a pilgrimage to the Holy Land which can be plausibly dated to the end of the 4th c. AD. The writer, a Spanish nun, is quite innocent of the artificialities of classical rhetoric, and her simple narrative style contains many features of syntax and idiom that can be directly linked with Romance and must reflect the spoken language.

The Empire was divided between East and West for administrative purposes by Diocletian in AD 293. On the European side of the Mediterranean, the boundary passed through the emperor's own native province of Illyria at its narrowest point (it still survives as the boundary between Serbia and Bosnia), and very approximately divided the Greek-speaking East from the Latin-speaking West, though the eastern Adriatic coast was Latin-speaking, and remnants of the local Romance dialect survived in Dalmatia until the late 19th c. (see *Dalmatian). Constantine established his new capital at Byzantium, renamed Constantinople (AD 324), in

Greek-speaking Asia Minor. Latin survived in the Eastern Empire, at any rate as an official language, for a considerable time. In the 6th c., the *Digest* of Roman law was compiled in Latin at Constantinople under Justinian's direction, and Latin words of command were still in use in the Byzantine army in the time of the Emperor Mauricius (*c.* AD 600). Spoken Latin evidently had some effect on Byzantine Greek, and hence on Modern Greek: e.g. the modern 'demotic' word σπίτι (*spiti*) 'house' derives from a late colloquial usage of Latin *hospitium*.

From Latin to Romance

At this period, however, the history of Latin as a living language is largely the history of Latin in western Europe, where the boundaries of the Latin or Romance-speaking area have remained broadly the same since the end of Roman imperial rule in the 5th c. AD. The former Empire was broken up into a number of smaller successor states ruled by Germanic kings. These states were still largely populated by Romans (defined linguistically as speakers of Latin or Romance: the difference is merely terminological) and the culture of western Europe was still Latin-based, even in the darkest periods of the so-called 'Dark Ages'. But the varieties of Roman speech in different parts of Europe will inevitably have continued to diverge.

As regards the outlying provinces, Gothic invasions on the Danube border had led to the abandonment of the province of Dacia (AD 270); the apparent survival of spoken Latin there does not lend itself to easy historical explanation, since the language simply disappears from the evidence until its re-emergence as ***Romanian** in the late Middle Ages. Britain was abandoned by the Roman government more than a century later; the works of a writer such as Gildas demonstrate the persistence in 6th-c. Britain of written Latin, whatever may have happened to the spoken language, and the spread of Christianity brought Latin to Ireland, the scholars of which country were to be a vital influence in preserving Latin learning and spreading it through Europe in succeeding centuries. The English learned Latin largely from the Irish, and a high degree of mastery of written Latin was achieved by English scholars such as Bede. The preservation of relatively pure standards of classical Latin in these peripheral areas was no accident. Not being native speakers of the language of the Romans, the Irish and Anglo-Saxons could learn to write a conservative version of Latin 'by the book', with no danger of interference from everyday speech; indeed, that was the only practical way which they could learn Latin. In contrast, in the Romance-speaking area of Europe, as spoken usage diverged more and more from the classical norm, changes in the written language inevitably ensued, giving the impression of a decline in grammatical standards.

By the 8th c. there are signs of awareness that the spoken language of the Romans had changed so much from Latin that it could no longer be regarded merely as a variety of it, but must be counted as a different language; it is occasionally referred to as *lingua romana* or *rustica romana lingua*, as opposed to *lingua latina*. When Charlemagne established his European empire at the beginning of the 9th c., one of his concerns was to re-establish Latin as a universal language, and he employed an English scholar, Alcuin of York, to assist in this enterprise. The Carolingian standardization of Latin pronunciation could only reinforce the differences between the written language and the spoken varieties. Soon after this came the first extant example of a serious attempt to write a variety of the spoken language phonetically, in the 'Strasbourg Oaths' of AD 842 (see *French, 'Origins and earliest attestations'). For the later history of the vernaculars see the **Romance languages**.

Medieval, Renaissance and later Latin

The Latin thus revived and purified persisted as Medieval Latin, which all medieval scholars and clerics in Europe could read and write (with differing degrees of accomplishment). Though it was nobody's native language, many could also speak it as an international medium of communication; there was a renewal of interest in many branches of classical literature; and Latin was used not only for formal, official and academic purposes but also for original literature in a variety of genres. Arguably the most notable literary development in medieval Latin was the introduction of rhymed accentual verse. Classical verse-forms had been derived from Greek and based on patterns of syllabic quantity. Distinctions of quantity in both vowels and syllables were already disappearing from spoken Latin by the 3rd c. AD and were uniformly lost in Romance; Latin as pronounced in the Middle Ages was a stressed language like Italian or Spanish. The classical rules of versification continued to be operated, but only as a theoretical system that had to be learnt laboriously, while the new accentual verse-forms arose naturally out of the way in which the language was by then pronounced. The lyric poems in such collections as the *Carmina Burana* may count among the highlights of Latin literature, and the new verse-forms also lent themselves appropriately to satire and burlesque.

Latin remained in official use in the succeeding centuries, and it was the language of Renaissance humanism as it had been of medieval scholarship; there was no basic change in the status of the language, although it is in the Renaissance that we see the beginnings of the rivalry between Latin and the vernaculars that was eventually to end in victory for the latter. As regards the use of the language itself, the humanists reasserted classical standards and models against what they saw as the corruptions of medieval usage. Latin literature from the Renaissance onwards is often termed 'Neo-Latin'. Often it is artificial and imitative, but the best of Neo-Latin prose writing (such as the works of Erasmus or Thomas More) can stand beside the classics of earlier ages, and the technical brilliance of some Renaissance Latin poetry is unsurpassed.

One particularly important aspect of the later history of Latin is the use of the language for scientific writings. Many of the most influential works of early modern science (e.g. those of Copernicus or Newton) were written in Latin, and as a consequence most modern scientific and technical terminology is derived from Latin (or from Latinized Greek). Although Latin has been replaced as a medium of scientific discourse by modern languages such as English, the terminology remains Latin-based. This is particularly obvious, in, for example, the Linnaean nomenclature of plant and animal species and in the terminology of the anatomy of the human body.

The Latin language is still used for a limited range of religious, ceremonial and monumental purposes. It remained as the universal liturgical language of the Roman Catholic Church until the Second Vatican Council (1962–5) and is still used as an official language for papal encyclicals, etc. It is worth commenting also that the expansion of western European culture has carried Latin far beyond Europe. Latin literature, along with Greek and other aspects of the culture of the ancient world, is taught in schools and universities and is appreciated by a wider public in translation. But apart from this, the presence of Latin as one of the formative ingredients of European culture cannot be escaped. Although no longer the basis of all education in Europe, Latin is likely to remain a subject of perennial interest and educational value.

Note on the pronunciation of Latin

Traditional pronunciations of Latin in the various European countries generally mirrored the changes in sound–spelling relationship that took place in the vernacular. This led to results that were little short of grotesque, in countries like England, where the relationship of letters to phonemes was widely different from what it had been in ancient Rome (so e.g. *caelum* became [si:lʌm]). In areas of Roman Catholic influence outside Italy, an Italianate pronunciation (*caelum* = [tʃe:lum]) has often existed as a rival to the traditional local one. During the 20th c. a largely successful attempt has been made to impose a reconstructed ancient pronunciation (in which *caelum* = [kailum]) for use in the study of the Classical language and its literature. Minor national variations still inevitably remain, but are by and large no longer a hindrance to mutual comprehension. No reconstructed pronunciation can aim to do justice either to the exact phonetics of Classical Latin or to the historical, regional and social variations in the language as it was spoken, but the so-called 'Revised' pronunciation gives a fair impression of what the language may roughly have sounded like in the time of Cicero.

Allen, W. S. 1978. *Vox Latina: A Guide to the Pronunciation of Classical Latin*, 2nd edn. Cambridge.
Devoto, G. 1940. *Storia della lingua di Roma*. Bologna.
Glare, P. G. W. (ed.) 1982 *Oxford Latin Dictionary*. Oxford.
Hammond, M. 1976. *Latin: A Historical and Linguistic Handbook*. Cambridge, MA, and London.
Kennedy, B. H. 1962. *The Revised Latin Primer*, ed. and further revised by Sir J. Mountford, new edn. London.
Kenney, E. J. (ed.) 1982. *Cambridge History of Classical Literature*: vol. 2, *Latin Literature*. Cambridge.
Leumann, M., Hofmann, J. B. and Szantyr, A. 1963–72. *Lateinische Grammatik*, 2 vols. Munich.
Meillet, A. 1977. *Esquisse d'une histoire de la langue latine*, new edn with bibliography by J. Perrot. Paris.
Niermeyer, J. F. 1976. *Mediae Latinitatis Lexicon Minus* ('Dictionary of Medieval Latin'). Leiden.
Palmer, L. R. 1954. *The Latin Language*. London.
Väänänen, V. 1967. *Introduction au latin vulgaire*, 2nd edn. Paris.
Wright, F. A. and Sinclair, T. A. 1931. *A History of Later Latin Literature*. London.

J. G. F. POWELL

Latino sine flexione (see under *Artificial languages*)

Latvian

One of the two living members (the other being ***Lithuanian**) of the eastern group of the ***Baltic languages**, spoken principally in Latvia itself but also by communities elsewhere in eastern and northern Europe (including Britain), North America and Australia.

Origins

The differentiation of the Eastern Baltic dialects from proto-Baltic is considered to have taken place before the 5th c. BC. Latvian was initially the language of only one of the Eastern Baltic tribes, mention of which in historical sources dates from the 11th c. AD. The process of formation of the Latvian nation began about the end of the first millennium with a gradual merging of separate Baltic tribes, Latgallians, Curonians, Zemgalians and Selians. The close linguistic relationship of the different tribes and internal migration facilitated the formation of a common language, a process that was complete by the end of the 16th c. The Livs, whose language is not ***Indo-European** but ***Finno-Ugrian**, were also gradually assimilated (see ***Livonian**).

Latvian and Lithuanian developed side by side till the 6th or 7th c., which explains the considerable similarity between them. Of the two languages, Lithuanian is the more conservative, Latvian the more innovative, especially in morphology and with a more marked tendency towards analytical syntactical constructions.

Earliest attestations

The earliest written attestations date back to the 13th c. when Latvian place-names and personal names appear in Henry of Livonia's *Origines Livoniae* and in the Latin texts of a number of Curonian contracts. The earliest texts in Latvian date from the 16th c. and are all religious in character. The oldest manuscript (now at Uppsala) is Ghisbert's version of the Lord's Prayer in the Catholic *Agenda siu Bene Dictionale* (1507). The first printed book in Latvian, of which however no copies are extant, was a Lutheran manual of 1525. The earliest surviving printed text is Hasentöter's Lord's Prayer published in Sebastian Münster's *Cosmographei oder Beschreibung aller Länder [. . .]* ('Cosmography or Description of all Countries') (Basle, 1550), while the first printed books are a Catholic catechism of 1585 and a Lutheran catechism of 1586. These were followed, but not until half a century later, by the first dictionary (Latvian–German), *Lettus das ist Wortbuch samt engehängtem täglichen Gebrauch der lettischen Sprache [. . .]* (1638) by G. Mancelius, and the first grammar (in Latin), J. G. Rehehusen's *Manuductio ad linguam lettonicam [. . .]* (1644). The publication of a translation of the Bible (New Testament, 1685; Old Testament, 1689) had a significant impact on the vocabulary and orthography of Latvian, setting a standard that affected the development of the written language for centuries.

The literary language

The origins of the national literary language are not homogeneous. Its main sources are Latvian folklore, Old Latvian literature, and the living language of the people.

The 'folk literary' variant reflects a variety of grammatical forms and constructions, including archaisms which owe their preservation to the metrical system of folk songs. The lexicon of folk literature also incorporates a number of foreign borrowings.

But, although folklore embodies the ethical and aesthetic values of the Latvian nation, it cannot, because of the limited range of poetic vocabulary, serve as the only basis for a literary language. The literary language was at first intended to meet primarily the needs of the clergy and to serve as a means of communication between Latvian peasants and their German landlords. Already in its early stages, the vocabulary was supplemented with abstract terminology and words for notions beyond the scope of everyday peasant speech. The basis for the further elaboration of morphology and syntax and for the development of a scientific style was also created.

The evolution of the written language has gone through three periods: Old Latvian (16th c.–mid-19th c.), 'New Latvian' (*jaunlatviešu*) (mid 19th c. to the 1880s), and the modern literary language (from the 1880s onwards).

Although the existence of one Latvian nation speaking one common language had been mentioned as early as 1649 by P. Einhorn in his *Historia Lettica*, it was the National Awakening movement in the mid-19th c. that finally laid the foundations of the national literary language. The 'New Latvians' (the Latvian intelligentsia), representing the spirit of national awareness, brought the literary and the spoken language closer together. The systematic collection and preserving of folklore from the middle of the century onwards culminated in the compilation of the most complete collection of folk songs (1894–1916), which is a unique literary monument in world literature. The first conscious efforts of Latvians themselves to foster their language led to the coining of new words and the differentiation of meanings. Principles for the borrowing and adaptation of foreign words were worked out, and the vocabulary was supplemented with a range of international terms. Certain non-native syntactical features were eliminated with a view to bringing the literary language closer to that of the people.

The development of the literary language was furthered by poets and other writers and by linguists, who attempted to purify and enrich the language. In that sense, the origins of the modern literary language and of a truly national literature can be said to date from the 1880s and 1890s. The norms of this literary language are clearly distinct both from the dialects and from the popular colloquial style. It has a fully developed range of functional styles and is completely adequate for all communicative purposes throughout Latvia.

Orthography

From the beginning, the Latin alphabet was used (in printing, German influence is revealed in the use of Gothic type) and the orthography was based on phonetic principles. G. Mancelius was the first to introduce the morphological principle into orthography. Under Russian rule, within the framework of the policy of attempted Russification of the Baltic provinces in the second half of the 19th c., attempts were made to introduce ***Cyrillic** script but in 1908 the Latin alphabet, supplemented by diacritics <ā, č, ē, ğ, ī, ķ, ļ. ŋ, š, ū, ž>, and an orthography based on phonetic-morphological principles were adopted. The contemporary orthography is based on this, as reformed in 1937.

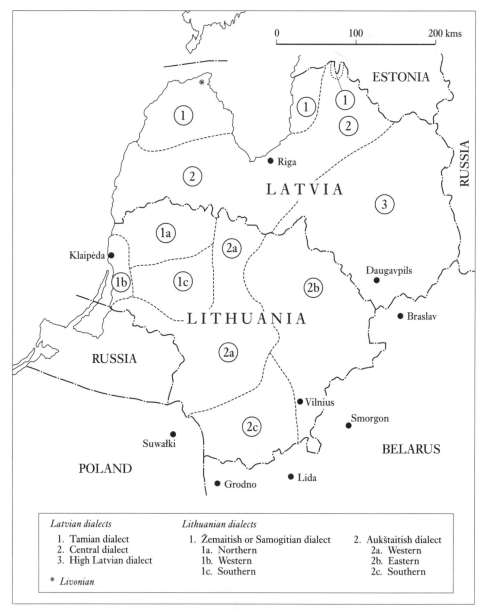

Map 12   Latvia and Lithuania: languages and dialects

Dialects

The process of formation of the Latvian language and contact with non-Baltic tribes, principally Livs, resulted in the emergence of three main dialects (see map 12): (i) the Central dialect, spoken in central and south-western Latvia; (ii) the 'High Latvian' (Latgallian, Selian) of eastern and southern Latvia; (iii) the Tamian dialects of north-western Latvia and the north-eastern coastal area (the ancestors of speakers of this dialect were Livs). The feudal administrative division of the territory led to the growth of a considerable number of subdialects, 512 of which have been identified, which makes it difficult to draw up clear dialectal boundaries.

The Central dialect, which has preserved an archaic phonetic system, has formed the basis for the common standard language. This process was encouraged by the fact that there were several important economic and cultural centres in the central regions of Latvia and that the Central dialect has been less affected than other dialects by foreign influences. Upland Latvian or Latgallian has preserved more archaic grammatical features than other dialects, whereas its sound system displays a number of relatively recent changes. This dialect developed its own written form (using Latin script) in the 18th c. and has sometimes been considered as a separate language. The main publications were religious works, the earliest being a Catholic hymnal of 1730. In the 19th and, especially, the first half of the 20th c., secular works were published, including both literary works and periodicals. The third National Awakening of the 1990s brought about a revival in the publication of Latgallian literature. The Tamian dialect, characterized by a simplification of grammatical structure resulting from word-shortening, is occasionally reflected in writing, for example in humorous verse.

Foreign influences

The territory of Latvia has been under the domination of Germans, Danes, Poles, Russians and Swedes and this is reflected in the lexicon in particular. Latvian has borrowed from the ***Germanic**, ***Slavonic** and **Finno-Ugrian** languages (though most loan-words from **Livonian** and ***Estonian** have only local currency). To the oldest stratum of borrowings belong terms relating to the church, the law and commerce. During the period of Soviet occupation there was large-scale borrowing of Russian terms. Latvian has also borrowed, for more than a century, from English (at first via German or Russian), and there has been a significant increase in English influence in the late 20th c. There has been some German influence, dating from the earliest period of the Latvian written language, on phraseology and syntax.

Present situation

Latvian is the first language of some 1,425,000 people in Latvia itself (data as of 1995), where some 400,000 people of other ethnic origins (Russian, Belarusian, Polish, Lithuanian, Jewish, Gypsy, German, Estonian) also use it mainly as a second language. About 9,000 Latvian-speakers remain in the former USSR (6,000 in Russia, the rest in Belarus). There are also small Latvian-speaking communities in neighbouring Estonia and Lithuania, and it is estimated that about a third of the

Latvian emigrants abroad still use Latvian as a first or second language, in North America (75,000–85,000), Australia (30,000+), Britain (9,000), Germany (9,000) and Sweden (4,000).

In the Republic of Latvia, Latvian had the status of official state language during the period of independence between the wars but, during the period of Soviet occupation, Russian was introduced in the state administration and in practically all other spheres of life and Latvian became a minority language in the country, continually losing its position as a result both of in-migration from Russia and of official language policy. Latvian became once more an official state language in 1989 and, since the country declared its independence in 1990, has come to function in all spheres of public life, in the fields of administration, education, religion (except in Orthodox parishes), the legal system and the mass media.

Endzelīns, J. 1951. *Latviešu valodas gramatika* ('Grammar of the Latvian Language'). Riga.
Fennel, T. G. H. 1980. *A Grammar of Modern Latvian*, 3 vols. The Hague.
Mülenbach, K. and Endzelīns, J. 1923–32. *Lettisch–Deutsches Wörterbuch* ('Latvian–German Dictionary'), 4 vols. Riga.
Rūķe-Draviņa, V. 1977. *The Standardization Process in Latvian, XVI Century to the Present*. Stockholm.
Veisbergs, A. 1997. *Latvian–English Dictionary*. Riga.

MAIJA BRĒDE

Laz (see under *Caucasian languages. V. South Caucasian family*)

Lechitic
A term applied to the westernmost group of the western ***Slavonic languages**, including ***Polish** (east Lechitic), ***Cassubian** (a central variety), and west Lechitic dialects that, apart from ***Polabian**, which became extinct in the 18th c., died out in the Middle Ages and of which little remains other than place-names.

Lemnian
A 7th- or 6th-c. BC funerary stele found in 1885 at Kaminia on the Greek island of Lemnos (and now in the Greek National Museum at Athens) bears an inscription of 33 words (198 characters in all) in an alphabet similar to that of ***Etruscan**. The language thereof may legitimately be termed 'Lemnian', since there is no reason to suppose that the stele originated from elsewhere than the island itself, and since similar characters have also been found scratched on pottery fragments of local origin. Although largely unintelligible, the language can be shown to have affinities with Etruscan, though how close these affinities might have been is undemonstrable.

Lepontic
An extinct member of the ***Celtic** branch of ***Indo-European** and probably closely akin to ***Gaulish** (see ***Continental Celtic**). The remnants of Lepontic have been found in the area of the great lakes in northern Italy, the centre of which is the Lake of Lugano (see map 10). The 70 or so inscriptions and coin-legends may be dated

approximately to between the 6th and 1st centuries BC. They provide only a fragmentary knowledge of the language. Lepontic is the oldest known Celtic language.

The appearance of Lepontic is usually associated with the Golasecca culture, which was present in the region from the 7th c. BC onwards.

The inscriptions are brief (one to seven words) and most contain stereotyped phrases. They are written in the so-called 'Lugano alphabet', which is a variant of the North *Etruscan alphabet.

There are a number of funerary steles inscribed with the name of the deceased and, often, with the word *pala*, which presumably means 'stele'. Three longer inscriptions have come to light. The Prestino Stone (from near Como) and the Vergiate Stone (now in Milan) each contain one complete sentence and mention the name of the deceased as well as the person responsible for erecting the monument. A vase found in a grave in Ornavasso probably contained 'wine from Naxos' (*uinom našom*) as a gift for the deceased, Latumaros and Sapsuta.

Campanile, E. (ed.) 1981. *I Celti d'Italia*. Pisa.
Lejeune, M. 1971. *Lepontica* (in French). Paris.

PETER SCHRIJVER

Lettish, see *Latvian*

Lëtzebuergesch, see *Luxemburgish*

Lezgi (Lezgian) (see under *Caucasian languages. IV. North-East Caucasian family*)

Liburnian
During the Roman period, the Liburni occupied the coast of modern Croatia between the rivers Raša (on the east side of the Istrian peninsula) and Krka (near Sibenik). If, which is uncertain, their *Illyrian-type speech was sufficiently distinct to have constituted a separate language, the evidence of place-names from the area suggests that it was similar to *Venetic.

Ligurian (Ancient)
By the 3rd c. BC, the territories (formerly much more widespread) occupied by the Ligurians stretched along the Mediterranean coast from the Rhône to the Arno and some way into the mountainous hinterland (see map 10). Evidence for their language is well described by Pulgram (1958: 175) as 'extraordinarily meager (mainly local names, a few words, and no connected text)' and seems insufficient to enable one to determine whether or not it was *Indo-European (though some scholars conclude that it was).

Pulgram, E. 1958. *The Tongues of Italy*. Cambridge, MA.

Ligurian (Modern) (see under *Italy. III. Northern Italy*)

Linear A

'Linear A' is the script of a number of inscriptions dating from approximately the 19th to the 15th centuries BC, mainly from a site near the village of Agia Triada (see fig. 9) in southern Crete but also from a number of other sites on the island. They include inscriptions on clay tablets and others on stone, metal (including one on a gold pin in the museum at Agios Nikolaos), or painted on earthenware jars. Most of these can be seen in the Archaeological Museum at Iraklion or in other museums in Crete, but the Ashmolean Museum at Oxford also has some. Linear A may derive from the ***Cretan pictographic script** and is probably itself a source of the ***Linear B** syllabary, but its links with neither are clear. It seems probable that the language it represents is the unknown pre-Greek Minoan language of Crete but none of the claims made by different scholars to have deciphered the script have met with general acceptance.

Chadwick, J. 1987. Linear A. In Id., *Linear B and Related Scripts*, London, 44–9.
Godart, L. and Olivier, J. -P. 1976–85. *Recueil des inscriptions en linéaire A*, 5 vols. Paris.

Fig. 9 Tablet in Linear A script from Agia Triada, Crete. From Florian Coulmas, *The Blackwell Encyclopedia of Writing Systems* (Oxford, Blackwell, 1996).

Linear B

A syllabic script that is clearly related to and probably derives, at least in part, from the so far undeciphered *Linear A script. It is known mainly from over 4,000 clay tablets from Knossos in Crete and, on the Greek mainland, Pylos in the SW Peloponnese (see fig. 10), Thebes (NW of Athens), with a few from Mycenae and elsewhere, together with a small number of inscriptions painted on vases found at Thebes and elsewhere. The Knossos tablets (most of which are in the Archaeological Museum at Iraklion, Crete, though some are in the Ashmolean Museum in Oxford, the British Museum, and other museums) probably date from the 14th c. BC, those from Pylos (now at the National Museum in Athens) from the late 13th c. Long a mystery, the script was finally deciphered by Michael Ventris in 1952 and the language demonstrated to be an early form of *Greek.

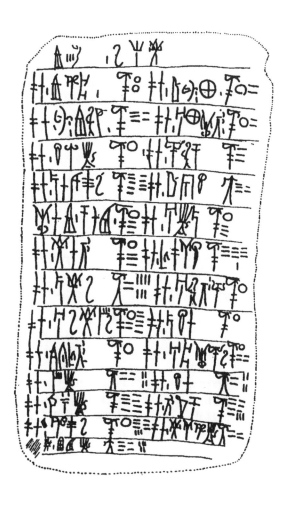

Fig. 10 (a) Tablet in Linear B script from Pylos. From Florian Coulmas, *The Blackwell Encyclopedia of Writing Systems* (Oxford, Blackwell, 1996).

Chadwick, J. 1967. *The Decipherment of Linear B*, 2nd edn. Cambridge.

—— 1987, *Linear B and Related Scripts*. London.

—— et al. 1986–90. *Corpus of Mycenaean Inscriptions from Knossos*, 2 vols. Cambridge.

Fig. 10 (b) The basic syllabary of Linear B. From John Chadwick, *Linear B and Related Scripts* (London, British Museum Press, 1987) (also in J. T. Hooker, *Reading the Past*, London, British Museum Press, 1990). Copyright the Trustees of the British Museum, British Museum Press.

Lingua Franca

The original Lingua Franca was a ***pidgin language** used for communication between ***Romance**-speaking western Europeans on the one hand and Arabs (and later Turks) on the other around the shores of the Mediterranean from at least the

14th c. onwards. In Algiers at least, it survived into the late 19th c. It is 'the earliest documented, and, by several centuries, the longest-lived of all pidgins [. . .] and it may well be the basis, whether by imitation or direct relexification, of many European-based pidgins and creoles' (Whinnom 1977).

The name 'Lingua Franca' is probably an Italianization of Byzantine Greek and Arabic forms meaning 'Frankish language', i.e. 'language of western Europeans', especially French, Occitan, Catalan and Italian (since the Byzantines and the Arabs had applied the term 'Franks' to all the Crusaders whatever their ethnic origins). Because it is essentially a spoken pidgin, our knowledge of the language is necessarily very limited, depending to some extent on passages purporting to be in Lingua Franca used (usually to comic ends) in various literary texts in western European languages from *c.*1300 onwards, most notably in Molière's *Le Bourgeois gentilhomme* (1670), and from phrases noted down by travellers and diplomats. An important source is a hastily compiled grammar, dictionary and phrase-book, *Dictionnaire de la langue franque ou petit mauresque*, published in 1830 for the use of members of the French expeditionary force that took Algiers in that year.

Though its exact origins are unknown, Lingua Franca certainly derives from the Romance languages of the Mediterranean, mainly Italian. It has the highly simplified grammatical structure typical of pidgin languages. The vocabulary is largely of regional (especially northern) Italian origin, with an important contribution from Spanish, particularly in its Algerian attestations; there are also some Provençal elements and a very few Arabic and other words.

The very existence of a Lingua Franca being used over such a wide territory and for such a long span of time has recently been disputed by a number of scholars. They have argued that what direct attestations have come down to us do not, in effect, constitute a pidgin but are attempts at reproducing Italian or an Italian-based Romance on the part of Arabs and Turks, attempts abetted by the Europeans' custom (when they could not speak Arabic or Turkish) of using a simplified 'foreigners' talk' in communicating with Orientals. Whether or not this is the case, it is certain that, over the whole of the Ottoman Empire during the 16th and 17th centuries, the language favoured in diplomatic and commercial transactions between western Europeans and Orientals was Italian.

The term 'Lingua Franca' has now come to be used with reference to a language widely used for intercommunication among different linguistic groups (e.g. Akkadian in the Middle East in the 2nd millennium BC, Greek in Classical and Christian times, Latin in much of medieval Europe, Swahili in East Africa, English in many parts of the globe). For this reason, the Lingua Franca proper is nowadays frequently referred to as the 'Mediterranean Lingua Franca'.

Cifoletti, G. 1989. *La lingua franca mediterranea*. Padua.
Kahane, H. and Kahane, R. 1976–7. Lingua franca: the story of a term. *Romance Philology*, 30: 25–41.
Minervini, L. 1996. La lingua franca mediterranea. *Medioevo Romanzo*, 20: 231–301.
Schuchardt, H. 1980. The Lingua Franca, translated by G. G. Gilbert in Id., *Pidgin and Creole Languages, Selected Essays by Hugo Schuchardt*, Cambridge, 65–88 (Originally published in German, 1909).

Wansbrough, J. 1996. *Lingua Franca in the Mediterranean*. Richmond, Surrey.
Whinnom, K. 1977. Lingua Franca: historical problems. In Valdman, A. (ed.), *Pidgin and Creole Linguistics*, Bloomington and London, 295–310.

JOSEPH CREMONA

Lithuanian

One of the two living members (the other being ***Latvian**) of the eastern group of the ***Baltic languages**, spoken principally in Lithuania itself (see map 12) but also by communities in neighbouring countries and by emigrant communities in western Europe (including Britain), North America and Australia.

Origins and geographical spread

The eastern limits of the Lithuanian linguistic territory in the past are not easy to establish. The earliest direct contacts with the eastern Slavs, mainly the Krivichi and the Dregovichi tribes who lived along almost the entire border of the territory inhabited by the Lithuanians, date from the 9th c. AD. In the second half of the 12th c. the Lithuanian state expanded into extensive parts of Kievan Rus and incorporated Kiev itself into its domain. In quite a wide stretch of what is now Belarusian territory, around Grodno, Ščučin, Lida, Kreva, Braslav, and other towns, the Lithuanian language became dominant. Historical data about the borders of the Lithuanian-speaking territory in the 13th c. are controversial. The study of toponyms and personal names of Lithuanian origin indicates that the eastern limit, established in the 14th c., had hardly moved until the Union of Lublin (1569), at which time the Lithuanian-speaking area must have encompassed the regions of Braslav and of Druya (at least the western part thereof), and have reached as far as Grodno and Ščučin and nearly to Novogrudok, Voložin and Smorgon. The furthest extent of the area covered by Lithuanian (or by Lithuanianized Baltic peoples) was close to Orša in eastern Belarus, some 200 kilometres from the Lithuanian heartland. In fact, the eastern border of Lithuanian at that time fluctuated greatly but the Lithuanian-speaking area must have covered more than 100,000 square km. By the 16th c., or perhaps a little later, Lithuanian was spoken only in the western area, i.e. in ethnic Lithuania, and, beyond its borders, mostly only by the nobility and landed gentry. The use of Lithuanian was considerably reduced in the 16th c. because of Polonization.

The 18th c. was the period of the greatest decline of literary and spoken Lithuanian. After the third partition of the Polish–Lithuanian Commonwealth in 1795, the greater part of ethnic Lithuania fell to Russia. The area to the south-west of the Nemunas river (the future Suvalkai region) went first to Prussia but was allocated to Russia in 1815. Under Russian rule, the eastern borders of ethnic Lithuania were extensively Belarusified (***Belarusian** being considered by the Russian authorities as a dialect of Russian). The eastern limit of Lithuanian shifted significantly to the west, no longer reaching Grodno, Lida, Ašmena, Smorgon, Svir and Braslav. Belarusian approached Vilnius and Trakai and to the north encroached even further.

It was at this period that Lazūnai (now Lazduny) and Gervėčiai (now Gervyaty), where there are still about a thousand Lithuanian-speakers, became isolated Lithuanian areas surrounded by Belarusian-speaking areas. At the end of the 19th and the beginning of the 20th c., the Lithuanian-speaking area retreated significantly to the west. In 1920 Poland annexed a third of Lithuania's territory (including the capital, Vilnius), in breach of the treaty of Suvalkai of 7 October 1920, and it was only in 1939 that Lithuania regained Vilnius and about a quarter of the territory occupied by Poland. In 1940 Lithuania also regained two small areas of ethnic Lithuania (around Druskininkai and Švenčionys respectively) that had been allocated to Byelorussia (Belarus). 'Common' Belarusian and the local Polish dialect (*polszczyzna litéwska*), beside Lithuanian and Russian, still play an important part in SE Lithuania today. In the Punsk (Punskas), Sejny (Seinai) and part of the Suwałki (Suvalkai) districts, which were incorporated into Poland but where there are still some Lithuanian-speakers, it was forbidden to speak Lithuanian in public until 1950 (and on the telephone until 1990), and it was only in the 1950s that the teaching of Lithuanian was introduced as a subject in schools.

Establishing the linguistic boundary with the Old *Prussian neighbours of the Lithuanians to the south-west poses a number of problems because of contradictory data and because it is difficult to distinguish between Lithuanian and Prussian elements in toponyms and personal names. Lithuanians inhabited the entire Scalovia and Nadrovia areas and even others further to the west, at least from the 16th c., and the Lithuanian element was augmented by immigrants from Lithuania itself and by Lithuanianized Prussians, Curonians, and even some Germans and Poles. It was in this unique Lithuanian area (then under Prussian and, after 1871, German rule), later to be termed 'Lithuania Minor', that the first printed book in Lithuanian (1547) and the first grammar (1653) (see below, 'Earliest attestations') appeared, and also the work of the important 18th-c. writer Donelaitis, whose poetical work *Metai* ('Seasons') (1765–75) was the first Lithuanian literary work to receive international acclaim. At that period, the use of Lithuanian was more widespread in public life in Lithuania Minor (then under German control) than in Lithuania itself and Germanization was relatively weak. In the mid-19th c., however, Lithuanian was banished from the schools, governmental institutions, and public life generally. In 1923 the northern part of Lithuania Minor, the Klaipėda region (in German, Memel), was allocated to Lithuania while the rest, the greater part, remained as the German province of East Prussia. After the Second World War, East Prussia was divided: in the northern part which went to the Soviet Union, remaining as a detached portion of the Russian Federation, Russian toponyms (even hydronyms) replaced not only Germanized names but Lithuanian and Old Prussian names which had existed since early times; in the southern part which was allocated to Poland, many names of Baltic origin were also replaced by Polish forms. East Prussian Lithuanian was annihilated.

To the north, the linguistic boundary between Lithuanian and Latgallian (see under *Latvian) formerly passed to the north of the present Latvian border. There are many vestiges of Lithuanian (including toponyms) along the edge of southern

Latgallia as far as the Daugava river, in the Daugavpils and Krāslava districts, and
even beyond it in the Drisa district.

Earliest attestations

The earliest Lithuanian texts date from the beginning of the 16th c. Though manuscripts of a religious character doubtless existed from the period following the
introduction of Christianity into Lithuania in the late 14th and early 15th centuries
(1387 in Aukštaitija, 1413 in Žemaitija), the oldest extant manuscript (now at the
University of Vilnius) is an anonymous text of a prayer written on the last page of
the Latin *Tractatus sacerdotalis* published in Strasbourg in 1503. The first printed
book, of which two copies remain, one in the library of the University of Vilnius and
the other at Torun in Poland, was Martynas Mažvydas's catechism of 1547, written
in the southern Žemaitish dialect (see below, 'Dialects'), a text of great importance
in the history of the formation of the Lithuanian written language. The first dictionary (the only surviving copy of which lacks its title-page) is K. Sirvydas's
Latin–Polish–Lithuanian *Dictionarium trium linguarum* of 1620. This was followed
by the first grammar (in Latin), Danielius Kleinas's *Grammatica litvanica* of 1653,
the publication of which set a standard for the written language and laid a solid foundation for the orthography.

The literary language

The beginnings of the Lithuanian literary language date from the early 16th c. when
the first written texts appear. Its development was determined by complex historical
conditions. Martynas Mažvydas, whose catechism dates from 1547 (see above), is
considered the father of the literary language. Lithuanian was used both in the Duchy
of Prussia, where its development was fostered by Baltramiejus Vilentas and Jonas
Bretkūnas, and in the grand Duchy of Lithuania, where important figures include
Mikalojus Daukša, Merkelis Petkevičius and Konstantinas Sirvydas. The literary
language in Prussia was based on the western Aukštaitish subdialect (see below,
'Dialects') and Danielius Kleinas's two grammars (1653, 1654) laid a firm foundation both for the written language in Prussia and for the formation of contemporary
standard Lithuanian. In the Grand Duchy there were two variants of the literary
language, the eastern and the central. However, the modern literary language in the
Grand Duchy developed only in the last decades of the 19th c. and is based on the
western Aukštaitish subdialect. The process of codification, purification and standardization of the literary language was later furthered by a number of linguists and
writers and continued up to the First World War and later until finally, in the 1910s
and 1920s, it was universally accepted.

Scripts

There was no written Lithuanian before the coming of Christianity in the late 14th c.
In the Grand Duchy of Lithuania (13th–18th centuries), Latin was in widespread
use for the purpose of maintaining contacts with western countries and especially
with Poland. Alongside Latin, the Grand Duchy's Slavonic chancellery language and

*Cyrillic script were extensively used for written communication with other nations to the east, in particular with Moscow. The earliest manuscript and printed texts (the anonymous prayer, Mažvydas's catechism – see above) used Gothic script. In the second half of the 17th c. the Latin antiqua (round letter) script was adopted though, in German-controlled East Prussia, Gothic script remained in use until the Second World War. Under Czarist Russian rule (from 1795 to 1915) the use of the Latin alphabet was forbidden and attempts were made to impose a Cyrillic orthography but, because of fierce resistance to this, the use of the Latin alphabet was restored to use in 1904. The contemporary orthography, as reformed at the end of the 19th c., uses the Latin alphabet supplemented by diacritics, <ą, ę, ė, į, ū, ų, č, š, ž>, giving a total of 32 characters.

Dialects

The process of dialectal differentiation began as early as the 6th or 7th c. when the Lithuanian language separated from that of other eastern Balts. Local differences began to develop within Lithuanian itself and in the 13th–14th centuries two main dialects emerged, each giving rise later to a number of subdialects: (i) Aukštaitish, with western, southern and eastern varieties, and (ii) Žemaitish, with western, northern and southern varieties. The two main dialects have the same grammatical categories and the same core lexicon. The principal differences between them are phonetic, Aukštaitish (and particularly the western subdialect, which forms the basis of the common standard language – see above, 'The literary language') being more archaic than Žemaitish (characterized *inter alia* by a shift of stress from the final to the initial syllable), though they also differ in respect of morphology (where Aukštaitish is also more archaic, Žemaitish being characterized *inter alia* by a reduction of endings), syntax and vocabulary.

The archaic nature of the closely related western and southern varieties of Aukštaitish was determined by the fact that almost the entire area was once inhabited by *Yatvingian western Balts, while the eastern subdialect was subject to *Selian (Selonian) and *Slavonic linguistic influences. The present-day dialect of the capital, Vilnius, falls within this eastern area and formed the basis of the eastern variant of the old Lithuanian literary language. The formation of the Žemaitish dialect was determined by *Curonian influence, probably in the 15th and 16th centuries.

Foreign influences

Lithuanian inherited a rich and extensive vocabulary from Indo-European, including terms for family relationships, animals, birds, trees, celestial bodies (sun, moon, etc.). Other strata date from the Proto-Baltic period (names of animals, flora, implements, metals, etc.) or are specific to eastern Baltic generally (terms referring to parts of the body, living creatures, natural phenomena, clothing, food, etc.). When the Slavonic chancellery language came into use in the Grand Duchy of Lithuania (13th c. onwards) the number of Slavisms and words acquired via the Slavs increased. From the end of the 14th c. these were supplemented by borrowings, mainly biblical and other religious terms, from Polish when Lithuania's grand Duke Jogaila became King of Poland and began to draw the two countries more closely together. From the 13th c., in consequence of contacts with the Teutonic Order and the presence in Lithuania of German artisans and merchants, German words began to make their way into Lithuanian, the most widespread of which are associated with the administrative, military and economic fields. In the late 19th and early 20th centuries, during periods of Polonization, Germanization and Russianization, the number of borrowings increased considerably. During the period of Soviet occupation (1941–90) the lexicon of spoken Lithuanian became permeated with Russianisms, the use of Russian cases, reflexive, forms, prefixes and prepositions was widespread, and Russian influence even affected word order and other aspects of syntax. Since the restoration of independence in 1990, there has been a significant increase in lexical borrowings from English.

There has also been influence in the other direction, with borrowings from Lithuanian being found both in Slavonic languages (Old Russian, Belarusian, Ukrainian, Polish) and in German (particularly in the German dialects of East Prussia).

Present situation

Lithuanian is the first language of 3,023,000 people, i.e. 81.4% of the population (data as of 1996), in Lithuania itself, where people of other ethnic origins (Russians, Poles, Belarusians and others) use it as a second language. It is also spoken by communities in Latvia (35,000+), Poland (12,000+), Belarus (7,000+), Estonia (3,000+), Ukraine (10,000+) and the Russian Federation (60,000+), by a large emigrant community in the USA (300,000+) and smaller communities in the United Kingdom (9,000+), Germany (7,000+), Canada (18,000+) and Australia (10,000+).

Lithuanian was adopted as the official language of the state in 1922. During the period of Soviet occupation, beginning in 1941, it lost this protected status but regained it in 1989 and it now functions in all spheres of public life, administration, the legal system, education, religion (except in Orthodox parishes) and the mass media.

Klimas, A., Dambriūnas, V. and Schmalstieg, W. 1939. *Introduction to Modern Lithuanian*. Chicago.
Piesarskas, B. and Svecevičius, B. 1979. *Lietuvių-Anglų kalbų Žodynas* ('Lithuanian–English Dictionary'). Vilnius.
Press, I. and Ramonienė, M. 1996. *Colloquial Lithuanian*. London.

LINARA BARTKUVIENĖ

Liv, see *Livonian*

Livonian

Livonian (also known as Liv) is a member of the **Baltic-Finnic** subgroup of the **Finno-Ugrian languages**. It is most closely related to **Estonian** but is not mutually intelligible with it.

External history

The first mention of the Livonians in written sources is in the *Chronicle of Henry of Livonia*, which deals with the conquest of their territory by the Teutonic Knights in the late 12th and early 13th centuries and their conversion to Christianity. At the time of the *Chronicle*, the Livonians' territory extended along the coast of the Gulf of Riga from the present Estonian border southward beyond Riga.

No written sources in the language exist from before the 19th c. Assimilation with Latvian-speakers and administrative domination by German-speaking colonizers was already under way at the time of Henry's *Chronicle*.

Bilingualism in Livonian and Latvian has been known for centuries – all known Livonian-speakers have also been fluent in Latvian. Livonian fisherfolk have throughout history traded, interacted and intermarried with the agricultural Latvians further inland and so it is no wonder that Latvian (a genetically unrelated ***Indo-European language**) has profoundly affected the phonology and lexis, and to a lesser extent the grammar (including the syntax), of Livonian. The most obvious phonological convergence has been the very recent loss in Livonian of the rounded vowels [ø] and [y] which are lacking in Latvian and which have become [e] and [i] respectively.

The written language

Livonian does not appear to have been committed to writing before it became an object of study by outsiders. The first systematic study of the language, and the first attempt at an orthography (based on the Latin alphabet supplemented by diacritics), was the work of a Finn, A. J. Sjögren (1794–1855), continued after his death by F. J. Wiedemann. This orthography was the basis of that used in the first printed book, a translation of St Matthew's Gospel, published in 1863.

A meagre body of work in the language has been published since, but only during the periods of Latvian independence, from 1918 to 1940 and again since 1990. The orthography is not fundamentally different from that of the New Testament published in 1938 under the supervision of the Finnish scholar Lauri Kettunen, whose definitive Livonian–German dictionary (see below) appeared in the same year.

The Livonian language never enjoyed any official status and no stable written standard has emerged. Writing in the language has been confined to almanacs, school readers, some poetry, and journalism on a small scale. The Livonian Cultural Association, re-established in 1990, publishes a monthly newspaper, which however is mostly in Latvian. Unlike the other Baltic-Finnic languages, Livonian has no large body of preserved oral literature on which to draw as the basis for a national literary tradition.

Dialects

Dialect differences are known to have existed within Livonian. The extinct Salis variant is recorded only scantily, but marked differences were evident from the

Kurzeme (Courland) variety which itself exhibits small differences that prompted Kettunen (1938) to distinguish between 'Eastern' and 'Western' dialects.

Present situation

The geographical shrinkage of Livonian to a narrow coastal strip at the northern tip of Curonia (see map 12) was a fact by the mid-19th c. Further recession was occasioned by the evacuation of the entire population during both World Wars. Revival was made impossible by the Soviet authorities, for whom the region was of strategic importance, and the collectivization of the fishing industry decimated the Livonian way of life. The area was closed even to Latvians until 1990. Since independence, the government has established a special 'Livonian Coast' (Latvian *Lībiešu Krasts*, Livonian *Līvõd Rānda*) cultural-historical territory near the village of Mazirbe. Nevertheless, the villages are by now mostly deserted.

The few remaining speakers are mostly dispersed in other parts of Latvia. All fluent native speakers (fewer than ten at the time of writing) are aged over 70. Though the language has not been passed on to younger generations in most cases, attempts are being made to teach it to younger people in an organized way, including summer camps for children in Livonian villages.

Livonian nationality is provided for and recognized in current and pending Latvian legislation on citizenship.

Kettunen, L. 1938. *Livisches Wörterbuch* ('Livonian Dictionary'). Helsinki.
Posti, L. 1942. *Grundzüge der livischen Lautgeschichte* ('Essentials of the Phonetic History of Livonian'). Helsinki.
Sjögren, A. J. 1861. *Livische Grammatik nebst Sprachproben* ('Livonian Grammar with Specimens of the Language') (ed. F. J. Wiedemann). St Petersburg.

CHRISTOPHER MOSELEY

Lombard (see under *Italy. III. Northern Italy*)

Lucanian (see under *Oscan*)

Ludian (Lud, Lude, Ludic) (see under *Karelian*)

Lusatian Serb, see *Sorbian*

Lusitanian

Lusitanian is an extinct *Indo-European language, of which only a few inscriptions remain. The three longest inscriptions, which may date back to the 1st or 2nd c. AD, were found in the mountainous area between the rivers Douro and Taag in present-day Portugal and western Spain. In antiquity, this region was inhabited by the Lusitani, hence the name of the language.

The Lusitanians submitted to Rome in 139 BC after the assassination of their leader, Viriathus, who for a decade had put up effective resistance. The land became part of the Roman province of Hispania Ulterior. Under Augustus, the imperial province of Lusitania was created, which roughly corresponded in size to modern-day Portugal.

All inscriptions are written in the Latin alphabet.

The inscription of Cabeço das Fráguas (near Guarda, Portugal) was found at the end of the 1950s. It contains 16 words, among them the words for 'sheep', 'pig', 'bull' as well as a number of presumed names of divinities.

The interpretation of the contents of the inscriptions of Arroyo de Cáceres (now lost; around 35 words) and of Lamas de Moledo (around 15 words) remains obscure, although valuable grammatical information can be gleaned from them.

The preservation of the Indo-European sound *p-* and the use of *indi* 'and' seem to rule out the possibility that Lusitanian is a Celtic language (see *Celtiberian).

Tovar, A. 1964–6. L'inscription du Cabeço das Fráguas et la langue des Lusitaniens. *Études celtiques*, 11: 239–69.

PETER SCHRIJVER

Lusitanian, South, see *South Lusitanian*

Luxemburgish

Luxemburgish (Luxembourgian) is a *German dialect spoken in the Grand Duchy of Luxembourg, the Belgian areas of Arlon and St-Vith, and in the districts of France and Germany which border on the Grand Duchy. A law of 1984 recognizes Luxemburgish as the national language of the Grand Duchy but French as the language of legislation.

Written language

Although the first works in the language might be regarded as the *Echternach Glosses* (9th–10th c.), the *Trier Capitular* (*c.*910) and *Iolande van Vianden* (*c.*1290), the language appeared in its first modern form in 1824. The first written collection of poetry appeared in 1829, newspaper satire in 1848, and plays with music and song in 1855. The novel and short story appeared at the end of the 19th c. Classic works are the plays of Edmond de la Fontaine (1823–91, known as 'Dicks'), the verse epic *Renert* (1872) by Michel Rodange (1827–76), the poetry of Michel Lenz (1820–93) and the prose of Caspar Matthias Spoo (1837–1914).

The first linguistic study of Luxemburgish appeared in 1843, the first dictionary in 1847, the first bilingual dictionary (German to Luxemburgish) in 1974. However, Luxemburgish is as yet still primarily a spoken language. The dictionary of 1950–77 (Tockert et al.) and the grammar of 1955 (Bruch) are in no sense prescriptive. The introduction of the new official spelling in 1975 (see below, 'Orthography') has, however, been seen by some as an attempt to engineer the language and lead to a situation in which the koine would be taught prescriptively in schools. Opinion on the desirability of this is strongly divided.

Orthography

Since 1829 there have been various spelling systems, based largely on the model of standard German, though modified with diacritics. The classic 19th-c. orthography is that of the poet Edmond de la Fontaine (1855). Because of its complexity, this gave way to a system devised by René Engelmann (1912) and published by Nikolaus Welter (1914). Spelling based on phonetic principles was introduced in 1946 (Margue-Feltes). While this was the first system to be officially adopted for government and educational use, it was overshadowed by the German-based spelling of the *Luxemburger Wörterbuch* (1950), which with modifications replaced it as from 10 October 1975.

Regional varieties

Luxemburgish belongs to the West Moselle Franconian subgroup of the dialects of German, within the larger grouping of Central Franconian. It has affinities with the Transylvanian German dialects of Bistriţa/Bistritz, where peasants from the Moselle Franconian area settled in the 12th c. Regional varieties within Luxembourg are very marked. One may identify the north (Luxemburg Ardennes, known locally as the Oesling or Éislek), the east (Echternach), the south-east (Remich, Moselle), the south-west (Esch-sur-Alzette and surrounding district), and the inner city of Luxembourg itself. A supraregional koine has been developing since the late 19th c. This is seen to be based on a levelled-out form of the language spoken in the valley of the Alzette river between Dudelange and Schieren.

Luxemburgish is open to lexical influence from French and German, though the latter is stronger, also affecting idiom and hypotaxis.

Present situation

In all areas except the Grand Duchy itself, where the language is exceptionally strong, the language is in decline. The number of resident native speakers in the Grand Duchy is about 275,000, with a further 119,000 foreign nationals, many of whom have grown up in the Grand Duchy and command the language with native competence. There are a further several thousand speakers in the areas bordering the Grand Duchy. The few villages in the Grand Duchy which up to the 1930s still had active speakers of Belgo-Romance and French have now gone over to Luxemburgish. In the 19th c., Luxemburgish was taken by emigrants to the Dubuque (Iowa) area of the USA.

The domains of use of Luxemburgish, French and German in the Grand Duchy are well defined for both speech and writing. French is used in most government documentation, and in written form is the language of initial contact. The use of German has very much receded in written form, though it is still the chief medium of daily newspapers. Spoken French is used on very formal occasions, or as a teaching language in the upper classes of secondary schools; spoken German is used by and large only in lower schools, and to varying degrees by the Church. The reading of Luxemburgish texts in schools was introduced in 1912. Luxemburgish has been used in parliamentary debate since 1945, and its wider written use in administrative documentation became possible under Constitutional revisions of 1984. The use of spoken Luxemburgish is, however, universal. Luxemburgish-language TV broadcasting was introduced in 1968.

In the Grand Duchy, Luxemburgish is a national language ranked alongside French and German for use by the administration and judiciary. While French remains the language of legislation, the concept of 'official languages' does not figure in the 1984 Constitutional revision. Within the European Union, Luxemburgish is neither an official nor a working language, though it has featured in the *Lingua* programme.

Up to 1795 the country was known in German as *Lützemburg* and in French as *Luxembourg*. Since 1849, *Luxembourg* has been the official spelling, with *Luxemburg* as the German variant. According to the 1975 orthography (see above), the name of the country appears as Lëtzebuerg /ˈlətsəbuərç/ and that of the national language as Lëtzebuergesch /ˈlətsəbuərjeʃ/.

Berg, G. 1993. *'Mir wëlle bleiwe, wat mir sin.' Soziolinguistische und sprachtypologische Betrachtungen zur luxemburgischen Mehrsprachigkeit* ('"We wish to remain what we are." Reflections on the Sociolinguistics and Linguistic Typology of Multilingualism in Luxembourg'). Tübingen.

Bruch, R. 1955. *Précis populaire de grammaire luxembourgeoise/Luxemburger Grammatik in volkstümlichem Abriß*. Luxembourg.

Christophory, J. 1982. *English–Luxemburgish Dictionary*. Luxembourg.

Hoffman, F. 1964–7. *Geschichte der Luxemburger Mundartdichtung* ('History of Luxemburgish Dialect literature'), 2 vols. Luxembourg.

—— 1979. *Sprachen in Luxemburg* ('Languages in Luxembourg'). Wiesbaden and Luxembourg.

Newton, G. (ed.) 1996. *Luxembourg and Lëtzebuergesch: Language and Communication at the Crossroads of Europe*. Oxford.

Tockert, J., Bruch, R., Palgen, H. et al. (eds) 1950–77. *Luxemburger Wörterbuch* ('Luxemburgish Dictionary') (reprinted 1995 as *Lëtzebuerger Dixionär*). Luxembourg.

GERALD NEWTON

M

Macedonian (Ancient)

The long-extinct native language of the inhabitants of ancient Macedonia. It should not be confused with modern *Macedonian, a south *Slavonic language. The homeland of the ancient Macedonians was situated north of Mount Olympus (Greece) and west of Ohrid (Republic of Macedonia), approximately east of the river Strimon (Greece, Bulgaria) and perhaps south of Skopje (Republic of Macedonia). Their territory greatly expanded as a result of the conquests of Philip II and his son Alexander the Great, in the latter half of the 4th c. BC. Macedonian bordered on *Greek in the south, Thracian (see *Daco-Thracian) and perhaps *Phrygian in the north and east, and ***Illyrian** in the west, but the linguistic situation in the area may actually have been more complicated.

Our knowledge of Macedonian is extremely fragmentary: place-names, personal names, and a few nouns surviving as glosses in Greek sources. These have given rise to hot and often politically inspired debates concerning its linguistic affiliation, which are far from settled. The sources can be divided into three categories: (1) Greek words and names; some of these are Attic and were undoubtedly borrowed (Attic Greek was the official language at the court of the Macedonian kings); others are not Attic but show possible resemblances to northern Greek dialects; (2) words which have Greek (and sometimes wider ***Indo-European**) cognates but whose sound structure differs markedly from any known Greek dialect (e.g. *danos* 'death', Greek *thánatos*); (3) words which have no known Greek cognates and usually no convincing Indo-European etymology (e.g. *bedu* 'air').

Crossland, R. A. 1982. The language of the Macedonians. In Boardman, J. et al. (eds), *The Cambridge Ancient History*, vol. 3 part 1, Cambridge, 843–7.
Katičić, R. 1976. Macedonia. In Id., *Ancient Languages of the Balkans*, The Hague, part 1, 100–16.

PETER SCHRIJVER

Macedonian (Modern)

A member, with ***Serbo-Croat**, ***Slovene** and ***Bulgarian**, of the southern subgroup of the ***Slavonic languages**. It is the official language of the former Yugoslav Republic of Macedonia which declared independence in 1991.

Affiliation

The two members of the eastern branch of the southern Slavonic languages, Macedonian and Bulgarian, form together with the non-Slavonic languages ***Romanian**, ***Greek** and ***Albanian** the so-called Balkan 'Sprachbund' ('Language league'). These languages share several striking grammatical features usually called 'Balkanisms'. Since these features were not originally present in the languages from which the languages of the Sprachbund derive, either their origin has been sought in some extinct language such as Thracian (see ***Draco-Thracian**) or ***Illyrian**, or they have been seen as features shared in common as a result of evolutionary convergence.

History

The history of Macedonian is divided into two periods, the old and the modern. The dividing line is conventionally placed in the 15th c. For several centuries after the break-up of Common Slavonic (9th c.), the Macedonian dialects belonged to the inherited linguistic type, but the process of Balkanization transformed the old structure and by the 15th c. the new Balkan linguistic model had gained ascendancy. The earliest texts showing specifically Macedonian phonetic features are Old ***Church Slavonic** classical texts written in Glagolitic (see ***Cyrillic and Glagolitic scripts**) which date from the 10th–11th centuries (*Codex Zographensis, Codex*

Assemanianus, Euchologium Sinaiticum, Psalterium Sinaiticum), but by the 12th c. Church Slavonic Cyrillic had become the main alphabet.

Texts reflecting vernacular Macedonian features appear in the second half of the 16th c. (the so-called 'Damaskin literature', i.e. translations of the sermons of the Greek writer Damascene Studite). The first literary texts in Macedonian date from the 19th c. (see below).

At the end of the 19th c., the process of modernization of the Macedonian Cyrillic alphabet and orthography took place under the influence of the phonetic principle of Serbian orthographic reforms.

A standard language, based on the dialect of the west-central region (see below, 'Dialects and geographical spread'), began to take shape in the 1860s and 1870s. Macedonians, at this period of greater educational freedom, attended Bulgarian schools, not only because the language of their Bulgarian neighbours was closer to their own than was Serbian but also because these schools were more available. It was soon realized, however, that the Bulgarian standard taught in schools, which was codified on the basis of NE Bulgarian dialects, was too remote from the Macedonians' own dialects. Macedonian intellectuals envisaged a Bulgarian standard based on a Bulgarian–Macedonian dialectal compromise, but Bulgarian codifiers did not wish to compromise and insisted on the eastern standard they operated with. The only alternative was a distinct Macedonian language. In 1903, K. P. Misirkov in his book *Za makedonckite raboti* ('On Macedonian Matters') outlined the principles of this language based on the Titov Veles-Prilep-Bitola dialect group of the west-central region. These dialects were in many respects the most highly differentiated from both Bulgarian and Serbian. Misirkov did, however, allow features from other dialects, whenever west-central features were too specific or archaic for general acceptance.

The partition of Macedonia between Serbia and Bulgaria in 1913 led to the suppression of Macedonian in public life in favour of the official language of the partitioning state, and Macedonian was either considered a Serbian or a Bulgarian dialect or its very existence was denied (in Greece).

Macedonian was not recognized as an independent literary language until 1944 when it was declared to be the official language of the Yugoslav Republic of Macedonia. The present orthography was established in 1945 and, in the course of the ten years following the recognition of the language, the literary language was standardized. The codifiers took Misirkov's choice of a west-central dialectal base for granted and the standard then elaborated has been accepted with relatively few modifications.

Macedonian as a literary language

At the beginning of the 19th c., J. Krčovski and K. Pejčinovik introduced the vernacular into literature and, in the second half of the 19th c., poetry written in Macedonian dialects made its appearance, the most famous poets being K. Miladinov and R. Žinzifov. Despite the fact that the language was not officially recognized (see above), nevertheless there was limited literary activity between the two world wars as attested in the dramas of V. Ilojski, A. Panov and R. Krle and the poetry of K. Racin and K. Nedelkovski. Since official recognition in 1944, Macedonian has consolidated itself culturally and is the language of literature of every genre.

Dialects and geographical spread

Macedonian comprises a group of dialects located in the southernmost part of Slavonic-speaking territory extending into northern Greece as far as the river Bistrica (Aliakmon in Greek) on the border of Thessaly (an area known as Aegean Macedonia). The dialects on which Macedonian is based form part of a continuum with Serbian and Bulgarian dialects and it is not possible to draw distinct boundaries between them. Macedonian is also spoken in the Blagoevgrad district in SW Bulgaria (an area known as Pirin Macedonia) and in some 60 to 70 villages in eastern Albania.

For historico-political reasons, Macedonian is not recognized in either Bulgaria or Greece. In Bulgaria it is considered a dialectal variant or 'regional norm' of Bulgarian, and in Greece the term 'Macedonian' can be used with reference only to the Greek dialects of (Greek) Macedonia or to Ancient ***Macedonian**.

Present situation

According to Yugoslav census figures for 1981 and other estimates, the total number of native speakers of Macedonian is approximately 2 million, many of whom have emigrated to Australia, Canada or the USA.

Having been first officially recognized in 1944 as an official language in the Yugoslav Republic of Macedonia, Macedonian is now the official language of the independent Republic of Macedonia and the language of public life, education and the mass media.

Crvenkovski, D. and Gruik, B. 1993. *Англиско–Македонски. Македонско–Англиски Речник (English–Macedonian, Macedonian–English Dictionary)*. Skopje.

Friedman, V. A. 1993. Macedonian. In Comrie, B. and Corbett, G. G. (eds), *The Slavonic Languages*, London, 249–305.

Koneski, B. 1965. *Историја на македонскиот јазик* ('History of the Macedonian Language'). Skopje and Belgrade.

Lunt, H. G. 1952. *A Grammar of the Macedonian Language*. Skopje.

PETER HERRITY

Macedo-Romanian, see *Aromanian*

Malay (see under *Community languages (Netherlands)*)

Malinka (see under *Community languages (France)*)

Maltese

A ***Semitic language**, historically a dialect of ***Arabic** (Maghreb group), sufficiently different from other Arabic dialects in script, phonology, lexis, grammar and social status to constitute a distinct language. It is spoken in all three inhabited islands

(Malta, Gozo, Comino) of the Republic of Malta, some 60 miles off the southern coast
of Sicily.

History

Apart from the names of Malta and Gozo, only one or two place-names can be tentatively ascribed to periods preceding the Arab conquest of AD 870. This lends weight
to the theory that the islands were uninhabited or supported a much reduced population during most of the Arab domination (*c*.870–1090). Between their capture by
the Norman rulers of Sicily and the arrival of the Knights of St John of Jerusalem
(1090–1530), the islands were a dependency of the Sicilian Crown. In the second half
of this period, Sicilian (see under *Italy. IV. **Central and southern Italy**) was
widely spoken by the upper echelons of laity and church, and probably also by skilled
tradesmen and craftsmen. The vocabulary of present-day Maltese is replete with
Sicilianisms: the lexicon pertaining to certain activities such as fishing or building is
largely of Sicilian origin.

Early samples of the lexis survive in place-names and nicknames found in notarial
and other documents (written in Sicilian or Latin) dating back to the late 14th c.
Further indications of what the late medieval language was like may be obtained from
an examination of contemporary Judaeo-Arabic documents of Maltese origin,
though it would be rash to equate the language of these texts with Maltese.

The coming of the Knights in 1530 followed closely the Tuscanization of Sicily
and from that date onwards a Tuscan-based Italian supplanted Sicilian as the
language of culture and administration in the islands. Italian played this role
throughout the period of the Knights (1530–1798) and well into the subsequent
British colonial years (1800–1964), but was gradually displaced by English in the
19th c. as the language of administration. The relative position of Italian, English and
Maltese was hotly debated in the first decades of the 20th c., the language question
becoming one of the issues dividing the political parties. The debate coincided with
the codification of the language by writers in Maltese, whose attitude led them to
follow puristic lines, i.e. to avoid Italian words and constructions where possible,
favouring the dialects of the (monolingual) country areas rather than that of the
(bilingual) middle classes. This policy was considered by their opponents to constitute a betrayal of the national cultural heritage. To complicate matters, the Malta
'language question' formed a main plank in the irredentist programme pursued by
Italian fascism in the 1930s. In 1936, Britain's revocation of the 1921 Constitution
abolished all remaining official uses of Italian (including its use in the law courts) and
established the use of Maltese. Modern Maltese is rich in Italian and English loan-
words pertaining to practically every sphere of modern life, abstract and concrete,
and contains several grammatical traits that are clearly traceable to Italian (note that
Sutcliffe (1936) ignores the Romance element).

Maltese as a literary medium

The earliest text in Maltese is a poem of 20 lines, Petro de Caxaro's *Cantilena*,
composed *c*.1460–85. Other texts are extant from about the second half of the 17th c.,

but it was not till some hundred years later that Maltese began to be written down systematically. The 19th c. witnessed the adoption of Maltese as a literary medium of obvious utility, encouraged by local writers and foreign administrators (e.g. J. Hookham Frere). The early 20th c. saw the maturation and fixing of a generally accepted standard in grammar and orthography by the *Għaqda tal-Kittieba tal-Malti* ('Society of Writers in Maltese') and the appearance of authors acknowledged to be of major status (e.g. Dun Karm Psaila, 1871–1961, regarded as Malta's national poet). Since independence in 1964, the pace, breadth and standard of publications in Maltese have grown remarkably. Several dailies and weeklies (and other periodicals) are published in Maltese (with three dailies and three Sunday papers in English). Several writers enjoy a wide local readership, one or two a modest international reputation (e.g. Francis Ebejer, Oliver Friggieri).

The written language and its study

The script is a modified Roman, fixed in the 1920s and officially adopted in 1934. It makes use of diacritics, digraphs and the redundant letters of the Roman alphabet to denote sounds not conventionally represented by the latter: <ċ> and <ġ> represent [tʃ] and [dʒ], <ż> is [z], <h> is not pronounced but <ħ> represents the voiceless pharyngeal fricative [ħ] (with dialectal variations), <għ> represents a consonant not pronounced in most positions and in most dialects of Maltese, but one which tends to lengthen an accompanying vowel, and <x> represents [ʃ].

Sporadic attention to Maltese dates back to the 16th and 17th centuries (e.g. Hieronymus Megiser 1588, Giovanni Francesco Abela 1647, Sir Philip Skippon 1664). Interest gathers momentum with Thezan's *Regole per la Lingua Maltese* (probably 17th c.), the work of Agius de Soldanis (1750) and especially that of Mikiel Anton Vassalli, first in publishing the view that Maltese should become the national language of Malta (from 1790). The first modern study of the language is generally considered to be Hans Stumme's 'Maltesische Studien' (in *Semitische Studien* (Leipzig), 1–4, 1904).

Dialects

Despite the smallness of the territory of the Republic of Malta (316 sq. km), dialectal variation is conspicuous, especially in the phonology. Two main groups of dialects can be discerned. The first comprises the prestigious dialect(s) of the educated classes, found in the capital, Valletta, and in the populous, largely middle-class residential areas of Sliema and environs. Frequent switching between Maltese and English is one of its main characteristics. The second group, spoken in the largely agricultural villages and in the industrial districts surrounding the Grand Harbour, is characterized by differences in the vowel system, the preservation, in one or two cases, of individual consonants characteristic of Arabic 'core' dialects and lost by the other Maltese dialects, and the preservation of more words of Arabic origin.

Present situation

Maltese is spoken by virtually the whole of the 376,000-strong population of the Maltese islands (1995 census). It is the country's national language and one of its two official languages, the other being English. It is also spoken by emigrant families abroad: in Australia (*c*.85,000 speakers), where there is a small number of periodicals and radio broadcasts wholly or partly in Maltese, in the UK, the USA (New York, Detroit, California) and Canada. There are no data on the extent to which Maltese is known among second- or third-generation migrants.

Maltese is used in the Maltese Parliament, the law courts and in church services and is the medium of instruction in state primary and secondary schools. Some private schools on the other hand tend to favour English and this also applies to most departments in the University of Malta. English (Maltese English) is widely used as a second language among the middle and upper classes (occasionally as a first language) and in the numerically important section of the work-force servicing the tourist industry. It is common to hear speakers switching from one language to the other. English is less well known among manual workers living in country districts. A knowledge of Italian is widespread among the educated classes, especially in some professional families. Moreover, Italian is widely taught in schools as a third language. This and the popularity of Italian television programmes, accessible to Maltese viewers for well over a generation, have enhanced the position of Italian that had suffered considerably because of the Second World War.

Aquilina, J. 1965. *Teach Yourself Maltese*. London.
—— 1987–90. *Maltese–English Dictionary*, 2 vols. Malta.
Arberry, A. J. 1960. *A Maltese Anthology*. Oxford.
—— and Grech, P. 1961. *Dun Karm, Poet of Malta*. Cambridge.
Borg, A. and Azzopardi-Alexander, M. 1997. *Maltese*. London.
Isserlin, B. S. J. 1990. The Maltese language. In Bosworth, C. E., Van Donzel, E., Lewis, B. and Pellat, C. (eds), *The Encyclopædia of Islam*, Leiden, vol. 6, 295–8.
Sutcliffe, E. F. 1936. *A Grammar of the Maltese Language, with Chrestomathy and Vocabulary*. Oxford (reprinted Malta, 1960.)

JOSEPH CREMONA

Mamertinian (see under *Oscan*)

Manx

Manx, earlier written 'Manks', is a member of the Goidelic or *Gaelic subgroup of the *Celtic languages, calling itself *Gailck* whereas the English name is a variant of the Norse *Mansk*. Before the separation of Common Gaelic into the three languages of the Goidelic group, no geographical designation was necessary; as they divided in the later part of the Middle Ages, Manx became the name of a distinctive variant of Gaelic, that spoken in the Isle of Man in the centre of the north Irish Sea, not inappropriately called in Old Irish *muir Manann* 'the sea of Man'.

The language in its earliest state, while still not distinct from Common Gaelic, is found in a handful of inscriptions in the ogham or *ogam script, in one case side by side with a parallel inscription in Latin letters, betokening, it is thought, the co-existence of speakers of the Goidelic and *Brittonic forms of Celtic. During the Norse period similar funerary inscriptions are found in *runes, the language being *Norse, but with a mixture of Norse and Goidelic personal names.

Manx shares with *Scottish Gaelic the shift of the inflected Gaelic present tense into future meaning, and the creation of a new periphrastic present, features which have sometimes been attributed in both languages to a Brittonic substratum. While Scottish Gaelic retained the Common Gaelic initial stress of uncompounded words, with consequent shortening of the long vowels of derivative syllables, and *Irish partly allowed these long vowels to attract the stress, Manx has a mixture of both systems, apparently on a prosodic basis, and with some reduction of root syllables when unstressed.

The commoner *Latin and *Anglo-Norman loan-words in Irish are also found in Manx, no doubt diffused during the period before the languages separated, together with loans from Middle and Early Modern English, but with very few words of Norse origin. Dialect differentiation undoubtedly existed in Manx while it was widely spoken, and may be reflected in the English dialect of the island, but the limitations of the evidence allow only a few broad features to be identified. Emigration from the island during the 19th c. produced for a time Manx-speaking communities abroad, notably at Cleveland, Ohio, but these did not continue long.

The earliest reasonably datable composition in Manx dates from the early 16th c. but is extant only in manuscripts of the third quarter of the 18th. The earliest writing in Manx to survive in a manuscript contemporaneous with its composition, or nearly so, is the translation of the English Book of Common Prayer completed in 1611, in a fair copy of *c*.1630, but which remained unpublished. The orthography here, as in all later writing and printing, has entirely parted company with the Gaelic conventions.

The most productive period for published work in Manx was the second half of the 18th c., though the first printed book, a Manx–English bilingual catechism, dates from 1707. From this century come the published Prayer Book, the Bible, various catechisms and tracts and late in the century, translations of hymns. The most notable 'literary' piece is the abridgement of Milton's *Paradise Lost* in about 4,000 lines of rhymed verse; the principal body of 'popular' verse is also religious, the carvals, but there is also a small surviving body of secular songs, both original and adapted. The 18th c. may therefore be regarded as the 'classical' period of the language, setting the standard of orthography which was continued by the lexicographers; the spelling of manuscript material, however, particularly in the collections of carvals, continued to be personal and irregular.

The use of Manx began to decline in the 19th c. under combined pressure from education, immigration (and emigration), the need to qualify for employment outside the island (e.g. trade, the merchant service and the Royal Navy) and the tourist industry. Although it had been used as a matter of necessity in the church and the courts, the language of record in both had been English, with some Latin in ecclesiastical contexts, from the 15th c., so that the official status of the language was low and the educational system had never included it, the Manx-speaking clergy receiving their academic and professional education in the island through English. By the end of the century Manx-speaking parents were deliberately not teaching the language to their children, fearing that it would prove a handicap to them. Professor John Rhŷs, collecting phonetic information from native speakers in the 1880s, remarked on encountering only one Manx-speaking child in the course of his researches. The decline was sharpest in Douglas, less so in the small towns and villages, least of all in the countryside.

Material relating to the language was collected by various scholars, beginning with Edward Lhuyd *c*.1700, Rhŷs as above, and Marstrander in the 1920s, and both sound recordings and phonetic notation were used. They exhibit a great variety of pronunciation, a decline in the grammatical usage of the language compared with the 18th c., and some confusion of similar lexical items. A question on the knowledge of the language has been included in the decennial census for some time now, but the figures, relying as they do on the self-assessment of the respondents, should be treated with reserve. In the census of 1991 the number claiming a knowledge of the language, out of a population of about 71,000, was 650. The last person who could claim to be a native speaker, Ned Maddrell, died aged 97 in 1974. There has been a movement, of varying strength and enthusiasm, for the revival of the language since the beginning of the 20th c., producing and reprinting texts and aids to acquiring Manx, and arranging classes; the most recent development has been the introduction of the language as an option within the school system.

There is still no satisfactory grammar of the language. The morphology is conveniently summarized in Goodwin (1966), and the syntax is dealt with in a running commentary on a text in Thomson (1981). The most reliable dictionary is that of Cregeen (1835).

Broderick, G. 1984–6. *A Handbook of Late Spoken Manx*, 3 vols. Tübingen.
Cregeen, A. 1835 (with frequent reprints). *A Dictionary of the Manks Language*. Douglas.
Goodwin, E. 1966. *First Lessons in Manx*, 3rd edn. Douglas.
Jackson, K. H. 1951. Common Gaelic: the evolution of the Goidelic languages. *Proceedings of the British Academy*, 37: 71–97.
Jenner, H. 1876. The Manx language: its grammar, literature and present state. *Transactions of the Philological Society*, 1875–6: 172–97.
Thomson, R. L. 1981. *Lessoonyn Sodjey 'sy Ghailck Vanninagh*. Douglas.
—— 1992a. Manx language and literature. In Price, G. (ed.), *The Celtic Connection*, Gerrards Cross, 154–70.
—— 1992b. The Manx language. In MacAulay, D. (ed.), *The Celtic Languages*, Cambridge, 100–36.

R. L. THOMSON

Mari

Mari, also known as Cheremis, is the northernmost representative (the other being ***Mordvinian**) of the Volga Finnic group of the ***Finno–Ugrian languages**. A considerable ***Chuvash** influence is recognizable in the language. The majority of the Mari live in the Mari Republic (capital, Yoshkar Ola) (Russian Federation) north of the Volga; 670,868 speakers were enumerated in 1989.

In the 6th c., the historian Jordanes in his 'Getica' names several peoples subjugated by the Goths, among them the 'Merens' (an extinct people closely related to the Mari) and the 'Imniscaris', who are probably the Mari or Cheremis themselves. After the 7th c. the Mari came under Volga Bolgar influence. In 10th-c. Khazar documents, their name appears as 'Zarmis'. There are four dialects: (i) Hill Mari, along the river Sura, to the west of the Volga; (ii) a north-western dialect, around the towns of Sharanga, Tonshaevo and Yaransk in the Nizhny Novgorod and Kirov districts; (iii) Meadow Mari, to the east of the Volga in an area bordered by the rivers Vyatka and Vetluga; and (iv) eastern or Ufa Mari, beyond the boundaries of the Republic on the rivers Ufa and Belaya in Bashkiria. Two separate standard languages have been created, for Hill Mari and Meadow Mari respectively. Since approximately 80% of the Mari speak Meadow Mari, there is a tendency to use this dialect everywhere. At least two authors deserve a mention, Sergey Chavayn (1888–1942) and J. Mayorov (1898–1937), who wrote under the pseudonym Shketan.

Bereczki, G. 1990. *Chrestomathia Ceremissica*. Budapest.
Collinder, B. 1957. Cheremis. In Id., *Survey of the Uralic Languages*, Stockholm, 247–71.
Saarinen, S. 1985. Die Dialekte des Tscheremissischen ('The dialects of Cheremis'). In Veenker, W. (ed.), *Dialectologia Uralica. Materialien des ersten internationalen Symposions zur Dialektologie der uralischen Sprachen*, Wiesbaden, 195–9.

WOLFGANG GRELLER

Marrucinian

The Marrucini were a small tribe occupying territory on the Adriatic coast of central Italy (see map 10), their chief town being Teate (modern Chieti). Apart from a small number of very brief inscriptions, our knowledge of it derives entirely from a 35-word inscription in an early form of the Latin alphabet and dating from the 3rd c. BC, found at Rapino and now in the Museum of Antiquities in Berlin. Although the interpretation of this inscription is far from certain, it is enough to demonstrate that Marrucinian is an *Italic language, probably closely related to *Paelignian.

Coleman, R. 1986. The central Italic languages in the period of Roman expansion. *Transactions of the Philological Society*, 1986: 100–31.
Pulgram, E. 1978. Marrucinian. In Id., *Italic, Latin, Italian: 600 BC to AD 1260: Texts and Commentaries*, Heidelberg, 144–9.

Marsian

The Marsi inhabited an area (which includes the modern town of Luco ne' Marsi, some 80 kilometres east of Rome) near the Fucine Lake (drained in the 19th c.) in the central Apennine massif (see map 10), with their capital at Marruvium (modern San Benedetto). Marsian is an *Italic language, and therefore related to *Latin. It is known to us from, at most, only about half a dozen inscriptions, in the Latin alphabet, and the status even of some of these is disputed. The most recent authoritative assessment (Coleman 1986) accepts as Marsian only three short inscriptions, from 300–150 BC, including one the language of which is probably a dialect of Marsian but could perhaps be *Volscian, and, from the same period, seven inscriptions in a dialectal Latin marked by Marsian features.

Coleman, R. 1986. The central Italic languages in the period of Roman expansion. *Transactions of the Philological Society*, 1986: 100–31.

Megeb (see under *Dargwa* under *Caucasian languages. IV. North-East Caucasian family*)

Megleno-Romanian

A dialect of *Romanian (also known as Vla(c)h), sometimes considered to be a distinct language, spoken in a few villages in northern Greece and by small communities elsewhere in the Balkans; the name comes from that of the Meglen district north of the Gulf of Salonica. Estimates of numbers of speakers formerly ranged from 12,000 to 26,000 but have recently (Atanasov 1989) been revised downwards to about 5,000; given the intolerant attitude towards linguistic minorities shown by the Greek state, which goes so far as to deny their existence, it is impossible to obtain reliable information of any kind. A few collections of popular literature, intended primarily as illustrations of the dialect for linguistic purposes, have been published by scholars.

Atanasov, P. 1984. Meglenoromână ('Megleno-Romanian'). In Rusu, V. (ed.), *Tratat de dialectologie românească* ('Treatise on Romanian Dialectology'), Craiova, 423–76.
—— 1989. *Le mégléno-roumain de nos jours*. Hamburg.
Capidan, Th. 1925–35. *Meglenoromâni* ('The Megleno-Romanians'), vol. 1, *Istoria și graiul lor* ('Their History and Language'); vol. 2, *Literatura populară la meglenoromâni* ('Popular Literature among the Megleno-Romanians'); vol. 3, *Dicționar meglenoromân* ('Megleno-Romanian Dictionary'). Bucharest.
Caragiu-Marioțeanu, M. 1972. La romanité sub-danubienne: l'aroumain et le mégléno-roumain. *La Linguistique*, 8: 105–22.
Dahmen, W. 1989. Meglenorumänisch. In Holtus, G., Metzeltin, M. and Schmitt, C. (eds), *Lexikon der Romanistischen Linguistik*, Tübingen, vol. 3, 436–47.
Wild, B. 1983. *Meglenorumänischer Sprachatlas* ('Megleno-Romanian Linguistic Atlas'). Hamburg.

GLANVILLE PRICE

Megrel(ian) (see *Mingrelian* under *Caucasian languages. V. South Caucasian family*)

Messapic

An *Indo-European language spoken in the last centuries of the pre-Christian era in SE Italy, in an area corresponding approximately to modern Puglia, i.e. the 'heel' of Italy and its extension northwards (see map 10). It is known from over 300 inscriptions dating from the 6th to the 1st centuries BC, a few of them in the Greek alphabet but most of them in a characteristic Messapic alphabet derived from that of Greek. These are found in tombs, on coins, and on a variety of objects of bronze, stone, pottery, etc. They are mainly very brief, many of them consisting of only one or two words, and are insufficient to reveal much about the structure of the language. It used to be considered that Messapic had been introduced to the area at some undetermined period from across the Adriatic and that it was descended from *Illyrian or was even itself a form of Illyrian. However, given that we know even less about Illyrian than we do about Messapic, this is at best an unproven theory.

de Simone, C. 1964. Die messapischen Inschriften und ihre Chronologie ('The Messapic inscriptions and their chronology'). In Krahe, H. (ed.), *Die Sprache der Illyrier* ('The Language of the Illyrians'), Wiesbaden, vol. 2, 1–151, 215–361.
Orioles, V. 1981. Il messapico. In Campanile, E. (ed.), *Nuovi materiali per la ricerca indoeuropeistica*, Pisa, 139–60.
Parlangeli, O. and Santaro, C. 1978. Il meṣsapico. In Prosdocimi, A. L. (ed.), *Popoli e civiltà dell'Italia antica*, vol. 4, *Lingue e dialetti*, Rome, 913–47.

Mingrel(ian) (see under *Caucasian languages. V. South Caucasian family*)

Minoan
Virtually nothing is known of the language (sometimes referred to as 'Eteo-Cretan') spoken in Crete by the Minoans before the coming of the Greeks. It appears that a small number of words were borrowed from it by Greek, e.g. *thalassa* 'sea'. Minoan may be represented by one or more of the so far undeciphered scripts discovered in the island (see *Cretan pictographic script, *Linear A, *Phaistos disc).

Mirandese
A Leonese dialect (see under *Spanish) spoken by some 10,000–12,000 people in and around the town of Miranda do Douro in NE Portugal in the valley of the Douro (Duero) where it forms the border with Spain. It is taught to some extent in primary and secondary schools and moves are afoot to establish written norms and draw up a standardized grammar. (See also under *Portuguese, 'Dialects'.)

Moesian (see under *Daco-Thracian*)

Moksha (see under *Mordvinian*)

Moldavian
The name 'Moldavian language' (in Russian, молдавский язык 'moldavskii iazyk'; in Romanian, *limbă moldovenească*, or, in Cyrillic characters, лимбз молдовсняскз) was applied in the Soviet Union, as during earlier periods of Russian occupation of the area in question, to the *Romance language used in the Moldavian Soviet Socialist Republic (corresponding more or less to the formerly Romanian territory of Bessarabia, annexed by the Soviet Union in 1940). In reality, 'Moldavian' is nothing other than the *Romanian language as spoken in Moldavia, i.e. both east of the river Prut in Bessarabia (now the Republic of Moldova) and west of the Prut in that part of the former province that remains as part of Romania. Claims made in

the post-Second World War period by Soviet linguists that 'Moldavian' should be recognized as a distinct Romance language were not taken seriously by western scholars.

Under Soviet domination, the *Cyrillic alphabet was in use in the Moldavian SSR until the passing of a law on 31 August 1989 (i.e. before the break-up of the Soviet Union) proclaiming Moldavian as the official language of the Republic and the use of Latin script. Apart from a few lexical differences (mainly technical terms borrowed from Russian rather than, as in standard Romanian, from western languages), the written language was thenceforth indistinguishable from that in use in Romania and moves are afoot to harmonize the technical terminology of Moldova with that adopted in Romanian specialized dictionaries.

After the Republic of Moldova declared its independence of the Soviet Union in 1991, its Constitution (1994) declared that the official language was *limba moldovenească* 'the Moldavian language'. At the time of writing, moves to have this amended to *limba română* 'the Romanian language' have not yet succeeded.

Heitmann, K. 1989. Moldauisch. In Holtus, G., Metzeltin, M. and Schmitt, C. (eds), *Lexikon der Romanistischen Linguistik*, Tübingen, vol. 3, 508–21.

GLANVILLE PRICE

Monégasque

The national but not the official language (the official language being French) of the Principality of Monaco. Monégasque is basically a **Ligurian** dialect (see under *Italy. III. Northern Italy), introduced when the territory came under Genoese control in the 13th c. Arveiller (1967) estimated that the vocabulary was still two-thirds Ligurian, the remainder consisting mainly of borrowings from *Occitan (and more specifically from the Niçois dialect of Provençal), *Italian and *French. Very few speakers remain. The development of the Casino and the coming of the railway in the 1860s, as a result of which Monégasque speakers were overwhelmed by outsiders, led to a rapid decline in the use of Monégasque. Notari (1927) says that by that time there were no more than a few dozen speakers of 'authentic Monégasque' left. When Arveiller studied the language in the 1940s and 1950s, he could trace only 20 reliable informants of whom most were dead by 1961. Although in his book (1967) he is able to study in detail the lexicon and the phonology, he asserts that it was already too late to make a systematic study of the syntax.

A few Monégasque sentences are preserved in a notarial document of 1484 and a variety of words and phrases are quoted in letters (otherwise composed in French) written by Antoine Grimaldi, Prince of Monaco, between 1724 and 1731. Two brief texts in Monégasque exist in 19th-c. collections of Italian dialectal texts. All of these documents, together with a translation of the Parable of the Prodigal Son by Louis Notari, are reproduced by Arveiller (1967: 383–95).

There was no Monégasque literature until, in 1927, Notari published his *Santa Devota*, a poem of over 1,500 lines. A few pieces of prose and verse have since been produced by others.

Monégasque has virtually no public presence in the Principality other than on bilingual street-names introduced in the old city of Monaco on 'the Rock', but not in newer areas such as Monte Carlo, in the 1980s.

Arveiller, R. 1967. *Étude sur le parler de Monaco*. Monaco.
Barral, L. 1983. *Dictionnaire français–monégasque*. Monaco.
Frolla, L. 1960. *Grammaire monégasque*. Monaco.
—— 1963. *Dictionnaire monégasque–français*. Monaco.
Notari, L. 1927. *Santa Devota*. Monte Carlo.

GLANVILLE PRICE

Mordvinian (Mordvin)

One of the two members (the other being *Mari) of the Volga Finnic group of the *Finno-Ugrian languages.

Distribution

The Mordvinians are one of the most numerous of the Finno-Ugrian languages but, on the other hand, one of the most scattered. Of the 1,153,987 Mordvinian-speakers enumerated in 1989, only 28% lived within the boundaries of the Mordvinian Republic (capital, Saransk) (Russian Federation), where they accounted for about 37% of the population. A further 22% were to be found in the neighbouring districts of Penza, Ulyanovsk, Nizhny Novgorod and Saratov, and in the Chuvash Republic, and 23% on the other side of the Volga in the districts of Samara (Kuybyshev), Orenburg and Perm and in the Tatar and Bashkir Republics. The remaining 27% live scattered from Ukraine and Moscow to the Caucasus and from the Altay mountains to Khabarovsk and Sakhalin Island.

Dialects and literary languages

Two dialectal groupings can be distinguished, each with several subdivisions: (i) an eastern dialect, Erza, in and around the valley of the Sura, accounting for some two-thirds of the Mordvinians; (ii) a western dialect, Moksha, around the river Moksha. The dialectal separation of the two groups is reckoned to date from the 7th or 8th c. As a result of later migrations, mixed dialects emerged. Differences in phonetic structure, morphology and syntax between the two main dialectal groupings are such that intercommunication is difficult and for this reason two standard languages have been created. It was only in 1920 that Mordvinian became a written language. Zahar Dorofeyev (1890–1952) is seen as the founder of Mordvinian literature. Other writers are Dmitriy Morskoy (1897–1956), Mihail Bezborodov (1907–35) and Tyimofey Raptanov (1906–36). There is also contemporary literature of note and two literary magazines are published, *Moksha* in the dialect of the same name and *Syatko* in the Erza dialect.

Collinder, B. 1957. Mordvin. In Id., *Survey of the Uralic Languages*, Stockholm, 227–46.
Keresztes, L. 1985. Kriterien zur Klassifizierung des Mordvinischen ('Criteria for the classification of Mordvinian'). In Veenker, W. (ed.) *Dialectologia Uralica. Materialien des ersten internationalen*

Symposions zur Dialektologie der uralischen Sprachen, Wiesbaden, 173–87.

—— 1990. *Chrestomathia Morduinica*. Budapest.

WOLFGANG GRELLER

Mountain Tatar, see *Karachay-Balkar*

Mozarabic

The name 'Mozarabic' is given to those varied descendants of popular Latin which were spoken in the Middle Ages (often bilingually with *Arabic) in Islamic Spain, or in territories recently reconquered from Islamic Spain by one or other of the Christian kingdoms of Spain. These varieties were spoken not only by Mozarabs (Christians living under Moorish rule), but also by Muslims and Jews living in the same territories at the same time.

Since writing in Mozarabic was rare, no standard language emerged, and there must have been wide differences between the Mozarabic speech of such widely separated cities as, say, Valencia, Cordoba and Lisbon. Some of this variation is observable in the surviving sources of information, which consist of: *Ibero-Romance poems written in Arabic or *Hebrew script and incorporated into longer poetic compositions in the Arabic or Hebrew languages; words and word-lists, written in Arabic script, included in Arabic treatises, especially those by herbalists; certain medieval and early modern Arabic–Latin and Arabic–Spanish dictionaries, in which the Hispano-Arabic component reveals borrowings from Mozarabic; place-names which resisted modification towards the incoming prestige languages after the Reconquest; and certain post-Reconquest legal documents.

Because of close contact with Arabic, the high-prestige official language, Mozarabic was especially prone to borrowing from this source, but lacks the loans from *French and *Occitan which passed into northern varieties of Ibero-Romance.

Mozarabic varieties were probably mutually comprehensible with the varieties of *Portuguese, Castilian (see *Spanish) and *Catalan with which they came into contact after the Reconquest of each area where Mozarabic was spoken. They were then probably modified, feature by feature, in the direction of the newly dominant language, disappearing as separately identifiable dialects by the 13th c. Some have argued that, during this process of absorption, Mozarabic exercised influence on the expanding northern languages, but the only clear evidence of such influence belongs to the field of vocabulary, where small numbers of Mozarabisms have been recognized in Spanish, etc. It is also likely that many of the Arabisms present in Spanish, Portuguese and Catalan reached these languages through the mediation of Mozarabic.

Entwistle, W. J. 1936. Mozarabic dialects. In Id., *The Spanish Language, together with Portuguese, Catalan and Basque*, London, 111–25.

Galmés de Fuentes, Á. 1983. *Dialectología mozárabe*. Madrid.

RALPH PENNY

Mukhad (see *Rutul* under *Caucasian languages. IV. North-East Caucasian family*)

Mysian (see under *Daco-Thracian*)

N

Nakh languages (see under *Caucasian languages. III. North Central Caucasian family*)

Nenets

Nenets (otherwise known as Yurak) is a member of the northern group of the ***Samoyedic languages** and is the only Samoyedic language spoken in Europe. Within Europe, where the majority of speakers live, it is found mainly in the Nenets National District (main town, Nar'yan Mar) in the Archangel Region. Further east, its territory extends across the tundra region of western Siberia as far as the lower Yenisey.

Although its small number of speakers (34,665 in 1989) are spread over a huge territory approximately the size of Scandinavia, the Nenets language has remained astonishingly homogeneous. The reason for this is to be seen in the nomadic way of life of the Nenets. Two main dialects are distinguished: (i) Tundra Nenets, the only one to be spoken west of the Urals; and (ii) Forest Nenets. The differences are primarily phonetic but there are also lexical differences, mainly in respect of loan-words (of ***Russian**, ***Komi** or Ostyak origin).

Our earliest knowledge of the language dates from the beginning of the 18th c. (word-lists collected by Philip Johann Strahlenberg, Johann Eberhard Fischer and others). Since 1937 an adaptation of the ***Cyrillic** alphabet has been used but earlier texts, consisting largely of folk tales collected by western travellers, were written in the Latin alphabet.

Hajdu, P. 1968. *Samoyed Peoples and Languages*, 2nd edn. Bloomington, IN.
—— 1989. *Chrestomathia Samoiedica*. Budapest.

WOLFGANG GRELLER

Nogay

A member of the Aralo-Caspian subgroup of the Kipchak or NW ***Turkic languages**. A few small groups of Nogay live in the northern Crimea near Krasnoperekopsk but the greatest number are found in the Chechen-Ingush and Daghestan Republics in the northern Caucasus where they inhabit the so-called 'Nogayskaya Steppe' in the north-easternmost part of these territories between the plains of the Kuma river and the Caucasus mountains. Nogay are also found as far afield as Moldavia and in the Constanţa district in the Romanian Dobruja. Some 75,181 speakers were enumerated in 1989 on the territory of the former Soviet Union. The Romanian census of 1977, which did not distinguish between Crimean Tatars and Nogay, enumerated 23,107 'Tatars' (on the confusion surrounding the use of the ethnonym 'Tatar', see under *Tatar).

Nogay shows strong signs of influence from other languages, mainly *Slavonic and Cherkess (see **Circassian** under *Caucasian languages. II. North-West Caucasian family). Its closest relative is *Kazakh. The language is usually divided into three dialects: (i) Kara-Nogay or Black Nogay, in the south-east; (ii) central Nogay, which is the basis of the standard language; (iii) Ak-Nogay or White Nogay, a somewhat archaic NW dialect. The dialect of the Crimean Nogay and the Nogay of the Dobruja are close to Kara-Nogay.

'Nogay' was originally the Mongolian name, meaning 'dog', for the people in question, probably since the dog was their totem. The Nogay Tatars seem to have originated from a tribal group under the Emir Nogay of the Golden Horde (*c*.1290). Up to the 19th c. they lived all over the Ponto-Caspian steppes.

Nogay has been a written language only since 1940 when an adaptation of the *Cyrillic alphabet was introduced.

Menges, K. H. 1959. Die aralo-kaspische Gruppe ('The Aralo-Caspian group'). In Deny, J. et al. (eds), *Philologiae Turcicae Fundamenta*, Wiesbaden, 434–89.

Schöpflin, G. 1993. The Turkic peoples of Romania. In Bainbridge, M. (ed.), *The Turkic Peoples of the World*, London and New York, 201–7.

WOLFGANG GRELLER

Norman-French, see *Anglo-Norman*

Norn

Norn was a member of the North Germanic or *Scandinavian subgroup of the *Germanic languages. It was spoken in Orkney, Shetland and in various parts of mainland Scotland.

Definition

While there is little doubt about the origin of the term 'Norn' (it is a reflex of ON *norrœnn* 'Norwegian, West Norse', *norrœna* 'Norwegian, West Norse language'), its use since the first recorded occurrence in *c*.1485 has varied, and it therefore requires definition. Scandinavian speech was brought to the Northern Isles, the Hebrides and parts of the mainland of Scotland by 9th-c. Viking settlers, who came principally from Norway. 'Norn' seems at one time to have been applied indiscriminately to the various speech communities the settlers established, but as their form or forms of language gradually died out in the Hebrides and on the mainland (possibly between the 13th and the 15th centuries) the term came to be restricted almost entirely to the Scandinavian of Orkney and Shetland (although 'Caithness Norn' has made an appearance in the work of one or two modern scholars). Since so little is known of Hebridean and mainland-Scottish Scandinavian speech, this article will only deal with Norn in its Northern Isles context. Norn will mean the spoken Scandinavian of Orkney and Shetland and its written manifestations. All other senses will be excluded, including the confusing usage whereby forms of Orkney or Shetland dialect heavily impregnated with Scandinavian words may be referred to as Norn.

Origins

It is uncertain what linguistic situation confronted the Norse settlers when they first arrived in the Northern Isles in about AD 800, though it seems likely that the principal language was *Pictish (possibly a non-*Indo-European language, but according to some a form of P-Celtic (see *Celtic languages)). In the course of a century or two, however, the settlers' form of western Scandinavian seems to have become completely dominant, wiping out virtually all traces of earlier languages. Orkney and Shetland place-names, for example (with the exception of recently introduced Scots names), are almost entirely Scandinavian in origin.

Written sources

The dearth of information on the speech of the indigenous inhabitants of the Northern Isles is to some extent paralleled by the scarcity of written sources from the period of Scandinavian ascendancy. Orkney can boast 52 runic inscriptions (see *Runes) of Viking-Age or medieval origin, but 33 of these are found in the prehistoric chambered cairn of Maeshowe. Most if not all of the Maeshowe inscriptions are probably the work of visiting Norwegians, who seem to have forced their way into the mound some time in the early 1150s. Shetland is even less well endowed: only seven runic artefacts have so far been discovered in the islands. Maeshowe aside, the inscriptions are almost all brief or fragmentary; few of them can be satisfactorily dated, and only some seven or eight have yielded anything approaching a comprehensible text. The corpus thus provides few clues to linguistic development in the islands. Where interpretation is reasonably certain the language cannot be shown to be different from that in contemporary inscriptions in Norway.

Scandinavian-language documents in the Roman alphabet which either give an Orkney or Shetland locality as their place of origin or whose Northern Isles provenance can be safely inferred from the contents are also few in number. Orkney has four spanning the years 1329–c.1425 and Shetland eleven, the earliest from 1299 and the latest from 1586. The linguistic affiliation of these documents is disputed, but if they do contain local forms they are certainly few and far between: what is reflected is in the main simply the changing written idiom of Norway.

Decline and late attestations

Norn had thus not achieved the status of a literary medium by the time of the pledging of the Northern Isles to King James III of Scotland in 1468–9. After this, it was too late. Even before the pledging, steady immigration from the Scottish lowlands (especially into Orkney) and the succession of the Scots-speaking Sinclairs to the Earldom of Orkney (1379) had ensured that *Scots would ultimately become the dominant tongue. After the pledging, the position of Norn seems to have declined rapidly. By the 17th c., most if not all Orkneymen and Shetlanders were probably bilingual, and Norn had become very much a language of work and the home.

Our knowledge of Norn stems chiefly from brief comments in the accounts of travellers or in general descriptions of the Northern Isles. Most authors offer only passing references, and it is usually unclear on what their information is based. However, one of their number, George Low, a keen and reliable observer, not only described in detail the linguistic situation he found on the outlying island of Foula during a visit to Shetland in 1774, but appended three specimens of Norn: the Lord's Prayer, a list of some 30 everyday words and a 35-stanza ballad (see Low 1879: 104–14). Low himself did not understand Norn, and seems not to have known any other form of Scandinavian, but it is nevertheless possible to make good sense of most of what he wrote down. His little collection now constitutes our principal source of information on the language while it was still remembered and possibly used by native speakers. Low's account of what he observed on Foula unfortunately does not allow us to draw firm conclusions about the state of Norn at the time. His account can be read to mean that it was a living language, but can just as easily imply that it was only dimly remembered, not having been spoken for some years. The character of Low's specimens of Foula Norn is clearly west Scandinavian. The phonology and morphology seem to be most closely related to *Faroese, west *Norwegian dialects, and *Icelandic – in that order. There is occasional evidence of interference from Scots, but its significance is hard to gauge.

The only other continuous piece of Norn to emerge from the period when it may still have been a living language is an Orkney version of the Lord's Prayer (printed in Wallace 1700: 68–9; no manuscript version exists). This, as well as the odd snatches of Norn and large numbers of words of Norn origin, collected in Shetland and Orkney in the late 19th and early 20th c. respectively, exhibits a phonologically less firmly west Scandinavian type of language than the Foula material. There thus seems to have been dialectal variation within Shetland. There is also slight evidence of linguistic divergence between Shetland and Orkney.

Barnes, M. P. 1984. Orkney and Shetland Norn. In Trudgill, P. (ed.), *Language in the British Isles*, Cambridge, 352–66.

—— 1994. *The Runic Inscriptions of Maeshowe, Orkney* (Runrön 8). Uppsala.

—— 1996. The origin, development and decline of Orkney and Shetland Norn. In Nielsen, H. F. and Schøsler, L. (eds), *The Origins and Development of Emigrant Languages (Proceedings from the Second Rasmus Rask Colloquium)*, Odense, 169–99.

Hægstad, M. 1900. *Hildinakvadet* ('The Hildina Ballad'; Videnskabsselskabets Skrifter. II. Historisk-filosofiske Klasse, 1900, no. 2). Christiania.

Jakobsen, J. 1928–32. *An Etymological Dictionary of the Norn Language in Shetland*, 2 vols. London (reprinted Lerwick 1985).

Low, G. 1879. *A Tour through the Islands of Orkney and Schetland*. Kirkwall (reprinted Inverness [no date]).

Marwick, H. 1929. *The Orkney Norn*. London.
Wallace, J. 1700. *An Account of the Islands of Orkney*. London.

MICHAEL P. BARNES

Norse, Old

Old Norse (ON) was a member of the North Germanic or *Scandinavian subgroup
of the *Germanic languages. It was spoken in the Viking Age and the early
medieval period in Denmark, Norway, Sweden and in the Norse colonies that arose
as a result of Viking expansion (*c.* AD 800–1000) – principally: the Greenland settlements, Iceland, Faroe, Shetland, Orkney, the Hebrides, coastal areas of mainland
Scotland, Man, coastal areas of Ireland (especially the towns), north-west England
and the Danelaw, Normandy, coastal areas of Finland and Estonia, the developing
Russian towns.

Definition

Since ON is a stage in the development of the Scandinavian languages, the dates
given for the beginning and end of its period of existence can vary, depending on
the criteria adopted by individual scholars. Runic inscriptions (see *Runes)
constitute our chief source of direct evidence for linguistic change in Scandinavia
c. AD 200–1150, and though these often cannot be dated more closely than to within
a century (if that), their cumulative testimony is that a form of language not unlike
the ON we know from manuscript texts of the 12th c. and later was in use in at least
parts of Denmark, Norway and Sweden by *c.*700. This language is sometimes
known as Common Scandinavian, on the assumption that it was subject to little, if
any, local variation, but many scholars operate with a binary division into East and
West Norse, some of the distinguishing characteristics of which seem to go back to
at least AD 700.

It is probably sensible to set the date for the end of ON to the period when the
inflectional system of the Scandinavian languages began to show signs of simplification – in Denmark in the 12th c., in Sweden towards the middle of the 14th, and in
Norway a generation or so later. This criterion will not do for the Norse colonies,
however. In Iceland the inflectional system remained more or less as it was, and here
the Reformation (1541), which signified a change of culture, forms a convenient cut-
off point. Records from the other areas to which ON was exported are too sparse to
allow judgements about stages of linguistic development to be made. In Faroe,
Shetland and Orkney, where ON became the sole medium of communication, and
forms of Scandinavian thus endured – in Faroe to the present day, in Shetland and
Orkney until *c.*1800 – arbitrary cut-off points have to be selected. In Faroe the
Reformation constitutes a natural break since the lack of Reformation literature in
Faroese was probably in large measure the reason why Danish thereafter became the
written medium of the islands – a situation that persisted until the 19th c. The succession to the Earldom of Orkney of the *Scots-speaking Sinclairs in 1379 seems a
convenient date at which to set the end of the ON period in the Northern Isles. It is

probably from that time on that Scots began to gain a firm foothold, a situation that led to the decline (doubtless with associated linguistic interference) and ultimate demise of Scandinavian speech in both Orkney and Shetland. In Finland and Estonia the situation is more complex in that there seem to have been further waves of immigration from Sweden after the Viking Age, and an unbroken tradition of Scandinavian speech is not guaranteed. If a date for the end of the ON period in these areas is to be given, it can hardly be other than the one suggested for Sweden – but the concept is purely notional. Elsewhere it is simplest to view the end of ON as coinciding with the date at which Scandinavian speech died out – in Normandy probably after a few generations, in Russia perhaps in the late 11th or the 12th c., in England seemingly in the late 12th c. but possibly somewhat later, in Ireland perhaps early in the 13th c., in Man, the Scottish coastal areas and the Hebrides probably in the 14th c., but conceivably as late as the beginning of the 15th, and in Greenland with the extinction of the Norse colony early in the 16th c.

The problem of defining ON is exacerbated by the differing ways in which the term is used. In the foregoing the net has been cast as widely as possible. To some, however, ON is simply the spoken and written language of Norway and Iceland *c*.1000–1350, i.e. 'classical' ON, the language of Eddaic and scaldic verse and of the sagas. To the extent to which it is useful to distinguish the latter form of language, some term other than ON should preferably be employed: a generic is needed for the totality of Viking-Age and early medieval Scandinavian, and the designations of the earliest observable products of Scandinavian dialect branching, 'East Norse' and 'West Norse', are based on the assumption that both are (Old) Norse.

ON as here defined was clearly a multi-faceted language. It grew out of Primitive or Early Scandinavian, the earliest demonstrable form of North Germanic, which was itself doubtless not dialect-free. The uniformity there can appear to be is probably an illusion, for the signs of linguistic variety stand in more or less direct proportion to the availability of source material. It is in any case hard to think that people living as far apart as, for example, Russia, Greenland and Ireland – most of them subject to differing linguistic influences – could have maintained uniformity of speech for very long.

Runic inscriptions and complementary evidence

Although runic inscriptions constitute our chief source of evidence for ON in the period before the Roman alphabet was employed for writing the vernaculars (Iceland and Norway up to *c*.1150, Denmark and Sweden *c*.1250), these are complemented (a) by Eddaic and scaldic verse (written down post-1150, but some of it much older), (b) by personal and place-names in the works of foreign authors (notably Anglo-Saxon and Irish) and in works written in Latin in Scandinavia (post *c*.1100), and (c) by loan-words in other languages. Runes were an epigraphic script and were used for carving memorial inscriptions (on stone), brief messages (mostly on wood or bone), magic formulas and incantations (on different types of material including metal), and casual graffiti (on anything that came to hand). By nature runic inscriptions are laconic, but most consist of at least one sentence, and many are somewhat longer. They can thus provide information on phonology, morphology and syntax. Even after the Roman alphabet was adopted for writing the vernaculars, people continued to use runes, in some areas until well after the end of the ON period. These later inscriptions also have value as linguistic source material because of the relatively orthophonic nature of runic writing. Eddaic and scaldic verse likewise provide large numbers of complete sentences, but their language is very stylized and the age of individual poems and verses can be hard to determine. Other sources of information on pre-manuscript ON rarely offer more than isolated words, whose form is often influenced by the fact that they are preserved in foreign-language environments.

Use of the Roman alphabet

The Roman alphabet came to the Scandinavian-speaking peoples with organized Christianity. When and to what extent the Norsemen who settled in already Christianized areas learnt to use Roman script is unclear, but there is scarcely any evidence that they employed it for writing their own language, though a number of them left behind runic inscriptions in ON. Denmark became Christian in the later half of the 10th c., Iceland and Norway *c*.1000, and Sweden probably at some point in the 11th c. The Danes and the Swedes seem to have been slow to adopt the Roman alphabet for writing the vernacular, whereas there is evidence that the Norwegians and Icelanders, the former, at least, apparently under Anglo-Saxon influence, began to compile manuscripts in ON using the Roman alphabet as early as the second half of the 11th c.

Literary texts

ON was the bearer of an extensive and sophisticated literary culture. Early (i.e. 11th-c.) writings appear chiefly to have been of a legal and religious nature – oral laws committed to parchment, saints' lives, homilies, etc. It is not until the 12th c. that there is evidence for wider literary activity in the vernacular (historical, scientific, diplomatic), and only in the 13th c. does saga literature really come into its own. Vernacular writing in Denmark and Sweden followed much the same pattern, though some 100–150 years later. Here, however, there was a rather greater dependence on foreign models and originals, and no native literature to compare with the (mainly Icelandic) sagas.

Foreign influences

Prior to the advent of Christianity, little foreign influence can be seen in ON, but thereafter Scandinavia became part of medieval European culture, and this left numerous traces on the language, particularly in the form of loan-words. Later there was to be even heavier influence from Low German, the language of the Hanseatic traders, but that marks the end of the ON period and the beginning of the road to modern Scandinavian. Iceland and Faroe were much less exposed to Low German, and that is one of the main causes of the split into mainland and island branches which characterizes Scandinavian in the post-ON period.

Barnes, M. P. 1993. Language. In Pulsiano, P. and Wolf, K. (eds), *Medieval Scandinavia. An Encyclopedia*, New York, 376–8.

Gordon, E. V. 1957. *An Introduction to Old Norse*. London.

Haugen, E. 1976. *The Scandinavian Languages. An Introduction to Their History*. London.

Hreinn Benediktsson 1965. *Early Icelandic Script*. Reykjavík.

Jansson, S. B. F. 1987. *Runes in Sweden*. [Stockholm].

Moltke, E. 1985. *Runes and Their Origin. Denmark and Elsewhere*. Copenhagen.

Valfells, S. and Cathey, J. 1981. *Old Icelandic. An Introductory Course*. London.

MICHAEL P. BARNES

North Picenian

North Picenian is the label attached to the language of about four inscriptions found near the Adriatic coast, approximately between Rimini and Ancona (see map 10). It should not be confused with *South Picenian. The most important document is the sandstone stele from Novilara, which dates from the 6th or 5th c. BC. On one side, the stele shows an inscription, in the *Etruscan alphabet (see fig. 6), of nearly 50 words. On the other side is carved what looks like a hunting scene. Not a single word or grammatical feature has received a convincing explanation; hence none of the various claims that North Picenian is a non-*Indo-European, non-Italic Indo-European or *Italic Indo-European language can be endorsed.

Poultney, J. W. 1979. The language of the Northern Picene inscriptions. *Journal of Indo-European Studies*, 7:49–64.

PETER SCHRIJVER

Norwegian

Norwegian forms, together with *Icelandic and *Faroese, the western division of the *Scandinavian group of languages, collectively the northern branch of *Germanic. Norwegian is spoken by some 4.2 million inhabitants of Norway, and by Norwegian emigrants and guest-workers abroad, now principally in Sweden, Denmark and the USA. There are two written forms, Nynorsk and Bokmål (see below), before 1929 known respectively as Landsmål and Riksmål.

From Old Norse to Middle Norwegian

The transition from Old *Norse to Middle Norwegian is generally dated to *c*.1350, and from Middle Norwegian to Modern Norwegian to *c*.1536. Both dates are of immediate political rather than linguistic significance, and represent stages in the decline of Norwegian as a medium of written communication. Nevertheless the transition from Old Norse to Middle Norwegian in the spoken language was marked. In Old Norse stressed syllables could be either long or short: in Middle Norwegian they became invariably long. Significant dialectal differences arose from whether the vowel or following consonant was lengthened. In addition the complex inflections of Old Norse were greatly simplified in Middle Norwegian, even in conservative dialects in the interior of the country. The loss of many inflections resulted in a more fixed syntax. The subjunctive was largely lost.

Decline of the written language

The economic base of medieval aristocratic society in Norway was terminally weakened by the end of the 13th c., and from 1319 the country found itself as the minor partner in a series of political unions with Sweden, Denmark, or both. The political centre of the country moved outside its borders, and from 1389 there was no longer a Norwegian Chancery in Oslo. None the less Norwegian was used in correspondence from the monarch and Chancery in Copenhagen to Norwegians until 1450. From 1478 all such correspondence was conducted in *Danish. Norwegian survived at lower levels of secular administration until *c.*1500. One factor in its relative longevity was the protracted use of the laws written down in Old Norse during the reign of Håkon V (1299–1319). Norwegian vanished from use in the Catholic Church only in 1510; in that year the last Norwegian-born archbishop died. Letters in something recognizable as Norwegian from peasants survive from some time into the 16th c. By far the greatest part of the extant material in Middle Norwegian has been published in the series *Diplomatarium Norvegicum*.

Norwegian society, already in decline before 1350, was dealt a fatal blow by the Black Death, in which a third of the population perished, large areas of the country were abandoned and the vernacular literate learning of the priesthood was largely lost. Given the enduring strength of the Old Norse literary tradition in the 13th c., the extreme paucity of original literature in Norwegian in the 14th is remarkable. The increasingly dialectal nature of writing in the 14th and 15th centuries is evidence of the gradual breakdown of the written tradition, of central authority generally, and bears witness to extensive foreign influence. From the 14th c. foreign trade was controlled by the Low German speakers of the Hanseatic League, and what was left of the Norwegian aristocracy became increasingly intermarried with Swedes. In the 15th c. royal policy deliberately transplanted Danes and north Germans to administer Norway. Cultural and translation loans and Low German affixes rapidly became established in Middle Norwegian writing, which was soon replaced by often heavily Germanized Danish. Much of this Low German/Danish material entered the dialects, particularly those of the towns and of the areas facing Denmark or otherwise in particularly close trading relations with Hanseatic and urban settlements. Isolated inner fjord and mountain areas, on the other hand, preserved more of the lexical material and morphological structure of Norwegian. The consequences for Norwegian of borrowing from Low German have been profound, comparable in scale and effect to the impact of Norman French on English.

Literature

As a literary medium Norwegian is of some significance, although the three best-known literary Norwegians all wrote essentially in Danish: Holberg (1684–1754), Ibsen (1828–1906) and Hamsun (1859–1952). The lyrical tradition has always been particularly strong in Nynorsk; Olav H. Hauge (1908–94) was a major 20th-c.

European poet, although little known abroad. Nynorsk derives a particular lyrical expressiveness from its concreteness, from the unsullied lexical resources of the dialects, and from its easy accommodation of the rhythms of speech. Nynorsk has no strong dramatic tradition, although paradoxically the best equipped, newest, largest and most innovative theatre in Oslo stages works exclusively in Nynorsk. There have been few great epic writers in Nynorsk: exceptions were Olav Duun (1876–1939) and Kristoffer Uppdal (1878–1961). As befits its function as a perpetual alternative, Nynorsk has more often been the medium of the picaresque (Kjartan Fløgstad (1944–)), the experimental (Rolf Sagen (1940–)), the early Edvard Hoem (1950–) and the critical. The dramatic tradition in Bokmål has never recaptured the grandeurs of Ibsen. Neither are there many significant poets writing in Bokmål; exceptions are Jan Erik Vold (1939–) and Rolf Jacobsen (1907–94). Bokmål has had an impressively strong prose tradition, from the early feminist novels of Sigrid Undset (1882–1949) to the Socialist Realism and Post-Realism of Dag Solstad (1941–).

Script

Writers on parchment and vellum during the Middle Norwegian period used Latin script. This had been introduced from England at some point during the mid-11th c.; the Modern Norwegian alphabet consists of the 26 standard Latin characters with three additions, <æ, ø, å>. There is limited use of diacritics. Runic writing had been practised in Norway from at least the 4th c. AD, and survived as 'everyman's alphabet' (Haugen 1976a: 191) into the Middle Norwegian period (see **Runes**). Runic writing survived into the 18th c. in archaic communities such as Oppdal (and the neighbouring region in Sweden), although in general little was produced after the 14th c. A Swedish manual of runology appeared in 1599, after which time runic writing may be the product of indigenous tradition or of book-learning.

Dialects

Topography and traditionally poor internal communications ensured that the dialectal differences which arose during the Old Norse and Middle Norwegian periods grew into modern times. Since the Second World War, increased geographical and social mobility have tended as elsewhere towards the emergence of regional spoken variants and of mixed-dialect speakers. Use of dialect in educated speech is normal and expected in Norway. Periodic attempts in the last century and a half to introduce the notion of a standard spoken language have failed. As early as the 1870s legislation enshrined the right of young schoolchildren to be taught in a spoken form adapted to their own dialect.

The central dialectal division is between east and west Norwegian. The eastern area covers all of SE and east Norway, the Midland mountain areas to the east of the watershed, and Trøndelag with the northernmost part of west Norway. These three areas supply the three principal subvariants of the dialect. West Norwegian is spoken in all of west Norway west of the watershed and along the south coast to a point about 90 km NW of Kristiansand. The dialects of north Norway also belong to the western group. Each of these two western groups contains three main subvariants. Dialectal differences within each of the two main groups are great, and are readily apprehended by native speakers.

Norwegian is, apart from *Swedish, the only indigenous European tonal language. Phonetically identical words are distinguished semantically by means of accent, called 'one' and 'two'. Accent one (low–high) is historically mono-syllabic, accent two (high–low–high) polysyllabic. All Norwegian dialects make the distinction with the exception of an area around Bergen, another in the extreme south of northern Norway and a larger area in the north of northern Norway. The contours of the accents vary considerably between dialects. In most of Trøndelag a so-called 'circumflex' form of accent two has developed in monosyllables which were historically polysyllabic, but were shortened by the loss of final unstressed syllables.

Revival

As a written medium Norwegian died out and was replaced by Danish in the Middle Norwegian period. The history of Modern Norwegian writing has two strands: the attempt to resuscitate Norwegian, and the attempt to Norwegianize written Danish.

The idea that the lost Norwegian written language could somehow be excavated from living peasant speech led to sporadic pre-scientific attempts from the 17th c. onwards to compile glossaries of conservative dialects. National Romanticism, spurred on by Norway's re-emergence as an administrative entity in 1814 as it was transferred from Denmark to union with Sweden, stimulated debate of the language issue. Three basic positions emerged. One accepted that Norwegian was historically redundant, and sought to cultivate the civilizing graft of linguistic union with Denmark. Alternatively, Norwegian could act as a lexical resource to produce a Dano-Norwegian hybrid for use in Norway. Thirdly, a norm could be created on the basis of one of the more archaic dialects to restore the language to its pristine splendour. Characteristically, none of these solutions addressed itself to the needs of a rapidly expanding and increasingly immiserated peasantry which, since the introduction of obligatory confirmation in 1739, had been forced by the State to literacy in a foreign language, Danish.

Nynorsk

It took a brilliant peasant autodidact, Ivar Aasen (1813–96), to formulate a written norm based on contemporary peasant speech. This he called 'Landsmaal', an ambiguous term which Aasen intended to mean 'national language' but which can be wilfully misunderstood as 'country language'. Aasen saw the language as a nec-essary precondition for the non-revolutionary emancipation of the mass of the people, but he skilfully exploited National Romantic rhetoric to win bourgeois sup-port for his project, at least in its earlier phases. The foundations of his work are the first (largely descriptive) and second (normative) editions of his Norwegian gram-mar (1848, 1864) and Norwegian–Danish dictionary (1850, 1873). Aasen published the first book in Landsmål in 1853, *Prøver af Landsmaalet i Norge* ('Specimens of the Norwegian National Language'). This contained texts in disparate dialects as well as normalized texts, ranging from folk tales and proverbs to translations of Shakespeare and Schiller. Aasen was also active as a dramatist, essayist and poet. A broadly based social movement grew up around Aasen's norm from 1868, and it was soon adopted by a number of belletristic writers, particularly those with a rural background. Even in its infancy Aasen's Landsmål was widely modified according to the dialect background of the writer. It was perceived by many as archaic and too closely based on west Norwegian; these valid criticisms can be explained by Aasen's own background, by the role he gave Old Norse when reconstructing supra-dialectal forms, and by coincidence. In 1885 Parliament gave Landsmål notionally equal official status with Danish. As during the National Romantic period, Landsmål benefited from its 'national' credentials at a moment of crisis and con-comitant bourgeois identity politics. Theoretical equality had far-reaching consequences and underpinned the subsequent introduction of Landsmål into all areas of public life. Orthographical reforms in 1901, 1917 and 1938 and the intro-duction of a complicated system of optional forms made Landsmål increasingly accessible to inhabitants of east and north Norway, and led, at least temporarily, to an increase in the number of writers of Landsmål (later Nynorsk) there. In 1892 the use of Landsmål as a medium of education in schools was permitted, and in 1906 an organization was established to propagate the use of Landsmål and defend the rights of its adherents. In 1930 a law was passed which gave the individual the right to receive from public authorities correspondence in whichever form of Norwegian s/he had addressed them.

Bokmål

Bokmål (known until 1929 as Riksmål) grew directly out of the Danish written tradi-tion. The folk-tale collectors Asbjørnsen and Moe Norwegianized the syntax of written Danish as early as the 1840s. The principal theorist of Riksmål was Knud Knudsen (1812–95), whose orthophonist reforms were based on the Norwegianized phonology of Danish as it was spoken by the bourgeoisie of Kristiania (later Oslo). In 1862 the first minor orthographical reform of Danish in Norway took place, partly as a result of Knudsen's agitation. By 1886 Knudsen was proposing Norwegianisms so radical that even today they would not be acceptable in Bokmål. During the latter half of the 19th c. most writing in Norway remained resolutely Danish. Social and cultural conservatism were responsible, as was the literary common market with Denmark. All major Norwegian writers published there, and generally sold better there than at home. Pressure to Norwegianize the written language in the spirit (if not the letter) of Knudsen's proposals came from schools, particularly after the publi-cation of Nordahl Rolfsen's reader in 1892. This contained Norwegianisms the children were not themselves permitted to use in written work. In 1907 the first substantial orthographical reform of Riksmål took place in an idealogical climate fired by Norway's newly gained independence. The reforms of 1917 and 1938 were both motivated by the aspiration ultimately of merging the two written forms of

Norwegian. They were set in train by Liberal and Socialist governments respectively, and both explicitly held up Norwegian popular speech as the arbiter of normalization. This caused few problems in Nynorsk, except in relation to marginal traditionalist groups. The 1938 reform of Bokmål, however, caused some upheaval, delayed until the early 1950s by the German occupation and post-war reconstruction period. Major protests, marches, book-burnings and campaigns to 'correct' school textbooks ensued, especially in the more salubrious western suburbs of Oslo; the protesters found the new forms intolerably plebeian. For the first time, historically Danish forms found in bourgeois Norwegian speech were forbidden in children's school writing. The Labour government took fright, and in 1959 a new norm for use in school textbooks was produced for both forms of Norwegian which implicitly abandoned the project of merger.

Bokmål has, like Nynorsk, a broad pallet of alternative forms. Unlike Nynorsk, Bokmål has a natural geographical and social centre, the middle class of Oslo and SE Norwegian towns. The economic and political influence of this group, and the relative centralization of Norwegian cultural life, produced an ascendant conservative variety of Bokmål with a relatively stable norm. More popular forms of Bokmål are relegated to imaginative writing. In current terminology, 'riksmål' is used to denote the most conservative variety of Bokmål; this contains a number of forms banned from the official orthography between 1938 and 1981.

Language policy

Today Nynorsk and Bokmål have equal legal status in Norway, at least in theory. Around 25% of Norwegians now living received their primary education in Nynorsk, but the number using it habitually is lower, despite the fact that 70–75% of the population speak dialects more closely represented by Nynorsk than by Bokmål. It is the public sector, where language legislation applies, which ensures the continued use of Nynorsk. In primary schools the voters in each school's catchment area can decide by referendum what the main form taught in the school will be (see map 13). Provision exists for parallel classes taught in the other form if a minimum of ten children can be found for the new class. School language referenda are fiercely fought. At present 17% of children have Nynorsk as their main form, 83% Bokmål; the minority is heavily concentrated in west Norway and in the mountain areas of east Norway which abut it. The percentage of children taught in Nynorsk declined from a maximum of 34.1% in 1944 to 16.4% in 1977, but has now increased slightly and stabilized due mainly to parallel classes in towns in west Norway. The first ever Nynorsk class in Oslo started in 1993. Textbooks for upper schools are supposed to be available in either form or, increasingly, are produced in a single edition in both. The principle that all public bodies should be functionally 'bilingual' in Norwegian necessitates the teaching of both forms to all children from the age of 15. From the same age pupils choose whether Nynorsk or Bokmål is to be their personal main form.

Local authorities decide whether they wish to receive correspondence from the central administration in Nynorsk or Bokmål, or to classify themselves as

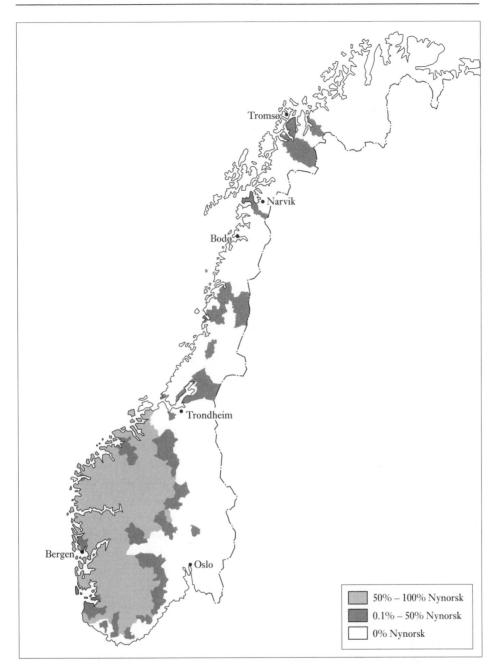

Map 13   Nynorsk and Bokmål in Norway. The map shows the percentage of schools in which the medium of instruction in 1991 was Nynorsk. In the great majority of other schools (and, in the south, in all other schools), the medium of instruction will have been Bokmål, but in some schools in the north it could have been Sámi or Finnish.

linguistically 'neutral'. By 1993, 169 authorities had opted for Bokmål, 115 for Nynorsk, and 118 were neutral.

Around a third of all newspapers are registered as using Nynorsk, two-thirds Bokmål. The position of Nynorsk is strongest in the local press in west and central Norway, less so elsewhere.

Regional newspapers often contain a mixture of Nynorsk and Bokmål, whilst national media are dominated by Bokmål. The State broadcasting organization NRK is bound by Act of Parliament to provide at least 25% of its programming in either form of Norwegian; in fact well over 80% of broadcasts in recent years have been in Bokmål.

The private and commercial sectors of the economy are dominated completely by Bokmål, except for the cooperative movement in west Norway. Language legislation has never applied to the private sector.

Since 1952 an official State body (*Norsk språknemnd*, from 1972 *Norsk språkråd* 'Norwegian Language Council') has existed to consider and advise on possible orthographical changes, approve school textbooks, consider new terminology, monitor the functioning of the linguistic legislation and respond to enquiries from the public. The Council is divided into two sections, one for each form of the language, nominated by a wide range of interested organizations. Whilst the remit of *Norsk språknemnd* was to bring the two forms closer together, *Norsk språkråd* has institutionalized the official policy post-1959 of peaceful co-existence between them.

Norwegian outside Norway

In the Middle and Modern Norwegian periods the language has extended little beyond Norway's borders. The Norwegian colony on the shores of the Kola peninsula in NW Russia was repatriated after 1917, although it is immortalized in the place-name Murmansk (cf. Norwegian *nordmann*, a Norwegian person). Only in North America did significant Norwegian colonies exist as a result of mass emigration. Only Ireland lost a larger proportion of its population to America than Norway, which over a quarter of a million people left in the century from 1815. Mass emigration persisted until the early 1920s, and temporary migration was common in rural areas until the 1960s. The Norwegian-language press flourished above all in the cities and small towns of the Mid-West and North-West, and still survives residually. In spite of the fact that many emigrants came from areas of Norway where Landsmål had won support, nearly all Norwegian-language publishing in the USA was in Riksmål. As late as 1950 there were purportedly three-quarters of a million Norwegian-speakers in the USA, or about 20% of the world total at the time. This figure, if ever reliable, is now greatly diminished.

Berulfsen, B. 1963. *Norwegian Grammar* [Bokmål], Oslo.
—— and Svenkerud, H. (eds) 1968. *Cappelens store engelsk–norsk ordbok* ('Cappelen's Large English–Norwegian Dictionary') [Bokmål]. Oslo.
Haugen, E. 1966. *Language Conflict and Language Planning: The Case of Modern Norwegian*. Cambridge, MA.
—— 1976a. *The Scandinavian Languages: An Introduction to Their History*. London.

—— 1976b. *Norsk–engelsk ordbok* ('Norwegian–English Dictionary'), 2nd edn. Oslo.

Moen, P. and Pedersen, P. -B. 1983. *Norwegian Grammar – Nynorsk*. Oslo.

—— 1992. *Engelsk–nynorsk blå ordbok* ('English–Nynorsk Blue Dictionary'). Oslo.

STEPHEN J. WALTON

Nostratic languages

The 'Nostratic hypothesis' seeks to show (on the basis of elements that they are claimed to share) that some of the major language families of Europe, Asia and northern Africa derive from a common origin. Among the families thus classified as Nostratic languages are ***Indo-European**, Afro-Asiatic (including ***Semitic**), Kartvelian (see ***Caucasian languages. V**), ***Altaic** and Dravidian (a group of languages spoken mainly in southern India). Some would also add other families. In the present state of knowledge, the hypothesis can be neither proved nor disproved though it has a certain plausibility.

Salmons, J. C. and Joseph, B. D. (eds) 1998. *Nostratic: Sifting the Evidence*. Amsterdam and Philadelphia, PA.

Novial (see under *Artificial languages*)

Nynorsk (see under *Norwegian*)

O

Occitan

Occitan (otherwise known as *la langue d'oc* or, less appropriately, Provençal) is the generic name for those ***Gallo-Romance** idioms which are native mainly to southern France (see map 6), although it is debatable whether ***Gascon** should be included or differentiated as one of three constituents of 'Occitano-Romance', viz. Occitan, Gascon and ***Catalan**.

Earliest attestations

Whether Occitan first appears in legal or in literary texts is uncertain. Traces occur in Latin charters before 1100. Of these, the earliest known (from Lautrec, Tarn) are dated 985 and 989. The first known document entirely in Occitan was written 117 years later (1102) in Saint-Rome-de-Berlière, Aveyron. The earliest literary use of Occitan may occur in a six-line fragment of a poem on the Passion, probably composed in Strasbourg in the late 10th c., or else in the problematic, apparently vernacular two-line refrain of a Latin dawn-song added in the 10th or 11th c. to a manuscript in Fleury-sur-Loire (Nièvre) but composed possibly in the Midi, although the refrain could be in ***Italo-Romance** or in garbled Low Latin. Indisputably Occitan are the 593-line hagiographic *Canczon de sancta Fides d'Agen* ('Song of St Fides of Agen'), composed near Narbonne *c*.1030–1070, and the *Boeci*, a 258-line fragment on Boethius in Limousin scripta composed almost certainly before 1150, probably *c*.1070–1115 and possibly earlier. A manuscript from St Martial de Limoges contains four 11th-c. religious verse texts in Poitevin scripta (three of them alongside Latin). Occitan administrative scripta appears *in extenso* *c*.1103 in Provence, *c*.1120 in the Limousin, and subsequently in the Gévaudan (1134), the Vivarais (1177), Périgord (*c*.1185), and in the Auvergne proper (1195).

Occitan as a literary medium

Although the earliest Occitan literature dates from the late 10th or 11th c., the language only achieved full international recognition as a literary medium in the 12th and 13th centuries with the lyric poetry of the troubadours, of whom some 450 are known. Their work was disseminated and influential throughout Europe for centuries, long after the troubadours themselves had fallen silent. Occitan writing, especially in verse, has continued to the present in an unbroken tradition with sustained high points in the late 16th and 17th centuries (Loïs Bellaud de la Bellaudière, Guilhem Ader, Pèire Godolin, Glaudi Brueis, Francés de Corteta) and again in the last century and a half, largely thanks to the Félibrige movement (launched in 1854), the Institut d'Estudis Occitans (founded in 1945) and, particularly before 1914, the local and regional press. Notable writers in this modern period include Frédéric Mistral, Théodore Aubanel, Joseph d'Arbaud, Sully-André Peyre, Jean Boudou (Joan Bodon), Max Rouquette, Robert Lafont and Yves Rouquette.

Codification

Faced with the usual Romance problem of accommodating a Latin-based writing system to a (regionally varied) phonology diverging considerably from Latin, 12th- and 13th-c. troubadours and their scribes adopted a type of koine which eclectically incorporated Southern and Northern Occitan features and was acceptable throughout Occitania and beyond. More precisely localizable dialectalisms appear in other medieval Occitan literary, administrative, religious and scientific texts, although the 14th-c. treatise *Las Leys d'Amors* recommends general use of Languedocian in preference to Gascon or Provençal. For centuries after 1560 anarchy prevailed in Occitan spelling, influenced by French, local dialect and authors' own idiosyncracies. Though the Alpine lexicographer S.-J. Honnorat (1783–1852) advocated a return to the pre-1560, more etymologically based writing system, the Félibrige led by Mistral (see above) instead promoted an orthographical system based on that of French, adapted to the distinctive Provençal of Arles and Avignon. As the literary movement spread through Occitania, so its orthographic reform met resistance, first in the Limousin (J. Roux, 1876), then in western Languedoc where, from 1904 on, the schoolteachers Prosper Estieu and Antonin Perbosc, following Honnorat, jointly advocated a simplified form of the troubadours' koine, usable throughout the Midi. Hostile Provençal reaction led to a polarization of positions and an enduring perception of rivalry between Provence and Occitania. In practice, Estieu and Perbosc preserved many dialectal pronunciations. More rigorous orthographic simplification was applied by the Languedocian grammarian and lexicographer Louis Alibert (1884–1959), whose system was adopted by the Societat d'Estudis Occitans in 1936 and the Institut d'Estudis Occitans in 1945 and has since been adapted to Provençal (1951), Gascon (1952), Auvergnat (1971) and Limousin (1974).

Geographical spread and dialects

Geographically, Occitan is bounded to the north and east by French, ***Francoprovençal** and ***Italian** dialects, and to the west and south by the Atlantic, ***Basque**, Aragonese (see under ***Spanish**), the Catalan of Roussillon, and Gascon (sometimes, as mentioned above, considered to be itself an Occitan dialect), though neither the interface with Italo-Romance nor that with ***Ibero-Romance** is very sharply defined. Linguistic evidence suggests that in Merovingian times proto-Occitan was spoken as far north as the Loire but that the frontier zone between the *langue d'oc* and the ***langue d'oïl** (i.e. French) subsequently retreated southwards before stabilizing in approximately its present-day position during the 13th c., so that Poitou, Aunis and Saintonge are now in the *langue d'oïl* area. Occitan was demonstrably spoken in central Poitou (including Poitiers itself) at least until 1150. Vestigial pockets of Occitan still survive in French-speaking Charente south of Angoulême where numerous villages retain a distinctively Limousin type of speech.

The present northern limit of Occitan snakes across France showing resistance to French advance in the high Limousin plateaux and the mountainous Auvergne and Dauphiné but recession due to easier communications in the west (in the lowlands of Poitou, Aunis and Saintonge) and in the east (in the Rhône valley). Along the curved northern perimeter between central Charente and the eastern Puy-de-Dôme runs a long crescent-shaped intermediate zone between French and Occitan which has remained fairly static since the Middle Ages.

Dialectalisms, apparent in the earliest texts, are considerably attenuated (or obfuscated by polymorphism) in later copyists' scripta and in the literary and legal Occitan koine adopted by 12th- and 13th-c. troubadours and notaries. The underlying dialectal patchwork re-emerges, however, from the mid-14th c. on, when written forms correspond approximately to the main isoglossic divisions of today. Southern Occitan is now spoken in the Languedoc and Provence while northern varieties occur in the Limousin and *Périgord blanc*, Auvergne, and the Vivarais and Alpine regions extending into some Piedmontese valleys. Alternatively, because Languedocian shares some (mainly phonetic) features only with Gascon, these two can be considered as forming an Aquitano-Pyrenean group distinct from an Arverno-Mediterranean group comprising Limousin, Auvergnat, Vivaro-Alpine and Provençal.

Territorially, the most extensively spoken dialect is Languedocian whose wedge-shaped zone covers all or part of 14 *départements*. Provençal and Vivaro-Alpine each occupy all or part of six *départements*, while Limousin and Auvergnat are found in all or part of five and four *départements* respectively.

A variety of Piedmontese Occitan known as Gardiol is still spoken today in parts of Calabria (especially Guardia Piemontese) which were settled before 1400 by Waldensian emigrants from the Val Chisone, Val Germanasca and Val Pellice.

Interrelationship with other languages

Romanization was more intensive in the south of Gaul than in the north since Roman involvement with the territory of Gallia Narbonensis lasted nearly seven centuries (219 BC to AD 475) and towns in the southern Dioecesis Viennensis (established in the late 3rd c.) were generally more prosperous and stable than those in the northern Dioecesis Galliae. Occitan consequently remains closer to its Vulgar Latin (see under *Latin) roots than do other varieties of Gallo-Romance. Like these, nevertheless, it incorporates some elements of pre-Roman lexis (principally Celtic toponyms and terms for the countryside, plants, farming, clothing, administration, animal and human anatomy) and various Germanic borrowings (e.g. anthroponyms, toponyms, and words for wild and domestic animals, trades, emotions, physical activity, habitation, warfare and government) attributable to *Visigothic settlement in Aquitaine and Septimania (the region between the Rhône, the Pyrenees and the Massif central) and to Frankish rule. The Arab occupation of Septimania (719–59), Mediterranean trade and piracy, *Mozarabic Spain and the Crusades gave Occitan scientific, technical, culinary, agricultural and exotic terms assimilated from or via *Arabic, often indirectly through Ibero- and Italo-Romance. *Greek borrowings appropriated during the Crusades (nautical and oriental terms) are outnumbered by those absorbed through Classical, Vulgar and Low Latin (nautical, meteorological, architectural and Christian vocabulary). Place-names from *Agde* (< *Agathe*) to *Monaco* (< *[Heracles]-Monoikos*) attest to pre-Roman Hellenization spreading from the first Phocaean settlement of Marseilles (< Latin *Massilia* < Greek *Massalia*), founded *c*.600 BC.

Contact between Occitan and other *Romance languages has regularly resulted in two-way lexical borrowing, exchanges with French being particularly numerous through social migration and changing patterns of cultural, social, administrative and technological superiority. The diglossic situation in the Midi results in Occitan pronunciation and lexis being marked by Gallicisms (despite the efforts of Mistral and the Félibrige – see above, 'Occitan as a literary medium'), in regional French characterized by Occitanisms (affecting lexis, pronunciation and morphosyntax), and in hybrid Franco-Occitan speech varieties known as *francitan*. The close relationship between Catalan and Occitan (especially the Aquitano-Pyrenean variety) is partly due to three centuries of trans-Pyrenean Visigothic rule and 200 years of shared Frankish dominion in the formative period of Romance, followed by the union of Catalonia and Provence (1113–1245). Already in Roman times communications between Tarraconensis and Gallia Narbonensis were excellent.

Number of speakers

In the absence of official statistics, estimates of the number of Occitan-speakers must be treated with caution. In the 1970s it was sometimes claimed that there were about 2 million regular Occitan-speakers, while a further 4 to 10 million were thought to have some knowledge of the language. In 1992 it was reckoned that there were 750,000 active speakers in Provence and between 1 and 1.5 million who understood Provençal; while in 1991 a representative sample of 939 interviewees surveyed in four *départements* of the Languedoc (Aude, Hérault, Lozère and Gard, with a total population of 1,751,178) indicated that 48% of the population understood Occitan and 28% could speak it, although only 9% did so daily.

Role and official status

Since the Middle Ages French has increasingly supplanted Occitan in administrative, literary and eventually popular use, working its way down the social scale. The process began with the Albigensian Crusade and accelerated between 1450 and 1600 after the Hundred Years War and the Edict of Villers-Cotterêts (1539), which prescribed the use of French in official documents. In the 19th and 20th centuries it has been further boosted by the development of centralizing policies (e.g. in education), military service and the influence of Parisian mass media.

Nevertheless, Occitan has received a certain status through the award of the Nobel Prize for literature to Mistral in 1904, its adoption by both Vichy and the Resistance forces in the Second World War, and its use in various popular left-wing demonstrations and strikes (1907, 1953, 1961–2, 1975–6, 1989–90). Militant educationalists have, in recent decades, promoted various measures giving an optional place in the French school curriculum to the minority languages of France. After numerous unsuccessful or timid attempts at legislation from 1870 onwards, the *loi Deixonne* of 1951 authorized optional courses in regional languages at all levels of state education, although the *baccalauréat* (school-leaving examination) did not include Occitan among optional languages until 1970. This legislation has been gently reinforced by the *loi Haby* of 1975 and the *circulaire Savary* of 1982. Even so, the place of Occitan in the school curriculum is rarely assured. Only since 1992 have secondary teachers' training qualifications (the CAPES) in Occitan been awarded. From the late 1980s parents have been able to choose to have their children taught elementary mathematics and science through Occitan in state infant and primary schools in some areas, monolingual Occitan or bilingual (Occitan and French) teaching for children of the same age-group having been available gratis in scattered semi-independent schools (*calandretas*) since 1979. Occitan evening classes held in several towns from autumn to spring are complemented by a few Occitan summer holiday camps for children and, for adults, by the Occitan Summer School and University held annually in Villeneuve-sur-Lot and Nîmes respectively.

In July 1994, the French Minister for Education signed an agreement promoting the use of Occitan and Gascon in education and the media. *Inter alia*, this doubled the number of CAPES (see above) in these languages, allowed history and geography to be taught through them, and opened up the possibility of daily TV programmes in Occitan or Gascon in the regions of Aquitaine, Midi-Pyrénées and Languedoc-Roussillon. In practice, these widely acclaimed measures have not as yet been fully implemented and, given that TV programmes in Provençal from Nice and Marseilles have either been discontinued or are under threat, the future of such programmes in Occitan is generally uncertain. However, more local radio stations now broadcast (often dull) programmes than in the 1950s.

Of the many Occitan folk and pop groups, two (The Fabulous Troubadours of Toulouse and Massilia Sound System of Marseilles) have achieved international reputations. Since its foundation in 1987, the Association GEMP/La Talvera, which covers the Midi-Pyrénées region, has produced over 50 video- or sound-recordings of Occitan folk song and folk tales. An approved Roman Catholic missal and ritual in Provençal appeared in 1972, followed by a standardized Languedocian equivalent in 1979 and a short Languedocian version in the Agenais subdialect in 1985. July 1994 saw the celebration of an exceptional Auvergnat mass in Pierrefort (Cantal) and the first mass in the peripheral subdialect of Menton (Alpes-Maritimes).

Bazalgues, G. 1975. *L'Occitan lèu-lèu e plan. L'Occitan selon le parler languedocien* (with two audio-cassettes). Paris.

Bec, P. 1973. *Manuel pratique d'occitan moderne* (with LP record). Paris.

—— 1986. *La Langue occitane*, 5th rev. edn. Paris.

Blanchet, P. 1992. *Le Provençal. Essai de description sociolinguistique et différentielle*. Louvain-la-Neuve.

Decomps, D. and Gonfroy, G. 1979. *L'Occitan redde e ben: lo lemosin. L'occitan selon le parler limousin* (with two audio-cassettes). Paris.

Fernández González, J. R. 1985. *Gramática histórica provenzal*. Oviedo.

Jeanjean, H. 1992. *De l'utopie au pragmatisme? (Le mouvement occitan 1976–1990)*. Perpignan.

Kremnitz, G. *Das Okzitanische. Sprachgeschichte und Sociologie* ('The History and Sociology of Occitan'). Tübingen.

Mistral, F. 1878–86. *Lou Tresor dóu Felibrige ou dictionnaire provençal–français embrassant les divers dialectes de la langue d'oc moderne*, 2 vols. Aix-en-Provence (reprinted 1979, Raphèle-lès-Arles).

Nowakowski, B. 1988. *Zu Sprache und Sprachideologie bei Vertretern der okzitanischen Renaissance in der Provence. Ergebnisse einer Befragung* ('Language and Linguistic Ideology among Representatives of the Occitan Renaissance in Provence. Results of an Inquiry'). Trier.

Ronjat, J. 1930–41. *Grammaire istorique* [sic] *des parlers provençaux modernes*, 4 vols. Montpellier (reprinted 1980, Geneva and Marseilles).

Teulat, R. 1985. *Uèi l'occitan* ('Occitan Today'). Bedous.

[Various authors] 1991. Okzitanisch. In Holtus, G., Metzeltin, M. and Schmitt, C. (eds), *Lexikon der Romanistischen Linguistik*, Tübingen, vol. 5.2, 1–126 (9 articles, 5 in French, 4 in German).

P. V. DAVIES

Ogam (ogham)

Ogam (or ogham), in which a number of very brief early *Irish inscriptions are written, was an alphabetic script of originally 20 characters (others were added later) in which vowels were represented by from one to five notches cut along the edge of a stone slab (and perhaps also on wood, though no examples survive) and consonants by grooves cut along one side or other of the edge or obliquely across it (see fig. 11). The inventor of ogam may have been inspired by an antique cipher for the Latin alphabet, in which the five Latin vowels were represented by from one to five dots. But as a whole the ogam alphabet was not a cipher on the Latin alphabet since it omitted letters such as <p> and <x> which were not needed for Primitive Irish, and probably included symbols for Irish phonemes such as the voiced labiovelar, unlike Latin which used the diagraph <gu>. Moreover, whereas the earliest manuscript Irish in Latin script denoted sounds such as [d] and [g] by <t> and <c> in non-initial position, the ogam inscriptions use the 'D' and 'G' symbols for these phonemes irrespective of position.

There is no reasonable doubt that ogam originated in Ireland, or an Irish settlement in Britain, in the 4th or 5th c. AD. The great majority (well over 300) of known inscriptions are found in Ireland, mainly in the south-west, and those found in the Isle of Man (six), Wales (40) and Cornwall and Devon (eight) are also all in Irish and can be attributed to Irish-speakers who settled in those areas in the 4th to 6th centuries. The bulk of the extant inscriptions on stone date from about the 5th to the 7th c. but it is clear from treatises on ogam contained in medieval manuscripts that knowledge of the system was maintained throughout the Middle Ages and beyond; the ogam alphabet provided the increasingly inappropriate framework for the discussion of the phonemes of Irish.

There are also in Scotland, dating from (probably) the 8th and 9th centuries, a couple of dozen enigmatic inscriptions in ***Pictish** in a stylistically different form of

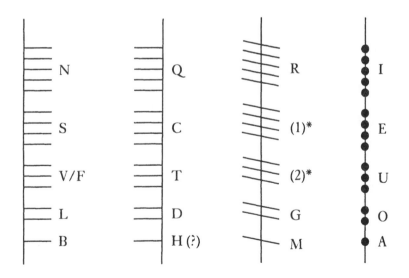

Fig. 11 The original ogam alphabet. Most reference works transcribe (1) as <Z> and (2) as <Ng> respectively, but Sims-Williams (1993) argues cogently that (1) represented [sw] or possibly a reflex, of uncertain phonetic value, of Indo-European [st], and that (2) represented [gʷ].

ogam in which the base-line for the grooves is not the edge of a stone but a line drawn on the face of it.

Jackson, K. H. 1983. Ogam stones and the early Christian Latin inscriptions. In Thomson, D. S. (ed.), *The Companion to Gaelic Scotland*, Oxford, 220–1.

McManus, D. 1991. *A Guide to Ogam*. Maynooth.

—— 1996. Ogham. In Daniels, P. T. and Bright, W. (ed.), *The World's Writing Systems*, New York and Oxford, 340–5.

Sims-Williams, P. 1992. The additional letters of the ogam alphabet. *Cambridge Medieval Celtic Studies*, 23: 29–75.

—— 1993. Some problems in deciphering the early Irish ogam alphabet. *Transactions of the Philological Society*, 91: 133–80.

GLANVILLE PRICE

Old Church Slavonic, see *Church Slavonic*

Old European

'Old European' (German *alteuropäisch*) is the term applied by Hans Krahe (1962) and, after him, by others to a Bronze Age (i.e. 2nd millennium BC) *Indo-European language assumed, on the basis of hydronymy or river-names, to have existed over much of northern Europe before the arrival of the *Celtic-, *Germanic-, *Italic- and *Baltic-speaking peoples and other Indo-Europeans. Nicolaisen (1982) postulates, for example, for Britain elements such as *kar- 'hard, stony?', reflected in the *Cart* (Renfrewshire), the *Carrant* (Gloucestershire), the *Ceri* (Radnorshire), with cognates in mainland Europe including the *Horund* in Norway and the *Charente* and the *Cher* in France, or *neid-/nid- 'to flow?' in the *Nedd* (English *Neath*) in South Wales and the *Nidd* (Yorkshire), with cognates in the *Nidda* (Germany) and the *Nied* (Lorraine). Vennemann's thesis (1994) that the language of Krahe's hydronymy was not Indo-European but *Pre-Indo-European is effectively countered by Kitson (1996) who argues persuasively that 'the linguistic material of the *alteuropäisch* river-names is Indo-European'.

Kitson, P. R. 1996. British and European river-names. *Transactions of the Philological Society*, 94: 73–118.

Krahe, H. 1963. *Die Struktur der alteuropäischen Hydronomie*. Wiesbaden.

Nicolaisen, W. F. L. 1982. The 'Old European' names in Britain. *Nomina*, 6: 37–42.

Vennemann, T. 1994. Linguistic reconstruction in the context of European prehistory. *Transactions of the Philological Society*, 92: 215–84.

GLANVILLE PRICE

Old Norse, see *Norse, Old*

Old Prussian, see *Prussian, Old*

Old Sabellic (see under *East Italic*)

Olonets (see under *Karelian*)

Oscan

An extinct member of the *Sabellian or *Osco-Umbrian branch of the *Italic languages. Linguistically, Oscan closely resembles *Umbrian and a number of smaller Sabellian languages (*Marsian, *Volscian, *Aequian, *Sabine, *South Picenian). Oscan was spoken by Samnitic tribes, who lived throughout the southern half of Italy (see map 10), excluding the extreme south-east (*Messapic) and Sicily (*Sicel, *Elymian; but Messina was occupied by the Oscan Mamertinians). In the north-west, Oscan bordered upon Volscian and *Latin, and in the north-east upon Umbrian, *Marrucinian and *Vestinian. The Oscans in the strict sense (Old Latin *Opsci*, Greek *Opikoí*) were a tribe in Campania (i.e. SW of Naples) but, following the Roman tradition, the linguistic label 'Oscan' is usually attached to the language of all Samnitic tribes. Oscan in the wider sense covers various Sabellian dialects, which seem to differ from one another only slightly in so far as the scanty evidence allows us to decide: Vestinian, Marrucinian, *Paelignian, Campanian, Samnitic (in the strict sense), Hirpinian, Frentanian, Lucanian, Bruttian and Mamertinian. The Samnite tribes nearly crushed the Roman aspirations to hegemony over Italy. It took Rome decades of fierce battle to subdue them (the three Samnite wars, from 370 to 290 BC).

The Oscan language (in the wider sense) is known through hundreds of inscriptions, most of which are brief and fragmentary. These date from around 400 BC (coins) to the 1st c. AD (graffiti in Pompeii). The use of Oscan in official documents, some of which survive, seems to cease at the beginning of the 1st c. BC.

Most inscriptions are written in the so-called 'national alphabet', which was derived from *Etruscan. Some inscriptions use the Latin and a number from southern Italy and Sicily the *Greek alphabet (there were important Greek colonies in southern Italy).

The *Cippus Abellanus* (now in Nola), a stone tablet, is inscribed (in the national alphabet) on two sides and contains over 180 words. It contains an agreement between the cities of Nola and Abella concerning the use and status of a temple dedicated to Hercules, which belonged to both cities. It may date from around 150 BC.

The longest surviving document is the *Tabula Bantina* (Banzi, near Potenza; now in the Museo Nazionale, Naples), which contains nearly 400 words and is inscribed in the Latin alphabet. It is a fragment of a bronze tablet, of which only the middle third of one of the original two columns survives. The *Tabula* contains a number of municipal by-laws of the town of Bantia. It may perhaps date from the end of the 2nd c. BC.

From Pompeii come a number of inscriptions: dedications and inscriptions on public buildings (2nd c BC?); the 'eituns' inscriptions, which probably functioned as signposts; graffiti dating from the 1st c. AD.

Other important inscriptions derive from Capua: the 'Vibia curse' (a lead plate) and the 'iovilae' inscriptions (dedications to Iuppiter). Finally, the archaic bronze tablet of Agnone (now in the British Museum) must be mentioned.

Buck, C. D. 1928. *A Grammar of Oscan and Umbrian*, 2nd edn. Boston.

Vetter, E. 1953. *Handbuch der italischen Dialekte* ('Handbook of the Italic Dialects'). Heidelberg.

PETER SCHRIJVER

Osco-Umbrian languages

A subgroup of the *Italic branch of the *Indo-European languages, consisting of *Oscan, *Umbrian and a number of lesser languages (see *Sabellian languages).

Ossetic

A member of the *Iranian subgroup of the *Indo-European languages, and considered to derive from the language of the Scythians of antiquity (see *Scythian). The Ossetes, numbering some half a million in all, live in the northern central part of the Caucasus region, in North Ossetia (in the Russian Federation) and South Ossetia (in Georgia). There are two main dialects, an eastern one, Iron, and a western one, Digor. Iron is the more widely spoken of the two and is also the basis of the literary language codified in the late 19th c. by the poet Kosta Khetagurov and now written in the **Cyrillic** alphabet. See also *Alanic, *Yassic.

Abaev, V. I. 1964. *A Grammatical Sketch of Ossetic.* Bloomington, IN and The Hague.

Kasaev, A. M. (ed.) 1962. Осетинско–русский словарь ('Ossetic–Russian Dictionary'), 2nd edn. Ordzhonikidze.

P

Paelignian

The Paelignians dwelt in an area in east central Italy that now falls within the Abruzzi region (see map 10), with their capital at Corfinium (modern Corfinio). Paelignian is an *Italic language closely related to *Oscan (and may even be derived from Oscan). It is known from some 40 inscriptions, mainly dating from the 1st c. BC and in the Latin alphabet, from around Corfinio and Sulmona (Classical Sulmo, the birthplace of Ovid) where many of them may be seen in the museum.

Coleman, R. 1986. The central Italic languages in the period of Roman expansion. *Transactions of the Philological Society*, 1986: 100–31.

Vetter, E. 1953. Paeligner. In Id., *Handbuch der italischen Dialekte* ('Handbook of the Italic Dialects'), Heidelberg, 140–53.

Paeonian

The Paeones were a people living in early Classical times on the Axios river (north of Thessalonica) with the town of Amydon as their capital. Virtually nothing is known of their language: on the basis of one gloss in Aristotle, *monapos* 'bison', and a number of names of individuals, tribes and places, scholars have variously concluded that it was connected with ***Greek**, or ***Illyrian**, or Thracian (see ***Daco-Thracian**), or ***Phrygian**.

Katičić, R. 1976. Paeonia. In Id., *Ancient Languages of the Balkans*, The Hague, part 1, 117–20.

Palaeo-Sardinian

The term 'Palaeo-Sardinian' has been applied to the language or languages (other than ***Phoenician** in Phoenician colonies in the south) spoken in Sardinia before the Romans took possession of the island in 238 BC. On the basis of the evidence, on the one hand, of a number of words of unknown origin that seem to have parallels in Basque and in non-Romance elements in the ***Ibero-Romance languages** and, on the other hand, of place-names, it seems likely that we are dealing with more than one language, one of which had links with ***Iberian** while another was in some way connected with North African languages.

Palaree, see *Polari*

Panjabi (see under *Community languages (Britain)*)

Pannonian

In Roman times, the Pannonii occupied territory in the valleys of the Danube downstream from Carnuntum (near Bratislava) and the Sava and some of its tributaries. Their ***Illyrian**-type speech may or may not have been sufficiently distinct from Illyrian to have constituted a separate language.

Papiamentu (see under *Community languages (Netherlands)*)

Parlyaree, see *Polari*

Patwa (see under *Creoles*)

P-Celtic (see under *Celtic languages*)

Pelasgian

The name 'Pelasgian', from that of a people referred to by Homer and other Greek writers as *Pelasgoi*, has been applied, appropriately or inappropriately, to an ***Indo-European language** spoken in Greece before the coming of the Greeks (for which reason the name 'Pre-Hellenic' has also been suggested). Although no direct evidence of the language (such as inscriptions) remains, it is plausibly argued that a number of Greek words (e.g. *pyrgos* 'tower', *rhodon* 'rose') and proper names (e.g. those containing the sequence *-nth-*, such as that of the island of Zakynthos) that cannot be explained on the basis of the historical phonology of Greek were borrowed from it.

Georgiev, V. I. 1966. La scoperta della lingua 'pelasgica' ('The discovery of the "Pelasgian" language').
    In Id., *Introduzione alla storia delle lingue indeuropee*, Rome, 107–19.
Van Windekens, A. 1957. *Le pélasgique*. Louvain.

Pelignian, see *Paelignian*

Permic languages
A subgroup of the ***Finno-Ugrian languages**, including ***Komi** and ***Udmurt**.

Permyak (see under *Komi*)

Peul (see under *Community languages (France)*)

Phaistos disc
In 1908, excavations on the site of the Minoan palace at Phaistos in southern Crete
brought to light a baked clay disc, some 160 mm in diameter, with, on each side, an
inscription (different on each side) running spirally from the edge to the centre.
There are 45 different signs, 242 in all. Given the probable period of the destruction
of the palace, the disc must be dated not later than the end of the 18th c. BC. Though
the signs are generally representational, they are too few in number (even allowing
for the brevity of the text) to constitute a pictographic script and so probably represent a syllabic script. The signs are not cut or drawn but, by a process analogous to
printing, stamped into the clay by means of punches (which is proved by the fact that
every instance of a given sign is identical).

Among the many problems posed by this text is not only that of its decipherment
but also that of its provenance since it could have been imported from elsewhere.
Chadwick (1987) points out, for example, that it would be highly unlikely that the
punches necessary for the production of the inscription would have been prepared
just for this one document and yet no others produced by the same process have come
to light. This suggests to him, particularly in view of the fact that some of the characters have a non-Minoan appearance, that the disc may have been imported,
possibly from Anatolia. It is claimed, on the other hand, by Sakellarakis (1994: 30)
that 'there can be no doubt' that the script and unknown language of the disc are
those of the Minoans since 'the same script' figures on a bronze axe, of undisputed
Cretan origin, from a sanctuary in a cave at Arkalochori in central Crete. It is true
that some of the 15 characters engraved on the axe bear a resemblance to some of
those on the disc or to ***Linear** A characters, but the most recent and most thorough
discussion of the disc argues (Godart 1995: 145–9) that the characters on the axe are
no more than a 'pseudo-inscription' engraved by an illiterate in uncomprehending
imitation of authentic Linear A characters on other similar axes. Godart dismisses
'categorically any association between the signs on the disc and the signs of the other
Cretan scripts', i.e. the ***Cretan pictographic script**, Linear A and ***Linear B**.
Nevertheless, comparison of the signs with archaeological evidence from the eastern
Mediterranean reconciles him to 'the purely Aegean provenance of many represen-

tations on the disc'. If that is so, then the script and unknown language of the disc can legitimately be claimed as European.

Chadwick, J. 1987. *Linear B and Related Scripts*, London, 57–61.
Godart, L. 1995. *The Phaistos Disc. The Enigma of an Aegean Script*. Athens.
Sakellarakis, J. A. 1994. *Herakleion Museum*. Athens.

GLANVILLE PRICE

Phoenician

A *Semitic language, closely akin to *Hebrew. The term 'Punic', which has come to be specialized in the sense of 'Carthaginian', derives from a Latinization of the Greek 'Phoinike' and so refers to the same language.

Phoenicia, towards the end of the second millennium BC, occupied a territory corresponding roughly to modern Lebanon and having as its main sites Byblos, Sidon, and Tyre which in due course came to predominate. Westward expansion from Tyre began in the 9th c. BC with the establishment of a colony at Kition, near Larnaka, on the south coast of Cyprus. According to a tradition that can be neither proved nor disproved, Tyre's principal colony of Carthage, which was in due course to control much of the western Mediterranean, was founded in 814 BC. In the 8th c. BC or a little earlier or later, other colonies were founded either from Tyre or from Carthage elsewhere on the northern coast of Africa, and in Europe, from west to east, at Gadir (Cádiz), along the Mediterranean coast of Andalusia from the Bay of Algeciras to east of Almería, on the island of Ibiza, in southern Sardinia, in western Sicily, and on Malta. For a variety of economic and military reasons, Phoenician influence in the area began to decline from the 6th c. BC onwards and came to an end with the conquest and destruction of Carthage by the Romans in 146 BC.

The earliest of the few Phoenician inscriptions found in Europe is a stele, dating probably from the end of the 9th c., from Nora in Sardinia. Others are known from Malta and Cyprus, and the discovery in 1964 of a Phoenician and a longer but corresponding *Etruscan inscription on gold tablets at Pyrgi, the port of ancient Caere (modern Cerveteri) north-west of Rome, proves the existence of a Phoenician presence (but not of a colony) in this area in the late 6th c. BC.

Phoenician is of particular importance for the later evolution of European civilization in that the Phoenician alphabet of 22 characters, which derived from earlier non-alphabetic scripts (possibly via now lost alphabetic scripts), is the earliest alphabet known to us, first found on the sarcophagus of Ahiram, king of Byblos (now in the museum in Beirut), which probably dates from *c*.1000 BC. This is a completely consonantal script, i.e. it contains no signs for vowels, and is usually written from right to left. From it derive various other alphabets, including the Hebrew and the *Greek, from the latter of which derive, *inter alia*, the Latin alphabet (via Etruscan) and the *Cyrillic alphabet.

Aubet, M. E. 1993. *The Phoenicians and the West*. Cambridge.
Culican, W. 1991. Phoenicians in the west. In Boardman, J. et al. (eds), *The Cambridge Ancient History*, 2nd edn, Cambridge, vol. 3, part 2, 485–540.

GLANVILLE PRICE

Phrygian

Apart from a number of words quoted in Greek texts, the only direct evidence for Phrygian comes from outside Europe in the form of inscriptions from NW Anatolia (where the Phrygians had their capital at Gordium). These represent two stages of the language, the first (which has come to be known as Old Phrygian) dating from the 8th to the 3rd c. BC, the later (New Phrygian) from the early centuries of the Christian era (3rd c. at latest), though Brixhe (1994: 175) suggests that the language may have survived for considerably longer, perhaps even into the 7th c. There seems no reason not to accept statements by the Greek historians Herodotus and Strabo to the effect that the Phrygians had once dwelt in parts of the Balkans, and Phrygian may therefore be counted as a European language. The likelihood is that the Phrygians emigrated to Asia Minor early in the first millennium BC.

The inscriptions are in Greek characters (an early form thereof in the case of the Old Phrygian inscriptions), and so present no problems of decipherment. They provide enough evidence, mainly lexical but some on grammatical features, for it to be agreed that Phrygian was an ***Indo-European language**. Views differ, however, as to its degree of kinship with other Indo-European languages: it has been variously suggested that it may have been connected in some way with ***Greek**, or (less probably) ***Armenian**, Thracian (see under ***Daco-Thracian**), ***Italic** or ***Celtic**.

Brixhe, C. 1994. Le phrygien. In Bader, F. (ed.), *Langues indo-européennes*, Paris, 165–78.
—— and Lejeune, M. 1984. *Corpus des inscriptions paléo-phrygiennes*. Paris.
Masson, O. 1991. The Phrygian language. In Boardman, J. et al. (eds), *The Cambridge Ancient History*, 2nd edn, Cambridge, vol. 3, part 2, 666–9.

Picard

A variety of the ******langue d'oïl** that is generally considered as just a dialect of ***French** but which is sufficiently different from standard French for some to have claimed for it the status of a language. Though it is not possible to define dialectal limits in the *langue d'oïl* area with great precision, even a fairly restrictive definition of the Picard area would include in it the French *départements* of the Nord (apart from the ***Dutch**-speaking area between Dunkirk and Hazebrouck), Pas-de-Calais and the Somme, the NW of the Aisne, much of the Oise, and the extreme north of Seine-Maritime, together with the western part of French-speaking Belgium (most of which falls within the ***Walloon** area), from the French frontier west of Tournai to somewhere east of Mons and Soignies. (The Picard dialect of Belgium is frequently known as 'Rouchi'.) No reliable estimates for the number of Picard-speakers are available but it can be asserted with confidence that Picard is no longer spoken by the majority of the inhabitants of its traditional area, especially in urban areas.

Many important Old French texts, though by no means written in pure Picard, are strongly marked by Picard linguistic features. They include the earliest known poem in French, the 29-line 'Séquence de Ste Eulalie' (*c.*880), and, from the early 13th c., Robert de Clari's chronicle of the Fourth Crusade and the plays of Jean Bodel of Arras. A few mid-17th.-c. texts have come down to us but the modern literary tradition dates from the mid-19th c., with the works of, among others, the poets A. Desrousseaux (1820–92) and J. Watteeuw (1849–1947). More recent writers include the poets G. Libbrecht (1891–1976) and F. Couvreur (b. 1932) and the short-story writer C. Dessaint (1875–1941). A more or less standardized orthography exists.

Carton, F. and Lebègue, M. 1989. *Atlas linguistique et ethnographique de la Picardie*, vol. 1. Paris.

Debrie, R. 1983. *Éche picard bèl é rade (Le picard vite et bien)*, with two cassettes. Paris.

Éloy, J. -M. 1997. *La Constitution du picard: une approche de la notion de langue*. Louvain-la-Neuve.

Flutre, L. -F. 1977. *Du moyen picard au picard moderne*. Amiens.

Gossen, C. T. 1976. *Grammaire de l'ancien picard*, new edn. Paris.

Ruelle, P. 1992. Le picard de Wallonie. In Bal, W. (ed.), *Limes I. Les langues régionales romanes en Wallonie*, Brussels, 51–69.

GLANVILLE PRICE

Picenian (see under *East Italic, North Picenian, South Picenian*)

Pictish

Pictish was the language spoken in Britain north of the Forth–Clyde line during the period of the historical Picts. There is some slight evidence that this, the northern offshoot of *Brittonic, was already diverging from the British spoken further south by the time of our earliest evidence (1st c. BC) (Koch 1983: 216). To Bede, a Northumbrian writing at the beginning of the 8th c., Pictish was a separate language. From at least the 5th c., *Gaelic-speaking immigrants from Ireland occupied Argyll, on the western borders of Pictish territory. This colony expanded politically, culturally and linguistically, especially after the mid-9th c. when a Gaelic dynasty secured hegemony over former Pictland. There is scant evidence with which to chart the decline of Pictish in the face of Gaelic expansion, though it appears from the comments of a contemporary writer in England that the language had disappeared totally by the 12th c. Several important features of Modern *Scottish Gaelic syntax have been tentatively identified as the result of Pictish ('British') influence.

The evidence for Pictish is almost entirely onomastic. For the early (Old Celtic) period there are the place-names and personal and ethnic names preserved in Classical texts; for the early medieval period (Neo-Celtic) there are names recorded in contemporary or near-contemporary writings from Ireland, Wales and Anglo-Saxon England. The place-names of modern Scotland constitute another important body of evidence. No Pictish manuscripts have been preserved, and only one text has survived, a king-list, extant in garbled form in Gaelicized sources. Though the evidence is comparatively meagre and much of it has passed through at least one 'linguistic filter' to appear in its present form, there is sufficient material to demonstrate that Pictish was a P-Celtic language (see *Celtic languages), akin to though distinct from *Cumbric, *Welsh, *Cornish and *Breton. Earlier writers, including Jackson (1955: 152), stressed correspondences between Pictish and *Gaulish, and identified the former as an independent member of a Gallo-Brittonic branch of Celtic. The relationship between the Insular and *Continental Celtic languages continues to generate controversy, and more recent writers on Pictish have tended to emphasize its position as part of a British linguistic continuum.

The final body of evidence is a small corpus of inscriptions in the Roman and the *ogam alphabets, numbering seven and 32 examples respectively. There are considerable archaeological and epigraphic difficulties in their interpretation, and many are too fragmentary to yield linguistic information. Of those that can be read with certainty, some contain clearly Celtic personal names, others stubbornly resist explanation. This handful of, as yet, unintelligible inscriptions forms the only compelling evidence in favour of Jackson's view that there were in fact two languages spoken in Pictland – the P-Celtic language described above, and a second, non-*Indo-European language. In a recent challenge to the orthodoxy of the 'two Pictishes' it has been argued that, in the face of the much greater body of positive evidence in favour of a single Brittonic Pictish, these few inscriptions are insufficient justification for positing two separate languages (Forsyth, forthcoming). Pictish may have incorporated an unusual degree of pre-Celtic substrate influence but this remains to be demonstrated.

Forsyth, K. 1995. Language in Pictland, spoken and written. In Nicoll, E. H. (ed.), *A Pictish Panorama: The Story of the Picts, and a Pictish Bibliography*, Balgavies, Forfar, 7–10 (and references therein).
—— (forthcoming). *Language in Pictland: The Case Against 'Non-Indo-European Pictish'* (Studia Hameliana, 2). Utrecht.
Jackson, K. 1955. The Pictish language. In Wainwright, F. T. (ed.), *The Problem of the Picts*, Edinburgh (reprinted 1980, Perth), 129–66.
Koch, J. T. 1983. The loss of final syllables and loss of declension in Brittonic. *Bulletin of the Board of Celtic Studies*, 30: 201–33 (section on Pictish, 214–20).

KATHERINE FORSYTH

Pidgin languages

Pidgins are 'contact vernaculars' that arise for purposes of intercommunication, frequently in a trading context but sometimes for other reasons (e.g. communication between masters and servants or slaves), in situations involving speakers of two or more languages, each of which contributes something of its pronunciation, grammar or lexicon to the pidgin. Pidgins are restricted languages in the sense that their range of functions and their vocabulary are significantly more limited than those of more conventional languages and that they have a simplified grammar lacking many of the features of the languages from which they derive. Nevertheless, a pidgin is not unstructured but obeys widely accepted conventions of pronunciation, grammar and lexical meaning. A pidgin that comes into use as the first language of a community and thereby develops an expanded vocabulary and frequently a more elaborate grammar has, by that process, evolved into a *creole.

The vast majority of pidgins have evolved outside Europe, especially in situations in which western European traders and others came into contact with speakers of indigenous languages. Strictly European pidgins are constituted by *Russenorsk and *Basque–Icelandic pidgin and, if indeed it ever existed, *Franco-Icelandic pidgin.

For further information, including the geographical distribution of the major pidgins, and bibliographical references, see under *Creoles.

GLANVILLE PRICE

Piedmontese (see under *Italy. III. Northern Italy*)

Polabian

An extinct west *Slavonic language of the *Lechitic subgroup spoken until the mid-18th-c. in the vicinity of Dannenberg, Lüchow and Wustrow in the Lüneburg Wendland in Germany (see map 18). The westernmost variety of Lechitic, it is thought to have been the language of the Slavonic tribe recorded in 1004 as the Drevani. In German it was called *wendisch* and in Polabian *slüvenst'ě* or *venst'ě*. Apart from toponyms, the only written records, dating from the late 17th and early 18th centuries, consist of vocabularies (see below), disconnected sentences and phrases, prayers, and one folk song. About 2,800 lexical items are recorded, of which about 20% are borrowings from Middle Low German. In the grammar too, German influence is in evidence. The spelling, based on that of German, is fairly capricious, but a standardized transcription has been devised for scholarly purposes. The main sources, consisting of three vocabularies, are: (i) Hennig von Jessen's *Vocabularium Venedicum* (*c*.1705); (ii) Johann Friedrich Pfeffinger's French–Polabian *Vocabulaire vandale* (1711); and (iii) a German–Polabian glossary included in a chronicle of the village of Süthen written in 1724 or 1725 by Johann Parum Schultze (the only native speaker to have left a record). Each of these represents one of the three dialects, which are those of Süthen (Schultze), Lüchow (Pfeffinger) and Klennow (von Jessen). Long after Polabian was dead, traces of it remained in the form of loan-words and other features in the Low German dialect of the Wendland.

Polański, K. 1993. Polabian. In Comrie, B. and Corbett, G. G. (eds), *The Slavonic Languages*, London and New York, 795–824.
—— and Sehnert, J. A. 1967. *Polabian–English Dictionary*. The Hague and Paris.

GERALD STONE

Polari

It is a moot point whether Polari (Parlyaree, Palaree) can properly be described as a language. Surviving now only as a collection of some 80 to 100 in-words in the language mainly of show-business, it arose according to Partridge (1950) among showmen, circus folk and strolling players. Its origins may, however, go back to the Mediterranean *Lingua Franca. It is considered by Hancock (1984: 390–1) to be the result either of 'gradual language loss or decay, or else of large-scale interference from another language upon an already existing English cant'. The name probably derives from Italian *parlare* 'to speak' and much of its word-stock seems to derive from, *inter alia*, *Italian or Lingua Franca. A few Polari words (e.g. *ponce* 'pimp', *scarper* 'run away') have passed into wider currency.

Hancock, I. 1984. Shelta and Polari. In Trudgill, P. (ed.), *Language in the British Isles*, Cambridge, 384–403.
Partridge, E. 1950. Parlyaree. In Id., *Here, There and Everywhere*, 2nd edn, London, 116–25.

Polish

The eastern and by far the most widely spoken member of the *Lechitic branch of the western subgroup of the *Slavonic languages. It is the state language of the Polish Republic, where it has 35–40 million speakers.

Origins

The history of the Polish nation and statehood goes back to the 10th c., hence celebrations of the Polish *Tysiąclecie* ('Millennium') in 1966, one thousand years after the acceptance of Christianity in its Roman Catholic version under Mieszko I. The acceptance of Roman Catholicism accounts for the importance of Latin as an official language in the ensuing centuries. The name of the nation and the language is traced back to Polanie, Slav tribes living in most of the area bounded by the Rivers Odra (Oder) and Bug, the Carpathians and the Baltic Sea in the 8th to the 10th centuries.

Periods in the history of Polish

The history of the language can be divided into four periods. In the prehistoric period, when Polish tribes were forming their first political organisms, which ultimately produced a Polish state under princes of the Piast dynasty, Polish is not available to direct investigation. This period continued until the second half of the 12th c.

This prehistoric period was followed by the Old Polish period, which continued until the turn of the 15th to the 16th c., when Polish was restricted in its functions, and not homogenized as a standard language. A large amount of private correspondence from the early 16th c. survives, but Polish still had to compete with Latin in that area. Borrowings and calques (loan translations) from Latin, German and *Czech were common.

The subsequent Middle Polish period stretches to the late 18th c., which saw the development of education and extension of the functions of Polish in public life.

Modern Polish is regarded as having emerged in the second half of the 18th c. Polish was being taught and developed, and the period of subjugation following 1795 did not halt the process. (The territory of the Polish Republic was divided between Russia, Prussia and Austria in 1772, between Russia and Prussia in 1793 and again between the three in 1795.) Attempts by the partitioning powers to suppress or discourage Polish in the 19th c. produced some purism as a reaction, but Polish purism was moderate compared to, for example, Czech or Hungarian purism. Poland became an independent state again in 1918, which allowed Polish to flourish in education, press and radio. After the Second World War, television and population movements increased the homogeneity and versatility of the language. Some elements previously regarded as colloquial came to be accepted as standard.

Earliest attestations

The earliest attestations of Polish are in place-names, tribal names and personal names found in Latin documents from the 9th c. onwards. The Papal Bull of Gniezno (1136) contains over 400 names and the Bull of Wrocław (Breslau) (1155) 50. The first recorded Polish sentence is quoted to explain a place-name in the Latin history of the Cistercian monastery of Henryków near Wrocław (*c.*1270).

This kind of material is supplemented from 1386 onwards by Latin court records in which, even before 1500, over 8,000 sworn depositions are cited in the original Polish. These sources are joined by many others, including *Biblia Królowej Zofii* ('Queen Sophia's Bible'), a manuscript of most of the Old Testament, dating from before 1455, by a number of translators working from Latin and showing considerable reliance on Czech versions.

The emergence of Polish as a standard and literary language

Polish has existed as a literary language in a broadly standardized form from the early 16th c. onwards, exhibiting increasingly the homogeneity of form and plurality of function characteristic of standard languages. Mikołaj Rej (1505–69) advocated the wider use of Polish, rather than Latin, in literature and in church. The language of Rej's works (and some of Jan Kochanowski's) was described in the first grammar of Polish, *Polonicae grammatices institutio* (1568), written by Piotr Stojeński-Statorius, a Polonized Frenchman. This Golden Age also produced dictionaries, most notably the *Lexicon latinopolonicum* of Jan Mączyński (1520–87), which appeared in Königsberg in 1564 and contained nearly 21,000 Polish words. Łukasz Górnicki (1527–1603) urged the use of Polish expressions in preference to the fashionable habit of borrowing from Latin, Czech (whose refinement and advanced state of development he readily acknowledged) and other western European languages.

The Union of Lublin in 1569 (uniting Poland with the Grand Duchy of Lithuania) expanded Polish influence into Lithuania, Belorussia and Ukraine to the east, and brought traces of *Ukrainian into Polish when Ukrainian nobles adopted Polish. Polish enjoyed a Golden Age in the late 16th c., which produced Jan Kochanowski (1530–84), whose *Treny* ('Laments'), *Psalmy* ('Psalms') and poetry are still widely read, and Piotr Skarga (1536–1612), author of *Kazania Sejmowe* ('Sermons to Parliament').

The regional basis of the standard language

The language of 16th-c. Polish literature contains features characteristic of the Wielkopolska area, as well as features associated with the Małopolska area (see below, 'Dialects'). The dialect base of the standard language has been the subject of much argument among Polish linguists. The view put forward in 1948 by Zdzisław Stieber has many adherents: the early history of Poland as a state was connected both with Gniezno and Poznań in the Wielkopolska dialect area, on the one hand, and with Kraków in Małopolska on the other. The two dialect areas together provided the basis for a standard language, used in literature, but many issues were decided by reference to Czech, whose influence had been strong ever since Bohemia passed Western Christianity on to Poland. The present capital, Warsaw, is in Mazovia (Mazowsze), which did not join Poland until the 16th c., and was thus too late to contribute to the basis of the standard language.

After the Golden Age

In the 17th and 18th centuries, the language is felt to have suffered with Poland itself from wars with Muscovy and Sweden, as well as the Thirty Years' War. Polish literature came under strong French influence in the latter 17th c. By the mid-18th c., before the First Partition of Poland in 1772, Polish language and education had enjoyed some revival. In 1778 Father Onufry Kopczynski's long influential *Gramatyka dla szkół narodowych* ('Grammar for National Schools'), repeatedly reprinted until 1839, began to appear. The six volumes of Samuel Bogumil Linde's (1771–1847) dictionary of Polish appeared between 1807 and 1815 (second edition 1854–60, reprinted in 1951); they covered Polish vocabulary from the early 16th c. to their own time, and illustrated meanings with quotations from Polish writers from Kochanowski onwards. The 19th c. produced Romantic poets like Adam Mickiewicz (1798–1855), Juliusz Słowacki (1809–49) and Cyprian Norwid (1821–83), and writers of ornate prose like Stefan Żeromski (1864–1925) or Władysław Reymont (1867–1925) or the much more terse Bolesław Prus (1845–1912). Writers using the medium of Polish have recently won two Nobel Prizes for literature, Czesław Miłosz and Wisława Szymborska, the latter in 1996.

Printing

Printing began in Poland in the early 16th c., carried out chiefly by Germans such as Jan Haller (1467–1525), Hieronim Wietor (1480?–1548/9) and Florian Ungler (d. 1536), who had become Polish subjects. Their work was centred in Kraków.

Alphabet

Polish has used the Latin alphabet throughout its history. Jan Parkoszowic's *Traktat o ortografii polskiej* ('Treatise on Polish Orthography') (*c*.1440) had recommended the use of double letters to indicate long vowels. In contrast to Czech, where an acute accent <′> was used to mark long vowels, early printed Polish marked some vowels with <′> to distinguish quality rather than length.

The modern Polish alphabet is normally said to use 32 letters, including <ą, ć, ę, ł, ń, ó, ś, ź, ż>. The letters <q>, <v> and <x> are restricted to foreign words and are thus excluded from the count, though <x> is increasingly common in words like *fax*.

Dialects

There are five basic dialect regions: Wielkopolska (including Poznań and Bydgoszcz), Małopolska (including Łódź, Kraków, Lublin and Rzeszów), Mazowsze (including Warsaw, Białystok and Olsztyn), Silesia (including Katowice and Opole) and, most distinct, to the extent that many regard the dialects in question as a separate language, **Cassubian** (Kashubian) (including Gdańsk). Population movements following the end of the Second World War created areas of 'new mixed dialects' in the west of Poland (including Koszalin, Szczecin, Zielona Góra and Wrocław) and the north (east of Gdańsk and north of Olsztyn). Polish dialects are said to be mutually intelligible.

Interrelationship with other languages

Polish has been willing to borrow material from, and to be influenced by, other languages. Modern Polish still contains items borrowed by proto-Slavs from outside the Slavonic language area, such as *deska* 'board', *misa* 'bowl' and *pieniądz* 'money, coin'. Czech influence continued into the 16th c. Czech not only provided vocabulary, but also frequently contributed to the phonetic shape of some words which would have developed differently if they had simply followed the regular course of sound-changes in Polish. Latin influence was strongest from the 16th to the 18th c., especially in specialized and abstract terminology. German influence was strong in the 13th and 14th centuries, and affected particularly the vocabulary of trade, craft, building and military life. It became strong again during the period of the Partitions, providing terms used in administration and industry. Italian influence was mainly confined to the 16th and 17th centuries, contributing substantially to the vocabulary of costume, music, horticulture and cuisine. French influence was felt towards the end of the 16th c., and was strong in the 17th, 18th and early 19th centuries. It is reflected in the language of courtly life, building and the military. **Ukrainian** and **Belarusian** influences were strong in the 16th and 17th centuries, especially in camp terminology and pejoratively marked vocabulary (*hołota* 'rabble', *rubaszny* 'coarse'). They also acted as an intermediary for **Turkish** influence on Polish, particularly noticeable in the 17th c. in names for costume, but also in terms for political, social and commercial relations. In the 16th c. and at the turn of the 17th, Polish also benefited from **Hungarian** borrowings. Surprisingly for such a closely related language, **Russian** has had relatively little influence on Polish, even after 1945. English influence goes back to at least the 19th c. and is currently very strong. English has provided nautical, sporting and travel terms and is now contributing richly to the Polish of science and technology, politics, trade, industry, entertainment, computing, and domestic and social life.

Present situation

In the period between the two world wars Polish co-existed with other languages in the newly restored Polish state. Of the 32,107,000 people recorded in the 1931 census, as few as 21,993,000 claimed to be native speakers of Polish. The 1946 census held within Poland's post-war borders showed a population of 23,930,000. The population has continued to grow, and national minorities appear to make up less than 1% of the population of Poland. Polish minorities in other countries are frequently large, and tend to maintain a strong Polish identity, often developing a specific local variety of Polish, borrowing vocabulary from the local language and adapting it to the Polish grammatical and word-forming systems. Thus, in addition to having 35–40 million speakers in the Polish Republic itself, where it is the language of all state functions, Polish is also spoken by an estimated 10 million Poles abroad in Britain, France, Germany, the countries of the former USSR, and outside Europe, for example in North and South America and in Israel.

Brooks, M. 1975. *Polish Reference Grammar*. The Hague.
Fisiak, J. (ed.) 1996. *Collins Polish Dictionary*. Glasgow and Warsaw.
Rothstein, R. A. 1993. Polish. In Comrie, B. and Corbett, G. G. (eds), *The Slavonic Languages*, London and New York, 686–758.
Schenker, A. 1980. Polish. In Schenker, A. and Stankiewicz, E. (eds), *The Slavic Literary Languages: Formation and Development*, New Haven, CT, 195–210.
Swan, O. E. 1983. *A Concise Grammar of Polish*, 2nd edn. Lanham, MD.
Westfal, S. 1966. *The Polish Language*. Rome.

NIGEL GOTTERI

Polissian (see under *Belarusian*)

Pomak
The Pomaks are a Muslim minority in western Thrace in Greece, speaking a *Slavonic dialect closely related to *Macedonian and *Bulgarian. Like other minority languages in Greece, it has no official status whatsoever and no public presence. Estimates for the number of speakers range from 18,000 to 27,000.

Portuguese
A member of the *Ibero-Romance subgroup of the *Romance languages. In Europe it is spoken in continental Portugal (see map 19) (population 9.5 million) and the dependent islands of Madeira and the Azores, and in a small number of linguistic enclaves in Spain; there are also significant emigrant Portuguese communities in Germany, France and Great Britain. The largest Portuguese-speaking country is Brazil (population 159 million) which guarantees Portuguese its position as one of the six most widely spoken languages in the world. Portuguese has been an official language of the European Community since Portugal's accession in 1985.

History

Portuguese is a dialect of *Galician, the two languages originating in the Romance of the NW Iberian Peninsula, and diverging only with the political separation of Galicia and Portugal. In common with the rest of the Iberian Peninsula, the west is known to have been populated by the non–Indo-European Iberians and by pre-existent *Basque-speakers, and at a later date the region was colonized by Celtic tribes. The conquest of the Iberian Peninsula by Rome began in 218 BC. The central and southern part of what is now Portugal belongs to an area which was most rapidly colonized, named Lusitania (land of the Lusitani whose name gave the forms *Luso* and *Lusitano* subsequently used as synonyms of Portuguese). The territory further north, now Galicia and northern Portugal, resisted until 16 BC, eventually forming the region of Gallaecia (of the Gallaeci). The two areas underwent distinctly different patterns of Romanization, with Lusitania being quickly Romanized and assimilating Latin culture from an educated Roman population, while Gallaecia was colonized more slowly and the native population preserved their language for much longer. The Germanic invasions of the 5th to 7th centuries, under which the region belonged to the empire of the Suevi in the 5th c. and to that of the Visigoths in the 6th and 7th, failed to impose any linguistic unity on the region.

The influence of pre-Roman tribes on Portuguese is a matter of debate. The slow Romanization of the NW of the peninsula, compared with the rapid progress of Latin among the populations of the south, has been advanced as a reason for expecting considerable effect of Basque and Celtic as substrate languages on the Romance of Galicia and northern Portugal. Explanations of this kind have been advanced for distinctive phonological developments of Galician-Portuguese such as nasalization (*bonu(m)* > OPtg *bõo* > *bom* [bõ] 'good', *centu(m)* > *cento* [sẽtu] '100'), the extension of lenition to intervocalic laterals and nasals, where geminates were reduced and single consonants were lost (*dolore(m)* > OPtg *door* > *dor* 'pain', *villa(m)* > *vila* 'town'; *manu(m)* > *mão* 'hand', *senu(m)* > OPtg *sẽo* > *seio* 'breast', *pannu(m)* > *pano* 'cloth'), and the palatalization of initial *pl- cl- fl-* (*plorare* > *chorar* 'weep', *clave(m)* > *chave* 'key', *flamma(m)* > *chama* 'flame'), but a conclusive case for such substrate influences over natural phonological developments remains to be made. There are nevertheless clear effects of these languages on toponymy (*Coimbra* < *Conimbriga*, incorporating the Celtic *-briga* suffix; *Ambrões* and *Lamego*, relating to the Celtic tribe of the Ambrones) and vocabulary (*veiga* 'plain', *esquerda* 'left', believed to be cognate with Basque *ibaiko* 'bank' and *eskerra* 'left' respectively). Similarly, the Germanic superstrate is evident in anthroponyms (*Rodrigo* and its derivative *Rui*, *Gonçalo*, *Afonso*), in toponyms derived from them (*Guimarães* < *Vimaranis*, relating to a Count Vimara), and in basic vocabulary items such as *roupa* 'clothes', *luva* 'glove', which are common to other Hispanic languages.

The Arab invasion of the Iberian Peninsula in 711 left almost all of this territory south of the river Mondego in Islamic hands, with the territory between the Douro and the Mondego a disputed zone, subject to successive depopulation and repopulation. The Christian kingdom of Galicia was thus reduced to the area north of the Douro, which became the source of the Galician-Portuguese which would spread southwards with the Christian Reconquest of the 11th and 12th centuries. In the Arabic south, the presumably bilingual Christian populations continued to speak *Mozarabic. The influence of the *Arabic adstrate is less strong than in Spanish, and is mainly detectable in the lexicon, in particular in the fields of agriculture (*alface* 'lettuce', *algodão* 'cotton', *rabadão* 'shepherd'), commerce (*armazém* 'store', *quilate* 'carat', *alvanel* 'stonemason') and administration (*alfândega* 'customs', *alvará* 'decree', *bairro* 'district'); its prominence is decreasing as traditional terms fall into disuse, such as the old measures of the *arroba* and *arrátel* equivalent to 15 kilograms and 459 grams in modern terms. The major dialect boundaries (discussed below) clearly perpetuate the pre-Reconquest borders, suggesting that the development of southern varieties was a product of the repopulation of the south by northern speakers and the contact of northern dialects with the Mozarabic of the south;

nevertheless, the distinctive features of southern Portuguese cannot be attributed directly to Arabic influence (with the possible exception of simplification of the sibilant system). A few grammatical forms are traceable to Arabic: *oxalá* 'would that' from Arabic *wa šā llâh* 'may God will', *até* 'until' (blending *atées* < *(ad) tenus* and *ata* < Arabic *hátta*).

The nationhood of Portugal and the independence of Portuguese have their origins in Reconquest politics of the late 11th c. As the Christian Reconquest was gaining momentum, Coimbra having already been retaken in 1064, Alfonso VI of Castile attempted to reinforce his position by marrying his daughters Urraca and Teresa (Tarejia) to two Burgundian counts, Raymond and Henry (Henrique). He initially granted the kingdom of Galicia to Urraca and Raymond; in 1095 he gave the county of Portugal (Portucale, named after the towns of Porto and Cale (modern Gaia) on the mouth of the Douro) as an independent region to Teresa and Henrique, who resisted Urraca's later attempts to reunify the kingdoms. The county of Portugal only became clearly independent from the kingdom of Galicia in 1128, when D. Afonso Henriques seized power from his mother, taking the title of King in 1139 after a resounding victory over the Moors at Ourique. The Reconquest of Portugal was completed swiftly: Lisbon was retaken in 1147, with the aid of English Crusaders, and by 1168 only parts of the Algarve held out, the kingdom of Faro falling finally in 1249, nearly two and a half centuries before the fall of Granada completed the Castilian Reconquest.

From the 13th c. onwards the political and administrative centre of Portugal moved away from the northern heartland to the cities of Lisbon and Coimbra, as an increasingly less nomadic monarchy established Lisbon as the capital, and set up the first university there in 1288, though the institution had no permanent location until its establishment as the University of Coimbra in 1537. The city of Lisbon played a crucial role in the revolution of 1383, by which John of Aviz, the illegitimate son of King Pedro I, supported by the bourgeoisie of the cities but opposed by most of the nobility, was proclaimed King John I in defiance of the claims of the king of Castile, who had married the only daughter of the recently deceased King Fernando.

The overseas expansion of Portugal began with the capture of the north African town of Ceuta in 1415, followed by the colonization of Madeira in 1420 and the discovery of the Azores in 1427. From the 1420s the Infante Henrique (Prince Henry the Navigator), son of John I and Queen Phillippa of Lancaster, developed the exploration of the West Coast of Africa, beginning the voyages of discovery which were to culminate in the discovery of Brazil by Nuno Álvares Cabral in 1496, the voyage to India of Vasco da Gama in 1498, and the circumnavigation of the globe by Fernando de Magalhães (Magellan) in 1500. Until the late 16th c. Portugal was at the forefront of European expansion, establishing colonies and trading links in Africa, Asia and South America, and charting many other regions, including Australia, which it did not colonize. This vast enterprise was halted by the disastrous expedition of King Sebastian to North Africa which ended with his death at the battle of Alcazarquivir in 1578, leading to the annexation of Portugal by Spain in 1580. The restoration of Portuguese sovereignty in 1640 did not protect its Asian empire from encroachment by other European powers, notably England and the Netherlands, though it retained control over Brazil until 1822. In 1807 the Portuguese court took up residence in Rio de Janeiro, to escape the threat of the Napoleonic Wars, with the result that the distinctive palatalized final sibilants of European Portuguese became part of the speech of central and northern Brazil. The proclamation of a Portuguese Republic in 1910 was followed by dictatorship in 1926, lasting until the restoration of democracy in 1974, which brought with it the independence of Portugal's African colonies.

The Portuguese voyages of discovery led to language contact with African, Asian and South American languages which has yielded many lexical items (e.g. *bunda* 'buttocks', *carimbo* 'stamp' from Kimbundu; *chávena* 'cup', *louro* 'parrot' from Malay; *piranha* 'piranha fish', *maracujá* 'passion fruit' from Tupi). It also resulted in the emergence of a large number of Portuguese-based *creoles, originating either in local language contact situations or by the implantation of a version of a Portuguese-based lingua franca or reconnaissance language widely used by traders of all nations. It has been seriously suggested that many English- and Spanish-based creoles have a similar Portuguese origin. The colonization of Brazil resulted in the large-scale transportation of African slaves via São Tomé to the new colony, where they constituted over 50% of the population from the 1770s until the end of the 19th c. In Brazil itself, a form of the indigenous Tupi language, known as *Língua Geral* or 'Common Language', was used and taught as a lingua franca, constituting the principal language of three-quarters of the population until the 18th c. Popular Brazilian Portuguese displays enough features common to creole languages to suggest that creolization was one influence on its development. The divergence of European and Brazilian Portuguese reflects phonological innovations in both varieties (segmental in Brazilian Portuguese, prosodic in European Portuguese), and a preponderance in Brazilian Portuguese of lexical items originating in Amerindian languages such as Tupi and in the African languages of the former slave population. There has always been cultural contact between the two varieties, most recently in the opening up of Portuguese media to Brazilian television programmes.

Periods of the language

A distinction is usually made between Old Portuguese (*português antigo, português arcaico*), referring to the period from the earliest texts to 1540, Classical Portuguese (1540–1850), and Modern Portuguese (1850 to the present). There is sometimes a further subdivision of the Old Portuguese period into a Galician-Portuguese period (origins to 1350), during which the linguistic and cultural unity of Galicia and Portugal remained strong, and the Old Portuguese period proper (1350–1540). The 15th c. was the period in which major changes in Portuguese pronunciation took place, though the change in prosodic organization of European Portuguese, resulting in European Portuguese becoming a stress-timed language while Brazilian remained largely syllable-timed, was an 18th-c. development. The 16th c. saw a large-scale renewal of the literary vocabulary through relatinization and borrowing, under the twin influences of literary Classicism and Portuguese–Castilian bilingualism, though the roots of this current of lexical expansion are to be found in 15th-c. writers and translators.

The earliest documents entirely in Portuguese are the *Notícia de Torto*, a notary's draft of a legal complaint, of uncertain date but now judged to have been written between 1211 and 1216, and two versions of the first will of King Alfonso II, produced by simultaneous dictation on 27 June 1214, the other 11 copies produced at the time being lost. (Two other documents, the *Auto de partilhas* (a property deed) and the related will of Elvira Sanches, which bear the dates of 1192 and 1193 respectively, have been demonstrated to be late 13th-c. copies, presumably of original documents in Latin.) Many earlier documents ostensibly in Latin contain greater or lesser quantities of recognizably Portuguese forms, indicating a co-existence of Latin and Romance graphic codes to notate what was undoubtedly Romance linguistic material. Alfonso III (1248–69) was the first monarch under whom Portuguese was systematically used for chancery documents, though it was under his son Dinis (1269–1325) that Portuguese replaced Latin as the language of administration. Galician-Portuguese is the medium used for a vast body of lyrics of the 13th and 14th centuries, though some poems have been assigned dates of composition earlier than 1200. They were composed by *trovadores* from most of Iberia, including King Dinis of Portugal and King Alfonso X of Castile, in a number of genres: the courtly *cantiga de amor*, which drew on Provençal lyric devices and vocabulary and European conventions of courtly love, the *cantiga de amigo*, expressing female emotions and reflecting long-standing popular traditions which may also be evident in the *kharjas* (short pieces of verse in Romance embedded in Arabic poetry) which for some scholars bear a resemblance to them, and the satirical and bawdy *cantigas de escarnho*. The main body of Galician-Portuguese poems is preserved only in two 16th-c. Italian copies, the *Cancioneiro da Biblioteca Nacional* (formerly the *Cancioneiro Colocci-Brancuti*) and the *Cancioneiro da Biblioteca Vaticana*; contemporary copies do exist, notably the 14th-c. *Cancioneiro da Ajuda*, and two single sheets of parchment, the *Pergaminho Sharrer*, discovered in 1990, containing seven poems by King Dinis, and the *Pergaminho Vindel* which contains the seven known poems of the Galician Martin Codax. (Also in Galician, but with no discernible Portuguese elements, are the *Cantigas de Santa Maria*, poems in praise of the Virgin Mary, compiled by Alfonso X of Castile in the late 13th c.)

The first printed books in Portuguese (all translations) date from the end of the 15th c., with the *Tratado de Confissom* of 1489, the *Vita Christi* of 1495 and the *Historia do mui nobre Vespasiano* of 1496; the first grammars of Portuguese, by Fernão de Oliveira and João de Barros, appeared in 1536 and 1540 respectively. Notable among Portuguese literary works of the 16th c. are the plays of Gil Vicente, who also wrote in Spanish, João de Barros's *Ásia* chronicling the Portuguese discoveries in the East, and Fernão Mendes Pinto's more imaginative *Peregrinação*, and the poetry of Antonio Ferreira and Luis de Camões. Camões's epic *Os Lusíadas*, commemorating the voyage of Vasco da Gama to India in 1498, is often credited with the classical renewal of the Portuguese language, though it did little more than reflect contemporary developments.

19th-c. Romanticism, reflected in the works of Almeida Garrett (born João Baptista da Silva Leitão) and Alexandre Herculano, and Realism, most notably in the novels of José Maria de Eça de Queirós, strengthened the cultural influence of English and French on Portuguese language and literature, with Queirós in particular an intensive user of Gallicisms. The dominant figure of 20th-c. Portuguese literature is the modernist poet Fernando Pessoa (d. 1935), educated in Durban (South Africa), who wrote in four different identities, creating the heteronyms Alberto Caeiro, Álvaro de Campos and Ricardo Reis.

Orthography

Portuguese orthography uses the Latin alphabet, though only 23 of its letters are part of the central orthography. <k>, <w> and <y> are now restricted to foreign or classical terms, though <y> has at some periods been used as an alternative <i>; in Old Portuguese <i>, <j> and <y> were equivalent, as were <u> and <v>. The distinctive use of the til <˜> to indicate nasality is a direct continuation of the medieval scribal representation of superscript <n>; the use of <h> (in the digraphs <nh>, <lh>) to indicate palatal consonants reflects medieval representations of yod by <h>, and was probably borrowed from Provençal scribal practice before being officially adopted by the Portuguese Royal Chancery in the late 13th c. A common orthography has been seen as one of the principal features binding Portuguese and Brazilian language and culture, with the effect that several attempts have been made in the 20th c. to formulate a unified orthography. Proposals formulated in 1986, involving the abandonment of distinctive practices on both sides, were rejected as too radical; a less drastic solution recognizing the differences between the two varieties still awaits formal ratification.

Dialects

The major division of Portuguese dialects, established by M. L. F. Lindley Cintra in 1970, opposes a conservative northern area, retaining close affinity with Galician, to an innovative central and southern area corresponding largely to the territory reconquered from the Arabs after the 11th c., and thus more affected by the Arabic superstrate. Inside the northern area it is customary to distinguish Minhoto, of the northernmost Minho province; in the south, the Alentejo and the Algarve have distinct dialects. Beirão (the dialects of the central regions of Beira Alta and Beira Baixa, characterized by the extensive use of the apical sibilants known as the *s beirão*) straddles the two areas. The NE region of Trás-os-Montes retains a set of dialects (Mirandês, Sendinês, Rionorês and Guadramilês) which are more properly considered a form of Leonese, and which are gradually acquiring regional autonomy. Portuguese is spoken in several enclaves on the Spanish side of the eastern border, notably Ermesinde in the province of Zamora, Olivenza (which was Portuguese territory until 1801), and in Barrancos.

No single body sets linguistic standards in Portugal. The Academia das Ciências de Lisboa, founded in 1779, has been involved in lexicography and orthographic reform, rather than in language planning. Southern Portuguese, represented by the cultured speech of the university cities of Coimbra and Lisbon, has been the accepted standard since at least the 18th c. In the 20th c. the importance of Lisbon as capital has established Lisbon pronunciation as the norm for broadcasting and the teaching of Portuguese as a foreign language, though Coimbran speech is still widely considered more cultured.

Portuguese outside Portugal

Outside Europe, Portuguese is the national language of Brazil. Brazilian Portuguese lacks a clear standard, but is dominated by the speech of Rio de Janeiro (Carioca) and São Paulo (Paulista). Portuguese also retains the status of a national language in a number of African states (known as PALOP = Países Africanos de Língua Oficial Portuguesa). In Angola and Mozambique it is the official language despite being spoken by a minority of the population, no native African language having emerged as standard. In Cape Verde, where there are no indigenous African languages, a Portuguese-based creole stands beside Portuguese as a national and literary language, and forms a post-creole continuum with it. Similarly in São Tomé and Príncipe, the main creoles (Forro, Moncó) are the first language of most speakers, together with Angolar, a variety of the Umbundu spoken in Angola; Portuguese is the language of education but has no monolingual native speakers. In Guinea-Bissau there is a more complex multilingual situation, with a creole widely spoken but not recognized as a language of education or administration, beside African languages and Portuguese spoken by a small minority.

In Asia, Portuguese is still spoken in India in the former colonies of Goa, Damão and Diu, in Timor, and in Macau. Portuguese-based creoles are found in Malacca (*papiá kristang*), Sri Lanka (a form related to the almost extinct Indian creoles of Tellicherry, Cananor and Cochin), Korlai, Hong Kong (where it was brought by emigrants from Macau) and Java (Tugu); other Atlantic creoles such as Fa d'Ambu (Annobonese, spoken on the island of Annobon) and Papiamentu (spoken in Curaçao) (see under *Community languages (Netherlands)) retain signs of Portuguese influence.

Câmara, J. M. 1972. *The Portuguese Language*. Chicago.
Congress 1985. *Congresso sobre a situação actual da língua portuguesa no mundo, Lisboa: 1983, Actas* ('Congress on the Current Situation of Portuguese in the World'), vol. 1. Lisbon.
Cunha, C. and Cintra, L. F. L. 1984. *Nova Gramática do Português Contemporâneo* ('A New Grammar of Modern Portuguese'). Lisbon and Rio de Janeiro.
Hundertmark-Santos Martins, M. T. 1982. *Portugiesische Grammatik*. Tübingen.
Hutchinson, A. P. and Lloyd, J. 1996. *Portuguese: An Essential Grammar*. London.
Parkinson, S. 1988. Portuguese. In Harris, M. and Vincent, N. (eds), *The Romance Languages*, London, 131–69.
Taylor, J. L. 1970. *A Portuguese–English Dictionary*. London and Stanford.
Teyssier, P. 1980. *Histoire de la langue portugaise*. Paris.
—— 1984. *Manuel de langue portugaise (Portugal-Brésil)*, 2nd edn. Paris.
[Various authors] 1994. Portugiesisch. In Holtus, G., Metzeltin, M. and Schmitt, C. (eds), *Lexikon der Romanistischen Linguistik*, vol. 6.2, *Galegisch, Portugiesisch*, Tübingen, 130–692 (40 articles, 17 in Portuguese, 16 in German, 6 in French, 1 in Italian.)
Vázquez Cuesta, P. and Luz, M. A. M. 1971. *Gramática Portuguesa*, 3rd edn. Madrid.

STEPHEN PARKINSON

Pre-Hellenic, see *Pelasgian*

Pre-Indo-European

It is a reasonable assumption that a population of some kind existed in northern Europe in the period following the last Ice Age, some 10,000 years ago. Though we can never hope to know very much about the language or languages spoken by these people, serious attempts have recently been made by eminent scholars to reconstruct something thereof from possible surviving elements in known languages. Hamp (1990), for example, hypothesizes a number of phonological, morphological and lexical features. On the basis of a study of river-names, which tend to reflect the oldest strata in the toponymy of an area (see also *Old European), Vennemann (1994) constructs a bold hypothesis sketching the possible phonological structure of such a language and its apparent rules for word-formation and thence its word-order and inclines to the view that, though not itself *Basque, his hypothesized language belonged to 'the same linguistic stock' as Basque. More recently, however, Kitson (1996) has argued for the *Indo-European character of these 'Old European' river-names.

Hamp, E. P. 1990. The pre-Indo-European language of northern (central) Europe. In Markey, T. L. and Greppin, J. A. C. (eds), *When Worlds Collide: The Indo-Europeans and the Pre-Indo-Europeans*, Ann Arbor, 291–309.

Kitson, P. R. 1996. British and European river-names. *Transactions of the Philological Society*, 94: 73–118.

Vennemann, T. 1994. Linguistic reconstruction in the context of European prehistory. *Transactions of the Philological Society*, 92: 215–84.

Pre-Samnitic

Pre-Samnitic is the name given to the language of from four to seven brief inscriptions on vases (two to seven words, mostly personal names) found in Campania (southern Italy, south of Naples: see map 10). The two earliest inscriptions date from the 6th c. BC and are written in the *South Picenian alphabet. The others are in the *Etruscan alphabet and probably date from before 438 BC, the traditional date of the arrival of the Samnitic (Oscan) tribes in Campania. Linguistically, Pre-Samnitic is closest to *Umbrian and hence belongs to the *Sabellian branch of the *Italic languages.

Meiser, G. 1986. Katalog der 'praesamnitischen' Inschriften ('Catalogue of the "pre-Samnitic" inscriptions'). In Id., *Lautgeschichte der Umbrischen Sprache* ('Historical Phonology of the Umbrian Language'), Innsbruck, 19–21.

PETER SCHRIJVER

Prussian, Old

A West *Baltic language (in contrast to East Baltic *Latvian and *Lithuanian) which became extinct at about the end of the 17th c. It was spoken on the shores of the Baltic Sea in the area of what is now the Russian province of

Kaliningrad (formerly Königsberg) and the Polish province of Olsztyn, which together correspond to the former German region of East Prussia.

The earliest reference to the Prussians by name (*c.*956) is found in the accounts of an Arab traveller from Spain, Ibrahim ibn-Iakub, who mentions a people whom he calls the B(u)rūs. This name subsequently appears in several variant forms, including Pruzze, Prousi and Borussus. Even earlier, references are found in the *Geographia* of the Greek Claudius Ptolomaeus (Ptolemy) to tribes called the Galindai and the Soudinoi. These tribes are now commonly associated with the Galindians (who appear as the Goliad' in the Primary Chronicles of Rus', living in the 12th c. around Smolensk near the frontier between Russia and Belarus) and Sudovians (perhaps the same as the Yatvingians mentioned in the East Slavonic Hypatian Chronicle). Mention of the Goliad' and the Yatvingians provides at least some evidence that the area of Baltic speech was considerably greater than today. These two tribes must have adopted East *Slavonic dialects very early, whereas the related Prussians retained their separate identity in the face of German pressure for longer.

Old Prussian is known from five documents and various fragments, personal names and place-names. The oldest document, known as the Elbing vocabulary, consists of a list of 802 words in German and Old Prussian. The second is a list of 100 words contained in the Prussian Chronicle of Simon Grunau, dating from 1517–26. The most valuable documents are three catechisms printed at Königsberg, two of them in 1545, the third, also known as the Enchiridion, in 1561. The complete text of the first two and the first part of the Enchiridion can be found in Schmalstieg (1965). The scribes were German-speakers who, having not surprisingly had no training in phonetics, relied entirely on intuition and an orthographic system based on German. Nevertheless, detailed textual study has yielded important results, not only for Baltic linguistics but also for the study of *Indo-European in general.

Mažiulis, V. 1988– . *Prūsų kalbos etimologijos žodynas* ('An Etymological Dictionary of the Prussian Language'). Vilnius.
Schmalstieg, W. R. 1965. *Readings in Old Prussian*. University Park, PA.
—— 1974. *An Old Prussian Grammar: The Phonology and Morphology of the Three Catechisms*. University Park, PA, and London.
Toporov, V. N. 1975– . *Лрусский язык. Словарь* ('The Prussian Language. A Dictionary'). Moscow.

JIM DINGLEY

Punic, see *Phoenician*

Punjabi (see *Panjabi*, under *Community languages (Britain)*)

Puter (see under *Romansh)*

Q

Q-Celtic (see under *Celtic languages*)

R

Raetic

A language related to Etruscan. It may also be related to **Camunic, but this is less
certain.

Raetic is attested in some 200 inscriptions found in the Italian provinces of
Bozen/Bolzano, Trento, Verona, Vicenza, Padua and Treviso (see map 10), in the
Tyrol in Austria, in the Swiss canton of the Grisons (Graubünden) and in Slovenia.
The bulk of the inscriptions have been found in the provinces of Trento and
Bozen/Bolzano. It can be concluded that Raetic was the main, if not the only, lan-
guage of this nuclear area. The Raetic inscriptions date back to a time roughly
between 500 and 15 BC, in which year the Alps were finally conquered by the Romans.
All are written in alphabets derived more or less directly from the Etruscan alphabet.
The main collections of Raetic inscriptions can be found at the Museo provincial
d'arte and the Museo tridentino di scienze naturali, both in Trento, the Stadtmuseum
of Bozen/Bolzano and the Tiroler Landesmuseum Ferdinandeum in Innsbruck.

As for the affiliation of Raetic, it is now certain that it is related to Etruscan. There
are obvious correspondences both in verbal and in nominal morphology, from which
we can conclude that Raetic and Etruscan can be traced back to one protolanguage.
Roman historians maintain that the tribes of the Raeti go back to Etruscans who fled
to the Alps after the invasion of northern Italy by Gaulish tribes (400 BC), but this is
a mere myth based on a traditional motif of Classical writing. The relationship
between Raetic and Etruscan is more distant and they must have separated much
earlier, perhaps about 1200 BC.

On an archaeological level, the Raetic inscriptions belong to the cultural group of
Fritzens-Sanzeno, a civilization that is markedly different from, though influenced
by, the neighbouring contemporary civilizations, viz. the La Tène culture of central
Europe, the Este culture of north-eastern Italy, and the Etruscan culture of central
and northern Italy. In the nuclear area of the La Tène culture – i.e. southern
Germany and eastern France – **Gaulish* was spoken and in the area of the Este
culture **Venetic* was spoken.

Most inscriptions are very brief and contain only a few words. They are found on
objects of various kinds, e.g. ritual objects (bronze statuettes, pieces of stagshorn),
bronze vessels and ladles used for the mixing and drinking of wine, and stone steles.

Some refer to the owner of the object. Others commemorate its dedication to a deity and contain the names of the persons dedicating the object, sometimes in the framework of formulaic expressions. If the stone steles are tombstones, they must refer to persons buried underneath.

Schumacher, S. 1992. *Die rätischen Inschriften. Geschichte und heutiger Stand der Forschung* ('The Raetic Inscriptions. History and Present Position of Research'). Innsbruck.

—— 1998. Sprachliche Gemeinsamkeiten zwischen Rätisch und Etruskisch ('Linguistic correspondences between Raetic and Etruscan'). *Der Schlern*, 72.

STEFAN SCHUMACHER

Raeto-Romance, see *Rhaeto-Romance*

Ragusan (see under *Dalmatian*)

Rhaeto-Romance

The term 'Rhaeto-Romance' (or 'Raeto-Romance') is an umbrella term covering the *Romance speech varieties of three separate areas in Switzerland and northern Italy (see map 14), viz.:

  (1) the *Romansh dialects (often referred to in German as 'Bündnerromanisch'), numbering at most some 50,000 speakers, of the upper Rhine and Inn valleys and some of their tributary valleys in the canton of Graubünden (Grisons) in SE Switzerland;
  (2) (Dolomitic) Ladin (see under *Italy. III. Northern Italy), with some 30,000 speakers in all, in five valleys in the Dolomites;
  (3) Friulian (see under *Italy. III. Northern Italy), spoken over much of the Friuli-Venezia Giulia region in NE Italy and numbering perhaps as many as half a million speakers.

The three areas, though not geographically contiguous, are not far removed from one another – at their closest points, the Swiss and Dolomitic areas are separated by only about 80 kilometres, and the Dolomitic and Friulian areas by about 50 kilometres. But it must be borne in mind that communications in these Alpine regions are difficult and that the three areas are divided by territory where the prevailing speech is either a northern Italian dialect or else German.

If one considers all three varieties as branches of one Rhaeto-Romance language, as many scholars do, the implication is that all three are remnants of a once unitary linguistic continuum. Those who do not accept this view point out that there is no evidence that any such continuum ever existed in post-Roman times (more specifically, since the incursions of Germanic-speaking tribes in the 5th to the 8th centuries) and that each of the Rhaeto-Romance varieties in some respects resembles one or other variety of *Italo-Romance or *Gallo-Romance rather than other varieties of Rhaeto-Romance. Though some would go so far as to deny the validity of the concept of 'Rhaeto-Romance', others who do not accept that one Rhaeto-Romance language ever existed would nevertheless agree, on the basis of the shared

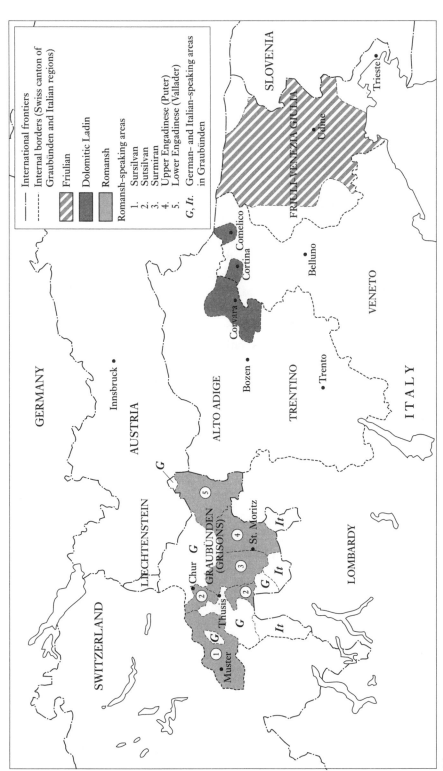

Map 14 Rhaeto-Romance areas. Some localities in the traditionally Romansh-speaking parts of the canton of Graubünden (Grisons) in Switzerland are by now largely and in some cases almost entirely Germanized; for a more detailed map of this area, see map 20, 'Linguistic zones in Switzerland'.

preservation of a number of conservative linguistic features, to the categorization of all three varieties as 'Rhaeto-Romance languages'.

Haiman, J. and Benincà, P. 1992. *The Rhaeto-Romance Languages*. London.
Holtus, G., Metzeltin, M. and Schmitt, C. (eds) 1989. *Lexikon der Romanistischen Linguistik*, vol. 3. Tübingen. ('Friaulisch', 8 articles in Italian, 563–645; 'Ladinisch', 10 articles, 3 in Italian, 7 in German, 646–673; 'Bündnerromanisch', 8 articles in German, 764–912.)

GLANVILLE PRICE

Riksmål (see under *Norwegian*)

Romagnol (see *Emilian-Romagnol*, under *Italy. III. Northern Italy*)

Romance languages

The languages derived from *Latin. Except in so far as they have, in the later periods of their development, been influenced by lexical borrowings from Classical Latin, they go back not to the highly codified and cultivated language that Classical Latin was but to 'Vulgar Latin', i.e. to the everyday spoken language.

There is no universal agreement either as to the number of varieties of Romance speech that are to be ranked as 'languages' rather than as dialects, or as to the classification of those that are ranked as languages.

Until quite recently, the majority of specialists would have recognized the following Romance languages:

   (1) *Portuguese
   (2) *Spanish
   (3) *Catalan
   (4) *Occitan
   (5) *French
   (6) *Rhaeto-Romance
   (7) Sardinian (see *Italy, V. Sardinian)
   (8) Italian (see *Italy, II. Italian)
   (9) *Dalmatian (extinct since the end of the 19th c.)
  (10) *Romanian

and many would have been prepared to include also:

  (11) *Francoprovençal.

Nowadays, there is increasing awareness of the separate linguistic identity of:

  (12) *Galician

and:

  (13) *Corsican.

This relatively simple pattern is, however, complicated by a number of debatable cases. In particular:

(a) Separate status is sometimes claimed (as in this encyclopedia) for ***Gascon,** otherwise classed as an Occitan dialect.
(b) ***Picard** and, more especially, ***Walloon,** although traditionally considered as the extreme northern dialects of French, are sometimes claimed as separate languages.
(c) Attitudes to Rhaeto-Romance vary greatly; there are, on the one hand, those who would deny any of the three major varieties in question (see ***Rhaeto-Romance**) the status of a 'language' and, on the other, those who recognize the Swiss, Dolomitic and Friulian varieties as separate languages.
(d) The status as 'dialects' of some of the major speech varieties of Italy (e.g. Piedmontese) is challenged by those who consider them to be 'languages'.
(e) A case can be made for considering the sub-Danubian varieties of Romanian, viz. ***Istro-Romanian,** ***Aromanian** and ***Megleno-Romanian,** as languages rather than dialects.

Further problems arise when one attempts to classify the Romance languages. Widely different classifications can be arrived at depending on the relative importance attached to such factors as historical development, typological (particularly phonetic and grammatical) features, geographical distribution and cultural factors.

Basing himself on features of phonetic and morphological evolution, the Swiss scholar Walther von Wartburg argued (1950) that a major dividing line within the Romance-speaking area in Europe followed the line of the Apennines from La Spezia on the west coast of Italy to Rimini on the east coast (so, unsurprisingly, it has come to be termed 'the La Spezia–Rimini line'). This led him to divide the Romance languages into an eastern group, which included central and southern Italian dialects and the standard Italian language, extinct Dalmatian, and Romanian, and a western group which included all the rest except Sardinian which does not fall neatly into either group. This classification, though widely accepted, has serious weaknesses; in particular, it groups Italian, the grammar of which is broadly similar to that of Spanish, Catalan, Portuguese, Occitan, and to a lesser extent French, with Romanian, whose grammar has evolved very differently.

A widely accepted geographically based classification, not necessarily incompatible with Wartburg's, divides the Romance-speaking part of Europe into five main areas:

(1) the ***Ibero-Romance** (or Hispano-Romance) area, including Portuguese, Galician, Spanish and Catalan;
(2) the ***Gallo-Romance** area, including French, Occitan together with Gascon (if it is considered to be a separate language) and Francoprovençal, and, in some versions of the system, northern Italian dialects;
(3) the Italo-Romance area, including standard Italian, the dialects of mainland Italy (with or without the northern dialects – see (2) above), Corsican and Sardinian;
(4) the Rhaeto-Romance area, including (whether or not one regards them as forms of the same language – see ***Rhaeto-Romance**) Swiss Romansh, Dolomitic Ladin and Friulian;
(5) Daco-Romance, i.e. Romanian (or, alternatively, to make room also for Dalmatian, 'Balkan Romance').

The major weakness of this classification is that it separates Catalan ('Ibero-Romance') and Occitan ('Gallo-Romance') which have a great deal in common.

A different approach identifies both French and Romanian as having sharply defined characteristics (phonetic, grammatical and/or lexical) that serve to distinguish them from the main block of languages (Portuguese, Spanish, Catalan, Occitan, Italian, to mention only the major ones) that have more in common with one another than with the more idiosyncratic (and, in a very geographical sense, peripheral) ones we have mentioned. Others would add to the list of languages to be distinguished from the main block Portuguese and/or Sardinian and/or Romansh (especially the Surselvan dialect thereof).

It is debatable whether these and other classifications in fact serve any very useful purpose.

Two Romance languages, French and Spanish, count among the world's major international languages and the number of those, throughout the world, who have a Romance language as their mother tongue has been estimated as high as 580 million.

Bec, P. 1971. *Manuel pratique de philologie romane*, 2 vols. Paris.
Bourciez, É. 1967. *Éléments de linguistique romane*, 5th edn. Paris.
Elcock, W. D. 1975. *The Romance Languages*, 2nd edn. London.
Iordan, I. 1970. *An Introduction to Romance Linguistics, its Schools and Scholars*, revised with a supplement, 'Thirty years on', by R. Posner. Oxford.
—— and Manoliu, M. 1972. *Manual de lingüística románica*, 2 vols. Madrid.
Malkiel, Y. 1978. The classification of Romance languages. *Romance Philology*, 31: 467–500.
Posner, R. 1996. *The Romance Languages*. Cambridge.
Posner, R. and Green, J. G. (eds) 1980–93. *Trends in Romance Linguistics and Philology*, 5 vols. The Hague and Berlin.
Wartburg, W. von 1950. *Die Ausgliederung der romanischen Sprachräume* ('The Break-up of the Romance Linguistic Area'). Bern. (French translation, 1967: *La Fragmentation linguistique de la Romania*. Paris.)

GLANVILLE PRICE

Romani

Romani (Romany, Romanes, 'Gypsy') is a Balkanized neo-Indo-Aryan language (see ***Indic languages**) spoken outside of India, principally in Europe and the Americas. It retains much of its Indic morphology, phonology and basic lexicon, but has undergone substantial syntactic reconstruction as a result of prolonged contact with Balkan languages, Byzantine Greek in particular. These features also characterize those dialects spoken outside of the Balkans.

Linguistic affinity

The ultimate linguistic affinity of Romani remains unestablished. In its lexicon and phonology in particular, it demonstrates a Central Indian core, but with greater evidence from North-western Indian and to some extend Dardic. Such linguistic clues support the most current theory of the origin of the population itself, which is that the ancestors of the Roma descend from a composite population assembled as a military force at the beginning of the 11th c. to resist the Islamic invasions led by

Mohammed of Ghazni. History suggests that this army, called the Rajputs, was intentionally drawn from non-Aryan populations, in particular the Aryan-speaking Dravidians from the Śudra caste, and the Pratihara who had settled in northern India from the north-west and who were related to the Alans and Ossetes. A more recent suggestion is that an East African element might also be considered, traceable to the Siddhis or Africans brought in by both the Muslim and the Hindu armies as mercenaries on both sides (see Hancock 1995).

Outside influences

On to this Indic core, surviving in perhaps 900 lexical items in modern Romani, have been grafted layers of Persian and *Kurdish (some 120 items), about 50 words from *Armenian and just three from Georgian (see *Caucasian languages. VI. Georgian), and Byzantine *Greek which has not only given over 250 words to Romani but has also provided most of the grammatical paradigm for the post-European (or 'athematic') lexicon. Items acquired between India and Europe generally conform to Indic (or 'thematic') grammatical rules.

The fact that a few items of apparent Burushaski origin, and at least one of Mongol origin, also turn up in Romani, helps determine the migratory route of the original Roma. Burushaski is spoken in the far north of the Hindu Kush, where the nearest passes out of India are at Shandur and Baroghil. The Mongol language could only have been encountered in the southern Caucasus and the north-eastern part of Persia later than AD 1250, when this area was occupied by the Golden Horde. It is also significant that there was no substantial influence from either Arabic or Turkish on the early lexicon. We can hypothesize, then, that the migration out of India took place between AD 1000 and 1027, from the far north of India almost directly west to the southern shore of the Caspian Sea, then up its western shoreline to the southern Caucasus, and from there directly west to the north coast of what is today Turkey, from there along the shoreline of the Black Sea to the Dardanelles, and thence up into the Balkans in Europe, probably between 1250 and 1300. The well-established theory that the original population split into three before reaching Europe, yielding what are today the European Romani, the Syrian Domari and the Armenian Lomavren populations, does not hold up under scrutiny. While the language of the Lom may be related to Romani, the language of the Dom almost certainly is not, descending from a separate migration out of India some five and a half centuries earlier.

Fragmentation and dialects

After arrival in Europe, the original population began to fragment almost immediately. A substantial number remained in the Balkans, where in Moldavia and Wallachia they had become enslaved by the middle of the 14th c. This was the result of a need for their skills (especially metalworking skills) in a damaged economy, and was not abolished until the second half of the 19th c. As a consequence, the Romani language developed during those centuries in isolation, and in close linguistic contact with *Romanian, and to a lesser extent *Hungarian and *Slavonic. This has subsequently become a distinct dialect cluster within the language, called today 'Vlax' (i.e. 'Vlach, Wallachian'). Not all of the Roma were enslaved; the rest of the migration continued north into Europe, fanning out and reaching most of the continent by 1500.

Romani is still most closely related lexically to Hindi and other North-western Indian languages, though its core phonology shows influences from Dardic (especially Phalura), Armenian and Greek, and the post-Byzantine dialects all demonstrate interference in all areas from the surrounding European language(s).

Romani dialects were originally divided into 'Vlax' and 'non-Vlax', though today we recognize three (or perhaps five) main branches, each divided further; altogether, some 60 distinct dialects have been recorded. In some countries, notably Britain and Spain, Romani has become restructured, consisting of a core of Romani lexical items in the grammatical and phonological framework of the national language, i.e. English or Spanish (Acton and Kenrick 1984).

Earliest attestations and scripts

The earliest samples of the language known to us date from 1542, from Britain, although Andrew Boorde who recorded them thought he was recording 'Egyptian' and accompanied them with a description of Egypt. Only four or five other examples of Romani from that early period have been located so far, and it was not until the 19th c. that longer texts began to appear in any number. These consisted mainly of collections of vocabulary lists, folk tales and gospel translations. Because of its composite linguistic nature, Romani did not inherit any single one of the Indian scripts, and remained unwritten (except by non-Romani academics) until the 20th c. Most of its various writing systems have been based upon the national orthography of the country in which the particular Romani dialect has been spoken, although a Slavic-based system, employing the wedge accent, has gained widest acceptance. Since the 1980s, the Linguistic Commission of the International Romani Union has devised an international standard orthography, and an increasing number of publications are appearing in it. Because it includes a number of non-traditional letters, it has not found universal acceptance so far; its most distinctive characteristic is the use of the morphographemic symbols <θ>, <q> and <ç> to represent phonetically distinct phonemes, thus *la manuśnàqe* 'for the woman' (= [la manušnjake]), *le manuśnànqe* 'for the women' (= [le manušnjange]).

Literary varieties and 'Common' Romani

The main dialects of Romani which have produced literatures are (i) the Northern, best represented by the Russian dialect, (ii) the Central, best represented by the Hungarian–Slovak group, (iii) Vlax, best represented by Kalderash, and (iv) Balkan, best represented by dialects spoken in Macedonia. But of all of these, Kalderash is emerging as the international dialect by default, being most widely spoken geographically and having the greatest number of speakers (*c.*2.5 million). It is upon the Vlax dialects that an International or 'Common' Romani is being modelled. This draws upon other dialects for words and grammatical rules lost in the Vlax group, e.g. *rukh* 'tree', replaced by *kašt* 'wood' in Vlax, or *tablo* 'warm', which is *tatičóso* in Vlax (i.e. 'hot' plus a modifying morpheme of Romanian origin). It also seeks to purge the language of its lexical adoptions, except for international items such as *tiléfono* or *integrácija*, and to expand the lexicon using various techniques such as metaphor (e.g. *drakhin* 'network', literally 'grapevine').

Recent developments

Since most of the world's Romani-speakers live in eastern Europe, it has only been since the collapse of communism in 1989 that contact with communities in the West has flourished. The increasing use of the language as a lingua franca has seen the proliferation of literally dozens of Romani publications, e.g. the magazines *Patrin* (Slovakia), *Informaciaqo Lil* and *Rrom po Drom* (Poland), *Buhazi* (USA), *Džaniben* (the Czech Republic). Poets such as Leksa Manus, Rajko Djurić and Sejdo Jašarov are producing works in Romani of the highest quality. The participation of eastern European Roma in the international political arena has increased sharply the need for a standardized dialect. The International Romani Union and the Roma National Congress use the language for all their internal correspondence. This has also led to the publication of several new linguistic descriptions of Romani (e.g. Boretzky, Hancock, Kochanowski, Matras, Sărau). Another side-effect of the collapse of communism and the resulting mobility of eastern European populations has been evidence of the reacquisition of Romani by groups for whom it had been lost. Thus in Hungary, where most of the country's nearly one million Roma abandoned the language because of Maria Theresa's legislation against it over two centuries ago, Vlax is gradually being relearnt. Additionally, the Romani Union has instituted a successful Romani Language Summer School, attended each year by a growing number of individuals, Roma and non-Roma, who wish to learn the language, and the Soros-Roma Foundation (Switzerland) is developing a programme to teach Romani to Roma who do not speak it. The Project on Ethnic Relations Romani Advisory Council (USA) has similar plans.

Despite having lived in the West for over 700 years, Roma remain fundamentally an Asian people, who speak an Asian language through which the Romani culture and world-view are expressed; thus for a diaspora population of between 9 and 12 million, at least half of whom speak varieties of Romani, the maintenance and cultivation of the language is a vital key to both political and ethnic survival.

Acton, T. and Kenrick, D. (eds) 1984. *Romani Rokkeripen To-Divvus* ('Romani Language Today'). London.

Boretzky, N. 1994. *Romani: Grammatik des Kalderaš mit Texten und Glossar* ('Grammar of Kalderash Romani with Texts and Glossary'). Wiesbaden.

Hancock, I. 1988. The development of Romani linguistics. In Jazyery, M. A. and Winter, W. (eds), *Languages and Cultures: Studies in Honor of Edgar C. Polomé*, Berlin and New York, 183–223.

—— 1995. *A Handbook of Vlax Romani*. Columbus, OH.

Holzinger, D. 1995. *Rómanes (Sinti)*. Munich and Newcastle.

Kochanowski, V. de G. 1994. *Parlons tsigane: histoire, culture et langue du peuple tsigane*. Paris.

Matras, Y. 1994. *Untersuchungen zu Grammatik und Diskurs des Romanes* ('Researches into Romani Grammar and Discourse'). Wiesbaden.

Sărau, Gh. 1991. *Limba romani* ('The Romani Language'). Bucharest.
Tcherenkov, L. and Heinschink, M. 1997. *Kalderaš (Romani)*. Munich and Newcastle.

IAN HANCOCK

Romanian

A **Romance language*, spoken principally in Romania and the Republic of
Moldova. Dialects (**Aromanian*, **Istro-Romanian*, **Megleno-Romanian*)
differing markedly from the language of Romania itself are spoken in various parts
of the Balkans, including Bulgaria, Greece, and most of the republics of the former
Yugoslavia.

Origins

The Roman province of Dacia was founded by the Emperor Trajan in AD 106, after
a military campaign that had begun in 101. Its precise limits are uncertain but it seems
to have included Wallachia, Oltenia, the Banat, at least the south of Transylvania,
and part of Moldavia. In 118–19, under Hadrian, the area was divided into two
provinces, Dacia Superior (in the north and centre) and Dacia Inferior (in the south),
and later (*c*.167–9) into three. There is evidence that the territory was colonized by
settlers brought in from many parts of the Roman Empire who, together with the
military and civil administration, introduced the widespread use of the **Latin*
language. It appears that the indigenous inhabitants, of Geto-Dacian stock, were
relatively rapidly Romanized, perhaps by the middle of the 3rd c., abandoning their
own language in favour of Latin.

   The Dacian provinces were frontier provinces in an area in which Rome was
frequently involved in warring with such peoples as the free Dacians (i.e. those who
remained outside the borders of the empire) and the Goths and, after only 165 years,
the decision was taken, in 271 or 272, during the reign of Aurelian, to withdraw from
the greater part of the area; the remainder, the south-west, was given up in 275. It is
not, however, entirely certain what happened to the Romanized civilian population,
of mixed Dacian and Roman ethnic origins, when the Roman legions and civil administration withdrew. According to the so-called 'sub-Danubian hypothesis', this
Romanized population also abandoned the area and withdrew south of the Danube;
it is claimed, in that case, that the ancestors of the present-day Romanians moved
back north across the Danube and the Carpathians and into Transylvania from other
parts of the Balkans in the 11th and 12th centuries. The balance of evidence,
however, seems to favour the 'hypothesis of continuity', according to which much,
if not all, of the rural population remained in at least parts of the area north of the
Danube, in which case the present-day Romanian-speaking population represents
the continuation of an unbroken linguistic tradition in the area. The linguistic,
toponymic and archaeological evidence, which each side seeks to interpret to its own
advantage, is unfortunately not enough to allow one to come to undisputed conclusions and the question therefore remains open.

   Whatever the truth of the history of the language during the 'dark period', it is certainly the case that Romanian evolved in very different circumstances from its western sister languages. Whereas all the other Romance languages evolved in a cultural context dominated by the Roman Catholic Church and the Latin language, the development of Romanian was profoundly affected by very different influences: the Orthodox Church, the Greek and Slavonic languages, and the Ottoman Empire.

Dialects

It is undisputed that there are four quite distinct varieties of Romanian. While these are often considered to be dialects of one Romanian language, it can also be argued that the differences between them are such that they would be better classified as distinct languages (as they are in this encyclopedia). The four varieties in question are:

(1) Daco-Romanian, the language of an area corresponding very roughly to the former Dacia, i.e. the Romanian of Romania itself and of contiguous areas, in particular the Republic of Moldova; dialectal distinctions exist within Daco-Romanian, though opinions as to dialectal areas vary: most would recognize a northern area (Moldavia – i.e. both that part of Moldavia which is part of Romania and the Republic of Moldova – and northern Transylvania), a southern area (southern Transylvania and Wallachia, which includes the capital, Bucharest), and a south-western area (the Banat), while some distinguish up to five dialects;

and three sub-Danubian dialects, i.e. those spoken south of the Danube:

(2) Istro-Romanian,
(3) Aromanian or Macedo-Romanian,
(4) Megleno-Romanian.

It is possible that what is termed 'common Romanian', i.e. the language of the period before it fragmented into the four main dialects, was spoken (in some areas alongside other languages) over an extensive area both south and (if one accepts the 'hypothesis of continuity') north of the Danube up till perhaps the 8th c. or later, and that the present dialectal divisions originate in a split between northern and southern varieties that occurred not later than the 10th c., quite possibly as a consequence of the arrival in the area of Slavonic-speaking peoples. Of the two southern varieties, Megleno-Romanian is probably an offshoot of Aromanian, while Istro-Romanian presumably originated north of the Danube and began to diverge from Daco-Romanian by the 13th c. or earlier.

Contact with other languages

It is agreed by most, though not all, specialists that some 80 or so Romanian words (some authorities argue for twice that number) are of Dacian origin (see under ***Daco-Thracian**). These include *balaur* 'dragon, monster', *mal* 'shore, bank', *vatră* 'hearth'.

Long and close contacts with ***Slavonic languages**, ranging from the liturgical use of ***Church Slavonic** and relations with neighbouring peoples (Bulgarians,

Serbs, Poles, Ukrainians) to more recent exposure to the influence of *Russian, have meant that a high proportion of Romanian words, probably at least 20% (some estimates are appreciably higher), and many of them among the basic elements of everyday vocabulary, are of Slavonic origin. They include such highly varied words as *ceas* 'hour', *gâscă* 'goose', *gât* 'throat', *glas* 'voice', *(a) iubi* '(to) love', *nevastă* 'wife', *nevoie* 'need', *oţet* 'vinegar', *pod* 'bridge', *pridvor* 'church porch', *prieten* 'friend', *primejdie* 'danger', *sfânt* 'holy', *slugă* 'servant', *smântână* 'cream', *sută* 'hundred', *târg* 'market (town)', *(a) trăi* '(to) live' and *zăpadă* 'snow'.

Romanian has also, over the centuries, acquired a number of words from the languages of other peoples and cultures with which it has been in close contact, in particular *Greek (e.g. *buzunar* 'pocket' < *bouzounara, proaspăt* 'fresh' < *proaspatos, trandafir* 'rose' < *triandafyllo*), *Hungarian (e.g. *(a) cheltui* '(to) spend' < *költeni, (a) făgădui* '(to) promise' < *fogadni, fel* 'kind, sort' < *féle, gând* 'thought' < *gond, oraş* 'town' < *város*), *Turkish (e.g. *cafea* 'coffee' < *kahve, cioban* 'shepherd' < *çoban, duşman* 'enemy' < *düşmen, papuc* 'slipper' < *pabuç*) and *German (e.g. *cartof* 'potato' < *Kartoffel, chelner* 'waiter' < *Kellner*).

In the course of the 19th and 20th centuries, vast numbers of words have been borrowed from western languages, in particular from *French (e.g. *(a) ambala* '(to) wrap up' < *emballer, avion* 'aeroplane' < *avion, birou* 'desk, office' < *bureau, creion* 'pencil' < *crayon, (a) deranja* '(to) disturb' < *déranger, (a) exploata* '(to) exploit' < *exploiter, nuanţă* 'shade, nuance' < *nuance, şansă* 'chance, luck' < *chance, şantaj* 'blackmail' < *chantage, teren* 'piece of ground' < *terrain*) and now, increasingly, from *English (e.g. *computer, gem* 'jam', *manager, marketing, meci* '(sporting) match', *standard*). A calculation made after the Second World War concluded that over 38% of words were of international (mainly French) origin.

Earliest attestations

What can with some justification be claimed to be the earliest recorded example of Romanian, or at any rate of the Balkan Romance from which it developed, is the brief utterance *torna, torna, fratre* ('Return [or turn back], brother') recorded (in Greek script) in a Byzantine chronicle of AD 587. Various Romanian proper names occur in Slavonic medieval texts from the area but the first extant text in Romanian itself is a brief document in *Cyrillic script, of some 200 words, dating from 1521; it is a letter from a nobleman, one Neacşu of Câmpulung (a town in the Carpathians NW of Bucharest) to a magistrate in Braşov in SE Transylvania, warning him that the Sultan had left Sofia and that his ships were on the Danube. It has been argued that the letter has a well-defined orthography which perhaps implies that, though nothing else of the period remains (or has yet come to light), a tradition of writing in Romanian already existed. However that may be, there is nothing else for over 40 years, when we have a deed of sale from 1563 or 1564. For the period between that date and the end of the century, we have a steadily increasing body of material with, in all, and from all parts of the Romanian-speaking territory, i.e. from Moldavia, Wallachia and Transylvania, well over a hundred non-literary texts (legal documents, letters, etc.). More significantly, the same period also saw the production of important translations (from Slavonic) of biblical texts, among them the Codex of Voroneţ (a translation of parts of the Acts of the Apostles), and the Psalters of Scheia, Voroneţ and Hurmuzaki, that all show a characteristic phonetic feature of northern dialects, namely rhotacization, i.e. the change of intervocalic [n] to [r], as in *bire* for *bine* (from Latin *bene* 'well').

Printing

There is ample contemporary evidence to indicate that the earliest printed book in Romanian was a catechism produced at Sibiu in 1544. Unfortunately, no copy of this remains. The earliest printed texts we have are due to a deacon of the Orthodox Church, Coresi, who, between 1559 and 1580, printed at Braşov 11 religious texts, beginning with a catechism of *c*.1560 of which only one (incomplete) copy is known, and continuing with, *inter alia*, a translation of the Gospels (*c*.1561), an Orthodox Liturgy (1570) and a Psalter (1577). Whereas, as we have seen, contemporary manuscript texts illustrate a northern rhotacizing tendency, Coresi's printed texts are basically in the language of southern Transylvania and Wallachia.

Romanian as a literary language

The earliest surviving original literary compositions in Romanian date from the 17th c. Foremost among them are prose chronicles of Moldavia by Grigore Ureche (1590?–1647?) and his continuer, Miron Costin (1633–91) (who was also one of the first Romanian poets whose name is known to us) and of Wallachia by Constantin Cantecuzino (*c*.1650–1716). The same century also saw the continued production of biblical translations and other religious texts, culminating in the first complete translation of the Bible (based to some extent on earlier partial translations), the Bucharest Bible of 1688 which marked an important stage in the development of a standard, national literary language. Other secular works from the period include juridical texts and Nicolae Milescu's accounts of his travels in the east, 'A Siberian Itinerary' and 'A Description of China'.

The foremost literary name in 18th-c. Romania was, beyond doubt, that of the important Enlightenment figure, Dimitrie Cantemir (1673–1723), who, in addition to numerous philosophical and historical works in Latin, Greek and Romanian, wrote what has been considered to be the first Romanian novel, *Istoria hieroglifică* ('Story in Hieroglyphs') (1705) and a three-volume 'Chronicle of the Ancient History of the Romanian-Moldavian-Wallachians' (1719–22).

From the period of the Romantics onwards, writing in Romanian comes to form a current of mainstream European literature. The national poet is Mihai Eminescu (1850–89). Other major figures are:

(1) poets: Vasile Alecsandri (1821–90), George Coşbuc (1866–1918), Tudor Arghezi (1880–1967), Octavian Goga (1881–1938), Lucian Blaga (1895–1961);
(2) dramatists: Vasile Alecsandri, I. L. Caragiale (1832–1912);
(3) short-story writers: Costache Negruzzi (1808–68), I. L. Caragiale, Ion Creangă (1837?–89), Ioan Slavici (1848–1925), Mihai Sadoveanu (1880–1961);
(4) novelists: Liviu Rebreanu (1885–1944), Camil Petrescu (1894–1957), George

Călinescu (also a critic) (1899–1965), Zaharia Stancu (1902–74), Marin Preda (1922–80);

(5) and the critic, historian and statesman, Nicolae Iorga (1871–1940).

Orthography and standardization

For the first three centuries during which Romanian was written, the Cyrillic alphabet was in general use, though the number of characters used was gradually reduced from 43 to 28. However, as early as the late 16th c., the Roman alphabet was used in some Romanian texts printed in Transylvania, which was then under Hungarian rule and where the Roman alphabet was used for Hungarian (indeed, the orthography of the Romanian texts in question is influenced by the orthographical conventions of Hungarian). The first to argue the need for a common literary language for all the Romanian-speaking provinces was the Metropolitan of Transylvania, Simeon Ştefan, in his preface to the first complete Romanian translation (by a number of priests and scholars) of the New Testament, published (in Cyrillic script) at Bălgrad (now Alba Iulia), in Transylvania, in 1648.

The final triumph of the Roman alphabet over the Cyrillic was largely due to the activity of the writers of the 'Transylvanian School' (*Şcoala ardeleană*) and to that of Ion Heliade (or Eliade) Rădulescu.

The members of the Transylvanian School were a group of young intellectuals who, by their writings on history and language, sought to foster among their compatriots an awareness of their national identity and of the Latin origins of the Romanian people and language. The principal members of the group were Samuil Micu (1745–1806), Gheorghe Şincai (1754–1816), Ion Budai-Deleanu (1760–1820) and Petru Maior (1761–1821). Micu's *Carte de rogacioni* ('Book of Prayers', Vienna, 1779) was the first Romanian book to be printed in the Latin alphabet. He and Şincai then brought out the first Romanian grammar to be published, *Elementa linguae daco-romanae sive valachicae* ('Elements of the Daco-Romanian or Wallachian Language', Vienna, 1780) which, despite its Latin title, was written in Romanian.

Ion Heliade Rădulescu (1802–72) was a poet, journalist (in 1829 he launched the first Romanian periodical, *Curierul românesc* 'The Romanian Courier') and publisher, and an indefatigable worker in the cause of promoting the Romanian language. In the Romanian grammar (*Gramatica românească*) that he published in 1828, he adopted a simplified version of the Cyrillic alphabet, dropping characters that were unnecessary for the adequate notation of Romanian. Then, in 1837, in his *Julia* (a translation of Rousseau's *la Nouvelle Éloïse*) he introduced what has come to be known as the 'transitional' orthography, consisting of 19 Cyrillic or modified Cyrillic characters, ten Latin ones <a, d, e, m, n, r, s, t, x, z>, and two <i, o> that could be either. This was widely used by many writers for over 20 years until the Latin alphabet was officially adopted in Wallachia in 1860 and in Moldavia in 1863.

There is, however, another aspect to the problem of orthography which is quite distinct from (though it can be influenced by) the question of what script one uses. The decision the reformers had to take was whether to adopt an orthography that was basically phonetic, i.e. designed solely or primarily for the purpose of rendering acceptably the sounds and forms of the Romanian language (and for this purpose either Cyrillic or Latin script could serve), or whether the orthography should reflect the Latin origins of the language or its associations with other Romance languages such as Italian. This consideration had not arisen for so long as Cyrillic script was in use but, once one opted for a Latin-based orthography, it became a live issue.

The members of the Transylvanian School strove for the renewal, modernization and standardization of the language, but adopted a highly purist attitude. They advocated the use not only of Latin characters but of an etymologizing spelling, in which the form of Romanian words was to be as close as possible to that of their Latin equivalents, and the elimination of non-Latin elements from the vocabulary. Gaps created by the banning of such foreign words or by the need to supplement the language to render it capable of dealing with the modern world would be filled by borrowing from Latin or from other Romance languages. This was, in general, the characteristic attitude of members of the School. However, in his second edition of *Elementa linguae daco-romanae* (see above) in 1805, Șincai took up a less extreme position and moved some distance in the direction of a phonetically based orthography.

The question was to remain unresolved for several decades, and was complicated by the fact that Heliade Rădulescu, who had at first advocated a phonetically based orthography, took up an Italianizing attitude. In 1869 the Romanian Academic Society, an association of writers and scholars, came out in favour of an etymologically based, Latinizing orthography, but in 1881 the recently founded Romanian Academy decided on a phonetically based system, with, however, some concessions to etymology. Modifications were introduced in 1932, 1904, 1953, 1965, and most recently in 1993 when some of the 1953 decisions were reversed.

The present situation is that Romanian has a standardized literary language, based primarily on the dialect of Wallachia and the capital, Bucharest, and a well devised, phonetically based orthography that is admirably adapted to the needs of the language.

In Bessarabia, during the period when, as the Moldavian Soviet Socialist Republic, it formed part of the Soviet Union, the Russian alphabet (i.e. a different form of Cyrillic from that in use in Romania generally up to the 19th c.) was imposed. In 1989, however, i.e. shortly before the break-up of the Soviet Union and Moldova's declaration of independence, the Latin orthography, in the form in use in Romania, was re-adopted.

Present situation

Romanian (i.e. Daco-Romanian, see above under 'Dialects') is the official language of Romania and of the Republic of Moldova (Moldavia) (where it is at present referred to as 'the *Moldavian language', *limba moldovenească*). There is a substantial Romanian-speaking minority (perhaps as many as 400,000) in Ukraine (in northern Bukovina which, between the wars, formed part of Romania), a small one (perhaps 25,000) in Hungary, and large communities in North America and Israel (in both of which various Romanian-language periodicals are published) and

Australia. Total numbers of speakers are estimated at about 25 or 26 million, including perhaps 2,000,000 (mainly Hungarian-, *Romani- or German-speakers) in Romania for whom it is not a first language. Speakers of other dialects remain in scattered communities throughout south-east Europe (see above under 'Dialects').

Academia Republicii Socialiste Române 1966. *Gramatica limbii române* ('Grammar of the Romanian Language'), 2nd edn, 2 vols. Bucharest.

Cioranescu, A. 1958–61. *Diccionario etimológico rumano*. La Laguna.

Close, E. 1974. *The Development of Modern Rumanian. Linguistic Theory and Practice in Muntenia, 1821–1838*. Oxford.

Deletant, D. 1995. *Colloquial Romanian*, 2nd edn. London.

Densuşianu, O. 1901–38. *Histoire de la langue roumaine*, vol. 1, *Les Origines*; vol. 2, *Le Seizième Siècle*. Paris.

Leviţchi, L. 1973. *Dicţionar român–englez* ('Romanian–English Dictionary'), 3rd edn. Bucharest.

—— and Bantaş, A. 1971. *Dicţionar englez–român* ('English–Romanian Dictionary'). Bucharest.

Lombard, A. 1974. *La Langue roumaine*. Paris.

Rosetti, A. 1973. *Brève histoire de la langue roumaine des origines à nos jours*. The Hague and Paris.

—— 1986. *Istoria limbii române. De la origini pînă la începutul secolului al XVII-lea* ('History of the Romanian Language. From its Origins up to the Beginning of the 17th Century'), 3rd edn. Bucharest.

—— Cazacu, B. and Onu, L. 1971. *Istoria limbii române literare* ('History of the Romanian Literary Language'). Bucharest.

Rusu, V. (ed.) 1984. *Tratat de dialectologie românească* ('Treatise on Romanian Dialectology'). Craiova.

[Various authors] 1989. Rumänisch. In Holtus, G., Metzeltin, M. and Schmitt, C. (eds), *Lexikon der Romanistischen Linguistik*, Tübingen, vol. 3, 1–521 (42 articles, 18 in French, 24 in German).

GLANVILLE PRICE

Romansh

A group of *Rhaeto-Romance dialects spoken in the canton of Graubünden (Romansh *Grischun*, Italian *Grigioni*, French *Grisons*) in SE Switzerland (see maps 14 and 20) by some 50,000 people.

Origins and history

When the Romans conquered the region, which then included what is now western Austria, in AD 15, it was named Provincia Raetia after the Illyrian (or possibly Etruscan) tribe that is supposed to have lived there. Romanization was thorough and a variety of spoken Latin became the local vernacular. In the 5th c., the Alemanni, a Germanic tribe, conquered the 'Austrian' Romance-speaking region which soon became almost totally Germanized. The rest of Raetia held out against the Alemanni for decades but was then subdued by the Ostrogoths. In the 6th c., the Franks conquered the area and began the process of Germanization that was to lead to the geographical separation of what were to become the different Romansh-speaking populations.

Dialects

A consideration of the dialectal fragmentation of Romansh is a necessary preamble to a discussion of the external history and literary tradition of the language.

Almost every village has its own vernacular, and five varieties have been successfully normalized in a written form. Two of these are closely related dialects spoken in the valley of the Vorderrhein (the more westerly of the two headwaters of the Rhine), namely Sursilvan (Surselvan) (*c*.20,000 speakers) upstream of the Flims forest, and Sutsilvan (Sutselvan) (*c*.1,500 speakers) below the forest and around the town of Andeer in the Hinterrhein. Sutsilvan is very close to Sursilvan and was established as a written language only in the mid-20th c. In the Engadine (i.e. the valley of the Inn), between St Moritz and the Austrian border, we have two forms of Ladin (also known as Engadinese), namely Upper Engadinese, otherwise known as Puter (*c*.3,500 speakers) in the south-west (the upper part of the valley), and Lower Engadinese or Vallader (*c*.6,000 speakers) in the north-east, i.e. downstream. The subdialect of Vallader spoken in the Val Müstair (Münstertal) is sometimes regarded as a separate dialect. The Bargaiot subdialect of Puter spoken in the Maira valley south-west of St Moritz to some extent constitutes a transitional dialect between Ladin and Lombard (see under *Italy, III. **Northern Italy**). Between these two main groups in the valleys of the Rhine and the Inn respectively is the Surmiran dialect (*c*.3,500 speakers) spoken in the Julia and Albula districts of central Graubünden.

Differences between the dialects are mainly lexical, though there are also significant phonetic and morphological differences. They are, however, mutually intelligible, at least with some effort. They have undergone considerable German and Italian influence which has affected about 5% of the vocabulary and also, to a minor extent, phonology and syntax. In Sursilvan, there is a curious difference between Catholics and Protestants in some features of their religious vocabulary, e.g. Catholic *gloria*, Protestant *gliera* 'glory'.

External history

Between 1367 and 1436, the people of present-day Graubünden united in three 'leagues' (one of them, in the NW area which includes Chur, the present capital of the canton, being the Grauer Bund 'Grey League', whence the name 'Graubünden'). Chur was largely destroyed by fire in 1464 and the reconstruction was carried out by German-speakers who settled there, with the result that the town became and has remained predominantly German-speaking. This loss of Chur to German language and culture prevented the development of Romansh as the dominant administrative language and facilitated the spread of German.

In the Middle Ages, Romansh immigrants spread along neighbouring valleys in Austria and as late as 1239 it is reported that many of the inhabitants of Innsbruck were Romansh-speakers. In the mid-16th c., the Engadinese Reformer Durich Chiampel ascertained the existence of a Romansh-speaking population in Vintschgau, partly along the Inn valley and the Paznaun valley in Austria. In the absence of reliable evidence, it is difficult to establish how far eastwards Romansh spread and exactly when and how it disappeared, though the lack of any evidence to the contrary seems to imply that Romansh was replaced by German not long after Chiampel's visit.

Graubünden became Protestant in the first half of the 16th c., but most of the Sursilvan- and Sutsilvan-speakers were later converted back to Catholicism by the Counter-Reformation. This confessional division of the Romansh-speakers has until recently been a major hindrance to any kind of linguistic or political unification of the Romansh-speaking communities.

In 1794 the Three Leagues decided that German, Italian and two varieties of Romansh, Sursilvan and Ladin, were to be recognized as official languages. In 1803, during the Napoleonic period, Graubünden joined what was then the Helvetic Republic and was later to become the Swiss Confederation. It was not until 1938 that, in the face of claims by Italian Irredentists that Romansh was an Italian dialect and that the area should therefore be ceded to Italy, Romansh was recognized by referendum as the fourth 'national' language of Switzerland. On the present situation, see below.

Earliest attestations

The oldest written attestation of Romansh consists of five words in a codex (now at Würzburg) and dating from the 10th or 11th c. The first real text is an early 12th-c. 14-line translation of a Latin homily in a manuscript now at Einsiedeln.

Literary tradition

The literary tradition begins with three Upper Engadinese texts, the rimed chronicle of Joan Gian Travers (1527) and Jachiam Bifrun's translations of a Protestant catechism (1557) (the first printed book in Romansh) and of the New Testament (1560). These were followed by Durich Chiampel's Lower Engadinese translation of the Psalms (1562), Daniel Bonifaci's Sursilvan Protestant catechism (1601), and, in 1611, by Gion Antoni Calvenzano's Catholic catechism in Sutsilvan and Steffan Gabriel's *Ilg Vêr Sulaz da pievel giuvan* ('The True Comfort of Young People'), a book of devotion for young Protestants written in Sursilvan. Although several books were published in both Sursilvan and Engadinese in the following centuries, it was not until the end of the 19th c. that there was a real literary awakening. The Sursilvan poet Giachen Caspar Muoth (1844–1906) and the Engadinese writer Peider Lansel (1863–1943) are possibly the best-known literary figures of this period. It was Lansel who formulated the often used slogan *Ni Talians, ni Tudais-chs, Rumantschs vulains restar!* ('Neither Italians nor Germans, Romansh we will remain!'). The 13-volume *Rätoromanische Chrestomatie* (1896–1919), a collection of stories, poems, popular plays and other literary texts edited by Caspar Decurtins, is an impressive and quite invaluable work. More recent literature has consisted especially of poetry and short stories, and some novels, treating especially nature, country life, and man's condition in the conflict between countryside, village and town. No real Romansh theatre has so far been founded but amateur performances take place with a certain regularity. In 1946 the Uniun da Scripturs Rumantschs ('Union of Romansh Writers') was founded.

Present situation

Almost all Romansh-speakers are bilingual with German as their second language. The number of speakers in Graubünden has remained more or less static at around 36,000 for the past century but, owing to the increase in the number of German- and Italian-speakers, the proportion of Romansh-speakers has declined from 40% to 22%. There has also been constant out-migration to other parts of Switzerland and, in the country as a whole, the actual number of Romansh-speakers increased from 46,430 in 1880 to about 51,000 in 1983.

The recognition of Romansh in 1938 as a fourth 'national language' (see above, 'External history') had the effect of rendering the language eligible for federal subsidies for cultural and other educational purposes. Within the canton of Graubünden, Romansh (together with German and Italian) was already an official language and could be used in proceedings in cantonal courts and in dealings with the cantonal authorities (though, in practice, it appears the language mainly used is German). Further progress at national level was made on 10 March 1996 when a referendum approved a constitutional change conferring on Romansh the status of 'official language for relations between the Confederation and Romansh-speaking citizens'.

In 1919 a cultural and linguistic society for Romansh was founded, the Ligia Romontscha (in Sursilvan) or Lia Rumantscha (in Ladin). Its main objectives are to represent the Romansh people, to coordinate the work of its associated societies, to organize the teaching of Romansh in nursery schools (*scolletas*), to elaborate dictionaries and publish other books, and to distribute subsidies. The fact that there is this officially recognized organization representing their culture is of great symbolic and practical importance to the Romansh people.

Romansh is widely taught in the first six years of elementary school, but in later years for only two or three hours a week, if that. Each village decides, on the basis of referenda, whether the medium of instruction in its school is to be only Romansh until German is introduced in the 4th grade, or German with only two or three hours a week in Romansh. There is no provision for Romansh outside the Romansh-speaking area apart from a training college at Chur with a section for Romansh teachers, professorships of Romansh at the universities of Freiburg and Zürich, and some provision for Romansh at university level in Bern, Geneva and St Gallen.

Four newspapers are published in Romansh, each appearing once or twice a week, namely *Gasetta Romontscha* (Sursilvan, Catholic), *La Casa Paterna/la Pùnt* (Sursilvan, Protestant), *la Pagina de Surmeir* (Surmiran), and *Fögl Ladin* (Ladin). There are also other monthly or irregularly published periodicals and the annuals of different societies. There is a steady, if limited, stream of books (both school-books and literary publications – see above).

Even the army has recognized the existence of the language; there are four Romansh-speaking companies, and military manuals have been translated into the language.

There have been radio broadcasts in Romansh since 1924, but on a regular basis only since 1943. There is now a daily ten-minute nation-wide news programme and, in Graubünden itself, four hours a day (since 1987), mainly of speech with some musical programmes. The radio programme 'Radioscola' has been of great importance in educating Romansh-speakers of all ages. TV programmes are limited to a couple of hours a week.

As we have seen above, there is no generally accepted unified literary language but, instead, five more or less standardized literary dialects (Sursilvan, Sutsilvan, Surmiran, Puter, Vallader) (attempts have also been made to promote standardized written forms of other subdialects). After several earlier attempts to create a unified language had failed, the Lia/Ligia decided in 1978 to make a new effort and, with a view to ensuring impartiality between the different dialects, entrusted the task to the non-Romansh linguist Heinrich Schmid. In 1982, he presented the outlines of 'Rumantsch Grischun' which is based not on any dialect but on a statistical approach, based on a comparison of the vocabularies of Sursilvan, Surmiran and Vallader. When all three use the same word, there is no problem but when one dialect uses a different word or form from the other two, the latter is used as the basis of the norm, e.g.:

Sursilvan	*Surmiran*	*Vallader*	*Rumantsch Grischun*	
clav	clav	clav	clav	'key'
plonta	planta	planta	planta	'plant, tree'
roda	roda	rouda	roda	'bicycle'
fil	feil	fil	fil	'thread'

In this way, Schmid attempted to create a normalized language based on words and forms enjoying the most widespread use throughout the Romansh-speaking territory and that most Romansh-speakers would understand without difficulty and without having to learn it. The intention is that Rumantsch Grischun should be used solely for administrative purposes, where there is need for a single language intelligible to all Romansh-speakers, while the existing standardized varieties continue in use for literary purposes. Despite many protests against this 'artificial' new standard, it has led to a 20-fold increase in the number of official publications and signs in Romansh and, consequently, has enhanced the prestige and use of the language.

Billigmeier, R. H. 1979. *A Crisis in Swiss Pluralism*. The Hague.
Gregor, D. B. 1982. *Romontsch, Language and Literature*. Cambridge.
Haiman, J. and Benincà, P. 1992. *The Rhaeto-Romance Languages*. London.
Liver, R. 1982. *Manuel pratique de romanche. Sursilvan–vallader*. Chur.
Lutz, F., Arquint, J. C. and Camartins, I. 1982. Die rätoromanische Schweiz ('Raeto-Romance Switzerland'). In Schläpfer, R. (ed.), *Die viersprachige Schweiz* ('Quadrilingual Switzerland'), Zürich and Cologne, 253–347.
Mützenberg, G. 1974. *Destin de la langue et de la littérature rhéto-romanes*. Lausanne.
Peer, O. 1979. *Dicziunari rumantsch, ladin–tudais-ch* ('Romansh Dictionary, Ladin-German'), 2nd edn. Chur.

[Various authors] 1989. Bündnerromanisch. In Holtus, G., Metzeltin, M. and Schmitt, C. (eds), *Lexikon der Romanistischen Linguistik*, Tübingen, vol. 3, 764–912 (8 articles in German).

Vieli, R. and Decurtins, A. 1962. *Vocabulari romontsch sursilvan–tudestg* ('Sursilvan–German Dictionary'). Chur.

INGMAR SÖHRMAN

Rumanian, see *Romanian*

Runes

Runes (see fig. 12) are the constituent characters of an alphabetic form of writing used at one time or another by many or most of the *Germanic-speaking peoples. Runic writing, which is almost exclusively epigraphic, goes back at least as far as the 2nd c. of the Christian era, but may be somewhat older. The earliest archaeologically dated artefacts bearing runic inscriptions are from shortly before or around AD 200 (the allegedly runic Meldorf fibula, from *c.* AD 25, may well be inscribed with Roman capitals). The bulk of the earliest inscriptions comes from present-day Denmark (with Meldorf, northern Germany, only a little way to the south), although examples also hail from as far afield as southern Norway, Gotland, the north-east of what is now France and eastern Europe. On the basis of this dating and distribution, it has been suggested that runic writing originated in Jutland or the Danish islands *c.* AD 100. The peoples living there at the time, it is argued, were in regular contact with the Roman Empire, and so learnt of the Romans' ability to record language. They were, however, distant and independent enough to devise their own system of writing rather than simply adopting the Roman alphabet – notwithstanding that several of the original runic characters are clearly based on Roman capitals (e.g. ᚱ ᚺ ᛒ). This interpretation has by no means gained general acceptance, and many rival theories exist about the origin of the runes. While all sensible scholars concede that they must be derived from one or more Mediterranean alphabets, there is controversy about time, place and the particular alphabet(s) involved.

There is equal uncertainty about the original purpose of runic writing. Some urge an exclusively or primarily religious, others a mercantile function. The early inscriptions themselves are too laconic, and many too hard to interpret, to cast much light on the question. Personal names (owners' or makers' marks? dedications?) occur frequently on loose objects, while a number of stone inscriptions seem to be of memorial type. There is, though, nothing in the extant material from the first centuries of runic writing indicative either of pagan rituals and beliefs or of a firm link with trade. Indeed, some have wondered whether the Germanic peoples had serious need of a writing system at all.

In many parts of the Germanic-speaking world runic writing can only have survived for a few hundred years at the most. In Germany it seems to have continued until the 8th c., in Frisia perhaps until the 9th. Only in Anglo-Saxon England and above all in Scandinavia did it exist side by side with Roman-alphabet writing for any length of time. The Anglo-Saxons were a two-script community between *c.* AD 650 and 900, and the Scandinavians between *c.*1000 and 1400 – indeed in a few parts of Scandinavia runes were still in use as late as the 18th c.

Once introduced, neither the runic alphabet nor runic writing practices remained static. The original alphabet contained 24 characters, arranged in an order quite unlike that of the Phoenician–Greek–Latin tradition (as is illustrated by the fact that an alternative name for 'runic alphabet' is *fuþark*, after the first six characters), and

Fig. 12 Forms of the runic alphabet: (a) the older *fuþark*; (b) the Anglo-Saxon *fuþorc*; (c) the long-branch younger *fuþark*; (d) the short-twig younger *fuþark*. Illustration by courtesy of Anne Haavaldsen, University of Bergen.

each rune had a Germanic name. The writing could run left to right, right to left, or boustrophedon. The Anglo-Saxons ultimately increased the number of characters to 31 to take account of sound changes in their language, altered the shapes and possibly the names of a few characters, and began to write consistently from left to right. The Scandinavians, too, adopted left-to-right as the sole direction of writing, but otherwise went entirely their own way, reducing the number of characters to 16 and simplifying the shapes of many of them. This revolution seems to have happened *c.*700, and the resulting alphabet is known as the younger *fuþark* to distinguish it from the Germanic (or older) *fuþark* and the Anglo-Saxon *fuþorc*.

The decrease in the number of runes coincided with a considerable increase in the phonemic inventory of the developing Scandinavian language. Viking-Age Scandinavian inscriptions thus render only crudely the speech sounds of Old *Norse. Nevertheless, the Scandinavians used variants of the younger *fuþark* for almost three centuries to write everything from complex memorial inscriptions to brief messages on wood. It was only with the coming of the Roman alphabet *c.*1000 that some attempt was made to provide for a more exact representation of sound (initially by the use of a diacritic dot); the gradual expansion in the number of characters that led to what is often known as the medieval *fuþark* was not complete until about 1200. In those parts of Scandinavia where runes continued in use after the Reformation, they tended to become diluted with letters of the Roman alphabet.

Elliott, R. W. V. 1989. *Runes. An Introduction*, 2nd edn. Manchester.
Page, R. I. 1973. *An Introduction to English Runes*. London.
—— 1987. *Runes*. London.

MICHAEL P. BARNES

Russenorsk

A *Norwegian- and *Russian-based *pidgin language that evolved in northern Norway in the late 18th c. for purposes of intercommunication between Russian traders and Norwegian fishermen. It lasted until the First World War.

Broch, I. and Jahr, E. H. 1983. Russenorsk: a new look at the Russo-Norwegian pidgin in northern Norway. In Ureland, P. S. and Clarkson, I. (eds), *Scandinavian Language Contacts*, Cambridge, 21–65.

Russian

A member of the eastern group of the *Slavonic languages and a close relation of *Ukrainian and *Belarusian, Russian is now spoken principally on the territory of the Russian Federation and is known in the other successor states of the former Soviet Union and in the countries of the former Soviet bloc.

Earliest attestations, inscriptions, manuscripts, printed texts

Literature began in Russia as a result of the introduction of Orthodox Christianity in 988–9, bringing the country a religion, an alphabet and a written language. However, the Slavonic liturgy and translations of parts of the Scriptures were probably brought to Russia well before the conversion, from Moravia, Bohemia, Bulgaria or Constantinople. At any rate, medieval Russian literature grew out of translations of the Greek liturgy and Scriptures into Old ***Church Slavonic**.

Old Church Slavonic (with East Slavonic dialectal features) was the language of early religious literature, while secular documents used local vernaculars. Kiev, the main cultural centre until 1240, was never a strongly centralized state like Muscovy, its successor, and many of its texts were characterized by regional variations.

The earliest preserved manuscript is the *Остромѝрово еванˢгелие* (*Ostromírovo evángelie* 'Ostromir Gospel Book'), a translation of the Gospels copied for the governor of Novgorod in 1056–7. Other documents in Old Church Slavonic include treaties between Kiev and Constantinople dated 911, 944 and 971 (preserved in a manuscript no earlier than the 14th c., however), Svyatoslav's anthology or *Изборник* (*Izbórnik*) of Christian literature dated 1073, and the *Новгородские служебные минеѝ* (*Novgoródskie sluzhébnye minéi* 'Novgorod Minaea') of 1095–7, collections of church canticles or lives of the saints for all the days of each month. Other manuscripts, such as Hilarion's *Слово о законе и благодати* (*Slóvo o zakóne i blagodáti* 'Sermon on Law and Grace') of the 1040s, in praise of the Christianization of Russia, a further anthology by Svyatoslav dated 1076, *Хождение игумена Даниила* (*Khozhdénie igúmena Daniíla* 'Abbot Daniel's Pilgrimage [to the Holy Land]'), dated about 1106–8, and an inscription on a cross made for Princess Euphrosyne of Polotsk (1161), are written mainly in a Russian recension of Old Church Slavonic.

Some documents were written in a hybrid of Church Slavonic and the vernacular: Vladimir Monomakh's *Поучение* (*Pouchénie* 'Admonition'), a moral disquisition for his sons (*c*.1110–25); *Повесть временных лет* (*Póvest′ vremennýkh let* 'Primary Chronicle'), completed *c*.1113, giving the history of the Slavs to the end of the 11th c. (one version survives in the Laurentian Chronicle of 1377, another in the Hypatian Chronicle of *c*.1425); *Слово о полку Ѝгореве* (*Slóvo o polkú Ígoreve* 'Lay of Igor's Campaign'), perhaps *c*.1185, an account, of still-disputed authenticity, of Prince Igor's campaign against the Polovtsians. Prince Mstislav Volodomirovich's *Дарственная грамота* (*Dárstvennaya grámota* 'Deed of Gift') to the St George Monastery in Novgorod (*c*.1130) is the earliest surviving secular document. A pure form of Old Russian (East Slavonic) is found in the *Русская Правда* (*Rússkaya Právda* 'Russian Law Code'), possibly of the 1020s.

The *Берестяные грамоты* (*Berestyanýe grámoty* 'Birchbark writs', 11th–15th c.), incised with a stylus on bast and found during excavations, begun in 1951, in Novgorod, Smolensk, Vitebsk, Pskov and Staraya Russa, contain domestic and commercial letters, with echoes of live popular speech, and provide evidence of a considerable spread of literacy in Novgorod, extending beyond the clergy, feudals and merchants. Some 11th-c. texts were inscribed on stone, coins or domestic utensils. Graffiti dating from 1052 and 1054 have been discovered on the walls of the Cathedral of St Sofia in Kiev. The Tmutorokan′ Stone of 1068 (of disputed authenticity) describes how Prince Gleb Svyatoslavich measured the distance across the straits of Kerch′ on the ice.

Most of the early texts derive from Kiev or Novgorod, but from the 14th c. the area of production extends to Pskov, Yaroslavl', Ryazan', and above all Moscow, whose mushroom growth ensured its status as undisputed centre of Russia.

Printing

Church Slavonic books for the East Slavs had been printed in Kraków in 1491, but printing began in Moscow only in the 1550s, the earliest dated book with a Moscow imprint being the epistle-book Апостол (*Apóstol*) printed by I. Fëdorov and P. Mstislavets in 1563–4. The two printers were sponsored by Ivan IV and Metropolitan Makary at a time when the government was anxious to standardize the texts of church books by publishing them in printed form. Fëdorov further published an Азбука (*Ázbuka*, 1574), the first Slavonic primer, in L'vov, then, in Ostrog, a Greek–Old Church Slavonic chrestomathy and a folio edition of the Old Church Slavonic Bible (1581). Printing in Moscow resumed in 1589, and in 1614 the Moscow Printing House opened, publishing primers, a treatise on infantry, and the Уложёние (*Ulozhénie* 'Civil Law Code', 1649). Under Peter I, St Petersburg broke the near monopoly of Moscow printing, and a new civic script was introduced to serve printing needs, originally for important scientific literature.

Scripts

On the origins and early development of the Cyrillic alphabet, in which Russian has been written throughout its recorded history, see *Cyrillic and Glagolitic scripts.

In the 14th c. the Metropolitan Cyprian, a Bulgarian, introduced reforms designed to restore earlier South Slavonic usage (the 'second South Slavonic influence' – the first being represented by Old Church Slavonic and the Cyrillic alphabet). In order to 'improve' Russian Church Slavonic, partly under the influence of the practice of Serbian and Bulgarian refugees from the Turkish-occupied Balkans, forms were adapted to contemporary Bulgarian usage, with a restoration of some obsolete letters.

The civic alphabet, introduced under Peter I in 1710, discarded a number of letters and simplified others. Meanwhile, spelling remained chaotic until the late 18th c., when the morphological principle favoured by M. Lomonosov (1711–65) and the Imperial Academy of Sciences finally took precedence over the phonetic principle advocated by V. Tredyakovsky (1703–68). In 1797 the letter <ë> was proposed, purportedly by N. Karamzin (1766–1826), to denote [jo] in alternation with [je]: сел0/сёла. Lomonosov, in his Россійская граммáтика (*Rossíyskaya grámmatika* 'Russian Grammar', 1755), retained the letter < ѣ > ('yat''), which, though almost identical in pronunciation with <e>, still helped to distinguish certain homophones.

The simplification of spelling was widely discussed in the 19th c., and in the early 20th c. the Imperial Academy set up its own Orthographical Commission, which proposed reforms that were carried out in December 1917. Where two letters had the same value, one was dropped; this involved the replacement of < ѣ > by <e>, <θ> by <ф> and <i> by <и>. The recommended spelling <ë> for [jo] was, however, omitted in the final version of the reform. The hard sign <ъ> was henceforth to be used only as a separative (<ь>, silent since *c.*1200, had long been redundant, albeit fulfilling a function in the 18th c. by indicating the end of a word; in the Soviet period an apostrophe was proposed in its stead, but <ь> prevailed). The spelling of certain prefixes and endings and of some pronominal forms was also reformed.

Literary and standard registers

Writing was practised in Rus' after the conversion of 988, and Russianized Church Slavonic was used as a literary language in religious and learned texts, with varying admixtures of the vernacular, a virtually pure form of which was used for legal, administrative and other secular documents. The second South Slavonic influence (14th–15th centuries), which aimed to restore a 'purer' Church Slavonic, prevented a fusion of learned and popular elements and perpetuated functional dualism until the 18th c. The relationship between the vernacular and Church Slavonic was much discussed in the 18th c., when literary Russian was still in a state of flux, with archaic, vernacular, chancery elements and loan-words rubbing shoulders uneasily in the absence of stabilizing factors still to be introduced. Peter I's alphabetic reform had further restricted the sphere of influence of Church Slavonic.

M. Lomonosov's *О пóльзе книг церкóвных в россúйском языкé (О pól'ze knig tserkóvnykh v rossíyskom yazyké* 'On the Use of Church Books in Russian', 1757) tackled the problems of (a) the co-existence of Old Church Slavonic lexis and the Russian vernacular in the literary language, (b) stylistic differentiation, and (c) the codification of current practice in the theory of three styles. The high style, in Lomonosov's definition, was dominated by Church Slavonic lexis (though not by its syntax), and was to be used for odes, epics and dignified orations; the middle style, based on educated colloquial usage, with some admixture of Slavonicisms, was for satires, eclogues, prose and drama (tragedy, however, could be written in the high style); the low style, colloquial and entirely Russian, was for comedies, epigrams, songs, letters and accounts of everyday matters.

A further step towards the creation of the literary language was taken by N. Karamzin. Strongly influenced by French lexis and syntax, Karamzin tried to approximate the literary language to the speech of the aristocracy, excluding Slavonicisms and introducing new words and calques based on western European languages, especially French. He meant to distance literary Russian from Slavonic and Latin and bring it closer to French, the language of polite society and secular knowledge, and strove to write elegant Russian on the basis of the language of educated society, replacing Lomonosov's heavy Germanic syntax by a more elegant French style. Karamzin distilled western European and Slavonic elements into an intermediate style based on the language of the court, in practice reducing Lomonosov's three styles to one, the middle style. In modified form his language formed the basis of the literary language of the 19th c. and the spoken language of the intelligentsia. However, Karamzin's style lacked elements of living speech, and it is A. Pushkin (1799–1837) who is credited with fusing the three historical elements of literary Russian – Church Slavonic, western European practice and the vernacular – into a balanced whole, retaining the elegance and polish of Karamzin's courtly language, but invigorating it through a judicious use of colloquial and folk elements. In the later 19th c., the language drew on western sources in the creation of a vocabulary designed for a literary medium dominated by the influence of philosophy and sociology.

Russian literature came on to the world stage in the early 19th c. The country's greatest poet, Alexander Pushkin, wrote not only verse but prose and drama, while his younger contemporary, Mikhail Lermontov (1814–41), is best known for the cyclical novel *Hero of Our Time* (1840). Novelists of the second half of the century include Ivan Turgenev (1818–83) (*Rudin* 1856, *Nest of Gentlefolk* 1859, *On the Eve* 1860, *Fathers and Sons* 1862), Ivan Goncharov (1812–91) (*Oblomov* 1859), Leo Tolstoy (1828–1910) (*War and Peace* 1865–9, *Anna Karenina* 1875–7, *Resurrection* 1899) and Fëdor Dostoevsky (1821–81) (*Crime and Punishment* 1866, *The Idiot* 1868–9, *The Devils* 1871–2, *The Brothers Karamazov* 1879–80). Nikolai Gogol' (1809–52) wrote plays (*The Inspector General* 1836), cycles of short stories and the novel *Dead Souls* (1842). Anton Chekhov (1860–1904), a writer of short stories and lyrical dramas (*The Seagull* 1896, *Uncle Vanya* 1897, *The Three Sisters* 1901, *The Cherry Orchard* 1904), bridged the two centuries, as did Maxim Gorky (1868–1936) with his novel *Foma Gordeev* (1899), the play *The Lower Depths* (1902) and the autobiographical *Childhood* (1913–14).

Poets of the early post-1917 period include Anna Akhmatova (1889–1966), the Symbolist Alexander Blok (1880–1921), the peasant poet Sergey Esenin (1895–1925), the Acmeist Osip Mandelshtam (1891–1938) and the Futurist poet Vladimir Mayakovsky (1894–1930), who also wrote plays. Main prose writers of the period were Isaac Babel' (1894–1938) (*Red Cavalry* 1926), Evgeniy Zamyatin (1884–1937) (*We*, written 1920–1), Mikhail Bulgakov (1891–1940) (*The White Guard* 1924, *The Heart of a Dog* 1925, *The Master and Margarita* 1928–40) and Mikhail Sholokhov (1905–84) (*Quiet Flows the Don* 1928–40, *Virgin Soil Upturned* 1931). In the post-Stalin period, prose is represented by Boris Pasternak (1890–1960) (*Dr Zhivago* 1958) and Alexander Solzhenitsyn (b. 1918) (*One Day in the Life of Ivan Denisovich* 1962, *The First Circle* 1968, *Cancer Ward* 1968, *August 1914* 1971, *The Gulag Archipelago* 1973–5), as well as by the so-called 'village-prose' writers of the 1960s–1970s, and verse by the poet best known in the West, Evgeniy Evtushenko (b.1933). Writing of the late 1980s and 1990s has been remarkable for the rise of interesting women writers, of whom the most talented is Tatyana Tolstaya.

Geographical spread and recession

Since Russian may be assumed to have encroached, in varying degrees, on all territories occupied by the Russian state, this section takes the form of an account of territorial expansion and recession over 1,000 years.

The first Russian state, Kievan Rus', bordered in the west on the West Slavs, in the NW on the ancestors of the Lithuanians and Latvians, and in the east on **Turkic**-speaking peoples who had established states on the middle and lower Volga. The principalities of Kievan Rus' were centred in southern towns such as Galich, Turov, Vladimir Volynsky, Pereyaslavl' and Novgorod Seversky, in the north in Polotsk, Smolensk, Pskov and Novgorod. In 1240 Kievan Rus' became part of the Mongol Empire, and principalities such as Kiev and Chernigov fell to Lithuania, whose union with Poland (1386) extended Polish influence into west Russia. Meanwhile, the principality of Moscow, 500 square miles in area in 1301, had begun to expand, a process accelerated by its Grand Princes.

Ivan III (ruled 1462–1505) and Vasily III (1505–33) seized all the eastern lands, including Tver' and the city-republic of Novgorod, as well as principalities such as Yaroslavl', Rostov and Ryazan'. Ivan III made some headway against Lithuania in the Dnieper area, while Vasily III took Smolensk and annexed Pskov. Ivan IV (1533–84) seized the territories of the Kazan' khanate (1552) and Astrakhan' (1554), thus opening the way to Siberia and giving Moscow control of the Volga to the Caspian Sea.

During the so-called 'Time of Troubles' (1598–1613), Moscow and Novgorod were for a time under foreign domination. However, in the 1640s the Romanovs, whose House had been established in 1613, pushed through Siberia to the Pacific Ocean and the Amur river basin, while Tsar Alexei Mikhailovich (1645–76) restored much of present-day Belarus and Ukraine to Muscovite control. The Treaty of Nystadt (1721), which concluded the Great Northern War against Sweden, secured for Peter I a foothold on the Baltic from Riga to Vyborg, as well as Estonia, Livonia (the larger part of present-day Latvia) and part of Karelia. The city of St Petersburg was founded in 1703. Catherine II (1762–96) established control over the north coast of the Black Sea, annexing the Crimea in 1783 and Odessa in 1791. As a result of the third partition of Poland (1795), Russia obtained Lithuania, Courland (the part of Latvia that lies south of the Western Dvina), the province of Volynia and the greater part of Belorussia. After the Napoleonic Wars the Duchy of Warsaw was given to the Russian Crown.

By the mid-19th c. the empire was at its greatest extent, larger even than the USSR was destined to be. Russia had gained Bessarabia, Daghestan and other parts of Transcaucasia and the Black Sea littoral from the Ottoman Empire early in the century, while in the late 1820s Transcaucasia and Azerbaijan were incorporated after a war with Persia. By the 1870s Russia ruled the whole of the Caucasus and had acquired Sakhalin and founded the far-eastern towns of Blagoveshchensk and Khabarovsk. In the later 19th c. the Central Asian khanates of Bukhara and Khiva became Russian protectorates, Tashkent was taken in 1865, in 1867 the capital of Kazakhstan was established at Verny (Alma-Ata from 1921, also Almaty since 1993), Samarkand was acquired in 1868, Khiva in 1873 and Kokand in 1876. Russia also expanded into Korea and Manchuria, where a railway was needed to link Russian Asia with Vladivostok. However, the Russo-Japanese War of 1904–5 halted Russian expansion in the Far East until 1945. Alaska, annexed to Russia in the 1730s, was sold to the USA in 1867.

The Treaty of Brest-Litovsk (1918) ceded vast areas of Russia to Germany, including the Baltic republics and Ukraine, and by 1922 Poland, Finland and the Baltic republics had declared independence, while Bessarabia had been annexed by Romania. However, the Soviet Constitution of 1923 incorporated the Ukrainian,

Belorussian and Transcaucasian republics into the USSR, followed in due course by five Central Asian republics. In 1940 the Baltic republics were annexed and Russia wrested Bessarabia from Romania, joining it to the Moldavian autonomous republic and establishing the Moldavian Soviet Socialist Republic. After 1945 and the victory over Nazi Germany, Soviet frontiers were advanced almost to the former Tsarist boundaries, as the USSR moved the frontier west to include all historical Ukrainian and Belorussian lands, and the Kurile Islands in the North Pacific became Russian again in accordance with the Yalta agreement of February 1945.

After the collapse of the USSR in 1991 and the declaration of independence by its former republics, the Russian Federation was established, occupying approximately the same territory as the Russian Soviet Federative Socialist Republic (17,075,400 sq. km). Access to the Black Sea via Odessa and Sevastopol′ came under Ukrainian control, and the Baltic republics controlled much of the former Soviet Baltic seaboard. Countries of the former Soviet bloc also declared independence. It is now policy in most of these countries to encourage the study of languages other than Russian, but it seems likely that the language will continue to be used as a lingua franca for some time to come.

Dialects

Dialects divide broadly into those north of Moscow and those south of Moscow, though there are 'islands' in the dialect map, due to population mobility resulting from expansion, resettlement and displacement.

The northern group, deriving from the small NW area about Novgorod, whose lexis is permeated by Finnic loans (see ***Finno–Ugrian languages**), covers an area including Novgorod, Vologda, Archangel, Yaroslavl′, Kostroma, Vyatka, Perm′, Nizhny Novgorod, Vladimir, and the southern group an area including Kaluga, Tula, Ryazan′, Orёl, Kursk and Voronezh. North–South dialectal differences in pronunciation and grammar are not great, nor are dialectal features completely uniform across either of the two areas; however, *g* is pronounced as a plosive in most northern dialects, but as a fricative in the south, while the pronunciation of *ch* as [ts] is common in the north, and the northern infinitive + nominative construction may have originated in the Novgorod area, possibly from its Finnic (***Estonian**) substratum, since there is a parallel construction in that language. In most southern dialects, *o* in an initial or pretonic syllable is pronounced [ʌ], and some dialects have lost the neuter gender.

There are significant lexical differences between north and south, particularly in agricultural lexis and the names of some domestic utensils, e.g. northern *izbá*, southern *kháta* 'hut'; northern *ukhvát*, southern *rogách* 'oven fork'; northern *kvashnyá*, southern *dézha* 'kneading trough'; northern *boronovát′*, southern *skorodít′* 'to harrow'; northern *lémekh*, southern *sóshnik* 'ploughshare'; northern *kuznéts*, southern *kovál′* 'smith'; northern *petúkh*, southern *kóchet* 'cockerel' (the northern form in each case corresponding to the national standard norm). *Orát′* 'to plough', now obsolescent, was found only in northern dialects, for standard *pakhát′* (cf. northern *pakhát′* 'to sweep').

Northern dialects subdivide into the eastern or Vologda-Vyatka group (the largest of the groups); the northern or Pomeranian, which shares some features with dialects of the Karelian peninsula and the area of the river Onega; and the western or Novgorod group (the dialect of Novgorod is the only one whose characteristics can be followed consistently from the beginning of the literate period to the present day; it shares a Finnic substratum with Pskov, which, in addition, also has a ***Baltic** component).

Southern dialects are much more varied than northern, and comprise the SW or Kursk-Orël group, cognate Cossack dialects and dialects of the Don area, the eastern or Ryazan'-Voronezh group and the NW or Tula group.

Northern and southern dialects are separated by a narrow band of central dialects, extending from Pskov in the west through Moscow to Penza, in some of which southern forms dominate, in others northern.

The Moscow dialect, which by the 16th c. had become the Russian standard, adopted some northern and southern forms, e.g. northern [t] rather than southern [t'], e.g. [si'dit] for *sidít* 'sits' (southern [si'dit']), and southern [ʌ] for [o] (which characterizes northern dialects) in initial and pretonic syllables, e.g. [vʌ'da] for *vodá* 'water' (northern [vo'da]) (this latter feature ('akan'e') was known in Moscow dialect as early as the 14th c. and was received pronunciation by the early 17th c.). The transfer of the capital to St Petersburg in 1710 had little effect on standard pronunciation, except that [ʃtʃ] for <ш> was preferred to long [ʃʃ].

Present situation

In the 1989 census, 163,578,000 (out of a Soviet population of 285,743,000) gave Russian as their native language and 69,010,000 as their second language. Native speakers of Russian in the Russian Federation, which was established after the collapse of the USSR in 1991, are estimated at 119,866,000, with 27,156,000 speaking it as a second language, a total of 147,022,000.

Article 68 of the constitution of the Russian Federation (which includes 21 republics) (12 December 1993) reads:

(1) Russian is the state language of the Russian Federation over the whole of its territory.
(2) The republics are entitled to establish their own state languages, which are used side by side with Russian in local authorities and state institutions.
(3) The Russian Federation guarantees to all its peoples the right to preserve their native language and create conditions for its study and development.

Russian has official status as a working language in all organizations of the United Nations Organization, in the Organization for Security and Cooperation in Europe, and in UNESCO.

All former republics of the USSR have included an article in their constitution specifying their titular language as the state language. A Soviet Law on the Languages of the USSR (24 April 1990), requiring the compulsory teaching of Russian, as the official Soviet language, became irrelevant after the collapse of communism. Nevertheless, a knowledge of Russian survives in former republics. Belarus, where Russian is used in the legal system and in public life, has Russian special schools and Russian TV channels, books and newspapers. Knowledge of Russian is widespread in other former republics, also in Mongolia (which has a Russian newspaper, *Новости Монголии* 'Mongolian News'). In Latvia, many schools are Russian-language orientated, there are Russian TV programmes, newspapers, library holdings and theatres, and Russian is used in law by mutual agreement. In Ukraine, the use of Russian is guaranteed under article 10 of the Constitution adopted on 28 June 1996.

In the countries of the former Soviet bloc, the study of Russian was compulsory at school and, to a lesser extent, at tertiary level. However, the language was often regarded as a medium for ideological propaganda and standards were low. Many of the newly independent states are replacing Russian with western European languages, especially English, to a lesser extent German, French and Spanish. In Slovakia, Russian is still taught as a second or third language in secondary schools. In Hungary, Russian-teachers are converting to teach English, German, French or Spanish; in Poland, Russian is finding its level as a normal means of economic and cultural contact. In the former East Germany, 'second language' command of Russian is claimed for students (two to three thousand per annum) and trade officials who spent protracted periods in Russia. In Romania, there are 9,000 Russians and 31,000 Lippovans (Russian Old Believers who fled from persecution to the Danube delta in the 18th c.) and Russian is used in services by the Christian Cult of the Ancient Rite; Russian ceased to be a compulsory subject in schools as long ago as 1964, but may still be taught as a first or second foreign language. In Bulgaria, Russian is now optional in many schools, and some teachers of Russian are being retrained as teachers of other languages; the language is well established in the universities of Sofia, Veliko Turnovo and Plovdiv.

Russian is also kept alive in some émigré communities, notably in Paris, where there have been three waves of immigrants since 1917 and the community is now in its fifth generation. Books in Russian are published by YMCA Press and by the Institut des langues slaves. The Orthodox Church has played a major part in preserving the language, but services are often held in French, for the benefit of younger Parisians of Russian descent. Long-standing Russian-speaking communities in Australia (18,000), Canada (32,000) and America (461,000) have now been joined by a substantial Russian-speaking community in Israel.

Auty, R. and Obolensky, D. (eds) 1977. *An Introduction to Russian Language and Literature (Companion to Russian Studies*, vol. 2). Cambridge.

Chernykh, P. Ya. 1962. *Историческая грамматика русского языка* ('Historical Grammar of Russian'). Moscow.

de Bray, R. G. A. 1969. *Guide to the Slavonic Languages*, revised edn. London.

Entwistle, W. J. and Morison, W. A. 1949. *Russian and the Slavonic Languages*. London.

Falla, P. (ed., English–Russian), Wheeler, M. and Unbegaun, B. (eds, Russian–English) 1993. *The Oxford Russian Dictionary*, revised and updated by C. Howlett. Oxford and New York.

Filin, F. P. (ed.) 1979. *Русский язык. Энциклопедия* ('Russian. An Encyclopedia'). Moscow.

Kirkwood, M. 1993. Soviet Language Laws: 1989–90. In P. J. S. Duncan and M. Rady (eds), *Towards a New Community. Culture and Politics in Post-Totalitarian Europe*, London, 147–60.

Matthews, W. K. 1960. *Russian Historical Grammar*. London.

Timberlake, A. 1993. Russian. In Comrie, B. and Corbett, G. G. (eds), *The Slavonic Languages*, London, 827–86.

Vlasto, A. P. 1988. *A Linguistic History of Russia to the End of the Eighteenth Century*. Oxford.

Wade, T. 1992. *A Comprehensive Russian Grammar*. Oxford.

—— and Ryazanova-Clarke, L. 1999. *The Russian Language Today*. London.

TERENCE WADE

Rusyn, see *Ruthenian*

Ruthenian (Rusyn)

Ruthenian (Rusyn) is a term used to describe a number of essentially different languages. The one factor that these languages share is a set of features that mark them out as clearly *Slavonic, and predominantly in the Eastern group, although this will have to be modified in one particular instance.

The word 'Ruthenian' (but *not* 'Rusyn') has been used to refer to the chancery language of the Grand Duchy of Lithuania, a written language that shows features of both *Ukrainian and *Belarusian with a strong admixture of *Polish. This language was in use in the 16th and 17th centuries. With more geographical than linguistic accuracy, this language has also been called 'West Russian' (see Stang 1935). For a full analysis, see Pugh 1996.

The modern usage of the term is fraught with political overtones that make the whole question very delicate. The problem arises out of the mixture of dialects spoken by people living in the area of the Carpathian mountains, and out of the bewildering variety of religious and national allegiances to be found there. The nature of the problem is set out in Dézső 1967. The very existence of a separate Rusyn nation and language is denied by many scholars. It is, however, a fact that a language called Ruthenian (Rusyn) is spoken by some 25,000 people (descendants of immigrants from eastern Slovakia) in Serbian Vojvodina where it has acquired official status and is used to a limited extent in education and the mass media. It is sometimes referred to as the Bačka language (or Bačka dialect of Ukrainian) after the district of Vojvodina where most of the speakers live. The first book in this language, by the priest Hawryil Kostel'nyk, was published in 1904. Kostel'nyk also published a grammar in 1923. The language has been described as a mixture of Ukrainian, Polish and *Slovak elements, which places it on the margins of both Eastern and Western Slavonic. The vocabulary has been heavily influenced by *German, *Hungarian and Serbian (see *Serbo-Croat). Attempts have been made to forge a specific Rusyn (i.e. not Ukrainian) identity among certain communities in the USA, in Poland (among the Lemko Ukrainians), and even in the Transcarpathian province of Ukraine itself.

Most importantly the term 'Rusyn' must now be used to refer to what was proclaimed on 27 January 1995 as 'the literary language of Rusyns in Slovakia'. No grammar of this form of the language has yet appeared (though Magocsi 1976 may serve as a language to be taught in schools. With no grammars and only a limited range of dictionaries available as yet (see Magocsi 1996), it is not possible to say how this norm differs from the Rusyn of Serbia. There are some contributions in Rusyn in Magocsi 1993. The issue remains delicate. The new language is not accepted by all those who might be called Rusyns. With an independent Ukraine to the east gaining in strength and self-confidence, the attraction of literary Ukrainian as a means of communication must be strong indeed.

Bidwell, C. 1971. *The Language of Carpatho-Ruthenian Publications in America*. Pittsburgh.

Dézső, L. (Laslo Dezhe) 1967. *Очерки по истории закарпатских говоров* ('Studies on the History of the Transcarpathian Dialects'). Budapest.

Gustavsson, S. 1992. Between East, West and South Slavic: Rusyn language planning. In Bugarski, R. and Hawkesworth, C. (eds), *Language Planning in Yugoslavia*, Columbus, OH, 223–5.

Horbach, O. 1984. Bačka dialect. In Kubijovič, V. (ed.), *Encyclopedia of Ukraine*, Toronto, vol. 1, 157–8.

Lutskay, M. 1830, *Gramatica Slavo-Ruthena seu Vetero-Slavicae, et actu in montibus Carpathicis Parvo-Russicae, ceu dialecti vigentis linguae* ('Slavo-Ruthenian or Old Slavic Language [. . .]'). Buda (reprinted with an afterword by O. Horbatsch, Munich, 1979).

Magocsi, P. 1976. *Let's Speak Rusyn [. . .]. Prešov Region Edition*. Englewood, NJ.

—— (ed.) 1993. *The Persistence of Regional Cultures: Rusyns and Ukrainians in Their Carpathian Homeland and Abroad*. New York.

—— 1996. *A New Slavic Language is Born: The Rusyn Literary Language of Slovakia*. New York.

Pugh, S. 1996. *Testament to Ruthenian. A Linguistic Analysis of the Smotryc'kyj Variant*. Cambridge, MA.

Stang, Ch. 1935. *Die Westrussische Kanzleisprache des Grossfürstentums Litauen* ('The West Russian Chancery Language of the Grand Duchy of Lithuania'). Oslo.

JIM DINGLEY

Rutul (see under *Caucasian languages. IV. North-East Caucasian family*)

S

Saami, see *Sámi*

Sabellian languages

The term 'Sabellian' has been used in at least two different senses, both of them relating to subgroups of the *Italic languages. For some scholars, as for Peter Schrijver in this encyclopedia (see *Oscan, *Umbrian), it is synonymous with *Osco-Umbrian. Other scholars (including Coleman 1986) restrict it to a group of minor Osco-Umbrian languages, consisting of *Aequian, *Marrucinian, *Marsian, *Paelignian, *Sabine, *Vestinian and *Volscian.

Coleman, R. 1986. The central Italic languages in the period of Roman expansion. *Transactions of the Philological Society*, 1986: 100–31.

Sabellic, Old (see under *East Italic*)

Sabine

The territory of the Sabines lay to the north-east of Rome having as its chief town Reate (modern Rieti) (see map 10). Earlier, until the southern and lower-lying part of their territory was conquered by Rome in 449, their lands also included Cures (modern Corese) and, within 20 km of Rome itself, Nomentum (modern Mentana) and Fidenae (modern Castel Giubileo). No inscriptions of undisputed Sabine provenance have so far come to light; a six-word inscription previously assigned by some scholars to Sabine has recently and authoritatively been judged to be *Vestinian (Coleman 1986). The limited evidence provided by a few Sabine words quoted by Latin writers (e.g. *fasena* corresponding to Latin *harena* 'sand') is enough to indicate beyond doubt that Sabine was an *Italic language, but its precise relationship to such languages as *Oscan, *Umbrian, *Volscian and *Faliscan remains uncertain.

Bruno, M. G. 1961–2. I Sabini e la loro lingua ('The Sabines and their language'). Istituto Lombardo, *Rendiconti. Classe di Lettere e Scienze Morali e Storiche*, 95: 501–44, 96: 413–42, 565–640.

Coleman, R. 1986. The central Italic languages in the period of Roman expansion. *Transactions of the Philological Society*, 1986: 100–31.

Sámi (Lapp)

A member of the *Finno-Ugrian branch of the *Uralic languages. Its precise classification within Finno-Ugrian is problematic but it is closely related to the *Baltic-Finnic languages.

Origins and history of the Sámi

The origin of the Sámi is much debated. It has been argued that they were of a different race from the Finns and only relatively late in their development adopted a Finno-Ugrian language. Recent genetic research has led to the opinion that the Sámi stand anthropologically between the Samoyeds (see *Samoyedic) and the Europeans but linguistically they are Finno-Ugrians. It has been variously suggested that the change of language may have taken place in the Proto-Finno-Ugrian period, in the Volga Finnic period, and in the early Baltic-Finnic period; in view of the great similarities between Lapp and the Baltic-Finnic languages, it is now generally accepted that Sámi is an offspring of Early Proto-Finnish.

The nomad Sámi people originally extended over a much wider area than that they now occupy and only slowly withdrew northwards. The people called 'Fenni' in Tacitus's *Germania* in the 1st c. AD are usually identified as Sámi and, in the 2nd c., Ptolemy knew of two different Finnish peoples, one of them (presumably the Sámi) living in the north of Scandinavia. Up to the 14th c., a group of Sámi lived as far south as eastern Karelia and as late as the 17th c. Sámi were also found in the central inland regions of Finland.

Distribution and dialects

The Sámi language extends over the whole of northern Scandinavia, covering some 400,000 square kilometres. Of the overall number of approximately 65,000 Sámi, some 34,000 speak the language but, because of the different ways in which census data are collected and presented in the various countries, widely differing figures are quoted. The great majority of speakers, some 22,000, live in Norway with 8,500 in Sweden and smaller communities in Finland (1,734 in 1990) and Russia (1,890 in 1989).

The language is divided into several dialects with considerable differences in grammar and lexicon, with the result that the different dialects are not easily mutually comprehensible. There are eight major dialects falling into three groups: (i) eastern Sámi, spoken mainly in the northern part of the Kola peninsula in Russia, with three subdivisions, Kola Sámi in the east (i.e. the Kildin and Ter dialects), Skolt Sámi or Kolta Sámi between Murmansk and the Finnish border, and Inari Sámi around Lake Inari in northern Finland; (ii) the central or northern dialect group, used by about three-quarters of Sámi-speakers, also with three subdivisions, namely northern Sámi in northern Norway, Sweden and Finland as far south as a line from Narvik (Norway) to Sodankylä (Finland), and Lule Sámi and Pite Sámi in northern Sweden around the rivers Lule and Pite which run into the Gulf of Bothnia; and (iii) southern Sámi, consisting of two varieties, one (Ume Sámi) spoken along the upper part of the river Ume in central Sweden and the other (South Sámi proper) extending from Ume as far as Trondheim in Norway.

The literary language

From the 17th c. on, there have been several attempts to create a standard language. Nowadays there are five literary languages with different orthography and alphabets. The most flourishing of these is Northern Sámi in which we find magazines such as *Min Aigi*, *Áššu*, *Sápmelaš* and *Nuorttanaste*. The first novel in Sámi was written by Anders Larsen (1870–1949). Modern authors are, among others, Nils Aslak Valkeapää, Kirsti Paltto and Nils Viktor Aslaksen. In 1978, a special linguistic commission of the Sámi Council approved common orthographical standards for the Northern Sámi dialect in Norway, Sweden and Finland.

Aarseth, B. 1993. *The Sámi – Past and Present*. Oslo.
Greller, W. 1997. *Provision and Regulation of the Sámi Languages*. Aberystwyth.
Korhonen, M. 1988. The Lapp language. In Sinor, D. (ed.), *Handbuch der Orientalistik*, vol. 8, *The Uralic Languages: Description, History and Foreign Influences*, Leiden, 41–57.
Larsson, L. -G. 1985. Kriterien zur Klassifizierung der lappischen Dialekte in Schweden ('Criteria for the classification of the Lapp dialects in Sweden'). In Veenker, W. (ed.) *Dialectologia Uralica. Materialien des ersten internationalen Symposions zur Dialektologie der uralischen Sprachen*, Wiesbaden. 159–73.

WOLFGANG GRELLER

Samnitic (see under *Oscan*)

Samoyedic languages

One of the two branches, the other being ***Finno-Ugrian**, of the ***Uralic languages**. They are mainly spoken east of the Urals and comprise only some 40,000 speakers in all. They are traditionally classified into (i) northern Samoyedic, i.e. ***Nenets** (the only Samoyedic language spoken in Europe), Nganass and Enets, and (ii) southern Samoyedic, the only living representative of which is Selkup.

Janurik, T. 1985. Kriterien zur Klassifizierung der Dialekte der samojedischen Sprachen ('Criteria for the classification of the dialects of the Samoyedic languages'). In Veenker, W. (ed.) *Dialectologia Uralica. Materialien des ersten international Symposions zur Dialektologie der uralischen Sprachen*, Wiesbaden, 283–303.

WOLFGANG GRELLER

Sardinian (Ancient), see *Palaeo-Sardinian*

Sardinian (Modern) (see under *Italy. V. Sardinian*)

Sark French (Sercquiais)

The variety of ***Channel Islands French** spoken on the island of Sark. Although Sark forms part of the Bailiwick of Guernsey, its patois is basically a form of ***Jersey French**, and particularly of that of the parish of St Ouen in western Jersey. The reason for this is that the island, which had been abandoned nearly 200 years before, was granted in 1563 to Hélier de Carteret as an adjunct to his fief of St Ouen and settled in 1565 by tenants from that parish.

According to a report sent to John Wesley by one of his missionaries in 1787, not a single family on Sark at that time understood English. The Anglicization of the island probably stems from the bringing in of English-speaking miners from 1835 onwards and from the development shortly thereafter of a flourishing tourist industry. Although the language seems to have been well maintained as recently as the 1930s, it is likely that fewer than 10% of the resident population of some 600, and few if any children, now speak it.

Liddicoat, A. 1994. *A Grammar of the Norman French of the Channel Islands. The Dialects of Jersey and Sark*. Berlin.

GLANVILLE PRICE

Sarnami (see under *Community languages (Netherlands)*)

Saterlandic (see under *Frisian*)

Scandinavian languages

The northern group of the ***Germanic languages**. Originally, Common ***Norse** was spoken throughout Scandinavia, and even as late as Viking times Scandinavians considered that they possessed a common language, *dansk tunga* ('Danish tongue'), though by this time dialect differences were beginning to appear. There are therefore many shared characteristic features, such as the enclitic definite article (e.g. *dag* 'day'/*dagen* 'the day') and a passive in *-s* (*kallas* 'be called'), that differentiate them from the other Germanic languages, as well as a large core vocabulary.

The main dialect split, dating from *c.* AD 1000, which divided West Norse from East Norse, is still discernible in the modern languages; for example, the West Norse languages, *Icelandic, *Faroese, and *Norwegian Nyorsk, often have dipththongs where the East Norse languages, *Norwegian Bokmål, *Danish and *Swedish, have monophthongs (e.g. Icelandic and Nynorsk *leita*, Bokmål *lete*, Danish *lede*, Swedish *leta* 'to search'), and three grammatical genders (masc., fem., neuter) as opposed to the two genders (common and neuter) of East Norse.

Iceland was settled *c.* AD 900, mainly from Norway, and Icelandic, together with Faroese, is today the most archaic and purist of the Nordic languages.

Norway was for 350 years dominated by Denmark and lost its own written tradition in the late Middle Ages. Of the two varieties of modern Norwegian (see under *Norwegian), Bokmål originated from a Norwegianized written Danish and occupies a middle position between Danish and Swedish as regards orthography, lexicon and inflexion, while Nynorsk is a 19th-c. codification based on the dialects of the fiords and mountains and originally intended to answer a call for a Norwegian written language untainted by foreign influences.

Swedish, Norwegian and Danish share the same alphabet but differ in respect of some graphemes: Swedish <ä, ö> correspond to Norwegian and Danish <æ, ø>; these characters come at the end of the alphabet but the order differs, Swedish having <å, ä, ö> and Norwegian and Danish <æ, ø, å>.

Haugen, E. 1976. *The Scandinavian Languages. An Introduction to Their History*. London.
—— 1982. *Scandinavian Language Structures. A Comparative Historical Survey*. Tübingen.
Molde, B. and Karker, A. (eds) 1983. *Språken i Norden* ('Languages in Scandinavia'). Arlöv.
Vikør, L. 1993. *The Nordic Languages. Their Status and Interrelations*. Oslo.
Wessén, E. 1965. *De nordiska språken* ('The Nordic Languages'), 7th edn. Lund.

PHIL HOLMES

Schwyzertüütsch (see *Swiss German*, under *German*)

Scots

The *Germanic language most closely related to *English. It is derived partly from the Old English of the Angles of early Northumbria and partly from the Scandinavianized Middle English of immigrants into Scotland from medieval northern and central England. Originally spoken only in Lowland Scotland, it was also carried from there in the 17th c. to parts of Northern Ireland.

Origins and early expansion

Scots (see map 15), the vernacular language of the northern, eastern and southern Lowlands of Scotland since medieval times, and of parts of Northern Ireland since

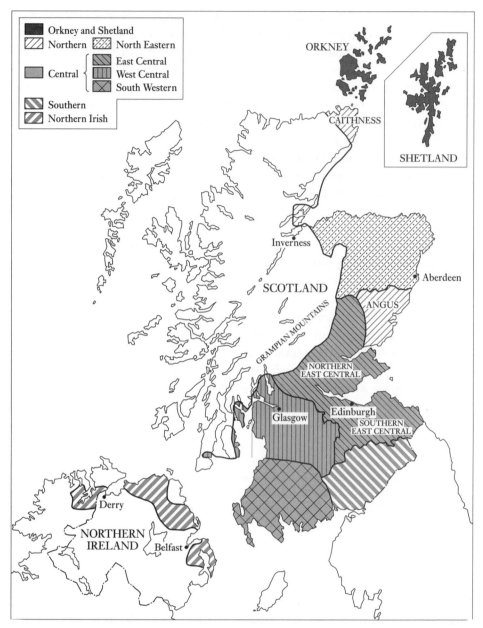

Map 15   Scots. The territory of Scots in Scotland and Ulster in the 19th and 20th centuries, with major dialectal divisions. Based, by permission of the Scottish National Dictionary Association, on a map in Mairi Robinson (editor-in-chief), *The Concise Scots Dictionary* (Aberdeen, Aberdeen University Press, 1985) and, by permission of the author, on Robert J. Gregg, *The Scotch-Irish Dialect Boundaries in the Province of Ulster* (Port Credit, Ont., Canadian Federation for the Humanities, 1985).

the early 17th c., is, in formal linguistic terms, a northern dialect of the family of dialects descended from Old English. It has its origins partly in the Northumbrian Old English of the Anglian people of the ancient kingdom of Bernicia, part of which, from the late 6th or early 7th c., lay in what is now southern Scotland. The other main source of Scots was the Scandinavian-influenced Middle English (or 'Anglo-Danish') of incomers from northern and central England in the 12th and early 13th centuries. The variety of northern English which crystallized out of these sources was at first known to its speakers as 'English' or, in a common medieval spelling, 'Inglis', and only later, from 1494, as 'Scots' ('Older Scots' to modern philologists). In due course, this early Scots spread out from the medieval burghs and the estates of Anglo-Norman lairds, where it was first most strongly established, and supplanted the *Gaelic and *Cumbric languages formerly spoken north of the Forth and south of the Clyde respectively.

Thereafter, from the 14th c. to the present day, Scots has been the common speech of the Scottish Lowlands everywhere south and east of the 'Highland Line' (the 'line' which marks the limit of the mountainous area of the Scottish mainland, extending from the Clyde estuary north-east to the Moray Firth). It is only, however, in the last hundred years that Scottish English (rather than Scots) has largely superseded Gaelic in the mainland Highlands themselves.

Scots in the later Middle Ages

In the 14th c. the Scottish baronage finally gave up its former Anglo-French speech for the Scots of the rest of the Lowland population. Scots was now, in the Lowlands, the spoken tongue of all ranks of Scottish society. By the late 17th c. or earlier, the last speakers of Gaelic in Galloway and Carrick in the south-west died out, leaving Scots as the sole vernacular there. The supplantation by Scots of the *Norn of Caithness, Orkney and Shetland, which began in the 14th c., was complete by the 18th c. In the course of the Plantation of Ulster in the 17th c., Scots was carried by Scottish settlers, many from western and south-western shires, into large enclaves of Northern Ireland.

The language of record and the literary language

In contrast with the situation in England, where French was much more dominant, almost the sole language of written record in Scotland throughout the medieval period was Latin (with some slight competition from French during the time of English hegemony in the late 13th and early 14th centuries and for some decades thereafter). Thus, until the late 14th c. the only glimpses we have of vernacular Scots consist of fragmentary snatches of legal, administrative and topographical terminology, and the terms making up newly coined place-names, all of these embedded in the Latin laws, deeds and records. These snatches suffice, however, to inform us that medieval Scots closely resembled northern Middle English in its phonology and morphology but that its vocabulary was already divergent in detail (in its unique Gaelic element and in other ways).

Except for a few early folk songs, the first continuous text in Scots was John

Barbour's heroic romance *The Brus*, on the exploits of the national hero. This was, however, followed almost immediately by many other writings in verse and prose, including, from 1424, the statutes of the Scottish Parliament. By the late 15th c., Scots had superseded Latin as the principal language of record and literary language of Scotland.

King's Scots

In the age of the Stewart monarchs of the 15th and 16th centuries, Scots was at its zenith, as the spoken, literary and record language of all ranks of the nation, and as the vehicle of a distinguished literature. This last encompassed the vivacious and stirring verse of Robert Henryson, William Dunbar and many other 'makars' (poets), and a substantial body of narrative and didactic prose. For the most part, the national and local statutes and records were also in Scots, as was a great mass of private writings – journals, letters and other documents. But this summit had hardly been reached when a decline set in, with a gradual loss of autonomy of the written, and in some speakers of the spoken, language and a falling away in the quality of the literature.

Anglicization

In its written and spoken modes, Scots was now progressively invaded by word-forms and spellings of English origin. The result was at first a mixed dialect, in which native Scots spellings and spelling-symbols co-occurred with corresponding English forms: *aith* and *oath*, *twa* and *two*, *gude* and *good*, *ony* and *any*, *gif* and *if*, *quh-* and *wh-* (e.g. *quhare* and *whare* 'where'), *-ei-* and *-ee-* or *-ea-* (e.g. *meit* and *meet* or *meat*), *-it* and *-ed* (e.g. *mendit* and *mended*, *leinit* and *leaned*), with the English options gradually gaining in popularity. Distinctively Scots items of vocabulary also gradually disappeared. This process, which began in a limited way in serious Scots verse in the 15th c., was also under way in prose from early in the 16th c., though some genres, notably local manuscript records, succumbed much later than others. Early in the 17th c. printing in Scots virtually ceased, and all new published work by Scots was now in English, but the elimination of Scots elements from writings in manuscript proceeded more gradually and fitfully through the 17th and into the 18th c. Spoken usage was in general more conservative, but it seems that already in the second half of the 16th c. the speech of most middle- and upper-class Scots featured occasional Anglicisms, and by the end of the next century most Scots aristocrats regularly spoke English not Scots, though with a Scottish accent and occasional Scots locutions. Among the several coincident conditions and causes which favoured this trend were the Scots' failure to produce a translation of the Bible in their own language and the reliance of Scottish Protestants, before and after the Reformation of 1560, on bibles and other religious literature in English, so that the religious language of Scotland was strongly influenced by English. The speaking of Anglicized Scots and, in due course, English was further stimulated by increasing contact between the Scots and English ruling classes before and, still more, after the Union of the Crowns in 1603.

'Correcting' Scots

While at lower social levels Scots continued in spoken use much as it formerly had, by the early 18th c. the formal or 'polite' speech of the educated classes of Scots, and indeed the informal speech of many of them, was no longer Scots but English. These people now eagerly subscribed to the Augustan culture of contemporary England, which attached great importance to 'propriety' and proscribed anything 'unrefined' or 'provincial'. The latter included Scots speech, 'a very corrupt dialect of the tongue we make use of [i.e. English]' (David Hume, 1757). Middle-class Scots, increasingly self-conscious over the supposed provinciality of their speech, now strove to rid themselves of Scots peculiarities and to acquire 'correct' (i.e. English) pronunciation, grammar and usage. Many of them now attended the courses of lectures and private classes on the correct pronunciation of English given in Edinburgh from 1748 onwards by a succession of English, Irish and Scottish elocutionists. As well as many new textbooks on correct English pronunciation and correct English grammar, many of them by Scottish authors and some published in Edinburgh or Glasgow, from 1752 onwards there appeared a fair number of collections of supposed solecisms of usage of Scots provenance known as 'Scotticisms', compiled expressly so that Scottish speakers and writers could learn to avoid them – such as *Scoticisms arranged in Alphabetical Order, designed to correct Improprieties of Speech and Writing* (1787). In most cases these endeavours were only partly successful, and the modern Scottish English descendant of the English of the 18th-c. Anglicizers retains many Scots-derived features, obtrusive and unobtrusive, of pronunciation, grammar, vocabulary and idiom. Many middle-class Scots of the late 18th c. also looked for a gradual 'improvement' (i.e. Anglicization) of the 'corrupt' Scots speech of the common people, leading, some hoped, to its total extinction (e.g. John Pinkerton, 1786).

'Reviving' Scots

In the following century, however, the attitude of the Scottish establishment towards Scots underwent a marked change, which indeed had been anticipated by a minority of 18th-c. intellectuals and literary men. It was now held to be regrettable that Scots was, as it had long been believed to be, 'dying'. At the same time the prevailing mood was one of resignation – 'This is all very sad, but it is the natural course' (Lord Cockburn, 1853). Apart from the compilation of dictionaries, the most notable of which were John Jamieson's *Etymological Dictionary of the Scottish Language* (1808, 1825) and *The Scottish National Dictionary* (in planning from 1907 and completed in 1976), the first practical steps to reverse this supposed decline of Scots were taken only in the early years of the 20th c. Competitions for schoolchildren and university students in performing and writing in Scots were sponsored by local Burns Clubs (which had existed since the early 19th c.), the Burns Federation, and by legacies from private individuals. At this time also there were calls for the creation of university chairs or lectureships in Scots, 'for its preservation' (D. McNaught, 1901).

Endeavours of these and other sorts to stimulate interest in Scots and support for its increased use in speech and writing, which continued and gradually expanded throughout the century, were massively boosted from the late 1960s onwards. Several new societies devoted to the promotion and/or study of Scots were now founded. University teaching about Scots at all its stages, which had existed since 1950 in Edinburgh University, was now considerably increased, and lectureships and courses on Scots language, once a visionary dream, are now well established in several of the ancient Scottish universities. The 1980s and 1990s have produced several important initiatives furthering the teaching of Scots language, no less than Scots literature, in schools. The most notable of these is the Scottish Language Project, supported by all the regional education authorities and the Scottish Office Education Department's Consultative Council on the Curriculum, the compilers of which have assembled from all the localities a massive resource pack or *Kist*, Gaelic *A' Chiste* ('chest') (which appeared in 1996) of texts and audiotapes in Scots and Gaelic for teachers of children aged 5 to 14. In 1985 the Scottish National Dictionary Association's *Concise Scots Dictionary*, perhaps the most valuable aid to the study of Scots that has so far appeared, was published with remarkable popular success, encapsulating in one comprehensive volume the great multi-volume historical dictionaries of Scots of the 20th c.

Another innovation is that whereas until lately Scots, unlike English and Gaelic, has enjoyed no government recognition whatever, since the late 1970s the Scottish Office, at first only indirectly through the Scottish Arts Council, more recently by direct albeit short-term grants, has provided substantial aid to several major projects in Scots philology. Also since the 1970s there have been occasional articles and broadcasts in Scots in the national media, though these initiatives have so far (1997) proved to be short-lived.

Dialects and the modern literature

The social and regional dialect variations which were developing within Scots from the 15th c. at first only occasionally show themselves, mostly in sporadic 'bad spellings'. But by the 19th c. five major regional dialect groupings (Orkney and Shetland, Northern, Central, Southern, and Northern Irish) are clearly displayed, in philological descriptions and in literature, each having its own literary representations. The 'standard', less obtrusively regional language of 'mainstream' literature is based on the Central dialect. This is the literature of Robert Burns, Walter Scott, Robert Louis Stevenson, Hugh MacDiarmid, and many other notable writers in a great variety of genres, including, recently, discursive prose. A notable branch of the 'mainstream' literature has been the poetry (and some prose) of the 'Scottish Renaissance' movement founded by Hugh MacDiarmid in the 1920s. Much of this is in the archaizing and dialectally eclectic subvariety of literary Scots at first called 'Synthetic Scots' (and, by hostile critics, 'Plastic Scots') and later, from the time of the Second World War, renamed 'Lallans' (a variant of Scots 'Lawland(s)', i.e. '(language of the) Lowlands').

In the course of the last two centuries the urban dialects have developed their own striking peculiarities, many of which are socially stigmatized. These, especially those of Glasgow and more recently Edinburgh, have since the 1960s been reproduced in verse, in dialogue and in monologue (including narrative) within prose fiction, in drama and in several kinds of comic writing, often in an untraditional, quasi–illiterate, orthography, intended to emphasize the demotic character of the underlying speech.

This whole literature, continuous since John Barbour in the 14th c., greatly excels the other regional literatures of the Anglophone world, in antiquity, copiousness, variety and distinction, except only that in standard English itself. In the 1990s it has flourished more vigorously than ever in all the genres already mentioned, perhaps most of all in novels and short stories.

Present situation

Since the late 17th c. the official language of Scotland has been not Scots but standard English. Though much of the terminology of Scots law, of the presbyterian churches of Scotland, of Scottish education, of local government and public administration is distinctive and largely derived from Older Scots, the language in which the business of these and all other institutions is normally carried out is English. And while Scots is widely used in 'art' literature, its use in prose for utilitarian or solemn purposes is all but unheard of – say for newspaper, radio or TV reports, announcements of deaths, academic prose, and (except for a few enthusiasts) private correspondence. The case of the student of Glasgow University who in 1994 submitted part of his Finals papers in Scottish literature in Scots was a first ever, that occasioned general astonishment.

In speech there has been since the 16th c. a continuum of more and less Scots varieties ranging across the wide linguistic distance from the fullest local working-class Scots (now confined to a small minority of rural people) to middle-class Scottish standard English. Even the latter, however, retains many Scots-derived features, and it is probably true that more Scotticisms are used by the Scots at all linguistic levels, more often and over virtually the entire social range, than similar vernacular elements are used elsewhere in the English-speaking world. It is, however, also true that, though novel words and idioms continue to be coined, the total trend is towards a slow diminution of the Scots element in Scottish speech as a whole.

As we have seen, many Scots-speaking and, even more so, middle-class Scottish-English-speaking Scots have long been conscious of the situation of Scots and some have wished to 'restore' it. But many others whose speech contains numerous Scots features, especially perhaps but not solely younger working-class people, remain largely unaware of the historical background of Scots and consider their language to be 'slang' or 'bad English'.

So, despite the continuing use of Scots in informal speech and in writing and efforts to promote it, it has no place in formal and official communication and its existence is virtually unrecognized by one substantial section of its constituency.

Numbers of speakers

It remains an arbitrary decision at what point along the scale of more or less Scots speech a speaker is to be classified as speaking Scots rather than Scotticized English.

Consequently, whereas the decennial national censuses have since 1881 included a question on the speaking of Gaelic, until very recently neither the national census nor anyone else has attempted to estimate the number of speakers of Scots.

But in February 1996, responding to persuasion from Scots language activists, the Scottish Office and the General Register Office for Scotland convened a one-day symposium on the desirability and feasibility of including in the Census a question on the speaking of Scots. Partly because of the difficulty of framing a question which, given the present complex linguistic situation, would be generally and consistently understood, the eventual decision was not to do so. However, GRO(S) did commission several surveys into the viability of such a question, one outcome of which was that about 30% of respondents said they could speak Scots. In 1995 a separate investigation had arrived at a much higher proportion, 255 of the 450 persons interviewed (57%) claiming to speak Scots. These surveys of course report only respondents' self-estimates, without addressing the question of what degree of Scottishness of usage constitutes 'speaking Scots'. This question will, however, be targeted in the North-East Language Project that is under way at the University of Aberdeen.

Of course, the number of speakers who use some Scots elements in their speech, a category which would include all speakers of Scottish English, doubtless comprises around 90% of the total population of nearly 5 million.

The diaspora

As a result of the Scots diaspora to the colonies of the British Empire from the 17th c. onwards, traces of Scots are to be found in many overseas varieties of English, such as some of the Midland dialects of the USA, Canadian English generally (and most of all, perhaps, the speech of Prince Edward Island), and the English of Otago in New Zealand.

What is special about Scots?

Scotland is a 'dialect-island': probably the most copious bunch of isoglosses in the Anglophone world is that running along the Scottish–English border. Scots elements, more and less obtrusive, are in common use across an exceptionally wide social range of Scottish speech. Other unique features of Scots are the many striking linguistic contrasts between it and standard English, its possession of a range of well-diversified dialects of its own, its own separate and well-documented history, matched only in these respects by that of standard English, and a distinguished literature. For these reasons, though it lacks several of the attributes of a full 'language', in particular that of being the normal language of public communication within the nation, Scots may claim to be much more than a mere 'dialect', and since the 16th c. many Scottish people, including many whose speech is only slightly tinged with Scots elements, have regarded it as their national tongue and as an important constituent of their identity as a nation, even though many have also long believed it to be 'dying'. The status of Scots as a language has been recognized by the inclusion of accounts of the situation of Gaelic and Scots in the 'European Languages' series of the European Bureau for Lesser Used Languages (Macleod and MacNeacail 1995).

Aitken, A. J. 1984. (a) Scottish accents and dialects, (b) Scots and English in Scotland. In Trudgill, P. (ed.), *Language in the British Isles*, Cambridge, 94–114, 517–32.
—— 1992. (a) Dialect in Scotland, (b) Scots, (c) Scottish English. In McArthur, T. (ed.), *The Oxford Companion to the English Language*, Oxford, 298–9, 893–9, 903–5.
Jones, C. (ed.) 1997. *The Edinburgh History of the Scots Language*. Edinburgh.
Kay, B. 1993. *Scots: The Mither Tongue*, rev. edn. Edinburgh.
Macleod, I. and MacNeacail, A. 1995. *Scotland: A Linguistic Double Helix*. Dublin.
McClure, J. D. 1988. *Why Scots Matters*. Edinburgh.
—— 1992. Scots literature. In McArthur, T. (ed.), *The Oxford Companion to the English Language*, Oxford, 899–900.
—— 1994. English in Scotland. In Burchfield, R. W. (ed.), *The Cambridge History of the English Language*, vol. 5. *English in Britain and Overseas*, Cambridge, 23–93.
Robinson, M. (ed.) 1985, *The Concise Scots Dictionary*. Aberdeen.

A. J. AITKEN

Scottish Gaelic

Scottish Gaelic (*Gàidhlig*) is a member of the *Gaelic or Goidelic subgroup of the *Celtic languages. It is spoken as a native language in the NW Highlands and Islands of Scotland (see map 16).

External history and the literary tradition

The Gaelic language having been brought to Scotland by settlers from NE Ireland in the 5th c. AD, Scottish Gaels shared the same literary language as Irish Gaels down to the 17th c. Some Old *Irish and Middle Irish texts were composed in Scotland – e.g. at the monastery of Iona – although they are mostly preserved in Ireland and are most often studied as part of Early Irish literature. Given the linguistic circumstances of Scottish speakers of Gaelic, whose links with Ireland continued at certain levels, but who came increasingly into contact with speakers of the other languages of northern Britain – *Pictish, *Cumbric and the Old *English of Northumbria – the spoken Gaelic of Scotland would have begun to diverge from that of Ireland at an early date, despite the unity of the literary language. Place-name evidence, vocabulary and some syntactic traits of Modern Scottish Gaelic suggest that this happened, but documentary evidence is lacking. Specifically Scottish traits have been descried by some in the 12th-c. Notitiae in the Book of Deer. They are undoubtedly present and visible in Early Modern Gaelic poems in the Book of the Dean of Lismore (early 16th c.). Distinctively Modern Scottish Gaelic verse texts are contained in the Fernaig MS (late 17th c.). A succession of biblical and related texts, beginning with the Classical Early Modern Irish of Bishop John Carswell's translation of the Book of Common Order (1567, the first Gaelic book published in Scotland) and ending with the publication of the full text of the Gaelic Bible (1787–1801), shows the emergence of Scottish Gaelic prose into the world of print. The first published collection of original Gaelic literary texts was *Aiseirigh na Sean Chanoin Albannaigh* ('The Resurrection of the Older Scottish Tongue', published in

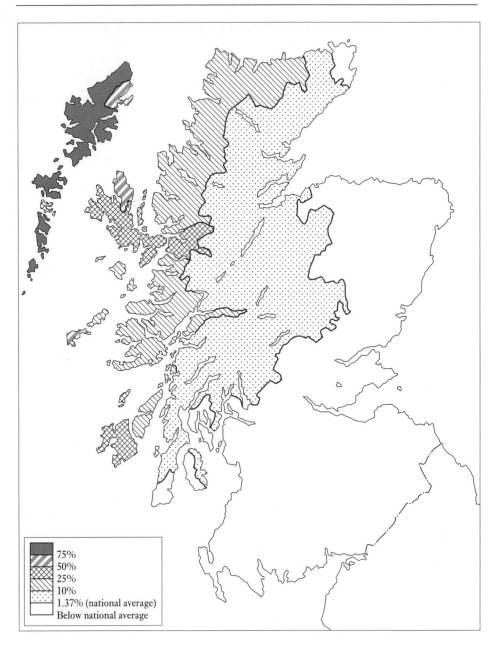

Map 16   Scottish Gaelic in 1991. Map based on data provided by the General
Register Office for Scotland's 1991 census of population. Percentages relate to the
proportion of the usually resident population aged 3 and over recorded as Gaelic-
speaking. The shaded areas are those that had a higher proportion of
Gaelic-speakers than that for Scotland as a whole (i.e. 1.37%). Map consultant,
Kenneth MacKinnon.

Edinburgh in 1751), i.e. the collected poetical works of the Jacobite poet Alexander MacDonald.

The scribes of the Gaelic manuscript tradition employed the *corr-litir* or Irish script, a direct descendant of the Hiberno-Saxon minuscule used by the clerics of the Celtic Church in the Early Christian period. This tradition survived into the 18th c. in Scotland. On the other hand, the vernacular Gaelic manuscripts and later collections used the Roman hand, in contemporary Scottish versions. The Roman alphabet was standard in print.

The Classical Early Modern literary dialect could not survive the disappearance of the Gaelic-speaking aristocracy which patronized it. However, the unifying and dignifying powers of a high register were recognized and cultivated equally by vernacular poets and by ministers of the Presbyterian Church. As a consequence, an orthodoxy as to the proper form of literary Scottish Gaelic gradually emerged during the 18th c., and norms of grammar and spelling were elaborated during the 19th. The collaborative efforts which led to the provision of the Scottish Gaelic Bible (see above) were crucial in this regard, as was the rise of Gaelic scholarship and publishing in the revivalist and activist context of the late 19th c. The standard language thus created survived for the best part of a century until in the 1960s the gap between spoken language and standard orthography began to seem irksome in a world in which the centre of gravity of Gaelic speaking had moved from the southern Highlands to the Hebrides, the power of the spoken media was steadily increasing, and literary fashion exalted informality.

Scottish Gaelic literature in the manuscript tradition (i.e. down to the early 18th c.) is largely as in Early Modern Irish. The verse preserved is mostly from the bardic tradition: eulogy and elegy, with an admixture of religious, satirical and courtly love poetry. Some heroic ballads (the genuine lays corresponding to James Macpherson's Ossianic 'versions') are also found. Prose literature consists of romances and some historical material. Much of the prose contained in Gaelic manuscripts is not literary but learned: the textbooks of the professional caste of physicians, lawyers, genealogists and poets. In Scotland the survival of medical manuscripts is particularly striking.

The vernacular literature began to appear in print in the second half of the 18th c.: collections of the poetry of living poets, and anthologies of the verse of older poets. The latter consisted mainly of clan poetry – i.e. poetry about the chiefs and their battles and politics – from the 16th and 17th centuries, preserved orally till it was written down. A body of folk poetry from the same period also exists, but it was not written down until the 19th c. or later. Folk tales (including vernacularized and orally preserved romances) were also collected from the later 19th c. They often imply originals in the 17th c. or earlier. However, written prose literature was initially dominated by religious tracts and sermons, and only gradually expanded from that base. Creative and intellectual domains of writing were opened up for Gaelic at the time of the Gaelic Revival of the 1870s. Currently there is a small but constant market for Gaelic literature in all the main genres of fictional and non-fictional writing, in which the short story has been powerfully developed, but poetry still ranks as the highest form of literary achievement.

Geographical spread

The evidence of place-names shows that at its widest extent, in the Middle Ages, Gaelic was spoken throughout what is now Scotland, although Gaelic-speakers were apparently only a superstratum in the far south-east of the country. Normanization of the Scottish court and nobility started a decline in the fortunes of Gaelic, and it gradually receded in Southern Scotland and up the East Coast. By the 15th c., the modern dichotomy of Gaelic-speaking Highlands and *Scots-speaking Lowlands was a *fait accompli* except for a Gaelic presence in Galloway, which lingered on until the 17th c. The pace of Anglicization increased from the 18th c. in a context of economic upheaval and linguistic imperialism under the banner of improvement and education. The mass emigration which resulted led to the creation of émigré Gaelic communities, both in the Scottish cities and further afield (see below). In the Highlands, while the so-called Highland Line (see under *Scots, 'Origins and early expansion') remained fairly static, the number of Gaelic-speakers declined steadily to just over 200,000 in 1901, and fell below 100,000 in 1951, according to the Census Reports for those years.

Dialects

The dialect map of Scottish Gaelic has been obscured by population movement, especially as a result of the Clearances and mass emigrations of the 18th and 19th centuries. More recently, the elimination of Gaelic by English in many localities at or near the periphery of the historical Gàidhealtachd (the Gaelic-speaking area) has further muddied the picture. Nevertheless, certain patterns of variation can be discerned. These include (1) an East–West divide, in which the western dialects (Western Isles and western seaboard) are characterized, for example, by morphological conservatism, as against eastern simplification; (2) a North–South divide in which the southern dialects (particularly the Argyllshire dialects) have certain features in common (e.g. extensive use of the glottal stop) which are not present in the more northerly dialects; and (3) a Central–Peripheral divide in which the most northerly, easterly and southerly dialects (in Sutherland, in central Inverness-shire and East Perthshire, and in Arran and Kintyre) have not shared in some of the most characteristic phonological developments of Scottish Gaelic, such as the preaspiration of historically voiceless stops closing stressed syllables.

Contacts with other languages

Scottish Gaelic is closely related to the other Goidelic languages, most notably (1) to *Manx Gaelic, and (2) to Ulster Irish. The terms Eastern Gaelic (i.e. Scottish Gaelic and Manx) and Western Gaelic (i.e. Irish) have been used to signify a special relationship between Scotland and the Isle of Man. Early contact between Gaels and the *Brittonic-speakers of Pictland and Strathclyde (see *Pictish, *Cumbric) is discernible in Scottish Gaelic lexis and, more controversially, syntax. On the

Germanic side, contact with ***Norse** occurred especially in the north and west, and took place principally between the 9th and 12th centuries. Significant English contact began in the Old English period with the intermingling of Gaels and Northumbrians in Southern Scotland, especially when the Gaelic-speaking Kings of Scots established control over Strathclyde and Lothian in the 11th and 12th centuries. Following on from this, contact between Gaelic and Scots was constant throughout the later Middle Ages, especially on the fringes of the Gàidhealtachd, until Scots gave way to English as the language of government and education. Thereafter, English influence became more important, and continues to the present, given the status of English as the language of administration, law and education, and as the predominant language of the media.

Present situation

Scottish Gaelic is currently spoken by the majority of the indigenous population of the Outer Hebrides, Skye and some of the Inner Hebrides, and the crofting townships of the NW coast from Sutherland down to North Argyll, together with isolated groups scattered throughout the rest of the Highlands. There are also substantial Gaelic communities in the Scottish cities. The emigration of Gaelic-speakers led to considerable Gaelic-speaking enclaves in Australia and New Zealand, the Carolinas, and especially in Canada. The only such enclave to retain Gaelic significantly to the present day is that of Cape Breton Island in Nova Scotia, where a sizeable set of Gaelic-speaking communities is only now disintegrating. The 1991 Census recorded the presence of 68,000 Gaelic speakers in Scotland, a drop of over 10,000 since the 1981 Census. Of these speakers, roughly half were resident in the traditional Gàidhealtachd areas described above, and the other half were divided between the cities and the rest of the country.

Gaelic has suffered over the centuries from governmental intolerance – exacerbated by the Highland associations of the Jacobite Risings, and enforced by the Church and educational system. Despite the slackening of these pressures and the gradual growth (especially since the 1970s) of effective support systems for the language, Scottish Gaelic still has no legal status in the United Kingdom. On the other hand, it is recognized as a Minority Language by the European Union, and receives official support from the Scottish Office as a school subject and, to a certain extent, as a medium for education. There has been a Gaelic radio service since the early days of broadcasting, which provides morning and evening programmes from the Islands, the Highlands and the cities. Both commercial and state television broadcast a certain number of Gaelic programmes per week. On the other hand, there is no wide-circulation Gaelic newspaper. There are Gaelic pressure groups and cultural organizations, but no national Gaelic language unit. Gaelic can be studied in the older Scottish universities but not the new. There are more jobs in the media and similar fields than ever before, and there are not enough Gaelic teachers to match demand. But some traditional strongholds of Gaelic, such as the Church, are in decline. In common with many other minority languages, Scottish Gaelic's most powerful enemy today is not the deliberate policy of government, nor rejection by its speakers, but the pervasive power of English as the language of administration, tourism and the media.

Clement, D. 1984. Scottish Gaelic. In Trudgill, P. (ed.), *Language in the British Isles*, London, 318–42.

Gillies, W. 1993. Scottish Gaelic. In Ball, M. J. (ed.), *The Celtic Languages*, London. 145–227.

MacAulay, D. 1992. The Scottish Gaelic language. In Id. (ed.), *The Celtic Languages*, Cambridge, 137–248.

MacKinnon, K. 1993. Scottish Gaelic today: social history and contemporary status. In Ball, M. J. (ed.), *The Celtic Languages*, London, 491–535.

Maclennan, M. 1979. *A Pronouncing and Etymological Dictionary of the Gaelic Language*, new edn. Aberdeen.

Watson, S. 1994. Gaeilge na hAlban ('Scottish Gaelic'). In McCone, K. et al. (eds), *Stair na Gaeilge* ('History of the Irish Language'), Maynooth, 661–702.

Withers, C. W. J. 1984. *Gaelic in Scotland 1698–1981: The Geographical History of a Language*. Edinburgh.

WILLIAM GILLIES

Scythian

The Scythians were a nomadic people or group of peoples of Iranian origin who figured largely in the history of eastern Europe throughout much of the first millennium BC. Penetrating Europe from the east, they occupied at one time or another extensive territories to the north and east of the Black Sea including much of what is now Ukraine, southern Russia and the Caucasus region and, at one stage, thrust westwards around the Black Sea as far as the Carpathians and the lower reaches of the Danube. It is generally accepted that they spoke a language belonging to the *Indo-Iranian branch of *Indo-European.

Selian (Selonian)

An extinct *Baltic language or dialect spoken in parts of Latvia and Lithuania and which may have been transitional between *Latvian and *Lithuanian. No written records remain. It probably died out in the 16th c.

Semigallian, see *Zemgalian*

Semitic languages

A large family of basically Middle Eastern and African languages some of which have come to be used in widely varying circumstances in Europe (see *Arabic, *Aramaic, *Assyrian, *Cypriot Arabic, *Hebrew, *Maltese, *Phoenician).

Serbian (see under *Serbo-Croat*)

Serbo-Croat

A member of the southern subgroup of the *Slavonic languages which, together with *Slovene, forms the western branch of this subgroup. The term 'Serbo-Croat' is normal in Western scholarship and was widely used in former Yugoslavia.

However, alongside this term we also find in Croatian linguistic usage the alternative terms 'Croato-Serbian' and 'Croatian or Serbian'. Speakers of the language, depending on their ethnic origin, often simply refer to the language as 'Serbian' or 'Croatian'.

Dialects

Serbo-Croat dialects are divided into three groups: Kajkavian, Čakavian and Štokavian which take their names from the interrogative pronoun 'what?', which differs in the three groups (i.e. *kaj, ča, što*). Some scholars also distinguish a fourth dialect, the Prizren-Timok dialect (also known as the Torlak dialect). This dialect, although belonging historically to the Štokavian group, has been structurally affected by so-called 'Balkanisms' similar to those found in neighbouring ***Macedonian** and ***Bulgarian**. One additional feature used to subdivide the three dialect groups is the reflex of the Common Slavonic phoneme ě *(jat')* which may be *(i)je, e* or *i*. This feature again gives three dialect types: *(i)jekavian, ekavian, ikavian*. The Kajkavian dialect is *ekavian* and is divided into six subdialects. It is spoken in the north of Croatia around Zagreb and shares several features with Slovene. The Čakavian dialect is spoken in Istria, on the Dalmatian coastal fringe and the Adriatic islands. It is either *ekavian* or *ikavian* or a mixed *ekavian/ikavian* and is divided into six subdialects. The main dialect is Štokavian, which may be *(i)jekavian, ekavian* or *ikavian*. The Štokavian dialect is divided into 11 subdialects and is spoken in the rest of Croatia, Bosnia and Hercegovina, Serbia, and Montenegro.

The Štokavian dialects may be further divided into Neo-Štokavian and Old Štokavian dialects. Neo-Štokavian dialects show two innovations: (1) a new shifted accentuation whereby the stress moved one syllable towards the beginning of the word creating two new rising tones, the length of which depended on the original length of the vowel in the syllable now bearing the tone; (2) syncretism of the dative/locative/instrumental plural oblique cases of nouns, pronouns and adjectives. These developments took place in the central Štokavian dialects (the east Hercegovinian dialect, the Šumadija-Vojvodinian dialect and the so-called 'Young *ikavian*' dialects, which are spoken in western Hercegovina, southern and central Bosnia, and Dalmatia between the rivers Neretva and Cetina; the Young *ikavian* dialect is also the dialect of the majority of Croats and Muslims in western Bosnia).

From an overall viewpoint Croats speak Kajkavian, Čakavian and Štokavian dialects whereas Serbs, Montenegrins, Bosnians and Muslims speak only Štokavian dialects. The Serbo-Croat literary language is based on the east Hercegovinian Neo-Štokavian *(i)jekavian* dialect. It was the result of a 'Literary Agreement' signed between leading Croats and Serbs in Vienna in 1850. Reactions to the 'Literary Agreement' varied – it aroused a certain hostility among some Croatian critics but gradually gained a measured support. However, since *ekavian* was used in most of Serbia this became the basis for the eastern form of the literary language. As a consequence there are today two acknowledged variants of the literary language: the eastern or Serbian variant which is *ekavian* with its cultural centre in Belgrade, and the western or Croatian variant which is *(i)jekavian* with its cultural centre in Zagreb.

However, the common use of the terms 'Serbian' and 'Croatian' variants does not in fact agree with the actual linguistic situation. The *ekavian* variant is used by Serbs within Serbia, but Serbs living in large areas outside Serbia use the *(i)jekavian* variant as do Montenegrins, Croats and Muslims. Apart from the reflex of the phoneme ě *(jat')*, the variants differ not so much as a result of the dialectal differences occurring within the Neo-Štokavian basis of the language as because of differences in the lexical superstructure which have arisen as a consequence of the diverse historical, religious and cultural backgrounds of the Serbs and the Croats. Since the 1970s certain scholars have also suggested that two further variants can be identified if usages in Bosnia and Hercegovina and in Montenegro are taken into account, because they are not identical with either of the standard variants.

Origins and early development of the literary language and scripts used

Before the Serbs and Croats reached agreement on a common literary language basis in 1850, there had been a great diversity of literary tradition. The beginnings of literature among the Serbs and Croats are associated with the adoption of Christianity and Old *Church Slavonic in the 9th c. From the 9th c. the Croatian Kingdom looked to Rome in religious matters, and, following the church schism of 1054 and the union of Croatia with the Hungarian crown in 1102, became Catholic. The early Serbian embryonic states of Duklja (later known as Zeta) and Raška came under Byzantine suzerainty and the medieval Serbian kingdom founded by Stefan Nemanje in the 12th c. continued to look towards Orthodox Constantinople. After the fall of Constantinople, Orthodox Serbia considered Moscow to be the centre of Orthodoxy. The invasion of the Turks in the late 14th c. led to large migrations of population, the contraction of some dialects, the expansion of others. In the 15th c. the Turks occupied Bosnia and Hercegovina, where large numbers of the population adopted Islam, and part of Montenegro, which remained Orthodox. When the Turks were finally expelled in 1878 Croatia was part of the Austro-Hungarian Empire, which also took over Bosnia and Hercegovina. Only in 1918 after the First World War were the Serbs, Montenegrins, Bosnians and Croats united for the first time in one kingdom.

The original alphabet used by both Serbs and Croats was Glagolitic (see *Cyrillic **and Glagolitic scripts** and fig. 5) and this tradition was continued in the Catholic West among some priests on the Dalmatian coast and islands right up to the beginning of the 20th c. In the areas which were Orthodox (Serbia, Bosnia, Dubrovnik), Glagolitic was replaced by Cyrillic (see figs. 4 and 5) from the late 12th c. onwards. In the 13th c. Cyrillic also replaced Glagolitic in some places in southern Dalmatia. In the 14th c. the Latin alphabet began to be used in documents written in various places on the Dalmatian coast and from then on the use of the Latin alphabet spread and gradually replaced Glagolitic and Cyrillic among Croats. Cyrillic, however, continued to be used in Orthodox areas (Serbia, Bosnia and Montenegro).

The earliest form of written language among Serbs and Croats was Church Slavonic, which had by the 12th c. under the influence of local speech habits developed into two recensions: Croatian Church Slavonic written in Glagolitic, and

Serbian Church Slavonic written in Cyrillic. In Croatia the Church Slavonic tradition lasted until about the 14th c. but in Serbia the Church Slavonic recension was used until the 18th c. The oldest evidence of written language dates from the 11th and early 12th centuries in the form of inscriptions on stone. The most famous of these are the Baška Tablet from the island of Krk, written in Glagolitic, and the Temnik inscription, in Cyrillic, from central Serbia. The earliest known Croatian Church Slavonic Glagolitic manuscripts are the *Glagolita Clozianus* and the *Vienna Folia* which date from the 11th c., while the oldest Cyrillic Church Slavonic manuscripts are the *Miroslav Gospel* and the *Vukan Gospel*, which date from the end of the 12th and beginning of the 13th c. respectively. Early on some texts show an admixture of dialect features, the most famous of these being the Štokavian-based *Charter of Ban Kulin* (12th c.) and Stefan Dušan's *Law Code* (14th c.). In the early period the alphabets of both recensions underwent a certain number of changes. The Glagolitic letters lost their rounded character and by the 13th c. were replaced by letters with an angular form, which survived in Croatian Glagolitic books until the beginning of the 20th c. For the most part, however, the Latin alphabet replaced Glagolitic from the 14th c. onwards. In the 14th c. in Orthodox areas the Cyrillic alphabet underwent reform under Bulgarian and Greek influence, while in Bosnia it developed into a special form known as 'Bosančica'. The first printed books appeared in the late 15th c. The first Glagolitic book, a Missal, was published in Vienna in 1483 and the first Cyrillic book, an *Oktoechos* (a collection of Orthodox liturgical hymns) was published in Montenegro in 1494.

The invasion of the Turks led to large numbers of the population moving to the north and north-west and the spread of the Štokavian dialect at the expense of the Kajkavian and Čakavian dialects. While most of Štokavian-speaking territory was at one time under the Turks or fell within the Austrian Military Frontier, the Čakavian and Kajkavian dialect areas remained outside Turkish control. The Turkish invasion led to the stagnation of Serbian Church Slavonic and it was sustained only in church usage. However, in areas not under Turkish rule vernacular literature began to flourish. Croatian Church Slavonic had in the period from the 12th to the 15th c. been influenced by the Čakavian dialect, and subsequently in the 16th c. a rich Čakavian-based vernacular literature made its appearance. At this period too literary activity flourished in the independent Republic of Dubrovnik to the south. Initially this Dubrovnik vernacular literature was Štokavian *(i)jekavian* with an admixture of Čakavian elements, but at its height in the 17th c. was basically Štokavian *(i)jekavian*. This literary language at the period of the Counter-Reformation (17th c.) spread to Bosnia, where it was also used in an *ikavian* variant under the influence of the western Neo-Štokavian dialects. From here its use spread to Dalmatia and then in the 18th c. in its *ikavian* form to Slavonia following Slavonia's liberation from the Turks. In the north the second half of the 16th c. saw the introduction of the Kajkavian dialect into literature. From the beginning this Kajkavian literary language contained some Čakavian and Štokavian elements which increased in number over the next two centuries. The names of the various literary languages differed from area to area. In Dalmatia the Čakavian-based language was called Croatian or Illyrian, in the north the Kajkavian-based language was initially known as Slovinski and later as Croatian, while in Bosnia the terms Slovinski, Illyrian and Bosnian and occasionally Croatian were used to describe the Štokavian-based language. By the end of the 18th c. Zagreb had become the cultural centre of Croatia and the Kajkavian literary language functioned very strongly in northern Croatia, but in other areas it was the Štokavian literary language that had acquired a general prestige, although it was used in both *ikavian* and *(i)jekavian* forms and had no codified norms. By this time too the Latin orthography, which had been Italian-based in Dalmatia and Hungarian-based in northern Croatia, was also beginning to show signs of stability with Bosnian practice as the regulator.

Serbian

In the Orthodox east the literary language had by the end of the 18th c. undergone a significant change. At the end of the 17th and beginning of the 18th c. very large numbers of Serbs moved across the Sava and Danube into what was then southern Hungary and is today the area of Serbia known as the Vojvodina. By this time the Štokavian vernacular had undergone significant changes in its various dialect forms, but the literary language was still the fossilized Serbian Church Slavonic, which had stagnated under Turkish rule and was confined to use in isolated monasteries. The Serbian Church, in order to resist the proselytizing activities of Catholic Hungary in the Vojvodina, decided to adopt Russian Church Slavonic as its literary language, seeing Russia as the guardian of Orthodoxy. This Russian Church Slavonic was first used for religious purposes, but in the second half of the 18th c. it also influenced the secular writing that appeared in the Vojvodina and Turkish-ruled Serbia. The linguistic result was a hybrid language known as Slaveno-Serbian, which freely mixed local dialect features and Russian (and Serbian) Church Slavonic features. This language was used for literary purposes in the last decades of the 18th and first decades of the 19th c., but its weakness was that it had no fixed norms and varied from writer to writer.

At the beginning of the 19th c. Vuk Karadžić, a largely self-taught scholar, proposed a reformed Serbian literary language based on a single dialect and the Štokavian koine of folk literature without Church Slavonic phonological or morphological features. The dialect he advocated was his own east Hercegovinian Neo-Štokavian *(i)jekavian* dialect (see above, 'Dialects'). He made his revolutionary proposals in his Serbian Dictionary (*Srpski rječnik*) of 1818, which also contained a grammar of the proposed language. He also introduced a new simplified version of the Cyrillic alphabet, using a single letter per sound and a phonemically based orthography. Resistance to these proposals was very fierce on the part of the Orthodox Church and some Serbian intellectuals, who objected to this peasant-based language and saw Vuk's introduction of the Latin letter <j> into the Cyrillic alphabet as a threat to Orthodoxy. However, after 50 years of polemics conducted by Vuk and his disciple Đuro Daničić, the newly independent Kingdom of Serbia in 1868 officially adopted his language and alphabet, although Vuk's *(i)jekavian* reflex of *jat'* gave way to the *ekavian* reflex which was typical of most of Serbia.

Croatian

The problem for the Croats in the 19th c. was different from that of the Serbs. They did not have to battle for the use of the vernacular, but had to resolve the problem as to which of the many vernacular-based literary languages should become the standard literary language for all Croats. In the 1820s and 1830s in the face of increasing Hungarian nationalism, a group of young intellectuals started the so-called 'Illyrian Movement' which initially sought the unity of all Southern Slavs including Bulgarians. They recognized three national names as generic, i.e. Croat, Serb and Slovene, and believed that Croat and South Slav unity could be best established by the use of the common, though artificial, name Illyrian. Their leader Ljudevit Gaj, a Kajkavian speaker, decided that the Štokavian dialect should be adopted as the standard language as this was the dialect known not only to Croats but also to Serbs, Bosnians and Montenegrins. It was also the idiom of Dubrovnik's great literary tradition, the language of early 18th-c. Bosnian Franciscan writers, and the dialect of a rich folk literature heritage. His rejection of his own Kajkavian, which did have a strong literary tradition, was based primarily on the fact that this dialect, although used in the Croatian cultural centre of Zagreb, was known to only a limited number of Croats and therefore had no wider appeal. In 1850 several Croatian literary figures made a 'Literary Agreement' with Vuk Karadžić and Đuro Daničić to use Vuk's Neo-Štokavian *(i)jekavian* dialect as the basis on which to standardize the literary language of both Serbs and Croats with the eventual aim of full integration. For the next 50 years there was resistance on the part of some Croatian writers and philologists to the acceptance of Vuk's form of Neo-Štokavian *(i)jekavian* and a phonetic orthography. They advocated instead the use of old plural case-endings to provide a link with Kajkavian and Čakavian, the use of Štokavian *ikavian* and an etymological orthography. By the end of the century, however, thanks to the efforts of his Croat supporters, Vuk's language finally gained full acceptance. Firstly, in 1892 I. Broz produced a 'Croatian Orthography' (*Hrvatski pravopis*) based on Vuk's principles, and then in 1899 T. Maretić published a 'Grammar and Stylistics of the Croatian or Serbian Literary Language' (*Gramatika i stilistika hrvatskoga ili srpskoga književnog jezika*) with a normative framework based on the writings of Vuk and Daničić. These were followed in 1901 by I. Broz and F. Iveković's 'Croatian Dictionary' (*Rječnik hrvatskog jezika*) which again was based mainly on the works of Vuk and Daničić.

Variants of the literary language

The period from 1850, however, witnessed the development of the two variants of the literary language. The 'Literary Agreement' could not at one fell swoop eliminate the centuries of division between different dialects, cultures and religions under different rulers. There remained the major task of adapting the chosen standard language to all the functions of a modern literary language. The Croats in the second half of the 19th c. went through a period of purism, rejecting Turkisms and international loan-words and preferring to adopt words from Czech or other Slavonic languages or to coin new domestic terms using native roots. The Serbs, on the other hand, were quite happy to retain Turkisms and adopt international terms. In both areas too we encounter differences in word-formation in new technical terms, because there was no one body to coordinate efforts in this field. The basic lexical fund for the Serbs was the enlarged 2nd edition of Vuk's *Srpski rječnik* (1852) based on the folk vocabulary of one dialect and containing many Turkisms. This vocabulary was subsequently enhanced in the second half of the 19th c. by international terms and new Serbian coinages. The major Croatian dictionary was B. Šulek's two-volume 'German–Croatian Dictionary' (*Njemačko–hrvatski rječnik*) of 1860, which included not only Štokavian material from Vuk's dictionary but also material from Kajkavian and Čakavian dialects. It also included numerous words borrowed from other Slavonic languages (mainly Czech, Russian and Slovene) and a large number of Šulek's own neologisms. This dictionary was subsequently largely ignored by the Croatian Academy's large-scale 'Dictionary of the Croatian or Serbian Language' (*Rječnik hrvatskoga ili srpskoga jezika*) which began to appear in 1880 (and was completed only in 1976). The original aim of the Academy dictionary's first editor, Vuk's disciple Đuro Daničić, was to include words from all three major dialects and the whole of Serbian and Croatian literature, but these aims were then modified, limiting Croatian literary sources and material from the Čakavian and Kajkavian dialects. This factor and the subsequent appearance of Broz–Iveković's 'Croatian Dictionary' in 1901, based primarily on Vuk's and Daničić's works, was to restrict still further the notion of what was standard vocabulary in Croatian.

In the early 20th c. there were suggestions that a compromise might be made in terms of the variants by the Serbs abandoning Cyrillic for Latin script and the Croats giving up *(i)jekavian* for *ekavian*. This idea, however, was rejected. In the Kingdom of the Serbs, Croats and Slovenes following the First World War there was strong resentment on the part of Croats against centralization and Serbianization with the infiltration of Serbian terms by means of civil administration, schools and the military. Belgrade's political centralism had a parallel linguistic direction with a preference for *ekavian*. New disputes arose over a new extreme phonetic orthography with no concessions to etymological spelling written by the Serb A. Belić, but people were more aware that the differences were not merely orthographic conventions.

The 20th c. saw in Croatia the revival of Kajkavian and Čakavian imaginative literature, and living practice curtailed those forms proposed by Vuk that were alien to Croatian and Serbian Neo-Štokavian idioms. Before the Second World War a dictionary appeared, suggesting some 3,000–4,000 lexical and stylistic differences between the Croatian and Serbian literary languages, and during the war itself the Croatian Pavelić dictatorship pursued a policy of exaggerated linguistic purism. In the postwar period in the new Yugoslavia an agreement was reached in 1954 in Novi Sad by scholars representing Serbs, Croats, Bosnians and Montenegrins which affirmed the equality of alphabets, and of *(i)jekavian* and *ekavian*, and stressed that their language was one language with two forms of pronunciation. They also agreed to produce a common orthography and dictionary and to establish a common scientific terminology. There was much dissatisfaction with the resulting dictionaries, and resistance by Croat scholars led them in 1965 to advocate the acknowledgement of two distinct variants of the literary language. Then in 1967 Croatian scholars and intellectuals issued a 'Declaration', which stated that Croatian and Serbian were separate languages. This statement produced an uproar especially as it seemed that the Serbian minority living in Croatia would have to use officially the Croatian form of the literary language. This sensitive issue led to a strong political clampdown by the central government. From that period, however, linguistic cooperation broke down and it has generally been accepted that there are two variants of the literary language.

The language question continued to be a touchy issue with rival claims being made by linguistic unitarists and supporters of local subvariants in increasingly mixed areas like Bosnia and Hercegovina. Since the 1970s the Croats have continued to use the term 'Croatian Literary Language' and now that Croatia has become an independent country this is the only term used. In Serbia even today the term Serbo-Croat is still used with a mind to the large minority of Croat-speakers in the new rump Yugoslavia. However, the simple term 'Serbian' is now more prevalent. At the present stage of development it is noticeable that some Croat scholars are actively emphasizing and encouraging the use of words that distinguish the variants/languages and in some areas new terms are again being coined or older dialectal words reactivated. There has also been some discussion on a return to an etymological orthography. In some countries such as Canada and Australia, with large émigré populations, Serbian and Croatian are now taught as two different languages. However, despite the lexical and stylistic differences that distinguish the variants, we are from a structural point of view still dealing with one language. It could well be, however, that within a certain period of time sociolinguistic pressures and language manipulation will lead us to talk of two separate languages. In this context it will be interesting to see what will happen to the ***Bosnian** Muslim variant of the language.

The language in the former Yugoslav republics

Serbo-Croat is spoken in Croatia, Bosnia and Hercegovina, Serbia, and Montenegro. Before 1991 these were all constituent republics of former Yugoslavia, as were Macedonia and Slovenia. Since the break-up of former Yugoslavia in 1991 all these republics have become independent countries, with Serbia and Montenegro merging to form a new Yugoslavia. Bosnia is still riven by the rival claims of three ethnic groups. Serbo-Croat is the native language of four ethnic groups: Serbs (8.5 million), Croats (4.5 million), Montenegrins (600,000) and Bosnian Muslims (2 million). In former Yugoslavia, Bosnian Muslims were recognized as a separate ethnic group on the grounds of religion. Historically they are descendants of Serbs and Croats who adopted Islam under the long Turkish occupation of Bosnia and Hercegovina. Countries and ethnic groups, however, coincide only in part. Serbia, predominantly inhabited by Serbs, has large Croat (150,000), Montenegrin (150,000) and Muslim (200,000) minorities. The population of Croatia is about four-fifths Croat, but it also has a Serb minority of almost half a million. Montenegro has small Muslim and Serb minorities. Bosnia and Hercegovina is a mixture of all four ethnic groups with 1.25 million Serbs and three-quarters of a million Croats living alongside the Bosnian

Muslims. As a result of historical migrations for economic and political reasons, large numbers of Serbo-Croat-speakers also live outside these countries in Burgenland in Austria, in Hungary, in Romania and in the Italian province of Molise. Several hundred thousand Serbo-Croat-speaking émigrés also live in the USA, Canada, Australia, Sweden and Germany. It should also be borne in mind that Serbo-Croat was the lingua franca for all the peoples of former Yugoslavia.

Benson, M. 1979. *Serbo-Croatian–English Dictionary*, 2nd edn. Belgrade.
—— 1986. *English–Serbo-Croatian Dictionary*, 2nd edn. Belgrade.
Brozović, D. 1974. Hrvatski jezik ('The Croatian Language'). In Flaker, A. and Pranjić, K. (eds), *Hrvatska književnost u evropskom kontekstu*, Zagreb, 9–83.
—— and Ivić, P. 1988. *Jezik srpskohrvatski/hrvatskosrpski, hrvatski ili srpski* ('The Serbo-Croat/Croato-Serbian, Croatian or Serbian Language'). Zagreb.
Drvodelić, M. 1989. *Croatian–English Dictionary*, 6th edn. Zagreb.
Filipović, R. 1993. *English–Croatian Dictionary*, 2nd edn. Zagreb.
Ivić, P. 1971. *Српски народ и његов језик* ('The Serbian Nation and Its Language'). Belgrade.
Magner, T. F. 1991. *Introduction to the Croatian and Serbian Language*, rev. edn. Pennsylvania.

PETER HERRITY

Sercquiais, see *Sark French*

Shelta

A 'secret language', varieties of which are spoken among Travellers in Ireland, Britain and America. The precise origins are unclear but, of the lexical items attested among the different communities using Shelta, many (2,000 to 3,000 according to Hancock (1984), which see also for bibliographical references) are of Irish origin, though the syntax is basically English with perhaps a very few Irish features. The origin of the name is unknown.

Hancock, I. 1984. Shelta and Polari. In Trudgill, P. (ed.), *Language in the British Isles*, Cambridge, 384–403.
Macalister, R. A. S. 1937. Shelta. In Id., *The Secret Languages of Ireland*, Cambridge, 130–224.

Sican (Sicanian)

The Sicani were a people who, according to ancient writers, dwelt in central Sicily and were distinguished from the Elymi to the west and the Siculi to the east (see map 10). They have been variously claimed to have been of Iberian or African origin, but nothing can be proved. Little if anything is known of their language – a 6th-c. BC inscription consisting of 58 Greek characters has been claimed as Sican but the attribution is far from certain and its meaning obscure, though it is probably non-*Indo-European.

Sicel (Siculan)

The Sicels or Siculi were a people who dwelt in eastern Sicily (to which they gave their name) in pre-Classical times (see map 10) and who, according to comments by Classical writers, at an earlier period occupied much of the Italian mainland as well.

Apart from a number of words quoted (rightly or wrongly) as Sicel by Greek or Latin writers and a few very brief inscriptions (of which only two or three may in fact be in Sicel), our knowledge of the Sicel language depends entirely on a 5th- or 4th-c. BC inscription on a clay vase found at Centuripae (modern Centuripe, some 25 km SW of Mount Etna) in 1824 and now in the Badisches Landesmuseum at Karlsruhe; this consists of 99 Greek letters (with one or at most two more missing at the end). Though the interpretation of the inscription is far from certain, many but not all scholars now agree that the language thereof is ***Indo-European**.

Pisani, V. 1964. Siculo. In Id., *Le lingue dell'Italia antica oltre il latino* ('The Languages of Ancient Italy other than Latin'), 2nd edn, Turin, 293–302.

Schmoll, U. 1958. *Die vorgriechischen Sprachen Siziliens* ('The Pre-Greek Languages of Sicily'). Wiesbaden.

Whatmough, J. 1933, Sicel. In Conway, R. S., Whatmough, J. and Johnson S. E., *The Prae-Italic Dialects of Italy*, London, vol. 2, 430–500.

Zamboni, A. 1978. Il siculo. In Prosdocimi, A. L. (ed.), *Popoli e civiltà dell'Italia antica*, vol. 4, *Lingue e dialetti*, Rome, 949–1012.

Sicilian (see under *Italy. IV. Central and southern Italy*)

Siculan, see *Sicel*

Sign languages

Some 30 sign languages used for visual, i.e. non-oral, communication among Deaf people and between Deaf people and 'hearing' people are in use in Europe, and adequate description of them all within the limits of the space available is impossible. We shall therefore concentrate on British Sign Language (BSL) (see fig. 13), which is the name given by 'hearing' linguists in the late 1970s to the various forms of sign language used in the United Kingdom that had been developed over the course of time by Deaf people themselves. Similar appellations have been devised for the sign languages of other European countries, e.g. *Langue des signes française* (LSF) for French Sign Language (on this, see for example Moody et al. 1983–6, Mottez 1988).

Sign languages are constructed from several elements. The first uses hands to create vocabulary; visual symbolism plays a significant role, although iconicity is much rarer than popularly supposed. The second uses facial expressions to create effect and also syntactic markers. The third uses signs to represent the alphabet, principally to incorporate loan-words from spoken languages.

The current consensus is that each sign language is autonomous, although there is a degree of lexical similarity between sign languages where their development parallels the sphere of influence of national languages, as, for example, between LSF and the lexical items of the sign languages of French-speaking Switzerland and Belgium or among the Scandinavian sign languages.

Some scholars hold that European sign languages have an affiliation to ***Indo-European languages** at the semantic level (which means that cultural

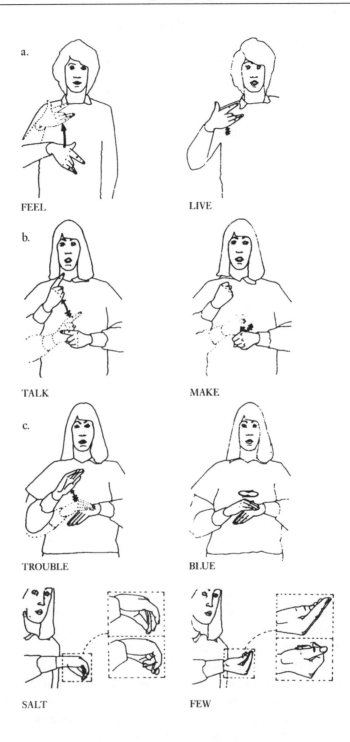

FEEL

LIVE

TALK

MAKE

TROUBLE

BLUE

SALT

FEW

Fig. 13 Examples of British Sign Language. Reproduced by permission from J. G. Kyle and B. Woll, *Sign Language* (Cambridge, Cambridge University Press, 1985). Illustrations by Bernard Quinn.

a. Durative verb
   Base sign

Slow reduplication

Fast reduplication

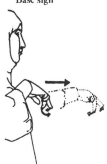

WALK

KEEP-ON-WALKING

WALK-OFTEN

b. Punctual verb
   Base sign

Slow reduplication

Fast reduplication

JUMP

JUMP-AGAIN-AND-AGAIN

JUMP-A-LOT

a. Base sign

b. Inhibiting

WALK

ABOUT-TO-WALK-BUT-DIDN'T

concepts from the spoken languages have to some extent been absorbed by Deaf communities and are reflected at a lexical level). However, the syntactic structures of sign languages are not only strikingly similar but appear to bear little resemblance to that of spoken languages.

The earliest attestations of sign languages in Europe can be found in Greece and Italy (and others are found in Israel). Hippocrates' references in the 5th c. BC were followed in succeeding centuries by descriptions by Aristotle and Socrates while, during the same period, the Talmud and the Mishnah make 387 references to Deaf people and their languages. Other references occur sporadically up to the 16th c. and more regularly thereafter. The earliest British references occur in Carew's *Survey of Cornwall* (1602), where four Deaf people are described, giving an indication of the degree of sophistication in the sign language of the time. The first purely sign-language-oriented accounts are to be found in Bulwer's *Chirologia: or the Natural Language of the Hand* (1644) and his *Philocophus: or the Deafe and Dumbe Man's Friend* (1648), which are also notable for their use of visual, if necessarily static, depiction of some of the lexical items in contemporary use, a number of which still form part of BSL today, which indicates a significant historical continuity.

Dialects within sign languages are perceived to be strong – the number of regional variations within BSL, for example, appears to exceed those of spoken English. This is attributed to at least two factors. The first is the development of Deaf schools from the late 18th c. onwards, each with its own set of signs. The second is the hostile attitude towards signs and Deaf teachers from the 19th c. until the late 20th which, though it did not halt the use of sign language, forced it underground. Thus the period in which English dialects declined as the result of a process of national standardization was not replicated in the Deaf community. This pattern appears to obtain throughout Europe, though smaller countries with fewer Deaf schools appear to have consequently less regional variation.

The process of standardization of sign languages is also different from that of spoken languages. In the case of BSL, a nationally agreed finger-spelling alphabet was certainly in place by the mid-19th c. (although, intriguingly, two letters differ from present-day usage) but numerical signs still vary widely (with at least five different sets existing in dialectal form and none as yet taking precedence). The development of Deaf television programmes in the 1980s began a process of standardization, in that signs used therein have obtained a degree of prestige and have begun to replace some of the dialectal vocabulary among younger people.

In the mid-19th c., British sign vocabulary was exported to other countries, usually by way of Deaf people establishing Deaf schools. The main examples are Australia and New Zealand where estimates of approximately 80% congruency with present-day BSL have been made. South Africa and India also share lexical items with BSL. Sign languages in these countries sometimes contain terms which have now almost disappeared in the UK. A similar historical dimension is apparent in the existence in the USA of a number of British signs which probably arrived there ahead of the formal establishment of American Sign Language (ASL) in 1816. There is little evidence of British influence in other European sign languages, though there is a significant degree of influence of LSF in Ireland and thence in Roman Catholic Scotland.

Since it cannot be adequately committed to print, BSL's chief literary forms parallel those found in 'oral' literatures, namely story-telling and poetry which have only recently come to be widely recognized, particularly since the advent of video created a basic medium of performance.

The continuing neglect of the Deaf community by statutory authorities has resulted in a lack of official statistics for numbers of BSL-users. Estimates of those for whom it is a first language vary from 30,000 to 100,000 and there are no estimates at all of the number of those who use it as a second or subsequent language. These figures serve, however, to confirm that BSL is, after *English and *Welsh, the third most widely used indigenous language in the UK. Numbers of European sign users, calculated according to the most comprehensive studies available (Schein and Delk 1974, Schein 1989), indicate an incidence of between one and two Deaf people per thousand.

Despite a number of campaigns from the 1980s onwards for linguistic minority status, there is as yet no official recognition of BSL although some government departments have implicitly recognized it by funding the translation of government information on to BSL videos. Likewise, research into BSL and the training of BSL–English interpreters have received limited funding. The legal system is at the present time in the process of acknowledging both the linguistic and the cultural aspects of BSL in courtroom situations.

Within the mass media, BSL is still largely confined to TV programmes for the Deaf and a handful of news programmes. In the print media, there has been little recognition of the language.

Undoubtedly, the most important sphere of activity for minority languages is within the education system, where policies determine whether such languages should be permitted to survive into the next generation. After a century of proscription, BSL and its users have begun to win their way back into the classroom, but only on a small scale. With the increase in theories of integration (strongly contested by Deaf people and their organizations), the number of Deaf schools has dwindled and at present only 6% of Deaf children are still educated in the traditional Deaf formal structures. This has led to widespread concern, not so much for the future of the language itself as for the quality of its use. A similar situation obtains in many other European countries. Scandinavia, however, has followed the Swedish government's lead in officially declaring Swedish Sign Language (SSL) to be the first language of the Deaf child, with the result that bilingual (Swedish–SSL) programmes and Deaf schools are the norm.

BSL has no international status. In so far as any sign language has gained a degree of internationality, it is American Sign Language (ASL) which has been disseminated. However, it is hearing professionals who have taken this approach which is currently resisted by Deaf Europeans.

The last years of the 20th c. have seen tremendous strides taken by European sign-language-users to liaise with each other, using what is referred to as International

Sign, which is in fact an *ad hoc* ***Pidgin** whose vocabulary varies according to the nationalities present in the liaison situation. Recent efforts have culminated in the official recognition of sign languages by the European Parliament. Such recognition is not, however, binding on individual states and the future development of the languages in question is therefore still uncertain.

Kyle, J. G. and Woll, B. 1985. *Sign Language*. Cambridge.
Miles, D. 1988. *British Sign Language*. London.
Moody, B. et al. 1983–6. *La Langue des signes*. Vol. 1, *Introduction à l'histoire et à la grammaire de la Langue des Signes;* vol. 2, *Dictionnaire bilingue élémentaire*. Paris.
Mottez, B. 1988. La langue des signes française. La Communauté linguistique des Sourds. In Vermes, G. (ed.), *Vingt-cinq communautés linguistiques de la France*, Paris, vol. 1, 360–80.
Sacks, O. 1989. *Seeing Voices*. Berkeley, CA.
Schein, J. D. 1989. *At Home among Strangers*. Washington, DC.
Schein, J. D. and Delk, M. 1974. *The Deaf People of the United States*. Silver Spring, MD.

PADDY LADD

Slaveno-Serbian (see under *Serbian*, under *Serbo-Croat*)

Slavonic, Church, see *Church Slavonic*

Slavonic languages

Common Slavonic, the parent of the Slavonic languages, existed for more than 3,000 years before disintegrating into individual languages over the period from the 6th to the 9th c. AD. For a considerable time Common Slavonic developed as an integrated dialect; however, in due course each branch of Slavonic developed from a dialect of the parent language. The expansion of the Slavs in the early centuries AD brought them from a compact area north of the Carpathians as far as the Elbe in the north-west, central Europe, the Balkans and the west of Russia, as a result of which the differences within Common Slavonic were magnified by loss of contact between the tribes.

Common Slavonic divided into three groups of languages, probably as the result of invasions by the Huns, then the Avars, who from the middle of the 4th c. pushed some tribes to the south in the direction of the Danube, others to the west, towards Volynia. The separate development of South Slavonic was caused by the settling of the Magyars in Hungary in the 10th c. and the Germanization of the Slavonic regions of Bavaria and Austria, while the eastward expansion of ***Romanian** led to a break between the South and East Slavonic groups in the 11th and 12th centuries. The languages may be categorized as follows (see map 17):

South Slavonic:	***Slovene, *Serbo-Croat, *Bulgarian, *Macedonian**, Old ***Church Slavonic;**
West Slavonic:	***Czech, *Slovak, *Polish**, Upper and Lower ***Sorbian** (Lusatian or Wendish), ***Cassubian** (regarded by some as a Polish dialect), ***Polabian** (extinct);
East Slavonic:	***Russian, *Ukrainian** and ***Belarusian.**

Map 17   Slavonic-speaking countries. **Note (i) that, within the Slavonic-speaking area, national boundaries and linguistic limits do not coincide exactly; (ii) that there are Slavonic-speaking minorities in some neighbouring countries; and (iii) that the Russian Federation and some other primarily Slavonic-speaking countries, especially Yugoslavia (i.e. Serbia and Montenegro), include communities (in some cases sizeable ones) whose first language is not Slavonic. See also map 18, 'Sorbian, Cassubian and Polabian'.**

The linguistic features that differentiate the three groups evolved during expansion, mainly in the 6th to the 10th centuries, but the languages remain close in root, formatives, syntax and semantics, with marked lexical unity, especially in family names, natural phenomena, parts of the body, cereals, domestic animals, stock-breeding, hunting, the making of clay pottery, weaving, physical properties, the names of actions, states, processes, numerals, pronouns, adverbs, some prepositions, conjunctions and particles. Some 300 words are the virtually unique common property of *Baltic and Slavonic, including some parts of the body and terms from the natural world: Lithuanian *ranka*, Russian *ruká* 'hand', Lithuanian *galva*, Russian *golová* 'head', Lithuanian *karvė*, Russian *koróva* 'cow', etc., due either to long proximity and mutual influence or to provenance from a common source.

The basic Slavonic word-stock was amplified by borrowing. Common Slavonic borrowed from *Iranian in prehistoric times, while East and South Slavonic subsequently borrowed from eastern languages, as a result of the political domination of the Tatars in Russia and the Turks in the Balkans. After the Renaissance, lexis derived from Classical and western European languages, especially French and German, but Church Slavonic remained the main source of lexical innovation in East Slavonic and some South Slavonic languages. Compounding, a productive word-formatory device in Church Slavonic, is still common in the creation of new terminology, though less so than affixation.

Fixed stress is characteristic of Czech, Slovak and South Cassubian (initial stress), Polish and East Slovak (penultimate stress), and literary Macedonian (pre-penultimate stress), while non-fixed stress in Serbo-Croat, Slovene, Bulgarian and East Slavonic languages reflects the distinction made in *Indo-European and Common Slavonic between non-fixed- and fixed-stress paradigms. Rising and falling intonation is retained in Serbo-Croat and Slovene.

Inflection is the main means of rendering grammatical meaning in Slavonic languages, with a potential seven cases in the singular and plural and three case forms in the dual (which is still preserved in Slovene and Sorbian). In Bulgarian and Macedonian, noun declension has been almost completely superseded by prepositional constructions. The languages have three noun genders, and many distinguish animate and inanimate noun forms in some cases.

The Slavonic aorist (denoting the completion of an action) and imperfect (denoting a continuing state or uncompleted action, usually in the past) survive in South Slavonic (except for Slovene) and Sorbian. The old Indo-European perfect tense has been largely superseded in Slavonic by forms based on a past active participle in -*l*-. The verb system is dominated by the concept of aspect, involving the existence of paired stems, one of which expresses the perfective (completed), the other the imperfective (uncompleted) aspect of a verb. The future can be expressed by conjugating a perfective verb or by using auxiliaries.

The first writing system used for Slavonic languages was Glagolitic (see *Cyrillic and Glagolitic scripts), subsequently replaced by Cyrillic, which is still used by the East Slavonic languages, and Bulgarian, Macedonian and Serbian. Other Slavonic languages are written in the Roman alphabet, combining letters or using diacritics to render distinctive Slavonic sounds (e.g. Polish<cz>, Czech <č> for [tʃ]).

Comrie, B. and Corbett, G. G. (eds) 1993. *The Slavonic Languages*. London.
Entwistle, W. J. and Morison, W. A. 1949. *Russian and the Slavonic Languages*. London.
Horálek, K. 1993. *An Introduction to the Study of the Slavonic Languages* (translated from the Czech and amended by P. Herrity). Nottingham.

TERENCE WADE

Slovak

A member, with *Czech, *Polish and *Sorbian, of the western subgroup of the *Slavonic languages. It is spoken mainly in the Slovak Republic (Slovakia), where it has the status of official language.

Pre-standardization history

The earliest attestations (isolated words, usually names of persons and places) in liturgical and, later, legal Latin or Old *Church Slavonic manuscripts, date from the 10th to the 13th centuries. Glosses of similar nature and content appear from the 14th c., after when Slovakisms in Czech texts of local provenance also begin to appear. Increasing numbers of 'accidental' Slovakisms continue to appear up to the 18th c. Slovakisms described contrastively first appear in *Grammaticae bohemicae [. . .] libri duo* ('Two Books of Bohemian Grammar') (1603) by Vavrinec Benedikt z Nedožier (Vavřinec Benedikti z Nudožer, 1555–1615). He sought to encourage his compatriots in Upper Hungary ('Slovakia' is still at that time an anachronism) to read more Czech, but not to compel them to speak or learn it; they should instead cultivate their own idiom. He does not call it Slovak, but his countrymen are described as 'mei gentiles Slavi'. Next in line is the Lutheran Tobiáš Masník's (1640–97) *Zpráva písma slovenského, jak se ma dobře psáti, čísti y tisknauti* ('Guide to Slovak writing, how to write, read and print properly') (1696). Masník, who deliberately vernacularized some of his writings to make them accessible to 'my nation and the Czechs', here describes the ideal of classical written Czech, although whenever he names the language it is as 'jazyk slovenský' – meaning Slavonic and contrasted with Hungarian and/or Latin. 'Literary' Slovenský/Slavonic means beyond question Czech. He quotes several of the same Bohemian–Moravian–Slovak oppositions mentioned by Vavrinec Benedikt z Nedožier, treating them as local variants, while some features which are specifically Slovak are described as plain errors (e.g. acc.pl. = gen.pl.). Masník's main sources were two 17th-c. Czech grammars: Šteyer's *Žáček* ('Pupil') (1668) and Rosa's *Čechořečnost* ('Czecholinguism') (1672), and his work has been described as the first handbook of Czech by a Slovak and published in 'Slovakia', serving as a makeshift for a full grammar for Slovaks until the appearance of Doležal's (1700–78) *Grammatica Slavico-Bohemica* (1746). The place of publication of Doležal's work, Bratislava, carries that little extra weight in interpretations of the Slovak elements in it. Like its predecessors, it is a grammar of Czech, but with clear acknowledgement of local discrepancies (Slovak features).

During 1635–1777 the south-western city of Trnava was home to the only surviving university in Hungary (transferred to Buda in 1777). Importantly, the university printery, while producing its own textbooks in Latin, also published some works in a version of 'Czech'. The university itself was a Jesuit foundation, and the language used in its non-Latin prints (and those of other printeries in the city) is now known as 'Jesuit Slovak'.

The eighteenth and nineteenth centuries

The activities of the post-university printers overlap with the life of Anton Bernolák (1762–1813), a Catholic priest and the man credited with the first standardization of Slovak. The Catholics had long been inclined to use a Slovakicized Czech as their written language, distancing themselves from the Slovak Protestant tradition with its roots in the Czech Reformation. All Bernolák's main grammatical works (published 1787–91) are inspired by the aim to normalize Slovak as a distinct language. Thus he set out not only to provide an appropriate and distinct spelling system, but also to eliminate all the 'errors' that crept into Slovak pronunciation and spelling from Czech, and to identify the genuine contemporary usage as he knew it, which was that of south-west Slovakia. The failings of this first standard Slovak were not only its hybrid and artificial nature, but the fact that, originating in an area close to the Czech-speaking area, it contained many grammatical and lexical features shared with Czech or easily domesticated from Czech, which were not present in the rest of Upper Hungary.

Despite contemporary opposition to Bernolák's 'Slovak', it had some short-term successes in publications (religious, educational and some 'higher' literature), but many books continued to appear in Czech. Many private individuals continued to write in Czech, but public documents of local significance began to show more and more Bernolákisms. There were learned societies propagating both languages, but usually only of local importance. When the effectiveness of Bernolák's Slovak dipped, it began to be artificially revived, in the 1830s and 1840s, from Pest, largely in association with the *Spolok milovníkov reči a literatúry slovenskej* ('Society of Friends of Slovak Language and Literature', 1834–50) and its almanach *Zora* ('Dawn', 1835–50).

Despite the strength of Catholic endeavours, personified by Bernolák, it was the Protestants who eventually carried the day when it comes to the modern standard language as we know it. Lutherans, though using Czech as their 'high style' written language, at least conversed in local versions of Slovak. For various reasons it was inevitable that differences had developed between standard Czech and the Czech used in Upper Hungary. Confessional antagonism remained an inhibiting factor in the creation of national unity, though a new standard language, applied throughout Slovakia, would help to cement the emerging nation (it would be inappropriate to say that the Slovak nation had already emerged; the intelligentsia that would speak in such terms was in fact a handful of Lutherans of non-aristocratic background).

The 1840s saw the culmination of a 'national revival' and the rise of a national political movement. The decade peaked in the 'revolutionary year' of 1848. Language as a reflection of nationhood, rather than a mere medium of communication for religious and similar purposes, had become a major issue. It had been one since 1832–6, when Latin was replaced by Hungarian as the official language throughout Hungary, irrespective of population structure. Hungary was to become a monolingual nation-state, and schools and public offices were all to be Magyarized.

The national Slovak language that did emerge is essentially the work of Ľudovít Štúr (1815–56), who was acutely interested in language and competent in many languages. Those who, like Štúr, wished to see the nation united were not satisfied with Bernoláčtina as a replacement for Czech. A language that would cut across the religious divide and be viable enough to sustain all the future nation's linguistic needs, especially for the planned nationwide newspaper, was a necessity. And Štúr busied himself with its creation. In a letter of 11 February 1843, when his work on the new grammar was almost complete, he refers to that date as 'the day of the resurrection of Slovak'.

In 1844, Štúr's Slovak (based on Central Slovak dialects) was adopted as the official language of communication by a new cultural association, Tatrín (founded at Liptovský Svätý Mikuláš). The same year saw the first publications in the 'new' 'literary' language, although Štúr's grammar, *Nauka reči slovenskej* ('Principles of the Slovak language'), did not itself appear until 1846. At the same time he laid the philosophical and political foundations for the Slovaks' nationhood (no mere Czech minority in Hungary, but a separate ethnic entity), based on the premise that they did possess a language having a social function and capable of literary development and were entitled to their own cultural, social and political development.

The twentieth century

Štúr's grammar survived, with various refinements by Štúr himself and others, especially M. M. Hodža, and is basically in use to this day, although never ceasing to be honed further. Mid-19th-c. opposition, centred on Ján Kollár's campaign favouring the continuing preferential status of Czech, eventually died out. However, new travails were in store with a purely Czechoslovak dimension. Czechoslovakia came into being in 1918 as a unitary nation-state and, inevitably, if the Czechoslovaks were one nation, there had to be one Czechoslovak language. The concession was that it might have two variants; thus, notwithstanding the 'Czechoslovak' policy, the Slovak variant sustained itself as separate and began to be provided with more and more descriptive and school grammars. Some Czechicization, especially of the vocabulary, did go on, but to little long-term effect. By the 1960s, Slovak linguists had largely sorted out what were Czechisms of various kinds, and so were to be rejected – though this is a highly fraught area and such purification processes continue today. Sometimes a word for a new idea is deliberately created different from Czech, such as the word for 'motorway' (*autostráda*, coll. *diaľnica*, Cz. *dálnice*), while sometimes a well-established Czech word is re-created as if it had gone through an evolution native to Slovak (*válenda* > *váľanda* 'divan'). Not every move to clean up Slovak is rewarded with either success or popular approval.

Dictionaries

The first proper dictionary of Slovak came from Bernolák. This was a five-volume work that gave translations in Czech, Latin, German and Hungarian (1825–7). It was a major undertaking, even if the language it represented was relatively short-lived in active use, but it appeared earlier than the first comparable Czech dictionary. The Slovaks then had to wait until the 1960s before another proper dictionary appeared, and then in a six-volume set that would scarcely sit 'on the shelf at home'. It was another quarter of a century before the Slovaks had the first one-volume dictionary of their own language (1987), rapidly republished with several revisions of substance in 1989.

Orthography

The earliest, 'primitive' or transcribed, orthography was ill-suited to Slovak, but since it is inappropriate to speak about Slovak as a language having definable contours until the late 18th c., this is of little interest. Texts in Slovakicized Czech, or Czech texts with random Slovakicisms, use the Czech orthography of the day. The first book in a 'conscious' Slovak, and the first book printed in what has to be called Slovak, although predating the birth of the modern language, was Ignác Bajza's novel (1783, the first Slovak novel), *René Mláďenca Príhodi a Skuſenoſti* ('The Adventures and Experiences of Young René'; in the modern language and orthography this would appear as *René mládenca príhody a skúsenosti*). However, the book recognized by Slovak historians as the first printed in the finally adopted Štúrian standard language is the second volume of the *Nitra* almanach (1844).

The modern orthography uses the Latin alphabet with four diacritics: the *mäkčeň* 'softener' <ˇ>, usually associated with palatalization past or present, also as <'> with letterpress lower case <d'>, <t'>, <l'> and with capital <Ľ> (<ˇ> being used with capital <Ď> and <Ť>); the *dĺžeň* 'length mark' (i.e. acute accent) over vowels or syllabic <l> or <r> to denote a long syllable; *dve bodky* 'two dots' (i.e. diaeresis) appearing over <a> in a short syllable after a labial where the vowel was originally nasal; and the *vokáň* 'circumflex', used over <o> and indicating the diphthong [uo]. Credit for the style of orthography using diacritics, though not in the form used today, is accorded to the 14th–15th-c. Czech religious reformer Jan (John) Hus, but the final version of the system, after variants used by Bajza and Bernolák, is due to refinements by Štúr and his successors between 1846 and 1851.

Contacts with other languages

During and after the Czech National Revival, when terminologies were being actively created for Czech, much borrowing and adaptation from other Slavonic languages, especially Polish and Russian, helped to fill some of the gaps; such borrowed items sat quite easily in the receiving language. And from Czech a large number were adopted, in a suitably adapted form, into Slovak. Lexical intrusions from other sources include a number of Sovietisms, transliterated or calqued, but now obsolete, and Anglicisms, most strongly in sport (early 20th-c.) and computer technology and business (late 20th c.), often mediated via German, and many Czechisms, often only at the colloquial level, since the codifiers, with varying success, have sought to eliminate many from the standard language. Slovak has been hospitable to a predictable range of cultural items from French and/or Italian, and a typical spread of internationalisms of Greek or Latin origin. Of earlier provenance is that section of the vocabulary associated with sheep-farming, which has many items encountered throughout the Balkans, from which sheep-farming spread. And from its long history of contiguity with Hungarian, within common state boundaries, Slovak acquired loan-words in such areas as public administration. 16th-c. Saxon colonization of the mining areas in particular also led to many German loans in the language of craft and early industry.

Demography and geography

Slovak in Europe is almost confined to the Slovak Republic (approximately 5 million speakers), though as a survival from the once united Czechoslovakia, about half a million Slovaks live in the Czech Republic, through work, marriage, etc. Elsewhere, from waves of migration largely within the Old Austrian Empire, scattered Slovak communities are to be found in Hungary, Romania and Croatia. Further afield, there are Slovak immigrant populations in parts of North America (Chicago, Pittsburgh, Toronto) and South America (Argentina), with more diffuse, more recent immigrant groups throughout western Europe and Australia. Some of the North and South American populations actively sustain the language, though with decreasing success. It is therefore difficult to assess just how many *native* speakers of Slovak there are world-wide: probably not more than 8 million.

As Slovakia's official language, Slovak is used throughout the legal, government and education systems, and in the media. It has no status internationally, though it may, as an echo of the recent past, be met in the neighbouring Czech Republic, where newspapers may even reproduce articles from the Slovak press without any perceived need for translation. The status of the language is protected by a language law and some subsidiary legislation.

Conclusion

'The rise, development and functions of the Slovak literary language are firmly connected with the rise of the Slovak nation. Since the Slovaks did not have a territorial sovereignty of their own, the formation of a literary language was the most evident symptom of the formation of their nation as a separate Slavic national entity. For this very reason, the language question, especially in the "nationalistic" nineteenth century, was ardently debated' (Ľubomír Ďurovič). Though much abated, and conducted in more modern terms, the debate is not over. Slovak is in many senses still coalescing as a language. While the general grammar, morphology and syntax of the standard language are now more or less stable, the vocabulary is constantly being enriched from the regions. An increasingly mobile population has brought regional language with it wherever it has gone, and key writers have hesitated less and less to use regionalisms in their works. The Ľudovít Štúr Linguistics Institute in Bratislava offers guidance on what might or might not be admitted to the standard lexicon. Yet even there, debates go on about the relative merits of this or that word or form, debates that still contain hints of either regional allegiance or even religious background: Central Slovak vs. Western Slovak, Nitra or Martin vs. Bratislava, even Lutheran vs. Catholic. Eastern Slovak barely enters the debate, for the easternmost dialects are now so distinct in so many ways that they are rather out on a limb. For a brief period in the early 1920s they became the basis of a local literary language, Slovjak.

Budovičová, V. 1987. Literary languages in contact: a sociolinguistic approach to the relation between Slovak and Czech today. In Chloupek, J., Nekvapil, J. et al., *Reader in Czech Sociolinguistics*, Amsterdam, Philadelphia, Prague, 156–75.

Ďurovič, Ľ. 1980. Slovak. In Schenker, A. M. and Stankiewicz, E. (eds), *The Slavic Literary Languages: Formation and Development*, New Haven, CT, 212–28, 278–80 (bibliography).

Habovštiaková, K. 1972. Le rôle de la langue tchèque dans la formation de la langue culturelle de la nationalité slovaque. *Recueil linguistique de Bratislava*, 3: 127–34.

Mistrík, J. 1985. The modernization of contemporary Slovak. In Stone, G. and Worth, D. (eds), *The Formation of the Slavonic Literary Languages*, Columbus, OH, 72–6.

Pynsent, R. B. 1994. *Questions of Identity. Czech and Slovak Ideas of Nationality and Personality*. Budapest, London, New York.

Short, D. 1993. Czech Republic and Slovak Republic: language situation. In Asher, R. E. (ed.), *The Encyclopedia of Language and Linguistics*, Oxford, vol. 2, 804–5.

—— 1993. Slovak. In Comrie, B. and Corbett, G. G. (eds), *The Slavonic Languages*, London, 533–92.

—— 1996. The use and abuse of the language argument in mid-nineteenth-century 'Czechoslovakism': an appraisal of a propaganda milestone. In Pynsent, R. B. (ed.), *The Literature of Nationalism: Essays on East European Identity*, Basingstoke, London, New York, 40–65.

D. SHORT

Slovene

A member of the southern subgroup of the *Slavonic languages and forming, together with *Serbo-Croat, the western branch of this subgroup. Standard literary Slovene is the official language of Slovenia which became an independent country in 1991.

Origins and early development of the literary language

The Slav tribes, who were the ancestors of the Slovenes, settled in the eastern Alps in the 6th c. AD. From the 8th c. onwards their lands were controlled by *Germanic-speakers and it was only in 1918 that the Slovenes gained a measure of independence within the newly created Kingdom of Serbs, Croats and Slovenes which from 1929 onwards was known as Yugoslavia. The 9th and 10th centuries saw the dissolution of Common Slavonic and the individualization of a Slovene language. The oldest texts that show Slovene features are the 'Freising Fragments' (written between 972 and 1039), which are normally included in the canon of Old *Church Slavonic texts. The first manuscripts which show distinctive Slovene dialect features are a few religious texts that appeared in the 14th and 15th centuries (the Rateče, Stična and Stara Gorska MS).

In 1550 the Reformation witnessed the publication of the first Slovene books by P. Trubar (a *Catechism* and an *Abecedarium*). Within the next 44 years Protestant writers had published a further 50 books. The main writers were S. Krelj, J. Dalmatin (who produced the first Slovene translation of the Bible in 1584) and A. Bohorič (the author of the first Slovene grammar, 1584). Trubar used the speech of Ljubljana (geographically just inside the Upper Carniolan dialect area, but with its own koine) with an admixture of his native Lower Carniolan Raščica dialect. Other writers, too, basically adhered to this language type although both Krelj and Dalmatin tried to broaden the literary base by introducing words from other Slovene dialects and Croatian dialects. Krelj also introduced forms from his native Inner Carniolan dialect. The Counter-Reformation saw a rapid decline in book production, but still an adherence by writers to the Trubar–Krelj–Dalmatin norm of the central dialects. In the 17th and 18th centuries, the number of writers from non-central areas increased and the production of texts for individual diocesan needs meant that by the mid-18th c. four additional dialects were in use in literature (Carinthian, Lower and East Styrian, Prekmurje). Writers from the central areas, however, continued to follow the old Protestant norm, at a time when the central role of Ljubljana in Slovene public life was increasing. This was important in terms of literary language continuity because the dialects had since the 16th c. undergone significant linguistic changes and there was a gap between the written and the spoken language. Beginning with the Enlightenment in the second half of the 18th c. the dialectal base of the language was broadened by a new generation of writers from Upper Carniola.

The literary language since 1808

J. Kopitar, in his grammar of 1808 (*Grammatik der slavischen Sprache in Krain, Kärnten und Steyermark* 'Grammar of the Slavonic Language in Carniola, Carinthia and Styria'), attempted to unite the speech of all Slovene regions purged of Germanisms on the basis of a synthesis of Upper and Lower Carniolan features. He accepted the Protestant heritage as the basis for the literary language, but stressed the primacy of the vernacular purged of Germanisms. At the beginning of the 19th c., debates on purism continued, new grammars appeared based on both Styrian and Lower Carniolan dialects, and attempts were made to improve the Latin alphabet of Bohorič (which used digraphs) by proposing a series of new graphemes from the *Cyrillic alphabet. It was only at this period that the name 'Slovene' as an ethnonym was firmly established (as opposed to the variety of terms previously used to describe the language: Carniolan, Styrian, Carinthian, Windisch). Slovene was still considered by some to be just a South Slavonic dialect and in the first half of the 19th c. came under pressure to merge with Croatian, Serbian (see *Serbo-Croat) and *Bulgarian into a new south Slavonic 'Illyrian' language. However, at this period the poetry of the greatest Slovene poet, F. Prešeren, and later the efforts of the great Slovene linguist Fr. Miklošič ensured the identity of a separate Slovene language. One result of resistance to Illyrianism was that some concessions were made by codifiers to Carinthian and Styrian dialects in terms of morphological features. Newspapers and magazines adopted the compromise norm still strongly linked to the central Carniolan dialects, and 'Gajica', the Croatian Latin alphabet that used diacritical marks and digraphs, replaced the old alphabet of Bohorič.

Two other important linguistic processes took place in the second half of the 19th c.: Slavization and archaization. Slavization introduced numerous words from other Slavonic languages in an attempt to eradicate Germanisms. Archaization using Church Slavonic as a model affected the grammatical structure of Slovene, introducing categories which had long been lost or weakened in the dialects, and indeed distinguish the literary language from the colloquial variants in use today.

This reconstructive, historical treatment of the literary language was superseded only at the turn of the 20th c., when new linguists embraced a more consistent synchronic approach putting a check on borrowings from other Slav languages and limiting archaic forms to those actually attested in older Slovene. When Slovenia became part of Yugoslavia in 1918 there was once more a puristic tendency, this time directed against Serbo-Croat words. There was a return to native resources, and this trend is evident even today in the new Slovenia.

Present situation

According to Yugoslav census figures for 1981 and other estimates, Slovene is spoken by nearly 2 million speakers in Slovenia and adjacent Slovene ethnic enclaves in Austria, Hungary and Italy, and by approximately 400,000 speakers in emigrant communities in the USA, Canada, Argentina, Germany and France. The standard language as presented in grammars and taught in schools and universities is to a large extent an artificial language in that its norm is modelled on an idealized Slavonic pattern which differs form the general colloquial language (as yet not adequately described) and does not agree in detail with any of the living dialects. The standard language is a composite of the dialects of several regions of Slovene linguistic territory, but is based primarily on the geographically central dialects of Upper and Lower Carniola (Gorenjska and Dolenjska) and to a lesser extent on the southwestern Inner Carniolan (Notranjsko) dialect. Slovene is unique among the Slavonic languages in the heterogeneity of its dialects especially in relation to the relatively small size of the Slovene-speaking area. The dialects are normally divided into seven major geographical groups although more recently a classification of eight has been proposed. Each of these groups embraces a number of subdialects which total 50 in all.

Derbyshire, W. W. 1993. *A Basic Reference Grammar of Slovene*. Columbus, OH.
Toporišič, J. 1991. *Slovenska Slovnica* ('A Slovene Grammar'), 3rd edn. Maribor.
Grad, A. and Leeming, H. 1993. *Slovensko–angleški slovar* ('Slovene–English Dictionary'). Ljubljana.
Grad, A., Škerlj, R. and Vitorovič, N. 1994. *Veliki angleško–slovenski slovar* ('Large English–Slovene Dictionary'). Ljubljana.
Lencek, R. L. 1982. *The Structure and History of the Slovene Language*. Columbus, OH.

PETER HERRITY

Slovincian (see under *Cassubian*)

Sorbian

Sorbian (or Wendish or Lusatian) (*serbšćina*) is a West *Slavonic language spoken in Lusatia (Ger. *Lausitz*) in the German *Länder* of Brandenburg and Saxony (see map 18). The northern varieties are referred to collectively as Lower Sorbian (spoken in Lower Lusatia) and the southern varieties as Upper Sorbian (in Upper Lusatia). Although there are separate Upper and Lower Sorbian *standard* languages, they are usually regarded as variants of one Sorbian language. The main urban centre of Lower Lusatia is Cottbus, that of Upper Lusatia is Bautzen. Most Sorbs (including all Lower Sorbs) are Lutherans, but there is a group of about 40 Catholic villages to the north and west of Bautzen (all Upper Sorbian).

The earliest known text is the oath by which citizens of Bautzen swore allegiance to the authorities (1532), but there is much older fragmentary evidence of the language in the form of isolated words, phrases, and even short sentences embedded in Latin and German documents. One of the main early sources of this kind is the Latin Chronicle of Bishop Thietmar of Merseburg, written in 1012–18. From the beginning the script and spelling system were based on the German model, but Jacobus Ticinus's *Principia linguae wendicae* ('Principles of the Wendish Language') (Prague, 1679) introduced an orthography based on *Czech which became the main distinguishing feature of a separate standard language for Catholics. All Sorbian was,

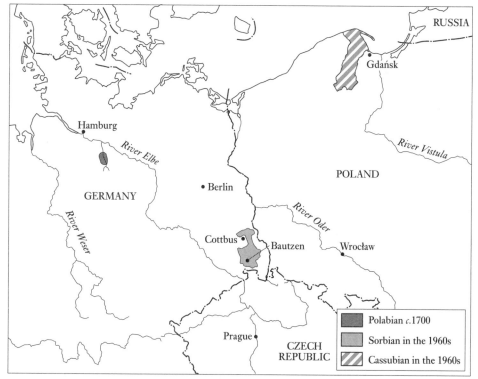

Map 18   Sorbian, Cassubian and Polabian

however, printed in Black Letter (*Fraktur*) until 1841, when a new spelling system based on Czech and *Polish and using Roman script began to be gradually introduced. *Fraktur* was last used in print in 1937. The earliest printed book is Albin Moller's Lower Sorbian *Wendisches Gesangbuch* ('Wendish Hymnal') (Bautzen, 1574). A manuscript New Testament of 1548, translated by Mikław š Jakubica into an east Lower Sorbian dialect, remained unpublished, but complete translations of the Bible into both Upper and Lower Sorbian were published during the 18th c. Before the 1840s Sorbian literature was overwhelmingly devotional in content.

Sorbian dialectology divides the language into three main zones: Lower Sorbian in the north, Upper Sorbian in the south, and a transitional zone between them. Centuries of close contact with German have left their trace on both the vocabulary and the syntax of Sorbian. In literary varieties the proportion of German loan-words is less than 5%, but colloquially as many as 50% of nouns may be of German origin. Since the 1840s there have been efforts to rid the literary languages of Germanisms and to introduce words and syntactic features from other Slavonic languages (mainly Czech).

In the 10th c., Sorbian was spoken in an area bounded by the rivers Saale in the west and Bober and Queis in the east. In the north it extended to where Berlin and Frankfurt-an-der-Oder now stand. Since then it has receded steadily and had by the early 20th c. been reduced, by and large, to what is today still regarded as the Sorbian speech area, though this is now predominantly German in speech. In the 16th and 17th centuries all texts were written in local varieties and intended solely for local use, but by the 18th c. there were three standard languages: (i) Lower Sorbian, (ii) Upper Sorbian for Protestants, (iii) Upper Sorbian for Roman Catholics. A united Upper Sorbian standard was achieved only after the Second World War.

Sorbian-speakers are today scattered throughout an area beginning about 80 km (50 miles) south-east of Berlin and stretching south from there for about 92 km (57 miles). Its southern limits are less than 8 km (5 miles) north of the Czech frontier. Within this area there are, here and there, small concentrations of Sorbian-speakers, the main concentration being in the Catholic area. There is no official figure for the number of speakers, but it was estimated in 1987 at 67,000 (23% Catholics; less than 20% Lower Sorbs). The Constitution of the German Democratic Republic (1949–90) guaranteed the cultural rights of the Sorbs, including the use of the Sorbian language. These rights are not guaranteed in the Constitution of the Federal Republic of Germany, but they were recognized in the treaty between the GDR and the Federal Republic preceding German re-unification (1990) and similar provisions have been included in the Constitutions of the new *Länder* of Brandenburg and Saxony. Funds continue to be provided to support Sorbian cultural and educational institutions. In 1993–4 Sorbian was being taught in 50 schools in Saxony and 16 in Brandenburg. In Saxony, 1,421 pupils were being taught in classes with Sorbian as the medium of instruction and a further 2,266 were studying it as a school subject. In Brandenburg, 829 pupils were studying Sorbian at school but none were being taught in Sorbian. In Brandenburg there is a half-hour television programme once a month in Lower Sorbian. In Saxony there is no Sorbian television broadcasting at all. Radio broadcasts (two hours daily) are mainly in Upper Sorbian. In Catholic churches there are regular and frequent services in Upper Sorbian. Lutheran services in Upper Sorbian are regular but less frequent. Lower Sorbian services (Lutheran) are held six to eight times a year. The Domowina publishing house, with official financial support, produces books, journals and newspapers in Sorbian. Bus and railway timetables, street signs, and some other public notices are (inconsistently) in both German and Sorbian, but the Sorbian element in public notices has recently declined. It is doubtful whether the theoretical right to use Sorbian for legal purposes and in dealings with the authorities is much exercised.

Faßke, H. (in collaboration with S. Michalk) 1981. *Grammatik der obersorbischen Schriftsprache der Gegenwart: Morphologie* ('Grammar of the Contemporary Upper Sorbian Written Language: Morphology'). Bautzen.

Janaš, P. 1984. *Niedersorbische Grammatik* ('Lower Sorbian Grammar'), 2nd edn. Bautzen.

Starosta, M. 1984. *Niedersorbisch–deutsches Wörterbuch* ('Lower Sorbian–German Dictionary'). Bautzen.

Stone, G. 1993. Sorbian (Upper and Lower). In Comrie, B. and Corbett, G. G. (eds), *The Slavonic Languages*, London and New York, 593–685.

Trofimovič, K. K. 1974. *Hornjoserbsko–ruski słownik/ Верхнелужицко–русский словарь* ('Upper Sorbian–Russian Dictionary'). Bautzen and Moscow.

GERALD STONE

Sorothaptic

The term 'Sorothaptic' (Spanish *sorotáptico*), from Greek *sorós* 'funerary urn' + *thaptós* 'buried', was coined by the Catalan scholar J. Corominas (Coromines) to refer to the presumably Indo-European pre-Celtic language of the Bronze Age people of the Urnfield culture in the Iberian Peninsula. Corominas claims to have identified Sorothaptic elements in etymologically problematic words in the *Ibero-Romance languages and in inscriptions (2nd c. AD?) on lead tablets found in a thermal spring at Amélie-les-Bains (formerly Bains-d'Arles) in the French *département* of Pyrénées-Orientales.

Corominas, J. 1954. Sorotáptico. In Id., *Diccionario crítico etimológico de la lengua castellana*, Madrid, vol. 4, 1081.

——— 1975. Les plombs sorathaptiques d'Arles. *Zeitschrift für romanische Philologie*, 91: 1–53.

——— 1976. Elementos prelatinos en las lenguas romances hispánicas. In Jordá, F. et al. (eds), *Actas del I Coloquio sobre lenguas y culturas prerromanas de la Península Ibérica*, Salamanca, 87–164.

Soso (see under *Community languages France)*)

South Lusitanian

The name 'South Lusitanian' has been widely applied, for want of a better one, to the language of some 70 pre-Roman inscriptions of uncertain date (possibly 7th–6th centuries BC) from the Algarve region of southern Portugal, written in a basically alphabetical but partly syllabic script similar to and perhaps derived from the so-called 'Iberian' script of eastern Spain. Two similar inscriptions are known from further east, one from the Guadalquivir valley upstream from Seville and one from Puente Genil about 100 km east of Seville. The language of these inscriptions is completely unknown and appears not to be the same as any of the other languages of pre-Roman Spain (though Untermann (1995) says that the possibility that it could be *Celtic cannot be totally excluded). There is a view that it could be connected with the city (or possibly region) of Tartessos referred to in Classical texts, which appears to have flourished in the 7th and 6th centuries BC, and the term 'Tartessian' has therefore sometimes been applied to it. However, Tartessos was probably sited in the lower valley of the Guadalquivir (though its exact location has not yet been identified) and the fact that no inscriptions have come to light in this area is a counter-indication.

Schmoll, U. 1961. *Die südlusitanischen Inschriften* ('The South Lusitanian Inscriptions'). Wiesbaden.
Untermann, J. 1995. Zum Stand der Deutung der 'tartessischen' Inschriften ('On the present position of the interpretation of the "Tartessian" inscriptions'). In Eska, J. F., Gruffydd, R. G. and Jacobs, N. (eds), *Hispano-Gallo-Brittonica*, Cardiff, 244–59.

South Picenian

In the ancient Italian district of Picenum, in the area located east of the Apennines, west of the Adriatic coast, between the rivers Chienti to the north and Sangro to the south (see map 10), a little over 20 South Picenian inscriptions have been found. They date from the 6th to the 4th c. BC. Together with *Pre-Samnitic, South Picenian is the earliest representative of the *Osco-Umbrian branch of *Italic. Around 250 years later, we find *Vestinian, *Paelignian and *Marrucinian in the territory formerly occupied by South Picenian. South Picenian should not be confused with *North Picenian. It seems to be closer to *Umbrian than to *Oscan, but it is not the ancestor of Umbrian. The relation between South Picenian and *Sabine may well be particularly close: the inscriptions of Penna Sant'Andrea indicate that at least some South Picenians labelled themselves *safino-*.

The inscriptions are written in an indigenous alphabet, which is ultimately cognate with the *Etruscan alphabet. The interpretation of some letters is still difficult. So is the interpretation of the text. Characteristically, fixed formulas are lacking and the syntax is complicated. The inscriptions are relatively long (up to 24 words) and show alliteration. Some inscriptions are undoubtedly funerary stones ('in this grave (?) lies . . .').

Most inscriptions were carved on oblong steles. The Steles of Penna Sant'Andrea (National Museum, Chieti), which above the text display a carved human head, are particularly fine examples. Remarkable objects are the famous inscribed Statue of the 'Capestrano warrior' (National Museum, Chieti) and the 'Canosa helmet' (Archaeological Museum, Florence).

Coleman, R. 1986. The central Italic languages in the period of Roman expansion. *Transactions of the Philological Society*, 1986: 100–31.
Marinetti, A. 1985. *Le iscrizioni sudpicene*, vol. 1, *Testi*. Florence.

PETER SCHRIJVER

South-east Asian languages (see under *Community languages (France)*)

Spanish

A member of the ***Romance** language family, most closely related to
*Portuguese, ***Galician** and ***Catalan** and, together with them, forming what is
often called the Hispano-Romance or ***Ibero-Romance** subgroup of that family.
Spanish is spoken throughout the Spanish state, including the Balearic Islands, the
Canaries, and Ceuta and Melilla (Spanish enclaves on the Mediterranean coast of
Morocco), by almost 100% of Spanish citizens, but not as a first language by all.
Some speakers in Galicia, rather more in the Basque Country and in Valencia, and
most in Catalonia, use Spanish as their second language, but most of these have
native control of the language. It is also spoken by most inhabitants of Gibraltar.
(See map 19.)

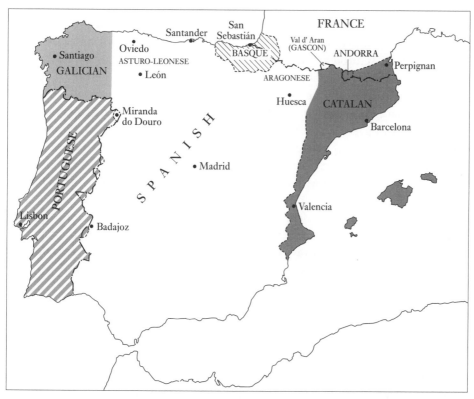

Map 19   Languages of the Iberian Peninsula. Divisions between dialects and, in
some cases, between languages are necessarily only approximate. Inhabitants of
those parts of Spain where languages other than Spanish are spoken are in general
either bilingual or else speak Spanish only.

Names

Since the standard variety of Spanish was elaborated in the medieval kingdom of Castile, this variety was referred to in the Middle Ages as (*romance*) *castellano* ('Castilian [Romance]'), and the name *castellano* continues to be used by many of those that speak it, especially by those from outside Castile proper (Catalonia, Galicia, Spanish America), since the term is often felt to lack the association with Spanish nationhood which is sometimes attached to the term *español* ('Spanish'). The latter term came into frequent use, as a synonym for *castellano*, after the late 15th-c. union of Castile (then also including Galicia, Asturias, León, the Basque Country and the Canary Islands) with Aragon (which also incorporated Catalonia, Valencia, the Balearic Islands and other Mediterranean territories). Since that time, the two terms have been used synonymously. In English, when referring to the national, standard language of Spain and of its daughter republics in America, there is no need to use any term other than 'Spanish'. The term 'Castilian' can be reserved for those varieties of speech used in that part of the Peninsula called Castile.

Early writing

Early medieval writing in Spain used the so-called Visigothic form of the Latin alphabet, progressively replaced by Carolingian script from the 11th c. Until the development of reformed spelling in the 13th c., writing in Castile, as in other Romance-speaking territories, was carried out on the basis of norms passed on, largely through scribal training within the Church, from late Roman times. Changes which took place in spoken language were not necessarily incorporated into the registers used in writing, so that the written language continued to contain morphological and lexical elements, in particular, which had ceased to be used in speech. The spelling of pre-13th-c. texts can also be described as essentially etymological, by which it is meant that the writer made an attempt to use a sanctioned sequence of letters for each word, without direct regard for pronunciation. However, such a *logographic* procedure naturally depended upon the writer's ability to identify, on the basis of his training, an appropriate sequence of letters for the word he was proposing to write, and this was not always possible, specifically in the case of words of non-Latin origin, such as Arabisms, borrowings from *Basque, or *Germanic personal names, as well as in the case of some Romance place-names. In writing such words, the scribe had to have recourse to informal equivalences between letter and sound, that is, he had to use phonological principles of writing. Thus, having noted that the initial letter of the spelling *caballus* corresponded to an initial [k] in his native pronunciation ([kaβáʎo]) of the local Romance word with appropriate meaning, he was free to use the graph <c> as part of the spelling of the Arabism [alkálde] 'judge, mayor', a word also belonging to his oral competence, and therefore to write *alcalde*, etc. This phonological principle could then be applied to the spelling of inherited vernacular words, that is, to those words which descended from Latin and which belonged to speech. Early examples of the application of the phonological principle to Spanish words and phrases (and occasional whole sentences) are the 11th-c. glosses inserted into Latin texts by monks working in the monasteries of San Millán de la Cogolla (western La Rioja) and Santo Domingo de Silos (NE Castile). Some regard these glosses as the earliest samples of written Spanish.

However, the implication of the foregoing discussion of early Spanish (and other Romance) spelling practice is that it is impossible to identify an earliest Spanish text. Texts which have the appearance of being written in Latin, because each word is written in accordance with the etymological principle, are in many cases better described as Spanish texts written in traditional spelling (Wright 1982). In fact, many pre-11th-c. texts, especially notarial texts, are written in a spelling which mixes the etymological and the phonological principles often chaotically. What then happens, in the very early 13th c., is the application to whole texts of the phonological principle, a move which was perhaps inspired by ultra-Pyrenean spelling practice, which for some centuries had been of a predominantly phonological type.

This is not to say that spelling immediately became self-consistent. On the contrary, early 13th-c. writing shows many cases of a single letter being used with several phonological values, and of the same sound being spelt with a variety of letters. However, during the reign of Alfonso X the Learned (1252–84) a high degree of consistency was achieved, and it can be said that total spelling reform was completed at this stage, under the direction of the king and his circle of scholarly advisers. This reformed spelling was put to use in the outpouring of literary, scientific, historiographical and other texts which flowed from the royal scriptorium, as well as in the administrative documents produced by the royal Chancery. Such texts henceforth provide the model, rapidly imitated elsewhere in the kingdom, for writing in Spanish.

Medieval expansion

Standard Spanish had its origins in a small segment of the dialect continuum which stretches from coast to coast across the northern third of the Peninsula. This array of dialects has traditionally been divided into five, labelled (from west to east) Galician-Portuguese, Asturian-Leonese, Castilian, Navarro-Aragonese, and Catalan. However, these divisions are based essentially upon political considerations (the boundaries between the medieval kingdoms of northern Spain) and are not justified on grounds of dialect boundaries, which do not exist in this area (see below). Within this dialect continuum, a few favoured groups of speech varieties, well separated one from another, gained special social prestige through association with the social groups that used them, and saw this prestige further enhanced by their preferential use in writing. In this way we can observe the creation of three separate Romance standards in the Peninsula. The Western type, based upon the speech of Santiago de Compostela, and the Eastern type, based upon that of Barcelona, are dealt with elsewhere in this volume (see *Galician, *Portuguese, *Catalan). The segment of the northern dialect continuum from which Spanish springs comprises those varieties spoken in and around the city of Burgos in the period up to the 11th c. These varieties were the ones which gradually dominated the mixture of dialects which occurred in central Spain as people

from northern Castile and other northern areas moved southwards and were resettled in territories recently reconquered from Islamic Spain. Probably the most
important reconquest, from a linguistic point of view, was that of Toledo, captured
by Alfonso VI of León and Castile in 1085. Toledo, which had been the capital of
the whole Peninsula during the period of Visigothic control (from the 5th c. AD to
the Islamic invasion of 711), became the new capital of Castile and León, and came
to be dominated, in the period following its reconquest, by varieties of Romance
brought by speakers from the Burgos area. These originally northern varieties consequently grew in social prestige and gave rise to a koine which was the vehicle for
the literary and scientific flowering, already referred to, which occurred under
Alfonso the Learned's direction.

Literary and official Spanish was firmly established, then, by the last quarter of
the 13th c., and within the Crown of Castile only Galician provided any competition.
This north-western variety achieved a substantially standardized form in the same
period, but was essentially limited to lyric poetry, and was otherwise used only in
certain chronicles and notarial documents. No other variety used within the kingdom
acquired literary or official status, although local (i.e. non-Toledan) features are
occasionally recognizable in literary texts written or copied after the end of the
13th c., and in non-literary texts for a good while longer.

At the spoken level, of course, wide variation must have remained, since we have
evidence of it many centuries later and can still observe it today (see below, 'Variation
within Peninsular Spanish'). However, there was a progressive Toledanization of
speech, which took the form of the outward spread, feature by feature or word by
word, of the characteristics of the educated usage of the capital. Evidence of this
spread is not confined to the Crown of Castile (where it can be seen, for example, in
the way in which local features in the notarial documents of, say, León are increasingly replaced by those of Central Castile), but can also be seen in texts written in the
Crown of Aragon, well before the Union of the Crowns of Castile and Aragon consequent upon the marriage of Isabella I of Castile to Ferdinand II of Aragon in 1469.
Already in the 14th c., the form of language used in literature produced at Saragossa
is heavily Castilianized, probably reflecting the way in which the speech of the
Aragonese elites had been modified towards the Castilian norm.

Following the 11th-c. Castilian reconquest of Central Spain (which led to the
extinction of the *Mozarabic varieties spoken in these areas), Castilian territorial
expansion continued into Andalusia, and by the middle of the 13th c. northern and
western Andalusia had been added to the Crown of Castile. This territory included
the major cities of Cordoba and Seville, as well as others such as Jaén and Cadiz, all
of which were rapidly resettled by speakers of Castilian. Islamic Spain was now
confined to the coastal Kingdom of Granada, which survived independently for a
further two and a half centuries, before succumbing to Isabella and Ferdinand in
1492. The subsequent redistribution of its lands gave rise to an influx of settlers from
other parts of Andalusia, who were therefore speakers of southern varieties of
Spanish. The extension of Spanish to the Kingdom of Granada was the last major
Peninsular advance of the language, but in the meantime the Canary Islands had been

discovered and had soon been assigned to Castile, bringing settlers mainly from the southern Atlantic ports who established their western Andalusian variety of Spanish there.

Later than all these events came the establishment of Madrid as the capital of Spain and the centre of linguistic fashion. After 1561, when Madrid became the seat of the Court and also underwent a dramatic increase in its population, largely as a result of an influx of northerners, the educated speech of the new capital, noticeably different (according to contemporary accounts) from that of earlier political centres such as Toledo, came to constitute the prestige norm.

In the late 20th c., following the establishment of a series of autonomous regions within the Spanish state, attempts have been made to produce a local linguistic standard in a number of regions where such a development had not occurred earlier, that is, in certain areas where standard Spanish has been used in writing since the Middle Ages, but where the local speech is felt to be significantly different from the national spoken standard. The most notable experiment of this kind has taken place in Asturias, where many Asturo-Leonese and other non-Castilian features have resisted Castilianization down to the present, at least in rural speech. Critics object that such proposed standards are uneasy mixes of dialect features drawn from several different varieties, but rarely shared by all, and it remains to be seen whether such experiments (a similar one has been made, more tentatively, in Aragon) will succeed, and whether serious writers will be persuaded to write in the proposed standard forms of Asturian and Aragonese.

Spanish as a literary medium

Spanish is the vehicle of an immense and varied literature. The first substantial texts date from the very early 13th c., and include the lengthy anonymous epic *Poema de Mío Cid*, which recounts the exploits of the Castilian hero Rodrigo Díaz de Vivar against both Moorish and Christian opponents, and the religious poetry of Gonzalo de Berceo, which comprises saints' lives and theological themes. The pace of literary creation quickened dramatically in the second half of the 13th c. and was inseparable from the creation of the standard form of the language, which took place under the auspices of Alfonso X the Learned (see 'Early writing', above). One of the most inventive and witty works of medieval European literature is the 14th-c. *Libro de Buen Amor* ('Book of Good Love'), by Juan Ruiz, Archpriest of Hita, and the transition from medieval to Renaissance modes of thought is marked by the appearance in print, probably in 1499, of the first edition of *Celestina*, a novel in dialogue by Fernando de Rojas.

In the 16th and 17th centuries, the Golden Age of Spanish letters, the enormous development of poetry, drama and prose went hand in hand with the power and prestige of Spain in Europe and America, but survived Spain's political decline to provide a wealth of creative writing, in all genres, which continued through the 19th c. and is unabated today, both in Spain and in Spanish America.

Variation within Peninsular Spanish

In a broad central band of territory, stretching from the northern coast in Cantabria to the Atlantic and Mediterranean coasts in the south, Spanish takes the form of a dialect continuum without sudden internal cleavages. This continuum includes such types of Spanish as the Andalusian varieties, with their rather distinctive characteristics. The area occupied by each of these features never coincides, however, with the territory defined as Andalusia.

Likewise, we have seen that northern Spanish forms part of a continuum which stretches from the Galician coast to the Costa Brava, again without abrupt transitions from one speech-type to another. The extremes of variation along this east–west axis across the north are considerably greater than those that can be heard down the central north–south axis, since the northern area includes the least Castilianized varieties of the Peninsula, such as the Asturian varieties, and extends seamlessly into territories where separate processes of standardization took place, namely those that gave rise to Galician-Portuguese and Catalan. However, it should be emphasized that the isoglosses which mark the line of abutment of one northern feature upon its competitors rarely (if ever) coincide one with another, and never coincide with the political boundaries which demarcate such geopolitical entities as Galicia, Asturias, Cantabria, La Rioja, Navarre, Aragon or Catalonia.

By contrast with this picture of seamlessly overlapping dialects, and as a result of the Christian reconquest of Islamic Spain and of the southward resettlement by speakers of northern varieties, the southern two-thirds of the Peninsula are today divided into three great dialectal blocs. Spanish forms the central bloc, containing within it the dialectal variation that we have observed, and abuts sharply upon Portuguese to the west and Catalan to the east. Only in these cases do we observe an abrupt cleavage between dialect territories; the line of abutment of Spanish upon Portuguese follows the political frontier closely (but not absolutely precisely, since the frontier has in places been moved since the linguistic boundary was established), while the line separating Spanish dialects from Catalan varieties corresponds to no political boundary and wanders southwards approximately parallel with the Mediterranean until it turns to meet the sea in the south of the province of Alicante.

Contacts with other languages

The varieties of Peninsular Romance from which standard Spanish grew, those of the Burgos area (see above), were spoken in an area which was adjacent to the territory where Basque was spoken. The Basque-speaking area has since contracted northwards, but it is likely that at least until the 11th c. Basque–Romance bilingualism was common not far to the east and north-east of Burgos. However, although some scholars have sought to explain some key characteristics of Spanish, particularly of pronunciation, as being due to contact between the two languages, the only undoubted cases of such influence are to be found in the vocabulary of Spanish, where a small number of words, including a few of quite high frequency, have been borrowed from Basque. These include, most strikingly, men's personal names such as *García, Íñigo, Javier, Gimeno, Sancho*.

A similar, rather slight, impact was exercised upon Spanish by the ancient and medieval Germanic languages. Most of the Germanic words which entered Spanish in the period up to the end of the Middle Ages are ones which entered common Romance in the period of the late Roman Empire, or formed part of the French word-stock which was passed to Spanish, especially from the 13th c. There are very few linguistic relics of the contact with the *Visigothic ruling class which dominated the Romance-speaking population of the Peninsula in the period from the 5th to the 7th c., although some common men's names again figure in the list, e.g. *Fernando/Hernando, Ramón*.

By contrast, the result of the contact between Spanish and *Arabic, because so intimate and long-lasting (more than seven centuries), is much more marked, although again restricted essentially to vocabulary. There are many hundreds of Arabisms in Spanish, most shared with Portuguese and Catalan, and some of these have high frequency in all varieties of the contemporary language. This indebtedness is due to the fact that, at least until the 11th c., Arabic was the vehicle of a culture which was technologically and culturally in advance of European cultures. Arabic therefore enjoyed the prestige which is usually associated with those languages from which others borrow heavily; and Arabic names were adopted by Spanish as Hispanic culture absorbed the many material and non-material innovations which reached Christian Spain through the mediation of the Islamic world, including Islamic Spain. Among borrowings from Arabic are such frequent words as *aceite* '(olive) oil', *adobe* 'sun-dried brick', *ahorrar* 'to save (money)', *alcalde* 'mayor', *alcatraz* 'gannet', *alcohol* 'alcohol', *aldea* 'village', *alfombra* 'carpet', *álgebra* 'algebra', *arroz* 'rice', *azul* 'blue', *barrio* 'quarter (or a town)', *hasta* 'until', *mazapán* 'marzipan', *naranja* 'orange'.

Intra-Romance contacts have, of course, been intense, and the Spanish vocabulary is indebted, in particular, to *French (in the Middle Ages, also to *Occitan) and to *Italian. French and Occitan influence was particularly felt from the 11th c. onwards, as a result of the influx of *Gallo-Romance speakers into Castile and the other Peninsular kingdoms, to help further the Reconquest, as semi-permanent settlers along the pilgrim way to Santiago, as part of the Cluniac monastic reform, and for other purposes. Italian influence is seen especially in the period of the Renaissance and of the 16th-c. military involvement of Spain in Italy.

Spanish in Flanders

Between the abdication in 1555 of Charles V as Holy Roman Emperor and the Treaty of Utrecht in 1713, all or part of the Low Countries, together with parts of northern France, belonged to the Spanish Crown. Spanish was the official language of this territory, in both its Dutch-speaking and French-speaking parts, and was spoken not just by the Spanish governing class, but also, most usually bilingually, by members of the local aristocratic and bureaucratic classes. The flourishing Flemish printing-presses also produced a steady stream of Spanish books, although the very large majority of their authors were Spaniards. However, following the collapse of Spanish power in Flanders, the Spanish language ceased to be used as either a written or a spoken medium.

Spanish in America

The dramatic expansion of Spanish outside the Peninsula began in 1492, following the European discovery of America, and the expulsion of those Jews who declined to be converted to Christianity. The latter development is the starting-point for the development of Judeo-Spanish, but here we shall discuss the first.

Settlement and conquest of America by Spanish-speakers began immediately after the discovery. Before the end of the 15th c., a number of settlements had been established in the Greater Antilles (Puerto Rico, La Española (modern Haiti and the Dominican Republic) and Cuba), consisting largely but not exclusively of people from Andalusia and Extremadura. In this way, from the beginning, a southern Spanish character was established in the speech of the new colonies, and although subsequent waves of settlers were drawn from all over the Peninsula (but always, it seems, with a substantial Andalusian component) the Andalusian character of American Spanish was nowhere entirely ousted and in most areas remains clearly evident to this day. A few Andalusian features (such as *seseo*, the use of a single sibilant [s] where Central and Northern Peninsular Spanish distinguish between two, [s] and [θ], as in *casa* 'house' vs. *caza* 'hunt') are universal in Spanish America, while others (such as *yeísmo*, the merger of the palatal *l* [ʎ] with [j], so that *pollo* 'chicken' comes to be pronounced like *poyo* 'stone bench') are very widespread. The universal Spanish-American use of an undifferentiated form of second-personal plural address (*ustedes* + third-person plural verb), to indicate both deference and solidarity, also has its roots in (Western) Andalusia, almost all Peninsular Spanish continuing to distinguish between *ustedes* + third-person plural verb, to express deference, and *vosotros* + second-person plural verb, to express solidarity.

The colonial, ecclesiastical and academic organization of the American colonies helped to bring features of standard Peninsular Spanish into competition with the Andalusian characteristics brought by the earliest colonists, and the result of this competition was different in each district of the Americas. Where the standard input was powerful, as in the seats of colonial administration such as Mexico City and Lima, the Andalusian character of the Spanish in use was somewhat lessened, while in areas distant from such cultural centres the Andalusian component remained correspondingly dominant.

Contact with the Amerindian languages in the Americas brought into Spanish the names of many concepts (mostly related to material objects, but also to social organization) which were foreign to Europeans. Many of these new words were transmitted back to the Peninsula and became part of the everyday vocabulary there, and a portion of these were further borrowed by other European languages as the new items and experiences were spread from one country to another. The Amerindian languages from which most borrowings were taken were the Carib and Arawak languages of the Antilles, Nahuatl (the language of the Aztec civilization) and Quechua (the main language of the Inca Empire). From Carib, Spanish took *canoa* 'canoe', *hamaca* 'hammock', *huracán* 'hurricane', *maíz* 'maize', *sabana* 'savannah', and, from Arawak, *caníbal* 'cannibal' and *curare* 'curare'. From Nahuatl we have *cacao* 'cocoa', *chile* 'chili', *chocolate* 'chocolate', *tomate* 'tomato', and many others, while from Quechua come *coca* 'coca plant', *cóndor* 'the American eagle', *guano* 'bird-lime fertilizer', *llama* 'llama', *papa* 'potato', *puma* 'puma', and many more.

Numbers of speakers

Speakers of Spanish, in the world, number close to 350 million. Of these, a little under 40 million live within the Spanish State, including some 1,250,000 in the Canary Islands, and some 150,000 in Ceuta and Melilla, the two Spanish enclaves in Morocco. A portion of the population of mainland Spain and the Balearic Islands speaks Spanish bilingually with another language. The population of Gibraltar (some 30,000) is largely Spanish-speaking, and there are also undefined numbers of Spanish-speakers living in other European countries, such as Germany, France and Britain, often as economic migrants.

The large majority of Spanish-speakers are therefore to be found outside Europe, principally in the Americas, but also in Africa (Equatorial Guinea, where an undefined proportion of the 300,000 inhabitants are Spanish-speakers) and Asia (the Philippines, with up to 2 million speakers). The few thousand remaining speakers of *Judeo-Spanish are to be found mainly in the Balkans, Turkey, Israel and the USA.

Spanish is the first language of all or most of the population in each of the republics which sprang from Spain's American Empire, as well as in the Commonwealth of Puerto Rico. In addition to being the language of Puerto Rico, the Dominican Republic and Cuba, Spanish is spoken in all of the countries in America south of the USA, with the exception of Surinam, Brazil and former or present British or French territories. In some of these Spanish-speaking countries, including the most populous, such as Argentina and Mexico, Spanish is the only language of all or almost all of the population, while in some other countries, such as Paraguay, Bolivia and Peru, there is a substantial bilingual Amerindian minority which uses one or other of the native American languages as its main means of local communication and Spanish for communication with the wider world. In addition, a Spanish-based *Creole, Papiamentu (see under *Community languages (Netherlands)), is spoken by most of the population (some 300,000) of the island of Curaçao, part of the Netherlands Antilles; this language, which is largely unintelligible to speakers of Spanish, has a written form which is used in publications of various sorts, and unsurprisingly reveals some indebtedness to the official language of the territory, namely Dutch.

There are more than 25 million first-language speakers of Spanish in the USA, concentrated in the south-western states and in certain northern urban centres, such as New York, but with small communities also in Louisiana. Most of this population results from 20th-c. migration from Spain and, above all, Spanish America, but the south-western area includes Spanish-speaking communities which survive from the period when this area was part of the Mexican state and, before that, of Spain's

American Empire, while the main Louisiana groups result from 18th-c. migration from the Canaries.

Official and international status

Spanish is the official language in all the territories which make up the Spanish State, and this status is enshrined in the current constitution, where it is stated that every citizen has the duty to know Spanish. However, the people of some autonomous regions have the constitutional right to use another language, namely Galician in Galicia, Basque in the Basque Country, and Catalan in Catalonia, Valencia and the Balearic Islands, since the constitutions of these regions specifically give official status to the language concerned, and since the national constitution acknowledges this local right.

In Equatorial Guinea, in Puerto Rico, and in the ex-Spanish American republics, Spanish is either the official language enshrined in the constitution or is effectively official, in the sense that it is the language of government, education, the Church, etc. It is only in the Philippines and in the USA (where we have seen that there is a Spanish-speaking minority, substantial in the latter case) that Spanish lacks this status.

Spanish is one of the working languages of the European Union, and is an official language of the United Nations Organization.

Since the 18th c., linguistic taste in Spain has been regulated by the Real Academia Española (Royal Spanish Academy), which publishes successive editions of its dictionary, its grammar, and of its orthographical norms. Each of the ex-Spanish American republics now also has its Academy, as does Puerto Rico, and prescriptions are now usually issued only after consultation among Academies. The weight of such recommendations is considerable; the most recently published spelling norms are followed in printed texts throughout the Spanish-speaking world.

Butt, J. and Benjamin, C. 1994. *A New Reference Grammar of Modern Spanish*, 2nd edn. London.

de Bruyne, J. 1995. *A Comprehensive Spanish Grammar* (adapted with additional material by C. J. Pountain). Oxford.

Entwistle, W. J. 1936. *The Spanish Language, together with Portuguese, Catalan and Basque*. London.

Green, J. N. 1988. Spanish. In Harris, M. and Vincent, N. (eds), *The Romance Languages*, London, 79–130.

Holtus, G., Metzeltin, M. and Schmitt, C. (eds) 1992. *Lexikon der Romanistischen Linguistik*, vol. 6.1, *Aragonesisch/Navarresisch, Spanisch, Asturianisch/Leonesisch*. Tübingen. (52 articles, 42 in Spanish, 10 in German.)

Jarman, B. and Russell, R. (eds) 1994. *The Oxford Spanish Dictionary: Spanish–English, English–Spanish*. Oxford.

Lipski, J. M. 1994. *Latin-American Spanish*. London and New York.

Lloyd, P. M. 1987. *From Latin to Spanish: Historical Phonology and Morphology of the Spanish Language*. Philadelphia.

Penny, R. 1991. *A History of the Spanish Language*. Cambridge.

Wright, R. 1982. *Late Latin and Early Romance in Spain and Carolingian France*. Liverpool.

RALPH PENNY

Sranan (see under *Community languages (Netherlands)*)

Surmiran (see under *Romansh*)

Sursilvan (Surselvan) (see under *Romansh*)

Susu (see under *Community languages (France)*)

Sutsilvan (Sutselvan) (see under *Romansh*)

Svan (see under *Caucasian languages. V. South Caucasian family*)

Swabian

The Swabians (Suebi, Suevi) were a Germanic people, speaking a West *Germanic language, who, having in the previous two years traversed and devastated Gaul, in 409, together with the Alans and the Vandals, crossed the Pyrenees. In 411 they took possession of the north-western part of the Iberian Peninsula (corresponding broadly to the modern Spanish provinces of Galicia, Asturias and León, and northern Portugal) where they established a kingdom which lasted until it was subdued by the Visigoths in 585. Their language has left few traces in the present-day *Romance languages of the area (Portuguese *britar* 'to break', Galician *laverca* 'lark' are two instances). Their name is recalled in such Galician place-names as *Suevos, Suegos*, as well as in that of the district of Schwaben (Swabia) in SW Bavaria.

Swedish

A North *Germanic (*Scandinavian) language spoken in Sweden and parts of Finland, in both of which countries it is an official language.

Periods

The history of the Swedish language is usually divided for the sake of convenience into the following periods:

Runic Swedish	*c*.800 to *c*.1225
Classical Old Swedish	*c*.1225 to *c*.1375
Later Old Swedish	*c*.1375 to 1526
Early Modern Swedish	1526 to 1732
Later Modern Swedish	1732 to the present day

Runic Swedish

The oldest texts in Swedish are runic inscriptions (see *Runes) from the 9th c., the most notable of which is found on the Rök Stone (Östergötland, Sweden) with its 850 runes. No fewer than 3,500 runic inscriptions are to be found in Sweden, most of them in the later 16-letter 'futhark' (or runic alphabet) (see fig. 12) and many on standing stones erected in the 11th c., their stereotyped inscriptions commemorating farmers and Viking warriors. Runes were employed well into the Middle Ages for personal and trade communication, but the fact that they were mainly used on wood (often on message sticks) has meant that relatively few texts have survived. The Latin alphabet (supplemented by the characters <æ>, <ø>, <þ>, the last of these from the futhark) was introduced with Christianity, which had become widespread in central Sweden.

Classical Old Swedish

The oldest written texts in Swedish found in a modified Latin alphabet are two medieval law texts – a fragment of the *Older West-Gothic Law* from the 1220s and the full text of this law code (Codex Holmiensis B5, comprising some 55 pages) from the 1280s. Law codes from a number of provinces (notably also Östergötland and Uppland) form the main source of our knowledge of medieval Swedish. They are the product of a long oral tradition. This is case law composed in a style that is simple and direct and that the peasants could understand, free from loan-words and with Scandinavian syntax. The use of rhythm, word pairs and stereotypical phrases betrays its oral tradition as the law man had to remember the text and recite the law at the meetings of the 'þing' or court. Some religious prose, largely in translation from Latin, includes the *Fornsvenska legendariet* based primarily on *Legenda aurea*. Later came poetry in the verse-form known as knittel, notably the *Eric Chronicle* (4,543 pair-rhyming lines depicting Swedish history from 1220 to 1319)) and the 'Eufemia poems', based on Norman French originals and including *Flores och Blanzeflor* from *c*.1300.

The language of this period is highly inflected: nouns have three genders and both nouns and adjectives retain the four cases nominative, accusative, genitive and dative; an increasing number of verbs have the same form throughout the singular (*iak/þu/han skiuter* 'I/you/he shoot(s)'), but all retain separate forms in the plural (*vi skiutum, I skiutin, þe skiuta* 'we/you/they shoot').

Later Old Swedish

Religious prose emanating from the monastery of St Birgitta at Vadstena is a major influence on written Swedish in this period, as is an officialese showing traces of Latin and Low German. During political domination by Denmark in the 1400s (under the Nordic Union) *Danish influences are also strong.

The lexicon shows major changes at this time. Latin and Greek loans are brought in by the church: *brev* 'letter' < Latin *breve scriptum*, *kyrka* 'church' < Greek *kyriakon*, *kloster* 'monastery' < Latin *claustrum*, *biskop* 'bishop' < Greek *episkopos*, *präst* 'priest' < Latin *presbyter*. A very large number of Low German loan-words are introduced in the areas of trade and services: *frakt* 'freight' < *vracht*, *ränta* 'interest' < *rente*, *skräddare* 'tailor' < *schräder*, *skomakare* 'shoemaker' < *schômaker*, *verkstad* 'workshop' < *werkstede*; new goods: *tyg* 'cloth' < *tuch*, *krydda* 'spice' < *krûde*, *ättika* 'vinegar' < *etik*; town organization: *rådhus* 'town hall' < *râthûs*, *borgmästare* 'mayor' < *borgemêster*, *fogde* 'steward' < *voget*; and the world of chivalry: *herre* 'lord' < *hêrro*, *fröken* 'miss' < *vrôuken*. Word-formation elements loaned from Low German lend a new flexibility to the language, e.g. prefixes *an-*, *be-*, *und-*, and the suffixes *-het*, *-bar*, *-aktig*, as in *anlägga* 'establish' (LG *anleggen*), *berätta* 'tell' (LG *berichten*), *undvika* 'avoid' (LG *entwiken*), *falskhet* 'falseness' (LG *valscheit*), *uppenbar* 'obvious' (LG *openbâr*), *varaktig* 'enduring' (LG *werachtich*). Common features are lexical replacement, e.g. *bliva* 'become' < LG *blîven* for Old Swedish *vardha*, *sådan* 'such' < *sodân* for Old Swedish *þolikin*, and semantic extension, e.g. *stad* 'place' acquires the meaning 'town' from LG *stat*.

The gradual change from a synthetic to an analytical language is completed with the disappearance of dative and accusative forms of nouns and of congruence in adjectives.

Early Modern Swedish

The advent of printing marks the beginning of a new period – the first printed book in Swedish, *Aff dyäfwlsens frestelse* ('On Temptation by the Devil'), appearing in 1495 – with the standardization of orthography and punctuation that such mass production entails. The most important printed works are the Reformation Bible translations *Nya testamentet* from 1526 and *Gustav Vasas bibel* from 1541. The extent of the influence of the first Bible available widely in the native tongue cannot be underestimated, and this version – with only orthographic changes – was used until as recently as 1917, thus providing a written norm for a very long period. In its striving for a worthy and formal style, *GVB* often reveals archaic forms, especially in inflexions, as well as some German influences, notably on the lexicon and in subordinate clause constructions.

A Swedish poetic language develops in the 17th c. under the influence of Georg Stiernhielm, and Swedish begins to be used at the University of Uppsala. Both Stiernhielm and Samuel Columbus cultivate the language consciously, with Stiernhielm reintroducing lexis from Old Swedish words and Old *Norse in the introductory fragment of his planned dictionary *Gambla Swea och Götha Måles fatebur* (The Storehouse of the Tongue of the Ancient Swedes and Goths') from 1643 and in the influential hexameter epic *Hercules* from 1658. Some that have survived are *alster* 'product' (OSw *alster*), *slöjd* 'handicraft' (OSw *sløghþ*), *snille* 'genius' (OSw *snille*). Columbus argues in *En swensk Orde-Skötsel* ('The Cultivation of Swedish Words'), *c*.1680, for a renewal of the written language from the spoken, influenced in this by the Frenchman Vaugelas's *Remarques sur la langue françoise*.

In the 16th and early 17th centuries, loans from High German are prevalent, culminating in the period of the Thirty Years' War (1618–48) in which Sweden was deeply involved. Many military terms are borrowed, e.g. *korpral*, *infanteri*, *pistol*, though mining terms are also heavily influenced, e.g. *schakt* 'shaft' < Ger. *Schacht*, *skikt* 'bed' < Ger. *Schicht*, *blyerts* 'graphite' < Ger. *Bleiertz* as well as terms from other areas.

As a result of strong cultural and political contacts, French loans begin to enter Swedish in large numbers, especially during the reign of Louis XIV (1643–1715), a phenomenon culminating in the mid-18th c. Areas where this is evident are the world of diplomacy (*allians, ambassadör*), the family (*kusin, mamma*), food and good living (*champinjon, sås* 'sauce', *karamell, paraply, parfym, peruk, möbel*), the arts (*balett, pjäs* 'play' < Fr. *pièce, poesi*) and business (*affär, kredit, kommers*).

Later Modern Swedish

This period usually dates from Olof von Dalin, the founder (in 1732) and sole author of the first newspaper in Sweden, *Then Swänska Argus* ('The Swedish Argus'), who introduced a clearer, less formal and more concise written style. The travelogues of the botanist Carl von Linné proved that Swedish could be used for accurate factual and scientific description in place of Latin. Another influential document is *Sweriges Rikes Lag* ('The Law of the Kingdom of Sweden') from 1734. An interest in cultivating and normalizing the language developed, with the publication of, for instance, Abraham Sahlstedt's *Swensk Grammatika* ('Swedish Grammar') of 1769 and his *Swensk Ordbok med latinsk uttolkning* ('Swedish Dictionary with Latin Translation') from 1773 in which usage is the predominant influence, albeit the usage of educated circles in the capital. This growing interest culminated in the foundation of the Swedish Academy by King Gustaf III in 1786 along the same lines as the Académie française. The Academy's primary task was 'to work for the purity, strength and nobility of the Swedish language, in the Sciences as especially with regards to Poetry and Oratory in all its parts, as in that which serves to interpret the Heavenly Truths'. The Academy was given the task of publishing a dictionary, and the book was eventually begun in 1893 but still remains unfinished. C. G. Leopold's normative treatise for the Academy (in 1801) on the adaptation of French loans to Swedish spelling has, however, proved important. So too has *Svenska Akademiens ordlista över svenska språket* ('The Swedish Academy Word-List of the Swedish Language'), published at regular intervals, most recently in the 12th edition of 1997, which provides guidance on correct spelling and inflexion.

In the modern era there has been an explosion of literacy and literature. There has been a flourishing literary production, from the still popular national poet and songwriter Carl Michael Bellman in the 1790s, via a Golden Age of Swedish writing in the 1880s and 1890s with the work of the polymath August Strindberg (novelist, autobiographer, storyteller and poet as well as prolific dramatist) and of the novelist Selma Lagerlöf, prominent both in Sweden and abroad. More recently Swedish-language film has been internationally prominent, not least the work of director Ingmar Bergman.

Literacy rates are very high; newspapers and magazines are read avidly, excellent public libraries receive generous funding and relatively inexpensive books of all kinds are readily available.

The great population movements of the last century, primarily from countryside to towns, and the general expansion of all kinds of communications have had two main effects on the language. Firstly, there has been a growing influence of the written language on the spoken, especially on pronunciation and forms. Secondly, the development of a standard spoken language has taken place with a corresponding decline in the influence of the dialects.

The last 150 years have also seen the growing influence of British and American English (see below).

Script

The oldest written texts in Swedish (apart from runic texts) employ a Latin alphabet modified by the addition of the letters <æ>, <ø>, and <þ> (more rarely <ð>). The script now in use is a modified Latin alphabet of 29 letters including (at the end of the alphabet) <å>, <ä> and <ö>. The graphemes <q>, <w> are only found in names. The grapheme <å> (introduced with printing in the late 1400s) developed from medieval <aa>, and <ä> developed from <æ> at this time. The new grapheme <ö> corresponds to <ø> in medieval Swedish (still found in present-day Danish and *Norwegian).

Dialects and the national language

The present national language is based largely on the dialects of central Sweden, i.e. the Lake Mälaren–Uppsala–Stockholm area which has been the seat of power and administration since the Middle Ages. The language of the Reformation Bibles played a great part in the formation of a national written standard by the end of the 1600s, and this norm, together with the spoken language of this core area, has contributed to the development of a national spoken language. Since the 1600s this has grown at the expense of the dialects; in the 1800s and the 1900s the process accelerated and the pronunciation of the standard spoken language has increasingly been influenced by the written norm.

Dialectal features are still retained in many localities but have been modified dramatically, and in some areas, notably in the south, a regional spoken and written Swedish has developed. The following dialect groups are usually identified:

(1) South Swedish dialects (the three southernmost provinces) have a different tone system from that in central Swedish and show considerable lexical influence from Danish. (Danish philologists also – with some justification – claim them as 'Eastern Danish'.)

(2) Göta dialects (south central Sweden) are intermediate in features, possessing some features of South Swedish and some of the Svea dialects.

(3) Svea dialects (central Sweden around Lake Mälaren) are difficult to distinguish now as they have formed the basis for standard spoken Swedish.

(4) Norrland dialects (northern Swedish, north of River Dalälven) have different word stress patterns from standard Swedish, and local dialects show very archaic phonological and morphological features.

(5) Gotlandic (the Baltic island of Gotland) displays very archaic features.

(6) Eastern Swedish (Finland-Swedish) dialects have many loan-words from *Finnish and *Russian as well as neologisms not found in mainland Swedish (see also 'Finland-Swedish' below).

The influence of British and American English

English loans into Swedish date back to the 17th c. but have been growing in numbers since the mid-1800s. They are found in many fields, notably in communications (*lok, sliper, bicykel, radio, container, motell, television, transistor*), sport (*bridge, krocket, sport, träna* 'to train'), food and drink (*paj* 'pie', *biff, whisky, fiskpinnar* 'fish fingers', *juice, ketchup*) and clothing (*blazer, bikini, jeans, jumper, overall, shorts*). Types of modern English loans include direct loans retaining their original meaning (*team, image*) and those in which some semantic change has taken place (*city* in Swedish refers only to the town centre, *kex* are not 'cakes' but 'biscuits', *soul* is only a kind of music). New English formations are also found where a neologism is based on English patterns but does not originate from English: *freestyle* is not a style of swimming but a personal stereo or 'walkman'; *en babysitter* is not someone who looks after a baby but a kind of baby chair. Loan-translations may be either a partial translation (*grapefrukt*) or a complete translation which is literal (*kedjerökare* 'chain smoker', *mjukvara* 'software', *utvärdera* 'evaluate', *släppa katten ur säcken* 'let the cat out of the bag'), or a 'free' translation (*bandspelare* 'tape recorder', *brädsegling* 'sail boarding', *allsång* 'community singing'). Semantic extension is also found in colloquial usage (*Det är inte min huvudvärk om du inte köper mitt argument* 'It's not my headache if you don't buy my argument'). Construction loans include the introduction of the English apostrophe (Swedish usually has no apostrophe before the genitive *-s*), e.g. *Köp maten hos Kalle's!* 'Buy your food at Kalle's!' and the writing of compounds as two separate words (Swedish usually integrates compounds), e.g. *Sko mässa* 'Shoe Fair'.

Adaptation of pronunciation and spelling is common (*sweater* is often pronounced as 'sweeter'). Plural forms of nouns in *-s* may occasionally be retained (*jeans, shorts, bestsellers*) but are commonly adapted to Swedish inflexional patterns (*revolvrar, guider, jobb*) or even double plurals (*babysar*).

Present situation

Swedish is spoken as mother tongue by approximately 8 million of the 8.6 million inhabitants of Sweden and slightly less than 300,000 in Finland (see below, 'Finland-Swedish'). In 1944, upon the occupation of Estonia by Soviet forces, some 7,000 Swedish-speaking Estonians fled to Sweden. It is an official language in both Sweden and Finland, and an official working language of the European Union.

Descendants of earlier Swedish and Finland-Swedish emigrants to the USA, Canada, Brazil, Uruguay and Argentina have now largely abandoned the use of Swedish as a functional language.

Since 1944 the responsibility for cultivating the language has lain with the body *Nämnden för svensk språkvård* whilst for Finland-Swedish it rests with *Svenska språknämnden i Finland*, founded in 1942.

Finland-Swedish

Swedish is spoken as first language by nearly 300,000 Finnish citizens or 6% of the population (a figure that has halved in the 20th c.), and is found especially on the coast of Ostrobothnia, in Nyland (including Helsinki/Helsingfors) and Åboland. Finland-Swedes often talk of such areas collectively as 'Swedish Finland'. The Åland islanders (entirely Swedish-speaking) do not consider themselves to be Finland-Swedes. For 600 years to 1809 Finland was part of Sweden, and Swedish was the only official language until 1863. It retains an official status in the republic today based in the 1919 constitution.

The ethnic background of Finland-Swedes is very varied as is their class background, with many belonging to lower social groups, contrary to the popular Finnish stereotype of a Finland-Swede as an individual of wealth and influence. In the capital, this stereotype may have some small justification but it is not the case in the provinces. Local municipalities may be classified as either monolingual Swedish (10 on the mainland and 16 in Åland), monolingual Finnish (399), bilingual with a Finnish majority (17) or bilingual with a Swedish majority (22). A bilingual district is defined as one having more than 8% or at least 3,000 inhabitants speaking the other language, and monolingual as one having less than 8%. The linguistic classification of municipalities is reviewed every ten years.

There is a national Swedish-language radio station and several local stations, a special television channel from Sweden, and Swedish-language programmes also constitute 15% of the total of broadcasts on Finnish television. The newspaper *Hufvudstadsbladet* is a national daily for the minority Swedish-speaking community. A number of Finland-Swedish writers are prominent in Swedish writing, and in the 1910s and 1920s Finland-Swedish Modernist poets such as Edith Södergran and Elmer Diktonius made major contributions.

As regards lexicon, common Finlandisms (Swedish words or phrases not found in standard Swedish) have been estimated at about a thousand, often comprising loans from Finnish or older Swedish words no longer current in Sweden. Examples are *aktionär* 'shareholder' (Sw. *aktieägare*), *gravgård* 'graveyard' (Sw. *kyrkogård*), *morgonmat* 'breakfast' (Sw. *frukost*). There are also many loan-translations from Finnish: *alkobutik* 'liquor store' (Sw. *systembutik*), *arbetskraftbyrå* 'job centre' (Sw. *arbetsförmedling*), *fjärrsamtal* 'long-distance call' (Sw. *rikssamtal*), and much official nomenclature that differs from standard Swedish: *befolkningsskydd* 'civil defence' (Sw. *civilförsvar*), *mellanstadiet* 'Sixth Form College' (Sw. *gymnasieskolan*). Some Swedish loans have undergone a semantic shift under the influence of equivalent Finnish words: *batteri* (in Sweden with the same meaning as English) in Finland means 'radiator' (Finnish *patteri*).

Pronunciation also clearly distinguishes Finland-Swedish from standard spoken Swedish. Among other features, sentence intonation also differs (perhaps as a result of Finnish influence), vowel length differs in that many words have short syllables (a short vowel followed by a single consonant or no consonant) where the standard Swedish vowel would be long, and there are differences in the pronunciation of certain initial consonants.

Spoken Finland-Swedish is less influenced by the written language than is standard Swedish, and it is unusual to hear the inflexional endings pronounced in e.g. *kallade* 'called', *skrivit* 'written', *barnet* 'the child', or the final consonant in *och* 'and', *är* 'is, are'. Some nouns have a different gender from standard Swedish, e.g. *en nummer* (non-neuter gender) 'a number' (in Sweden, *ett nummer* (neuter)), and prepositional use differs in some cases, e.g. *i året* 'per year' (Sweden *om året*).

Bergman, G. 1973. *A Short History of the Swedish Language*, 2nd edn. Lund.

Holmes, P. and Hinchcliffe, I. 1993. *Swedish. A Comprehensive Grammar*. London.

Norstedts stora engelsk–svenska ordbok ('Norstedt's Large English–Swedish Dictionary'), 2nd edn. 1993. Stockholm.

Norstedts stora svensk–engelska ordbok ('Norstedt's Large Swedish–English Dictionary'), 2nd edn. 1993. Stockholm.

Wessén, E. 1945. *Våra folkmål* ('Our Dialects'), 2nd edn. Stockholm.

—— 1968. *Svensk språkhistoria* ('Swedish Language History'), 3 vols, 8th edn. Lund.

PHIL HOLMES

Switzerland

Of the four national languages of Switzerland (see map 20), *German, according to the 1991 census, was the first language of 63.6% of the total population of nearly seven million, *French of 19.2%, *Italian of 7.6%, and *Romansh of 0.6% (the remaining 9% is accounted for by foreign permanent residents, seasonal workers and other foreigners). The cantons of Geneva, Vaud, Neuchâtel and Jura are largely French-speaking. The cantons of Fribourg and Valais are divided between French (the majority language) and German. Italian is the first language of the canton of Ticino, apart from a small German-speaking area in the west. Graubünden (Grisons) is the only trilingual canton, with German as the dominant language, three Italian-speaking areas in the south, and a geographically and dialectally fragmented population of some 40,000 to 50,000 Romansh-speakers, virtually all of whom also speak German. Apart from a French-speaking area in the north-west of the canton of Bern, the other 18 cantons are almost entirely German-speaking.

Though Romansh was recognized as a 'national' language after a referendum in 1938, German, French and Italian remained the only 'official' languages. However, under a change to the federal constitution approved by referendum on 10 March 1996, Romansh was accorded enhanced status as 'the official language for relations between the Confederation and Romansh-speaking citizens'.

GLANVILLE PRICE

Sylheti (see under *Community languages (Britain)*)

Syriac (see under *Assyrian*)

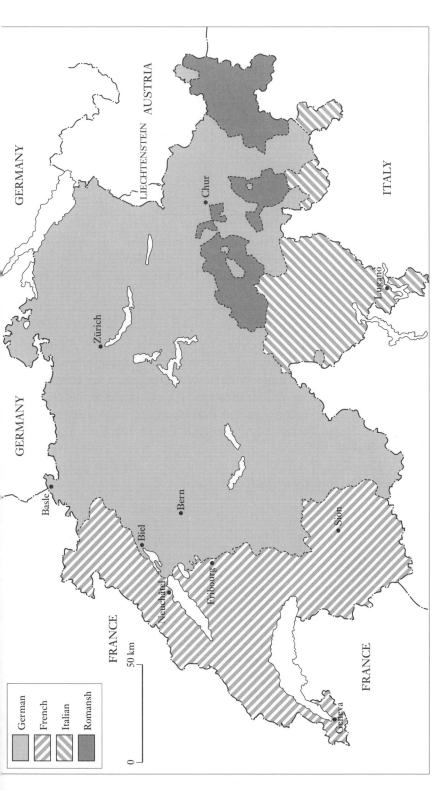

Map 20   Linguistic zones in Switzerland. This map illustrates the distribution of the four national languages of Switzerland by first language or mother tongue according to data provided by the census of 1980. It should be noted, however, that virtually all Romansh-speakers are also fluent in German. On the other hand, substantial numbers of Romansh-speakers remain in parts of the canton of Graubünden (Grisons) that are here indicated as German-speaking.

T

Tabasaran (see under *Caucasian languages. IV. North-East Caucasian family*)

Talishi (Talesh, Talysh)
An *Iranian language spoken mainly in SE Azerbaijan (where one estimate puts the total number of speakers at 130,000), and also in NW Iran. There is no written tradition, despite an unsuccessful attempt in the 1930s to create a literary language.

Tartessian see *South Lusitanian*

Tat (Tati, Takestani)
An *Iranian language spoken mainly in Iran but also in Azerbaijan (where there are two different communities, one Jewish and the other Muslim, each having perhaps 20,000 or more speakers, though estimates vary considerably), and by some further north in Daghestan (Russian Federation). Its written tradition dates only from the 1920s.

Tatar
A member of the Volga-Kama (Uralic) group of the Kipchak or NW *Turkic languages. Its closest relative is *Bashkir. The term 'Tatar' was originally used in various ways for Turkic- and non-Turkic-speaking peoples before the coming of Islam, and Russians later tended to call all Muslims 'Tatars'. In the former Soviet Union, the term was applied to several scattered Turkic peoples, the two major such communities being the Kazan Tatars and the Crimean Tatars. The Turkic peoples of Siberia, i.e. the Khakass, the Shors, etc., were formerly denoted collectively as 'Siberian Tatars'. The name 'Tatar' was also used in connection with the Nogay. Nowadays, it is applied exclusively to the Kazan Tatars.

History

First accounts of the Tatars come from the Codex Cumanicus of 1303. Earlier, in Old Turkic inscriptions and in Chinese chronicles, the name is used for a non-Turkic people, probably of Mongolian origin. After the Mongol invasion, it was used for the mixture of peoples who lived within the realm of the Golden Horde, especially the Turkic Kipchaks or Cumans who were the forefathers of the modern Tatars. In Old Russian chronicles the Cumans are generally called 'Polov'tsii'. The language of the Codex Cumanicus, a Low Latin–Persian–Cuman glossary compiled by Franciscan friars in the Crimea and Volga region, is closely related to Kazan Tatar of which it can be seen as the direct forerunner. After the fall of the Kipchak realm of the Golden Horde, the Khanate of Kazan (1445–1552) took its place in the Volga-Kama region.

The oldest Kazan Tatar texts go back to the 15th c. The Islamic literary language,

*Chaghatay, written in the Arabic alphabet, was used up to the second half of the 19th c. when it was finally replaced by the modern Tatar language, also written in Arabic script until 1927. The Latin alphabet was then adopted for a brief period but was replaced by *Cyrillic in 1939. The basis of a literary Tatar language was laid by Qayum Nasiri (1824–1902). From the 1880s on, a rich literary tradition in the national language developed, some of the more important writers being A. Ishaqi, S. Maqsudi, A. A. Kemal and A. Ibrahim.

Distribution

Within the Russian Federation, Tatar is spoken in the Tatar Republic (capital, Kazan) in the Volga-Kama region, where about a quarter of the entire Tatar population live. There is another large contingent in the adjacent Bashkir Republic and about 20% of the total live in the central Asian republics of Uzbekistan and Kazakhstan. Sizeable contingents of Tatars are also known in the Ural mountains, in the region of the Vyatka river (north of the Tatar Republic), in the northern Caucasus and in NW Russia, and, east of the Urals, there are scattered groups throughout southern Siberia between the Urals and the Sayan mountains, mainly along the upper Irtysh and the Tobol rivers. The total figure for Tatar-speakers in the former Soviet Union in 1989 was given as 6,648,760.

Dialects

The dialectology of the Tatar language has not yet been thoroughly discussed, but there seems to be a general acceptance of a fourfold division into: (i) western dialects, in and around Nizhny-Novgorod, Kasimov, Ryazan, Penza, Saratov and Kuybyshev; (ii) central dialects, i.e. Kazan Tatar, on which the standard language is based; (iii) eastern dialects, in western Siberia; and (iv) Baraba, which occupies a special position being further removed from the standard language and having therefore been taken by a few scholars as belonging to the northern Turkic languages.

Gabain, A. von 1959. Die Sprache des Codex Cumanicus ('The language of the Codex Cumanicus'). In Deny, J. et al. (eds), *Philologiae Turcicae Fundamenta*, Wiesbaden, 46–74.
Thomsen, K. 1959. Das Kasantatarische und die westsibirischen Dialekte ('Kazan-Tatar and the West Siberian dialects'). In Deny, J. et al. (eds), *Philologiae Turcicae Fundamenta*, Wiesbaden, 407–21.

WOLFGANG GRELLER

Tati, see *Tat*

Teutonic

The Teutoni or Teutones were a people from Jutland who, together with the Cimbri (see *Cimbrian), moved southwards and westwards in the late 2nd c. BC and, in or about 110 BC, arrived in Gaul. In 102 BC they were defeated by the Romans in a battle near Aix-en-Provence in which they were virtually all killed or captured. Nothing remains of their language but, despite claims sometimes made that they were Celts, there is little doubt that they were a Germanic-speaking people.

Their name was sometimes applied by Latin writers to Germanic peoples in general, whence the modern (but now unfashionable) use of the term 'Teutonic languages' as a synonym for '***Germanic languages**'.

Thracian (see under *Daco-Thracian*)

T'indi (see under *Caucasian languages. IV. North-East Caucasian family*)

Ts'akhur (see under *Caucasian languages. IV. North-East Caucasian family*)

Tsakonian

A dialect of Greek spoken in a number of villages in the SE Peloponnese between Mount Parnon and the Argolic Gulf. Whereas all other modern Greek dialects derive more or less directly from the ancient Attic-based Koine (see under ***Greek**), Tsakonian, though subject to Koine influence at various times, is the sole surviving remnant of the Laconian or Spartan form of the ancient Doric dialect. Not being mutually intelligible with other dialects, it has sometimes (though not usually) been reckoned to be a distinct language. It is in decline but there may still be a few thousand speakers left (nearly all of whom also speak standard modern Greek).

Anagnostopulos, G. P. 1926. *Tsakonische Grammatik*. Heidelberg.
Pernot, H. 1934. *Introduction à l'étude du dialecte tsaconien*. Paris.

Tsez (see under *Caucasian languages. IV. North-East Caucasian family*)

Turkic languages

The Turkic languages are spoken by some 130 million people, mainly in Asia with the biggest concentration in Turkey and others in the central Asian republics of Uzbekistan, Kazakhstan, Turkmenia and Kirgizia. Within Europe, Turkic-speaking peoples are found mainly in the central and southern Urals, parts of the Caucasus and the Crimean peninsula, and in Turkey in Europe.

The Turkic languages are relatively close to one another and mutual comprehension between most of them seems possible. Consequently, the thin line between dialect and language is sometimes difficult to draw and some scholars make more detailed distinctions than others. According to a widely accepted classification, the Turkic languages fall into five branches: (i) Hunno-Bolgar, with its sole living representative, ***Chuvash**, and its historical predecessor, Volga-Bolgar; (ii) Oghuz or southern Turkic, comprising ***Turkish**, ***Gagauz**, ***Azeri** and (in Asia) Turkmen, with material dating from the 11th c. onwards; (iii) Kipchak or NW Turkic, subdivided into (a) the Uralic or Volga-Kama group, i.e. ***Tatar** and ***Bashkir** (historically, Old Tatar is identical with the language of the Kipchaks or Cumans recorded from the beginning of the 14th c.), (b) the Ponto-Caspian group, consisting of ***Karaim**, ***Karachay-Balkar**, ***Kumyk** and ***Crimean Tatar**, and (c) the Aralo-Caspian group, consisting of ***Nogay**, ***Kazakh** and (in Asia) Karakalpak; (iv) eastern Turkic, including (in Asia) ***Chaghatay**, which was also used as a literary language by Turkic-speaking peoples in European Russia from the 15th to the 19th c., Uzbek, and Uygur (Uighur) (with a wealth of historical material going as far back as the 8th–9th centuries); and (v) northern Turkic, including (in Asia) Yakut, Dolgan, Khakass, Shor, Altay and Tuva, and perhaps Kirgiz (considered by some, however, to belong to the Kipchak group) – to this northern group belong the earliest surviving attestations of the Turkic languages, the Orkhon and Yenisey runic inscriptions dating from the 7th–8th centuries.

Although the Proto-Altaic hypothesis, which postulated a common origin for the Turkic, Mongolian and Manchu-Tungus languages, is still adhered to by some scholars, the linguistic evidence is insufficient to prove such a connection at present. Historically, the Turkic peoples had emerged as a recognizable ethnic unity of the Mongolian steppe by the 6th c. AD. During their migrations, they gradually adopted Islam though some became Christians or converted to Judaism. Through their constant rivalry with Russia, they came increasingly under the influence of the Slavs.

Benzing, J. 1959. Classification of the Turkic languages. In Deny, J. et al. (eds), *Philologiae Turcicae Fundamenta*, Wiesbaden, 1–10.

Dewdney, J. C. 1993. The Turkic peoples of the USSR. In Bainbridge, M. (ed.), *The Turkic Peoples of the World*, London and New York, 215–97.

Gabain, A. von 1963. Charakteristik der Türksprachen. In *Handbuch der Orientalistik*, Leiden and Cologne, part 1, vol. 5, 3–26.

Menges, K. H. 1995. *The Turkic Languages and Peoples*, 2nd edn. Wiesbaden.

WOLFGANG GRELLER

Turkish

Turkish (*Türkçe*), a member of the Oghuz or south-western subgroup of ***Turkic languages**, is spoken in Turkey, Cyprus (120,000), and various parts of the Balkans.

Origins of the Turkic peoples and the Turks in Europe

The earliest history of the Turkic-speaking peoples can be traced back to Inner Asia, to the area of modern Mongolia. Reports about northern barbarians appear increasingly in the Chinese sources from the 3rd c. BC. Although there remains some uncertainty concerning the languages of these tribal confederations, there is general consensus that they included Turkic and other Altaic groups. Towards the end of the 10th c. AD, the Oghuz Turkic tribes were organized by Seljuk, who converted to Islam and consolidated his power in what is today western Persia. Seljuk's successors expanded their power to the west and in 1071 Alparslan defeated the Byzantine army at Manzikert. This Turkic expansion threatened Byzantium and the Holy Land, and the first Crusades were launched against the Turks. The gradual expansion of Turkic power and of Islam in Anatolia culminated in the emergence of the Ottoman dynasty at the end of the 13th c. Consistent attempts to expand into the Balkans began during the reign of Murad I, a process which led to direct Ottoman threats to Hungary and to the principalities of Moldavia and Wallachia. The conquest of Constantinople by Mehmed the Conqueror in 1453 finally opened the way to European expansion. Ottoman victories in the Balkans were followed by the occupation of a large part of Hungary and renewed conflicts with Poland. The Turks threatened Vienna in 1529, but Ottoman expansion came to a halt after the middle of the 16th c. and they suffered significant losses on the European front after the second unsuccessful siege of Vienna in 1683. The decline of the Ottoman Empire entailed the loss of most of its European lands and, following the Balkan Wars of 1912–13, only Constantinople and its hinterland were retained.

While the spread of Turkish-speakers in Europe owes much to historical developments during Ottoman times, labour migration during the 1960s and 1970s has also brought large numbers of Turkish-speakers into western Europe.

Earliest attestations

The Orkhon inscriptions and other early Inner Asian Turkic documents, including outstanding Islamic works in Turkic, are considered by most Turkic-speaking groups as their common cultural heritage. Among the early Islamic works the best-known are the *Kutadğu Bilig*, a long didactic poem (1069–70) by Yusuf Hass Hacib, and the *Divan-ül Luğat at-Türk* (1072–3) by Mahmud Kaşgari. The latter contains a wealth of information about the languages, history and ethnography of the contemporary Turkic-speaking world and many early examples of their oral traditions.

The periodization of Turkish

The history of Anatolian Turkish can be divided into four periods; Old Ottoman (13th to mid-15th centuries), Middle Ottoman (mid-15th to 18th centuries), New Ottoman (19th c), Modern Turkish (from the language reform of 1928 onwards).

Although the first large concentrations of Turkish-speakers appeared in Anatolia in the 11th c., the first Anatolian Turkish documents, such as Ahmed Fakih's poem entitled *Çarhname*, Turkish couplets in Celaleddin Rumi's *Mesnevi*, and the poetic output of Şeyyad Hamza, Dehhani, Sultan Veled and Yunus Emre, date from the 13th c. Most of these early works were inspired by Islamic mysticism. The number of collections of poems increased from the 14th c. onwards alongside translations and reinterpretations of themes from Persian and Arabic literature. Prose writing also started to develop, and from the 15th c. onwards the plain (*sade nesir*) and ornamental (*süslü nesir*) styles can be distinguished.

Scripts

Literacy among the Turkic peoples has a long history. The earliest examples of Turkic literacy are memorial inscriptions in the runic script found by the Orkhon river (Mongolia), dating from the 8th c. AD. Shorter inscriptions on metal objects, pottery, paper and wood have also survived from even earlier times. From the 9th to the 13th centuries, Turkic texts were produced in the Brahmi script, while some Buddhist texts were committed to writing in the Tibetan and Uighur (Uygur) scripts. Conversion to Islam entailed the use of the Arabic script which, until 1928, remained the most widely used script in Anatolia, though there also exists a body of documents in the *Armenian (see fig. 1), Georgian (see under **Caucasian languages. VI. Georgian**, and fig. 2), *Greek, *Hebrew, *Cyrillic, Latin and Syriac scripts. The Uighur script was also used in Anatolia until the 15th c. Research into the early development of Ottoman Turkish has relied on indigenous manuscripts written in the Arabic script. Another important source of diachronic language research is provided by the so-called transcription-texts produced by Europeans. These texts afford many insights into the spoken language and the history of Turkish phonology.

Printing

Although printing was practised in Ottoman lands by minorities from the late 15th c. onwards, the first Turkish-language books were printed in Constantinople by the Hungarian renegade Ibrahim Müteferrika, who between 1729 and 1742 published 17 books dealing with history, geography and language.

Interrelationship with other languages and language reform

Throughout the Ottoman centuries, Turkish remained the language of the Anatolian peasants but, among the educated, Persian enjoyed the highest prestige, while *Arabic was the language of liturgy. From its beginnings Ottoman Turkish was influenced by these two languages. The many translations from these languages resulted in further borrowings, the outcome of which was a composite language with a high content of Arabic and Persian words and even syntactic elements. An attempt to stop this influx of foreign elements in the late 15th c., the *Türk-Basit* ('Simple Turkish') movement, failed.

Early attempts to describe the Turkish language were influenced by either Arabic or Latin grammar. Deny's *Grammaire de la langue turque (dialecte osmanli)* (1921), though based on diachronic materials, was the first reference grammar.

The question of language reform was raised repeatedly during the 19th c., in the context of discussions of how to bridge the considerable gap between the written language and the vernacular. It was also believed that a reform of the script was essential to eliminate illiteracy. An important argument in favour of script reform was the inability of the Arabic script to reflect the vowel system of Turkish. The move towards the creation of a national language was accompanied by the publication of grammars and dictionaries, one of which, Süleyman Paşa's *Sarf-'ı Türkı* published in 1874, denoted the language as Turkish rather than Ottoman. Because the literary language was becoming more or less unintelligible to the speakers of the vernacular, reforms in the legal, administrative and educational systems in the 19th c. during the *Tanzimat* ('Reform') Period, an era of intensifying contacts with the West, led to a recognition of the need for language reform. While Turkish newspapers published during the 19th c. contributed to the formulation of a simpler written style, it was during the decade of the Young Turks (1908–18) that the most significant developments took place. Writers of a Salonika literary paper, *Genç Kalemler* ('Young Pens'), drew up rules for a purer style. The move towards a simple written language close to the vernacular of the common people culminated in the script reform, followed immediately by the language reform, which became important components of the nationalist ideology of Mustafa Kemal (Atatürk). The script change, i.e. the replacement of the Arabic script by the Latin alphabet, was implemented in 1928.

Atatürk's language revolution (*dil devrimi*) called for a complete break with the Islamic past, which meant the eradication of Arabic and Persian elements, the invention of new words from original Turkic stems (*Öz-Türkçe*), the abolition of the Arabic alphabet and its replacement with a suitably modified Latin script. The aim of the Turkish Linguistic Society (*Türk Dil Kurumu*), founded in 1932, was to promote this new Turkish language. The early phase of the language reform (mid-1930s) was characterized by a radical approach which tried to eliminate all Arabic and Persian vocabulary from the literary language, even those items which had become integral parts of the spoken and written languages. However, such an elimination could not be achieved and a more moderate and realistic approach was adopted by the Turkish Linguistic Society during the late 1940s and 1950s. The overall result of the reforms was that the number of Arabic and Persian loan-words was dramatically reduced and many innovations have become accepted. The sources of lexical innovations were diverse: new words were derived from Anatolian dialects, manuscripts, pre-Islamic Turkic inscriptions and documents, Turkish Koran commentaries, historical works, popular poetry and dictionaries of contemporary Turkic languages. Thanks to simultaneous reforms of the education system and the means of communication, the previously existing gap between the written and spoken languages was more or less successfully bridged. The 1950s saw a slowing-up of the language reform, but after 1961 the Turkish Linguistic Society resumed its activities with more vigour. From about this time onward, language reform became more than an expression of Turkish nationalism. It was an important arena for ideological battle between left-wing intellectuals who stood for further reform and conservatives who opposed it.

Modern standard Turkish is based on the dialect spoken in Istanbul, the former capital which is still the cultural capital of Turkey. As such, it emerged as the direct continuation of Ottoman Turkish. Due to the multi-ethnic and multilingual character of the Ottoman Empire, its Turkish vocabulary had also been influenced by ***Greek**, ***Armenian**, ***Romanian**, ***Slavonic** and ***Italian** elements. An influx of ***French** loan-words dominated the 19th c., while ***English** has been comparably prominent in the late 20th c. At the same time, Turkish has also influenced many of the languages with which it came into contact.

Geographical spread and numbers of speakers

Turkish is spoken in the Republic of Turkey (45 million), in the Turkish Republic of Northern Cyprus (120,000), in Bulgaria (where unofficial estimates put the number of Turkish-speakers anywhere between 900,000 and 1,550,000, the largest concentrations being in the Dobruja), Greece (100,000, with the largest concentration in Western Thrace), and the former Yugoslavia (100,000, mostly in Macedonia and Kossovo). The Turkish-speaking community of Romania (estimated at 23,303 in 1977) is concentrated in the Dobruja region.

Dialects

The classification of modern Turkish dialects remains unsatisfactory. For general guidance, the following dialect groups can be distinguished: (i) Istanbul, or Rumelian; (ii) South-east Anatolian; (iii) Middle Anatolian; (iv) South Anatolian or Mediterranean which also includes the Turkish spoken in Cyprus; (v) South-eastern (Adana, Gaziantep, Urfa); (vi) East Anatolian (east of Erzurum); (vii) North-eastern (Black Sea region, east of Samsun); (viii) North-western (Black Sea region and Kastamonu); (ix) Karamanlı; (x) the West-Rumelian dialect spoken in western Bulgaria and Macedonia, which has been exposed to Slavonic influences and shows similarities with the north-eastern Anatolian dialects. The Turkish spoken in other areas of the Balkans is close to the Istanbul dialect and therefore to the modern standard.

Bainbridge, M. (ed.) 1993. *The Turkic Peoples of the World*. London.

Boeschoten, H.-L. V. (ed.) 1991. *Turkish Linguistics Today*. Leiden.

Gabain, A. von 1963. Die Südwest-Dialekte des Türkischen ('The south-western dialects of Turkish'). In *Handbuch der Orientalistik*, Leiden and Cologne, part 1, vol. 5, 174–80.

Hazai, G. 1978. *Kurze Einführung in das Studium der Türkischen Sprache* ('Brief Introduction to the Study of the Turkish Language'). Budapest.

—— (ed.) 1990. *Handbuch der Türkischen Sprachwissenschaft* ('Handbook of Turkish Linguistics'), part 1. Wiesbaden.

Hegyi, K.-V. Zimányi 1989. *The Ottoman Empire in Europe* (translated by C. and I. Hann). Budapest.

Heyd, U. 1954. *Language Reform in Modern Turkey*. Jerusalem.

Iz, F. and Hony, H. C. 1978. *The Oxford English–Turkish Dictionary*, 2nd edn. Oxford.

Kornfilt, J. 1990. Turkish and the Turkic languages. In Comrie, B. (ed.), *The Major Languages of Eastern Europe*, London, 227–52.

Lewis, G. L. 1988. *Turkish Grammar*. Oxford.

Mansuroğlu, M. 1959. *Das Altosmanische* ('Old Ottoman'). In Deny, J. et al. (eds), *Philologiae Turcicae Fundamenta*, Wiesbaden, vol. 1, 161–81.

Róna-Tas, A. 1991. *An Introduction to Turkology*. Szeged.

Underhill, R. 1976. *Turkish Grammar*. Cambridge, MA.

ILDIKÓ BELLÉR–HANN

Tuscan (see under *Italy*, (i) *II. Italian*, (ii) *IV. Central and southern Italy*)

U

Ubykh (see under *Caucasian languages. II. North-West Caucasian family*)

Udi (see under *Caucasian languages. IV. North-East Caucasian family*)

Udmurt

Udmurt, otherwise known as Votyak, belongs, together with *Komi, to the Permic group of the *Finno-Ugrian languages. The Udmurts live south of the Komi, mainly in an area between the Vyatka and Kama rivers, though some settlements occur beyond these rivers. The majority of them (746,793 speakers according to the 1989 census) live in the Udmurt Republic (capital, Izhevsk).

Udmurt is closely related to Komi, the two languages having some 80% of their vocabulary in common. It has been strongly influenced however, by the *Turkic languages, especially *Chuvash and *Tatar, and has also been in close contact with neighbouring *Mari. Dialectal differences are few and speakers of different dialects have no difficulty in understanding one another and the standard language. The dialects can be grouped into: (i) northern, along the river Chepsta; (ii) the Besserman dialect, which lies amidst the northern dialects close to Glazov; (iii) central, in the area of the rivers Kil'mez and Izh and westwards as far as the Vyatka; (iv) southern, in the south of the Udmurt Republic, around the town of Yelabuga on the river Kama in the Tatar Republic and elsewhere in that Republic, and near the town of Malmyzh.

Early works and collections of folk tales were written in the Latin alphabet, but now an adaptation of the *Cyrillic alphabet is used. Important writers in Udmurt include Gerd Kuzebay (1898–1941) and Ashalchi Oki (1898–1973).

Austerlitz, R. 1964. *Permian (Votyak-Zyrian) Manual*. Cleveland, OH.

Collinder, B. 1957. Votyak. In Id., *Survey of the Uralic Languages*, Stockholm, 273–95.

Csúcs, S. 1985. Kriterien zur Klassifizierung der Dialekte des Wotjakischen ('Criteria for the classification of the dialects of Votyak'). In Veenker, W. (ed.), *Dialectologia Uralica. Materialien des ersten internationalen Symposions zur Dialektologie der uralischen Sprachen*, Wiesbaden, 201–9.

—— 1990. *Chrestomathia Votiatica*. Budapest.

WOLFGANG GRELLER

Ugric languages

Speakers of the Ugric languages are assumed to have been the first to leave the Proto-*Finno-Ugrian community. They settled between the Urals and the Ob River in western Siberia. It seems probable that the Magyars or Hungarians were the southernmost of these. They migrated to eastern Europe and the Carpathian basin, where they finally settled during the 10th c. AD. In consequence, *Hungarian was separated from the other two Ugric languages which are still spoken by communities of a few thousand each in the neighbourhood of the Ob river and form the so-called Ob-Ugric group, namely Ostyak or Hanti and Vogul or Mansi, and which later underwent strong influences from neighbouring *Turkic languages especially *Tatar.

WOLFGANG GRELLER

Ukrainian

A member of the eastern branch of the ***Slavonic languages** and the sole state language of the Ukrainian Republic.

Early history

The earliest written language on what is now Ukrainian territory was the primarily liturgical language of the Orthodox Church, known variously as Old ***Church Slavonic** or Old Bulgarian. Scribal errors in the manuscripts give some insight into the actual local pronunciation of the day. In more secular texts several features can be identified that are still present in modern Ukrainian, although it is impossible to talk of a linear evolution of the literary language from medieval Kyiv (Kiev) to modern times. The absorption of the Ukrainian lands into the Grand Duchy of Lithuania, a process that began in the 14th c., led to the establishment of an administrative, or chancery, language (sometimes known as ***Ruthenian**) with features common to both Ukrainian and ***Belarusian**. Although undoubtedly based in part on the spoken language, it showed increasing influences from ***Polish**, especially after 1569 when the Ukrainian lands were removed from the Grand Duchy of Lithuania and placed under the control of the Polish crown.

The early modern period

The literary language of Ukraine in the 17th and 18th centuries was a local form of Church Slavonic with a considerable admixture of Polish forms. The importance of Kyiv, specifically the Mohyla Academy, as a centre of learning did not lead to the development of a Ukrainian literary language; the languages of eduction were Church Slavonic, Greek and Latin. Indeed, it was not until the end of the 18th c. that any literature appeared in a language closely resembling modern Ukrainian, viz. the Aeneid travesty of Ivan Kotliarevs'kyi (1769–1838). One of the other major figures of Ukrainian culture of the period, the philosopher Hryhory Skovoroda (1722–94), wrote in a language closely resembling ***Russian**.

The nineteenth century

Increasing use of Ukrainian in the 19th c. marked the growth of a greater sense of national identity. The key figure in this development is without doubt Taras Shevchenko (1814–61); his poetry kindled a sense of 'Ukrainianness' in a way unmatched by any other writer of the day. Yet even Shevchenko used Russian for most of his prose writings. The difficulty of establishing a literary language that would unite all Ukrainians was intensified by the fact that they lived in two countries with very different policies. The Russian imperial authorities were hostile to any form of writing in Ukrainian; in fact the use of the language in printed form was banned almost entirely in 1876. The ban remained in force until after 1905. Austria had acquired the western Ukrainian territories (principally Galicia and the city of L'viv (L'vov)) at the end of the 18th c. as a result of the partitions of the Polish Commonwealth, and the government was prepared to permit a certain degree of Ukrainian national self-expression, if only as a counterbalance to the political role of the Poles. Even so, it was not before the end of the 19th c. that Ukrainian found acceptance as a literary medium among the majority of Ukrainians in Galicia.

Dialects and the establishment of the modern literary language

Largely because of the two major centres in which literary Ukrainian developed in the 19th and early 20th centuries, Kyiv in the Russian Empire and L'viv in the Austrian Empire, it is hardly surprising that the modern language in many ways represents a fusion of eastern (Kyiv and Poltava) and western (Galicia) dialects. A crucial role in the establishment of a common norm was played by two dictionaries, those of E. Zhelekhiv'skyi (L'viv 1886) and of B. Hrynchenko (Kyiv 1907–9). In Ukraine itself the eastern dialects played a more important role; outside Ukraine the linguistic situation was largely determined by population movement. The Ukrainians who emigrated to Canada in the second half of the 19th c. and were to play an important role in maintaining Ukrainian culture in the Soviet period came in the main from Austrian Galicia. They had never known Russian domination and their language differed in several respects from that of Ukraine, in morphology as well as lexis. The northern and south-western dialects are regarded as the most archaic. The northern dialects are spoken in the Polisse region bordering on Belarus, an area that was difficult of access until relatively recent times. The south-western dialects include many subgroups spoken in the area of the Carpathian mountains and Bukovina. The question of modern ***Ruthenian**, or Rusyn, is examined in a separate article.

The twentieth century

Ukrainian independence in the aftermath of the Russian Revolution of 1917, although fragile and short-lived, greatly assisted the development of a language that could be used in all spheres of education and state administration. This trend continued even after the establishment of Soviet power in Ukraine in the early 1920s. The 'Ukrainianization' policy, including the development of terminology, was put into reverse by Stalin at the beginning of the 1930s. Using Ukrainian became tantamount to nationalist deviation. The period after 1945 saw no improvements; by the 1960s all university-level institutions were teaching in Russian. The dissident movement in Ukraine focused particularly on matters connected with the preservation of Ukrainian language and culture.

Present situation

Renewed independence for Ukraine in 1991 brought with it opportunities for the re-establishment of Ukrainian as a state language, rather than a domestic language of inferior social status. However, a number of areas of Ukraine are predominantly Russian-speaking (the Black Sea coastal region, the eastern provinces – especially the major industrial cities, and the Crimea), and even the number of Ukrainian-speakers recorded in the most recent census can be misleading. The majority of the population of 52 million claim a knowledge of Ukrainian, but just as national self-identity can shift, so can language use. In any case, 'knowing' Ukrainian does not necessarily mean the ability or willingness to use it in all situations. Ukrainian is the sole state language of the republic and its position in the education system is probably assured, but in the legal system and public administration it is somewhat weaker, although undoubtedly gaining ground. The use of the language in religion is complicated by the number of churches competing for allegiance (Ukrainian Uniate, Ukrainian Autocephalous Orthodox, Ukrainian Orthodox under Moscow) and the role of Church Slavonic.

Outside Ukraine there are large numbers of speakers in Russia and other republics of the former Soviet Union (nearly 900,000 in Kazakhstan alone, according to the 1989 census), and smaller numbers in Poland, Slovakia and Romania. There are significant émigré communities in western Europe, especially the United Kingdom, France and Germany, in Canada, the USA, South America (Brazil, Argentina and Paraguay), Australia and New Zealand (total estimates vary between 1,200,000 and 2,500,000).

Andrusyshen, C. H. and Krett, J. N. 1955. *Ukrainian–English Dictionary* (5th printing, 1993). Saskatoon.
Bekh, O. and Dingley, J. 1997. *Teach Yourself Ukrainian*. London.
Nin'ovs'kyi, V. 1993. *Ukrainian–English* and *English–Ukrainian Dictionary*. Kyiv.
Press, I. and Pugh, S. 1994. *Colloquial Ukrainian*. London.
Shevelov, G. Y. 1993. Ukrainian. In Comrie, B. and Corbett, G. G. (eds), *The Slavonic Languages*, London, 947–98.

JIM DINGLEY

Umbrian

A long-extinct language belonging to the *Sabellian or *Osco-Umbrian subgroup of the *Italic branch of *Indo-European. Its closest cognates are *Volscian, *South Picenian and *Pre-Samnitic. The linguistic differences from *Oscan and the other minor Sabellian languages are only slightly greater. Umbrian was spoken in present-day Umbria (Italy), in a narrow region between the Apennines and the Tiber (see map 10). Originally the Umbrians also lived in Tuscany, whence they were expelled by the incoming Etruscans. Around 300 BC the Umbrians lost their independence and became subject to Rome; this must have been the beginning of the Latinization which ultimately led to the disappearance of Umbrian.

Our knowledge of the language is based almost entirely on seven inscribed bronze plates of irregular size (approximately 40 x 35 cm), the so-called Tabulae Iguvinae, which were unearthed in 1444 in Gubbio (the ancient Iguvium) and are now in the Palazzo dei Consoli in the city. The plates originally numbered nine, but two were lost soon after discovery. They contain about 750 different words. Most plates are inscribed on both sides. The Tabulae are written in two different alphabets. The oldest portions (Old Umbrian) are written in the so-called 'national alphabet', which is a derivative of the *Etruscan alphabet; in the later portions (Late Umbrian), the Latin alphabet is used. The Tabulae cannot be accurately dated: the Late Umbrian sections were probably written in the 1st c. BC, the Old Umbrian sections may date back to the 5th c. BC.

Although a number of obscure passages remain, the language of the Tabulae can be read and understood. They contain the prescriptions of the brotherhood of the 'Atiedian priests' and mention various detailed rules concerning sacrifices, auspices, purification, donations to the brotherhood, etc.

There are nearly 30 shorter inscriptions, consisting of from one to about 20 words, some of which may not be Umbrian at all. These may be dated between the 5th and 1st centuries BC.

A few Umbrian words can be found in *Latin texts. Only five of these are explicitly stated to be Umbrian. A somewhat larger number of Umbrian words, both common nouns and names, have been traced in Etruscan, but their identification and interpretation throw up numerous problems.

It is not clear whether there once existed an Umbrian literature. The Umbrian Plautus, who died in 184 BC, wrote his comedies in Latin.

Buck, C. D. 1928. *A Grammar of Oscan and Umbrian*, 2nd edn. Boston.

Meiser, 1986. *Lautgeschichte der Umbrischen Sprache* ('Historical Phonology of the Umbrian Language'). Innsbruck.

Vetter, E. 1953. *Handbuch der italischen Dialekte* ('Handbook of the Italic Dialects'). Heidelberg.

PETER SCHRIJVER

Uralic languages

The Uralic languages comprise two major groups, the ***Finno-Ugrian languages** and the ***Samoyedic languages**. In older works, the term 'Finno-Ugrian' covered both. The name 'Uralic' refers to the assumed proto-homeland of the peoples in question in the Ural mountain range. The original Uralic territory may have stretched as far west as the Volga or even the Baltic Sea. The Uralic languages are spoken by some 24 million people in all, the most widespread by far being ***Hungarian**. Except in Hungary, Estonia and Finland, where they have national status, the Uralic languages are minority languages in Russia or Scandinavia.

During the proto-Uralic period, the Uralic people must have been in contact with Indo-Europeans, as can be seen in loan-words of *Indo-European origin that seem to have entered the Uralic proto-language. The oldest known text in a Uralic language, namely Hungarian, dates only from the beginning of the 13th c.

The origins of comparative Finno-Ugrian linguistics are relatively old. Apart from a few earlier observations, one of the first to compare the different languages was the German Martin Fogl, who, in the 17th c., posits some etymologies and points to structural correspondences.

Hajdu, P. and Domokos, P. 1980. *Die uralischen Sprachen und Literaturen* ('The Uralic Languages and Literatures'). Hamburg.

WOLFGANG GRELLER

Urartian

Urartu was a kingdom that flourished in the 9th–6th centuries BC in eastern Anatolia, extending in the north-east as far as Lake Sevan in present-day Armenia and therefore into Europe as defined in this encyclopedia. The Urartian language is believed to have been related to the non-*Indo-European Hurrian language spoken in the 2nd millennium BC in eastern Anatolia and northern Mesopotamia. It is probable that a number of non-Indo-European words in *Armenian are of Urartian origin.

Urdu (see under *Community languages (Britain)*)

V

Valencian (see under *Catalan*)

Vallader (see under *Romansh*)

Vandalic

The Vandals were a Germanic people, speaking an East *Germanic language, who, having originally come from further east, crossed the Rhine together with the Alans and the Swabians on 31 December 406 and within three years entered the Iberian Peninsula, where their stay was to be of short duration. Some settled at first in the north-west, in Galicia, but within a few years moved to join the other Vandals in the south, in Baetica (modern Andalusia). In 429, under pressure from the Visigoths, they crossed into Africa. At various times they attacked the Mediterranean islands and the European mainland, sacking Rome in 455, but established no lasting settlements before their power was finally broken by Byzantium in 533. Their language left little trace in the languages of the areas where they had settled but their name is perhaps recalled in that of Andalusia (Spanish *Andalucía*), from Arabic *Al-Andalus*.

Vegliote (see under *Dalmatian*)

Veinakh languages (see under *Caucasian languages. III. North Central Caucasian family*)

Venetan (see under *Italy. III. Northern Italy*)

Venetic

A language spoken before and during the Roman period in the hinterland of the NW Adriatic, north of the Adige river (see map 10). It is known from over 200 brief inscriptions written in varieties of the northern *Etruscan alphabet and dating from the 6th to the 1st centuries BC. Most of these are from sites at Este (the ancient Ateste), while others come from Padua (the ancient Patavium, the chief city of the Veneti) and elsewhere. These include votive inscriptions (containing much duplication) on bronze or stone tablets or on bronze styluses, funerary inscriptions on stone, and very brief inscriptions (often limited to names) on pottery. It seems certain that Venetic was *Indo-European but opinions differ as to whether it was an *Italic dialect or whether it should be considered as a separate branch of Indo-European. The view that it was closely related to *Illyrian is now abandoned. After the founding in 181 BC of an important Roman colony at Aquileia (some 30 km NW of Trieste), which grew into a major city and commercial centre, the area was gradually Romanized, but it is not known how long Venetic survived.

Lejeune, M. 1974. *La Langue vénète*. Heidelberg.

Pellegrini, G. B. and Prosdocimi, A. L. 1967. *La lingua veneta*, 2 vols: vol. 1, *Le iscrizioni:* vol. 2, *Studi*. Florence.

Prosdocimi, A. L. 1978. Il veneto. In Id. (ed.), *Popoli e civiltà dell'Italia antica*, vol. 4, *Lingue e dialetti*, Rome, 257–380.

Veps

A member of the *Baltic-Finnic group of the *Finno-Ugrian languages, and closely related to *Karelian. The main area where Veps is spoken lies north-east of St Petersburg, roughly in the middle of a triangle formed by Lake Ladoga, Lake Onega and Lake Beloye, with a further group on the SW shore of Lake Onega around the town of Seltozero. According to the 1989 census, 12,501 (i.e. 51%) of the Veps spoke their national language as their mother tongue. The language falls into four dialects: (i) northern, around the shores of Lake Onega; (ii) central, on the upper Oyat river; (iii) southern, from the Oyat southwards; (iv) eastern, near Lake Beloye.

Veps has only recently developed a standard literary language although some attempt had already been made in the 1930s. Veps language teaching has now also been introduced into the educational system. In the few reading primers and other publications that have been produced, the Latin alphabet is used. A Veps–Russian dictionary was published in 1972.

Viitso, T. -R. 1985. Kriterien zur Klassifizierung der Dialekte der ostseefinnischen Sprachen ('Criteria for the classification of the Baltic-Finnic languages'). In Veenker, W. (ed.), *Dialectologia Uralica. Materialien des ersten internationalen Symposions zur Dialektologie der uralischen Sprachen*, Wiesbaden, 89–97.

WOLFGANG GRELLER

Vestinian

The Vestini occupied an area between the Gran Sasso d'Italia (the highest point in the Apennines), about 100 km NE of Rome, and the Adriatic (see map 10), their principal town being Pinna (modern Penne). Vestinian was an *Italic language, closely related to *Oscan and *Umbrian and less closely so to *Latin, and little of it remains. Coleman (1986) recognizes as Vestinian only three brief inscriptions (one of which has been claimed by other scholars to be *Sabine), in the Latin alphabet and all dating from the period 250–100 BC, and considers that another that has been taken to be Vestinian is more probably Oscan.

Coleman, R. 1986. The central Italic languages in the period of Roman expansion. *Transactions of the Philological Society*, 1986: 100–31.
Pulgram, E. 1978. Vestinian. In Id., *Italic, Latin, Italian: 600 BC to AD 1260: Texts and Commentaries*, Heidelberg, 149–51.

Vietnamese (see under *Community languages (France)*)

Visigothic

After proceeding from the Balkans via Italy, the *Germanic-speaking Visigoths or Western Goths entered southern Gaul and established a kingdom south of the Loire that lasted some 80 years until they were defeated by the Franks at Vouillé near Poitiers in AD 507. Meanwhile, other Visigoths had crossed the Pyrenees into Spain in AD 415 where they founded a kingdom which extended over much of the Peninsula and lasted until the Arab conquest of 711–18. Within a few generations, the Visigoths seem to have abandoned their *Gothic tongue for the *Romance speech of the area in which they had settled and where a few words of Gothic origin remain, especially in the languages of the Iberian Peninsula, *Spanish, *Catalan and *Portuguese, with a handful also remaining in *Occitan, e.g. Sp., Port., Cat., Oc. *bramar* 'to roar'; Sp., Port., Cat. *estaca*, Oc. *estac* 'stake'; Old Sp., Port., *elmo*, Cat. *elm* 'helmet'; Sp. *ropa*, Port. *roupa*, Cat. *roba* 'clothing'; Sp., Port. *frasco* 'bottle', *ganso* 'goose', *sacar* 'to pull out, extract'. The presence of the Goths is also recalled in the names of a number of localities in the Peninsula, e.g. *Godos, Godones, Valdegodos* 'valley of the Goths'.

Thompson, E. A. 1969. *The Goths in Spain*. Oxford.
Todd, M. 1992. *The Early Germans* ('The Visigoths', 153–76). Oxford.

Vla(c)h, see (a) *Aromanian*, (b) *Megleno-Romanian*

Volapük (see under *Artificial languages*)

Volga-Bolgar (see under *Chuvash*)

Volga-Finnic languages

A subgroup of the *Finno-Ugrian languages, including *Mordvinian and *Mari.

Volscian

The area of southern Latium, south-east of Rome, inhabited by the Volsci (see map 10) included among others the towns of Velitrae (modern Velletri) some 30 km from Rome at the foot of the Alban Hills, Tarracina (Volscian Anxur, modern Terracina) on the coast, and Sora and Arpinum (modern Arpino), the birthplace of Cicero, in the valley of the Liris. Volscian is an ***Italic language,** and so related to ***Latin,** and is known to us from at most three inscriptions, only one of which is indisputably Volscian; this is a 30-word text from Velitrae inscribed in an early form of the Latin alphabet on a bronze plate, dating from the early 3rd c. BC and now in the Naples Museum; while agreeing that it is the text of a decree relating to the goddess Declona, specialists are divided as to its precise meaning. Of the other two inscriptions, one is considered by Coleman (1986) to be more likely to be ***Marsian** while the other, discovered as recently as 1977 on the site of ancient Satricum (modern Conca), has generally been taken to be Latin though Coleman argues convincingly that it cannot be Latin and that there is 'nothing incompatible with a Volscian attribution'.

Coleman, R. 1986. The central Italic languages in the period of Roman expansion. *Transactions of the Philological Society*, 1986: 100–31.
Pulgram, E. 1978. Volscian. In Id., *Italic, Latin, Italian: 600 BC to AD 1260: Texts and Commentaries*, Heidelberg, 151–7.

Votic (Vot, Vote)

A member of the **Baltic-Finnic** group of the ***Finno-Ugrian languages.** The Votes lived in a few villages scattered between NE Estonia and St Petersburg. During the Second World War, the population of the Vote territory was deported to Germany where many died or disappeared. No figures for numbers of speakers of Votic are given in post-war Soviet censuses. In the 1940s there were still some 500 speakers in West Ingermanland around Luga Bay on the Baltic Sea west of St Petersburg and in 1980 it was estimated that 20 elderly speakers were still alive, but the language is probably now extinct. It has been argued that Votic was originally a NE dialect of ***Estonian** which, through isolation, developed into a separate language. Dialects, which differed markedly from village to village, are generally divided into two groups, western and eastern. The Ingricized dialect (see ***Ingrian**) of the village of Kukkosi was a special case. Votic had no standardized form.

The extinct ***Krevinian** language of Latvia derived from the language of Votes deported to the area in the 15th c.

Ariste, P. 1968. *A Grammar of the Votic Language*. Bloomington, IN.
Suhonen, S. 1985. Wotisch oder Ingrisch? ('Votic or Ingrian?'). In Veenker, W. (ed.), *Dialectologia Uralica. Materialien des ersten internationalen Symposions zur Dialektologie der uralischen Sprachen*, Wiesbaden, 139–49.

WOLFGANG GRELLER

Votyak, see *Udmurt*

W

Walloon

The dialect of the *langue d'oïl* (i.e. **French**) indigenous to the greater part, but not the whole, of Wallonia, the French-speaking part of Belgium; in the west of Wallonia, from west of Tournai to east of Mons and Soignies, a **Picard** dialect (sometimes termed Rouchi) is spoken while in small areas of the south-east the dialects are Champenois (Sugny and three other villages) or the Gaumais subdialect of Lorrain (around Virton). Walloon is also spoken in a small part of the French *département* of the Ardennes (18 villages stretching from Fumay to Givert, in the valley of the Meuse leading into Belgium) and in a tiny portion of NW Luxembourg (the hamlets of Doncols and Sonlez, just over the Belgian border from Bastogne), though in this last area it is dying out. In North America, a small Walloon-speaking community, the descendants of 19th-c. immigrants, survives in the Green Bay and Door Peninsula area of NE Wisconsin.

On the basis of a number of (generally conservative) phonetic, grammatical and lexical features serving to distinguish it markedly from other *langue d'oïl* dialects, it is sometimes claimed that Walloon should be considered as a separate language from French.

While a number of medieval French literary texts exhibit Walloon linguistic features, the Walloon literary tradition as such dates from around the year 1600, since when there has been extensive use of the language in a variety of genres but especially in poetry and drama. Important figures include the lyric poet Nicolas Defrecheux (1825–74) and the dramatist Édouard Remouchamps (1836–1900).

A standardized orthography devised by Jules Feller at the beginning of the 20th c. at the request of the Société liégeoise de littérature wallonne (now the Société de langue et littérature wallonnes) is in general use.

It has been estimated that, of the total population of Wallonia of over 3 million, some 800,000 can at least understand Walloon, of whom perhaps 200,000 use it on a regular basis.

The teaching of Walloon in schools was first authorized in 1983 and was confirmed by a decree of the French Community of Belgium dated 24 December 1990 aimed at encouraging the maintenance of *langues régionales endogènes* (unspecified but, in practice, Walloon, Champenois and Lorrain together with the **Luxemburgish** dialect of the Arlon district). Such teaching is carried out on a limited scale, and on a strictly voluntary basis since no financial provision has been made, in a number of primary schools but apparently not in secondary schools. There is some provision for Walloon in the broadcasting media and weekly chronicles in it appear in a number of local newspapers.

Bal, W. (ed.) 1992. *Limes 1. Les langues régionales romanes en Wallonie*. Brussels.
—— and Maquet, A. 1986. *Littérature dialectale de la Wallonie*. Liège.

Germain, G. and Pierret, J. -M. 1990. La Wallonie. In Holtus, G., Metzeltin, M. and Schmitt, C. (eds), *Lexikon der Romanistischen Linguistik*, Tübingen, vol. 5.1, *Französisch/Le français*, 595–604.

Haust, J. 1933. *Dictionnaire liégeois* (reprinted 1972). Liège.

Lechanteur, J. et al. (eds) 1990–2. *Petit atlas linguistique de la Wallonie*. Liège.

Pierret, J. -M. 1992. Le wallon. In Bal 1992, 70–132.

Remacle, L. 1948. *Le Problème de l'ancien wallon*. Liège.

—— 1953–60. *Syntaxe du parler wallon de La Gleize*, 3 vols. Paris.

—— Legros, É. et al. (eds) 1953- . *Atlas linguistique de la Wallonie*. Liège (vols 1–5 and 9 so far published).

GLANVILLE PRICE

Welsh

A member of the *Brittonic subgroup of the *Celtic languages, spoken by over half a million people in Wales and with unknown numbers of speakers in England and elsewhere.

Origins and early attestations

At the time of the Roman invasion in the 1st c. AD, the Brittonic Celtic language from which Welsh is descended was spoken over most or all of Britain south of the Forth–Clyde valley and perhaps north of it as well (on the situation north of the line, see *Pictish). It is probably by about the 6th c. that the language in the western part of the island had evolved to a stage at which it can properly be termed 'Welsh'; this stage of the language is represented by the forms of some personal names in Latin inscriptions dating probably from the 7th c. The earliest inscription actually written in Welsh and dating probably from the 8th c. is on a stone now in the parish church at Tywyn (Gwynedd). The earliest known manuscript text, with which we enter the Old Welsh period (the language of earlier inscriptions has been referred to as 'Primitive Welsh'), is a brief legal memorandum incorporated in a Latin gospel book, the Book of St Chad, now in Lichfield cathedral. The first literary text properly so called consists of two sets of brief poems (12 in all) in a 9th-c. manuscript (known as the Juvencus manuscript) in the Cambridge University Library, followed by a 23-line 10th-c. prose text known as the 'Computus Fragment' relating to the method of recording the course of the moon through the signs of the zodiac. From this early period we also have numerous glosses, personal names, etc., included in various Latin manuscripts.

Welsh as a literary language

It is possible that the origins of Welsh literature go back considerably further than the brief texts referred to above. Many scholars have argued that some of the material attributed to the 6th-c. poets Aneirin and Taliesin, which is known to us only in 13th-c. manuscripts, probably dates in its essentials (though not in the form in which we have it, since it had been modernized and otherwise modified in the course of the centuries) from the time of the poets in question and that it can plausibly be assumed to be their work.

It is beyond the scope of this article to attempt even the briefest sketch of a history of Welsh literature. What is strictly relevant to our present purposes, however, is the fact that Welsh has one of the longest literary traditions of any European language and that that tradition has remained vital and unbroken to the present day. We must mention in particular two of the outstanding highlights of Welsh medieval literature, namely the prose tales known collectively as the *Mabinogi* (known in two late medieval manuscripts but probably originating from a much earlier period) and the poetry of Dafydd ap Gwilym (13th c.).

What is almost certainly the first printed book in Welsh (1547), containing among other things translations of the Creed, the Lord's Prayer and the Ten Commandments, is known, since it has no title, by its opening words, *Yn y lhyvyr hwnn* 'In this book'; the only extant copy is in the National Library of Wales at Aberystwyth. This was followed in the same year by a book of proverbs, and four years later by two works both due to William Salesbury, a Welsh–English dictionary and a translation of the Epistles and Gospels from the Anglican prayer-book. Translations of the Book of Common Prayer and of the New Testament (most of it by Salesbury) appeared in 1567 and, in 1588 (23 years before the publication of the English 'Authorized Version'), there followed the complete Bible, consisting of Bishop William Morgan's translation of the Old Testament and his revision of Salesbury's New Testament. This was to constitute a decisive factor in both the literary and the linguistic history of Wales. Morgan based his language on that of traditional Welsh poetry as maintained in the bardic schools and thereby laid the foundations for a dignified modern literary language in a way that could not have been achieved had he attempted to base himself on the unstandardized spoken tongue of his day. A revised edition of the 1588 translation was published in 1620 and for three and half centuries (until the publication of a modern translation of the New Testament in 1975 and of the complete Bible in 1988) this version, regularly reprinted, was the model for the standard literary language. The fact that Welsh thereby acquired a literary standard that was both firmly based and universally accepted was to prove of inestimable benefit, sparing Wales as it did from the bitter quarrels about the principles and practices to be followed that have all too often bedevilled attempts to codify such languages as ***Breton** and ***Occitan**. It is, however, true that this literary language is somewhat archaic in some respects, but recent decades have seen largely successful attempts to bring the literary language closer to the spoken language.

Official status

The Act of 1536 by which Wales was incorporated in England stipulated that no Welsh-speaking person should occupy any office within the King's dominions 'unless he or they use and exercise the speech or language of English' – in other words, a command of English was an essential qualification for public office. However, though Welsh had no legal or official status, it was not proscribed and, since the majority of Welsh-speakers were ignorant of English, the use of the language in courts of law seems to have continued throughout the centuries when there was no alternative. The first measure granting a minimal degree of recognition to Welsh was the Welsh Courts Act of 1942, passed in response to a national petition organized on the eve of the Second World War. This repealed that section of the 1536 Act which was held to restrict unduly 'the right of Welsh speaking persons to use the Welsh language in courts of justice in Wales', but its only practical provision was to allow the use of Welsh in the courts 'by any party or witness who considers that he would be otherwise be at any disadvantage by reason of his natural language of communication being Welsh'. This fell far short of allowing a party or witness to speak in Welsh merely out of preference and it was to be another quarter of a century before a substantial improvement in the official and legal status of Welsh was achieved. An Act of 1964 legalizing the provision of Welsh versions of forms used in connection with local or parliamentary elections was followed in 1967 by the Welsh Language Act which enacted that 'in any legal proceeding in Wales [. . .] the Welsh language may be spoken by any party, witness or other person who desires to use it'. It also authorized (but did not require) appropriate Ministers to prescribe a Welsh version of any official document or form of words and stipulated that 'anything done in Welsh' on the basis of any such document 'shall have the like effect as if done in English'. While not going so far as to provide for full equality of Welsh with English, the Act therefore enshrined in law what had come to be known as 'the principle of equal validity'. Partly in consequence of the 1967 Act and partly in response to other pressures, in particular to campaigns waged from 1962 onwards by Cymdeithas yr Iaith Gymraeg ('The Welsh Language Society'), numerous official and other bodies (including government ministries, local government authorities, the Post Office, banks, the police, the National Trust, transport undertakings, supermarkets) have come to make greatly increased use of Welsh. Among other developments, the use of bilingual road-signs and other public announcements instead of the previous English-only versions has become general since the early 1970s and some local councils have begun to encourage the use of Welsh in their meetings (introducing simultaneous translation facilities for the benefit of members who may not have adequate command of the language). While some (though by no means all) of this is little more than tokenism, the result is that, since the early 1970s, the 'public presence' of the language has become very noticeable, even in parts of Wales where the language has long since ceased to be a normal spoken medium.

In 1993, a new Welsh Language Act established a Welsh Language Board, the members of which are appointed by the Secretary of State for Wales. The Board's function is defined in the Act as being that of 'promoting and facilitating the use of the Welsh language', and in particular by advising the Secretary of State on matters concerning the Welsh language and by advising others on ways of giving effect 'to the principle that, in the conduct of public business and the administration of justice in Wales, the English and Welsh languages should be treated on a basis of equality'. Further, all public bodies (including local government councils, police, fire and health authorities, school governors, and others) are required to prepare schemes specifying the measures they propose to take with a view to giving effect to that principle. It is as yet too early to determine how effective the Act will be in practice.

Welsh in the churches and in education

Ever since the Reformation, Welsh has played an important part in the life and worship of most branches of the Christian church, many of which led the field in publishing throughout the centuries considerable numbers of books, pamphlets and periodicals in Welsh (as we have seen, the Anglican Book of Common Prayer and the Bible were both translated very early). This fact has served to confer an element of dignity on the language and ensure that its position has never been totally restricted to low-status roles. Welsh is still the sole or primary medium of worship and other activities in many churches and chapels. After the Second Vatican Council (1962–5), the Roman Catholic missal was translated into Welsh and a Welsh version of the Liturgy of the Russian Orthodox Church also exists.

Various Christian bodies also played an important role in the 18th and 19th centuries in fostering literacy in Welsh, both through 'circulating schools', in which an itinerant teacher would spend up to three months in a locality teaching children and adults to read the Scriptures in Welsh, and through Sunday schools. The role of state education, when it came into being, was at first much less creditable. The Elementary Education Act of 1870, which related to both England and Wales, took no cognizance of the special situation in Wales and no place was therefore accorded to the Welsh language in the schools that came into being as a result of the Act. Over the next half-century the situation gradually improved, particularly as a result of various provisions in the early 1890s allowing for the use of bilingual textbooks and for the teaching of Welsh as an optional subject. By the 1930s, the use of Welsh as a medium of instruction in primary schools was by no means unusual but it was not until 1947 that the first officially Welsh-medium primary school was established (in Llanelli) within the state system. Since the early 1950s some dozens of such schools have been set up, not only in predominantly Welsh-speaking areas but also, where parents have pressed for it, in certain predominantly English-speaking areas. From 1956 onwards, Welsh-medium instruction has also spread to secondary schools, with over 40 in many parts of the country being now either 'designated' Welsh-medium schools (in which most subjects, usually with the exception of sciences, are taught through the medium of Welsh and Welsh is the administrative language of the school) or bilingual schools. Under the provisions of the 1988 Education Act, secondary schools in Wales (a small number have been exempted from the provision) are required to teach Welsh to all pupils in at least the lower forms.

The last quarter of the 20th c. has also seen spectacular growth in the provision (largely thanks to the efforts of a voluntary movement) of Welsh-language nursery schools.

At the other end of the educational spectrum, there has been some expansion in the use of Welsh in the various Colleges of the University of Wales. Previously, teaching through the medium of Welsh existed only in Departments of Welsh and, in some Colleges, in such departments as Welsh History and Biblical Studies. From the late 1960s onwards, however, a small number of staff have been appointed to a range of other departments (mainly Arts departments) with special responsibility for providing courses through the medium of Welsh. In 1980, the University of Wales at Aberystwyth inaugurated a scheme whereby Welsh-medium courses for external students could be combined in such a way as to enable them to graduate having followed all their courses through the medium of Welsh but, with this exception and that of internal students studying Welsh and closely related subjects, it is not possible to complete a degree course in any subject without following at least some courses in English. There is no realistic possibility that demands for an all-Welsh College within the University can be met.

Welsh in the media

As far as its use in the written and spoken mass media is concerned, Welsh is in a stronger position than many other minority languages in western Europe, including all the other Celtic languages. While publishing books in Welsh could not nowadays, with few exceptions, be an economically self-sustaining undertaking, the provision of subsidies from, *inter alia*, government sources (channelled through the Welsh Books Council set up in 1958) and such other bodies as the Welsh Joint Education Committee and the Welsh Arts Council has meant that, in recent years, well over 200 books on average are published annually. There has never been a daily paper in Welsh but, in many cases also aided by subsidies, a wide range of weeklies, monthlies and other periodicals are available.

Radio broadcasting in Welsh had existed on a modest scale before the Second World War and there was significant expansion of the service in the late 1940s and 1950s, though by 1971–2 there were still only a little over 11 hours of Welsh per week. A substantial improvement came in 1977 with the inauguration of Radio Cymru, a BBC channel that now broadcasts in Welsh for some 90 hours a week. More recently, local broadcasting stations (some operated by the BBC, some of them independent) have accorded a significant role to the Welsh language.

Welsh-language television began on a small scale on the BBC in 1952 and on independent (commercial) television in 1958. Output in Welsh from the two stations rose to about 11.5 hours a week by the 1960s but was in the main restricted to unsocial late-night hours with no peak-hour viewing. A most significant, and a highly influential, development came with the establishment in Britain in 1980 of a fourth national television channel which, in Wales, is devoted in part to transmitting, mainly at peak hours, some 30 hours per week of Welsh-language programmes appealing to a wide variety of tastes and interests.

Numbers and geographical distribution of speakers

Although figures for language use derived from censuses must be treated with caution, since they can be influenced both by the way the questions are phrased and by speakers' attitudes to the language or languages concerned, they nevertheless provide valid bases of comparison for assessing the strength of a given language in different areas and at different censuses. A question relating to Welsh was first put in the British decennial census in 1891, when it emerged that over 900,000 persons, or over 54% of the population over the age of 2, were recorded as being able to speak

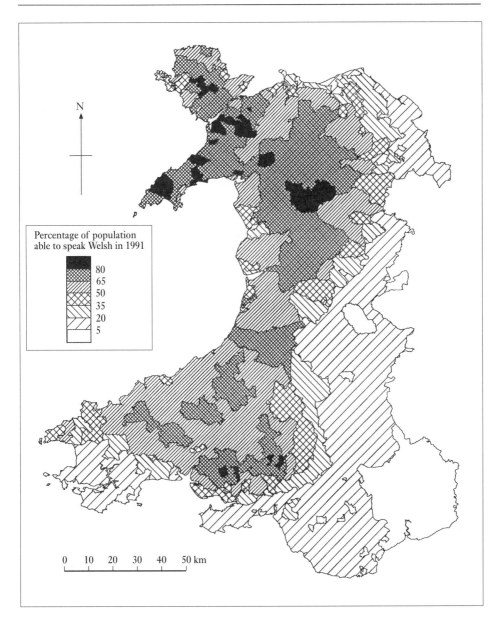

Percentage of population
able to speak Welsh in 1991

80
65
50
35
20
5

0 10 20 30 40 50 km

Map 21   The Welsh language in 1991. Map based on data provided by the 1991
census of population. From John Aitchison and Harold Carter, *A Geography of the
Welsh Language 1961–1991* (Cardiff, University of Wales Press, 1994).

the language. Because of the way the question was worded, too much reliance should not perhaps be placed on this result. The figures for later censuses, i.e. those from 1901 onwards, are likely to be more dependable. These show a drop in the numbers of those recorded as able to speak Welsh from 929, 824 (or 50% of the population aged 3 years or over) in 1901 to 508,098 (or 18.6%) in 1991. The numbers (included in those given above) of those recorded as able to speak only Welsh declined from 280,905 (or 15%) in 1901 to a mere 21,583 (1%) in 1981 (no question relating to competence in English was asked at the 1991 census). It is clear that, if Welsh is to survive, it has do so in a bilingual context in which there are no monoglot Welsh-speakers, and that all strategies devised for ensuring its survival must be based on that assumption.

There are also substantial emigrant Welsh-speaking communities, for which no figures are available, in England, North America and other parts of the English-speaking world, and a small bilingual Welsh–Spanish community, dating from a colony established in 1865, in Patagonia.

The beginnings of the geographical recession of Welsh go back at least to the 13th c. when the southern part of Pembrokeshire and parts of the Gower peninsula and the Vale of Glamorgan became the domains of Anglo-Norman lords. Elsewhere, Welsh seems to have maintained its position well for several centuries and was even spoken over the border in several parishes in Herefordshire and Shropshire until the 17th c. and, in one small part of Shropshire, still is to some extent. An analysis of the data provided by reports made to their bishops by Anglican clergy in Wales as to the language or languages used in their churches (see Pryce 1978) reveals that, as late as 1750, most of rural Wales was still Welsh in speech. A century later, there is good evidence that English had ousted Welsh from most if not all of Radnorshire and other eastern parts and had largely (but not totally) overwhelmed Monmouthshire and parts of Glamorgan, and by 1900 it was spreading in strength along the North Wales coast and outwards into the Welsh-speaking heartland from partly Anglicized towns such as Holyhead, Bangor, Aberystwyth and Carmarthen. Nevertheless, according to the results of the 1991 census (see map 21), there remain both in the north-west and (with the exception of southern Pembroke) in the south-west substantial areas (but, in general, areas of low population density) where a majority of the population still speaks Welsh, including many wards where the proportion rises to 65% and a few where it reaches 80%.

Dialects

There is considerable regional variation in spoken Welsh, affecting pronunciation and vocabulary and to some extent grammar. But though a native speaker can usually be readily localized, and often very precisely so, there are no sharp dialectal divisions. However, the eminent Celticist Sir John Rhŷs proposed a century ago a classification into four main dialects, to which he gave names derived from those of the Celtic tribes that occupied approximately the areas in question in the early centuries of the Christian era, viz. Venedotian (north-west), Ordovician (north-east), Demetian (south-west), and Silurian (south-east) (Rhŷs's map is reproduced as a frontispiece to A. R. Thomas 1973). The general validity of this classification has been upheld by recent research (A. R. Thomas 1980).

Aitchison, J. and Carter, H. 1994. *A Geography of the Welsh Language 1961–1991*. Cardiff.
Ball, M. J. (ed.) 1988. *The Use of Welsh*. Clevedon.
Davies, J. 1993. *The Welsh Language*. Cardiff.
Evans, D. S. 1964. *A Grammar of Middle Welsh*. Dublin.
Griffiths, B. and Jones, D. G. 1995. *The Welsh Academy English–Welsh Dictionary*. Cardiff.
Jenkins, G. H. (ed.) 1997. *The Welsh Language before the Industrial Revolution*. Cardiff.
—— 1998. *Language and Community in the Nineteenth Century*. Cardiff.
Jones, R. O. 1993. The sociolinguistics of Welsh. In Ball, M. J. (ed.), *The Celtic Languages*, London, 536–605.
Pryce, W. T. R. 1978. Welsh and English in Wales, 1750–1971: a spatial analysis based on the linguistic affiliation of parochial communities. *Bulletin of the Board of Celtic Studies*, 28: 1–36.
Thomas, A. R. 1973. *The Linguistic Geography of Wales. A Contribution to Welsh Dialectology*. Cardiff.
—— 1980. *Areal Analysis of Dialect Data by Computer: A Welsh Example*. Cardiff.
Thomas, R. J. et al. (eds) 1950– . *Geiriadur Prifysgol Cymru. A Dictionary of the Welsh Language*. Vol.1, A–FFYSUR, 1950–67; vol. 2, G–LLYYS, 1968–87; vol. 3, M–RHYWYR, 1987–98; vol. 4, S– , 1999– .
Thorne, D. A. 1993. *A Comprehensive Welsh Grammar*. Oxford.
Watkins, T. A. 1993. Welsh. In Ball, M. J. (ed.), *The Celtic Languages*, London, 289–348.

GLANVILLE PRICE

West Russian (see under *Ruthenian*)

White Russian (White Ruthenian), see *Belarusian*

Wolof (see under *Community languages (France)*)

Y

Yassic

An *Iranian language very close to *Ossetic. It is known only from a 15th-c. list of 40 words found in Hungary where its presence presumably reflects the stay in that area of the Yas or Alans (see *Alanic) who probably arrived there in the 13th c. A few *Hungarian words of apparent Ossetic origin may derive from Yassic.

Németh, G. 1959. Eine Wörterliste der Jassen, der ungarländischen Alanen ('A word-list of the Yas, the Alans of Hungary'). *Abhandlungen der Deutschen Akademie der Wissenschaften zu Berlin: Klasse für Sprache, Literatur und Kunst*. Berlin.

Yatvingian (Yotvingian)

An extinct *Baltic language or dialect spoken in SW Lithuania and the neighbouring part of Poland. No written records remain. It probably died out in the 16th or 17th c. See also under (Old) *Prussian.

Yiddish

Yiddish is a fusion language comprising an intricate linguistic union of three components: (the quantitatively dominant) *Germanic (from medieval urban varieties of Middle High *German), *Semitic (from post-classical *Hebrew and *Aramaic), and, in the modern dialects, *Slavonic (from *Polish, *Ukrainian, *Belarusian, *Russian). In addition to vocabulary, all the components have contributed varying degrees of phonology, morphology, syntax and semantics, and they have all impacted on each other profoundly. The language is well known for the fine-tuned semantic nuancing enabled by the multiplicity of near-synonyms.

Origins

The traditional language of the Ashkenazim (Jews of central European origin) arose on the banks of the Rhine and (especially) the Danube about a thousand years ago, when the first settlers merged their Hebrew and Aramaic (and a trickle of *Romance) with select portions of local German varieties. Their new Jewish civilization was known as Ashkenaz. The term initially meant 'Germany' but came to signify all the contiguous lands settled by the Ashkenazim, and ultimately, their culture *per se*. Very early on, Ashkenaz broke away from the collapsing centres of rabbinic authority in the Near East and developed along autonomous lines. Its symbolic declaration of independence from the Orient was the edict against polygamy, issued roughly at the turn of the millennium by Rabeynu Gershom (*c*.960–1028).

Yiddish is one of three Ashkenazic languages taking part in an exotic trilingualism that includes Hebrew and Aramaic, which were brought into central Europe by the first Ashkenazic settlers. Yiddish was the only vernacular. All three were used in writing, Yiddish initially for secular works and private communication; Hebrew for communal correspondence, biblical commentaries and a wide range of genres; Aramaic for the two 'most learned' genres: legalistic treatises (especially commentaries on the Talmud and on other commentaries) and Kabbalah (Jewish mysticism).

External history

A series of catastrophic persecutions, including the Crusades (from 1096), the Rindfleisch massacres of 1298, the riots following the Black Death (1348–9), and a host of 'blood libels' all contributed to increased migration. Many Ashkenazim emigrated to the Slavonic and Baltic lands, which offered relative racial and religious tolerance. In the 'new Ashkenaz' of eastern Europe, Yiddish acquired its Slavonic component.

At its geographic zenith in the 16th c., Yiddish stretched from Holland and Italy in the west, deep into Russia in the east. Western Yiddish, the older branch, comprises North-western (Holland, northern Germany and Denmark), Mid-western (central Germany) and South-western Yiddish (Alsace, Switzerland, southern Germany). Eastern Yiddish also has three major dialects: North-eastern (Lithuania, Belarus, Latvia; popularly 'Lithuanian'); Mid-eastern (Poland,

Hungary; popularly 'Polish'); and South-eastern (Ukraine, Romania; 'Ukrainian' or 'Volhynian').

From about 1500 onward, Eastern Yiddish began its ascent, ultimately to become the dominant branch. In the West, lower population concentrations and attrition to German were taking a toll, especially in the 18th c. Late in that century, the 'Berlin Enlightenment' of Moses Mendelssohn and his circle, which despised Yiddish and sought to stamp it out as a blot on Jewish prospects for integration, added a campaign against the language. Western Yiddish declined and largely died out, although 'islands' were discovered in the 1950s in Switzerland. Individual speakers of Alsatian and Dutch Yiddish survived through to the late 20th c.

Eastern Yiddish, by contrast, experienced dramatic linguistic, literary and demographic development. By the 1880s there were 7 million Ashkenazim in the world, with the greatest concentrations in the Russian and Austro-Hungarian empires, i.e. the territories of the three eastern dialects (which are, in effect, the three dialects that can be heard today). Massive migration brought Yiddish to all the world's continents. The greatest single concentration of immigrants was to be found in New York City.

Literary tradition

The story of Yiddish literature is one of ever-increasing literary functions of the vernacular. The earliest authenticated attestations are from 1096 (proper names), 1272 (one sentence) and 1382 (an extensive literary manuscript). Many early works entail the fusion of ancient Jewish (often biblical) themes with the European epic poem. The greatest work of old Yiddish literature, however, is Elijah Levita's early 16th c. *Bovo d'Antona*. Based on an Italian work, it contains the first use in any Germanic language of *ottava rima*. From around 1600 onwards, a new tide of pietistic works rooted in Jewish law and ethics predominated.

Pivotal shifts were under way during the 19th c. Western Yiddish more or less 'fell off the map' while Eastern Yiddish leaped to previously inconceivable heights. The very East European adherents of the Berlin Enlightenment, who realized that they had to use Yiddish in their campaign for modernization, secularization, and popular education, ended up themselves remoulding the literary language into a powerful and multifaceted tool capable of producing masterpieces. Early on in the century, they had discarded both the old standard language, which had become hopelessly archaic, as well as its characteristic font. They began to write books using the flourishing spoken dialects of eastern Europe, and published them in square Hebrew characters. A stylistic dialectic developed between the more literary authors, who tapped the wealth of the dialects, and the more journalistically and didactically inclined, who imported a host of 19th-c. German words.

The most dramatic development was the 'reinvention' of Sholem-Yankev Abramovitsh (*c*.1836–1917), a Hebrew didactic writer, as Mendele Moykher Sforim, whose Yiddish prose debut on 24 November 1864 is regarded as the symbolic birthdate of modern Yiddish literature. He was joined later in the century by Y. L. Peretz (1852–1916) and Sholem Aleichem (1859–1915). The three collectively established a classical tradition.

Yiddish was quickly undergoing transformation from folk tongue to a powerful medium of literary and political expression. By the turn of the century, various of the revolutionary movements (and particularly the socialist Bund) were turning to Yiddish as a practical tool, but many writers turned from politics to art. In 1908 three symbolically potent developments transpired. In New York, a group of young poets rebelled against the labour movement's control of literature by establishing an avant-garde journal dedicated to poetry for its own sake. In Vilna, the first really modern literary monthly was launched. And in Chernowitz (Bukovina, now Chernovtsy, Ukraine), the first Yiddish language conference was called. Its final resolution, proclaiming Yiddish to be a national language of the Jewish people, inspired many young writers to Yiddish.

At the end of the First World War, new circles of modernist Yiddish literature arose in New York, Warsaw, Berlin and in the Soviet Union. During the interwar period, Yiddish prose and poetry had grown into a world-class literature producing talents of the calibre of Isaac Bashevis Singer (1904–91), who started writing in Warsaw in the 1920s, and eventually won the Nobel Prize for Literature (1978). A number of sophisticated works emanated from the Soviet Union.

Script and printing

Yiddish is written in the historical Jewish (Hebrew) alphabet. Historically that alphabet has only consonants. From an early stage, Yiddish recycled unused letters (ancient Semitic consonants that had fallen out of use) as vowels, thereby achieving a phonetic representation that was perfected over the centuries.

The extensive development of Yiddish printing in the 1540s brought with it a pan-European standard language. It was a much watered-down 'lowest common denominator' designed to make for easy comprehension (and good book sales) in both western and eastern Ashkenaz. It was set in a special font (known as 'mashkit') which distinguished it from both square Hebrew and rabbinic cursive ('Rashi'). It survived until the early 19th c. in both the western and eastern sectors.

The twentieth century

The Yiddish-speaking civilization of eastern Europe was at a zenith when the Second World War brought it to a crushing and brutal end. Five and a half of the six million Jewish civilians murdered by the Nazis and their collaborators were Yiddish-speakers. The language was forever wiped out on its native territory.

After the war, Stalin's regime, which had begun before the war to repress literary freedom and arrest prominent writers, closed down Yiddish schools and publications altogether. The campaign culminated in the shooting of the 24 leading Yiddish writers and cultural leaders on 12 August 1952.

Secular Yiddish culture elsewhere has been in steady decline. The émigré generation, that had set up impressive cultural institutions and publications in the USA, Canada, Argentina, western Europe and elsewhere, failed to transmit the culture to coming generations. Linguistic acculturation to attractive, free and affluent societies was the order of the day.

From the 1960s onward, however, a growing number of enthusiasts born after the war (including a sizeable proportion of non-Jews) have taken up the cause of Yiddish. There are several thousand scattered in small groups internationally. In western Europe, the leading centres are Paris and Oxford. In 1995 the Council of Europe passed a resolution calling for the perpetuation of Yiddish language and culture.

Yiddish continues to thrive as a natural vernacular among many groups of 'ultra-Orthodox' Hasidic Jews (chasidim) who preserve Ashkenaz as a civilization in its entirety. Successful resistance to assimilation and high birth rates lead demographers to predict a million Yiddish-speaking chasidim a hundred years hence. They have substantial communities in Antwerp, London and Manchester (among others) which maintain close ties with the major centres in America and Israel.

Birnbaum, S. A. 1979. *Yiddish. A Survey and a Grammar*. Manchester and Toronto.
Fishman, J. A. (ed.) 1981. *Never Say Die! A Thousand Years of Yiddish in Jewish Life and Letters*. The Hague.
Katz, D. (ed.) 1987. *Origins of the Yiddish Language*. Oxford.
—— (ed.) 1988. *Dialects of the Yiddish Language*. Oxford.
Weinreich, M. 1980. *History of the Yiddish Language*. Chicago and London.

DOVID KATZ

Yurak, see *Nenets*

Z

Zan (see under *Caucasian languages. V. South Caucasian family*)

Zemgalian
An extinct *Baltic language or dialect spoken in parts of Latvia and Lithuania and which may have been transitional between *Latvian and *Lithuanian. No written records remain. It probably died out in the 16th c.

Zyrian (Ziryene), see *Komi*